P9-DJB-043

THE
LONGMAN
READER
Brief Edition

THE LONGMAN READER

Brief Edition

SEVENTH EDITION

Judith Nadell

John Langan
Atlantic Cape Community College

Eliza A. Comodromos
Rutgers, The State University of New Jersey

PEARSON
Longman

New York   San Francisco   Boston
London   Toronto   Sydney   Tokyo   Singapore   Madrid
Mexico City   Munich   Paris   Cape Town   Hong Kong   Montreal

Senior Vice President and Publisher: Joseph Opiela
Vice President and Publisher: Eben W. Ludlow
Development Manager: Janet Lanphier
Development Editor: Linda Stern
Marketing Manager: Deborah Murphy
Senior Supplements Editor: Donna Campion
Media Supplements Editor: Nancy Garcia
Production Manager: Douglas Bell
Project Coordination, Text Design, and Electronic Page Makeup: Elm Street
    Publishing Services, Inc.
Cover Designer/Manager: John Callahan
Cover and Interior Photo: Mount Assiniboine, British Columbia, courtesy of
    Alan Maichrowicz/Peter Arnold, Inc.
Senior Manufacturing Buyer: Dennis J. Para
Printer and Binder: R.R. Donnelley & Sons, Harrisonburg
Cover Printer: Coral Graphic Services

For permission to use copyrighted material, grateful acknowledgment is made to the copyright holders on pp. 499–501, which are hereby made part of this copyright page.

Library of Congress Cataloging-in-Publication Data
Nadell, Judith.
    The Longman reader / Judith Nadell, John Langan, Eliza A.
    Comodromos.—Brief [7th] ed.
        p. cm.
    Includes bibliographical references and index.
    ISBN 0-321-23641-6
    1. College readers. 2. English language—Rhetoric—Problems, exercises, etc.
    3. Report writing—Problems, exercises, etc. I. Langan, John, 1942– II. Comodromos,
    Eliza A. III. Title.

PE1417.N33 2005
808'.0427—dc22   2004002583

Copyright © 2005 by Pearson Education, Inc.

All rights reserved. No part of this publication may be reproduced, stored in a retrieval system, or transmitted, in any form or by any means, electronic, mechanical, photocopying, recording, or otherwise, without the prior written permission of the publisher. Printed in the United States.

Please visit us at http://www.ablongman.com/nadell.

ISBN 0-321-23641-6

1 2 3 4 5 6 7 8 9 10—DOH—07 06 05 04

ABOUT THE
AUTHORS

Judith Nadell was until several years ago Associate Professor of Communications at Rowan University (New Jersey). During her eighteen years at Rowan, she coordinated the introductory course in the Freshman Writing Sequence and served as Director of the Writing Lab. In the past several years, she has developed a special interest in grassroots literacy. Besides designing an adult-literacy project, a children's reading-enrichment program, and a family-literacy initiative, she has worked as a volunteer tutor and a tutor trainer in the programs. A Phi Beta Kappa graduate of Tufts University, she received a doctorate from Columbia University. She is author of *Becoming a Read-Aloud Coach* (Townsend Press) and coauthor of *Doing Well in College* (McGraw-Hill), *Vocabulary Basics* (Townsend Press), and *The Longman Writer.* The recipient of a New Jersey award for excellence in the teaching of writing, Judith Nadell lives with her coauthor husband, John Langan, near Philadelphia.

John Langan has taught reading and writing courses at Atlantic Cape Community College near the New Jersey shore for more than twenty years. He earned an advanced degree in reading at Glassboro State College and another in writing at Rutgers University. Active in a mentoring program, he designed a reading-enrichment program for inner-city high school students and wrote a motivational and learning skills guidebook, *Ten Skills You Really Need to Succeed in School,* for urban youngsters. Coauthor of *The Longman Writer* and author of a series of college textbooks on both reading and writing, he has published widely with McGraw-Hill Book Company, Townsend Press, and Longman. His books include *English Skills, Reading and Study Skills,* and *College Writing Skills.*

Eliza A. Comodromos has taught composition and developmental writing in the English Departments of both Rutgers University and John Jay College of Criminal Justice. After graduating with a B.A. in English and in French from La Salle University, she did graduate work at the City University of New York Graduate School and went on to earn an advanced degree at Rutgers University, New Brunswick. A freelance editor and textbook consultant, Eliza Comodromos has delivered numerous papers at language and literature conferences around the country. Currently, she teaches composition at Rutgers University and lives with her husband, Paul, and daughter, Anna Maria, near Philadelphia.

CONTENTS

3 DESCRIPTION   70

Gordon Parks   FLAVIO'S HOME   83
Having battled poverty and prejudice himself, writer-photographer
Gordon Parks visits a Brazilian slum and finds, among the wretched
thousands forgotten by the outside world, a dying yet smiling boy.

Gary Soto   THE JACKET   91
Everything that was wrong with the author's sixth-grade world could
be traced to a cheap, ugly jacket the color of day-old guacamole.

Maya Angelou   SISTER FLOWERS   96
Hidden deep within herself after the trauma of a rape, a young girl is
escorted back into life by the grand lady of a small town.

Additional Writing Topics   103

4 NARRATION   105

Bill Bryson   YOUR NEW COMPUTER   233
Anyone who has ever read a computer manual, trying to figure out whether to insert the red wire into the blue slot or the blue wire into the red slot, will sympathize with Bryson's humorous exasperation.

Clifford Stoll   CYBERSCHOOL   239
Ah, brave new world that relies on CD-ROMs, cubicles, and e-mails and dispenses with such old-fashioned notions as teachers, classrooms, and human interaction! Skeptical techie Stoll casts a jaundiced eye on the school of the future.

Caroline Rego   THE FINE ART OF COMPLAINING   245
Shoddy service and malfunctioning products afflict us all, but some of us complain more effectively than others.

Additional Writing Topics   251

8 COMPARISON-CONTRAST   253

Rachel Carson   A FABLE FOR TOMORROW   267
Ecologist Rachel Carson warns us that what seems like a nightmare will become all too real if we fail to protect the earth.

Joseph H. Suina   AND THEN I WENT TO SCHOOL   271
The author recollects painful memories of leaving his nurturing Native American home to attend the white man's school. Looking back years later, he confronts a harsh reality: he ultimately became an outsider in both worlds.

K. C. Cole ENTROPY   332

**Alexandra Robbins
and Abby Wilner** WHAT IS THE QUARTERLIFE CRISIS?   337

William Raspberry THE HANDICAP OF DEFINITION   345

Additional Writing Topics   349

11 ARGUMENTATION-PERSUASION   351

Yuh Ji-Yeon LET'S TELL THE STORY OF
                ALL AMERICA'S CULTURES   385

THEMATIC CONTENTS

ETHICS AND MORALITY

FAMILY AND CHILDREN

HUMOR AND SATIRE

MEANING IN LIFE

MEMORIES AND AUTOBIOGRAPHY

PREFACE

Since the first edition of this book, much has changed in education, with the Internet transforming the way students acquire and communicate information. The Internet has even changed the way many instructors teach. Nevertheless, despite the forward march of technology, some things in education remain the same, one being the need for students to develop sound writing skills. It's to this mission that we continue to be committed.

When we first began working on the original full version of *The Longman Reader,* we aimed for a different kind of text—one that would offer fresh examples of professional prose, one that would take a more active role in helping students become stronger readers, thinkers, and writers.

As in the full version, our primary goal in this brief edition has been to enliven the mix of selections commonly appearing in readers. Although *The Longman Reader,* Seventh Edition, Brief Edition includes widely read and classic essays, a number of our selections have not yet appeared in other anthologies. Among these are Beth Johnson's "Bombs Bursting in Air," Gordon Parks's "Flavio's Home," Caroline Rego's "The Fine Art of Complaining," and Bill Bryson's "Your New Computer." We've been careful to choose selections that range widely in subject matter and approach, from the humorous to the informative, from personal meditation to polemic. We've also made sure that each selection captures students' interest and clearly illustrates a specific pattern of development or combination of patterns.

Our second concern has remained the quality of instruction in the book. As before, our objective has been to help students bridge the gap between the product and process approaches to reading and writing. Throughout, we describe possible sequences and structures but emphasize that such steps and formats are not meant to be viewed as rigid prescriptions; rather, they are strategies for helping students discover what works best in a particular situation. Such an approach does indeed help students read more critically, think more logically, and write more skillfully.

Gratified by the enthusiasm for the many editions of *The Longman Reader* in its original long version, we decided not to tinker with the book's essential structure in creating this brief edition. The main changes we've made are that (1) a small handful of activities in the "Writing Process" chapter has been streamlined and (2) the number of reading selections has been reduced from five to three in each of the rhetorical chapters, and from six to three in the "Combined Patterns" chapter, yielding a total of 34 (as opposed to 58) highly engaging readings. Apart from these changes, the brief edition is otherwise exactly the same as the long version. The book's format remains as follows:

- **Chapter 1, "The Reading Process,"** is designed to reflect current theories about the interaction of reading, thinking, and writing. The chapter provides guided practice in a three-part process for reading with close attention and a high level of interpretive skill. This step-by-step process sharpens students' understanding of the book's selections and promotes the rigorous thinking needed to write effective essays. An activity at the end of the chapter gives students a chance to use the three-step process. First, they read an essay by journalist Ellen Goodman. The essay has been annotated both to show students the reading process in action and to illustrate how close critical reading can pave the way to promising writing topics. Then they respond to sample questions and writing assignments, all similar to those accompanying each of the book's selections. The chapter thus does more than just tell students how to sharpen their reading abilities; it guides them through a clearly sequenced plan for developing critical reading skills.
- **Chapter 2, "The Writing Process,"** introduces students to essay writing. To make the composing process easier for students to grasp, we provide a separate section for each of the following stages: prewriting, identifying a thesis, supporting the thesis with evidence, organizing the evidence, writing the first draft, and revising. From the start, we point out that the stages are fluid. Indeed, the case history of an evolving student paper illustrates just how recursive and individualized the writing process can be. Guided activities at the end of each section give students practice taking their essays through successive stages in the composing process.

  To illustrate the link between reading and writing, the writing chapter presents the progressive stages of a student paper written in response to Ellen Goodman's "Family Counterculture," the selection presented in Chapter 1. An easy-to-spot symbol in the margin (✎) makes it possible to locate—at a glance—this evolving student essay. Commentary following the student paper highlights the essay's strengths and points out spots that could use additional work. In short, by the end of the second chapter, the entire reading-writing process has been illustrated, from reading a selection to writing about it.

- **Chapters 3–11** of *The Longman Reader,* Seventh Edition, Brief Edition contain selections grouped according to **nine patterns of development:** description, narration, exemplification, division-classification, process analysis, comparison-contrast, cause-effect, definition, and argumentation-persuasion. The sequence progresses from the more personal and expressive patterns to the more public and analytic. However, because each chapter is self-contained, the patterns may be covered in any order. Instructors preferring a thematic approach will find the Thematic Contents helpful.

    The Longman Reader, Seventh Edition, Brief Edition treats the patterns separately because such an approach helps students grasp the distinctive characteristics of each pattern. At the same time, the book continually shows the way writers usually combine patterns in their work. We also encourage students to view the patterns as strategies for generating and organizing ideas. Writers, we explain, rarely set out to compose an essay in a specific pattern. Rather, they choose a pattern or combination of patterns because it suits their purpose, audience, and subject.

    Each of the nine pattern-of-development chapters follows this format:

1. **A detailed explanation of the pattern** begins the chapter. The explanation includes (a) a definition of the pattern, (b) a description of the way the pattern helps a writer accommodate his or her purpose and audience, and (c) step-by-step guidelines for using the pattern.
2. Next, we present **an annotated student essay** using the pattern. Written in response to one of the professional selections in the chapter, each essay illustrates the characteristic features of the pattern discussed in the chapter.
3. **Commentary** after each student essay points out the blend of patterns in the piece, identifies the paper's strengths, and locates areas needing improvement. "First draft" and "revised" versions of one section of the essay reveal how the student writer went about revising, thus illustrating the relationship between the final draft and the steps taken to produce it.
4. The **professional selections** in the pattern-of-development chapters are accompanied by these items.

- *A biographical note and "Pre-Reading Journal Entry"* give students a perspective on the author and create interest in the piece. The journal assignment "primes" students for the selection by encouraging them to explore—in a loose, unpressured way—their thoughts about an issue that will be raised in the selection. The journal entry thus motivates students to read the piece with extra care, attention, and personal investment.

- *Questions for Close Reading,* five in all, help students dig into and interpret the selection. The first question asks them to identify the selection's thesis; the last provides work on vocabulary development.

- *Questions About the Writer's Craft,* four in all, deal with such matters as purpose, audience, tone, organization, sentence structure, diction, and figures of speech. The first question in the series (labeled "The Pattern") focuses on the distinctive features of the pattern used in the selection. And usually there's another question (labeled "Other Patterns") that asks students to analyze the writer's use of additional patterns in the piece.

- *Writing Assignments,* five in all, follow each selection. Packed with suggestions on how to proceed, the assignments use the selection as a springboard. The first two assignments ask students to write an essay using the same pattern as the one used in the selection; the next two assignments encourage students to experiment with a combination of patterns in their own essay; the last assignment helps students turn the raw material in their pre-reading journal entries into fully considered essays. By the time students reach this final assignment, the rough ideas in their journals will have been enriched by a careful reading of the selection, setting the stage for more rigorously conceived essays. Frequently, the assignments are preceded by the symbol ∞, indicating a cross-reference to at least one other selection in the book. By encouraging students to make connections among readings, such assignments broaden students' perspective and give them additional material to draw on when they write. These "paired assignments" will be especially welcome to instructors stressing recurring ideas and themes. In other cases, assignments are preceded by the symbol ▣, indicating that students might benefit from conducting library and/or Internet research.

5. **Prewriting and revising activities,** placed in shaded boxes at the end of each chapter, help students understand the unique demands posed by the pattern being studied.

6. At the end of each pattern-of-development chapter are two sets of **Additional Writing Assignments:** "General Assignments" and "Assignments With a Specific Purpose, Audience, and Point of

View." The first set provides open-ended topics that prompt students to discover the best way to use a specific pattern; the second set develops their sensitivity to rhetorical context by asking them to apply the pattern in a real-world situation.

- **Chapter 12, "Combining the Patterns,"** offers a sample student essay as well as an essay by each of three very different prose stylists. Annotations on the student essay and on one of the professional selections show how writers often blend patterns of development in their work. The chapter also provides guidelines to help students analyze this fusing of patterns.
- **Appendix A, "A Concise Guide to Finding and Documenting Sources,"** provides guidelines for conducting library and Internet research and for citing print and electronic sources.
- **Appendix B, "Avoiding Ten Common Writing Errors,"** targets common problem areas in student writing and offers quick, accessible solutions for each.

The Longman Reader, Seventh Edition, Brief Edition also includes a glossary that lists all the key terms presented in the text.

WHAT'S NEW IN THE SEVENTH EDITION

In preparing this edition, we looked closely at the questionnaires completed by instructors using the full version. Their comments helped us identify new directions the book might take. Here are some of the new features of this brief edition of *The Longman Reader.*

- *One-third of the selections are new.* Many of these readings were suggested by instructors across the country; others were chosen after a lengthy search through magazines, nonfiction collections, newspapers, autobiographies, and the like. Whether written by a well-known figure such as Joan Didion ("Marrying Absurd") or a relative newcomer such as Adam Mayblum ("The Price We Pay"), the new selections are bound to stimulate strong writing on a variety of topics—family life, education, technology, race, mass culture, and morality, to name a few. When selecting new readings, we took special care to include pieces written from the first- and the second-person point of view (for example, Alexandra Robbins and Abby Wilner's "What Is the Quarterlife Crisis?") as well as those written from the third-person point of view (for example, James Barszcz's "Can You Be Educated From a Distance?"). Honoring the requests of many instructors, we also made an effort to find compelling pieces on education and on technology.

Clifford Stoll's "Cyberschool" and Jay Walljasper's "Our Schedules, Our Selves" are two among several such pieces.

- *Peer review receives greater attention.* The "Writing Process" chapter now discusses the usefulness of e-mail when students respond to each other's work during the revision stage. The chapter also presents a *sample peer review sheet, filled out by a student writer.* The filled-out form models one student's constructive response to a classmate's first draft. The commentary following the final draft highlights the way the peer reviewer's comments guided the student's revision. Further emphasis on peer review is provided in the *Peer Review/Revision checklists* that have been *added to each pattern chapter.* These easy-to-use checklists allow students to focus on the demands of specific patterns as they revise their own and others' writing.

- *Throughout the book, greater emphasis is placed on the way writers combine patterns of development. Most significant is the new student essay ("The Super-Sizing of America's Kids") in Chapter 12, showing how a student writer uses a variety of patterns in a paper.* Accompanied by marginal annotations and followed by detailed commentary, this new essay models for students how to draw upon multiple patterns in their own writing. Furthermore, the commentary accompanying the student essays in Chapters 3–11 now highlights the use of combined patterns. Finally, following every reading selection are the revised "Writing Assignments Combining Patterns of Development," which include assignments that encourage students to combine multiple patterns in their essays.

- *The "Reading Process" chapter discusses more fully techniques for annotating material when reading.* Adapting strategies described in Mortimer Adler's classic essay "How to Mark a Book," this expanded discussion provides students with hands-on techniques for interacting with text as they read.

- *A new section, "Avoiding Ten Common Writing Errors" (Appendix B), helps students brush up on useful rules and conventions of writing. This section identifies ten skill areas that give student writers the most trouble and provides explanations and corrected examples of each.* The areas covered are fragments, comma splices and run-ons, faulty subject-verb agreement, faulty pronoun agreement, misplaced and dangling modifiers, faulty parallelism, comma misuse, apostrophe misuse, confusing homonyms, and misuse of italics and underlining.

- *Writing in non-academic contexts receives greater emphasis.* The "Assignments With a Specific Purpose, Audience, and Point of View" at the end of each pattern chapter have been revised to focus on the way a particular pattern can be used in three different real-life writing contexts: "On Campus," "At Home or in the Community," and "On the Job."

- *The book's design is more user friendly than ever, with new checklists, boxes, and graphics throughout making key information more accessible.* Additionally, for quick and easy reference, the inside back cover now features an "Overview of Checklists in *The Longman Reader.*"
- *The value of collaborative learning is underscored more than ever.* Many assignments encourage students to investigate various sides of an issue by brainstorming with classmates, questioning friends, speaking with family members, or interviewing "experts." Such assignments help students formulate sound, well-reasoned opinions and steer them away from reflexive, off-the-cuff positions.
- *A greater number of linked assignments* (indicated by ∞) *help students make connections between selections,* thus broadening their perspectives and giving them additional material to draw upon when they write.
- *The argumentation-persuasion chapter, already more comprehensive than any comparable text's, expands coverage of refutation strategies by presenting a provocative new pair of professional essays, one written in rebuttal to the other.*
- The *research paper* has been *updated* to reflect the *most recent MLA guidelines regarding the use of electronic sources.*
- *Appendix A, "A Concise Guide to Finding and Documenting Sources," has been updated and expanded.* This chapter includes *up-to-date information on both library and Internet research, highlighting the most useful and authoritative research tools and sources.* It also provides more detailed guidance in methods for quoting sources. The sample MLA bibliographic entries have been revised to reflect the most recent guidelines regarding the documentation of print and electronic sources.

Supplements for Students and Instructors

A comprehensive *Instructor's Manual* contains the following: in-depth answers to the "Questions for Close Reading" and "Questions About the Writer's Craft"; suggested activities; pointers about using the book; a detailed syllabus; and an analysis of the blend of patterns in the selections in the "Combining the Patterns" chapter.

A *Companion Website* (http://www.ablongman.com/nadell), written by Karen Grandy, offers a number of helpful features, including review and writing exercises and thematic groupings of links to other sites of interest. The Instructor's Resources section includes links of interest to instructors, a sample syllabus, and sample grading kubrics.

ACKNOWLEDGMENTS

At Longman, our thanks go to Eben Ludlow for his perceptive editorial guidance and continued enthusiasm for *The Longman Reader.* We're also indebted to Linda Stern and to Heather Johnson of Elm Street Publishing Services, Inc., and Douglas Bell of Longman for their skillful handling of the never-ending complexities of the production process.

For help in preparing *The Longman Reader,* Seventh Edition, Brief Edition, we owe thanks to the insightful comments of these reviewers: Martha R. Bachman, Camden County College; Robert P. Berman, Wake Technical Community College; Carol Bledsoe, Florida Gulf Coast University; Susan Buchler, Montgomery County Community College; Amy M. Clarke, Sierra College; Lincoln Davis, Imperial Valley College; Raymond W. Foster, Scottsdale Community College; Scott P. Johnson, Bethel College; Elaine Kromhout, Indian River Community College; Jennifer Lane, Glendale Community College; Kristin LaTour, Central Texas College; Carol Liebscher, Montgomery County Community College; Robert Mugford, Scottsdale Community College; Allison Murray, Long Beach City College; Monique E. Neal, University of Delaware; Daniel Olson, North Harris College; Irene Schiller, Camden County College; Mary L. Simpson, Central Texas College; Sinéad Waters Turner, Wake Technical Community College; and Deanna M. White, University of Texas at San Antonio.

Our work on this edition was influenced too by the many students who took advantage of the questionnaire at the back of the sixth edition to tell us which selections they preferred.

Thanks also go to Jennifer Druce and the staff of very knowledgeable research librarians at the Camden County Library in Voorhees, New Jersey, for sharing their expertise on library and Internet research.

Some individuals from our at-home office deserve special thanks. During the preparation of the seventh edition, Joan Dunayer and Beth Johnson provided valuable assistance with the apparatus. Finally, as always, we're thankful to our students. Their reaction to various drafts of material sharpened our thinking and helped focus our work. And we are especially indebted to the eleven students whose essays are included in the book. Their thoughtful, carefully revised papers dramatize the potential of student writing and the power of the composing process.

Judith Nadell
John Langan
Eliza A. Comodromos

1
THE READING PROCESS

More than two hundred years ago, essayist Joseph Addison commented, "Of all the diversions of life, there is none so proper to fill up its empty spaces as the reading of useful and entertaining authors." Addison might have added that reading also challenges our beliefs, deepens our awareness, and stimulates our imagination.

Why, then, don't more people delight in reading? After all, most children feel great pleasure and pride when they first learn to read. As children grow older, though, the initially magical world of books is increasingly associated with homework, tests, and grades. Reading turns into an anxiety-producing chore. Also, as demands on a person's time accumulate throughout adolescence and adulthood, reading often gets pushed aside in favor of something that takes less effort. It's easier simply to switch on the television and passively view the ready-made images that flash across the screen. In contrast, it's almost impossible to remain passive while reading. Even a slick best-seller requires that the reader decode, visualize, and interpret what's on the page. The more challenging the material, the more actively involved the reader must be.

The essays we selected for this book call for active reading. Representing a broad mix of styles and subjects, the essays range from the classic to the contemporary. They contain language that will move you, images that will enlarge your understanding of other people, ideas that will transform your views on complex issues.

The selections serve other purposes as well. For one thing, they'll help you develop a repertoire of reading skills—abilities that will benefit you throughout life. Second, as you become a better reader, your own writing style will become more insightful and polished. Increasingly, you'll be able to draw on the ideas presented in the selections and employ the techniques that professional writers use to express such ideas. As novelist Saul Bellow has observed, "A writer is a reader moved to emulation."

In the pages ahead, we outline a three-stage approach for getting the most out of this book's selections. Our suggestions will enhance your understanding of the book's essays, as well as help you read other material with greater ease and assurance.

STAGE 1: GET AN OVERVIEW OF THE SELECTION

Ideally, you should get settled in a quiet place that encourages concentration. If you can focus your attention while sprawled on a bed or curled up in a chair, that's fine. But if you find that being very comfortable is more conducive to daydreaming and dozing off than it is to studying, avoid getting too relaxed.

Once you're settled, it's time to read the selection. To ensure a good first reading, try the following hints.

☑ FIRST READING: A CHECKLIST

❑ Start by reading the biographical note that precedes the selection. By providing background information about the author, the biographical note helps you evaluate the writer's credibility as well as his or her slant on the subject. For example, if you know that Clifford Stoll is a computer-savvy scientist, you can better assess whether he is a credible source for the analysis he presents in his essay "Cyberschool" (page 239).

❑ Do the *Pre-Reading Journal Entry* assignment, which precedes the selection. This assignment "primes" you for the piece by helping you to explore—in an easy, unpressured way—your thoughts about a key point raised in the selection. By preparing the journal entry, you're inspired to read the selection with special care, attention, and personal investment. (For more on pre-reading journal entries, see pages 14–16 and 492.)

❑ Consider the selection's title. A good title often expresses the essay's main idea, giving you insight into the selection even before you read it. For example, the title of Yuh Ji-Yeon's "Let's Tell the Story of All America's Cultures" (page 385) suggests that the piece will advocate multiculturalism. A title may also hint at a selection's tone. The student essay "Becoming a Videoholic" (page 225) is light in spirit, whereas Adam Mayblum's "The Price We Pay" (page 128) suggests a piece with a serious mood.

❑ Read the selection straight through purely for pleasure. Allow yourself to be drawn into the world the author has created. Just as you first see a painting from the doorway of a room and form an overall

---

impression without perceiving the details, you can have a preliminary, subjective feeling about a reading selection. Moreover, because you bring your own experiences and viewpoints to the piece, your reading will be unique. As Ralph Waldo Emerson said, "Take the book, my friend, and read your eyes out; you will never find there what I find."

❑ After this initial reading of the selection, focus your first impressions by asking yourself whether you like the selection. In your own words, briefly describe the piece and your reaction to it.

STAGE 2: DEEPEN YOUR SENSE OF THE SELECTION

At this point, you're ready to move more deeply into the selection. A second reading will help you identify the specific features that triggered your initial reaction.

There are a number of techniques you can use during this second, more focused reading. You may, for example, find it helpful to adapt some of the strategies that Mortimer Adler, a well-known writer and editor, wrote about in his 1940 essay "How to Mark a Book." There, Adler argues passionately for marking up the material we read. The physical act of annotating, he believes, etches the writer's ideas more sharply in the mind, helping readers grasp and remember those ideas more easily. And "best of all," Adler writes, the "marks and notes . . . stay there forever. You can pick up the . . . [material] the following week or year, and there are all your points of agreement, doubt, and inquiry. It's like resuming an uninterrupted conversation."

Adler goes on to describe various annotation techniques he uses when reading. Several of these techniques, adapted somewhat, are presented in the checklist below.

☑ SECOND READING: A CHECKLIST

Using a pen (or pencil) and highlighter, you might . . .

❑ Underline or highlight the selection's main idea, or thesis, often found near the beginning or end. If the thesis isn't stated explicitly, write down your own version of the selection's main idea.

❑ Place numbers in the margin to designate the main points that support the thesis.

❑ Circle or put an asterisk next to key ideas that are stated more than once.

❑ Take a minute to write "Yes," "No," or a brief comment beside points with which you strongly agree or disagree. Your reaction to these points often explains your feelings about the aptness of the selection's ideas.

❏ Return to any unclear passages you encountered during the first reading. The feeling you now have for the piece as a whole will probably help you make sense of initially confusing spots. However, this second reading may also reveal that, in places, the writer's thinking isn't as clear as it could be. If that's the case, you might put a question mark in the margin beside the unclear material.

❏ Put brackets around words whose meaning you need to check in a dictionary.

❏ Ask yourself if your initial impression of the selection has changed in any way as a result of this second reading. If your feelings *have* changed, try to determine why you reacted differently on this reading.

STAGE 3: EVALUATE THE SELECTION

Now that you have a good grasp of the selection, you may want to read it a third time, especially if the piece is long or complex. This time, your goal is to make judgments about the essay's effectiveness. Keep in mind, though, that you shouldn't evaluate the selection until after you have a strong hold on it. A negative or even a positive reaction is valid only if it's based on an accurate reading.

At first, you may feel uncomfortable about evaluating the work of a professional writer. But remember: Written material set in type only *seems* perfect; all writing can be fine-tuned. By identifying what does and doesn't work in others' writing, you're taking an important first step toward developing your own power as a writer. You might find it helpful at this point to get together with other students to discuss the selection. Comparing viewpoints often opens up a piece, enabling you to gain a clearer perspective on the selection and the author's approach.

To evaluate the essay, ask yourself the following questions.

☑ EVALUATING A SELECTION: A CHECKLIST

❏ *Where does support for the selection's thesis seem logical and sufficient? Where does support seem weak?* Which of the author's supporting facts, arguments, and examples seem pertinent and convincing? Which don't?

❏ *Is the selection unified? If not, why not?* Where does something in the selection not seem relevant? Where are there any unnecessary digressions or detours?

> ❏ *How does the writer make the selection move smoothly from beginning to end?* How does the writer create an easy flow between ideas? Are any parts of the essay abrupt and jarring? Which ones?
>
> ❏ *Which stylistic devices are used to good effect in the selection?* Which *pattern of development* or combination of patterns does the writer use to develop the piece? Why do you think those patterns were selected? How do paragraph development, sentence structure, and word choice contribute to the piece's overall effect? What *tone* does the writer adopt? Where does the writer use *figures of speech* effectively? (The next chapter and the glossary explain the terms shown here in italics.)
>
> ❏ *How does the selection encourage further thought?* What new perspective on an issue does the writer provide? What ideas has the selection prompted you to explore in an essay of your own?

It takes some work to follow the three-step approach just described, but the selections in *The Longman Reader: Brief Edition* are worth the effort. Bear in mind that none of the selections sprang full-blown from the pen of its author. Rather, each essay is the result of hours of work—hours of thinking, writing, rethinking, and revising. As a reader, you should show the same willingness to work with the selections, to read them carefully and thoughtfully. Henry David Thoreau, an avid reader and prolific writer, emphasized the importance of this kind of attentive reading when he advised that "books must be read as deliberately and unreservedly as they were written."

To illustrate the multi-stage reading process just described, we've annotated the professional essay that follows: "Family Counterculture" by Ellen Goodman. Note that annotations are provided in the margin of the essay as well as at the end of the essay. As you read Goodman's essay, try applying the three-stage sequence. You can measure your ability to dig into the selection by making your own annotations on Goodman's essay and then comparing them to ours. You can also see how well you evaluated the piece by answering the questions in "Evaluating a Selection: A Checklist" and then comparing your responses to ours on pages 9–10.

Ellen Goodman

The recipient of a Pulitzer Prize, Ellen Goodman (1941–) worked for *Newsweek* and the *Detroit Free Press* before joining the staff of the *Boston Globe* in the mid-1970s. A resident of the Boston area, Goodman writes a popular syndicated column that provides insightful commentary on life in the United States. Her pieces have appeared in a number of national publications, including *The Village Voice* and *McCalls*. Collections of her columns have been published in *Close to Home* (1979), *Turning Points* (1979), *At Large* (1981), *Keeping in Touch* (1985), *Making Sense* (1989), and *Value Judgments* (1993). Most recently, she coauthored *I Know Just What You Mean* (1999), a book that examines the complex nature of women's friendships, and *Paper Trail* (2004). The following selection is from *Value Judgments*.

Pre-Reading Journal Entry

Television is often blamed for having a harmful effect on children. Do you think this criticism is merited? In what ways does TV exert a negative influence on children? In what ways does TV exert a positive influence on youngsters? Take a few minutes to respond to these questions in your journal.

Marginal Annotations

Family Counterculture

Interesting take on the term "counterculture"

Time frame established

Light humor; easy, casual tone

Time frame picked up

Thesis, developed overall by cause-effect pattern

First research-based example to support thesis

Sooner or later, most Americans become card-carrying members of the counterculture. This is not an underground holdout of hippies. No beads are required. All you need to join is a child. 1

At some point between Lamaze and the PTA, it becomes clear that one of your main jobs as a parent is to counter the culture. What the media delivers to children by the masses, you are expected to rebut one at a time. 2

The latest evidence of this frustrating piece of the parenting job description came from pediatricians. This summer, the American Academy of Pediatrics called for a ban on television food ads. Their plea was hard on the heels of a study showing that one Saturday morning of TV cartoons contained 202 junk-food ads. 3

The kids see, want, and nag. That is, after all, the theory behind advertising to children, since few six-year-olds have their own trust funds. The end result, said the pediatricians, is obesity and high cholesterol. 4

Their call for a ban was predictably attacked by the   5
grocers' association. But it was also attacked by people
assembled under the umbrella marked "parental responsibility." We don't need bans, said these "PR" people, we

Relevant paragraph?
Identifies Goodman
as a parent, but
interrupts flow

need parents who know how to say "no."

Well, I bow to no one in my capacity for naysaying. I   6
agree that it's a well-honed skill of child raising. By the time
my daughter was seven, she qualified as a media critic.

Transition
doesn't work but
would if ¶6 were
cut

But it occurs to me now that the call for "parental   7
responsibility" is increasing in direct proportion to the irresponsibility of the marketplace. Parents are expected to protect their children from an increasingly hostile environment.

Series of questions
and brief answers
consistent with
overall casual tone

Are the kids being sold junk food? Just say no. Is TV   8
bad? Turn it off. Are there messages about sex, drugs, violence all around? Counter the culture.

Brief real-life
examples support
thesis

Mothers and fathers are expected to screen virtually   9
every aspect of their children's lives. To check the ratings on
the movies, to read the labels on the CDs, to find out if
there's MTV in the house next door. All the while keeping
in touch with school and, in their free time, earning a living.

Fragments

In real life, most parents do a great deal of this mon-   10
itoring and just-say-no-ing. Any trip to the supermarket

More examples

produces at least one scene of a child grabbing for something only to have it returned to the shelf by a frazzled
parent. An extraordinary number of the family arguments
are over the goodies—sneakers, clothes, games—that the
young know only because of ads.

Another weak
transition—no
contrast

But at times it seems that the media have become the   11
mainstream culture in children's lives. Parents have
become the alternative.

Restatement
of thesis

Barbara Dafoe Whitehead, a research associate at the   12
Institute for American Values, found this out in interviews

Second research-
based example to
support thesis

with middle-class parents. "A common complaint I heard
from parents was their sense of being overwhelmed by the
culture. They felt their voice was a lot weaker. And they

Citing an expert
reinforces thesis

felt relatively more helpless than their parents.

Restatement
of thesis

"Parents," she notes, "see themselves in a struggle   13
for the hearts and minds of their own children." It isn't
that they can't say no. It's that there's so much more to
say no to.

Without wallowing in false nostalgia, there has been a   14
fundamental shift. Americans once expected parents to raise
their children in accordance with the dominant cultural

Comparison-contrast pattern—signaled by "once," "Today," "Once," and "Now"

messages. Today they are expected to raise their children in opposition.

Once the chorus of cultural values was full of ministers, teachers, neighbors, leaders. They demanded more conformity, but offered more support. Now the messengers are Ninja Turtles, Madonna, rap groups, and celebrities pushing sneakers. Parents are considered "responsible" only if they are successful in their resistance.   15

Restatement of thesis

It's what makes child raising harder. It's why parents feel more isolated. It's not just that American families have less time with their kids. It's that we have to spend more of this time doing battle with our own culture.   16

Conveys the challenges that parents face

It's rather like trying to get your kids to eat their green beans after they've been told all day about the wonders of Milky Way. Come to think of it, it's exactly like that.   17

Annotations at End of Selection

Thesis: First stated in paragraph 2 (". . . it becomes clear that one of your main jobs as a parent is to counter the culture. What the media delivers to children by the masses, you are expected to rebut one at a time.") and then restated in paragraphs 11 ("the media have become the mainstream culture in children's lives. Parents have become the alternative."); 13 (Parents are frustrated, not because ". . . they can't say no. It's that there's so much more to say no to."); and 16 ("It's not just that American families have less time with their kids. It's that we have to spend more of this time doing battle with our own culture.").

First reading: A quick take on a serious subject. Informal tone and to-the-point style gets to the heart of the media vs. parenting problem. Easy to relate to.

Second and third readings:
1. Uses the findings of the American Academy of Pediatrics, a statement made by Barbara Dafoe Whitehead, and a number of brief examples to illustrate the relentless work parents must do to counter the culture.
2. Uses cause-effect overall to support thesis and comparison-contrast to show how parenting nowadays is more difficult than it used to be.
3. Not everything works (reference to her daughter as a media critic, repetitive and often inappropriate use of "but" as a transition), but overall the essay succeeds.
4. At first, the ending seems weak. But it feels just right after an additional reading. Shows how parents' attempts to counter the culture are as commonplace as their attempts to get kids to eat vegetables. It's an ongoing and constant battle that makes parenting more difficult than it has to be and less enjoyable than it should be.
5. Possible essay topics: A humorous paper about the strategies kids use to get around their parents' saying "no" or a serious paper on the negative effects on kids of another aspect of television culture (cable television, MTV, tabloid-style talk shows, and so on).

The following answers to the questions in "Evaluating a Selection: A Checklist" on pages 4–5 will help crystallize your reaction to Goodman's essay.

1. *Where does support for the selection's thesis seem logical and sufficient? Where does support seem weak?*

   Goodman begins to provide evidence for her thesis when she cites the American Academy of Pediatrics' call for a "ban on television food ads" (paragraphs 3–5). The ban followed a study showing that kids are exposed to 202 junk-food ads during a single Saturday morning of television cartoons. Goodman further buoys her thesis with a list of brief "countering the culture" examples (8–10) and a slightly more detailed example (10) describing the parent-child conflicts that occur on a typical trip to the supermarket. By citing Barbara Dafoe Whitehead's findings later on (12–13), Goodman further reinforces her point that the need for constant rebuttal makes parenting especially frustrating: Because parents have to say "no" to virtually everything, more and more family time ends up being spent "doing battle" with the culture (16).

2. *Is the selection unified? If not, why not?*

   In the first two paragraphs, Goodman identifies the problem and then provides solid evidence of its existence (3–4, 8–10). But Goodman's comments in paragraph 6 about her daughter's skill as a media critic seem distracting. Even so, paragraph 6 serves a purpose because it establishes Goodman's credibility by showing that she, too, is a parent and has been compelled to be a constant naysayer with her child. From paragraph 7 on, the piece stays on course by focusing on the way parents have to compete with the media for control of their children. The concluding paragraphs (16–17) reinforce Goodman's thesis by suggesting that parents' struggle to counteract the media is as common—and as exasperating—as trying to get children to eat their vegetables when all the kids want is to gorge on candy.

3. *How does the writer make the selection move smoothly from beginning to end?*

   The first two paragraphs of Goodman's essay are clearly connected: The phrase "sooner or later" at the beginning of the first paragraph establishes a time frame that is then picked up at the beginning of the second paragraph with the phrase "at some point between Lamaze and the PTA." And Goodman's use in paragraph 3 of the word *this* ("The latest evidence of *this* frustrating piece of the parenting job description . . .") provides a link to the preceding paragraph. Other connecting strategies can be found in the piece. For example, the words *once, Today, Once,* and *Now* in paragraphs 14–15 provide an easy-to-follow contrast between parenting in earlier times and parenting in this era. However, because paragraph 6 contains a distracting aside, the contrast implied by the word *But* at the beginning of paragraph 7 doesn't work. Nor does Goodman's use of the word *But* at the beginning of paragraph 11 work; the point there emphasizes rather than contrasts with the one made in paragraph 10. From this point on, though, the essay is tightly written and moves smoothly along to its conclusion.

4. *Which stylistic devices are used to good effect in the selection?*

   Goodman uses several patterns of development in her essay. The selection as a whole shows the *effect* of the mass media on kids and their parents. In paragraphs 3 and 12, Goodman provides *examples in the form of research data* to support her thesis, while paragraphs 8–10 provide a series of *brief real-life examples*. Paragraphs 12–15 use *contrast*, and paragraph 17 makes a *comparison* to punctuate Goodman's concluding point. Throughout, Goodman's *informal, conversational tone* draws readers in, and her *no-holds-barred style* drives her point home forcefully. In paragraph 8, she uses a *question-and-answer format* ("Are the kids being sold junk food? Just say no.") and *short sentences* ("Turn it off" and "Counter the culture") to illustrate how pervasive the situation is. And in paragraph 9, she uses *fragments* ("To check the ratings . . ." and "All the while keeping in touch with school . . .") to focus attention on the problem. These varied stylistic devices help make the essay a quick, enjoyable read. Finally, although Goodman is concerned about the corrosive effects of the media, she leavens her essay with dashes of *humor*. For example, the image of parents as counterculturists (1) and the comments about green beans and Milky Ways (17) probably elicit smiles or gentle laughter from most readers.

5. *How does the selection encourage further thought?*

Goodman's essay touches on a problem most parents face at some time or another—having to counter the culture in order to protect their children. Her main concern is how difficult it is for parents to say "no" to virtually every aspect of the culture. Although Goodman offers no immediate solutions, her presentation of the issue urges us to decide for ourselves which aspects of the culture should be countered and which should not.

If, for each essay you read in this book, you consider the preceding questions, you'll be able to respond thoughtfully to the *Questions for Close Reading* and *Questions About the Writer's Craft* presented after each selection. Your responses will, in turn, prepare you for the writing assignments that follow the questions. Interesting and varied, the assignments invite you to examine issues raised by the selections and encourage you to experiment with various writing styles and organizational patterns.

Following are some sample questions and writing assignments based on the Goodman essay; all are similar to the sort that appear later in this book. Note that the final writing assignment paves the way for a student essay, the stages of which are illustrated in Chapter 2.

Questions for Close Reading

1. According to Goodman, what does it mean to "counter the culture"? Why is this harder now than ever before?
2. Which two groups, according to Goodman, protested the American Academy of Pediatrics's ban on television food ads? Which of these two groups does she take more seriously? Why?

Questions About the Writer's Craft

1. What audience do you think Goodman had in mind when she wrote this piece? How do you know? Where does she address this audience directly?

2. What word appears four times in paragraph 16? Why do you think Goodman repeats this word so often? What is the effect of this repetition?

Writing Assignments

1. Goodman believes that parents are forced to say "no" to almost everything the media offer. Write an essay illustrating the idea that not everything the media present is bad for children.
2. Goodman implies that, in some ways, today's world is hostile to children. Do you agree? Drawing upon but not limiting yourself to the material in your pre-reading journal, write an essay in which you support or reject this viewpoint.

The benefits of active reading are many. Books in general and the selections in *The Longman Reader: Brief Edition* in particular will bring you face to face with issues that concern all of us. If you study the selections and the questions that follow them, you'll be on the way to discovering ideas for your own papers. Chapter 2, "The Writing Process," offers practical suggestions for turning those ideas into well-organized, thoughtful essays.

2

THE WRITING PROCESS

Not many people retire at age thirty-eight. But Michel Montaigne, a sixteenth-century French attorney, did exactly that. Montaigne retired at a young age because he wanted to read, think, and write about all the subjects that interested him. After spending years getting his ideas down on paper, Montaigne finally published his short prose pieces. He called them *essais*—French for "trials" or "attempts."

In fact, all writing is an attempt to transform ideas into words, thus giving order and meaning to life. By using the term *essais*—or *essays* in English—Montaigne acknowledged that a written piece is never really finished. Of course, writers have to stop at some point, especially if they have deadlines to meet. But, as all experienced writers know, even after they dot the final *i*, cross the final *t*, and say "That's it," there's always something that could have been explored further or expressed a little better.

Because writing is a process, shaky starts and changes in direction aren't uncommon. Although there's no way to eliminate the work needed to write effectively, certain approaches can make the process more manageable and rewarding. This chapter describes a sequence of steps for writing essays. Familiarity with a specific sequence develops your awareness of strategies and choices, making you feel more confident when it comes time to write. You're less likely to look at a blank piece of paper and think, "Help! Now what do I do?" During the sequence, you do the following:

1. Prewrite
2. Identify the thesis
3. Support the thesis with evidence
4. Organize the evidence
5. Write the first draft
6. Revise the essay

We present the sequence as a series of stages, but we urge you not to view it as a rigid formula that must be followed step by unchanging step. Most people develop personalized approaches to the writing process. Some writers mull over a topic in their heads and then move quickly into a promising first draft; others outline their essays in detail before beginning to write. Between these two extremes are any number of effective approaches. The sequence here can be streamlined, juggled around, or otherwise altered to fit individual writing styles as well as the requirements of specific assignments.

STAGE 1: PREWRITE

Prewriting refers to strategies you can use to generate ideas *before* starting the first draft of a paper. Prewriting techniques are like the warm-ups you do before going out to jog—they loosen you up, get you moving, and help you to develop a sense of well-being and confidence. Since prewriting techniques encourage imaginative exploration, they also help you discover what interests you most about your subject. Having such a focus early in the writing process keeps you from plunging into your initial draft without first giving some thought to what you want to say.

Prewriting can help in other ways, too. When we write, we often sabotage our ability to generate material because we continually critique what we put down on paper. During prewriting, you deliberately ignore your internal critic. Your purpose is simply to get ideas down on paper *without evaluating* their effectiveness. Writing without immediately judging what you produce can be liberating. Once you feel less pressure, you'll probably find that you can generate a good deal of material. And that can make your confidence soar.

Keep a Journal

Of all the prewriting techniques, keeping a journal (daily or almost daily) is the one most likely to make writing a part of your life. Some journal entries focus on a single theme; others wander from topic to topic. Your starting point may be a dream, a snippet of overheard conversation, a video on MTV, a political cartoon, an issue raised in class or in your reading—anything that surprises, interests, angers, depresses, confuses, or amuses you. You may also use a journal to experiment with your writing style—say, to vary your sentence structure if you tend to use predictable patterns.

Here is a fairly focused excerpt from a student's journal:

Today I had to show Paul around school. He and Mom got here by 9. I didn't let on that this was the earliest I've gotten up all semester! He got out of the car looking kind of nervous. Maybe he thought his big brother would be different after a couple of months of college. I walked him around part of the campus and then he went with me to Am. Civ. and then to lunch. He met Greg and some other guys. Everyone seemed to like him. He's got a nice, quiet sense of humor. When I went to Bio., I told him that he could walk around on his own since he wasn't crazy about sitting in on a science class. But he said "I'd rather stick with you." Was he flattering me or was he just scared? Anyway it made me feel good. Later when he was leaving, he told me he's definitely going to apply. I guess that'd be kind of nice, having him here. Mom thinks it's great and she's pushing it. I don't know. I feel kind of like it would invade my privacy. I found this school and have made a life for myself here. Let him find his own school! But it could be great having my kid brother here. I guess this is a classic case of what my psych teacher calls ambivalence. Part of me wants him to come, and part of me doesn't! (November 10)

Although some instructors collect students' journals, you needn't be overly concerned with spelling, grammar, sentence structure, or organization. While journal writing is typically more structured than freewriting (see page 22), you don't have to strive for entries that read like mini-essays. In fact, sometimes you may find it helpful to use a simple list (see the journal entry on page 21) when recording your thoughts about a subject. The important thing is to let your journal writing prompt reflection and new insights, providing you with material to draw upon in your writing. It is, then, a good idea to reread each week's entries to identify recurring themes and concerns. Keep a list of these issues at the back of your journal, under a heading like "Possible Essay Subjects." Here, for instance, are a few topics suggested by the preceding journal entry: deciding which college to attend, leaving home, sibling rivalry. Each of these topics could be developed in a full-length essay.

The Pre-Reading Journal.   To reinforce the value of journal writing, we've included a journal assignment before every selection in the book. This assignment, called *Pre-Reading Journal Entry,* "primes" you for the piece by encouraging you to explore—in a tentative fashion—your thoughts about an issue that will be raised in the selection. Here, once again, is the *Pre-Reading Journal Entry* assignment that precedes Ellen Goodman's "Family Counterculture" (page 6):

> Television is often blamed for having a harmful effect on children. Do you think this criticism is merited? In what ways does TV exert a negative influence on children? In what ways does TV exert a positive influence on youngsters? Take a few minutes to respond to these questions in your journal.

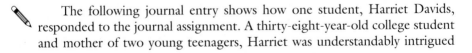

The following journal entry shows how one student, Harriet Davids, responded to the journal assignment. A thirty-eight-year-old college student and mother of two young teenagers, Harriet was understandably intrigued by the assignment. As you'll see, Harriet used a listing strategy to prepare her journal entry. She found that lists were perfect for dealing with the essentially "for or against" nature of the journal assignment.

TV's Negative Influence on Kids	TV's Positive Influence on Kids
Teaches negative behaviors (violence, sex, swearing, drugs, alcohol, etc.)	Teaches important educational concepts (Sesame Street, shows on The Learning Channel, etc.)
Cuts down on imagination and creativity	Exposes kids to new images and worlds (Dora the Explorer, Mister Rogers' Neighborhood)
Cuts down on time spent with parents (talking, reading, playing games together)	Can inspire important discussions (about morals, sexuality, drugs, etc.) between kids and parents
Encourages parents' lack of involvement with kids	Gives parents a needed break from kids
Frightens kids excessively by showing images of real-life violence (terrorist attacks, war, murders, etc.)	Educates kids about the painful realities in the world
Encourages isolation (watching screen rather than interacting with other kids)	Creates common ground among kids, basis of conversations and games
De-emphasizes reading and creates need for constant stimulation	Encourages kids to slow down and read books based on a TV series or show (the Arthur and the Clifford, the Big Red Dog series, The Bookworm Bunch, etc.)
Promotes materialism (commercials)	Can be used by parents to teach kids that they can't have everything they see

The journal assignment and subsequent journal entry do more than prepare you to read a selection with extra care and attention; they also pave the way to a full-length essay. Here's how. The final assignment following each selection is called *Writing Assignment Using a Journal Entry as a Starting Point*. This assignment helps you to translate the raw material in your journal entry into a thoughtful, well-considered essay. By the time you get to the assignment, the rough ideas in your journal entry will have been enriched by your reading of the selection. (For an example of a writing assignment that draws upon material in a pre-reading journal entry, turn to page 83.)

As you've just seen, journal writing can stimulate thinking in a loose, unstructured way; journal writing can also prompt the focused thinking required by a specific writing assignment. When you have a specific piece to write, you should approach prewriting in a purposeful, focused manner. You need to:

- Understand the boundaries of the assignment.
- Determine your purpose, audience, and tone.
- Discover your essay's limited subject.
- Generate raw material about your limited subject.
- Organize the raw material.

We'll discuss each of these steps in turn. But first, here's a practical tip: If you don't use a word processor during the prewriting stage, try using a pencil and scrap paper. They're less intimidating than pen, typewriter, and "official" paper; they also reinforce the notion that prewriting is tentative and exploratory.

Understand the Boundaries of the Assignment

You shouldn't start writing a paper until you know what's expected. First, clarify the *kind of paper* the instructor has in mind. Assume the instructor asks you to discuss the key ideas in an assigned reading. What does the instructor want you to do? Should you include a brief summary of the selection? Should you compare the author's ideas with your own view of the subject? Should you determine if the author's view is supported by valid evidence?

If you're not sure about an assignment, ask your instructor—not the student next to you, who may be as confused as you—to make the requirements clear. Most instructors are more than willing to provide an explanation. They would rather take a few minutes of class time to explain the assignment than spend hours reading dozens of student essays that miss the mark.

Second, find out *how long* the paper is expected to be. Many instructors will indicate the approximate length of the papers they assign. If no length requirements are provided, discuss with the instructor what you plan to cover and indicate how long you think your paper will be. The instructor will either give you the go-ahead or help you refine the direction and scope of your work.

Determine Your Purpose, Audience, and Tone

Once you understand the requirements for a writing assignment, you're ready to begin thinking about the essay. What is its *purpose?* For what *audience* will it be written? What *tone* will you use? Later on, you may modify your decisions about these issues. That's fine. But you need to understand the way these considerations influence your work in the early phases of the writing process.

Purpose.   The papers you write in college are usually meant to *inform* or *explain*, to *convince* or *persuade*, and sometimes to *entertain*. In practice, writing often combines purposes. You might, for example, write an essay trying to *convince* people to support a new trash recycling program in your community. But before you win readers over, you most likely would have to *explain* something about current waste disposal technology.

When purposes blend this way, the predominant one determines the essay's content, organization, emphasis, and choice of words. Assume you're writing about a political campaign. If your primary goal is to *entertain*, to take a gentle poke at two candidates, you might start with several accounts of one candidate's "foot-in-mouth" disease and then describe the attempts of the other candidate, a multimillionaire, to portray himself as an average Joe. Your language, full of exaggeration, would reflect your objective. But if your primary purpose is to *persuade* readers that the candidates are incompetent and shouldn't be elected, you might adopt a serious, straightforward style. Rather than poke fun at one candidate's gaffes, you would use them to illustrate her insensitivity to important issues. Similarly, the other candidate's posturing would be presented, not as foolish pretension, but as evidence of his lack of judgment.

Audience.   To write effectively, you need to identify who your readers are and to take their expectations and needs into account. An essay about the artificial preservatives in the food served by the campus cafeteria would take one form if submitted to your chemistry professor and a very different one if written for the college newspaper. The chemistry paper would probably be formal and technical, complete with chemical formulations and scientific data: "Distillation revealed sodium benzoate particles suspended in a gelatinous medium." But such technical material would be inappropriate in a newspaper column intended for general readers. In this case, you might provide specific examples of cafeteria foods containing additives—"Those deliciously smoky cold cuts are loaded with nitrates and nitrites, both known to cause cancer in laboratory animals"—and suggest ways to eat more healthily: "Pass by the deli counter and fill up instead on vegetarian pizza and fruit juices."

When analyzing your audience, ask yourself the following questions.

☑ ANALYZING YOUR AUDIENCE: A CHECKLIST

❑ What are my readers' age, sex, and educational level?

❑ What are their political, religious, and other beliefs?

❏ What interests and needs motivate my audience?

❏ How much do my readers already know about my subject?

❏ Do they have any misconceptions?

❏ What biases do they have about me, my subject, my opinion?

❏ How do my readers expect me to relate to them?

❏ What values do I share with my readers that will help me communicate with them?

Tone.   Just as your voice may project a range of feelings, your writing can convey one or more *tones,* or emotional states: enthusiasm, anger, resignation, and so on. Tone is integral to meaning; it permeates writing and reflects your attitude toward yourself, your purpose, your subject, and your readers. How do you project tone? You pay close attention to sentence structure and word choice.

Sentence structure refers to the way sentences are shaped. Although the two paragraphs that follow deal with exactly the same subject, note how differences in sentence structure create sharply dissimilar tones:

> During the 1960s, many inner-city minorities considered the police an occupying force and an oppressive agent of control. As a result, violence against police grew in poorer neighborhoods, as did the number of residents killed by police.

> An occupying force. An agent of control. An oppressor. That's how many inner-city minorities in the '60s viewed the police. Violence against police soared. Police killings of residents mounted.

Informative in its approach, the first paragraph projects a neutral, almost dispassionate tone. The sentences are fairly long, and clear transitions ("During the 1960s"; "As a result") mark the progression of thought. But the second paragraph, with its dramatic, almost alarmist tone, seems intended to elicit a strong emotional response; its short sentences, fragments, and abrupt transitions reflect the turbulence of earlier times.

Word choice also plays a role in establishing the tone of an essay. Words have *denotations,* neutral dictionary meanings, as well as *connotations,* emotional associations that go beyond the literal meaning. The word *beach,* for instance, is defined in the dictionary as "a nearly level stretch of pebbles and sand beside a body of water." This definition, however, doesn't capture individual responses to the word. For some, *beach* suggests warmth and relaxation; for others, it calls up images of hospital waste and sewage washed up on a once-clean stretch of shoreline.

Since tone and meaning are tightly bound, you must be sensitive to the emotional nuances of words. In a respectful essay about police officers, you wouldn't refer to *cops, narcs,* or *flatfoots;* such terms convey a contempt inconsistent with the tone intended. Your words must also convey tone clearly. Suppose you're writing a satirical piece criticizing a local beauty pageant. Dubbing the participants "livestock on view" leaves no question about your tone. But if you simply referred to the participants as "attractive young women," readers might be unsure of your attitude. Remember, readers can't read your mind, only your paper.

Discover Your Essay's Limited Subject

Once you have a firm grasp of the assignment's boundaries and have determined your purpose, audience, and tone, you're ready to focus on a limited aspect of the general assignment. Because too broad a subject can result in a diffuse, rambling essay, be sure to restrict your general subject before starting to write.

The following examples show the difference between general subjects that are too broad for an essay and limited subjects that are appropriate and workable. The examples, of course, represent only a few among many possibilities.

General Subject	Less General	Limited
Education	Computers in education	Computers in elementary school arithmetic classes
	High school education	High school electives
Transportation	Low-cost travel	Hitchhiking
	Getting around a metropolitan area	The transit system in a nearby city
Work	Planning for a career	College internships
	Women in the work force	Women's success as managers

How do you move from a general to a narrow subject? Imagine that you're asked to prepare a straightforward, informative essay for your writing class. Reprinted below is writing assignment 2 from page 11. The assignment, prompted by Ellen Goodman's essay "Family Counterculture," is an extension of the journal-writing assignment on page 6.

Goodman implies that, in some ways, today's world is hostile to children. Do you agree? Drawing upon but not limiting yourself to the material in your pre-reading journal, write an essay in which you support or reject this viewpoint.

You might feel unsure about how to proceed. But two techniques can help you limit such a general assignment. Keeping your purpose, audience, and tone in mind, you may *question* or *brainstorm* the general subject. These two techniques have a paradoxical effect. Although they encourage you to roam freely over a subject, they also help restrict the discussion by revealing which aspects of the subject interest you most.

1. Question the general subject.   One way to narrow a subject is to ask a series of *who, how, why, where, when,* and *what* questions. The following example shows how Harriet Davids, the mother of two young teenagers, used this technique to limit the Goodman assignment.

You may recall that, before reading Goodman's essay, Harriet had used her journal to explore TV's effect on children (see page 15). After reading "Family Counterculture," Harriet concluded that she essentially agreed with Goodman; like Goodman, she felt that parents nowadays are indeed forced to raise their kids in an "increasingly hostile environment." She was pleased that the writing assignment gave her an opportunity to expand preliminary ideas she had jotted down in her journal.

Harriet soon realized that she had to narrow the Goodman assignment. She started by asking a number of pointed questions about the general topic. As she proceeded, she was aware that the same questions could have led to different limited subjects—just as other questions would have.

General Subject: We live in a world that is difficult, even hostile to children.

Question	Limited Subject
<u>Where</u> do kids go to escape?	Television, which makes the world seem even more dangerous (violence, sex, etc.). Also malls and the Internet
<u>Who</u> is to blame for the difficult conditions under which children grow up?	Parents' casual attitude toward child-rearing
<u>How</u> have schools contributed to the problems children face?	Not enough counseling programs for kids in distress
<u>Why</u> do children feel frightened?	Divorce
<u>When</u> are children most vulnerable?	The special problems of adolescents
<u>What</u> dangers or fears should parents discuss with their children?	AIDS, drugs, alcohol, war, terrorism

2. Brainstorm the general subject.   Another way to focus on a limited subject is to list quickly everything about the general topic that pops into your mind. Working vertically down the page, jot down brief words, phrases, and abbreviations to capture your free-floating thoughts. Writing in complete sentences will slow you down. Don't try to organize or censor your ideas. Even the most fleeting, random, or seemingly outrageous thoughts can be productive.

Here's an example of the brainstorming that Harriet Davids generated in an effort to gather even more material on the Goodman assignment:

General Subject: We live in a world that is difficult, even hostile to children.

- TV--shows corrupt politicians, casual sex, drugs, alcohol, foul language, violence
- Real-life violence on TV, especially terrorist attacks and war, scares kids--have nightmares!
- Kids babysat by TV
- Not enough guidance from parents
- Kids raise themselves
- Too many divorces
- Parents squabbling over material goods in settlements
- Money too important
- Kids feel unimportant
- Families move a lot
- I moved in fourth grade--hated it
- Rootless feeling
- Nobody graduates from high school in the same district they went to kindergarten in
- Drug abuse all over, in little kids' schools
- Pop music glorifies drugs
- Kids not innocent--know too much
- Single-parent homes
- Day care problems
- Abuse of little kids in day care
- TV coverage of day care abuse frightens kids
- Perfect families on TV make kids feel inadequate

As you can see, questioning and brainstorming suggest many possible limited subjects. To identify especially promising ones, reread your material. What arouses your interest, anger, or curiosity? What themes seem to dominate and cut to the heart of the matter? Star or circle ideas with potential.

After marking the material, write several phrases or sentences summarizing the most promising limited subjects. These, for example, are just a few that emerged from Harriet Davids's questioning and brainstorming for the Goodman assignment:

- TV partly to blame for children having such a hard time
- Relocation stressful to children

- Schools also at fault
- The special problems that parents face raising children today

Harriet decided to write on the last of these limited subjects—the special problems that parents face raising children today. This topic, in turn, is the focus of our discussion in the pages ahead.

Generate Raw Material About Your Limited Subject

When a limited subject strikes you as having possibilities, your next step is to see if you have enough interesting and insightful things to say about the subject to write an effective essay. To find out if you do, you may use any or all of the following techniques.

1. Freewrite on your limited subject. *Freewriting* means jotting down in rough sentences or phrases everything that comes to mind. To capture this continuous stream of thought, write nonstop for ten minutes or more. Don't censor anything; put down whatever pops into your head. Don't reread, edit, or pay attention to organization, spelling, or grammar. If your mind goes blank, repeat words until another thought emerges.

Here is part of the freewriting that Harriet Davids generated about her limited subject, "The special problems that parents face raising children today":

Parents today have tough problems to face. Lots of dangers. Drugs and alcohol for one thing. Also crimes of violence against kids. Parents also have to keep up with cost of living, everything costs more, kids want and expect more. Television? The Internet? Another thing is Playboy, Penthouse. Internet sites featuring sex. Sexy ads on TV, movies deal with sex. Kids grow up too fast, too fast. Drugs. Witness real-life violence on TV, like terrorist attacks. Little kids can't handle knowing too much at an early age. Both parents at work much of the day. Finding good day care a real problem. Lots of latchkey kids. Another problem is getting kids to do homework, lots of other things to do. Especially playing on the computer and going to the mall! When I was young, we did homework after dinner, no excuses accepted by my parents.

2. Brainstorm your limited subject. Let your mind wander freely, as you did when using brainstorming to narrow your subject. This time, though, list every idea, fact, and example that occurs to you about your limited subject. Use brief words and phrases so you don't get bogged down writing full sentences. For now, don't worry whether ideas fit together or whether the points listed make sense.

To gather additional material on her limited subject for the Goodman assignment ("The special problems that parents face raising children today"), Harriet Davids brainstormed the following list:

- Trying to raise kids when both parents work
- Prices of everything outrageous, even when both parents work
- Commercials make kids want <u>more</u> of everything
- Clothes so important
- Day care not always the answer--cases of abuse
- Day care very expensive
- Sex everywhere--TV, movies, magazines
- Sexy clothes on little kids. Absurd!
- Sexual abuse of kids
- Violence on TV, especially images of real-life terrorist attacks--scary for kids!
- Violence against kids when parents abuse drugs
- Acid, "Ecstasy," heroin, AIDS
- Schools have to teach kids about these things
- Schools doing too much--not as good as they used to be
- Not enough homework assigned--kids unprepared
- Distractions from homework--malls, TV, phones, stereos, MTV, Internet, computer games

3. Use group brainstorming.   Brainstorming can also be conducted as a group activity. Thrashing out ideas with other people stretches the imagination, revealing possibilities you may not have considered on your own. Group brainstorming doesn't have to be conducted in a formal classroom situation. You can bounce ideas around with friends and family anywhere— over lunch, at the student center, and so on.

4. Map out the limited subject.   If you're the kind of person who doodles while thinking, you may want to try *mapping,* sometimes called *diagramming* or *clustering.* Like other prewriting techniques, mapping proceeds rapidly and encourages the free flow of ideas. Begin by expressing your limited subject in a crisp phrase and placing it in the center of a blank sheet of paper. As ideas come to you, put them along lines or in boxes or circles around the limited subject. Draw arrows and lines to show the relationships among ideas. Don't stop there, however. Focus on each idea; as subpoints and details come to you, connect them to their source idea, again using boxes, lines, circles, or arrows to clarify how everything relates.

5. Use the patterns of development.   Throughout this book, we show how writers use various patterns of development (narration, process analysis, definition, and so on), singly or in combination, to develop and organize their ideas. Because each pattern has its own distinctive logic, the patterns encourage you, when you prewrite, to think about a subject in different ways, causing insights to surface that might otherwise remain submerged.

The various patterns of development are discussed in detail in Chapters 3–11. At this point, though, you should find the following chart helpful.

It not only summarizes the broad purpose of each pattern but also shows the way each pattern can generate different raw material for the limited subject of Harriet Davids's essay.

Limited Subject: The special problems that parents face raising children today.

Pattern	Purpose	Raw Material
Description	To detail what a person, place, or object is like	Detail the sights and sounds of a glitzy mall that attracts kids
Narration	To relate an event	Recount what happened when neighbors tried to forbid their kids from going to a rock concert
Exemplification	To provide specific instances or examples	Offer examples of family arguments. Can a friend known to use drugs visit? Can a child go to a party where alcohol will be served? Can parents outlaw MTV?
Division-classification	To divide something into parts or to group related things in categories	Identify components of a TV commercial that distorts kids' values Classify the kinds of commercials that make it difficult to teach kids values
Process analysis	To explain how something happens or how something is done	Explain step by step how family life can disintegrate when parents have to work all the time to make ends meet
Comparison-contrast	To point out similarities and/or dissimilarities	Contrast families today with those of a generation ago
Cause-effect	To analyze reasons and consequences	Explain why parents are not around to be with their kids: Industry's failure to provide day care and inflexibility about granting time off for parents with sick kids Explain the consequences of absentee parents: Kids feel unloved; they're undisciplined; they take on adult responsibility too early
Definition	To explain the meaning of a term or concept	What is meant by "tough love"?
Argumentation-persuasion	To win people over to a point of view	Convince parents to work with schools to develop programs that make kids feel safer and more secure

(For more on ways to use the patterns of development in different phases of the writing process, see pages 32–33, 40, and 425–427.)

6. Conduct research.   Depending on your topic, you may find it helpful to visit the library and/or to go online to identify books and articles about your limited subject. (See pages 445–471 for hints on conducting research.) At this point, you don't need to read closely the material you find. Just skim and perhaps take a few brief notes on ideas and points that could be useful.

In researching the Goodman assignment, for instance, Harriet Davids could look under such headings and subheadings as the following:

> Day care
> Drug abuse
> Family
> Parent-child relationship
>> Child abuse
>> Children of divorced parents
>> Children of working mothers
> School and home

Organize the Raw Material

Once you generate the raw material for your limited subject, you're ready to shape your rough, preliminary ideas. Preparing a *scratch outline* or *scratch list* is an effective strategy. On pages 41–44, we talk about the more formal outline you may need later on in the writing process. Here we show how a rough outline or scratch list can impose order on the tentative ideas generated during prewriting.

Reread your exploratory thoughts about the limited subject. Cross out anything not appropriate for your purpose, audience, and tone; add points that didn't originally occur to you. Star or circle compelling items that warrant further development. Then draw arrows between related items, your goal being to group such material under a common heading. Finally, determine what seems to be the best order for those headings.

By giving you a sense of the way your free-form material might fit together, a scratch outline makes the writing process more manageable. You're less likely to feel overwhelmed once you actually start writing because you'll already have some idea about how to shape your material into a meaningful statement. Remember, though, the scratch outline can, and most likely will, be modified along the way.

The following scratch outline shows how Harriet Davids began to shape her brainstorming (page 23) into a more organized format. Note the way she eliminated some items (for example, the points about outrageous prices and about real-life TV violence), added others (for example, the point about video arcades), and grouped the brainstormed items under four main headings, with the appropriate details listed underneath. (If you'd like to see Harriet's more formal outline and her first draft, turn to pages 43–44 and 57–58.)

Limited Subject: The special problems that parents face raising children today.

1. Day care for two-career families
   • Expensive
   • Before-school problems
   • After-school problems

2. Distractions from homework
   • Stereos, televisions, and computers in room at home
   • Places to go--malls, video arcades, fast-food restaurants, rock concerts

3. Sexually explicit materials
   • Magazines and books
   • Television shows
   • Internet
   • MTV
   • Movies
   • Rock posters

4. Life-threatening dangers
   • AIDS
   • Drugs
   • Drinking
   • Violence against children (by sitters, in day care, etc.)

The prewriting strategies just described provide a solid foundation for the next stages of your work. But invention and imaginative exploration don't end when prewriting is completed. As you'll see, remaining open to new ideas is crucial during all phases of the writing process.

Activities: Prewrite

1. Number the items in each set from 1 (*broadest subject*) to 5 (*most limited subject*):

Set A	Set B
Abortion	Business Majors
Controversial social issue	Students' majors
Cutting state abortion funds	College students
Federal funding of abortions	Kinds of students on campus
Social issues	Why many students major in business

2. Which of the following topics are too broad for an essay of two to five type-written pages: soap operas' appeal to college students; day care; trying to

"kick" the junk-food habit; male and female relationships; international terrorism?

X. Use the techniques indicated in parentheses to limit each general topic listed below. Then, identify a specific purpose, audience, and tone for the one limited subject you consider most interesting. Next, with the help of the patterns of development, generate raw material about that limited subject. (You may find it helpful to work with others when developing this material.) Finally, shape your raw material into a scratch outline—crossing out, combining, and adding ideas as needed. (Save your scratch outline so you can work with it further after reading about the next stage in the writing process.)

Friendship (*journal writing*)
Malls (*mapping*)
Leisure (*freewriting*)
Television (*brainstorming*)
Required courses (*group brainstorming*)
Manners (*questioning*)

STAGE 2: IDENTIFY THE THESIS

The process of prewriting—discovering a limited subject and generating ideas about it—prepares you for the next stage in writing an essay: identifying the paper's *thesis,* or controlling idea. Presenting your opinion on a subject, the thesis should focus on an interesting and significant issue, one that engages your energies and merits your consideration. You may think of the thesis as the essay's hub—the central point around which all the other material revolves. Your thesis determines what does and does not belong in the essay. The thesis, especially when it occurs early in an essay, also helps focus the reader on the piece's central point.

Sometimes the thesis emerges early in the prewriting stage, particularly if a special angle on your limited topic sparks your interest or becomes readily apparent. Often, though, you'll need to do some work to determine your thesis. For some topics, you may need to do some library research. For others, the best way to identify a promising thesis is to look through your prewriting and ask yourself questions such as these: "What statement does all this prewriting support? What aspect of the limited subject is covered in most detail? What is the focus of the most provocative material?"

For a look at the process of finding the thesis within prewriting material, glance back at the scratch outline (page 26) that Harriet Davids prepared for the limited subject "The special problems that parents face raising children today." Harriet devised the following thesis to capture the focus of this prewriting: "Being a parent today is much more difficult than it was a generation ago." (The full outline for Harriet's paper appears on pages 43–44; the first draft on pages 57–58; the final draft on pages 65–66.)

Writing an Effective Thesis

What makes a thesis effective? Generally expressed in one or two sentences, a thesis statement often has two parts. One part presents your paper's *limited subject;* the other presents your *point of view,* or *attitude,* about that subject. Here are some examples of the way you might move from general subject to limited subject to thesis statement. In each thesis statement, the limited subject is underlined once and the attitude twice.

General Subject	Limited Subject	Thesis
Education	Computers in elementary school arithmetic classes	Computer programs in arithmetic can individualize instruction more effectively than the average elementary school teacher can.
Transportation	A metropolitan transit system	Although the city's transit system still has problems, it has become safer and more efficient in the last two years.
Work	College internships	College internships provide valuable opportunities to students uncertain about what to do after graduation.
Our anti-child world	Special problems that parents face raising children today	Being a parent today is much more difficult than it was a generation ago.

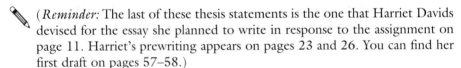

(*Reminder:* The last of these thesis statements is the one that Harriet Davids devised for the essay she planned to write in response to the assignment on page 11. Harriet's prewriting appears on pages 23 and 26. You can find her first draft on pages 57–58.)

Because identifying your thesis statement is an important step in writing a sharply focused essay, you need to avoid three common problems that lead to an ineffective thesis.

Don't make an announcement.   Some writers use the thesis statement merely to announce the limited subject of their paper and forget to indicate their attitude toward the subject. Such statements are announcements of intent, not thesis statements.

Compare the following three announcements with the thesis statements beside them.

Announcements	Thesis Statements
My essay will discuss whether a student pub should exist on campus.	This college should not allow a student pub on campus.
Handgun legislation is the subject of this paper.	Banning handguns is the first step toward controlling crime in the United States.
I want to discuss cable television.	Cable television has not delivered on its promise to provide an alternative to network programming.

Don't make a factual statement.   Your thesis and thus your essay should focus on an issue capable of being developed. If a fact is used as a thesis, you have no place to go; a fact generally doesn't invite much discussion.

Notice the difference between these factual statements and thesis statements:

Factual Statements	Thesis Statements
Many businesses pollute the environment.	Tax penalties should be levied against businesses that pollute the environment.
Nowadays, many movies are violent.	Movie violence provides a healthy outlet for aggression.
The population of the United States is growing older.	The aging of the U.S. population will eventually create a crisis in the delivery of health-care services.

Don't make a broad statement.   Avoid stating your thesis in vague, general, or sweeping terms. Broad statements make it difficult for readers to grasp your essay's point. Moreover, if you start with a broad thesis, you're saddled with the impossible task of trying to develop a book-length idea in an essay that runs only several pages.

The following examples contrast statements that are too broad with thesis statements that are focused effectively.

Broad Statements	Thesis Statements
Nowadays, high school education is often meaningless.	High school diplomas have been devalued by grade inflation.
Newspapers cater to the taste of the American public.	The success of *USA Today* indicates that people want newspapers that are easy to read and entertaining.

Broad Statements	Thesis Statements
The computer revolution is not all that we have been led to believe it is.	Home computers are still an impractical purchase for many people.

You have considerable freedom regarding the placement of the thesis in an essay. The thesis is often stated near the beginning, but it may be delayed, especially if you need to provide background information before it can be understood. Sometimes the thesis is reiterated—with fresh words—in the essay's conclusion or elsewhere. You may even leave the thesis unstated, relying on strong evidence to convey the essay's central idea.

One final point: Once you start writing your first draft, some feelings, thoughts, and examples may emerge that qualify, even contradict, your initial thesis. Don't resist these new ideas; they frequently move you toward a clearer statement of your main point. Remember, though, your essay must have a thesis. Without this central concept, you have no reason for writing.

Activities: Identify the Thesis

1. For the following limited subject, four possible thesis statements are given. Indicate whether each is an announcement (*A*), a factual statement (*FS*), too broad a statement (*TB*), or an effective thesis (*OK*). Then, for the effective thesis, identify a possible purpose, audience, and tone.

   Limited Subject: The ethics of treating severely handicapped infants

   Some babies born with severe handicaps have been allowed to die.

   There are many serious issues involved in the treatment of handicapped newborns.

   The government should pass legislation requiring medical treatment for handicapped newborns.

   This essay will analyze the controversy surrounding the treatment of severely handicapped babies who would die without medical care.

2. Below you'll find listed the key points in an essay. Using the information provided, prepare a possible thesis for the essay.

   - We do not know how engineering new forms of life might affect the earth's delicate ecological balance.
   - Another danger of genetic research is its potential for unleashing new forms of disease.
   - Even beneficial attempts to eliminate genetic defects could contribute to the dangerous idea that only perfect individuals are entitled to live.

3. Following are four pairs of general and limited subjects. Generate an appropriate thesis statement for each pair. Select one thesis, and determine which pattern of development would support it most effectively. Use that pattern to

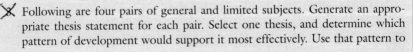

draft a paragraph developing the thesis. (Save the paragraph so you can work with it further after reading about the next stage in the writing process.)

General Subject	Limited Subject
Psychology	The power struggles in a classroom
Health	Doctors' attitudes toward patients
U.S. politics	Television's coverage of presidential campaigns
Work	Minimum-wage jobs for young people

Return to the scratch outline you prepared for activity 3 on page 27. After examining the outline, identify a thesis that conveys the central idea behind most of the raw material. Then, ask others to evaluate your thesis in light of the material in the outline. Finally, keeping the thesis—as well as your purpose, audience, and tone—in mind, refine the scratch outline by deleting inappropriate items, adding relevant ones, and indicating where more material is needed. (Save your refined scratch outline and thesis so you can work with them further after reading about the next stage in the writing process.)

STAGE 3: SUPPORT THE THESIS WITH EVIDENCE

After identifying a preliminary thesis, you should develop the evidence needed to support the central idea. Such supporting material grounds your essay, showing readers you have good reason for feeling as you do about your subject. Your evidence also adds interest and color to your writing. In college essays of five hundred to fifteen hundred words, you usually need at least three major points of evidence to develop your thesis. These major points—each focusing on related but separate aspects of the thesis—eventually become the supporting paragraphs in the body of the essay.

What Is Evidence?

By *evidence*, we mean a number of different kinds of support. *Examples* are just one option. To develop your thesis, you might also include *reasons, facts, details, statistics, anecdotes,* and *quotations from experts.* Imagine you're writing an essay with the thesis "People normally unconcerned about the environment can be galvanized to constructive action if they feel personally affected by an environmental problem." You could support this thesis with any combination of the following types of evidence:

- *Examples* of successful recycling efforts in several neighborhoods.
- *Reasons* why people got involved in a neighborhood recycling effort.
- *Facts* about other residents' efforts to preserve the quality of their well water.

- *Details* about the steps that people can take to get involved in environmental issues.
- *Statistics* showing the number of Americans concerned about the environment.
- An *anecdote* about your involvement in environmental efforts.
- A *quotation* from a well-known scientist about the impact that citizens can have on environmental legislation.

Where Do You Find Evidence?

Where do you find the examples, anecdotes, details, and other types of evidence needed to support your thesis? As you saw when you followed Harriet Davids's strategies for gathering material for an essay (pages 22–25), a good deal of evidence is generated during the prewriting stage. In this phase of the writing process, you tap into your personal experiences, draw upon other people's observations, perhaps interview a person with special knowledge about your subject. The library, with its abundant material, is another rich source of supporting evidence. In addition, the various patterns of development are a valuable source of evidence.

How the Patterns of Development Help Generate Evidence

On pages 23–24, we discussed the way patterns of development help generate material about a limited subject. The same patterns also help develop support for a thesis. The following chart shows how they generate evidence for this thesis: "To those who haven't done it, babysitting looks easy. In practice, though, babysitting can be difficult, frightening, even dangerous."

Pattern	Evidence Generated
Description	Details about a child who, while being babysat, was badly hurt
Narration	Story about the time a friend babysat an ill child whose condition was worsened by the babysitter's actions
Exemplification	Examples of potential babysitting problems: an infant rolls off a changing table; a toddler sticks objects in an electric outlet; a school-age child is bitten by a neighborhood dog
Division-classification	A typical babysitting evening divided into stages: playing with the kids; putting them to bed; dealing with their nighttime fears once they're in bed
	Classify kids' nighttime fears: of monsters under their beds; of bad dreams; of being abandoned by their parents

Process analysis	Step-by-step account of what a babysitter should do if a child becomes ill or injured
Comparison-contrast	Contrast between two babysitters: one well-prepared, the other unprepared
Cause-effect	Why children have temper tantrums; the effect of such tantrums on an unskilled babysitter
Definition	What is meant by a *skilled* babysitter?
Argumentation-persuasion	A proposal for a babysitting training program

(For more on ways to use the patterns of development in different phases of the writing process, see pages 23–24, 40, and 425–427.)

Characteristics of Evidence

No matter how it is generated, all types of supporting evidence share the characteristics described in the following sections. You should keep these characteristics in mind as you review your thesis and scratch outline. That way, you can make the changes needed to strengthen the evidence gathered earlier. As you'll see shortly, Harriet Davids focused on many of these issues as she worked with the evidence she collected during the prewriting phase.

The evidence is relevant and unified.   All the evidence in an essay must clearly support the thesis. It makes no difference how riveting material might be; if it doesn't *relate directly* to the essay's central point, the material should be eliminated. Irrelevant material can weaken your position by implying that no relevant support exists. It also distracts readers from your controlling idea, thus disrupting the paper's overall unity.

The following paragraph, taken from an essay illustrating recent changes in Americans' television-viewing habits, demonstrates the importance of unified evidence. The paragraph focuses on people's reasons for switching from network to cable television. As you'll see, the paragraph lacks unity because it contains points (underlined) unrelated to its main idea. Specifically, the comments about cable's foul language should be deleted. Although these observations bring up interesting points, they shift the paragraph's focus. If the writer wants to present a balanced view of the pros and cons of cable and network television, these points *should* be covered, but in *another paragraph*.

Nonunified Support

Many people consider cable TV an improvement over network television. For one thing, viewers usually prefer the movies on cable. Unlike network films, cable movies are often only months old, they have not been edited by censors, and they are not interrupted by commercials. Growing numbers of people also feel that cable specials are superior to the ones the networks grind out. Cable viewers may enjoy such pop stars as Billy Joel, Mariah Carey, or Chris Rock in concert, whereas the networks continue to broadcast tired variety shows and boring awards ceremonies. <u>There is, however, one problem with cable comedians.</u> <u>The foul language many of them use makes it hard to watch these cable specials</u> <u>with children. The networks, in contrast, generally present "clean" shows that</u> <u>parents and children can watch together.</u> Then, too, cable TV offers viewers more flexibility since it schedules shows at various times over the month. People working night shifts or attending evening classes can see movies in the afternoon, and viewers missing the first twenty minutes of a show can always catch them later. It's not surprising that cable viewership is growing while network ratings have taken a plunge.

Early in the writing process, Harriet Davids was aware of the importance of relevant evidence. Take a moment to compare Harriet's brainstorming (pages 21 and 23) and her scratch outline (page 26). Even though Harriet hadn't identified her thesis when she prepared the scratch outline, she realized she should delete a number of items on the reshaped version of her brainstorming—for example, the second item and third-to-last item ("prices of everything outrageous" and "schools doing too much"). Harriet eliminated these points because they weren't consistent with the focus of her limited subject.

The evidence is specific.   When evidence is vague and general, readers lose interest in what you're saying, become skeptical of your ideas' validity, and feel puzzled about your meaning. In contrast, *specific, concrete evidence* provides sharp *word pictures* that engage your readers, persuade them that your thinking is sound, and clarify meaning.

Consider, for example, the differences between the following two sentences: "The young man had trouble lifting the box out of an old car" and "Joe, only twenty years old but more than fifty pounds overweight, struggled to lift the heavy wooden crate out of the rusty, dented Chevrolet." The first sentence, filled with generalities, is fuzzy and imprecise while the second sentence, filled with specifics, is crisp and clear.

As the preceding sentences illustrate, three strategies can be used, singly or in combination, to make writing specific. First, you can provide answers to *who, which, what,* and similar *questions.* (The question "How does the car look?" prompts a change in which "an old car" becomes "a rusty, dented Chevrolet.") Second, you can use *vigorous verbs* ("had trouble lifting" becomes "struggled to lift"). Finally, you can replace *vague, abstract* nouns with *vivid, concrete* nouns or phrases ("the young man" becomes "Joe, only twenty years old but more than fifty pounds overweight").

Following are two versions of a paragraph from an essay about trends in the business community. Although both paragraphs focus on one such trend—flexible working hours—note how the first version's bland language fails to engage the reader and how its vague generalities leave the meaning unclear. What, for example, is meant by the term "flex-time scheduling"? The second paragraph answers this question (as well as several others) with clear specifics; it also uses strong, energetic language. As a result, the second paragraph is more informative and more interesting than the first.

Nonspecific Support

More and more companies have begun to realize that flex-time scheduling offers advantages. Several companies outside Boston have tried flex-time scheduling and are pleased with the way the system reduces the difficulties their employees face getting to work. Studies show that flex-time scheduling also increases productivity, reduces on-the-job conflict, and minimizes work-related accidents.

Specific Support

More and more companies have begun to realize that flex-time scheduling offers advantages over a rigid 9-to-5 routine. Along suburban Boston's Route 128, such companies as Compugraphics and Consolidated Paper now permit employees to schedule their arrival any time between 6 A.M. and 11 A.M. The corporations report that the number of rush-hour jams and accidents has fallen dramatically. As a result, employees no longer arrive at work weighed down by tension induced by choking clouds of exhaust fumes and the blaring horns of gridlocked drivers. Studies sponsored by the journal Business Quarterly show that this more mellow state of mind benefits corporations. Traffic-stressed employees begin their workday anxious and exasperated, still grinding their teeth at their fellow commuters, their frustration often spilling over into their performance at work. By contrast, stress-free employees work more productively and take fewer days off. They are more tolerant of coworkers and customers, and less likely to balloon minor irritations into major confrontations. Perhaps most importantly, employees arriving at work relatively free of stress can focus their attention on working safely. They rack up significantly fewer on-the-job accidents, such as falls and injuries resulting from careless handling of dangerous equipment. Flex-time improves employee well-being, and as well-being rises, so do company profits.

At this point, it will be helpful to compare once again Harriet Davids's brainstorming (page 21 and 23) and her scratch outline (page 26). Note the way she added new details to make her brainstorming more specific. For example, to the item "Distractions from homework," she added the new examples "video arcades," "fast-food restaurants," and "rock concerts." And, as you'll see when you read Harriet's first and final drafts (pages 57–58 and 65–66), she added many more vigorous specifics during later stages of the writing process.

The evidence is adequate.   Readers won't automatically accept your thesis; you need to provide *enough specific evidence* to support your viewpoint. On occasion, a single extended example will suffice. Generally, though, you'll need various kinds of evidence: facts, examples, reasons, personal observations, expert opinion, and so on.

Following are two versions of a paragraph from a paper showing how difficult it is to get personal, attentive service nowadays at gas stations, supermarkets, and department stores. Both paragraphs focus on the problem at gas stations, but one paragraph is much more effective. As you'll see, the first paragraph starts with good, specific support, yet fails to provide enough of it. The second paragraph offers additional examples, descriptive details, and dialogue—all of which make the writing stronger and more convincing.

Inadequate Support

Gas stations are a good example of this impersonal attitude. At many stations, attendants have even stopped pumping gas. Motorists pull up to a combination convenience store and gas island where an attendant is enclosed in a glass booth with a tray for taking money. The driver must get out of the car, pump the gas, and walk over to the booth to pay. That's a real inconvenience, especially when compared with the way service stations used to be run.

Adequate Support

Gas stations are a good example of this impersonal attitude. At many stations, attendants have even stopped pumping gas. Motorists pull up to a combination convenience store and gas island where an attendant is enclosed in a glass booth with a tray for taking money. The driver must get out of the car, pump the gas, and walk over to the booth to pay. Even at stations that still have "pump jockeys," employees seldom ask, "Check your oil?" or wash windshields, although they may grudgingly point out the location of the bucket and squeegee. And customers with a balky engine or a nonfunctioning heater are usually out of luck. Why? Many gas stations have eliminated on-duty mechanics. The skillful mechanic who could replace a belt or fix a tire in a few minutes has been replaced by a teenager in a jumpsuit who doesn't know a carburetor from a charge card and couldn't care less.

Now take a final look at Harriet Davids's scratch outline (page 26). You'll see that Harriet realized she needed more than one block of supporting material to develop her limited subject; that's why she identified four separate blocks of evidence (day care, homework distractions, sexual material, and dangers). When Harriet prepared her first and final drafts (pages 57–58 and 65–66), she decided to eliminate the material about day care. But she added so many more specific and dramatic details that her evidence was more than sufficient.

The evidence is accurate.   When you have a strong belief and want readers to see things your way, you may be tempted to overstate or downplay facts, disregard information, misquote, or make up details. Suppose you plan to write an essay making the point that dormitory security is lax. You begin supporting your thesis by narrating the time you were nearly mugged in your dorm hallway. Realizing the essay would be more persuasive if you also mentioned other episodes, you decide to invent some material. Perhaps you describe several supposed burglaries on your dorm floor or exaggerate the amount of time it took campus security to respond to an emergency call from a residence hall. Yes, you've supported your point—but at the expense of truth.

The evidence is representative.   Using representative evidence means that you rely on the typical, the usual, to show that your point is valid. Contrary to the maxim, exceptions don't prove the rule. Perhaps you plan to write an essay contending that the value of seat belts has been exaggerated. To support your position, you mention a friend who survived a head-on collision without wearing a seat belt. Such an example isn't representative because the facts and figures on accidents suggest your friend's survival was a fluke.

Borrowed evidence is documented.   If you include evidence from outside sources (books, articles, interviews), you need to acknowledge where that information comes from. If you don't, readers may consider your evidence nothing more than your point of view, or they may regard as dishonest your failure to cite your indebtedness to others for ideas that obviously aren't your own.

For help in documenting sources in brief, informal papers, turn to page 358. For information on acknowledging sources in longer, more formal papers, refer to Appendix A (pages 445–471).

Strong supporting evidence is at the heart of effective writing. Without it, essays lack energy and fail to convey the writer's perspective. Such lifeless writing is more apt to put readers to sleep than to engage their interest and convince them that the points being made are valid. Taking the time to accumulate solid supporting material is, then, a critical step in the writing process.

Activities: Support the Thesis With Evidence

X Below you'll find listed a thesis statement and four points of support. Identify the one point that is off target.

> *Thesis:* The United States is becoming a homogenized country.
>
> Regional accents vanishing
> Chain stores blanket country
> Americans proud of their ethnic identities
> Metropolitan areas almost indistinguishable from one another

X For each of the following thesis statements, develop three points of relevant support. Then use the patterns of development to generate evidence for each point of support.

Thesis: The trend toward disposable, throwaway products has gone too far.

Thesis: The local (or college) library fails to meet the needs of those it is supposed to serve.

Thesis: Television portrays men as incompetent creatures.

3. Choose one of the following thesis statements. Then identify an appropriate purpose, audience, and tone for an essay with this thesis. Using freewriting, mapping, or the questioning technique, generate at least three supporting points for the thesis. Last, using the appropriate pattern of development, write a paragraph about one of the points, making sure your evidence reflects the characteristics discussed in these pages. Alternatively, you may go ahead and prepare the first draft of an essay having the selected thesis. (If you choose the second option, you may want to turn to page 57 to see a diagram showing how to organize a first draft.) Save whatever you prepare so you can work with it further after reading about the next stage in the writing process.

- Teenagers should (or should not) be able to obtain birth-control devices without their parents' permission.
- Winning the lottery may not always be a blessing.
- All of us can take steps to reduce the country's trash crisis.
- Drug education programs in public schools are (or are not) effective.

4. Retrieve the paragraph you wrote in response to activity 3 on page 31. Keeping in mind the characteristics of effective evidence discussed in pages 32–37, make whatever changes are needed to strengthen the paragraph. (Save the paragraph so you can work with it further after reading about the next stage in the writing process.)

5. Look at the thesis and refined scratch outline you prepared in response to activity 4 on page 31. Where do you see gaps in the support for your thesis? By brainstorming with others, generate material to fill these gaps. If some of the new points generated suggest that you should modify your thesis, make the appropriate changes now. (Save this material so you can work with it further after reading about the next stage in the writing process.)

STAGE 4: ORGANIZE THE EVIDENCE

After you've generated supporting evidence, you're ready to *organize* that material. Even highly compelling evidence won't illustrate the validity of your thesis or achieve your purpose if readers have to plow through a maze of chaotic evidence. Some writers can move quickly from generating support to writing a clearly structured first draft. (They usually say they have sequenced their ideas in their heads.) Most, however, need to spend some time sorting out their thoughts on paper before starting the first draft; otherwise, they tend to lose their way in a tangle of ideas.

When moving to the organizing stage, you should have in front of you your scratch outline (see pages 25–26) and thesis plus any supporting material you've accumulated since you did your prewriting. To find a logical framework for all this material, you'll need to (1) determine which pattern of development is implied in your evidence, (2) select one of four basic approaches for organizing your evidence, and (3) outline your evidence. These issues are discussed in the pages ahead.

Use the Patterns of Development

As you saw on pages 23–25 and 32–33, the patterns of development (definition, narration, process analysis, and others) can help you develop prewriting material and generate evidence for a thesis. In the organizing stage, the patterns provide frameworks for presenting evidence in an orderly, accessible way. Here's how.

Each pattern of development has its own internal logic that makes it appropriate for some writing purposes but not for others. (You may find it helpful at this point to turn to pages 23–25 so you can review the broad purpose of each pattern.) Once you see which pattern (or combination of patterns) is implied by your purpose, you can block out your paper's general structure. Imagine that you're writing an essay *explaining why* some students drop out of college during the first semester. You might organize the essay around a three-part discussion of the key *causes* contributing to the difficulty that students have adjusting to college: (1) they miss friends and family, (2) they take inappropriate courses, and (3) they experience conflicts with roommates. As you can see, your choice of pattern of development significantly influences your essay's content and organization.

Some essays follow a single pattern, but most blend them, with a predominant pattern providing the piece's organizational framework. In our example essay, you might include a brief *description* of an overwhelmed first-year college student; you might *define* the psychological term "separation anxiety"; you might end the paper by briefly explaining a *process* for making students' adjustment to college easier. Still, the essay's overall organizational pattern would be *cause-effect* since the paper's primary purpose is to explain why students drop out of college. (For more information on the way patterns often blend in writing, see Chapter 12, "Combining the Patterns.")

Although writers often combine the patterns of development, your composition instructor may ask you to write an essay organized according to a single pattern. Such an assignment helps you understand a particular pattern's unique demands. Keep in mind, though, that most writing begins not with a specific pattern but with a specific *purpose*. The pattern or combination of patterns used to develop and organize an essay evolves out of that purpose.

Select an Organizational Approach

No matter which pattern(s) of development you select, you need to know four general approaches for organizing supporting evidence. These are explained below.

Chronological approach.   When an essay is organized *chronologically,* supporting material is arranged in a clear time sequence, usually starting with what happened first and ending with what happened last. Occasionally, chronological sequences can be rearranged to create flashback or flashforward effects, two techniques discussed in Chapter 4 on narration. Essays using narration (for example, an experience with prejudice) or process analysis (for instance, how to deliver an effective speech) are most likely to be organized chronologically. The paper on public speaking might use a time sequence to present its points: how to prepare a few days before the presentation is due; what to do right before the speech; what to concentrate on during the speech itself. (For examples of chronologically arranged student essays, turn to pages 113 and 225.)

Spatial approach.   When you arrange supporting evidence *spatially,* you discuss details as they occur in space, or from certain locations. This strategy is particularly appropriate for description. Imagine that you plan to write an essay describing the joyous times you spent as a child playing by a towering old oak tree in the neighborhood park. Using spatial organization, you start by describing the rich animal life (the plump earthworms, swarming anthills, and numerous animal tracks) you observed while hunkered down *at the base* of the tree. Next, you recreate the contented feeling you experienced sitting on a branch *in the middle* of the tree. Finally, you end by describing the glorious view of the world you had *from the top* of the tree.

Although spatial arrangement is flexible (you could, for instance, start with a description from the top of the tree), you should always proceed systematically. And once you select a particular spatial order, you should usually maintain that sequence throughout the essay; otherwise, readers may get lost along the way. (A spatially arranged student essay appears on page 77.)

Emphatic approach.   In *emphatic* order, the most compelling evidence is saved for last. This arrangement is based on the psychological principle that people remember best what they experience last. Emphatic order has built-in momentum because it starts with the least important point and builds to the most significant. This method is especially effective in argumentation-persuasion essays, in papers developed through examples, and in pieces involving comparison-contrast, division-classification, or causal analysis.

Consider an essay analyzing the negative effect that workaholic parents can have on their children. The paper might start with a brief discussion of relatively minor effects such as the family's eating mostly frozen or takeout foods. Paragraphs on more serious effects might follow: children get no parental help with homework; they try to resolve personal problems without parental advice. Finally, the essay might close with a detailed discussion of the most significant effect—children's lack of self-esteem because they feel unimportant in their parents' lives. (The student essays on pages 146, 260, and 325 all use an emphatic arrangement.)

Simple-to-complex approach.   A final way to organize an essay is to proceed from relatively *simple* concepts to more *complex* ones. By starting with easy-to-grasp, generally accepted evidence, you establish rapport with your readers and assure them that the essay is firmly grounded in shared experience. In contrast, if you open with difficult or highly technical material, you risk confusing and alienating your audience.

Assume you plan to write a paper arguing that your college has endangered students' health by not making an all-out effort to remove asbestos from dormitories and classroom buildings. It probably wouldn't be a good idea to begin with a medically sophisticated explanation of precisely how asbestos damages lung tissue. Instead, you might start with an observation that is likely to be familiar to your readers—one that is part of their everyday experience. You could, for example, open with a description of asbestos—as readers might see it—wrapped around air ducts and furnaces or used as electrical insulation and fireproofing material. Having provided a basic, easy-to-visualize description, you could then go on to explain the complicated process by which asbestos can cause chronic lung inflammation. (See page 292 for an example of a student essay using the simple-to-complex arrangement.)

Depending on your purpose, any one of these four organizational approaches might be appropriate. For example, assume that you planned to write an essay developing Harriet Davids's thesis: "Being a parent today is much more difficult than it was a generation ago." To emphasize that the various stages in children's lives present parents with different difficulties, you'd probably select a *chronological* sequence. To show that the challenges that parents face vary depending on whether children are at home, at school, or in the world at large, you'd probably choose a *spatial* sequence. To stress the range of problems that parents face (from less to more serious), you'd probably use an *emphatic* sequence. To illustrate today's confusing array of theories for raising children, you might take a *simple-to-complex* approach, moving from the basic to the most sophisticated theories.

Prepare an Outline

Do you, if asked to submit an outline, prepare it *after* you've written the essay? If you do, we hope to convince you that having an outline—a skeletal version of your paper—*before* you begin the first draft makes the writing process much more manageable. The outline helps you organize your thoughts beforehand, and it guides your writing as you work on the draft. Even though ideas continue to evolve during the draft, an outline clarifies how ideas fit together, which points are major, which should come first, and so on. An outline may also reveal places where evidence is weak, underscoring the need, perhaps, for more prewriting.

Like previous stages in the writing process, outlining is individualized. Some people prepare highly structured outlines; others make only a few informal jottings. Sometimes outlining will go quickly, with points falling easily into place; at other times you'll have to work hard to figure out how points are related. If that happens, be glad you caught the problem while outlining rather than while writing the first draft.

To prepare an effective outline, you should reread and evaluate your scratch outline and thesis as well as any other evidence you've generated since the prewriting stage. Then decide which pattern of development (description, cause-effect, and so on) seems to be suggested by your evidence. Also determine whether your evidence lends itself to a chronological, a spatial, an emphatic, or a simple-to-complex order. Having done all that, you're ready to identify and sequence your main and supporting points.

The amount of detail in an outline will vary according to the paper's length and the instructor's requirements. A scratch outline (like the one on page 26) is often sufficient, but for longer papers, you'll probably need a more detailed and formal outline. In such cases, the suggestions in the accompanying checklist will help you develop a sound plan. Feel free to modify these guidelines to suit your needs.

☑ OUTLINING: A CHECKLIST

- ❑ Write your purpose, audience, tone, and thesis at the top of the outlining page.
- ❑ Below the thesis, enter the pattern of development that seems to be implied by the evidence you've accumulated.
- ❑ Also record which of the four organizational approaches would be most effective in sequencing your evidence.
- ❑ Reevaluate your supporting material. Delete anything that doesn't develop the thesis or that isn't appropriate for your purpose, audience, and tone.
- ❑ Add any new points or material. Group related items together. Give each group a heading that represents a main topic in support of your thesis.
- ❑ Label these main topics with Roman numerals (I, II, III, and so on). Let the order of the numerals indicate the best sequence.

❑ Identify subtopics and group them under the appropriate main topics. Indent and label these subtopics with capital letters (A, B, C, and so on). Let the order of the letters indicate the best sequence.

❑ Identify supporting points (often, reasons and examples) and group them under the appropriate subtopics. Indent and label these supporting points with Arabic numbers (1, 2, 3, and so on). Let the numbers indicate the best sequence.

❑ Identify specific details (secondary examples, facts, statistics, expert opinions, quotations) and group them under the appropriate supporting points. Indent and label these specific details with lowercase letters (a, b, c, and so on). Let the letters indicate the best sequence.

❑ Examine your outline, looking for places where evidence is weak. Where appropriate, add new evidence.

❑ Double-check that all main topics, subtopics, supporting points, and specific details develop some aspect of the thesis. Also confirm that all items are arranged in the most logical order.

The sample outline that follows develops the thesis "Being a parent today is much more difficult than it was a generation ago." You may remember that this is the thesis that Harriet Davids devised for the essay she planned to write in response to the assignment on page 11. Harriet's scratch list appears on page 26. When you compare Harriet's scratch list and outline, you'll find some differences. On the whole, the outline contains more specifics, but it doesn't include all the material in the scratch list. For example, after reconsidering her purpose, audience, tone, and thesis, Harriet decided to omit from her outline the section on day care and the points about rock concerts, MTV, rock posters, and AIDS.

The plan shown below is called a *topic outline* because it uses phrases, or topics, for each entry. For a lengthier or more complex paper, a *sentence outline* would be more appropriate.

Purpose: To inform

Audience: Instructor as well as class members, most of whom are 18–20 years old

Tone: Serious and straightforward

Thesis: Being a parent today is much more difficult than it was a generation ago.

Pattern of development: Exemplification

Organizational approach: Emphatic order

  I. Distractions from homework
    A. At home

     1. Stereos, radios, tapes
     2. Television--esp. on MTV
     3. Computers--Internet
  B. Outside home
     1. Malls
     2. Video arcades
     3. Fast-food restaurants

II. Sexually explicit materials
  A. In print
     1. Sex magazines
       a. Playboy
       b. Penthouse
     2. Pornographic books
  B. In movies
     1. Seduction scenes
     2. Casual sex
  C. On television
     1. Soap operas
     2. R-rated comedians
     3. R-rated movies on cable
  D. Internet
     1. Easy-to-access adult chat rooms
     2. Easy-to-access pornographic websites

III. Increased dangers
  A. Drugs--peer pressure
  B. Alcohol--peer pressure
  C. Violent crimes against children

(If you'd like to see the first draft that resulted from Harriet's outline, turn to pages 58–59. Hints for moving from an outline to a first draft appear on page 46.)

Before starting to write your first draft, show your outline to several people (your instructor, friends, classmates). Their reactions will indicate whether your proposed organization is appropriate for your thesis, purpose, audience, and tone. Their comments can also highlight areas needing additional work. After making whatever changes are needed, you're in a good position to go ahead and write the first draft of your essay.

Activities: Organize the Evidence

1. The thesis statement below is followed by a scrambled list of supporting points. Prepare an outline for a potential essay, making sure to distinguish between major and secondary points.

Thesis: Our schools, now in crisis, could be improved in several ways.

Certification requirements for teachers
Schedules
Teachers
Longer school year
Merit pay for outstanding teachers
Curriculum
Better textbooks for classroom use
Longer school days
More challenging content in courses

2. Assume you plan to write an essay based on the following brief outline, which consists of a thesis and several points of support. Determine which pattern of development (page 39) you would probably use for the essay's overall framework. Also identify which organizational approach (pages 39–41) you would most likely adopt to sequence the points of support listed. Then, use one or more patterns of development to generate material to support those points. Having done that, review the material generated, deleting, adding, combining, and arranging ideas in logical order. Finally, make an outline for the body of the essay. (Save your outline so you can work with it further after reading about the next stage in the writing process.)

Thesis: Friends of the opposite sex fall into one of several categories: the pal, the confidant, or the pest.

- Frequently, an opposite-sex friend is simply a "pal."
- Sometimes, though, a pal turns, step by step, into a confidant.
- If a confidant begins to have romantic thoughts, he or she may become a pest, thus disrupting the friendship.

3. Retrieve the writing you prepared in response to activity 3 or 4 on pages 37–38. As needed, reshape that material, applying the organizational principles discussed in these pages. Be sure, for example, that you select the approach (chronological, spatial, emphatic, or simple-to-complex) that would be most appropriate, given your main idea, purpose, audience, and tone. (Save whatever you prepare so you can work with it further after reading about the next stage in the writing process.)

4. Look again at the thesis and scratch outline you refined and elaborated in response to activity 5 on page 38. Reevaluate this material by deleting, adding, combining, and rearranging ideas as needed. Also, keeping your purpose, audience, and tone in mind, consider whether a chronological, a spatial, an emphatic, or a simple-to-complex approach will be most appropriate. Now prepare an outline of your ideas. Finally, ask at least one person to evaluate your organizational plan. (Save your outline. After reading about the next stage in the writing process, you can use it to write the essay's first draft.)

STAGE 5: WRITE THE FIRST DRAFT

After prewriting, deciding on a thesis, and developing and organizing evidence, you're ready to write a *first draft*—a rough, provisional version of your essay. Because of your work in the preceding stages, the first draft may flow quite smoothly. But don't be discouraged if it doesn't. You may find that your thesis has to be reshaped, that a point no longer fits, that you need to return to a prewriting activity to generate additional material. Such stopping and starting is to be expected. Writing the first draft is a process of discovery, involving the continual clarification and refining of ideas.

How to Proceed

There's no single right way to prepare a first draft. Some writers rely heavily on their scratch lists or outlines; others glance at them only occasionally. Some people write the first draft in longhand; others use a typewriter or a computer.

However you choose to proceed, consider the suggestions in the following checklist when moving from an outline or scratch list to a first draft.

☑ TURNING OUTLINE INTO FIRST DRAFT: A CHECKLIST

❑ Make the outline's *main topics* (I, II, III) the *topic sentences* of the essay's supporting paragraphs. (Topic sentences are discussed later on page 48.)

❑ Make the outline's *subtopics* (A, B, C) the *subpoints* in each paragraph.

❑ Make the outline's *supporting points* (1, 2, 3) the key *examples* and *reasons* in each paragraph.

❑ Make the outline's *specific details* (a, b, c) the *secondary examples, facts, statistics, expert opinions,* and *quotations* in each paragraph.

(To see how one student, Harriet Davids, moved from outline to first draft, turn to pages 57–58.)
Although outlines and lists are valuable for guiding your work, don't be so dependent on them that you shy away from new ideas that surface during your writing of the first draft. If promising new thoughts pop up, jot them down in the margin. Then, at the appropriate point, go back and evaluate them: Do they support your thesis? Are they appropriate for your essay's purpose, audience, and tone? If so, go ahead and include the material in your draft.

It's easy to get bogged down while preparing the first draft if you try to edit as you write. Remember: A draft isn't intended to be perfect. For the time being, adopt a relaxed, noncritical attitude. Working as quickly as you can, don't stop to check spelling, correct grammar, or refine sentence structure. Save these tasks for later. One good way to help remind you that the first draft is tentative is to use scrap paper and pencil. Writing on alternate lines also underscores your intention to revise later on, when the extra space will make it easier to add and delete material. Similarly, writing on only one side of the paper can prove helpful if, during revision, you decide to move a section to another part of the paper.

What should you do if you get stuck while writing your first draft? Stay calm and try to write something—no matter how awkward or imprecise it may seem. Just jot a reminder to yourself in the margin ("Fix this," "Redo," or "Ugh!") to fine-tune the section later. Or leave a blank space to hold a spot for the right words when they finally break loose. It may also help to reread—out loud is best—what you've already written. Regaining a sense of the larger context is often enough to get you moving again. You might also try talking your way through a troublesome section. By speaking aloud, you tap your natural oral fluency and put it to work in your writing.

If a section of the essay strikes you as particularly difficult, don't spend time struggling with it. Move on to an easier section, write that, and then return to the challenging part. If you're still getting nowhere, take a break. Watch television, listen to music, talk with friends. While you're relaxing, your thoughts may loosen up and untangle the knotty section.

Because you read essays from beginning to end, you may assume that writers work the same way, starting with the introduction and going straight through to the conclusion. Often, however, this isn't the case. In fact, since an introduction depends so heavily on everything that follows, it's usually best to write the introduction *after* the essay's body.

When preparing your first draft, you may find it helpful to follow this sequence:

1. Write the supporting paragraphs.
2. Connect ideas in the supporting paragraphs.
3. Write the introduction.
4. Write the conclusion.
5. Write the title.

Write the Supporting Paragraphs

Drawn from the main sections in your outline or scratch list, each *supporting paragraph* should develop an aspect of your essay's thesis. Besides containing relevant, concrete, and sufficient evidence (see pages 33–37), a strong supporting paragraph is (1) often focused by a topic sentence and (2) organized around one or more patterns of development. We'll focus on both features in the pages ahead. As you read our discussion, though, keep in mind that you shouldn't expect your draft paragraphs to be perfect; you'll have a chance to revise them later on.

Use topic sentences.   Frequently, each supporting paragraph in an essay is focused by a *topic sentence* that functions as a kind of mini-thesis for the paragraph. Generally one or two sentences in length, the topic sentence usually appears at or near the beginning of the paragraph. However, it may also appear at the end, in the middle, or—with varied wording—several times within the paragraph.

Regardless of its length or location, the topic sentence states the paragraph's main idea. The other sentences in the paragraph provide support for this central point in the form of examples, facts, expert opinion, and so on. Like a thesis statement, the topic sentence *signals the paragraph's subject* and frequently *indicates the writer's attitude* toward that subject. In the topic sentences that follow, the subject of the paragraph is underlined once and the attitude toward that subject is underlined twice:

> Some students select a particular field of study for the wrong reasons.
> The ocean dumping of radioactive waste is a ticking time bomb.
> Several contemporary rock groups show unexpected sensitivity to social issues.
> Political candidates are sold like slickly packaged products.

As you work on the first draft, you may find yourself writing paragraphs without paying too much attention to topic sentences. That's fine, as long as you evaluate the paragraphs later on. When revising, you can provide a topic sentence for a paragraph that needs a sharper focus, recast a topic sentence for a paragraph that ended up taking an unexpected turn, even eliminate a topic sentence altogether if a paragraph's content is sufficiently unified to imply its point.

Use the patterns of development.   As you saw on page 39, an entire essay can be organized around one or more patterns of development (narration, process analysis, definition, and so forth). These patterns can also provide the organizational framework for an essay's supporting paragraphs. Assume you're writing an article for your town newspaper with the thesis "Year-round residents of an ocean community must take an active role in safeguarding the seashore environment." Your supporting paragraphs could develop this thesis through a variety of patterns, with each paragraph's topic sentence suggesting a specific pattern or combination of patterns. For example, one paragraph might start with the topic sentence "In a nearby ocean community, signs of environmental danger are everywhere" and go on to *describe* a seaside town with polluted waters, blighted trees, and diseased marine life. The next paragraph might have the topic sentence "Fortunately, not all seaside towns are plagued by such environmental problems" and continue by *contrasting* the troubled community with another, more ecologically sound shore town. A later paragraph, focused by the topic sentence "Residents can get involved in a variety of pro-environment activities," might use *division-classification* to elaborate on activities at the neighborhood, town, and municipal levels.

Connect Ideas in the Supporting Paragraphs

While writing the supporting paragraphs, you can try to smooth out the progression of ideas within and between paragraphs. In a *coherent* essay, the relationship between points is clear; readers can easily follow the development of your thoughts. (Sometimes, working on coherence causes a first draft to get bogged down; if this happens, move on, and wait until the revision stage to focus on such matters.)

The following paragraph lacks coherence for two main reasons. First, it sequences ideas improperly. (The idea about the toll attendants' being cut off from coworkers is introduced, dropped, then picked up again. References to motorists are similarly scattered throughout the paragraph.) Second, it doesn't indicate how individual ideas are related. (What, for example, is the connection between drivers who pass by without saying anything and attendants who have to work at night?)

Incoherent Support

Collecting tolls on the turnpike must be one of the loneliest jobs in the world. Each toll attendant sits in his or her booth, cut off from other attendants. Many drivers pass by each booth. None stays long enough for a brief "hello." Most don't acknowledge the attendant at all. Many toll attendants work at night, pushing them "out of synch" with the rest of the world. And sometimes the attendants have to deal with rude drivers who treat them like non-people, swearing at them for the long lines at the tollgate. Attendants also dislike how cut off they feel from their coworkers. Except for infrequent breaks, they have little chance to chat with each other and swap horror stories--small pleasures that would make their otherwise routine jobs bearable.

Coherent Support

Collecting tolls on the turnpike must be one of the loneliest jobs in the world. First of all, although many drivers pass by the attendants, none stays long enough for more than a brief "hello." Most drivers, in fact, don't acknowledge the toll collectors at all, with the exception of those rude drivers who treat the attendants like non-people, swearing at them for the long lines at the tollgate.

Then, too, many toll attendants work at night, pushing them further "out of synch" with the rest of the world. Worst of all, attendants say, is how isolated they feel from their coworkers. Each attendant sits in his or her booth, cut off from other attendants. Except for infrequent breaks, they have little chance to chat with each other and swap horror stories--small pleasures that would make their otherwise routine jobs bearable.

To avoid the kinds of problems found in the incoherent paragraph, use—as the revised version does—two key strategies: (1) a clearly *chronological, spatial, emphatic* ("*Worst of all,* attendants say . . ."), or *simple-to-complex* approach and (2) *signal devices* ("*First of all,* although many drivers pass by . . .") to show how ideas are connected. For a discussion of the four organizational approaches, see pages 39–41. The following paragraphs describe signal devices.

Once you determine a logical approach for presenting your points, you need to make sure readers can follow the progression of those points. Signal devices provide readers with cues, reminding them where they have been and indicating where they are going.

Aim to include some signals—however awkward or temporary—in your first draft. If you find you *can't*, that's probably a warning that your ideas may not be arranged logically. A light touch should be your goal with such signals. Too many call attention to themselves, making the essay mechanical and plodding. In any case, here are some signaling devices to consider.

1. Transitions.   Words and phrases that ease readers from one idea to another are called *transitions*. The following chart lists a variety of such signals. (You'll notice that some transitions can be used for more than one purpose.)

TRANSITIONS

Time

first	immediately	afterward
before	at the same time	after
earlier	simultaneously	finally
next	in the meantime	later
then	meanwhile	eventually
now	subsequently	

Addition (or Sequence)

moreover	one . . . another	next
also	and	finally
furthermore	also	last
in addition	too	
first, . . . second, . . . third	besides	

Space	**Examples**	
above	for instance	
below	for example	
next to	to illustrate	
behind	specifically	
	namely	

Contrast		**Comparison**
but	despite	similarly
however	even though	in the same way
yet	on the one (other) hand	also
in contrast	still	likewise
on the contrary	whereas	too
although	nevertheless	in comparison
otherwise	nonetheless	
conversely		

Cause or Effects	**Summary or Conclusion**
because	therefore
as a result	thus
consequently	in short
therefore	in conclusion
then	
so	
since	

Here's an earlier paragraph from this chapter. Note how the italicized transitions show readers how ideas fit together.

> *After* you've generated supporting evidence, you're ready to organize that material. Even highly compelling evidence won't illustrate the validity of your thesis or achieve your purpose if the readers have to plow through a maze of chaotic evidence. Some writers can move quickly from generating support to writing a clearly structured first draft. (They usually say they have sequenced their ideas in their heads.) Most, *however,* need to spend some time sorting out their thoughts on paper before starting the first draft; *otherwise,* they tend to lose their way in a tangle of ideas.

2. Bridging sentences. Although bridging sentences may be used within a paragraph, they are more often used to move readers from one paragraph to the next. Look again at the first sentence in the preceding paragraph.

Note that the sentence consists of two parts: The first part reminds readers that the previous discussion focused on techniques for generating evidence; the second part tells readers that the focus will now be the organization of such evidence.

3. Repeated words, synonyms, and pronouns.   The repetition of important words maintains continuity, reassures readers that they are on the right track, and highlights key ideas. Synonyms—words similar in meaning to key words or phrases—also provide coherence, while making it possible to avoid unimaginative and tedious repetitions. Finally, pronouns (*he, she, it, they, this, that*) enhance coherence by causing readers to think back to the original word the pronoun replaces (antecedent). When using pronouns, however, be sure there is no ambiguity about antecedents.

Reprinted here is another paragraph from this chapter. Repeated words have been underlined once, synonyms underlined twice, and pronouns printed in italic type to illustrate how these techniques were used to integrate the paragraph's ideas.

> The process of prewriting—discovering a limited subject and generating ideas about *it*—prepares you for the next stage in writing an essay: identifying the paper's thesis or controlling idea. Presenting your opinion on a subject, the thesis should focus on an interesting and significant issue, *one* that engages your energies and merits your consideration. You may think of the thesis as the essay's hub—the central point around which all the other material revolves. Your thesis determines what does and does not belong in the essay. The thesis, especially when *it* occurs early in an essay, also helps focus the reader on the piece's central point.

Write the Introduction

Many writers don't prepare an introduction until they have started to revise; others feel more comfortable if their first draft includes in basic form all parts of the final essay. If that's how you feel, you'll probably write the introduction as you complete your first draft. No matter when you prepare it, keep in mind how crucial the introduction is to your essay's success. Specifically, the introduction serves three distinct functions: It arouses readers' interest, introduces your subject, and presents your thesis.

The length of your introduction will vary according to your paper's scope and purpose. Most essays you write, however, will be served best by a one- or two-paragraph beginning. To write an effective introduction, use any of the following methods, singly or in combination. The thesis statement in each sample introduction is underlined.

Broad Statement Narrowing to a Limited Subject

For generations, morality has been molded primarily by parents, religion, and schools. Children traditionally acquired their ideas about what is right and wrong, which goals are important in life, and how other people should be treated from these three sources collectively. But in the past few decades, a single force--television--has undermined the beneficial influence that parents, religion, and school have on children's moral development. Indeed, <u>television often implants in children negative values about sex, work, and family life.</u>

Brief Anecdote

At a local high school recently, students in a psychology course were given a hint of what it is like to be the parents of a newborn. Each "parent" had to carry a raw egg around at all times to symbolize the responsibilities of parenthood. The egg could not be left alone; it limited the "parents'" activities; it placed a full-time emotional burden on "Mom" and "Dad." This class exercise illustrates a common problem facing the majority of new mothers and fathers. <u>Most people receive little preparation for the job of being parents.</u>

Idea That Is the Opposite of the One Developed

We hear a great deal about divorce's disastrous impact on children. We are deluged with advice on ways to make divorce as painless as possible for youngsters; we listen to heartbreaking stories about the confused, grieving children of divorced parents. Little attention has been paid, however, to a different kind of effect that divorce may have on children. <u>Children from divorced families may become skilled manipulators, playing off one parent against the other, worsening an already painful situation.</u>

Series of Short Questions

What happens if a child is caught vandalizing school property? What happens if a child goes for a joyride in a stolen car and accidentally hits a pedestrian? Should parents be liable for their children's mistakes? Should parents have to pay what might be hundreds of thousands of dollars in damages? Adults have begun to think seriously about such questions because the laws concerning the limits of parental responsibility are changing rapidly. <u>With unfortunate frequency, courts have begun to hold parents legally and financially accountable for their children's misdeeds.</u>

Quotation

Educator Neil Postman believes that television has blurred the line between childhood and adulthood. According to Postman, "All the secrets that a print culture kept from children . . . are revealed all at once by media that do not, and cannot, exclude any audience." <u>This media barrage of information, once intended only for adults, has changed childhood for the worse.</u>

Refutation of a Common Belief

Adolescents care only about material things; their lives revolve around brand-name sneakers, designer jeans, the latest fad in stereo equipment. They resist education, don't read, barely know who is president, mainline rock 'n' roll, experiment with drugs, and exist on a steady diet of Ring-Dings, nachos, and beer. This is what many adults, including parents, seem to believe about the young. The reality is, however, that young people today show more maturity and common sense than most adults give them credit for.

Dramatic Fact or Statistic

Seventy percent of the respondents in a poll conducted by columnist Ann Landers stated that if they could live their lives over, they would choose not to have children. This startling statistic makes one wonder what these people believed parenthood would be like. Most parents, it seems, have unrealistic expectations about their children. Parents want their children to accept their values, follow their paths, and succeed where they failed.

Introductory paragraphs sometimes end with a *plan of development:* a quick preview of the essay's major points in the order in which those points will be discussed. The plan of development may be part of the thesis (as in the first sample introduction) or it may immediately follow the thesis (as in the last sample introduction). Because the plan of development outlines the essay's organizational structure, it helps prepare the reader for the essay's progression of ideas. In a brief essay, readers can often keep track of the ideas without this extra help. In a longer paper, though, a plan of development can be an effective unifying device since it highlights the main ideas the essay will develop.

Write the Conclusion

You may have come across essays that ended with jarring abruptness because they had no conclusions at all. Other papers may have had conclusions, but they sputtered to a weak close, a sure sign that the writers had run out of steam and wanted to finish as quickly as possible. Just as satisfying closes are an important part of everyday life (we feel cheated if dinner doesn't end with dessert or if a friend leaves without saying goodbye), a strong conclusion is an important part of an effective essay. Generally one or two paragraphs in length, the conclusion should give the reader a feeling of completeness and finality. One way to achieve this sense of "rounding off" is to return to an image, idea, or anecdote from the introduction. Because people tend to remember most clearly the points they read last, the conclusion is also a good place to remind readers of your thesis. You may also use the conclusion to make a final point about your subject. Be careful, though, not to open an entirely new line of thought at the essay's close.

Illustrated briefly here are several strategies for writing sound conclusions. These techniques may be used singly or in combination. The first strategy, the summary conclusion, can be especially helpful in long, complex essays since readers may appreciate a review of your points. Tacked onto a short essay, though, a summary conclusion often seems boring and mechanical.

Summary

Contrary to what many adults think, most adolescents are not only aware of the important issues of the times but also deeply concerned about them. They are sensitive to the plight of the homeless, the destruction of the environment, and the pitfalls of rampant materialism. Indeed, today's young people are not less mature and sensible than their parents were. If anything, they are more so.

Prediction

The growing tendency on the part of the judicial system to hold parents responsible for the actions of their wayward children can have a disturbing impact on all of us. Parents will feel bitter toward their own children and cynical about a system that holds them accountable for the actions of minors. Children, continuing to escape the consequences of their actions, will become even more lawless and destructive. Society cannot afford two such possibilities.

Quotation

The comic W. C. Fields is reputed to have said, "Anyone who hates children and dogs can't be all bad." Most people do not share Fields's cynicism. Viewing childhood as a time of purity, they are alarmed at the way television exposes children to the seamy side of life, stripping youngsters of their innocence and giving them a glib sophistication that is a poor substitute for wisdom.

Statistic

Granted, divorce may, in some cases, be the best thing for families torn apart by parents who battle one another. However, in longitudinal studies of children from divorced families, psychologist Judith Wallerstein found that only 10 percent of the youngsters felt relief at their parents' divorce; the remaining 90 percent felt devastated. Such statistics surely call into question parents' claims that they are divorcing for their children's sake.

Recommendation or Call for Action

It is a mistake to leave parenting to instinct. Instead, we should make parenting skills a required course in schools. In addition, a nationwide hotline should be established to help parents deal with crises. Such training and continuing support would help adults deal more effectively with many of the problems they face as parents.

Write the Title

Some writers say that they began a certain piece with only a title in mind. But for most people, writing a title is a finishing touch. Although creating a title for your paper is usually one of the last steps in writing an essay, it shouldn't be done haphazardly. It may take time to write an effective title—one that hints at the essay's thesis and snares the reader's interest.

Good titles may make use of the following techniques: repetition of sounds ("Affirmative Action: The Price of Preference"); questions ("Can You Be Educated from a Distance?"); and irony ("The Ugly Truth About Beauty"). More often, though, titles are straightforward phrases derived from the essay's subject or thesis: "The Chase" and "The Ways We Lie," for example.

Pull It All Together

Now that you know how to prepare a first draft, you might find it helpful to examine the accompanying illustration to see how the different parts of a draft can fit together. Keep in mind that not every essay you write will take this shape. As your purpose, audience, and tone change, so will your

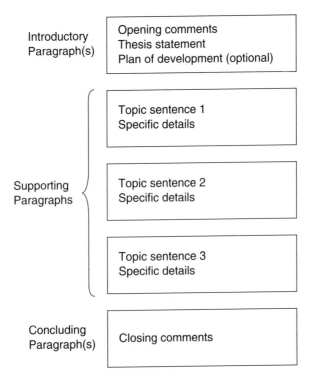

essay's structure. An introduction or conclusion, for instance, may be developed in more than one paragraph; the thesis statement may be implied or delayed until the essay's middle or end; not all paragraphs may have topic sentences; and several supporting paragraphs may be needed to develop a single topic sentence. Even so, the basic format presented here offers a strategy for organizing a variety of writing assignments—from term papers to lab reports. Once you feel comfortable with the structure, you have a foundation on which to base your variations. (This book's student and professional essays illustrate some possibilities.) Even when using a specific format, you always have room to give your spirit and imagination free play. The language you use, the details you select, the perspective you offer are uniquely yours. They are what make your essay different from everyone else's.

Sample First Draft

Here is the first draft of Harriet Davids's essay. (The assignment and prewriting for the essay appear on pages 11, 21–23, and 26.) Harriet wrote the draft in one sitting. Working at a computer, she started by typing her thesis at the top of the first page. Then, following the guidelines on page 46, she moved the material in her outline (pages 43–44) to her draft. Harriet worked rapidly; she started with the first body paragraph and wrote straight through to the last supporting paragraph.

By moving quickly, Harriet got down her essay's basic text rather easily. Once she felt she had captured in rough form what she wanted to say, she reread her draft to get a sense of how she might open and close the essay. Then she drafted her introduction and conclusion; both appear here, together with the body of the essay. The commentary following the draft will give you a clearer sense of how Harriet proceeded. (Note that the marginal annotations reflect Harriet's comments to herself about areas she needs to address when revising her first draft.)

Challenges for Today's Parents
by Harriet Davids

Thesis: Being a parent today is much more difficult than it was a generation ago.

ADD
SPECIFICS ———

Raising children used to be much simpler in the '50s and '60s. I remember TV images from that era showing that parenting involved simply teaching kids to clean their rooms, do their homework, and _____. But being a parent today is much more difficult because nowadays parents have to shield/protect kids from lots of things, like distractions from schoolwork, from sexual material, from dangerous situations.

Parents have to control all the new distractions/ temptations that turn kids away from schoolwork. These days many kids have stereos, computers, and televisions in their rooms. Certainly, my girls can't resist the urge to listen to MTV and go online, especially if it's time to do homework. Unfortunately, though, kids aren't assigned much homework and what is assigned too often is busywork. And there are even more distractions outside the home. Teens no longer hang out/ congregate on the corner where Dad and Mom can yell to them to come home and do homework. Instead they hang out at the mall, in video arcades, and fast-food restaurants. Obviously, parents and school can't compete with all this.

WEAK TRANS. — Also parents have to help kids develop responsible sexual values even though sex is everywhere. Kids see sex magazines and dirty paperbacks in the corner store where they used to get candy and comic books. And instead of the artsy nude shots of

SP? — the past, kids see ronchey, explicit shots in <u>Playboy</u> and <u>Penthouse</u>. And movies have sexy stuff in them today. Teachers seduce students and people treat sex casually/as a sport. Not exactly traditional values. TV is no better. Kids see soap-opera characters in bed and cable shows full of nudity by

FIX — just flipping the dial. Even worse is what's on the Internet. Too easy for kids to access chat rooms and websites dealing with adult, sometimes pornographic material. The situation has gotten so out of hand that maybe the government should establish guidelines on what's permissible.

Worst of all are the life-threatening dangers that parents must help children fend off over the years. With older kids,

AWK. — drugs fall into place as a main concern. Peer pressure to try drugs is bigger to kids than their parents' warnings. Other

WRONG WORD — kinds of warnings are common when children are small. Then parents fear violence since news shows constantly report stories of little children being abused. And when kids aren't

ADD SPECIFICS — much older, they have to resist the pressure to drink. Alcohol has always attracted kids, but nowadays they are drinking more and this can be deadly, especially when drinking is combined with driving.

REDO — Most adults love their children and want to be good parents. But it's difficult because the world seems stacked against young people. Even Holden Caufield had trouble dealing

SP? — with society's confusing pressures. Parents must give their children some freedom but not so much that the kids lose sight of what's important.

Commentary

As you can see, Harriet's draft is rough. Because she knew she would revise later on (page 60), she "zapped out" the draft in an informal, colloquial style. For example, she occasionally expressed her thoughts in fragments ("Not exactly traditional values"), relied heavily on "and" as a transition, and used slangy expressions such as "kids," "dirty paperbacks," and "lots of things." She also used slashes between alternative word choices and left a blank space when wording just wouldn't come. Then, as Harriet reviewed the printed copy of this rough draft, she made handwritten marginal notes to herself in capital letters: "REDO" or "FIX" to signal awkward sentences; "ADD SPECIFICS" to mark overly general statements; "WRONG WORD" after an imprecise word; "SP?" to remind herself to check spelling in the dictionary; "WEAK TRANS." to indicate where a stronger signaling device was needed. (Harriet's final draft appears on pages 65–66.)

Writing a first draft may seem like quite a challenge, but the tips offered in these pages should help you proceed with confidence. Indeed, as you work on the draft, you may be surprised how much you enjoy writing. After all, this is your chance to get down on paper something you want to say.

Activities: Write the First Draft

1. Retrieve the writing you prepared in response to activity 3 on page 45. Applying the principles just presented, rework that material. If you wrote a single paragraph earlier, expand the material into a full essay draft. If you prepared an essay, strengthen what you wrote. In both cases, remember to consider your purpose, audience, and tone as you write the body of the essay as well as its introduction and conclusion. (Save your draft so you can rework it even further after reading about the next stage in the writing process.)

2. Referring to the outline you prepared in response to activity 2 or activity 4 on page 45, draft the body of your essay, making your evidence as strong as possible. As you work, keep your purpose, audience, and tone in mind. After reading what you've prepared, go ahead and draft a rough introduction, conclusion, and title. Finally, ask at least one other person to react to your draft by listing its strengths and weaknesses. (Save the draft so you can work with it further after reading about the next stage in the writing process.)

STAGE 6: REVISE THE ESSAY

By now, you've probably abandoned any preconceptions you might have had about good writers sitting down and creating a finished product in one easy step. Alexander Pope's comment that "true ease in writing comes from art, not chance" is as true today as it was more than two hundred years ago. Writing that seems effortlessly clear is often the result of sustained work, not of good luck or even inborn talent. And much of this work takes place during the final stage of the writing process when ideas, paragraphs, sentences, and words are refined and reshaped.

Professional writers—novelists, journalists, textbook authors—seldom submit a piece of writing that hasn't been revised. They recognize that rough, unpolished work doesn't do them justice. What's more, they often look forward to revising. Columnist Ellen Goodman puts it this way: "What makes me happy is rewriting. . . . It's like cleaning house, getting rid of all the junk, getting things in the right order, tightening up."

In a sense, revision occurs throughout the writing process: At some earlier stage, you may have dropped an idea, overhauled your thesis, or shifted paragraph order. What, then, is different about the rewriting that occurs in the revision stage? The answer has to do with the literal meaning of the word *revision*—to resee, or to see again. Genuine revision involves casting clear eyes on your work, viewing it as though you're a reader rather than the writer. Revision means that you go through your paper looking for trouble, ready to pick a fight with your own writing. And then you must be willing to sit down and make the changes needed for your writing to be as effective as possible.

Revision is not, as some believe, simply touch-up work—changing a sentence here or a word there, eliminating spelling errors, preparing a neat final copy. Revision means cutting deadwood, rearranging paragraphs, substituting new words for old ones, recasting sentences, improving coherence, even generating new material when appropriate. With experience, you'll learn how to streamline the process so you can focus on the most critical issues for a particular piece of writing. (For advice on correcting some common writing errors, see Appendix B on pages 472–484.)

Five Revision Strategies

Because revision is challenging, you may find yourself unsure about how to proceed. Keep in mind that there are no hard-and-fast rules about the revision process. Even so, the following pointers should help get you going if you balk at or feel overwhelmed by revising.

- *Set your draft aside for a while* before revising. When you pick up your paper again, you'll have a fresh, more objective point of view.
- *Work from typed or computer-generated material* whenever possible. Having your essay in neutral typed letters instead of in your own familiar writing helps you see the paper impartially, as if someone else had written it. Each time you make major changes, try to print out a copy of that section so that you can see it anew.
- *Read your draft aloud* as often as you can. Hearing how your writing sounds helps you pick up problems that you passed by before: places where sentences are awkward, meaning is ambiguous, words are imprecise. Even better, have another person read aloud to you what you have written. If the reader slows to a crawl over a murky

paragraph or trips over a convoluted sentence, you know where you have to do some rewriting.

- *View revision as a series of steps.* Don't try to tackle all of a draft's problems at once; instead, proceed step by step, starting with the most pressing issues. Although there are bound to be occasions when you have time for only one quick pass over a draft, whenever possible, read your draft several times; each time focus on different matters and ask yourself different questions. Move from a broad view of the draft to an up-close look at its mechanics.

- *Evaluate and respond to instructor feedback.* Often, instructors collect and respond to students' first drafts. Like many students, you may be tempted to look only briefly at your instructor's comments. Perhaps you've "had it" with the essay and don't want to think about revising the paper to reflect the instructor's remarks. But taking your instructor's comments into account when revising is often what's needed to turn a shaky first draft into a strong final draft.

When an instructor returns a final draft graded, you may think that the grade is all that counts. Remember, though: Grades are important, but comments are even more so. They can help you *improve* your writing—if not in this paper, then in the next one. If you don't understand or agree with the instructor's observations, don't hesitate to request a conference. Getting together gives both you and the instructor a chance to clarify your respective points of view.

Peer Review/Revision Checklist

Many instructors include in-class or at-home peer review as a regular part of a composition course. Peer review—the critical reading of another person's writing with the intention of suggesting changes—accomplishes several important goals. First, peer review helps you gain a more objective perspective on your work. When you write something, you're often too close to what you've prepared to evaluate it fairly; you may have trouble seeing where the writing is strong and where it needs to be strengthened. Peer review supplies the fresh, neutral perspective you need. Second, reviewing your classmates' work broadens your own composing options. You may be inspired to experiment with a technique you admired in a classmate's writing but wouldn't have thought of on your own. Finally, peer review trains you to be a better reader and critic of your *own* writing. When you get into the habit of critically reading other students' writing, you become more adept at critiquing your own.

The Peer Review/Revision Checklist on the inside front cover of this book will help focus your revision—whether you're reworking your own paper or responding to a peer's. Your instructor may have you respond to all questions on the checklist or to several selected items. What follows is a peer review worksheet that Harriet Davids's instructor prepared to help students respond to first drafts based on the assignment on page 11. Wanting students to focus on four areas (thesis statement, support for thesis statement, overall organization, and signal devices), the instructor drew upon relevant sections from the Peer Review/Revision Checklist. With this customized worksheet in hand, Harriet's classmate Frank Tejada was able to give Harriet constructive feedback on her first draft (see pages 57–58). (*Note:* Because Harriet didn't want to influence Frank's reaction, the draft she gave him didn't include her marginal notations to herself.)

Peer Review Worksheet

Essay Author's Name: <u>Harriet Davids</u>   Reviewer's Name: <u>Frank Tejada</u>

1. What is the essay's thesis? Is it explicit or implied? Does the thesis focus on a limited subject and express the writer's attitude toward that subject?

   Thesis: "Being a parent today is much more difficult [than it used to be]." The thesis is limited and expresses a clear attitude. But the sentence the thesis appears in (last sentence of para. 1) is too long because it also contains the plan of development. Maybe put thesis and plan of development in separate sentences.

2. What are the main points supporting the thesis? List the points. Is each supporting point developed sufficiently? If not, where is more support needed?

   (1) Parents have to control kids' distractions from school.
   (2) Parents have to help kids develop responsible sexual values despite sex being everywhere.
   (3) Parents have to protect kids from life-threatening dangers.
      The supporting points are good and are explained pretty well, except for a few places. The "Unfortunately" sentence in para. 2 is irrelevant. Also, in para. 2, you use the example of your girls, but never again. Either include them throughout or not at all. In para. 3, the final sentence about the government guidelines opens a whole new topic; maybe steer away from this. The items in para. 4 seem vague and need specific examples. In the conclusion, omit Holden Caulfield; since he was from an earlier generation, this example undermines your thesis about parenting today.

3. What overall format (chronological, spatial, emphatic, simple-to-complex) is used to sequence the essay's main points? Does this format work? Why or why not? What organizational format is used in each supporting paragraph? Does the format work? Why or why not?

> The paper's overall emphatic organization seems good. Emphatic order also works in para. 3, and spatial order works well in para. 2. But the sentences in para. 4 need rearranging. Right now, the examples are in mixed-up chronological order, making it hard to follow. Maybe you should reorder the examples from young kids to older kids.

4. What signal devices are used to connect ideas within and between paragraphs? Are there too few signal devices or too many? Where?

> The topic sentence of para. 3 needs to be a stronger bridging sentence. Also, too many "and's" in para. 3. Try "in addition" or "another" in some places. I like the "worst of all" transition to para. 4.

As you can see, Frank flagged several areas that Harriet herself also noted needed work. (Turn to pages 57–58 to see Harriet's marginal comments on her draft.) But he also commented on entirely new areas (for example, the sequence problem in paragraph 4), offering Harriet a fresh perspective on what she needed to do to polish her draft. To see which of Frank's suggestions Harriet followed, take a look at her final draft on pages 65–66 and at the "Commentary" following the essay.

Becoming a skilled peer reviewer.   Even with the help of a checklist, preparing a helpful peer review is a skill that takes time to develop. At first, you, like many students, may be too easy or too critical. Effective peer review calls for rigor and care; you should give classmates the conscientious feedback that you hope for in return. Peer review also requires tact and kindness; feedback should always be constructive and include observations about what works well in a piece of writing. People have difficulty mustering the energy to revise if they feel there's nothing worth revising.

If your instructor doesn't include peer review, you can set up peer review sessions outside of class, with classmates getting together to respond to each other's drafts. Or you may select non-classmates who are objective (not a love-struck admirer or a doting grandparent) and skilled enough to provide useful commentary.

To focus your readers' comments, you may adapt the Peer Review/ Revision Checklist on the inside front cover of this book, or you may develop your own questions. If you prepare the questions yourself, be sure to solicit *specific* observations about what does and doesn't work in your writing. If you simply ask, "How's this?" you may receive a vague comment like "It's not very effective." What you want are concrete observations and suggestions: "I'm confused because what you say in the fifth sentence contradicts what you say in the second." To promote such specific responses, ask your readers targeted (preferably written) questions like "I'm having trouble moving from my second to my third point. How can I make the transition smoother?" Such questions require more than "yes" or "no" responses; they encourage readers to dig into your writing where you sense it needs work. (If it's feasible, encourage readers to *write* their responses to your questions.)

If you and your peer reviewer(s) can't meet in person, **e-mail** can provide a crucial means of contact. With a couple of clicks, you can simply send each other computer files of your work. Before you do so, determine whether your word-processing software is compatible; if so, you'll be able to send each other your computerized drafts as file attachments. If not, you can copy the text of your paper and paste it into the e-mail message box. (You'll likely lose the paper's format features, but the content is what matters most during peer review.) You and your reviewer(s) also need to decide exactly how to exchange comments about your drafts. You might conclude, for example, that you'll type your responses, perhaps in bold capitals, into the file itself. Or you might decide to print out the drafts and reply to the comments in writing, later exchanging the annotated drafts in person. No matter what you and your peer(s) decide, you'll probably find e-mail an invaluable tool in the writing process.

Evaluating and responding to peer review.   Accepting criticism isn't easy (even if you asked for it), and not all peer reviewers will be diplomatic. Even so, try to listen with an open mind to those giving you feedback. Take notes on their oral observations and/or have them fill out relevant sections from the Peer Review/Revision Checklist (on the inside front cover). Later, when you're ready to revise your paper, reread your notes. Which reviewer remarks seem valid? Which don't? Rank the problems and solutions that your reviewers identified, designating the most critical as number 1. Using the peer feedback, enter your own notes for revising in the margins of a clean copy of your draft. This way, you'll know exactly what changes need to be made in your draft as you proceed. Then, keeping the problems and remedies in mind, start revising. If you've been working on a computer, type in your changes, or handwrite changes directly on the draft above the appropriate line. (Rework extensive sections on a separate piece of paper.) When revising, always keep in mind that you may not agree with every reviewer suggestion. That's fine. It's *your* paper, and it's *your* decision to implement or reject the suggestions made by your peers.

STUDENT ESSAY

In this chapter, we've taken you through the various stages in the writing process. You've seen how Harriet Davids used prewriting (pages 21–23 and 26) and outlining (pages 43–44) to arrive at her first draft (pages 57–58). You've also seen how Harriet's peer reviewer, Frank Tejada, critiqued her first draft (pages 62–63). In the following pages, you'll look at Harriet's final draft—the paper she submitted to her instructor.

Harriet, a thirty-eight-year-old college student and mother of two teenagers, wanted to write an informative paper with a straightforward, serious tone. While preparing her essay, she kept in mind that her audience would include her course instructor as well as her classmates, many of them considerably younger than she. This is the assignment that prompted Harriet's essay:

> Goodman implies that, in some ways, today's world is hostile to children. Do you agree? Drawing upon but not limiting yourself to the material in your pre-reading journal, write an essay in which you support or reject this viewpoint.

Harriet's essay is annotated so that you can see how it illustrates the essay format described on page 56. As you read her essay, try to determine how well it reflects the principles of effective writing. The commentary following the paper will help you look at the essay more closely and give you some sense of the way Harriet went about revising her first draft.

Challenges for Today's Parents
by Harriet Davids

Introduction   Reruns of situation comedies from the 1950s and early   1
1960s dramatize the kinds of problems that parents used to have with their children. The Cleavers scold Beaver for not washing his hands before dinner; the Andersons ground Bud for not doing his homework; the Nelsons dock little Ricky's allowance because he keeps forgetting to clean his room. But **Thesis** — times have changed dramatically. Being a parent today is much more difficult than it was a generation ago. **Plan of development** — Parents nowadays must protect their children from a growing number of distractions, from sexually explicit material, and from life-threatening situations.

First supporting paragraph   Today's parents must try, first of all, to control all the new   2
distractions that tempt children away from schoolwork. At **Topic sentence** — home, a child may have a room furnished with a stereo, television, and computer. Not many young people can resist the urge to listen to CDs, go online, play computer games, or watch MTV--especially if it is time to do schoolwork. Outside the home, the distractions are even more alluring. Children no longer "hang out" on a neighborhood corner within earshot of Mom or Dad's reminder to come in and do homework. Instead, they congregate in vast shopping malls, buzzing video arcades, and gleaming fast-food restaurants. Parents and

Second
supporting
paragraph

Topic sentence —
with link to
previous
paragraph

Third supporting
paragraph

Topic sentence —
with emphasis
signal

Conclusion

References to ——
TV shows recall
introduction

school assignments have obvious difficulty competing with such enticing alternatives.

Besides dealing with these distractions, parents have to shield their children from a flood of sexually explicit materials. Today, children can find sex magazines and pornographic paperbacks in the same corner store that once offered only comics and candy. Children will not see the fuzzily photographed nudes that a previous generation did but will encounter the hard-core raunchiness of Playboy or Penthouse. Moreover, the movies young people attend often focus on highly sexual situations. It is difficult to teach children traditional values when films show teachers seducing students and young people treating sex as a casual sport. Unfortunately, television, with its often heavily sexual content, is no better. With just a flick of the dial, children can see soap-opera stars cavorting in bed or watch cable programs where nudity is common. But the sexually graphic content of TV shows is nothing compared to the seamy material on the Internet. Many parents report that their children, sometimes without intending to, access pornographic chat rooms and websites that haunt the youngsters for months afterward.

Most disturbing to parents today, however, is the increase in life-threatening dangers that face young people. When children are small, parents fear that their youngsters may be victims of violence. Every news program seems to carry a report about a mass murderer who preys on young girls, a deviant who has buried six boys in his cellar, or an organized child pornography ring that molests preschoolers. When children are older, parents begin to worry about their kids' use of drugs. Peer pressure to experiment with drugs is often stronger than parents' warnings. This pressure to experiment can be fatal. Finally, even if young people escape the hazards associated with drugs, they must still resist the pressure to drink. Although alcohol has always held an attraction for teenagers, reports indicate that they are drinking more than ever before. As many parents know, the consequences of this attraction can be deadly--especially when drinking is combined with driving.

Within one generation, the world as a place to raise children has changed dramatically. One wonders how yesterday's parents would have dealt with today's problems. Could the Andersons have kept Bud away from MTV? Could the Nelsons have shielded little Ricky from sexually explicit material on the Internet? Could the Cleavers have protected Beaver from drugs and alcohol? Parents must be aware of all these distractions and dangers yet be willing to give their children the freedom they need to become responsible adults. This is not an easy task.

3

4

5

COMMENTARY

Introduction and thesis.   The opening paragraph attracts readers' interest by recalling several vintage television shows that have almost become part of our cultural heritage. Harriet begins with these examples from the past because they offer such a sharp contrast to the present, thus underscoring the idea expressed in her *thesis:* "Being a parent today is much more difficult than it was a generation ago." Opening in this way, with material that serves as a striking contrast to what follows, is a common and effective strategy. Note, too, that Harriet's thesis states the paper's subject (being a parent) as well as her attitude toward the subject (the job is more demanding than it was years ago).

Plan of development.   Harriet follows her thesis with a *plan of development* that anticipates the three major points to be covered in the essay's support- ing paragraphs. When revising her first draft, Harriet followed peer reviewer Frank Tejada's recommendation (page 62) to put her thesis and plan of development in separate sentences. Unfortunately, though, her plan of devel- opment ends up being somewhat mechanical, with the major points being trotted past the reader in one long, awkward sentence. To deal with the problem, Harriet could have rewritten the sentence or eliminated the plan of development altogether, ending the introduction with her thesis.

Patterns of development.   Although Harriet develops her thesis primarily through *examples,* she also draws on two other patterns of development. The whole paper implies a *contrast* between the way life is now and the way it used to be. The essay also contains an element of *causal analysis* since all the factors that Harriet cites affect children and the way they are raised.

Purpose, audience, and tone.   Given the essay's *purpose* and *audience,* Harriet adopts a serious *tone,* providing no-nonsense evidence to support her thesis. But assume she had been asked by her daughters' school newspaper to write a humorous column about the trials and tribulations that parents face raising children. Aiming for a different tone, purpose, and audience, Harriet would have taken another approach. Drawing on her experience as a mother of two teenage daughters, she might have confessed how she survives MTV's flash and dazzle, as well as the din of stereos blasting rock music at all hours: she stuffs her ears with cotton, hides her daughters' CDs, and cuts off the electricity. This material—with its personalized perspective, exagger- ation, and light tone—would be appropriate.

Organization.   Structuring the essay around a series of *relevant* and *spe- cific examples,* Harriet uses *emphatic order* to sequence the paper's three main points: that a growing number of distractions, sexually explicit materials, and life-threatening situations make parenting difficult nowadays. The third supporting paragraph begins with the words "Most disturbing to parents today . . . ," signaling that Harriet feels particular concern about the physical dangers children face. Moreover, she uses basic organizational strategies to sequence the supporting examples within each paragraph. The details in the first supporting paragraph are organized *spatially*, starting with distractions at home and moving to those outside the home. The second supporting paragraph arranges examples *emphatically*. Harriet starts with sexually explicit publications and ends with the "seamy material on the Internet," which is even more disturbing than TV's "heavily sexual content." Note that Harriet followed Frank's peer review advice (page 62) about omitting her first-draft observation that kids don't get enough homework—or that they get too much busywork. The third and final supporting paragraph is organized *chronologically;* it begins by discussing dangers to small children and concludes by talking about teenagers. Again, Frank's advice—to use a clearer time sequence in this paragraph (page 62)—was invaluable when Harriet was revising.

The essay also displays Harriet's familiarity with other kinds of organizational strategies. Each supporting paragraph opens with a *topic sentence*. Further, *signal devices* are used throughout the paper to show how ideas are related to one another: *transitions* ("Instead, they congregate in vast shopping malls"; "Moreover, the movies young people attend often focus on highly sexual situations"); *repetition* ("sexual situations" and "sexual content"); *synonyms* ("distractions . . . enticing alternatives" and "life-threatening . . . fatal"); *pronouns* ("young people . . . they"); and *bridging sentences* ("Besides dealing with these distractions, parents have to shield their children from a flood of sexually explicit material").

Two minor problems.   Harriet's efforts to write a well-organized essay result in a somewhat predictable structure. It might have been better had she rewritten one of the paragraphs, perhaps embedding the topic sentence in the middle of the paragraph or saving it for the end. Similarly, Harriet's signal devices are a little heavy-handed. Even so, an essay with a sharp focus and clear signals is preferable to one with a confusing or inaccessible structure. As she gains more experience, Harriet can work on making the structure of her essays more subtle.

Conclusion.   Following Frank's suggestion, Harriet dropped from the final paragraph the first draft's problematic reference to Holden Caulfield (page 62). Having done that, she's able to bring the essay to a satisfying *close* by reminding readers of the paper's central idea and three main points. The final paragraph also extends the essay's scope by introducing a new but related issue: that parents have to strike a balance between their need to provide limitations and their children's need for freedom. Besides eliminating the distracting reference to Holden Caulfield, she replaced the shopworn opening sentence

("Most adults love their children . . . ") with three interesting and rhythmical questions ("Could the Andersons . . . ? Could the Nelsons . . . ? Could the Cleavers . . . ?"). Because these questions recall the essay's main points and echo the introduction's reference to vintage television shows, they help unify Harriet's paper and bring it to a rounded close.

These are just a few of the changes Harriet made when reworking her essay. Realizing that writing is a process, she left herself enough time to revise—and to carefully consider Frank Tejada's comments. Early in her composition course, Harriet learned that attention to the various stages in the writing process yields satisfying results, for writer and reader alike.

Activity: Revise the Essay

Return to the draft you wrote in response to either activity 1 or activity 2 on page 60. Also look at any written feedback you received on the draft. To identify any further problems in the draft, get together with several people (classmates, friends, or family members) and request that one of them read the draft aloud to you. Then ask your audience focused questions about the areas you sense need work, or use the checklist on the inside front cover to focus the feedback. In either case, summarize and rank the comments on a feedback chart or in marginal annotations. Then, using the comments as a guide, go ahead and revise the draft. Either type a new version or do your revising by hand, perhaps on a photocopy of the draft. Don't forget to proofread closely before submitting the paper to your instructor.

3

DESCRIPTION

WHAT IS DESCRIPTION?

All of us respond in a strong way to sensory stimulation. The sweet perfume of a candy shop takes us back to childhood; the blank white walls of the campus infirmary remind us of long vigils at a hospital where a grandmother lay dying; the screech of a subway car sets our nerves on edge.

Without any sensory stimulation, we sink into a less-than-human state. Neglected babies, left alone with no human touch, no colors, no lullabies, become withdrawn and unresponsive. And prisoners dread solitary confinement, knowing that the sensory deprivation can be unbearable, even to the point of madness.

Because sensory impressions are so potent, descriptive writing has a unique power and appeal. *Description* can be defined as the expression, in vivid language, of what the five senses experience. A richly rendered description freezes a subject in time, evoking sights, smells, sounds, textures, and tastes in such a way that readers become one with the writer's world.

HOW DESCRIPTION FITS YOUR PURPOSE AND AUDIENCE

Description can be a supportive technique that develops part of an essay, or it can be the dominant technique used throughout an essay. Here are some examples of the way description can help you meet the objective of an essay developed chiefly through another pattern of development:

- In a *causal analysis* showing the *consequences* of pet overpopulation, you might describe the desperate appearance of a pack of starving stray dogs.

- In an *argumentation-persuasion* essay urging more rigorous handgun control, you might start with a description of a violent family confrontation that ended in murder.
- In a *process analysis* explaining the pleasure of making ice cream at home, you might describe the beauty of an old-fashioned, hand-cranked ice-cream maker.
- In a *narrative essay* recounting a day in the life of a street musician, you might describe the musician's energy and the joyous appreciation of passersby.

In each case, the essay's overall purpose would affect the amount of description needed.

Your readers also influence how much description to include. As you write, ask yourself, "What do my particular readers need to know to understand and experience keenly what I'm describing? What descriptive details will they enjoy most?" Your answers to these and similar questions will help you tailor your description to specific readers. Consider an article intended for professional horticulturists; its purpose is to explain a new technique for controlling spider mites. Because of readers' expertise, there would be little need for a lengthy description of the insects. Written for a college newspaper, however, the article would probably provide a detailed description of the mites so student gardeners could distinguish between the pesky parasites and flecks of dust.

While your purpose and audience define *how much* to describe, you have great freedom deciding *what* to describe. Description is especially suited to objects (your car or desk, for example), but you can also describe a person, an animal, a place, a time, and a phenomenon or concept. You might write an effective description of a friend who runs marathons (person), a pair of ducks who return each year to a neighbor's pond (animals), the kitchen of a fast-food restaurant (place), a period when you were unemployed (time), the "fight or flight" response to danger (phenomenon or concept).

Description can be divided into two types: *objective* and *subjective*. In an objective description, you describe the subject in a straightforward and literal way, without revealing your attitude or feelings. Reporters, as well as technical and scientific writers, specialize in objective description; their jobs depend on their ability to detail experiences without emotional bias. For example, a reporter may write an unemotional account of a township meeting that ended in a fistfight. Or a marine biologist may write a factual report describing the way sea mammals are killed by the plastic refuse (sandwich wrappings, straws, fishing lines) that humans throw into the ocean.

In contrast, when writing a subjective description, you convey a highly personal view of your subject and seek to elicit a strong emotional response from your readers. Such subjective descriptions often take the form of reflective pieces or character studies. For example, in an essay describing the rich plant life in an inner-city garden, you might reflect on people's longing to connect with the soil and express admiration for the gardeners' hard work—an admiration you'd like readers to share. Or, in a character study of your grandfather, you might describe his stern appearance and gentle behavior, hoping that the contradiction will move readers as much as it moves you.

The *tone* of a subjective description is determined by your purpose, your attitude toward the subject, and the reader response you wish to evoke. Consider an essay about a dynamic woman who runs a center for disturbed children. If your goal is to make readers admire the woman, your tone will be serious and appreciative. But if you want to criticize the woman's high-pressure tactics and create distaste for her management style, your tone will be disapproving and severe.

The language of a descriptive piece also depends, to a great extent, on whether your purpose is primarily objective or subjective. If the description is objective, the language is straightforward, precise, and factual. Such *denotative* language consists of neutral dictionary meanings. If you want to describe as dispassionately as possible fans' violent behavior at a football game, you might write about the "large crowd" and its "mass movement onto the field." But if you are shocked by the fans' behavior and want to write a subjective piece that inspires similar outrage in readers, then you might write about the "swelling mob" and its "rowdy stampede onto the field." In the latter case, the language used would be *connotative* and emotionally charged so that readers would share your feelings.

Subjective and objective descriptions often overlap. Sometimes a single sentence contains both objective and subjective elements: "Although his hands were large and misshapen by arthritis, they were gentle to the touch, inspiring confidence and trust." Other times, part of an essay may provide a factual description (the physical appearance of a summer cabin your family rented), while another part of the essay may be highly subjective (how you felt in the cabin, sitting in front of a fire on a rainy day).

SUGGESTIONS FOR USING DESCRIPTION IN AN ESSAY

The following suggestions will be helpful whether you use description as a dominant or a supportive pattern of development.

1. Focus a descriptive essay around a dominant impression.   Like other kinds of writing, a descriptive essay must have a thesis, or main point. In a descriptive essay with a subjective slant, the thesis usually centers on the *dominant impression* you have about your subject. Suppose you decide to write an essay on your ninth-grade history teacher, Ms. Hazzard. You want the paper to convey how unconventional and flamboyant she was. The essay could, of course, focus on a different dominant impression—how insensitive she could be to students, for example. What's important is that you establish—early in the paper—the dominant impression you intend to convey. Although descriptive essays often imply, rather than explicitly state, the dominant impression, that impression should be unmistakable.

2. Select the details to include.   The power of description hinges on your ability to select from all possible details only those that support the dominant impression. All others, no matter how vivid or interesting, must be left out. If you're describing how flamboyant Ms. Hazzard could be, the details in the following paragraph would be appropriate.

> A large-boned woman, Ms. Hazzard wore her bright red hair piled on top of her head, where it perched precariously. By the end of class, wayward strands of hair tumbled down and fell into eyes fringed by spiky false eyelashes. Ms. Hazzard's nails, filed into crisp points, were painted either bloody burgundy or neon pink. Plastic bangle bracelets, also either burgundy or pink, clattered up and down her ample arms as she scrawled on the board the historical dates that had, she claimed, "changed the world."

Such details—the heavy eye makeup, stiletto nails, gaudy bracelets— contribute to the impression of a flamboyant, unusual person. Even if you remembered times that Ms. Hazzard seemed perfectly conventional and understated, most likely you wouldn't describe those times since they contradict the dominant impression.

You must also be selective in the *number of details* you include. Having a dominant impression helps you eliminate many details gathered during prewriting, but there still will be choices to make. For example, it would be inappropriate to describe in exhaustive detail everything in a messy room:

> The brown desk, made of a grained plastic laminate, is directly under a small window covered by a torn yellow-and-gold plaid curtain. In the left corner of the desk are four crumbled balls of blue-lined yellow paper, three red markers, two fine-point blue pens, an ink eraser, and four letters, two bearing special wildlife stamps. A green down-filled vest and a red cable-knit sweater are thrown over the back of the bright blue metal bridge chair pushed under the desk. Under the chair is an oval braided rug, its once brilliant blues and greens spotted by old coffee stains.

Readers will be reluctant to wade through such undifferentiated specifics. Even more important, such excessive detailing dilutes the focus of the essay. You end up with a seemingly endless list of specifics rather than with a carefully crafted picture in words. In this regard, sculptors and writers are similar—what they take away is as important as what they leave in.

Perhaps you're wondering how to generate the details that support your dominant impression. As you can imagine, you have to develop heightened powers of observation and recall. To sharpen these key faculties, it can be helpful to make up a chart with separate columns for each of the five senses. If you can observe your subject directly, enter in the appropriate columns what you see, hear, taste, and so on. If you're attempting to remember something from the past, try to recollect details under each of these sense headings. Ask yourself questions ("How did it smell? What did I hear?") and list each memory recaptured. You'll be surprised how this simple technique can tune you in to your experiences and help uncover the specific details needed to develop your dominant impression.

3. Organize the descriptive details.   Select the organizational pattern (or combination of patterns) that best supports your dominant impression. The paragraphs in a descriptive essay are usually sequenced *spatially* (from top to bottom, interior to exterior, near to far) or *chronologically* (as the subject is experienced in time). But the paragraphs can also be ordered *emphatically* (ending with your subject's most striking elements) or by *sensory impression* (first smell, then taste, then touch, and so on).

You might, for instance, use a *spatial* pattern to organize a description of a large city as you viewed it from the air, a taxi, and a subway car. A description of your first day on a new job might move *chronologically*, starting with how you felt the first hour on the job and proceeding through the rest of the day. In a paper describing a bout with the flu, you might arrange details *emphatically*, beginning with a description of your low-level aches and pains and concluding with an account of your raging fever. An essay about a neighborhood garbage dump, euphemistically called an "ecology landfill" by its owners, could be organized by *sensory impressions:* the sights of the dump, its smells, its sounds. Regardless of the organizational pattern you use, provide enough *signal devices* (for example, *about, next, worst of all*) so that readers can follow the description easily.

Finally, although descriptive essays don't always have conventional topic sentences, each descriptive paragraph should have a clear focus. Often this focus is indicated by a sentence early in the paragraph that names the scene, object, or individual to be described. Such a sentence functions as a kind of *informal topic sentence;* the paragraph's descriptive details then develop that topic sentence.

4. Use vivid sensory language and varied sentence structure.   The connotative language typical of subjective description should be richly evocative. The words you select must etch in readers' minds the same picture that you have in yours. For this reason, rather than relying on vague generalities, you must use language that involves readers' senses. Consider the difference between the following paired descriptions.

Vague	Vivid
The food was unappetizing.	The stew congealed into an oval pool of milky-brown fat.
The toothpaste was refreshing.	The toothpaste, tasting minty sweet, felt good against slippery teeth, free finally from braces.
Filled with passengers and baggage, the car moved slowly down the road.	Burdened with its load of clamoring children and well-worn suitcases, the car labored down down the interstate on bald tires and worn shocks, emitting puffs of blue exhaust and an occasional backfire.

Unlike the *concrete, sensory-packed* sentences on the right, the sentences on the left fail to create vivid word pictures that engage readers. While all good writing blends abstract and concrete language, descriptive writing demands an abundance of specific sensory language.

Keep in mind, too, that *verbs pack more of a wallop* than adverbs. The following sentence has to rely on adverbs (italicized) because its verbs are so weak: "She walked *casually* into the room and *deliberately* tried not to pay much attention to their stares." Rewritten, so that verbs (italicized), not adverbs, do the bulk of the work, the sentence becomes more powerful: "She *strolled* into the room and *ignored* their stares."

Figures of speech—nonliteral, imaginative comparisons between two basically dissimilar things—are another way to enliven descriptive writing. *Similes* use the words *like* or *as* when comparing; *metaphors* state or imply that two things being compared are alike; and *personification* attributes human characteristics to inanimate things.

The examples that follow show how effective figurative language can be in descriptive writing.

Moving as jerkily as a marionette on strings, the old man picked himself up off the sidewalk and staggered down the street. (*simile*)

Stalking their prey, the hall monitors remained hidden in the corridors, motionless and ready to spring on any unsuspecting student who dared to sneak into class late. (*metaphor*)

The scoop of vanilla ice cream, plain and unadorned, cried out for hot-fudge sauce and a sprinkling of sliced pecans. (*personification*)

Finally, when writing descriptive passages, you need to *vary sentence structure*. Don't use the same subject-verb pattern in all sentences. The second example above, for instance, could have been written as follows: "The hall monitors stalked their prey. They hid in the corridors. They remained motionless and ready to spring on any unsuspecting student who tried to sneak into class late." But the sentence is richer and more interesting when the descriptive elements are embedded, eliminating what would otherwise have been a clipped and predictable subject-verb pattern.

REVISION STRATEGIES

Once you have a draft of the essay, you're ready to revise. The following checklist will help you and those giving you feedback apply to description some of the revision techniques discussed on pages 59–61.

☑ DESCRIPTION: A REVISION/PEER REVIEW CHECKLIST

Revise Overall Meaning and Structure

❏ What dominant impression does the essay convey? Is the dominant impression stated or implied? Where? Should it be made more obvious or more subtle?

❏ Is the essay primarily objective or subjective? Should the essay be more emotionally charged or less so?

❏ Which descriptive details don't support the dominant impression? Should they be deleted, or should the dominant impression be adjusted to encompass the details?

Revise Paragraph Development

❏ How are the essay's descriptive paragraphs organized—spatially, chronologically, emphatically, or by sensory impression? Would another organizational pattern be more effective? Which one(s)?

❏ Which paragraphs lack a distinctive focus?

❏ Which descriptive paragraphs are mere lists of sensory impressions?

❏ Which descriptive paragraphs fail to engage the reader's senses? How could they be made more concrete?

Revise Sentences and Words

❏ What signal devices guide readers through the description? Are there enough signals? Too many?

❏ Where should sentence structure be varied to make it less predictable?

❏ Which sentences should include more sensory images?

❏ Which flat verbs should be replaced with vigorous verbs?

❏ Where should there be more or fewer adjectives?

❏ Do any figures of speech seem contrived or trite? Which ones?

STUDENT ESSAY

The following student essay was written by Marie Martinez in response to this assignment:

> The essay "Flavio's Home" is an evocative piece about a place that had a powerful impact on Gordon Parks. Write an essay about a place that holds rich significance for you, centering the description on a dominant impression.

While reading Marie's paper, try to determine how well it applies the principles of description. The annotations on Marie's paper and the commentary following it will help you look at the essay more closely.

Salt Marsh
by Marie Martinez

Introduction

In one of his journals, Thoreau told of the difficulty he had escaping the obligations and cares of society: "It sometimes happens that I cannot easily shake off the village. The thought of some work will run in my head and I am not where my body is--I am out of my senses. In my walks I . . . return to my senses." All of us feel out of our senses at times. Overwhelmed by problems or everyday annoyances, we lose touch with sensory pleasures as we spend our days in noisy cities and stuffy classrooms. Just as Thoreau walked in the woods to return to his senses, I have a special place where I return to mine: the salt marsh behind my grandparents' house.   1

Dominant impression (thesis)

Informal topic sentence: Definition paragraph

My grandparents live on the East Coast, a mile or so inland from the sea. Between the ocean and the mainland is a wide fringe of salt marsh. A salt marsh is not a swamp, but an expanse of dark, spongy soil threaded with saltwater creeks and clothed in a kind of grass called salt meadow hay. All the water in the marsh rises and falls daily with the ocean tides, an endless cycle that changes the look of the marsh--partly flooded or mostly dry--as the day progresses.   2

Informal topic sentence: First paragraph in a four-part spatial sequence

Simile

Heading out to the marsh from my grandparents' house, I follow a short path through the woods. As I walk along, a sharp smell of salt mixed with the rich aroma of peaty soil fills my nostrils. I am always amazed by the way the path changes with the seasons. Sometimes I walk in the brilliant green of spring, sometimes in the tawny gold of autumn, sometimes in the grayish tan of winter. No matter the season, the grass flanking the trail is often flattened into swirls, like thick Van Gogh brush strokes that curve and recurve in circular patterns. No people come here. The peacefulness heals me like a soothing drug.   3

Informal topic sentence: Second paragraph in the spatial sequence ——→ After a few minutes, the trail suddenly opens up to a view 4
that calms me no matter how upset or discouraged I might be:
a line of tall waving reeds bordering and nearly hiding the salt
marsh creek. To get to the creek, I part the reeds.

Informal topic sentence: Third paragraph in the spatial sequence ——→ The creek is a narrow body of water no more than fifteen 5
feet wide, and it ebbs and flows as the ocean currents sweep
toward the land or rush back toward the sea. The creek winds
in a sinuous pattern so that I cannot see its beginning or end,
the places where it trickles into the marsh or spills into the
open ocean. Little brown birds dip in and out of the reeds on
the far shore of the creek, making a special "tweep-tweep"
sound peculiar to the marsh. When I stand at low tide on the
shore of the creek, I am on a miniature cliff, for the bank of the
creek falls abruptly and steeply into the water. Below me,
green grasses wave and shimmer under the water while tiny
minnows flash their silvery sides as they dart through the
underwater tangles.

Informal topic sentence: Last paragraph in the spatial sequence ——→ The creek water is often much warmer than the ocean, so 6
I can swim there in three seasons. Sitting on the edge of the
creek, I scoop some water into my hand, rub my face and neck,
then ease into the water. Where the creek is shallow, my feet

Simile ——— sink into a foot of muck that feels like mashed potatoes mixed
with motor oil. But once I become accustomed to it, I enjoy
squishing the slimy mud through my toes. Sometimes I feel
brushing past my legs the blue crabs that live in the creek.
Other times, I hear the splash of a turtle or an otter as it slips
from the shore into the water. Otherwise, it is silent. The salty
water is buoyant and lifts my spirits as I stroke through it to
reach the middle of the creek. There in the center, I float
weightlessly, surrounded by tall reeds that reduce the world to
water and sky. I am at peace.

Conclusion   The salt marsh is not the kind of dramatic landscape found 7
on picture postcards. There are no soaring mountains, sandy
beaches, or lush valleys. The marsh is a flat world that some
consider dull and uninviting. I am glad most people do not
respond to the marsh's subtle beauty because that means I can

Echo of idea in introduction be alone there. Just as the rising tide sweeps over the marsh,
floating debris out to the ocean, the marsh washes away my
concerns and restores me to my senses.

COMMENTARY

The dominant impression.   Marie responded to the assignment by writing a moving tribute to a place having special meaning for her—the salt marsh near her grandparents' home. Like most descriptive pieces, Marie's essay is organized around a *dominant impression:* the marsh's peaceful solitude and gentle, natural beauty. The essay's introduction provides a context for the dominant impression by comparing the pleasure Marie experiences in the marsh to the happiness Thoreau felt in his walks around Walden Pond.

Combining patterns of development.   Before developing the essay's dominant impression, Marie uses the second paragraph to *define* a salt marsh. An *objective description,* the definition clarifies that a salt marsh—with its spongy soil, haylike grass, and ebbing tides—is not to be confused with a swamp. Because Marie offers such a factual definition, readers have the background needed to enjoy the personalized view that follows.

Besides the definition paragraph and the comparison in the opening paragraph, the essay contains a strong element of *causal analysis:* Throughout, Marie describes the marsh's effect on her.

Sensory language.   At times, Marie develops the essay's dominant impression explicitly, as when she writes "No people come here" (paragraph 3) and "I am at peace" (6). But Marie generally uses the more subtle techniques characteristic of *subjective description* to convey the dominant impression. First of all, she fills the essay with strong *connotative language,* rich with *sensory images.* The third paragraph describes what she smells (the "sharp smell of salt mixed with the rich aroma of peaty soil") and what she sees ("brilliant green," "tawny gold," and "grayish tan"). In the fifth paragraph, she tells us that she hears the chirping sounds of small birds. And the sixth paragraph includes vigorous descriptions of how the marsh feels to Marie's touch. She splashes water on her face and neck; she digs her toes into the mud at the bottom of the creek; she delights in the delicate brushing of crabs against her legs.

Figurative language, vigorous verbs, and varied sentence structure.   You might also have noted that *figurative language, energetic verbs,* and *varied sentence patterns* contribute to the essay's descriptive power. Marie develops a *simile* in the third paragraph when she compares the flattened swirls of swamp grass to the brush strokes in a painting by Van Gogh. Later she uses another simile when she writes that the creek's thick mud feels "like mashed potatoes mixed with motor oil." Moreover, throughout the essay, she uses lively verbs ("shimmer," "flash") to capture the marsh's magical quality. Similarly, Marie enhances descriptive passages by varying the length of her sentences. Long, fairly elaborate sentences are interspersed with short, dramatic statements. In the third paragraph, for example, the long sentence describing the circular swirls of swamp grass is followed by the brief statement "No people come here." And the sixth paragraph uses two short sentences ("Otherwise, it is silent" and "I am at peace") to punctuate the paragraph's longer sentences.

Organization.   We can follow Marie's journey through the marsh because she uses an easy-to-follow combination of *spatial, chronological,* and *emphatic* patterns to sequence her experience. The essay relies primarily on a spatial arrangement since the four body paragraphs focus on the different spots that Marie reaches: first, the path behind her grandparents' house (paragraph 3); then the area bordering the creek (4); next, her view of the creek (5); last, the creek itself (6). Each stage of her walk is signaled by an *informal topic sentence* near the start of each paragraph. Furthermore, *signal devices* (marked by italics here) indicate not only her location but also the chronological passage of time: "*As* I walk along, a sharp smell . . . fills my nostrils" (3); "*After* a few minutes, the trail suddenly opens up . . ." (4); "*Below* me, green grasses wave . . ." (5). And to call attention to the creek's serene beauty, Marie saves for last the description of the peace she feels while floating in the creek.

An inappropriate figure of speech.   Although the four body paragraphs focus on the distinctive qualities of each location, Marie runs into a minor problem in the third paragraph. Take a moment to reread that paragraph's last sentence. Comparing the peace of the marsh to the effect of a "soothing drug" is jarring. The effectiveness of Marie's essay hinges on her ability to create a picture of a pure, natural world. A reference to drugs is inappropriate. Now, reread the paragraph aloud, stopping after "No people come here." Note how much more in keeping with the essay's dominant impression the paragraph is when the reference to drugs is omitted.

Conclusion.   The concluding paragraph brings the essay to a graceful close. The powerful *simile* found in the last sentence contains an implied reference to Thoreau and to Marie's earlier statement about the joy to be found in special places having restorative powers. Such an allusion echoes, with good effect, the paper's opening comments.

Revising the first draft.   When Marie met with some classmates during a peer review session, the students agreed that Marie's first draft was strong and moving. But they also said that they had difficulty following her route through the marsh; they found her third paragraph especially confusing. Marie kept track of her classmates' comments on a separate piece of paper and then entered them, numbered in order of importance, in the margin of her first draft. Reprinted here is the original version of Marie's third paragraph.

Original Version of the Third Paragraph

As I head out to the marsh from the house, I follow a short trail through the woods. A smell of salt mixed with the aroma of soil fills my nostrils. The end of the trail suddenly opens up to a view that calms me no matter how upset or discouraged I might be: a line of tall waving reeds bordering the salt marsh creek. Civilization seems far away as I walk the path of flattened grass and finally reach my goal, the salt marsh creek hidden behind the tall waving reeds. The path changes with the seasons; sometimes I walk in the brilliant green of spring, sometimes in the tawny gold of autumn, sometimes in the quiet grayish tan of winter. In some areas, the grass is flattened into swirls that make the marsh resemble one of those paintings by Van Gogh. No people come here. The peacefulness heals me like a soothing drug. The path stops at the line of tall waving reeds, standing upright at the border of the creek. I part the reeds to get to the creek.

When Marie looked more carefully at the paragraph, she agreed it was confusing. For one thing, the paragraph's third and fourth sentences indicated that she had come to the path's end and had reached the reeds bordering the creek. In the following sentences, however, she was on the path again. Then, at the end, she was back at the creek, as if she had just arrived there. Marie resolved this confusion by breaking the single paragraph into two separate ones—the first describing the walk along the path, the second describing her arrival at the creek. This restructuring, especially when combined with clearer transitions, eliminated the confusion.

While revising her essay, Marie also intensified the sensory images in her original paragraph. She changed the "smell of salt and soil" to the "sharp smell of salt mixed with the rich aroma of peaty soil." And when she added the phrase "thick Van Gogh brush strokes that curve and recurve in circular patterns," she made the comparison between the marsh grass and a Van Gogh painting more vivid.

These are just some of the changes Marie made while rewriting her paper. Her skillful revisions provided the polish needed to make an already strong essay even more evocative.

Activities: Description

Prewriting Activities

1. Imagine you're writing two essays: One explains the *process* by which students get "burned out"; the other *argues* that being a spendthrift is better (or worse) than being frugal. Jot down ways you might use description in each essay.

2. Go to a place on campus where students congregate. In preparation for an *objective* description of this place, make notes of various sights, sounds, smells, and textures, as well as the overall "feel" of the place. Then, in preparation for a *subjective* description, observe and take notes on another sheet of paper. Compare the two sets of material. What differences do you see in word choice and selection of details?

Revising Activities

3. Revise each of the following sentence sets twice. The first time, create an unmistakable mood; the second time, create a sharply contrasting mood. To convey atmosphere, vary sentence structure, use vigorous verbs, provide rich sensory details, and pay special attention to words' connotations.

a. The card players sat around the table. The table was old. The players were, too.
b. A long line formed outside the movie theater. People didn't want to miss the show. The movie had received a lot of attention recently.
c. A girl walked down the street in her first pair of high heels. This was a new experience for her.

4. The following descriptive paragraph is from the first draft of an essay showing that personal growth may result when romanticized notions and reality collide. How effective is the paragraph in illustrating the essay's thesis? Which details are powerful? Which could be more concrete? Which should be deleted? Where should sentence structure be more varied? How could the description be made more coherent? Revise the paragraph, correcting any problems you discover and adding whatever sensory details are needed to enliven the description. Feel free to break the paragraph into two or more separate ones.

As a child, I was intrigued by stories about the farm in Harrison County, Maine, where my father spent his teens. Being raised on a farm seemed more interesting than growing up in the suburbs. So about a year ago, I decided to see for myself what the farm was like. I got there by driving on Route 334, a surprisingly easy-to-drive, four-lane highway that had recently been built with matching state and federal funds. I turned into the dirt road leading to the farm and got out of my car. It had been washed and waxed for the occasion. Then I headed for a dirt-colored barn. Its roof was full of huge, rotted holes. As I rounded the bushes, I saw the house. It too was dirt-colored. Its paint must have worn off decades ago. A couple of dead-looking old cars were sprawled in front of the barn. They were dented and windowless. Also by the barn was an ancient refrigerator, crushed like a discarded accordion. The porch steps to the house were slanted and wobbly. Through the open windows came a stale smell and the sound of television. Looking in the front door screen, I could see two chickens jumping around inside. Everything looked dirty both inside and out. Secretly grateful that no one answered my knock, I bolted down the stairs, got into my clean, shiny car, and drove away.

Gordon Parks

The son of deeply religious tenant farmers, Gordon Parks (1912–) grew up in Kansas knowing both the comforts of familial love and the torments of poverty and racism. Sent as a teenager to live with his sister in Minnesota after his mother's death, Parks was thrown out on his own in a frigid winter by his brother-in-law. To support himself, Parks worked as a janitor in a flophouse and as a piano player in a bordello. These and other odd jobs gave Parks the means to buy his first camera. Fascinated by photographic images, Parks studied the masters and eventually developed his own powers as a photographer. So evocative were his photographic studies that both *Life* and *Vogue* brought him on staff, the first Black photographer to be hired by the two magazines. Parks's prodigious creativity has found expression in filmmaking (*Shaft* in 1971), musical composition (both classical and jazz), fiction, nonfiction, and poetry (titles include *The Learning Tree, A Choice of Weapons, To Smile in Autumn, Arias in Silence, Glimpses Toward Infinity, A Star for Noon,* and *The Sun Stalker,* published, respectively, in 1986, 1987, 1988, 1994, 1996, 2000, and 2003.). But it is Parks's photographic essays, covering five decades of American life, that have brought him the most acclaim. In the following essay, taken from his 1990 autobiography, *Voices in the Mirror,* Parks tells the story behind one of his most memorable photographic works—that of a twelve-year-old boy and his family, living in the slums of Rio de Janeiro.

Pre-Reading Journal Entry

The problem of poverty has provoked a wide array of proposed solutions. One controversial proposal argues that the government should pay poor women financial incentives to use birth control. What do you think of this proposal? Why is such a policy controversial? Use your journal to explore your thinking on this issue.

Flavio's Home

I've never lost my fierce grudge against poverty. It is the most savage of all human afflictions, claiming victims who can't mobilize their efforts against it, who often lack strength to digest what little food they scrounge up to survive. It keeps growing, multiplying, spreading like a cancer. In my wanderings I attack it wherever I can—in barrios, slums and favelas.   1

Catacumba was the name of the favela[1] where I found Flavio da Silva. It was wickedly hot. The noon sun baked the mud-rot of the wet mountainside.   2

[1]Slums on the outskirts of Rio de Janeiro, Brazil, inhabited by seven hundred thousand people (editors' note).

Garbage and human excrement clogged the open sewers snaking down the slopes. José Gallo, a *Life* reporter, and I rested in the shade of a jacaranda tree halfway up Rio de Janeiro's most infamous deathtrap. Below and above us were a maze of shacks, but in the distance alongside the beach stood the gleaming white homes of the rich.

Breathing hard, balancing a tin of water on his head, a small boy climbed   3
toward us. He was miserably thin, naked but for filthy denim shorts. His legs resembled sticks covered with skin and screwed into his feet. Death was all over him, in his sunken eyes, cheeks and jaundiced coloring. He stopped for breath, coughing, his chest heaving as water slopped over his bony shoulders. Then jerking sideways like a mechanical toy, he smiled a smile I will never forget. Turning, he went on up the mountainside.

The detailed *Life* assignment in my back pocket was to find an impover-   4
ished father with a family, to examine his earnings, political leanings, religion, friends, dreams and frustrations. I had been sent to do an essay on poverty. This frail boy bent under his load said more to me about poverty than a dozen poor fathers. I touched Gallo, and we got up and followed the boy to where he entered a shack near the top of the mountainside. It was a leaning crumpled place of old plankings with a rusted tin roof. From inside we heard the babblings of several children. José knocked. The door opened and the boy stood smiling with a bawling naked baby in his arms.

Still smiling, he whacked the baby's rump, invited us in and offered us a   5
box to sit on. The only other recognizable furniture was a sagging bed and a broken baby's crib. Flavio was twelve, and with Gallo acting as interpreter, he introduced his younger brothers and sisters: "Mario, the bad one; Baptista, the good one; Albia, Isabel and the baby Zacarias." Two other girls burst into the shack, screaming and pounding on one another. Flavio jumped in and parted them. "Shut up, you two." He pointed at the older girl. "That's Maria, the nasty one." She spit in his face. He smacked her and pointed to the smaller sister. "That's Luzia. She thinks she's pretty."

Having finished the introductions, he went to build a fire under the   6
stove—a rusted, bent top of an old gas range resting on several bricks. Beneath it was a piece of tin that caught the hot coals. The shack was about six by ten feet. Its grimy walls were a patchwork of misshapen boards with large gaps between them, revealing other shacks below stilted against the slopes. The floor, rotting under layers of grease and dirt, caught shafts of light slanting down through spaces in the roof. A large hole in the far corner served as a toilet. Beneath that hole was the sloping mountainside. Pockets of poverty in New York's Harlem, on Chicago's south side, in Puerto Rico's infamous El Fungito seemed pale by comparison. None of them had prepared me for this one in the favela of Catacumba.

Flavio washed rice in a large dishpan, then washed Zacarias's feet in the   7
same water. But even that dirty water wasn't to be wasted. He tossed in a chunk of lye soap and ordered each child to wash up. When they were

finished he splashed the water over the dirty floor, and, dropping to his knees, he scrubbed the planks until the black suds sank in. Just before sundown he put beans on the stove to warm, then left, saying he would be back shortly. "Don't let them burn," he cautioned Maria. "If they do and Poppa beats me, you'll get it later." Maria, happy to get at the licking spoon, switched over and began to stir the beans. Then slyly she dipped out a spoonful and swallowed them. Luzia eyed her. "I see you. I'm going to tell on you for stealing our supper."

Maria's eyes flashed anger. "You do and I'll beat you, you little bitch." Luzia threw a stick at Maria and fled out the door. Zacarias dropped off to sleep. Mario, the bad one, slouched in a corner and sucked his thumb. Isabel and Albia sat on the floor clinging to each other with a strange tenderness. Isabel held onto Albia's hair and Albia clutched at Isabel's neck. They appeared frozen in an act of quiet violence.   8

Flavio returned with wood, dumped it beside the stove and sat down to rest for a few minutes, then went down the mountain for more water. It was dark when he finally came back, his body sagging from exhaustion. No longer smiling, he suddenly had the look of an old man and by now we could see that he kept the family going. In the closed torment of that pitiful shack, he was waging a hopeless battle against starvation. The da Silva children were living in a coffin.   9

When at last the parents came in, Gallo and I seemed to be part of the family. Flavio had already told them we were there. "Gordunn Americano!" Luzia said, pointing at me. José, the father, viewed us with skepticism. Nair, his pregnant wife, seemed tired beyond speaking. Hardly acknowledging our presence, she picked up Zacarias, placed him on her shoulder and gently patted his behind. Flavio scurried about like a frightened rat, his silence plainly expressing the fear he held of his father. Impatiently, José da Silva waited for Flavio to serve dinner. He sat in the center of the bed with his legs crossed beneath him, frowning, waiting. There were only three tin plates. Flavio filled them with black beans and rice, then placed them before his father. José da Silva tasted them, chewed for several moments, then nodded his approval for the others to start. Only he and Nair had spoons; the children ate with their fingers. Flavio ate off the top of a coffee can. Afraid to offer us food, he edged his rice and beans toward us, gesturing for us to take some. We refused. He smiled, knowing we understood.   10

Later, when we got down to the difficult business of obtaining permission from José da Silva to photograph his family, he hemmed and hawed, wallowing in the pleasant authority of the decision maker. He finally gave in, but his manner told us that he expected something in return. As we were saying good night Flavio began to cough violently. For a few moments his lungs seemed to be tearing apart. I wanted to get away as quickly as possible. It was cowardly of me, but the bluish cast of his skin beneath the sweat, the choking and spitting were suddenly unbearable.   11

Gallo and I moved cautiously down through the darkness trying not to   12
appear as strangers. The Catacumba was no place for strangers after sundown. Desperate criminals hid out there. To hunt them out, the police came
in packs, but only in daylight. Gallo cautioned me. "If you get caught up
here after dark it's best to stay at the da Silvas' until morning." As we drove
toward the city the large white buildings of the rich loomed up. The world
behind us seemed like a bad dream. I had already decided to get the boy
Flavio to a doctor, and as quickly as possible.

The plush lobby of my hotel on the Copacabana waterfront was   13
crammed with people in formal attire. With the stink of the favela in my
clothes, I hurried to the elevator hoping no passengers would be aboard.
But as the door was closing a beautiful girl in a white lace gown stepped in.
I moved as far away as possible. Her escort entered behind her, swept her
into his arms and they indulged in a kiss that lasted until they exited on the
next floor. Neither of them seemed to realize that I was there. The room I
returned to seemed to be oversized; the da Silva shack would have fitted
into one corner of it. The steak dinner I had would have fed the da Silvas
for three days.

Billowing clouds blanketed Mount Corcovado as we approached the   14
favela the following morning. Suddenly the sun burst through, silhouetting
Cristo Redentor, the towering sculpture of Christ with arms extended, its
back turned against the slopes of Catacumba. The square at the entrance to
the favela bustled with hundreds of favelados. Long lines waited at the sole
water spigot. Others waited at the only toilet on the entire mountainside.
Women, unable to pay for soap, beat dirt from their wash at laundry tubs.
Men, burdened with lumber, picks and shovels and tools important to their
existence threaded their way through the noisy throngs. Dogs snarled,
barked and fought. Woodsmoke mixed with the stench of rotting things. In
the mist curling over the higher paths, columns of favelados climbed like ants
with wood and water cans on their heads.

We came upon Nair bent over her tub of wash. She wiped away sweat   15
with her apron and managed a smile. We asked for her husband and she
pointed to a tiny shack off to her right. This was José's store, where he sold
kerosene and bleach. He was sitting on a box, dozing. Sensing our presence,
he awoke and commenced complaining about his back. "It kills me. The
doctors don't help because I have no money. Always talk and a little pink pill
that does no good. Ah, what is to become of me?" A woman came to buy
bleach. He filled her bottle. She dropped a few coins and as she walked away
his eyes stayed on her backside until she was out of sight. Then he was complaining about his back again.

"How much do you earn a day?" Gallo asked.   16

"Seventy-five cents. On a good day maybe a dollar."   17

"Why aren't the kids in school?"   18

"I don't have money for the clothes they need to go to school." 19

"Has Flavio seen a doctor?" 20

He pointed to a one-story wooden building. "That's the clinic right 21
there. They're mad because I built my store in front of their place. I won't
tear it down so they won't help my kids. Talk, talk, talk and pink pills." We
bid him good-bye and started climbing, following mud trails, jutting rock,
slime-filled holes and shack after shack propped against the slopes on shaky
pilings. We sidestepped a dead cat covered with maggots. I held my breath
for an instant, only to inhale the stench of human excrement and garbage.
Bare feet and legs with open sores climbed above us—evils of the terrible soil
they trod every day, and there were seven hundred thousand or more afflict-
ed people in favelas around Rio alone. Touching me, Gallo pointed to Flavio
climbing ahead of us carrying firewood. He stopped to glance at a man
descending with a small coffin on his shoulder. A woman and a small child
followed him. When I lifted my camera, grumbling erupted from a group of
men sharing beer beneath a tree.

"They're threatening," Gallo said. "Keep moving. They fear cameras. 22
Think they're evil eyes bringing bad luck." Turning to watch the funeral pro-
cession, Flavio caught sight of us and waited. When we took the wood from
him he protested, saying he was used to carrying it. He gave in when I hung
my camera around his neck. Then, beaming, he climbed on ahead of us.

The fog had lifted and in the crisp morning light the shack looked more 23
squalid. Inside the kids seemed even noisier. Flavio smiled and spoke above
their racket. "Someday I want to live in a real house on a real street with
good pots and pans and a bed with sheets." He lit the fire to warm leftovers
from the night before. Stale rice and beans—for breakfast and supper. No
lunch; midday eating was out of the question. Smoke rose and curled up
through the ceiling's cracks. An air current forced it back, filling the place
and Flavio's lungs with fumes. A coughing spasm doubled him up, turned
his skin blue under viscous sweat. I handed him a cup of water, but he waved
it away. His stomach tightened as he dropped to his knees. His veins
throbbed as if they would burst. Frustrated, we could only watch; there was
nothing we could do to help. Strangely, none of his brothers or sisters
appeared to notice. None of them stopped doing whatever they were doing.
Perhaps they had seen it too often. After five interminable minutes it was
over, and he got to his feet, smiling as though it had all been a joke. "Maria,
it's time for Zacarias to be washed!"

"But there's rice in the pan!" 24

"Dump it in another pan—and don't spill water!" 25

Maria picked up Zacarias, who screamed, not wanting to be washed. 26
Irritated, Maria gave him a solid smack on his bare bottom. Flavio stepped
over and gave her the same, then a free-for-all started with Flavio, Maria and
Mario slinging fists at one another. Mario got one in the eye and fled the
shack calling Flavio a dirty son-of-a-bitch. Zacarias wound up on the floor

sucking his thumb and escaping his washing. The black bean and rice breakfast helped to get things back to normal. Now it was time to get Flavio to the doctor.

The clinic was crowded with patients—mothers and children covered   27
with open sores, a paralytic teenager, a man with an ear in a state of decay, an aged blind couple holding hands in doubled darkness. Throughout the place came wailings of hunger and hurt. Flavio sat nervously between Gallo and me. "What will the doctor do to me?" he kept asking.

"We'll see. We'll wait and see."   28

In all, there were over fifty people. Finally, after two hours, it was   29
Flavio's turn and he broke out in a sweat, though he smiled at the nurse as he passed through the door to the doctor's office. The nurse ignored it; in this place of misery, smiles were unexpected.

The doctor, a large, beady-eyed man with a crew cut, had an air of impa-   30
tience. Hardly acknowledging our presence, he began to examine the frightened Flavio. "Open your mouth. Say 'Ah.' Jump up and down. Breathe out. Take off those pants. Bend over. Stand up. Cough. Cough louder. Louder." He did it all with such cold efficiency. Then he spoke to us in English so Flavio wouldn't understand. "This little chap has just about had it." My heart sank. Flavio was smiling, happy to be over with the examination. He was handed a bottle of cough medicine and a small box of pink pills, then asked to step outside and wait.

"This the da Silva kid?"   31

"Yes."   32

"What's your interest in him?"   33

"We want to help in some way."   34

"I'm afraid you're too late. He's wasted with bronchial asthma, malnu-   35
trition and, I suspect, tuberculosis. His heart, lungs and teeth are all bad." He paused and wearily rubbed his forehead. "All that at the ripe old age of twelve. And these hills are packed with other kids just as bad off. Last year ten thousand died from dysentery alone. But what can we do? You saw what's waiting outside. It's like this every day. There's hardly enough money to buy aspirin. A few wealthy people who care help keep us going." He was quiet for a moment. "Maybe the right climate, the right diet, and constant medical care might . . ." He stopped and shook his head. "Naw. That poor lad's finished. He might last another year—maybe not." We thanked him and left.

"What did he say?" Flavio asked as we scaled the hill.   36

"Everything's going to be all right, Flav. There's nothing to worry about."   37

It had clouded over again by the time we reached the top. The rain   38
swept in, clearing the mountain of Corcovado. The huge Christ figure loomed up again with clouds swirling around it. And to it I said a quick prayer for the boy walking beside us. He smiled as if he had read my thoughts. "Papa says 'El Cristo' has turned his back on the favela."

"You're going to be all right, Flavio." 39

"I'm not scared of death. It's my brothers and sisters I worry about. 40
What would they do?"

"You'll be all right, Flavio."[2] 41

——————————

[2]Parks's photo-essay on Flavio generated an unprecedented response from *Life* readers. Indeed, they sent so much money to the da Silvas that the family was able to leave the *favela* for better living conditions. Parks brought Flavio to the United States for medical treatment, and the boy's health was restored. However, Flavio's story didn't have an unqualifiedly happy ending. Although he overcame his illness and later married and had a family, Flavio continuously fantasized about returning to the United States, convinced that only by returning to America could he improve his life. His obsession eventually eroded the promise of his life in Brazil (editors' note).

Questions for Close Reading

1. What is the selection's thesis (or dominant impression)? Locate the sentence(s) in which Parks states his main idea. If he doesn't state the thesis explicitly, express it in your own words.
2. What is Flavio's family like? Why does Flavio have so much responsibility in the household?
3. What are some of the distinctive characteristics of Flavio's neighborhood and home?
4. What seems to be the basis of Flavio's fear of giving food to Parks and Gallo? What did Parks and Gallo understand that led them to refuse?
5. Refer to your dictionary as needed to define the following words used in the selection: *barrios* (paragraph 1), *jacaranda* (2), *jaundiced* (3), and *spigot* (14).

Questions About the Writer's Craft

1. **The pattern.** Without stating it explicitly, Parks conveys a dominant impression about Flavio. What is that impression? What details create it?
2. **Other patterns.** When relating how Flavio performs numerous household tasks, Parks describes several *processes*. How do these step-by-step explanations reinforce Parks's dominant impression of Flavio?
3. Parks provides numerous sensory specifics to depict Flavio's home. Look closely, for example, at the description in paragraph 6. Which words and phrases convey strong sensory images? How does Parks use transitions to help the reader move from one sensory image to another?
4. Paragraph 13 includes a scene that occurs in Parks's hotel. What's the effect of this scene? What does it contribute to the essay that the most detailed description of the *favela* could not?

Writing Assignments Using Description as a Pattern of Development

∞ 1. Parks paints a wrenching portrait of a person who remains vibrant and hopeful even though he is suffering greatly—from physical illness, poverty, overwork, and worry. Write a description about someone you know who has shown courage or other positive qualities during a time of personal trouble. Include, as Parks does, plentiful details about the person's appearance and behavior so that you don't have to state directly what you admire about the person. Maya Angelou's "Sister Flowers" (page 96) shows how one writer conveys the special quality of an admirable individual.

2. Parks presents an unforgettable description of the *favela* and the living conditions there. Write an essay about a region, city, neighborhood, or building that also projects an overwhelming negative feeling. Include only those details that convey your dominant impression, and provide—as Parks does—vivid sensory language to convey your attitude toward your subject.

Writing Assignments Combining Patterns of Development

3. The doctor reports that a few wealthy people contribute to the clinic, but the reader can tell from the scene in Parks's hotel that most people are insensitive to those less fortunate. Write an essay *describing* a specific situation that you feel reflects people's tendency to ignore the difficulties of others. Analyze why people distance themselves from the problem; then present specific *steps* that could be taken to sensitize them to the situation. John M. Darley and Bibb Latané's "Why People Don't Help in a Crisis" (page 304) will provide some perspective on the way people harden themselves to the pain of others.

4. Although Parks celebrates Flavio's generosity of spirit, the writer also *illustrates* the brutalizing effect of an impoverished environment. Prepare an essay in which you also show that setting, architecture, even furnishings can influence mood and behavior. You may, as Parks does, focus on the corrosive effect of a negative environment, or you may write about the nurturing effect of a positive environment. Either way, provide vivid *descriptive* details of the environment you're considering. Possible subjects include a park in the middle of a city, a bus terminal, and a college library.

Writing Assignment Using a Journal Entry as a Starting Point

5. Write an essay explaining why you think impoverished women should—or should not—be paid financial incentives to practice birth control. To help define your position, review your pre-reading journal entry, and interview classmates, friends, and family members to get their opinions. Consider supplementing this informal research with material gathered in the library and/or on the Internet. Weigh all the evidence carefully before formulating your position.

Gary Soto

Born and raised in Fresno, California, Gary Soto (1952–) is a prolific poet, essayist, playwright, and film producer. The son of Mexican-American farm laborers, he earned degrees from California State University in Fresno and the University of California. He has published dozens of collections of poetry, from *The Elements of San Joaquin* (1977) through *One Kind of Faith* (2003). In 1985, Soto found acclaim with his prose memoir *Living up the Street: Narrative Recollections.* His later memoirs and essay collections include *Small Faces* (1986) and *Lesser Evils: Ten Quartets* (1988). Soto's writing for adults has earned him prizes and honors including a Guggenheim Fellowship (1979) and a National Book Award (1995). In 1990, Soto published *Baseball in April and Other Stories,* named a Best Book for Young Adults by the American Library Association. Since then, he has written more than two dozen children's books in which he explores, sympathetically and often humorously, what it means to be Mexican-American in the United States. His juvenile novels include *Taking Sides* (1991), *Pacific Crossing* (1992), *Buried Onions* (1997), and *The Afterlife* (2003). His poetry for young readers includes *Neighborhood Odes* (1992) and *Fearless Fernie* (2002), as well as the picture book *Too Many Tamales* (1992). A professor of creative writing at the University of California, Riverside, Soto regularly visits area schools to promote reading. He lives in Berkeley, California, with his wife and daughter. The following essay originally appeared in *Small Faces.*

Pre-Reading Journal Entry

It's likely that, at some point, you have blamed someone or something else for a problem that you yourself caused, at least partially. In your pre-reading journal, jot down at least two or three such situations. If you're brave enough, consult family and friends. Write your thoughts as to why you placed blame elsewhere. Did you want to avoid embarrassment, punishment, or some other negative consequence of your behavior? Did you have trouble accepting your faults? Did you blame someone with whom you were angry, as a way of "getting back"? Consider how you would handle the same situations today. Discuss what you would, or would not, do differently.

The Jacket

My clothes have failed me. I remember the green coat that I wore in fifth 1
and sixth grade when you either danced like a champ or pressed yourself
against a greasy wall, bitter as a penny toward the happy couples.

When I needed a new jacket and my mother asked what kind I wanted, 2
I described something like bikers wear: black leather and silver studs, with
enough belts to hold down a small town. We were in the kitchen, steam on
the windows from her cooking. She listened so long while stirring dinner

that I thought she understood for sure the kind I wanted. The next day when I got home from school, I discovered draped on my bedpost a jacket the color of day-old guacamole. I threw my books on the bed and approached the jacket slowly, as if it were a stranger whose hand I had to shake. I touched the vinyl sleeve, the collar, and peeked at the mustard-colored lining.

From the kitchen mother yelled that my jacket was in the closet. I closed the door to her voice and pulled at the rack of clothes in the closet, hoping the jacket on the bedpost wasn't for me but my mean brother. No luck. I gave up. From my bed, I stared at the jacket. I wanted to cry because it was so ugly and so big that I knew I'd have to wear it a long time. I was a small kid, thin as a young tree, and it would be years before I'd have a new one. I stared at the jacket, like an enemy, thinking bad things before I took off my old jacket, whose sleeves climbed halfway to my elbow. 3

I put the big jacket on. I zipped it up and down several times and rolled the cuffs up so they didn't cover my hands. I put my hands in the pockets and flapped the jacket like a bird's wings. I stood in front of the mirror, full face, then profile, and then looked over my shoulder as if someone had called me. I sat on the bed, stood against the bed, and combed my hair to see what I would look like doing something natural. I looked ugly. I threw it on my brother's bed and looked at it for a long time before I slipped it on and went out to the backyard, smiling a "thank you" to my mom as I passed her in the kitchen. With my hands in my pockets I kicked a ball against the fence, and then climbed it to sit looking into the alley. I hurled orange peels at the mouth of an open garbage can, and when the peels were gone I watched the white puffs of my breath thin to nothing. 4

I jumped down, hands in my pockets, and in the backyard, on my knees, I teased my dog, Brownie, by swooping my arms while making bird calls. He jumped at me and missed. He jumped again and again, until a tooth sunk deep, ripping an L-shaped tear on my left sleeve. I pushed Brownie away to study the tear as I would a cut on my arm. There was no blood, only a few loose pieces of fuzz. Damn dog, I thought, and pushed him away hard when he tried to bite again. I got up from my knees and went to my bedroom to sit with my jacket on my lap, with the lights out. 5

That was the first afternoon with my new jacket. The next day I wore it to sixth grade and got a D on a math quiz. During the morning recess Frankie T., the playground terrorist, pushed me to the ground and told me to stay there until recess was over. My best friend, Steve Negrete, ate an apple while looking at me, and the girls turned away to whisper on the monkey bars. The teachers were no help: they looked my way and talked about how foolish I looked in my new jacket. I saw their heads bob with laughter, their hands half covering their mouths. 6

Even though it was cold, I took off the jacket during lunch and played kickball in a thin shirt, my arms feeling like braille from goose bumps. But when I returned to class I slipped the jacket on and shivered until I was 7 warm. I sat on my hands, heating them up, while my teeth chattered like a cup of crooked dice. Finally warm, I slid out of the jacket but put it back on a few minutes later when the fire bell rang. We paraded out into the yard where we, the sixth graders, walked past all the other grades to stand against the back fence. Everybody saw me. Although they didn't say out loud, "Man, that's ugly," I heard the buzz-buzz of gossip and even laughter that I knew was meant for me.

And so I went, in my guacamole-colored jacket. So embarrassed, so hurt, I couldn't even do my homework. I received C's on quizzes and forgot the state capitals and the rivers of South America, our friendly neighbor. Even the girls who had been friendly blew away like loose flowers to follow the boys in neat jackets. 8

I wore that thing for three years until the sleeves grew short and my forearms stuck out like the necks of turtles. All during that time no love came to me—no little dark girl in a Sunday dress she wore on Monday. At lunchtime I stayed with the ugly boys who leaned against the chainlink fence and looked around with propellers of grass spinning in our mouths. We saw girls walk by alone, saw couples, hand in hand, their heads like bookends pressing air together. We saw them and spun our propellers so fast our faces were blurs. 9

I blame that jacket for those bad years. I blame my mother for her bad taste and her cheap ways. It was a sad time for the heart. With a friend I spent my sixth-grade year in a tree in the alley, waiting for something good to happen to me in that jacket, which had become the ugly brother who tagged along wherever I went. And it was about that time that I began to grow. My chest puffed up with muscle and, strangely, a few more ribs. Even my hands, those fleshy hammers, showed bravely through the cuffs, the fingers already hardening for the coming fights. But that L-shaped rip on the left sleeve got bigger; bits of stuffing coughed out from its wound after a hard day of play. I finally Scotch-taped it closed, but in rain or cold weather the tape peeled off like a scab and more stuffing fell out until that sleeve shriveled into a palsied arm. That winter the elbows began to crack and whole chunks of green began to fall off. I showed the cracks to my mother, who always seemed to be at the stove with steamed-up glasses, and she said that there were children in Mexico who would love that jacket. I told her that this was America and yelled that Debbie, my sister, didn't have a jacket like mine. I ran outside, ready to cry, and climbed the tree by the alley to think bad thoughts and watch my breath puff white and disappear. 10

But whole pieces still casually flew off my jacket when I played hard, read quietly, or took vicious spelling tests at school. When it became so spotted that my brother began to call me "camouflage," I flung it over the fence into the alley. Later, however, I swiped the jacket off the ground and went inside to drape it across my lap and mope. 11

I was called to dinner: steam silvered my mother's glasses as she said grace; my brother and sister with their heads bowed made ugly faces at their 12 glasses of powdered milk. I gagged too, but eagerly ate big rips of buttered tortilla that held scooped-up beans. Finished, I went outside with my jacket across my arm. It was a cold sky. The faces of clouds were piled up, hurting. I climbed the fence, jumping down with a grunt. I started up the alley and soon slipped into my jacket, that green ugly brother who breathed over my shoulder that day and ever since.

Questions for Close Reading

1. What is the selection's thesis (or dominant impression)? Locate the sentence(s) in which Soto states his main idea. If he doesn't state the thesis explicitly, express it in your own words.
2. What was the economic status of Soto's family? Cite some details that support your answer.
3. When Soto was a child, what were his feelings toward his mother? What are his feelings toward her as an adult?
4. How do the narrator's feelings toward the jacket evolve over the course of the essay? What does he mean when, at the end, he calls the jacket "that green ugly brother who breathed over my shoulder that day and ever since" (paragraph 12)?
5. Refer to your dictionary as needed to define the following words used in the selection: *guacamole* (paragraph 2), *braille* (7), *palsied* (10), *camouflage* (11), and *tortilla* (12).

Questions About the Writer's Craft

1. **The pattern.** What organizational sequence does Soto use in describing the jacket and his relationship to it? Quote some transitional terms and phrases that help to establish this sequence.
2. At various points, Soto uses personification (page 75) to describe the jacket. Where and how does he do so? What does this figurative language imply about his feelings toward the jacket?
3. In paragraphs 4, 7, and 9, the narrator uses similes (page 75) to describe his appearance. Name the specific similes he uses. What do these similes imply about the way he felt as a child?
4. **Other patterns.** In paragraphs 2 and 9, Soto presents some key *contrasts*. What does he contrast in these paragraphs? How do these contrasts contribute to the essay's dominant impression?

Writing Assignments Using Description as a Pattern of Development

1. By describing a jacket and his feelings toward it, Soto reveals much about his personality and values. Write an essay describing some article of clothing that has had special meaning for you, either positive or negative. Like Soto, use sensory details and figures of speech to convey your feelings about this article of clothing. Unlike Soto, also write about what your feelings indicate about your personality and values.
2. In paragraph 7, Soto briefly describes his misery when he was cold. Recall a time when you were physically miserable—for example, exceedingly hungry, in pain, or

sleep-deprived. Write an essay that makes readers *feel* your misery. Describe how your body and your surroundings looked and felt. Also describe any sounds, tastes, and smells that contributed to your displeasure. Your tone can be humorous or serious. For other examples of writing describing an oppressive physical state or environment, consider reading Gordon Parks's "Flavio's Home" (page 83) and Joseph H. Suina's "And Then I Went to School" (page 271).

Writing Assignments Combining Patterns of Development

∞ 3. In his essay, Soto draws heavily upon his childhood conception of physical ugliness, epitomized by his "guacamole-colored" jacket. Write an essay in which you *define* "ugliness" in your own way. Your sense of ugliness might be primarily physical, emotional, or moral. For you, the epitome of ugly might be anything from an ugly place (an abandoned and vandalized house) to an ugly experience (being betrayed by a friend) to an ugly attitude (indifference to cruelty). Develop your definition with strong, specific *examples* of ugliness. Before writing your essay, you might consider reading K. C. Cole's "Entropy" (page 332) for a model of how an abstract term can be defined through concrete examples.

∞ 4. In "The Jacket," Soto narrates a time in his life when he felt alienated. In his childhood view, an ugly green jacket caused him to be alone and apart from his peers. Write an essay *narrating* a specific time in your life when *you* felt alienated. You might, for example, discuss when your family moved to a new place or when you started attending a new school. Analyze the various factors in your situation *causing* you to feel so alone. Langston Hughes's "Salvation" (page 124) and Joseph H. Suina's "And Then I Went to School" (page 271) offer compelling examples of writing that explores an alienating experience.

Writing Assignment Using a Journal Entry as a Starting Point

5. In "The Jacket," the narrator to a great extent blames his ugly green jacket for the problems he had in his youth. Using the material you generated in your pre-reading journal entry, select *one* situation in which you blamed someone or something else for a problem at least partly of your own making. Write an essay analyzing what you now recognize to have been the actual cause(s) of your problem. As you do so, analyze why you refused to acknowledge error at the time. You might conclude your essay with a commentary on how you could have handled the situation more constructively.

Maya Angelou

Born Marguerite Johnson in 1928, Maya Angelou spent her childhood in Stamps, Arkansas, with her brother, Bailey, and her grandmother, "Momma." Although her youth was difficult—she was raped at age eight and a mother at sixteen—Angelou somehow managed to thrive. Multi-talented, she later worked as a professional dancer, starred in an off-Broadway play, appeared in the television miniseries *Roots,* served as a coordinator for the Southern Christian Leadership Conference, and wrote several well-received volumes of poetry—among them *Oh Pray My Wings Are Gonna Fit Me Well* (1975) and *And Still I Rise* (1996). She has also written essay collections, such as *Even the Stars Look Lonesome* (1997), and children's books, including *My Painted House, My Friendly Chicken, and Me* (1994), and *Kofi and His Magic* (1996). A professor at Wake Forest University since 1991, Angelou delivered at the 1993 presidential inauguration a stirring poem written for the occasion. The recipient of numerous honorary doctorates, Angelou is best known for her series of six autobiographical books, starting with *I Know Why the Caged Bird Sings* (1970) and concluding with *A Song Flung Up to Heaven* (2002). The following essay is taken from *I Know Why the Caged Bird Sings.*

Pre-Reading Journal Entry

Growing up isn't easy. In your journal, list several challenges you've had to face in your life. In each case, was there someone who served as a "lifeline," providing you with crucial guidance and support? Who was that individual? How did this person steer you through the difficulty?

Sister Flowers

For nearly a year [after I was raped], I sopped around the house, the 1
Store, the school and the church, like an old biscuit, dirty and inedible. Then I met, or rather got to know, the lady who threw me my first life line.

Mrs. Bertha Flowers was the aristocrat of Black Stamps. She had the 2
grace of control to appear warm in the coldest weather, and on the Arkansas summer days it seemed she had a private breeze which swirled around, cooling her. She was thin without the taut look of wiry people, and her printed voile dresses and flowered hats were as right for her as denim overalls for a farmer. She was our side's answer to the richest white woman in town.

Her skin was a rich black that would have peeled like a plum if snagged, 3
but then no one would have thought of getting close enough to Mrs. Flowers to ruffle her dress, let alone snag her skin. She didn't encourage familiarity. She wore gloves too.

I don't think I ever saw Mrs. Flowers laugh, but she smiled often. A slow   4
widening of her thin black lips to show even, small white teeth, then the slow
effortless closing. When she chose to smile on me, I always wanted to thank
her. The action was so graceful and inclusively benign.

She was one of the few gentlewomen I have ever known, and has   5
remained throughout my life the measure of what a human being can be.

Momma had a strange relationship with her. Most often when she passed   6
on the road in front of the Store, she spoke to Momma in that soft yet carrying voice, "Good day, Mrs. Henderson." Momma responded with "How
you, Sister Flowers?"

Mrs. Flowers didn't belong to our church, nor was she Momma's famil-   7
iar. Why on earth did she insist on calling her Sister Flowers? Shame made
me want to hide my face. Mrs. Flowers deserved better than to be called
Sister. Then, Momma left out the verb. Why not ask, "How *are* you,
Mrs. Flowers?" With the unbalanced passion of the young, I hated her for
showing her ignorance to Mrs. Flowers. It didn't occur to me for many years
that they were as alike as sisters, separated only by formal education.

Although I was upset, neither of the women was in the least shaken by   8
what I thought an unceremonious greeting. Mrs. Flowers would continue
her easy gait up the hill to her little bungalow, and Momma kept on shelling
peas or doing whatever had brought her to the front porch.

Occasionally, though, Mrs. Flowers would drift off the road and down   9
to the Store and Momma would say to me, "Sister, you go on and play." As
she left I would hear the beginning of an intimate conversation. Momma
persistently using the wrong verb, or none at all.

"Brother and Sister Wilcox is sho'ly the meanest—" "Is," Momma?   10
"Is"? Oh, please, not "is," Momma, for two or more. But they talked, and
from the side of the building where I waited for the ground to open up and
swallow me, I heard the soft-voiced Mrs. Flowers and the textured voice of
my grandmother merging and melting. They were interrupted from time to
time by giggles that must have come from Mrs. Flowers (Momma never gig-
gled in her life). Then she was gone.

She appealed to me because she was like people I had never met person-   11
ally. Like women in English novels who walked the moors (whatever they
were) with their loyal dogs racing at a respectful distance. Like the women
who sat in front of roaring fireplaces, drinking tea incessantly from silver trays
full of scones and crumpets. Women who walked over the "heath" and read
morocco-bound books and had two last names divided by a hyphen. It would
be safe to say that she made me proud to be Negro, just by being herself.

She acted just as refined as whitefolks in the movies and books and she   12
was more beautiful, for none of them could have come near that warm color
without looking gray by comparison.

It was fortunate that I never saw her in the company of powhitefolks.   13
For since they tend to think of their whiteness as an evenizer, I'm certain

that I would have had to hear her spoken to commonly as Bertha, and my image of her would have been shattered like the unmendable Humpty-Dumpty.

One summer afternoon, sweet-milk fresh in my memory, she stopped   14
at the Store to buy provisions. Another Negro woman of her health and age would have been expected to carry the paper sacks home in one hand, but Momma said, "Sister Flowers, I'll send Bailey up to your house with these things."

She smiled that slow dragging smile, "Thank you, Mrs. Henderson. I'd   15
prefer Marguerite, though." My name was beautiful when she said it. "I've been meaning to talk to her, anyway." They gave each other age-group looks.

Momma said, "Well, that's all right then. Sister, go and change your   16
dress. You going to Sister Flowers's."

The chifforobe was a maze. What on earth did one put on to go to   17
Mrs. Flowers's house? I knew I shouldn't put on a Sunday dress. It might be sacrilegious. Certainly not a house dress, since I was already wearing a fresh one. I chose a school dress, naturally. It was formal without suggesting that going to Mrs. Flowers's house was equivalent to attending church.

I trusted myself back into the Store.   18

"Now, don't you look nice." I had chosen the right thing, for once. . . .   19

There was a little path beside the rocky road, and Mrs. Flowers walked   20
in front swinging her arms and picking her way over the stones.

She said, without turning her head, to me, "I hear you're doing very   21
good school work, Marguerite, but that it's all written. The teachers report that they have trouble getting you to talk in class." We passed the triangular farm on our left and the path widened to allow us to walk together. I hung back in the separate unasked and unanswerable questions.

"Come and walk along with me, Marguerite." I couldn't have refused   22
even if I wanted to. She pronounced my name so nicely. Or more correctly, she spoke each word with such clarity that I was certain a foreigner who didn't understand English could have understood her.

"Now no one is going to make you talk—possibly no one can. But bear   23
in mind, language is man's way of communicating with his fellow man and it is language alone which separates him from the lower animals." That was a totally new idea to me, and I would need time to think about it.

"Your grandmother says you read a lot. Every chance you get. That's   24
good, but not good enough. Words mean more than what is set down on paper. It takes the human voice to infuse them with the shades of deeper meaning."

I memorized the part about the human voice infusing words. It seemed   25
so valid and poetic.

She said she was going to give me some books and that I not only must   26
read them, I must read them aloud. She suggested that I try to make a sentence sound in as many different ways as possible.

"I'll accept no excuse if you return a book to me that has been badly   27
handled." My imagination boggled at the punishment I would deserve if in
fact I did abuse a book of Mrs. Flowers's. Death would be too kind and brief.

The odors in the house surprised me. Somehow I had never connected   28
Mrs. Flowers with food or eating or any other common experience of common people. There must have been an outhouse, too, but my mind never
recorded it.

The sweet scent of vanilla had met us as she opened the door.   29

"I made tea cookies this morning. You see, I had planned to invite you   30
for cookies and lemonade so we could have this little chat. The lemonade is
in the icebox."

It followed that Mrs. Flowers would have ice on an ordinary day, when   31
most families in our town bought ice late on Saturdays only a few times during the summer to be used in the wooden ice-cream freezers.

She took the bags from me and disappeared through the kitchen door.   32
I looked around the room that I had never in my wildest fantasies imagined
I would see. Browned photographs leered or threatened from the walls and
the white, freshly done curtains pushed against themselves and against the
wind. I wanted to gobble up the room entire and take it to Bailey, who
would help me analyze and enjoy it.

"Have a seat, Marguerite. Over there by the table." She carried a platter   33
covered with a tea towel. Although she warned that she hadn't tried her
hand at baking sweets for some time, I was certain that like everything else
about her the cookies would be perfect.

They were flat round wafers, slightly browned on the edges and butter-   34
yellow in the center. With the cold lemonade they were sufficient for childhood's lifelong diet. Remembering my manners, I took nice little lady-like
bites off the edges. She said she had made them expressly for me and that
she had a few in the kitchen that I could take home to my brother. So I
jammed one whole cake in my mouth and the rough crumbs scratched the
insides of my jaws, and if I hadn't had to swallow, it would have been a
dream come true.

As I ate she began the first of what we later called "my lessons in living."   35
She said that I must always be intolerant of ignorance but understanding of
illiteracy. That some people, unable to go to school, were more educated and
even more intelligent than college professors. She encouraged me to listen
carefully to what country people called mother wit. That in those homely
sayings was couched the collective wisdom of generations.

When I finished the cookies she brushed off the table and brought a   36
thick, small book from the bookcase. I had read *A Tale of Two Cities* and
found it up to my standards as a romantic novel. She opened the first page
and I heard poetry for the first time in my life.

"It was the best of times and the worst of times . . ." Her voice slid in   37
and curved down through and over the words. She was nearly singing. I

wanted to look at the pages. Were they the same that I had read? Or were there notes, music, lined on the pages, as in a hymn book? Her sounds began cascading gently. I knew from listening to a thousand preachers that she was nearing the end of her reading, and I hadn't really heard, heard to understand, a single word.

"How do you like that?"   38

It occurred to me that she expected a response. The sweet vanilla flavor   39
was still on my tongue and her reading was a wonder in my ears. I had to speak.

I said, "Yes, ma'am." It was the least I could do, but it was the most also.   40

"There's one more thing. Take this book of poems and memorize one   41
for me. Next time you pay me a visit, I want you to recite."

I have tried often to search behind the sophistication of years for the   42
enchantment I so easily found in those gifts. The essence escapes but its aura
remains. To be allowed, no, invited, into the private lives of strangers, and to
share their joys and fears, was a chance to exchange the Southern bitter
wormwood for a cup of mead with Beowulf[1] or a hot cup of tea and milk
with Oliver Twist.[2] When I said aloud, "It is a far, far better thing that I do,
than I have ever done . . ."[3] tears of love filled my eyes at my selflessness.

On that first day, I ran down the hill and into the road (few cars ever   43
came along it) and had the good sense to stop running before I reached the
Store.

I was liked, and what a difference it made. I was respected not as   44
Mrs. Henderson's grandchild or Bailey's sister but for just being Marguerite
Johnson.

Childhood's logic never asks to be proved (all conclusions are absolute).   45
I didn't question why Mrs. Flowers had singled me out for attention, nor did
it occur to me that Momma might have asked her to give me a little talking
to. All I cared about was that she had made tea cookies for *me* and read to
me from her favorite book. It was enough to prove that she liked me.

---

[1]The hero of an Old English epic poem dating from the eighth century (editors' note).
[2]The main character in Charles Dickens's novel *Oliver Twist* (1837) (editors' note).
[3]The last words of Sydney Carton, the selfless hero of Charles Dickens's novel *A Tale of Two
Cities* (1859) (editors' note).

Questions for Close Reading

1. What is the selection's thesis (or dominant impression)? Locate the sentence(s) in which Angelou states her main idea. If she doesn't state the thesis explicitly, express it in your own words.
2. Angelou states that Mrs. Flowers "has remained throughout my life the measure of what a human being can be" (paragraph 5). What does Angelou admire about Mrs. Flowers?

3. Why is young Angelou so ashamed of Momma when Mrs. Flowers is around? How do Momma and Mrs. Flowers behave with each other?

4. What are the "lessons in living" that Angelou receives from Mrs. Flowers during their first visit? How do you think these lessons might have subsequently influenced Angelou?

5. Refer to your dictionary as needed to define the following words used in the selection: *taut* (paragraph 2), *voile* (2), *benign* (4), *unceremonious* (8), *gait* (8), *moors* (11), *incessantly* (11), *scones* (11), *crumpets* (11), *heath* (11), *chifforobe* (17), *sacrilegious* (17), *infuse* (24), *couched* (35), and *aura* (42).

Questions About the Writer's Craft

1. **The pattern.** Reread the essay, focusing on the descriptive passages first of Mrs. Flowers and then of Angelou's visit to Mrs. Flowers's house. To what senses does Angelou appeal in these passages? What method of organization (see pages 39–41) does she use to order these sensory details?

2. To enrich the description of her eventful encounter with Mrs. Flowers, Angelou draws upon figures of speech (see page 75). Consider, for example, the similes in paragraphs 1 and 11. How do these figures of speech contribute to the essay's dominant impression?

3. **Other patterns.** Because Angelou's description has a strong *narrative* component, it isn't surprising that there's a considerable amount of dialogue in the selection. For example, in paragraphs 7 and 10, Angelou quotes Momma's incorrect grammar. She then provides an imagined conversation in which the young Angelou scolds Momma and corrects her speech. What do these imagined scoldings of Momma reveal about young Angelou? How do they relate to Mrs. Flowers's subsequent "lessons in life"?

4. Although it's not the focus of this selection, the issue of race remains in the background of Angelou's portrait of Mrs. Flowers. Where in the selection does Angelou imply that race was a fact of life in her town? How does this specter of racism help Angelou underscore the significance of her encounter with Mrs. Flowers?

Writing Assignments Using Description as a Pattern of Development

1. At one time or another, just about all of us have met someone who taught us to see ourselves more clearly and helped us understand what we wanted from life. Write an essay describing such a person. Focus on the individual's personal qualities, as a way of depicting the role he or she played in your life. Be sure not to limit yourself to an objective description. Subjective description, filled with lively language and figures of speech, will serve you well as you provide a portrait of this special person.

2. Thrilled by the spectacle of Mrs. Flowers's interesting home, Angelou says she wanted to "gobble up the room entire" and share it with her brother. Write an essay describing in detail a place that vividly survives in your memory. You may describe a setting that you visited only once or a familiar setting that holds a special place in your heart. Before you write, list the qualities and sensory impressions you associate with this special place; then refine the list so that all details support your dominant impression.

Writing Assignments Combining
Patterns of Development

∞ 3. When the young Angelou discovers, thanks to Mrs. Flowers, the thrill of acceptance, she experiences a kind of *epiphany*—a moment of enlightenment. Write an essay about an event in your life that represented a kind of epiphany. You might write about a positive discovery, such as when you realized you had a special talent for something, or about a negative discovery, such as when you realized that a beloved family member had a serious flaw. To make the point that the moment was a turning point in your life, start by *describing* what kind of person you were before the discovery. Then *narrate* the actual incident, using vivid details and dialogue to make the event come alive. End by discussing the importance of this epiphany in your life. For additional accounts of personal epiphanies, you might read Langston Hughes's "Salvation" (page 124) and Beth Johnson's "Bombs Bursting in Air" (page 160).

4. Think of an activity that engages you completely, one that provides—as reading does for Angelou—an opportunity for growth and expansion. Possibilities include reading, writing, playing an instrument, doing crafts, dancing, hiking, playing a sport, cooking, or traveling. Write an essay in which you *argue* the merits of your chosen pastime. Assume that some of your readers are highly skeptical. To win them over, you'll need to provide convincing *examples* that demonstrate the pleasure and benefits you have discovered in the activity.

Writing Assignment Using a Journal
Entry as a Starting Point

5. Write an essay about a time when someone threw you a much-needed "lifeline" at a challenging time. Review your pre-reading journal entry, selecting *one* time when a person's encouragement and support made a great difference in your life. Be sure to describe the challenge you faced before recounting the specific details of the person's help. Dialogue and descriptive details will help you recreate the power of the experience.

Additional Writing Topics

DESCRIPTION

General Assignments

Write an essay using description to develop any of the following topics. Remember that an effective description focuses on a dominant impression and arranges details in a way that best supports that impression. Your details—vivid and appealing to the senses—should be carefully chosen so that the essay isn't overburdened with material of secondary importance. When writing, keep in mind that varied sentence structure and imaginative figures of speech are ways to make a descriptive piece compelling.

1. A favorite item of clothing
2. A school as a young child might see it
3. A hospital room you visited or stayed in
4. An individualist's appearance
5. A coffee shop, a bus shelter, a newsstand, or some other small place
6. A parade or victory celebration
7. A banana, a squash, or another fruit or vegetable
8. A particular drawer in a desk or bureau
9. A houseplant
10. A "media event"
11. A dorm room
12. An elderly person
13. An attractive man or woman
14. A prosthetic device or wheelchair
15. A TV, film, or music celebrity
16. A student lounge
17. A once-in-a-lifetime event
18. The inside of something, such as a cave, boat, car, shed, or machine
19. A friend, a roommate, or another person you know well
20. An essential gadget or a useless gadget

Assignments With a Specific Purpose, Audience, and Point of View

On Campus

1. For an audience of incoming first-year students, prepare a speech describing registration day at your college. Use specific details to help prepare students for the actual event. Choose an adjective that represents your dominant impression of the experience, and keep that word in mind as you write.
2. Your college has decided to replace an old campus structure (for example, a dorm or dining hall) with a new version. Write the administration a letter of protest

describing the place so vividly and appealingly that its value and need for preservation are unquestionable.

3. As a staff member of the campus newspaper, you have been asked to write a weekly column of social news and gossip. For your first column, you plan to describe a recent campus event—a dance, party, or concert, or other social activity. With a straightforward or tongue-in-cheek tone, describe where the event was held, the appearance of the people who attended, and so on.

At Home or in the Community

4. As a subscriber to a community-wide dating service, you've been asked to submit a description of the kind of person you'd like to meet. Describe your ideal date. Focus on specifics about physical appearance, personal habits, character traits, and interests.

5. As a resident of a particular town, you're angered by the appearance of a certain spot and by the activities that take place there. Write the town council a letter describing in detail the undesirable nature of this place (a video arcade, an adult bookstore, a bar, a bus station, a neglected park or beach). End with some suggestions about ways to improve the situation.

On the Job

6. You've noticed a recurring problem in your workplace, and you want to bring it to the attention of your boss, who is typically inattentive. Write a letter to your boss describing the problem. Your goal is not to provide solutions, but rather, to provide vivid description—complete with sensory details—so that your boss can no longer deny the problem.

4

NARRATION

WHAT IS NARRATION?

Human beings are instinctively storytellers. In prehistoric times, our ancestors huddled around campfires to hear tales of hunting and magic. In ancient times, warriors gathered in halls to listen to bards praise in song the exploits of epic heroes. Things are no different today. Boisterous children invariably settle down to listen when their parents read to them; millions of people tune in day after day to the ongoing drama of their favorite soap operas; vacationers sit motionless on the beach, caught up in the latest best-sellers; and all of us enjoy saying, "Just listen to what happened to me today." Our hunger for storytelling is a basic part of us.

Narration means telling a single story or several related stories. The story can be a means to an end, a way to support a main idea or thesis. For instance, to demonstrate that television has become the constant companion of many children, you might narrate a typical child's day in front of the television—starting with frantic cartoons in the morning and ending with dizzy situation comedies at night. Or to support the point that the college registration process should be reformed, you could tell the tale of a chaotic morning spent trying to enroll in classes.

Narration is powerful. Every public speaker, from politician to classroom teacher, knows that stories capture the attention of listeners as nothing else can. Narration speaks to us strongly because it is about us; we want to know what happened to others, not simply because we're curious, but because their experiences shed light on the nature of our own lives. Narration lends force to opinions, triggers the flow of memory, and evokes places and times in ways that are compelling and affecting.

HOW NARRATION FITS YOUR PURPOSE AND AUDIENCE

Because narratives tell a story, you may think they are found only in novels or short stories. But narration can also appear in essays, sometimes as a supplemental pattern of development. For example, if your purpose in a paper is to *persuade* apathetic readers that airport security regulations must be followed strictly, you might lead off with a brief account of an armed terrorist who easily boarded a plane. In a paper *defining* good teaching, you might keep readers engaged by including satirical anecdotes about one hapless instructor, the antithesis of an effective teacher. An essay on the *effects* of an overburdened judicial system might provide—in an attempt to involve readers—a dramatic account of the way one clearly guilty murderer plea-bargained his way to freedom.

In addition to providing effective support in one section of your paper, narration can also serve as an essay's dominant pattern of development. In fact, most of this chapter shows you how to use a single extended narrative to convey a central point and share with readers your view of what happened. You might choose to narrate the events of a day spent with your three-year-old nephew as a way of revealing how you rediscovered the importance of family life. Or you might relate the story of your roommate's mugging, evoking the powerlessness and terror of being a victim. Any story can form the basis for a narrative essay as long as you convey the essence of the experience and evoke its meaning.

SUGGESTIONS FOR USING NARRATION IN AN ESSAY

The following suggestions will be helpful whether you use narration as a dominant or a supportive pattern of development.

1. Identify the conflict in the event.   The power of many narratives is rooted in a special kind of tension that "hooks" readers and makes them want to follow the story to its end. This narrative tension is often a by-product of some form of *conflict* within the story. Many narratives revolve around an internal dilemma experienced by a key person in the story. Or the conflict may be between people in the story or between a pivotal character and some social institution or natural phenomenon.

2. Identify the point of the narrative.   In *The Adventures of Huckleberry Finn*, Mark Twain warned: "Persons attempting to find a motive in this narrative will be prosecuted; persons attempting to find a moral in it will be banished; persons attempting to find a plot in it will be shot." Twain was, of course, being ironic; his novel's richness lies in its "motives" and "morals." Similarly, when you recount a narrative, it's your responsibility to convey the event's *significance* or *meaning*. In other words, be sure readers are clear about your *narrative point*, or thesis.

Suppose you decide to write about the time you got locked in a mall late at night. Your narrative might focus on the way the mall looked after hours and the way you struggled with mounting terror. But you would also use the narrative to make a point. Perhaps you want to emphasize that fear can be instructive. Or your point might be that malls have a disturbing, surreal underside. You could state this thesis explicitly. ("After hours, the mall shed its cheerful daytime demeanor and took on a more sinister quality.") Or you could refrain from stating the thesis directly, relying on your details and language to convey the point of the narrative: "The mannequins stared at me with glazed eyes and frozen smiles" and "The steel grates pulled over each store's entrance glinted in the cold light, making each shop look like a prison cell."

3. Develop only those details that advance the narrative point.   You know from experience that nothing is more boring than a storyteller who gets sidetracked and drags out a story with nonessential details. If a friend started to tell about the time his car broke down in the middle of an expressway—but interrupted his story to complain at length about the slipshod work done by his auto repair shop—you might clench your teeth in annoyance, wishing your friend would hurry up and get back to the interesting part of the story.

Brainstorming ("What happened? When? Where? Who was involved? Why did it happen?") can be valuable for helping you amass narrative details. Then, after generating the specifics, you cull out the nonessential and devote your energies to the key specifics needed to advance your narrative point. When telling a story, you maintain an effective narrative pace by focusing on that point and eliminating details that don't support it. A good narrative depends not only on what is included, but also on what has been left out.

But how do you determine which specifics to omit, which to treat briefly, and which to emphasize? Having a clear sense of your narrative point and knowing your audience are crucial. Assume you're writing a narrative about a disastrous get-acquainted dance sponsored by your college the first week of the academic year. In addition to telling what happened, you want to make a point; perhaps you want to emphasize that, despite the college's good intentions, such official events actually make it difficult to meet people. With this purpose in mind, you might write about how stiff and unnatural students seemed, all dressed up in their best clothes; you might narrate snatches of strained conversation you overheard; you might describe the way males gathered on one side of the room, females on the other—reverting to behaviors supposedly abandoned in fifth grade. All these details would support your narrative point.

Because you don't want to get waylaid by detours that lead away from that point, you would leave out details about the topnotch band and the appetizing refreshments at the dance. The music and food may have been surprisingly good, but since these details don't advance the point you want to make, they should be omitted.

You also need to keep your audience in mind when selecting narrative details. If the audience consists of your instructor and other students—all of them familiar with the new student center where the dance was held—specific details about the center probably wouldn't have to be provided. But imagine that the essay is going to appear in the quarterly magazine published by the college's community relations office. Many of the magazine's readers are former graduates who haven't been on campus for several years. They may need some additional specifics about the student center: its location, how many people it holds, how it is furnished.

As you write, keep asking yourself, "Is this detail or character or snippet of conversation essential? Does my audience need this detail to understand the conflict in the situation? Does this detail advance or intensify the narrative action?" Summarize details that have some importance but do not deserve lengthy treatment ("Two hours went by . . ."). And try to limit *narrative commentary*—statements that tell rather than show what happened—since such remarks interrupt the narrative flow. Focus instead on the specifics that propel action forward in a vigorous way.

Sometimes, especially if the narrative re-creates an event from the past, you won't be able to remember what happened detail for detail. In such a case, you should take advantage of what is called *dramatic license*. Using as a guide your powers of recall as well as the perspective you now have of that particular time, feel free to reshape events to suit your narrative point.

4. Organize the narrative sequence.   All of us know the traditional beginning of fairy tales: "Once upon a time. . . ." Every narrative begins somewhere, presents a span of time, and ends at a certain point. Frequently, you'll want to use a straightforward time order, following the event *chronologically* from beginning to end: first this happened, next this happened, finally this happened.

But sometimes a strict chronological recounting may not be effective—especially if the high point of the narrative gets lost somewhere in the middle of the time sequence. To avoid that possibility, you may want to disrupt chronology, plunge the reader into the middle of the story, and then return in a *flashback* to the beginning of the tale. You're probably familiar with the way flashback is used on television and in film. You see someone appealing to the main character for financial help, then return to an earlier time when both were students in the same class, before learning how the rest of the story unfolds. Narratives can also use *flashforward*. You give readers a glimpse of the future (the main character being jailed) before the story continues in the present (the events leading to the arrest). These techniques shift the story onto several planes and keep it from becoming a step-by-step, predictable account. Reserve flashforwards and flashbacks, however, for crucial incidents only, since breaking out of chronological order acts as emphasis. Here are examples of how flashback and flashforward can be used in narrative writing:

Flashback

Standing behind the wooden counter, Greg wielded his knife expertly as he shucked clams--one every ten seconds--with practiced ease. The scene contrasted sharply with his first day on the job, when his hands broke out in blisters and when splitting each shell was like prying open a safe.

Flashforward

Rushing to move my car from the no-parking zone, I waved a quick goodbye to Karen as she climbed the steps to the bus. I didn't know then that by the time I picked her up at the bus station later that day, she had made a decision that would affect both our lives.

Whether or not you choose to include flashbacks or flashforwards in an essay, remember to limit the time span covered by the narrative. Otherwise, you will have trouble generating the details needed to give the story depth and meaning. Also, regardless of the time sequence you select, organize the tale so that it drives toward a strong finish. Be careful that your story doesn't trail off into minor, anticlimactic details.

5. Make the narrative easy to follow. Describing each distinct action in a separate paragraph helps readers grasp the flow of events. Although narrative essays don't always have conventional topic sentences, each narrative paragraph should have a clear focus. Often this focus is indicated by a sentence early in the paragraph that directs attention to the action taking place. Such a sentence functions as a kind of *informal topic sentence;* the rest of the paragraph then develops that topic sentence. You should also be sure to use time signals when narrating a story. Words like *now, then, next, after,* and *later* ensure that your reader won't get lost as the story progresses.

6. Make the narrative vigorous and immediate. A compelling narrative provides an abundance of specific details, making readers feel as if they're experiencing the story being told. Readers must be able to see, hear, touch, smell, and taste the event you're narrating. *Vivid sensory description* is, therefore, an essential part of an effective narrative. Not only do specific sensory details make writing a pleasure to read—we all enjoy learning the particulars about people, places, and things—but they also give the narrative the stamp of reality. The specifics convince the reader that the event being described actually did, or could, occur.

Compare the following excerpts from a narrative essay. The first version is lifeless and dull; the revised version, packed with sensory images, grabs readers with its sense of foreboding:

That eventful day started out like every other summer day. My sister Tricia and I made several elaborate mud pies, which we decorated with care. A little later on, as we were spraying each other with the garden hose, we heard my father walk up the path.

That sad summer day started out uneventfully enough. My sister Tricia and I spent a few hours mixing and decorating mud pies. Our hands caked with dry mud, we sprinkled each lopsided pie with alternating rows of dandelion and clover petals. Later when the sun got hotter, we tossed our white T-shirts over the red picket fence--forgetting my grandmother's frequent warnings to be more ladylike. Our sweaty backs bared to the sun, we doused each other with icy sprays from the garden hose. Caught up in the primitive pleasure of it all, we barely heard my father as he walked up the garden path, the gravel crunching under his heavy work boots.

A caution: Sensory language enlivens narration, but it also slows the pace. Be sure that the slower pace suits your purpose. For example, a lengthy description fits an account of a leisurely summer vacation but is inappropriate in a tale about a frantic search for a misplaced wallet.

Another way to create an aura of narrative immediacy is to use *dialogue* while telling a story. Our sense of other people comes, in part, from what they say and from the way they sound. Conversational exchanges allow the reader to experience characters directly. Compare the following fragments of a narrative, one with dialogue and one without, noting how much more energetic the second version is.

When I finally found my way back to the campsite, the trail guide commented on my disheveled appearance.

When I finally found my way back to the campsite, the trail guide took one look at me and drawled, "What on earth happened to you, Daniel Boone? You look as though you've been dragged through a haystack backwards."

"I'd look a lot worse if I hadn't run back here. When a bullet whizzes by me, I don't stick around to see who's doing the shooting."

Note that, when using dialogue, you generally begin a new paragraph to indicate a shift from one person's speech to another's (as in the second example above).

Using *varied sentence structure* is another strategy for making narratives lively and vigorous. Sentences that plod along predictably (subject-verb, subject-verb) put readers to sleep. Experiment with your sentences by juggling length and sentence type; mix long and short sentences, simple and complex. Compare the following original and revised versions to get an idea of how effective varied sentence rhythm can be in narrative writing.

Original

The store manager went to the walk-in refrigerator every day. The heavy metal door clanged shut behind her. I had visions of her freezing to death among the hanging carcasses. The shiny door finally swung open. She waddled out.

Revised

Each time the store manager went to the walk-in refrigerator, the heavy metal door clanged shut behind her. Visions of her freezing to death among the hanging carcasses crept into my mind until the shiny door finally swung open and she waddled out.

Original

The yellow-and-blue-striped fish struggled on the line. Its scales shimmered in the sunlight. Its tail waved frantically. I saw its desire to live. I decided to let it go.

Revised

Scales shimmering in the sunlight, tail waving frantically, the yellow-and-blue-striped fish struggled on the line. Seeing its desire to live, I let it go.

Finally, *vigorous verbs* lend energy to narratives. Use active verb forms ("The boss *yelled at* him") rather than passive ones ("He *was yelled at* by the boss"), and try to replace anemic *to be* verbs ("She *was* a good basketball player") with more dynamic constructions ("She *played* basketball well").

7. Keep your point of view and verb tense consistent.   All stories have a *narrator*, the person who tells the story. If you, as narrator, tell a story as you experienced it, the story is written in the *first-person point of view* ("*I* saw the dog pull loose"). But if you observed the event (or heard about it from others) and want to tell how someone else experienced the incident, you would use the *third-person point of view* ("*Anne* saw the dog pull loose"). Each point of view has advantages and limitations. First person allows you to express ordinarily private thoughts and to re-create an event as you actually experienced it. This point of view is limited, though, in its ability to depict the inner thoughts of other people involved in the event. By way of contrast, third person makes it easier to provide insight into the thoughts of all the participants. However, its objective, broad perspective may undercut some of the subjective immediacy typical of the "I was there" point of view. No matter which point of view you select, stay with that vantage point throughout the entire narrative.

Knowing whether to use the *past* or *present tense* ("I *strolled* into the room" as opposed to "I *stroll* into the room") is important. In most narrations, the past tense predominates, enabling the writer to span a considerable period of time. Although more rarely used, the present tense can be powerful for events of short duration—a wrestling match or a medical emergency, for instance. A narrative in the present tense prolongs each moment, intensifying the reader's sense of participation. Be careful, though; unless the event is intense and fast-paced, the present tense can seem contrived. Whichever tense you choose, avoid shifting midstream—starting, let's say, in the past tense ("she skated") and switching to the present ("she runs").

REVISION STRATEGIES

Once you have a draft of the essay, you're ready to revise. The following checklist will help you and those giving you feedback apply to narration some of the revision techniques discussed on pages 59–61.

☑ NARRATION: A REVISION/PEER REVIEW CHECKLIST

Revise Overall Meaning and Structure

❏ What is the essay's main point? Is it stated explicitly or is it implied? Where? Could the point be conveyed more clearly? How?

❏ What is the narrative's conflict? Is it stated explicitly or is it implied? Where? Could the conflict be made more dramatic? How?

❏ From what point of view is the narrative told? Is it the most effective point of view for this essay? Why or why not?

Revise Paragraph Development

❏ Which paragraphs fail to advance the action, reveal character, or contribute to the story's mood? Should these sections be condensed or eliminated?

❏ Where should the narrative pace be slowed down or quickened?

❏ Where is it difficult to follow the chronology of events? Should the order of paragraphs be changed? How? Where would additional time signals help?

❏ How could flashback or flashforward paragraphs be used to highlight key events?

❏ Would dramatic dialogue or mood-setting description help make the essay's opening paragraph more compelling?

❏ What could be done to make the essay's closing paragraph more effective? Should the essay end earlier? Should it close by echoing an idea or image from the opening?

Revise Sentences and Words

❑ Where is sentence structure monotonous? Where would combining sentences, mixing sentence types, and alternating sentence length help?

❑ Where could dialogue replace commentary to convey character and propel the story forward?

❑ Which sentences and words are inconsistent with the essay's tone?

❑ Where do vigorous verbs convey action? Where could active verbs replace passive ones? Where could dull *to be* verbs be converted to more dynamic forms?

❑ Where are there inappropriate shifts in point of view or verb tense?

STUDENT ESSAY

The following student essay was written by Paul Monahan in response to this assignment.

> In "Salvation," Langston Hughes tells about an incident in which he felt pressured to act in a manner that ran counter to his better instincts. Write a narrative about a time when you faced a disturbing conflict and ended up doing something you later regretted.

While reading Paul's paper, try to determine how well it applies the principles of narration. The annotations on Paul's paper and the commentary following it will help you look at the essay more closely.

If Only
by Paul Monahan

Introduction	Having worked at a 7-Eleven store for two years, I 1 thought I had become successful at what our manager calls "customer relations." I firmly believed that a friendly smile and an automatic "sir," "ma'am," and "thank you" would see me through any situation that might arise, from soothing impatient or unpleasant people to apologizing for giving out
Narrative point (thesis)	the wrong change. But the other night an old woman shattered my belief that a glib response could smooth over the rough spots of dealing with other human beings.
Informal topic sentence	The moment she entered, the woman presented a sharp 2 contrast to our shiny store with its bright lighting and neatly arranged shelves. Walking as if each step were painful, she slowly pushed open the glass door and hobbled down the
Sensory details	nearest aisle. She coughed dryly, wheezing with each breath.

On a forty-degree night, she was wearing only a faded print dress, a thin, light beige sweater too small to button, and black vinyl slippers with the backs cut out to expose calloused heels. There were no stockings or socks on her splotchy, blue-veined legs.

After strolling around the store for several minutes, the old woman stopped in front of the rows of canned vegetables. She picked up some corn niblets and stared with a strange intensity at the label. At that point, I decided to be a good, courteous employee and asked her if she needed help. As I stood close to her, my smile became harder to maintain; her red-rimmed eyes were partially closed by yellowish crusts; her hands were covered with layer upon layer of grime, and the stale smell of sweat rose in a thick vaporous cloud from her clothes.   3

Informal topic sentence

Sensory details

Start of dialogue → "I need some food," she muttered in reply to my bright "Can I help you?"   4

"Are you looking for corn, ma'am?"   5

"I need some food," she repeated. "Any kind."   6

"Well, the corn is ninety-five cents," I said in my most helpful voice. "Or, if you like, we have a special on bologna today."   7

"I can't pay," she said.   8

Conflict established → For a second, I was tempted to say, "Take the corn." But the employee rules flooded into my mind: Remain polite, but do not let customers get the best of you. Let them know that you are in control. For a moment, I even entertained the idea that this was some sort of test, and that this woman was someone from the head office, testing my loyalty. I responded dutifully, "I'm sorry, ma'am, but I can't give away anything free."   9

Informal topic sentence → The old woman's face collapsed a bit more, if that were possible, and her hands trembled as she put the can back on the shelf. She shuffled past me toward the door, her torn and dirty clothing barely covering her bent back.   10

Conclusion Moments after she left, I rushed out the door with the can of corn, but she was nowhere in sight. For the rest of my shift, the image of the woman haunted me. I had been young, healthy, and smug. She had been old, sick, and desperate. Wishing with all my heart that I had acted like a human being rather than a robot, I was saddened to realize how fragile a hold we have on our better instincts.   11

Echoing of narrative point in the introduction

COMMENTARY

Point of view, tense, and conflict.   Paul chose to write "If Only" from the *first-person point of view,* a logical choice because he appears as a main character in his own story. Using the *past tense,* Paul recounts an incident filled with *conflicts*—between him and the woman and between his fear of breaking the rules and his human instinct to help someone in need.

Narrative point.   It isn't always necessary to state the *narrative point* of an essay; it can be implied. But Paul decided to express the controlling idea of his narrative in two places—in the introduction ("But the other night an old woman shattered my belief that a glib response could smooth over the rough spots of dealing with other human beings") and again in the conclusion, where he expands his idea about rote responses overriding impulses of independent judgment and compassion. All of the essay's *narrative details* contribute to the point of the piece; Paul does not include any extraneous information that would detract from the central idea he wants to convey.

Organization.   The narrative is *organized chronologically,* from the moment the woman enters the store to Paul's reaction after she leaves. Paul limits the narrative's time span. The entire incident probably occurs in under ten minutes, yet the introduction serves as a kind of *flashback* by providing some necessary background about Paul's past experiences. To help the reader follow the course of the narrative, Paul uses *time signals: "The moment* she entered, the woman presented a sharp contrast" (paragraph 2); "*At that point,* I decided to be a good, courteous employee" (3); "*For the rest of my shift,* the image of the woman haunted me" (11).

The paragraphs (except for those consisting solely of dialogue) also contain *informal topic sentences* that direct attention to the specific stage of action being narrated. Indeed, each paragraph focuses on a distinct event: the elderly woman's actions when she first enters the store, the encounter between Paul and the woman, Paul's resulting inner conflict, the woman's subsequent response, and Paul's delayed reaction.

Combining patterns of development.   This chronological chain of events, with one action leading to another, illustrates that the *cause-effect* pattern underlies the basic structure of Paul's essay. And by means of another pattern—*description*—Paul gives dramatic immediacy to the events being recounted. Throughout, he provides rich sensory details to engage the reader's interest. For instance, the sentence "her red-rimmed eyes were partially closed by yellowish crusts" (3) vividly re-creates the woman's appearance while also suggesting Paul's inner reaction to the woman.

Dialogue and sentence structure.   Paul uses other techniques to add energy and interest to his narrative. For one thing, he dramatizes his conflict with the woman through *dialogue* that crackles with tension. And he achieves a vigorous narrative pace by *varying the length and structure of his sentences.* In the second paragraph, a short sentence ("There were no stockings or socks on her splotchy, blue-veined legs") alternates with a longer one ("On a forty-degree night, she was wearing only a faded print dress, a thin, light beige sweater too small to button, and black vinyl slippers with the backs cut out to expose calloused heels"). Some sentences in the essay open with a subject and verb ("She coughed dryly"), while others start with dependent clauses or participial phrases ("As I stood close to her, my smile became harder to maintain"; "Walking as if each step were painful, she slowly pushed open the glass door") or with a prepositional phrase ("For a second, I was tempted").

Revising the first draft.   Comparing the final version of the essay's third paragraph, shown above, with the preliminary version reprinted below reveals some of the changes Paul made while revising the essay.

Original Version of the Third Paragraph

After sneezing and hacking her way around the store, the old woman stopped in front of the vegetable shelves. She picked up a can of corn and stared at the label. She stayed like this for several minutes. Then I walked over to her and asked if I could be of help.

After putting the original draft aside for a while, Paul reread his paper aloud and realized the third paragraph especially lacked power. So he decided to add compelling descriptive details about the woman ("the stale smell of sweat," for example). When revising, he also worked to reduce the paragraph's choppiness. By expanding and combining sentences, he gave the paragraph an easier, more graceful rhythm. Much of the time, revision involves paring down excess material. In this case, though, Paul made the right decision to elaborate his sentences. Furthermore, he added the following comment to the third paragraph: "I decided to be a good, courteous employee." These few words introduce an appropriate note of irony and serve to echo the essay's controlling idea.

Finally, Paul decided to omit the words "sneezing and hacking" because he realized they were too comic or light for his subject. Still, the first sentence in the revised paragraph is somewhat jarring. The word *strolling* isn't quite appropriate since it implies a leisurely grace inconsistent with the impression he wants to convey. Replacing *strolling* with, say, *shuffling* would bring the image more into line with the essay's overall mood.

Despite this slight problem, Paul's revisions are right on the mark. The changes he made strengthened his essay, turning it into a more evocative, more polished piece of narrative writing.

Activities: Narration

Prewriting Activities

1. Imagine you're writing two essays: One analyzes the *effect* of insensitive teachers on young children; the other *argues* the importance of family traditions. With the help of your journal or freewriting, identify different narratives you could use to open each essay.

2. For each of the situations below, identify two different conflicts that would make a story worth relating. Then prepare six to ten lines of natural-sounding dialogue for each potential conflict in *one* of the situations.

   a. Going to the supermarket with a friend
   b. Telling your parents which college you've decided to attend
   c. Participating in a demonstration
   d. Preparing for an exam in a difficult course

Revising Activities

3. Revise each of the following narrative sentence groups twice: once with words that carry negative connotations, and again with words that carry positive connotations. Use varied sentence structure, sensory details, and vigorous verbs to convey mood.

   a. The bell rang. It rang loudly. Students knew the last day of class was over.
   b. Last weekend, our neighbors burned leaves in their yard. We went over to speak with them.
   c. The sun shone in through my bedroom window. It made me sit up in bed. Daylight was finally here, I told myself.

4. The following paragraph is the introduction from the first draft of an essay proposing harsher penalties for drunk drivers. Revise this narrative paragraph to make it more effective. How can you make sentence structure less predictable? Which details should you delete? As you revise, provide language that conveys the event's sights, smells, and sounds. Also, clarify the chronological sequence.

   As I drove down the street in my bright blue sports car, I saw a car coming rapidly around the curve. The car didn't slow down as it headed toward the traffic light. The light turned yellow and then red. A young couple, dressed like models, started crossing the street. When the woman saw the car, she called out to her husband. He jumped onto the shoulder. The man wasn't hurt but, seconds later, it was clear the woman was. I ran to a nearby emergency phone and called the police. The ambulance arrived, but the woman was already dead. The driver, who looked terrible, failed the sobriety test, and the police found out that he had two previous offenses. It's apparent that better ways have to be found for getting drunk drivers off the road.

Annie Dillard

Pilgrim at Tinker Creek (1974) is probably Annie Dillard's best-known work. A collection of lyrical observations and reflections about the natural world, *Pilgrim* was awarded a Pulitzer Prize for general nonfiction. Born in 1945, Dillard is currently Adjunct Professor at Wesleyan University in Connecticut and a contributing editor at *Harper's*. Over the years, she has published a variety of books: *Tickets for a Prayer Wheel* (1974), a book of poetry; *Holy the Firm* (1978), *Teaching a Stone to Talk* (1982), *The Annie Dillard Reader* (1994), and *Mornings Like This* (1995), collections of essays; *Living by Fiction* (1982), literary criticism; *Encounters With Chinese Writers* (1984) and *For the Time Being* (1999), narrative nonfiction; *An American Childhood* (1987), an autobiography; and *The Writing Life* (1989), miscellaneous reflections on writing. Her first novel, *The Living*, was published to critical acclaim in 1992. The following selection is from *An American Childhood*.

Pre-Reading Journal Entry

Use your journal to reminisce about several of your memorable childhood and/or adolescent adventures that involved a confrontation with an adult. Some events may be amusing, while others may be serious. What happened? Who was involved? What was the outcome? Writing quickly, immerse yourself in your memories, recapturing as best you can your thoughts and feelings at the time of the incident.

The Chase

Some boys taught me to play football. This was fine sport. You thought 1
up a new strategy for every play and whispered it to the others. You went out
for a pass, fooling everyone. Best, you got to throw yourself mightily at
someone's running legs. Either you brought him down or you hit the
ground flat out on your chin, with your arms empty before you. It was all or
nothing. If you hesitated in fear, you would miss and get hurt: you would
take a hard fall while the kid got away, or you would get kicked in the face
while the kid got away. But if you flung yourself wholeheartedly at the back
of his knees—if you gathered and joined body and soul and pointed them
diving fearlessly—then you likely wouldn't get hurt, and you'd stop the ball.
Your fate, and your team's score, depended on your concentration and
courage. Nothing girls did could compare with it.

Boys welcomed me at baseball, too, for I had, through enthusiastic 2
practice, what was weirdly known as a boy's arm. In winter, in the snow,
there was neither baseball or football, so the boys and I threw snowballs at

passing cars. I got in trouble throwing snowballs, and have seldom been happier since.

On one weekday morning after Christmas, six inches of new snow had just fallen. We were standing up to our boot tops in snow on a front yard on trafficked Reynolds Street, waiting for cars. The cars traveled Reynolds Street slowly and evenly; they were targets all but wrapped in red ribbons, cream puffs. We couldn't miss.

I was seven; the boys were eight, nine, and ten. The oldest two Fahey boys were there—Mikey and Peter—polite blond boys who lived near me on Lloyd Street, and who already had four brothers and sisters. My parents approved Mikey and Peter Fahey. Chickie McBride was there, a tough kid, and Billy Paul and Mackie Kean too, from across Reynolds, where the boys grew up dark and furious, grew up skinny, knowing, and skilled. We had all drifted from our houses that morning looking for action, and had found it here on Reynolds Street.

It was cloudy but cold. The cars' tires laid behind them on the snowy street a complex trail of beige chunks like crenellated castle walls. I had stepped on some earlier; they squeaked. We could have wished for more traffic. When a car came, we all popped it one. In the intervals between cars we reverted to the natural solitude of children.

I started making an iceball—a perfect iceball, from perfectly white snow, perfectly spherical, and squeezed perfectly translucent so no snow remained all the way through. (The Fahey boys and I considered it unfair actually to throw an iceball at somebody, but it had been known to happen.)

I had just embarked on the iceball project when we heard tire chains come clanking from afar. A black Buick was moving toward us down the street. We all spread out, banged together some regular snowballs, took aim, and, when the Buick drew nigh, fired.

A soft snowball hit the driver's windshield right before the driver's face. It made a smashed star with a hump in the middle.

Often, of course, we hit our target, but this time, the only time in all of life, the car pulled over and stopped. Its wide black door opened; a man got out of it, running. He didn't even close the car door.

He ran after us, and we ran away from him, up the snowy Reynolds sidewalk. At the corner, I looked back; incredibly, he was still after us. He was in city clothes: a suit and tie, street shoes. Any normal adult would have quit, having sprung us into flight and made his point. This man was gaining on us. He was a thin man, all action. All of a sudden, we were running for our lives.

Wordless, we split up. We were on our turf; we could lose ourselves in the neighborhood backyards, everyone for himself. I paused and considered. Everyone had vanished except Mikey Fahey, who was just rounding the corner of a yellow brick house. Poor Mikey, I trailed him. The driver of the Buick sensibly picked the two of us to follow. The man apparently had all day.

He chased Mikey and me around the yellow house and up a backyard   12
path we knew by heart: under a low tree, up a bank, through a hedge, down
some snowy steps, and across the grocery store's delivery driveway. We
smashed through a gap in another hedge, entered a scruffy backyard and ran
around its back porch and tight between houses to Edgerton Avenue; we ran
across Edgerton to an alley and up our own sliding woodpile to the Halls'
front yard; he kept coming. We ran up Lloyd Street and wound through
mazy backyards toward the steep hilltop at Willard and Lang.

He chased us silently, block after block. He chased us silently over pick-   13
et fences, through thorny hedges, between houses, around garbage cans, and
across streets. Every time I glanced back, choking for breath, I expected he
would have quit. He must have been as breathless as we were. His jacket
strained over his body. It was an immense discovery, pounding into my hot
head with every sliding, joyous step, that this ordinary adult evidently knew
what I thought only children who trained at football knew: that you have to
fling yourself at what you're doing, you have to point yourself, forget yourself, aim, dive.

Mikey and I had nowhere to go, in our own neighborhood or out of it,   14
but away from this man who was chasing us. He impelled us forward; we
compelled him to follow our route. The air was cold; every breath tore my
throat. We kept running, block after block; we kept improvising, backyard
after backyard, running a frantic course and choosing it simultaneously, failing always to find small places or hard places to slow him down, and discovering always, exhilarated, dismayed, that only bare speed could save us—for
he would never give up, this man—and we were losing speed.

He chased us through the backyard labyrinths of ten blocks before he   15
caught us by our jackets. He caught us and we all stopped.

We three stood staggering, half blinded, coughing, in an obscure hill-   16
top backyard: a man in his twenties, a boy, a girl. He had released our jackets, our pursuer, our captor, our hero: he knew we weren't going anywhere.
We all played by the rules. Mikey and I unzipped our jackets. I pulled off
my sopping mittens. Our tracks multiplied in the backyard's new snow. We
had been breaking new snow all morning. We didn't look at each other. I
was cherishing my excitement. The man's lower pants legs were wet; his
cuffs were full of snow, and there was a prow of snow beneath them on his
shoes and socks. Some trees bordered the little flat backyard, some messy
winter trees. There was no one around: a clearing in a grove, and we the
only players.

It was a long time before he could speak. I had some difficulty at first,   17
recalling why we were there. My lips felt swollen; I couldn't see out of the
sides of my eyes; I kept coughing.

"You stupid kids," he began perfunctorily.   18

We listened perfunctorily indeed, if we listened at all, for the chewing   19
out was redundant, a mere formality, and beside the point. The point was

that he had chased us passionately without giving up, and so he had caught us. Now he came down to earth. I wanted the glory to last forever.

But how could the glory have lasted forever? We could have run through   20
every backyard in North America until we got to Panama. But when he trapped us at the lip of the Panama Canal, what precisely could he have done to prolong the drama of the chase and cap its glory? I brooded about this for the next few years. He could only have fried Mikey Fahey and me in boiling oil, say, or dismembered us piecemeal, or staked us to anthills. None of which I really wanted, and none of which any adult was likely to do, even in the spirit of fun. He could only chew us out there in the Panamanian jungle, after months or years of exalting pursuit. He could only begin, "You stupid kids," and continue in his ordinary Pittsburgh accent with his normal right-eous anger and the usual common sense.

If in that snowy backyard the driver of the black Buick had cut off our   21
heads, Mikey's and mine, I would have died happy, for nothing has required so much of me since as being chased all over Pittsburgh in the middle of win-ter—running terrified, exhausted—by this sainted, skinny, furious redheaded man who wished to have a word with us. I don't know how he found his way back to his car.

Questions for Close Reading

1. What is the selection's thesis (or narrative point)? Locate the sentence(s) in which Dillard states her main idea. If Dillard doesn't state the thesis explicitly, express it in your own words.
2. In the first paragraph, Dillard describes football as a "fine sport." Which aspects of the sport does she refer to when illustrating her point? Which aspect is most important? Why?
3. Why was the driver's decision to follow Dillard and Mikey "sensible"?
4. Dillard dubs her pursuer "our hero" (paragraph 16) and says he was "sainted" (21). What is it about the man that merits these words of praise?
5. Refer to your dictionary as needed to define the following words used in the selec-tion: *crenellated* (paragraph 5), *spherical* (6), *translucent* (6), *embarked* (7), *simul-taneously* (14), *dismayed* (14), *labyrinths* (15), *prow* (16), *perfunctorily* (18), and *redundant* (19).

Questions About the Writer's Craft

1. **The pattern.** Dillard draws upon sensory details, play-by-play action, varied sen-tence length, and repetition to create a narrative filled with drama and suspense. Locate examples of each of these techniques and explain how the strategy keeps readers on the edge of their seats.
2. What key word does Dillard repeat in paragraph 6? Why do you suppose she repeats this word? What is the effect?
3. **Other patterns.** In paragraphs 12 and 13, Dillard provides a number of *spatial* signals to help readers track the path she and Mikey followed. Identify the signals and comment on their effectiveness.

4. There is only one place in the essay where someone actually speaks. Locate this instance of dialogue. Why do you think Dillard chose to include only this one piece of dialogue?

Writing Assignments Using Narration as a Pattern of Development

∞ **1.** The chase tested Dillard—and she rose to the challenge. In a narrative of your own, write about a challenge that you responded to in a way that made you feel proud. Perhaps you triumphed over a serious illness, succeeded in a difficult sporting event, or worked hard not to lash out verbally at someone who had hurt you. Like Dillard, use vivid narrative details to convey how you reacted and why you felt good about your reaction. You might also consider first reading Adam Mayblum's "The Price We Pay" (page 128), an account of many people's noble actions in the face of a dire challenge.

∞ **2.** Like Dillard, most of us—at some point in our lives—have done something that crossed traditional gender lines. If you're female, you might have built some bookshelves. If you're male, you might have prepared a special dinner for friends. Write an essay about a time you engaged in what might be considered a "gender-bending" activity. Where appropriate, use sensory details and dialogue to convey how you and others felt about what you did. Before writing, you may want to read the following essays exploring gender-based behaviors: Barbara Ehrenreich's "What I've Learned From Men" (page 166) and Dave Barry's "The Ugly Truth About Beauty" (page 277).

Writing Assignments Combining Patterns of Development

3. Dillard believes that there are times we should "fling" ourselves at an experience and "dive" in with abandon. In an essay, *argue* the opposing point of view. Defend the position that there are times in life when a measured, thoughtful response is called for even though the common tendency is to act impulsively. Select convincing *examples* to support your position, showing how a more spontaneous approach could be harmful or counterproductive.

4. At one time or another, all children do things they shouldn't. Focus on *one* negative thing that children do in the classroom, at home, or in a public place, and write an essay showing that adults' typical *response* to the behavior is far from effective. *Contrast* adults' usual response with what you think adults should do to handle the problem behavior more effectively. Before writing, you might consider investigating your topic in the library and/or on the Internet.

Writing Assignment Using a Journal Entry as a Starting Point

∞ **5.** Reread your pre-reading journal entry, and choose the *one* memory that conveys most dramatically a collision between the world of children (or adolescents) and the world of adults. Write an essay about this event. Make the conflict real and immediate by providing rich sensory details about the place and people involved. Reveal, either implicitly or explicitly, your current perspective on the event. Before you begin writing, read Langston Hughes's "Salvation" (page 124) for inspiration in depicting this clash between child and adult worlds.

Langston Hughes

One of the foremost members of the 1920s literary movement known as the Harlem Renaissance, Langston Hughes (1902–67) committed himself to portraying the richness of Black life in the United States. A poet and a writer of short stories, Hughes was greatly influenced by the rhythms of blues and jazz. In his later years, he published two autobiographical works, *The Big Sea* (1940) and *I Wonder as I Wander* (1956), and he wrote a history of the National Association for the Advancement of Colored People (NAACP). The following selection is from *The Big Sea*.

Pre-Reading Journal Entry

Young people often feel pressured by family and community to adopt certain values, beliefs, or traditions. In your journal, reflect on some of the pressures that you've experienced. What was your response to these pressures? What have been the consequences of your response? Do you think your experience with these family or community pressures was unique or fairly common?

Salvation

I was saved from sin when I was going on thirteen. But not really saved. It happened like this. There was a big revival at my Auntie Reed's church. Every night for weeks there had been much preaching, singing, praying, and shouting, and some very hardened sinners had been brought to Christ, and the membership of the church had grown by leaps and bounds. Then just before the revival ended, they held a special meeting for children, "to bring the young lambs to the fold." My aunt spoke of it for days ahead. That night I was escorted to the front row and placed on the mourners' bench with all the other young sinners, who had not yet been brought to Jesus.

My aunt told me that when you were saved you saw a light, and something happened to you inside! And Jesus came into your life! And God was with you from then on! She said you could see and hear and feel Jesus in your soul. I believed her. I had heard a great many old people say the same thing and it seemed to me they ought to know. So I sat there calmly in the hot, crowded church, waiting for Jesus to come to me.

The preacher preached a wonderful rhythmical sermon, all moans and shouts and lonely cries and dire pictures of hell, and then he sang a song about the ninety and nine safe in the fold, but one little lamb was left out in the cold. Then he said: "Won't you come? Won't you come to Jesus? Young lambs, won't you come?" And he held out his arms to all us young sinners there on the mourners' bench. And the little girls cried. And some of them jumped up and went to Jesus right away. But most of us just sat there.

A great many older people came and knelt around us and prayed, old   4
women with jet-black faces and braided hair, old men with work-gnarled hands. And the church sang a song about the lower lights are burning, some poor sinners to be saved. And the whole building rocked with prayer and song.

Still I kept waiting to *see* Jesus.   5

Finally all the young people had gone to the altar and were saved, but   6
one boy and me. He was a rounder's son named Westley. Westley and I were surrounded by sisters and deacons praying. It was very hot in the church, and getting late now. Finally Westley said to me in a whisper: "God damn! I'm tired o' sitting here. Let's get up and be saved." So he got up and was saved.

Then I was left all alone on the mourners' bench. My aunt came and   7
knelt at my knees and cried, while prayers and songs swirled all around me in the little church. The whole congregation prayed for me alone, in a mighty wail of moans and voices. And I kept waiting serenely for Jesus, waiting, waiting—but he didn't come. I wanted to see him, but nothing happened to me. Nothing! I wanted something to happen to me, but nothing happened.

I heard the songs and the minister saying: "Why don't you come? My   8
dear child, why don't you come to Jesus? Jesus is waiting for you. He wants you. Why don't you come? Sister Reed, what is this child's name?"

"Langston," my aunt sobbed.   9

"Langston, why don't you come? Why don't you come and be saved?   10
Oh, Lamb of God! Why don't you come?"

Now it was really getting late. I began to be ashamed of myself, holding   11
everything up so long. I began to wonder what God thought about Westley, who certainly hadn't seen Jesus either, but who was now sitting proudly on the platform, swinging his knickerbockered legs and grinning down at me, surrounded by deacons and old women on their knees praying. God had not struck Westley dead for taking his name in vain or for lying in the temple. So I decided that maybe to save further trouble, I'd better lie, too, and say that Jesus had come, and get up and be saved.

So I got up.   12

Suddenly the whole room broke into a sea of shouting, as they saw me   13
rise. Waves of rejoicing swept the place. Women leaped in the air. My aunt threw her arms around me. The minister took me by the hand and led me to the platform.

When things quieted down, in a hushed silence, punctuated by a few   14
ecstatic "Amens," all the new young lambs were blessed in the name of God. Then joyous singing filled the room.

That night, for the last time in my life but one—for I was a big boy   15
twelve years old—I cried. I cried, in bed alone, and couldn't stop. I buried

my head under the quilts, but my aunt heard me. She woke up and told my uncle I was crying because the Holy Ghost had come into my life, and because I had seen Jesus. But I was really crying because I couldn't bear to tell her that I had lied, that I had deceived everybody in the church, and I hadn't seen Jesus, and that now I didn't believe there was a Jesus any more, since he didn't come to help me.

Questions for Close Reading

1. What is the selection's thesis (or narrative point)? Locate the sentence(s) in which Hughes states his main idea. If Hughes doesn't state the thesis explicitly, express it in your own words.
2. During the revival meeting, what pressures are put on the young Langston to get up and be saved?
3. How does Westley's attitude differ from Hughes's?
4. Does the narrator's Auntie Reed really understand him? Why can't he tell her the truth about his experience in the church?
5. Refer to your dictionary as needed to define the following words used in the selection: *revival* (paragraph 1), *knickerbockered* (11), *punctuated* (14), and *ecstatic* (14).

Questions About the Writer's Craft

1. **The pattern.** A narrative's power can often be traced to a conflict within the event being recounted. What conflict does the narrator of "Salvation" experience? How does Hughes create tension about this conflict?
2. What key role does Westley serve in the resolution of the narrator's dilemma? How does Hughes's inclusion of Westley in the story help us to understand the narrator better?
3. **Other patterns.** The thirteenth paragraph presents a *metaphor* of the church as an ocean. What images develop this metaphor? What does the metaphor tell us about Hughes's feelings and those of the church people?
4. The singing of hymns is a major part of this religious service. Why do you think Hughes has the narrator reveal the subjects and even the lyrics of some of the hymns?

Writing Assignments Using Narration
as a Pattern of Development

1. Like Hughes, we sometimes believe that deception is our best alternative. Write a narrative about a time you felt deception was the best way either to protect those you care about or to maintain the respect of those important to you.
2. Write a narrative essay about a chain of events that caused you to become disillusioned about a person or institution you had previously regarded highly. Begin as Hughes does by presenting your initial beliefs. Relate the sequence of events that changed your evaluation of the person or organization. In the conclusion, explain the short- and long-term effects of the incident. For more accounts of childhood disillusionment, read Beth Johnson's "Bombs Bursting in Air" (page 160) and Joseph H. Suina's "And Then I Went to School" (page 271).

Writing Assignments Combining Patterns of Development

3. Hughes writes, "My aunt told me that when you were saved, you saw a light, and something happened to you inside! And Jesus came into your life!" What *causes* people to change their beliefs? Do such changes come from waiting calmly, as Hughes tried to do in church, or must they come from a more active process? Write an essay explaining your viewpoint. You may use *process analysis, causal analysis,* or some other organizational pattern to develop your thesis. Be sure to include specific examples to support your understanding of the way beliefs change.

4. Write a *persuasive* essay *arguing* either that lying is sometimes right or that lying is always wrong. Apply your thesis to particular situations and show how lying is or is not the right course of action. Be sure to keep your *narration* of these situations brief and focused on your point. Remember to acknowledge the opposing viewpoint. William Lutz's "Doublespeak" (page 200) may help you define your position. You might even mention this author's perspective in your essay.

Writing Assignment Using a Journal Entry as a Starting Point

5. Review your pre-reading journal entry, and select *one* family or community pressure with which you've had to contend. Then write an essay examining the effect that this pressure has had on you. Refer to your journal as you prepare to explain the values, beliefs, or traditions that you were expected to adopt. Discuss your response to this pressure and how your reaction has affected you.

Adam Mayblum

On September 11, 2001, as thirty-five-year-old Adam Mayblum worked in his investment firm's office on the eighty-seventh floor of the World Trade Center's North Tower, a terrorist-hijacked plane crashed into the building. His presence of mind—and a great deal of good fortune—allowed him to escape from the tower before it collapsed. The day after the attacks, he sent an e-mail to friends and family describing his experiences. The e-mail, later titled "The Price We Pay," was soon being forwarded around the world and reprinted in newspapers and magazines and on websites. (Mayblum's account appears below in much the same form as when he sent it; it has not been corrected for grammar or mechanics.) Today, Mayblum works at a new firm located just a few blocks from the site of the former World Trade Center. He lives with his wife and two children in New Rochelle, New York.

Pre-Reading Journal Entry

The terrorist attacks against the United States on September 11, 2001, had a profound impact on people the world over. Where were you the morning of that fateful day? What was your reaction when you learned of the attacks? What was the reaction of those around you? How did your feelings change over time? How, if at all, did the event alter your perspectives about larger issues? Explore these questions in your pre-reading journal.

The Price We Pay

My name is Adam Mayblum. I am alive today. I am committing this to "paper" so I never forget. SO WE NEVER FORGET. I am sure that this is one of thousands of stories that will emerge over the next several days and weeks.

I arrived as usual a little before 8am. My office was on the 87th floor of 1World Trade Center, AKA: Tower 1, AKA: the North Tower. Most of my associates were in by 8:30am. We were standing around, joking around, eating breakfast, checking emails, and getting set for the day when the first plane hit just a few stories above us. I must stress that we did not know that it was a plane. The building lurched violently and shook as if it were an earthquake. People screamed. I watched out my window as the building seemed to move 10 to 20 feet in each direction. It rumbled and shook long enough for me to get my wits about myself and grab a co-worker and seek shelter under a doorway. Light fixtures and parts of the ceiling collapsed. The kitchen was destroyed. We were certain that it was a bomb. We looked out the windows. Reams of paper were flying everywhere, like a ticker tape parade. I looked down at the street. I could see people in Battery Park City looking up. Smoke started billowing in through the holes in the ceiling. I believe that there were 13 of us.

We did not panic. I can only assume that we thought that the worst was 3 over. The building was standing and we were shaken but alive. We checked the halls. The smoke was thick and white and did not smell like I imagined smoke should smell. Not like your BBQ or your fireplace or even a bonfire. The phones were working. My wife had taken our 9 month old for his check up. I called my nanny at home and told her to page my wife, tell her that a bomb went off, I was ok, and on my way out. I grabbed my laptop. Took off my tee shirt and ripped it into 3 pieces. Soaked it in water. Gave 2 pieces to my friends. Tied my piece around my face to act as an air filter. And we all started moving to the staircase. One of my dearest friends said that he was staying until the police or firemen came to get him. In the halls there were tiny fires and sparks. The ceiling had collapsed in the men's bathroom. It was gone along with anyone who may have been in there. We did not go in to look. We missed the staircase on the first run and had to double back. Once in the staircase we picked up fire extinguishers just in case. On the 85th floor a brave associate of mine and I headed back up to our office to drag out my partner who stayed behind. There was no air, just white smoke. We made the rounds through the office calling his name. No response. He must have succumbed to the smoke. We left defeated in our efforts and made our way back to the stairwell. We proceeded to the 78th floor where we had to change over to a different stairwell. 78 is the main junction to switch to the upper floors. I expected to see more people. There were some 50 to 60 more. Not enough. Wires and fires all over the place. Smoke too. A brave man was fighting a fire with the emergency hose. I stopped with two friends to make sure that everyone from our office was accounted for. We ushered them and confused people into the stairwell. In retrospect, I recall seeing Harry, my head trader, doing the same several yards behind me. I am only 35. I have known him for over 14 years. I headed into the stairwell with 2 friends.

We were moving down very orderly in Stair Case A. very slowly. No 4 panic. At least not overt panic. My legs could not stop shaking. My heart was pounding. Some nervous jokes and laughter. I made a crack about ruining a brand new pair of Merrells.[1] Even still, they were right, my feet felt great. We all laughed. We checked our cell phones. Surprisingly, there was a very good signal, but the Sprint network was jammed. I heard that the Blackberry 2-way email devices worked perfectly. On the phones, 1 out of 20 dial attempts got through. I knew I could not reach my wife so I called my parents. I told them what happened and that we were all okay and on the way

---

[1] A brand of men's shoes (editors' note).

down. Soon, my sister in law reached me. I told her we were fine and moving down. I believe that was about the 65th floor. We were bored and nervous. I called my friend Angel in San Francisco. I knew he would be watching. He was amazed I was on the phone. He told me to get out that there was another plane on its way. I did not know what he was talking about. By now the second plane had struck Tower 2. We were so deep into the middle of our building that we did not hear or feel anything. We had no idea what was really going on. We kept making way for wounded to go down ahead of us. Not many of them, just a few. No one seemed seriously wounded. Just some cuts and scrapes. Everyone cooperated.

Everyone was a hero yesterday. No questions asked. I had co-workers in   5 another office on the 77th floor. I tried dozens of times to get them on their cell phones or office lines. It was futile. Later I found that they were alive. One of the many miracles on a day of tragedy.

On the 53rd floor we came across a very heavyset man sitting on the   6 stairs. I asked if he needed help or was he just resting. He needed help. I knew I would have trouble carrying him because I have a very bad back. But my friend and I offered anyway. We told him he could lean on us. He hesitated, I don't know why. I said do you want to come or do you want us to send help for you. He chose for help. I told him he was on the 53rd floor in Stairwell A and that's what I would tell the rescue workers. He said okay and we left.

On the 44th floor my phone rang again. It was my parents. They were   7 hysterical. I said relax, I'm fine. My father said get out, there is third plane coming. I still did not understand. I was kind of angry. What did my parents think? Like I needed some other reason to get going? I couldn't move the thousand people in front of me any faster. I know they love me, but no one inside understood what the situation really was. My parents did. Starting around this floor the firemen, policemen, WTC K-9 units without the dogs, anyone with a badge, started coming up as we were heading down. I stopped a lot of them and told them about the man on 53 and my friend on 87. I later felt terrible about this. They headed up to find those people and met death instead.

On the 33rd floor I spoke with a man who somehow knew most of the   8 details. He said 2 small planes hit the building. Now we all started talking about which terrorist group it was. Was it an internal organization or an external one? The overwhelming but uninformed opinion was Islamic Fanatics. Regardless, we now knew that it was not a bomb and there were potentially more planes coming. We understood.

On the 3rd floor the lights went out and we heard & felt this rumbling   9 coming towards us from above. I thought the staircase was collapsing upon itself. It was 10am now and that was Tower 2 collapsing next door. We did not know that. Someone had a flashlight. We passed it forward and left the stairwell and headed down a dark and cramped corridor to an exit. We could not see at all. I recommended that everyone place a hand on the shoulder of the person in front of them and call out if they hit an obstacle so others would know to avoid it. They did. It worked perfectly. We reached another stairwell and saw a female officer emerge soaking wet and covered in soot. She said we could not go that way it was blocked. Go up to 4 and use the other exit. Just as we started up she said it was ok to go down instead. There was water everywhere. I called out for hands on shoulders again and she said that was a great idea. She stayed behind instructing people to do that. I do not know what happened to her.

We emerged into an enormous room. It was light but filled with smoke. 10
I commented to a friend that it must be under construction. Then we realized where we were. It was the second floor. The one that overlooks the lobby. We were ushered out into the courtyard, the one where the fountain used to be. My first thought was of a TV movie I saw once about nuclear winter and fallout. I could not understand where all of the debris came from. There was at least five inches of this gray pasty dusty drywall soot on the ground as well as a thickness of it in the air. Twisted steel and wires. I heard there were bodies and body parts as well, but I did not look. It was bad enough. We hid under the remaining overhangs and moved out to the street. We were told to keep walking towards Houston Street. The odd thing is that there were very few rescue workers around. Less than five. They all must have been trapped under the debris when Tower 2 fell. We did not know that and could not understand where all of that debris came from. It was just my friend Kern and I now. We were hugging but sad. We felt certain that most of our friends ahead of us died and we knew no one behind us.

We came upon a post office several blocks away. We stopped and looked 11
up. Our building, exactly where our office is (was), was engulfed in flame and smoke. A postal worker said that Tower 2 had fallen down. I looked again and sure enough it was gone. My heart was racing. We kept trying to call our families. I could not get in touch with my wife. Finally I got through to my parents. Relieved is not the word to explain their feelings. They got through to my wife, thank God and let her know I was alive. We sat down. A girl on a bike offered us some water. Just as she took the cap off her bottle we heard a rumble. We looked up and our building, Tower 1 collapsed. I did not note the time but I am told it was 10:30am. We had been out less than 15 minutes.

We were mourning our lost friends, particularly the one who stayed in 12
the office as we were now sure that he had perished. We started walking towards Union Square. I was going to Beth Israel Medical Center to be looked at. We stopped to hear the President speaking on the radio. My phone rang. It was my wife. I think I fell to my knees crying when I heard her voice. Then she told me the most incredible thing. My partner who had stayed behind called her. He was alive and well. I guess we just lost him in

the commotion. We started jumping and hugging and shouting. I told my wife that my brother had arranged for a hotel in midtown. He can be very resourceful in that way. I told her I would call her from there. My brother and I managed to get a gypsy cab to take us home to Westchester instead. I cried on my son and held my wife until I fell asleep.

As it turns out my partner, the one who I thought had stayed behind was behind us with Harry Ramos, our head trader. This is now second-hand information. They came upon Victor, the heavyset man on the 53rd floor. They helped him. He could barely move. My partner bravely/stupidly tested the elevator on the 52nd floor. He rode it down to the sky lobby on 44. The doors opened, it was fine. He rode it back up and got Harry and Victor. I don't yet know if anyone else joined them. Once on 44 they made their way back into the stairwell. Someplace around the 39th to 36th floors they felt the same rumble I felt on the 3rd floor. It was 10am and Tower 2 was coming down. They had about 30 minutes to get out. Victor said he could no longer move. They offered to have him lean on them. He said he couldn't do it. My partner hollered at him to sit on his butt and scooch down the steps. He said he was not capable of doing it. Harry told my partner to go ahead of them. Harry had once had a heart attack and was worried about this mans heart. It was his nature to be this way. He was/is one of the kindest people I know. He would not leave a man behind. My partner went ahead and made it out. He said he was out maybe 10 minutes before the building came down. This means that Harry had maybe 25 minutes to move Victor 36 floors. I guess they moved 1 floor every 1.5 minutes. Just a guess. This means Harry was around the 20th floor when the building collapsed. As of now 12 of 13 people are accounted for. As of 6pm yesterday his wife had not heard from him. I fear that Harry is lost. However, a short while ago I heard that he may be alive. Apparently there is a website with survivor names on it and his name appears there. Unfortunately, Ramos is not an uncommon name in New York. Pray for him and all those like him.[2]

With regards to the firemen heading upstairs, I realize that they were going up anyway. But, it hurts to know that I may have made them move quicker to find my friend. Rationally, I know this is not true and that I am not the responsible one. The responsible ones are in hiding somewhere on this planet and damn them for making me feel like this. But they should know that they failed in terrorizing us. We were calm. Those men and women that went up were heroes in the face of it all. They must have known what was going on and they did their jobs. Ordinary people were heroes too. Today the images that people around the world equate with power and democracy are gone but "America" is not an image it is a concept. That concept is only

[2]Sadly, it later was confirmed that Harry Ramos did not survive the collapse of the towers that day (editors' note).

strengthened by our pulling together as a team. If you want to kill us, leave us alone because we will do it by ourselves. If you want to make us stronger, attack and we unite. This is the ultimate failure of terrorism against The United States and the ultimate price we pay to be free, to decide where we want to work, what we want to eat, and when & where we want to go on vacation. The very moment the first plane was hijacked, democracy won.

Questions for Close Reading

1. What is the selection's thesis (or narrative point)? Locate the sentence(s) in which Mayblum states his main idea. If he doesn't state the thesis explicitly, express it in your own words.
2. Strong narrative involves conflict (see page 106). What is the main conflict in "The Price We Pay"?
3. What reason does Mayblum give for writing his account? What additional reasons might he have?
4. In Mayblum's view, the World Trade Center attacks were part of "the price we pay." What is it that he believes Americans paid for on September 11, 2001? Do you agree? Why or why not?
5. Refer to your dictionary as needed to define the following terms used in the selection: *aka* (2), *lurched* (2), *reams* (2), *ticker tape* (2), *succumbed* (3), *junction* (3), *ushered* (3), *retrospect* (3), *nuclear winter* (10), *fallout* (10), *debris* (10), *engulfed* (11), *commotion* (12), and *gypsy cab* (12).

Questions About the Writer's Craft

1. **The pattern.** As is common in narration, Mayblum tells his story primarily in past tense. However, he occasionally interjects present tense into his account. Identify some instances where he uses present tense. What effect does his use of present tense have on the narrative?
2. Mayblum's essay is marked by two clear stylistic characteristics: First, he uses many sentence fragments and short sentences, and second, he omits quotation marks around people's exact words. How do these choices affect the narrative?
3. Many of Mayblum's sentences begin with *We*—for example, "We did not panic" (3), "We all laughed" (4), and "We understood" (7). How does the prevalent use of *we* and *our* fit with Mayblum's theme?
4. Mayblum illustrates American freedom with three examples: the freedom to "decide where we want to work, what we want to eat, and when & where we want to go on vacation" (12). Do you find these examples effective and appropriate? Why or why not?

Writing Assignments Using Narration as a Pattern of Development

∞ 1. Mayblum tells a story of courage, compassion, and quick thinking in the face of horror. Think back on your own life and take a few moments to freewrite about a situation in which you experienced terror or alarm. Maybe you were snowbound in a blizzard, got lost in the woods, or witnessed a crime. Write an essay in which you recount your frightening situation. What exactly took place? How did you react? How did others react? What did you learn from the experience? Be sure to provide vivid details to recreate the sights, sounds, and feelings surrounding the event. For another account of weathering a harrowing situation, read Beth Johnson's "Bombs Bursting in Air" (page 160).

2. Americans cherish their personal liberties. Recall a time when, in your view, you were wrongly deprived of some freedom. Perhaps you were punished for expressing your opinion or ordered not to associate with particular people. Write an essay that narrates the unjust incident, focusing on the main conflict. What were the circumstances? Who was involved? Discuss your treatment and why you felt it was unjust. In addition, provide some thoughts on whether now, in retrospect, you have a different perspective on the event than you did at the time.

Writing Assignments Combining Patterns of Development

3. In an emergency, some people stay calm; others panic. Think of the person you would *most* want to be with in a crisis. Next, think of the person you would *least* want to be with. Freewrite thoughts about each of these people in your journal. Then, in a serious or humorous piece, *contrast* these two people's personalities, revealing why one would probably be a reliable partner in a crisis whereas the other would probably be a disastrous one. Be sure to provide *examples* of these people's behavior to *illustrate* why you regard each of them as you do.

4. Plans are currently in the works to erect new buildings on the site of the destroyed World Trade Center towers. Yet popular opinion on this topic remains divided: Some people still argue that the site should remain undeveloped as a memorial to September 11th, while others advocate rebuilding on the site as a symbol of American resilience. Where do you fall in this debate? Write an essay in which you *argue* that the site of the former Twin Towers should or should not be redeveloped. In either case, be sure to explain exactly what you think should be done with the land on which the towers once stood, *describing* what features the area should include. In the course of your essay, you should address opposing points of view. Research in the library and/or on the Internet can help you identify others' points of view, as well as give you a better idea of the landscape of the area in question.

Writing Assignment Using a Journal Entry as a Starting Point

5. It is clear from Mayblum's account that the events of September 11, 2001, had a profound impact on his life. But a person need not have been actively involved in the events to have felt their repercussions. Review the thoughts you recorded in your pre-reading journal. Then write an essay about how the events of that day have *affected* you. You might organize the essay by first considering your immediate response to the events, perhaps as part of a *narrative* of when and how you

found out. What kinds of emotions and thoughts did you experience at the time? Then you might proceed by discussing longer-term effects on your thoughts or feelings. For instance, has the attack made you feel any closer to your family and friends? Has it left you feeling unsafe or depressed? Has it changed your view of America or the rest of the world?

Additional Writing Topics

NARRATION

General Assignments

Prepare an essay on any of the following topics, using narration as the paper's dominant method of development. Be sure to select details that advance the essay's narrative purpose; you may even want to experiment with flashback or flashforward. In any case, keep the sequence of events clear by using transitional cues. Within the limited time span covered, use vigorous details and varied sentence structure to enliven the narrative. Tell the story from a consistent point of view.

1. An emergency that brought out the best or worst in you
2. The hazards of taking children out to eat
3. An incident that made you believe in fate
4. Your best or worst day at school or work
5. A major decision
6. An encounter with a machine
7. An important learning experience
8. A narrow escape
9. Your first date, first day on the job, or first anything
10. A memorable childhood experience
11. A fairy tale the way you would like to hear it told
12. A painful moment
13. An incredible but true story
14. A significant family event
15. An experience in which a certain emotion (pride, anger, regret, or some other) was dominant
16. A surprising coincidence
17. An act of heroism
18. An unpleasant confrontation
19. A cherished family story
20. An imagined meeting with an admired celebrity or historical figure

Assignments With a Specific Purpose, Audience, and Point of View

On Campus

1. Write an article for your old high school newspaper. The article will be read primarily by seniors who are planning to go away to college next year. In the article, narrate a story that points to some truth about the "breaking away" stage of life.
2. A friend of yours has seen someone cheat on a test, plagiarize an entire paper, or seriously violate some other academic policy. In a letter, convince this friend to

inform the instructor or a campus administrator by narrating an incident in which a witness did (or did not) speak up in such a situation. Tell what happened as a result.

At Home or in the Community

3. You have had a disturbing encounter with one of the people who seems to have "fallen through the cracks" of society—a street person, an unwanted child, or anyone else who is alone and abandoned. Write a letter to the local newspaper describing this encounter. Your purpose is to arouse people's indignation and compassion and to get help for such unfortunates.

4. Your younger brother, sister, relative, or neighborhood friend can't wait to be your age. Write a letter in which you narrate a dramatic story that shows the young person that your age isn't as wonderful as he or she thinks. Be sure to select a story that the person can understand and appreciate.

On the Job

5. As fund-raiser for a particular organization (for example, the Red Cross, the SPCA, Big Brothers/Big Sisters), you're sending a newsletter to contributors. Support your cause by telling the story of a time when your organization made all the difference—the blood donation that saved a life, the animal that was rescued from abuse, and so on.

6. A customer has written a letter to you (or your boss) telling about a bad experience that he or she had with someone in your workplace. On the basis of that single experience, the customer now regards your company and its employees with great suspicion. It's your responsibility to respond to this complaint. Write a letter to the customer balancing his or her negative picture by narrating a story that shows the "flip side" of your company and its employees.

5

EXEMPLIFICATION

WHAT IS EXEMPLIFICATION?

If someone asked you, "Have you been to any good restaurants lately?" you probably wouldn't answer "Yes" and then immediately change the subject. Most likely, you would go on to illustrate with *examples*. Perhaps you'd give the names of restaurants you've enjoyed and talk briefly about the specific things you liked: the attractive prices, the tasty main courses, the pleasant service, the tempting desserts. Such examples and details are needed to convince others that your opinion—in this or any matter—is valid. Similarly, when you talk about larger and more important issues, people won't pay much attention to your opinion if all you do is string together vague generalizations: "We have to do something about acid rain. It's had disastrous consequences for the environment. Its negative effects increase every year. Action must be taken to control the problem." To be taken seriously and to convince others that your point is well-founded, you must provide specific supporting examples: "The forests in the Adirondacks are dying"; "Yesterday's rainfall was fifty times more acidic than normal"; "Pine Lake, in the northern part of the state, was once a great fishing spot but now has no fish population."

Examples are equally important when you write an essay. It's not fuzzy generalities and highfalutin abstractions that make writing impressive. Just the opposite is true. Facts, anecdotes, statistics, details, opinions, and observations are at the heart of effective writing, giving your work substance and solidity.

HOW EXEMPLIFICATION FITS YOUR PURPOSE AND AUDIENCE

The wording of assignments and essay exam questions may signal the need for specific examples:

Soap operas, whether shown during the day or in the evening, are among the most popular television programs. Why do you think this is so? Provide specific examples to support your position.

Some observers claim that college students are less interested in learning than in getting ahead in their careers. Cite evidence to support or refute this claim.

A growing number of people feel that parents should not allow young children to participate in highly competitive team sports. Basing your conclusion on your own experiences and observations, indicate whether you think this point of view is reasonable.

Such phrases as "Provide specific examples," "Cite evidence," and "Basing your conclusion on your own experiences and observations" signal that each essay should be developed through examples.

Usually, though, you won't be told so explicitly to provide examples. Instead, as you think about the best way to achieve your essay's purpose, you'll see the need for illustrative details—no matter which patterns of development you use. For instance, to *persuade* skeptical readers that the country needs a national health system, you might mention specific cases to dramatize the inadequacy of our current health-care system: a family bankrupted by medical bills; an uninsured accident victim turned away by a hospital; a chronically ill person rapidly deteriorating because he didn't have enough money to visit a doctor. Or imagine a lightly satiric piece that pokes fun at cat lovers. Insisting that "cat people" are pretty strange creatures, you might make your point—and make readers chuckle—with a series of examples *contrasting* cat lovers and dog lovers: the qualities admired by each group (loyalty in dogs versus independence in cats) and the different expectations each group has for its pets (dog lovers want Fido to be obedient and lovable, whereas cat lovers are satisfied with Felix's occasional spurts of docility and affection). Similarly, you would supply examples in a *causal analysis* speculating on the likely impact of a proposed tuition hike at your college. To convince the college administration of the probable negative effects of such a hike, you might cite the following examples: articles reporting a nationwide upswing in student transfers to less expensive schools; statistics indicating a significant drop in grades among already employed students forced to work more hours to pay increased tuition costs; interviews with students too financially strapped to continue their college education.

Whether you use examples as the primary or a supplemental method of development, they serve a number of important purposes. For one thing, examples make writing *interesting*. Assume you're writing an essay showing that television commercials are biased against women. Your essay would be lifeless and boring if all it did was repeat, in a general way, that commercials present stereotyped views of women.

An anti-female bias is rampant in television commercials. It is very much alive, yet most viewers seem to take it all in stride. Few people protest the obviously sexist characters and statements in such commercials. Surely, these commercials misrepresent the way most of us live.

Without interesting particulars, readers may respond, "Who cares?" But if you provide specific examples, you'll attract your readers' attention:

Sexism is rampant in television commercials. Although millions of women hold responsible jobs outside the home, commercials continue to portray women as simple creatures who spend most of their time thinking about wax buildup, cottony-soft bathroom tissue, and static-free clothes. Men, apparently, have better things to do than fret over such mundane household matters. How many commercials can you recall that depict men proclaiming the virtues of squeaky-clean dishes or sparkling bathrooms? Not many.

Examples also make writing *persuasive*. Most writing conveys a point, but many readers are reluctant to accept someone else's point of view unless evidence demonstrates its validity. Imagine you're writing an essay showing that latchkey children are more self-sufficient and emotionally secure than children who return from school to a home where a parent awaits them. Your thesis is obviously controversial. Without specific examples—from your own experience, personal observations, or research studies—your readers would undoubtedly question your position's validity.

Further, examples *help explain* difficult, abstract, or unusual ideas. Suppose you're assigned an essay on a complex subject such as inflation, zero population growth, or radiation exposure. As a writer, you have a responsibility to your readers to make these difficult concepts concrete and understandable. If writing an essay on radiation exposure in everyday life, you might start by providing specific examples of home appliances that emit radiation—color televisions, computers, and microwave ovens—and tell exactly how much radiation we absorb in a typical day from such equipment. To illustrate further the extent of our radiation exposure, you could also provide specifics about unavoidable sources of natural radiation (the sun, for instance) and details about the widespread use of radiation in medicine (X rays, radiation therapy). These examples would ground your discussion, making it immediate and concrete, preventing it from flying off into the vague and theoretical.

Finally, examples *help prevent unintended ambiguity*. All of us have experienced the frustration of having someone misinterpret what we say. In face-to-face communication, we can provide on-the-spot clarification. In writing, however, instantaneous feedback isn't available, so it's crucial that meaning be as unambiguous as possible. Examples will help.

Assume you're writing an essay asserting that ineffective teaching is on the rise in today's high schools. To clarify what you mean by "ineffective," you provide examples: the instructor who spends so much time disciplining unruly students that he never gets around to teaching; the moonlighting teacher who is so tired in class that she regularly takes naps during tests; and the teacher who accepts obviously plagiarized reports because he's grateful that students hand in something. Without such concrete examples, your readers will supply their own ideas—and these may not be what you had in mind. Readers might imagine "ineffective" to mean harsh and punitive, whereas your concrete examples would show that you intend it to mean out of control and irresponsible. Such specifics help prevent misunderstanding.

SUGGESTIONS FOR USING EXEMPLIFICATION IN AN ESSAY

The following suggestions will be helpful whether you use examples as a dominant or a supportive pattern of development.

1. Generate examples.   Where do you get the examples to develop your essay? The first batch of examples is generated during the prewriting stage. With your purpose and thesis in mind, you make a broad sweep for examples, using brainstorming, freewriting, the mapping technique—whichever prewriting technique you prefer. During this preliminary search for examples, you may also read through your journal for relevant specifics, interview other people, or conduct library research.

Examples can take several forms, including specific names (of people, places, products, and so on), anecdotes, personal observations, expert opinion, as well as facts, statistics, and case studies gathered through research. While prewriting, try to generate more examples than you think you'll need. Starting with abundance—and then picking out the strongest examples—will give you a firm base on which to build the essay. If you have a great deal of trouble finding examples to support your thesis, you may need to revise the thesis; you may be trying to support an idea that has little validity. On the other hand, while prewriting, you may unearth numerous examples but find that many of them contradict the point you started out to support. If that happens, don't hesitate to recast your central point, always remembering that your thesis and examples must fit.

2. Select the examples to include.   Once you've used prewriting to generate as many examples as possible, you're ready to limit your examples to the strongest ones. Keeping your purpose, thesis, and audience in mind, ask yourself several key questions: "Which examples support my thesis? Which do not? Which are most convincing? Which are most likely to interest readers and clarify meaning?"

You may include several brief examples within a single sentence:

> The French people's fascination with some American literary figures, such as Poe and Hawthorne, is understandable, but their great respect for "artists" like comedian Jerry Lewis is a mystery.

Or you may develop a paragraph with a number of "for instances":

> A uniquely American style of movie-acting reached its peak in the 1950s. Certain charismatic actors completely abandoned the stage techniques and tradition that had been the foundation of acting up to that time. Instead of articulating their lines clearly, the actors mumbled; instead of making firm eye contact with their colleagues, they hung their heads, shifted their eyes, even talked with their eyes closed. Marlon Brando, Montgomery Clift, and James Dean were three actors who exemplified this new trend.

As the preceding paragraph shows, *several examples* are usually needed to make a point. An essay with the thesis "Rock videos are dangerously violent" wouldn't be convincing if you gave only one example of a violent rock video. Several strong examples would be needed for readers to feel you had illustrated your point sufficiently.

As a general rule, you should strive for variety in the kinds of examples you include. For instance, you might choose a *personal-experience example* drawn from your own life or from the life of someone you know. Such examples pack the wallop of personal authority and lend drama to writing. Or you might include a *typical-case example*, an actual event or situation that did occur—but not to you or to anyone you know. (Perhaps you learned about the event through a magazine article, newspaper account, or television report.) The objective nature of such cases makes them especially convincing. You might also include a speculative or *hypothetical example* ("Imagine how difficult it must be for an elderly person to carry bags of groceries from the market to a bus stop several blocks away"). You'll find that hypothetical cases are effective for clarifying and dramatizing key points, but be sure to acknowledge that the example is indeed invented ("*Suppose* that . . ." or "Let's for a moment *assume* that . . ."). Make certain, too, that the invented situation is easily imagined and could conceivably happen. Finally, you might create a *generalized example*— one that is a composite of the typical or usual. Such generalized examples are often signaled by words that involve the reader ("*All of us,* at one time or another, have been driven to distraction by a trivial annoyance like the buzzing of a fly or the sting of a paper cut"), or they may refer to humanity in general ("When *most people* get a compliment, they perk up, preen, and think the praise-giver is blessed with astute powers of observation").

Occasionally, *one extended example,* fully developed with many details, can support an essay. It might be possible, for instance, to support the thesis "Federal legislation should raise the legal drinking age to twenty-one" with a single compelling, highly detailed example of the effects of one teenager's drunken-driving spree.

The examples you choose must also be *relevant;* that is, they must have direct bearing on the point you want to make. You would have a hard time convincing readers that Americans have callous attitudes toward the elderly if you described the wide range of new programs, all staffed by volunteers, at a well-financed center for senior citizens. Because these examples *contradict,* rather than support, your thesis, readers are apt to dismiss what you have to say.

Make certain, too, that your examples are *accurate.* Exercise special caution when using statistics. An old saying warns that there are lies, damned lies, and statistics—meaning that statistics can be misleading. A commercial may claim, "In a taste test, 80 percent of those questioned indicated that they preferred Fizzy Cola." Impressed? Don't be—at least, not until you find out how the test was conducted. Perhaps the subjects had to choose between Fizzy Cola and battery acid, or perhaps there were only five subjects, all Fizzy Cola vice presidents.

Finally, select *representative* examples. Picking the oddball, one-in-a-million example to support a point—and passing it off as typical—is dishonest. Consider an essay with the thesis "Part-time jobs contribute to academic success." Citing only one example of a student who works at a job twenty-five hours a week while earning straight As isn't playing fair. Why not? You've made a *hasty generalization* based on only one case. To be convincing, you need to show how holding down a job affects *most* students' academic performance. (For more on hasty generalizations, see page 364.)

3. Develop your examples sufficiently.   To ensure that you get your ideas across, your examples must be *specific.* An essay on the types of heroes in American movies wouldn't succeed if you simply strung together a series of undeveloped examples in paragraphs like this one:

> Heroes in American movies usually fall into types. One kind of hero is the tight-lipped loner, men like Clint Eastwood and Humphrey Bogart. Another movie hero is the quiet, shy, or fumbling type who has appeared in movies since the beginning. The main characteristic of this hero is lovableness, as seen in actors like Jimmy Stewart. Perhaps the most one-dimensional and predictable hero is the superman who battles tough odds. This kind of hero is best illustrated by Sylvester Stallone as Rocky and Rambo.

If you developed the essay in this way—if you moved from one undeveloped example to another—you would be doing little more than making a list. To be effective, key examples must be expanded in sufficient detail. The examples in the preceding paragraph could be developed in paragraphs of their own. You could, for instance, develop the first example this way:

> Heroes can be tight-lipped loners who appear out of nowhere, form no permanent attachments, and walk, drive, or ride off into the sunset. In many of his Westerns, from the low-budget "spaghetti Westerns" of the 1960s to Unforgiven in 1992, Clint Eastwood personifies this kind of hero. He is remote, mysterious, and not talkative. Yet he guns down an evil sheriff, runs other villains out of town, and helps a handicapped girl--acts that cement his heroic status. The loner might also be Sam Spade as played by Humphrey Bogart. Spade solves the crime and sends the guilty off to jail, yet he holds his emotions in check and has no permanent ties beyond his faithful secretary and shabby office. One gets the feeling that he could walk away from these, too, if necessary. Even in The Right Stuff, an account of the United States's early astronauts, the scriptwriters mold Chuck Yeager, the man who broke the sound barrier, into a classic loner. Yeager, portrayed by the aloof Sam Shepard, has a wife, but he is nevertheless insular. Taking mute pride in his ability to distance himself from politicians, bureaucrats, even colleagues, he soars into space, dignified and detached.

(For hints on ways to make writing specific, see pages 33–35.)

4. Organize the examples.   If, as is usually the case, several examples support your point, be sure that you present the examples in an *organized* manner. Often you'll find that other patterns of development (cause-effect, comparison-contrast, definition, and so on) suggest ways to sequence examples. Let's say you're writing an essay showing that stay-at-home vacations offer numerous opportunities to relax. You might begin the essay with examples that *contrast* stay-at-home and get-away vacations. Then you might move to a *process analysis* that illustrates different techniques for unwinding at home. The essay might end with examples showing the *effect* of such leisurely at-home breaks.

Finally, you need to select an *organizational approach consistent* with your *purpose* and *thesis*. Imagine you're writing an essay about students' adjustment during the first months of college. The supporting examples could be arranged *chronologically*. You might start by illustrating the ambivalence many students feel the first day of college when their parents leave for home; you might then offer an anecdote or two about students' frequent calls to Mom and Dad during the opening weeks of the semester; the essay might close with an account of students' reluctance to leave campus at the midyear break.

Similarly, an essay demonstrating that a room often reflects the character of its occupant might be organized *spatially:* from the empty soda cans on the floor to the spitballs on the ceiling. In an essay illustrating the kinds of skills taught in a composition course, you might move from *simple* to *complex* examples: starting with relatively matter-of-fact skills such as spelling and punctuation and ending with more conceptually difficult skills such as formulating a thesis and organizing an essay. Last, the *emphatic sequence*—in which you lead from your first example to your final, most significant one—is another effective way to organize an essay with many examples. A paper about Americans' characteristic impatience might progress from minor examples (dependence on fast food, obsession with ever faster mail delivery) to more disturbing manifestations of impatience (using drugs as quick solutions to problems, advocating simple answers to complex international problems: "Bomb them!").

5. Choose a point of view. Many essays developed by illustration place the subject in the foreground and the writer in the background. Such an approach calls for the *third-person point of view*. For example, even if you draw examples from your own personal experience, you can present them without using the *first-person* "I." You might convert such personal material into generalized examples (see page 142), or you might describe the personal experience as if it happened to someone else. Of course, you may use the first person if the use of "I" will make the example more believable and dramatic. But remember: Just because an event happened to you personally doesn't mean you have to use the first-person point of view.

REVISION STRATEGIES

Once you have a draft of the essay, you're ready to revise. The following checklist will help you and those giving you feedback apply to exemplification some of the revision techniques discussed on pages 59–61.

☑ EXEMPLIFICATION: A REVISION/PEER REVIEW CHECKLIST

Revise Overall Meaning and Structure

❏ What thesis is being advanced? Which examples don't support the thesis? Should these examples be deleted, or should the thesis be reshaped to fit the examples? Why?

❏ Which patterns of development and methods of organization (chronological, spatial, simple-to-complex, emphatic) provide the essay's framework? Would other ordering principles be more effective? If so, which ones?

Revise Paragraph Development

❏ Which paragraphs contain too many or too few examples? Which contain examples that are too brief or too extended? Which include insufficiently or overly detailed examples?

❏ Which paragraphs contain examples that could be made more compelling?

❏ Which paragraphs include examples that are atypical or incorrect?

Revise Sentences and Words

❑ What signal devices introduce examples and clarify the line of thought?
  Where are there too many or too few of these devices?

❑ Where would more varied sentence structure heighten the essay's
  illustrations?

❑ Where would more concrete and specific words make the examples
  more effective?

STUDENT ESSAY

The following student essay was written by Michael Pagano in response to
this assignment:

> One implication in Beth Johnson's "Bombs Bursting in Air" is
> that, given life's unanticipated tragedies, people need to focus on
> what's really important rather than on trivial complications and dis-
> tractions. Observe closely the way you and others conduct your
> daily lives. Use your observations for an essay that supports or
> refutes Johnson's point of view.

While reading Michael's paper, try to determine how effectively it applies
the principles of exemplification. The annotations on Michael's paper and the
commentary following it will help you look at the essay more closely.

Pursuit of Possessions
by Michael Pagano

Introduction

In the essay "Bombs Bursting in Air," Beth Johnson   1
develops the extended metaphor of bombs exploding
unexpectedly to represent the tragedies that occur without
warning in our daily lives. Herself a survivor of innumerable
life bombs, Johnson suggests that in light of life's fragility, we
need to remember and appreciate what's really important to
us. But very often, we lose sight of what truly matters in our
lives, instead occupying ourselves with trivial distractions. In

Thesis — particular, many of us choose to spend our lives in pursuit of
material possessions. Much of our time goes into buying new

Plan of
development — things, dealing with the complications they create, and
working madly to buy more things or pay for the things we
already have.

Topic sentence ——▶ We devote a great deal of our lives to acquiring the   2
material goods we imagine are essential to our well-being.
Hours are spent planning and thinking about our future

The first of three paragraphs in a chronological sequence	purchases. We window-shop for designer jogging shoes; we leaf through magazines looking at ads for elaborate stereo equipment; we research back issues of <u>Consumer Reports</u> to find out about recent developments in exercise equipment. Moreover, once we find what we are looking for, more time is taken up when we decide to actually buy the items. How do we find this time? That's easy. We turn evenings, weekends, and holidays--time that used to be set aside for family and friends--into shopping expeditions. No wonder family life is deteriorating and children spend so much time in front of television sets. Their parents are seldom around.

Topic sentence ———→ As soon as we take our new purchases home, they begin   3
to complicate our lives. A sleek new sports car has to be
The second
paragraph in the
chronological
sequence

A paragraph
with many
specific
examples
washed, waxed, and vacuumed. A fashionable pair of overpriced dress pants can't be thrown in the washing machine but has to be taken to the dry cleaner. New stereo equipment has to be connected with a tangled network of cables to the TV, radio, and cassette deck. Eventually, of course, the inevitable happens. Our indispensable possessions break down and need to be repaired. The home computer starts to lose data, the microwave has to have its temperature controls adjusted, and the DVD player has to be serviced when a disc becomes jammed in the machine.

Topic sentence ———→ After more time has gone by, we sometimes discover that   4
our purchases don't suit us anymore, and so we decide to
The third
paragraph in the
chronological
sequence
replace them. Before making our replacement purchases, though, we have to find ways to get rid of the old items. If we want to replace our "small" 19-inch television set with a 35-inch one, we have to find time to put an ad in the classified section of the paper. Then we have to handle phone calls and set up times people can come to look at the TV. We could store the set in the basement--if we are lucky enough to find a spot that isn't already filled with other discarded purchases.

Topic sentence ———→ Worst of all, this mania for possessions often influences   5
with emphasis
signal
our approach to work. It is not unusual for people to take a second or even a third job to pay off the debt they fall into because they have overbought. After paying for food, clothing, and shelter, many people see the rest of their paycheck go to Visa, MasterCard, department store charge accounts, and time payments. Panic sets in when they realize there simply is not enough money to cover all their expenses. Just to stay afloat, people may have to work overtime or take on additional jobs.

Conclusion   It is clear that many of us have allowed the pursuit of   6
possessions to dominate our lives. We are so busy buying, maintaining, and paying for our worldly goods that we do not have much time to think about what is really important. We should try to step back from our compulsive need for more of

everything and get in touch with the basic values that are the real point of our lives.

COMMENTARY

Thesis, combining patterns of development, and plan of development. In "Pursuit of Possessions," Michael analyzes the mania for acquiring material goods that permeates our society. He begins by addressing an implication conveyed in Beth Johnson's "Bombs Bursting in Air"—that life's fragility dictates that we need to focus on what really matters in our lives. This reference to Johnson gives Michael a chance to *contrast* the reflective way she suggests we should live with the acquisitive and frenzied way many people lead their lives. This contrast leads to the essay's *thesis:* "[M]any of us choose to spend our lives in pursuit of material possessions."

Besides introducing the basic contrast at the heart of the essay, Michael's opening paragraph helps readers see that the essay contains an element of *causal analysis.* The final sentence of the introductory paragraph lays out the effects of our possession obsession. This sentence also serves as the essay's *plan of development* and reveals that Michael feels the pursuit of possessions negatively affects our lives in three key ways.

Essays of this length often don't need a plan of development. But since Michael's paper is filled with many *examples,* the plan of development helps readers see how all the details relate to the essay's central point.

Evidence.   Support for the thesis consists of numerous examples presented in the *first-person-plural point of view* ("*We* choose to clutter our lives . . . ," "*We* devote a great deal of our lives . . . ," and so on). Many of these examples seem drawn from Michael's, his friends', or his family's experiences; however, to emphasize the events' universality, Michael converts these essentially personal examples into generalized ones that "we" all experience.

These examples, in turn, are organized around the three major points signaled by the plan of development. Michael uses one paragraph to develop his first and third points and two paragraphs to develop his second point. Each of the four supporting paragraphs is focused by a *topic sentence* that appears at the start of the paragraph. The transitional phrase "Worst of all" (paragraph 5) signals that Michael has sequenced his major points *emphatically,* saving for last the issue he considers most significant: how the "mania for possessions . . . influences our approach to work."

Organizational strategies.   Emphatic order isn't Michael's only organizational technique. When reading the paper, you probably felt that there was an easy flow from one supporting paragraph to the next. How does Michael achieve such *coherence between paragraphs?* For one thing, he sequences paragraphs 2–4 *chronologically:* what happens before a purchase is made; what happens afterward. Secondly, topic sentences in paragraphs 3 and 4 include *signal devices* that indicate this passage of time. The topic sentences also strengthen coherence by *linking back* to the preceding paragraph: "*As soon as we take our new purchases home,* they . . . complicate our lives" and "*After more time has gone by,* we . . . discover that our purchases don't suit us anymore."

The same organizing strategies are used *within paragraphs* to make the essay coherent. Details in paragraphs 2 through 4 are sequenced chronologically, and to help readers follow the chronology, Michael uses *signal devices:* "*Moreover, once* we find what we are looking for, more time is taken up . . ." (2); "*Eventually,* of course, the inevitable happens" (3); "*Then* we have to handle phone calls . . ." (4).

Problems with paragraph development.   You probably recall that an essay developed primarily through exemplification must include examples that are *relevant, interesting, convincing, representative, accurate,* and *specific.* On the whole, Michael's examples meet these requirements. The third and fourth paragraphs, especially, include vigorous details that show how our mania for buying things can govern our lives. We may even laugh with self-recognition when reading about "overpriced dress pants [that] can't be thrown in the washing machine" or a basement "filled with other discarded purchases."

The fifth paragraph, however, is underdeveloped. We know that this paragraph presents what Michael considers his most significant point, but the paragraph's examples are rather *flat* and *unconvincing.* To make this final section more compelling, Michael could mention specific people who overspend, revealing how much they are in debt and how much they have to work to become solvent again. Or he could cite a television documentary or magazine article dealing with the issue of consumer debt. Such specifics would give the paragraph the solidity it now lacks.

Shift in tone.   The fifth paragraph has a second, more subtle problem; *a shift in tone.* Although Michael has, up to this point, been critical of our possession-mad culture, he has poked fun at our obsession and kept his tone conversational and gently satiric. In this paragraph, though, he adopts a serious tone and, in the next paragraph, his tone becomes even weightier, almost preachy. It is, of course, legitimate to have a serious message in a lightly satiric piece. In fact, most satiric writing has such an additional layer of meaning. But because Michael has trouble blending these two moods, there's a jarring shift in the essay.

Shift in focus.   The second paragraph shows another kind of shift—in *focus.* The paragraph's controlling idea is that too much time is spent acquiring possessions. However, starting with "No wonder family life is deteriorating," Michael includes two sentences that introduce a complex issue beyond the scope of the essay. Since these last two sentences disrupt the paragraph's unity, they should be deleted.

Revising the first draft.   Although the final version of the essay needs work in spots, it's much stronger than Michael's first draft. To see how Michael went about revising the draft, compare his paper's second and third supporting paragraphs with his draft version re-printed here.

Original Version of the Second Paragraph

Our lives are spent not only buying things but in dealing with the inevitable complications that are created by our newly acquired possessions. First, we have to find places to put all the objects we bring home. More clothes demand more closets; a second car demands more garage space; a home entertainment center requires elaborate shelving. We shouldn't be surprised that the average American family moves once every three years. A good many families move simply because they need more space to store all the things they buy. In addition, our possessions demand maintenance time. A person who gets a new car will spend hours washing it, waxing it, and vacuuming it. A new pair of pants has to go to the dry cleaners. New stereo systems have to be connected to already existing equipment. Eventually, of course, the inevitable happens. Our new items need to be repaired. Or we get sick of them and decide to replace them. Before making our replacement purchases, though, we have to get rid of the old items. That can be a real inconvenience.

When Michael looked more closely at this paragraph, he realized it rambled and lacked energy. He started to revise the paragraph by tightening the first sentence, making it more focused and less awkward. Certainly, the revised sentence ("As soon as we take our new purchases home, they begin to complicate our lives") is crisper than the original. Next, he decided to omit the discussion about finding places to put new possessions; these sentences about inadequate closet, garage, and shelf space were so exaggerated that they undercut the valid point he wanted to make. He also chose to eliminate the sentences about the mobility of American families. This was, he felt, an interesting point, but it introduced an issue too complex to be included in the paragraph.

Michael strengthened the rest of the paragraph by making his examples more specific. A "new car" became a "sleek new sports car," and a "pair of pants" became a "fashionable pair of overpriced dress pants." Michael also realized he had to do more than merely write, "Eventually, . . . our new items need to be repaired." This point had to be dramatized by sharp, convincing details. Therefore, Michael added lively examples to describe how high-tech possessions—microwaves, home computers, DVD players—break down. Similarly, Michael realized it wasn't enough simply to say, as he had in the original, that we run into problems when we try to replace out-of-favor purchases. Vigorous details were again needed to illustrate the point. Michael thus used a typical "replaceable" (a "small" 19-inch TV set) as his key example and showed the annoyance involved in handling phone calls and setting up appointments so people could see the TV.

After adding these specifics, Michael realized he had enough material to devote a separate paragraph to the problems associated with replacing old purchases. By dividing his original paragraph, Michael ended up with two well-focused paragraphs, neither of which has the rambling quality found in the original.

In short, Michael strengthened his essay through substantial revision. Another round of rewriting would have made the essay stronger still. Even without this additional work, Michael's essay provides an interesting perspective on an American preoccupation.

ACTIVITIES: EXEMPLIFICATION

Prewriting Activities

1. Imagine you're writing two essays: One is a serious paper analyzing the factors that *cause* large numbers of public school teachers to leave the profession each year; the other is a light essay *defining* "preppie," "head banger," or some other slang term used to describe a kind of person. Jot down ways you might use examples in each essay.

2. Use mapping or another prewriting technique to gather examples illustrating the truth of *one* of the following familiar sayings. Then, using the same or a different prewriting technique, accumulate examples that counter the saying. Weigh both sets of examples to determine the saying's validity. After developing an appropriate thesis, decide which examples you would elaborate in an essay.

   a. Haste makes waste.
   b. There's no use crying over spilled milk.
   c. A bird in the hand is worth two in the bush.

Revising Activities

3. The following paragraph is from the first draft of an essay about the decline of small-town shopping districts. The paragraph is meant to show what small towns can do to revitalize business. Revise the paragraph, strengthening it with specific and convincing examples.

> A small town can compete with a large new mall for shoppers. But merchants must work together, modernizing the stores and making the town's main street pleasant, even fun to walk. They should also copy the malls' example by including attention-getting events as often as possible.

4. Reprinted here is a paragraph from the first draft of a light-spirited essay showing that Americans' pursuit of change for change's sake has drawbacks. The
   paragraph is meant to illustrate that infatuation with newness costs consumers
   money yet leads to no improvement in product quality. How effective is the
   paragraph? Which examples are specific and convincing? Which are not? Do
   any seem nonrepresentative, offensive, or sexist? How could the paragraph's
   organization be improved? Consider these questions as you rewrite the paragraph. Add specific examples where needed. Depending on the way you revise,
   you may want to break this one paragraph into several.

   We end up paying for our passion for the new and improved. Trendy
   clothing styles convince us that last year's oufits are outdated, even though
   our old clothes are fine. Women are especially vulnerable in this regard. What,
   though, about items that have to be replaced periodically, like shampoo? Even
   slight changes lead to new formulations requiring retooling of the production
   process. That means increased manufacturing costs per item--all of which get
   passed on to us, the consumer. Then there are those items that tout new,
   trendsetting features that make earlier versions supposedly obsolete. Some
   manufacturers, for example, boast that their stereo or CD systems transmit an
   expanded-frequency range. The problem is that humans can't even hear such
   frequencies. But the high-tech feature dazzles men who are too naive to
   realize they're being hoodwinked.

Kay S. Hymowitz

A senior fellow at the Manhattan Institute and a contributing editor of the urban-policy magazine *City Journal*, Kay S. Hymowitz (1948–) writes on education and childhood in America. A native of Philadelphia, Hymowitz received an undergraduate English degree from Brandeis University and graduate degrees from Tufts University and Columbia University. She has taught English literature and composition at Brooklyn College and at Parsons School of Design. Hymowitz is the author of *Ready or Not: Why Treating Our Children as Small Adults Endangers Their Future and Ours* (1999) and is a principal contributor to *Modern Sex: Liberation and Its Discontents* (2001). In 2003, she published *Liberation's Children: Parents and Kids in a Postmodern Age*, a collection of her *City Journal* essays. Her work has appeared in publications including *The New York Times, The Washington Post,* and *The New Republic*. Hymowitz lives in Brooklyn with her husband and three children. The following essay appeared in the Autumn 1998 issue of *City Journal*.

Pre-Reading Journal Entry

Think back on your childhood. What were some possessions and activities that you cherished and enjoyed? Freewrite for a few moments in your pre-reading journal about these beloved objects and/or pastimes. What exactly were they? Why did you enjoy them so much? Did your feelings about them change as you matured into adolescence?

Tweens: Ten Going on Sixteen

During the past year my youngest morphed from child to teenager. 1
Down came the posters of adorable puppies and the drawings from art class; up went the airbrushed faces of Leonardo di Caprio and Kate Winslet. CDs of Le Ann Rimes and Paula Cole appeared mysteriously, along with teen fan magazines featuring glowering movie and rock-and-roll hunks. . . . She started reading the newspaper—or at least the movie ads—with all the intensity of a Talmudic scholar, scanning for glimpses of her beloved Leo or, failing that, Matt Damon. As spring approached and younger children skipped past our house on their way to the park, she swigged from a designer water bottle, wearing the obligatory tank top and denim shorts as she whispered on the phone to friends about games of Truth or Dare. The last rites for her childhood came when, embarrassed at reminders of her foolish past, she pulled a sheet over her years-in-the-making American Girl doll collection, now dead to the world.

So what's new in this dog-bites-man story? Well, as all this was going on, 2
my daughter was ten years old and in the fourth grade.

Those who remember their own teenybopper infatuation with Elvis or   3
the Beatles might be inclined to shrug their shoulders as if to say, "It was ever
thus." But this is different. Across class lines and throughout the country,
elementary and middle-school principals and teachers, child psychologists
and psychiatrists, marketing and demographic researchers all confirm the
pronouncement of Henry Trevor, middle-school director of the Berkeley
Carroll School in Brooklyn, New York: "There is no such thing as pre-
adolescence anymore. Kids are teenagers at ten."

Marketers have a term for this new social animal, kids between eight   4
and 12: they call them "tweens." The name captures the ambiguous reality:
though chronologically midway between early childhood and adolescence,
this group is leaning more and more toward teen styles, teen attitudes, and,
sadly, teen behavior at its most troubling.

The tween phenomenon grows out of a complicated mixture of biology,   5
demography, and the predictable assortment of Bad Ideas. But putting aside
its causes for a moment, the emergence of tweendom carries risks for both
young people and society. Eight- to 12-year-olds have an even more wobbly
sense of themselves than adolescents; they rely more heavily on others to tell
them how to understand the world and how to place themselves in it. Now,
for both pragmatic and ideological reasons, they are being increasingly
"empowered" to do this on their own, which leaves them highly vulnerable
both to a vulgar and sensation-driven marketplace and to the crass authority
of their immature peers. In tweens, we can see the future of our society taking shape, and it's not at all clear how it's going to work.

Perhaps the most striking evidence for the tweening of children comes   6
from market researchers. "There's no question there's a deep trend, not a
passing fad, toward kids getting older younger," says research psychologist
Michael Cohen of Arc Consulting, a public policy, education, and marketing
research firm in New York. "This is not just on the coasts. There are no real
differences geographically." It seems my daughter's last rites for her American Girl dolls were a perfect symbol not just for her own childhood but for
childhood, period. The Toy Manufacturers of America Factbook states that,
where once the industry could count on kids between birth and 14 as their
target market, today it is only birth to ten. "In the last ten years we've seen
a rapid development of upper-age children," says Bruce Friend, vice president of worldwide research and planning for Nickelodeon, a cable channel
aimed at kids. "The 12- to 14-year-olds of yesterday are the ten to 12s of
today." The rise of the preteen teen is "the biggest trend we've seen."

Scorning any symbols of their immaturity, tweens now cultivate a self-   7
image that emphasizes sophistication. The Nickelodeon-Yankelovich Youth
Monitor found that by the time they are 12, children describe themselves as
"flirtatious, sexy, trendy, athletic, cool." Nickelodeon's Bruce Friend reports
that by 11, children in focus groups say they no longer even think of themselves as children.

They're very concerned with their "look," Friend says, even more so   8
than older teens. Sprouting up everywhere are clothing stores like the chain
Limited Too and the catalog company Delia, geared toward tween girls who
scorn old-fashioned, little-girl flowers, ruffles, white socks, and Mary Janes[1]
in favor of the cool—black mini-dresses and platform shoes. . . . Teachers
complain of ten- or 11-year-old girls arriving at school looking like madams,
in full cosmetic regalia, with streaked hair, platform shoes, and midriff-
revealing shirts. Barbara Kapetanakes, a psychologist at a conservative Jewish
day school in New York, describes her students' skirts as being about "the
size of a belt." Kapetanakes says she was told to dress respectfully on Fridays,
the eve of the Jewish Sabbath, which she did by donning a long skirt and a
modest blouse. Her students, on the other hand, showed their respect by
looking "like they should be hanging around the West Side Highway,"
where prostitutes ply their trade.

Lottie Sims, a computer teacher in a Miami middle school, says that the   9
hooker look for tweens is fanning strong support for uniforms in her district.
But uniforms and tank-top bans won't solve the problem of painted young
ladies. "You can count on one hand the girls not wearing makeup," Sims
says. "Their parents don't even know. They arrive at school with huge bags
of lipstick and hair spray, and head straight to the girls' room."

Though the tweening of youth affects girls more visibly than boys, espe-   10
cially since boys mature more slowly, boys are by no means immune to these
obsessions. Once upon a time, about ten years ago, fifth- and sixth-grade boys
were about as fashion-conscious as their pet hamsters. But a growing minority have begun trading in their baseball cards for hair mousse and baggy jeans.
In some places, $200 jackets, emblazoned with sports logos like the warm-up
gear of professional athletes, are *de rigueur;* in others, the preppy look is popular among the majority, while the more daring go for the hipper style of
pierced ears, fade haircuts, or ponytails. Often these tween peacocks strut
through their middle-school hallways taunting those who have yet to catch on
to the cool look. . . .

Those who seek comfort in the idea that the tweening of childhood is   11
merely a matter of fashion—who maybe even find their lip-synching, hip-
swaying little boy or girl kind of cute—might want to think twice. There are
disturbing signs that tweens are not only eschewing the goody-goody childhood image but its substance as well. . . .

The clearest evidence of tweendom's darker side concerns crime.   12
Although children under 15 still represent a minority of juvenile arrests, their
numbers grew disproportionately in the past 20 years. According to a report
by the Office of Juvenile Justice and Delinquency Prevention, "offenders
under age 15 represent the leading edge of the juvenile crime problem, and

---

[1]Trademark name of patent-leather shoes for girls, usually having a low heel and a strap that fas-
tens at the side (editors' note).

their numbers are growing." Moreover, the crimes committed by younger teens and preteens are growing in severity. "Person offenses,[2] which once constituted 16 percent of the total court cases for this age group," continues the report, "now constitute 25 percent." Headline grabbers—like Nathaniel Abraham of Pontiac, Michigan, an 11-year-old who stole a rifle from a neighbor's garage and went on a shooting spree in October 1997, randomly killing a teenager coming out of a store; and 11-year-old Andrew Golden, who, with his 13-year-old partner, killed four children and one teacher at his middle school in Jonesboro, Arkansas—are extreme, exceptional cases, but alas, they are part of a growing trend toward preteen violent crime. . . .

The evidence on tween sex presents a troubling picture, too. Despite a 13 decrease among older teens for the first time since records have been kept, sexual activity among tweens increased during that period. It seems that kids who are having sex are doing so at earlier ages. Between 1988 and 1995, the proportion of girls saying they began sex before 15 rose from 11 percent to 19 percent. (For boys, the number remained stable, at 21 percent.) This means that approximately one in five middle-school kids is sexually active. Christie Hogan, a middle-school counselor for 20 years in Louisville, Kentucky, says: "We're beginning to see a few pregnant sixth-graders." Many of the principals and counselors I spoke with reported a small but striking minority of sexually active seventh-graders. . . .

Certainly the days of the tentative and giggly preadolescent seem to be 14 passing. Middle-school principals report having to deal with miniskirted 12-year-olds "draping themselves over boys" or patting their behinds in the hallways, while 11-year-old boys taunt girls about their breasts and rumors about their own and even their parents' sexual proclivities. Tweens have even given new connotations to the word "playground": one fifth-grade teacher from southwestern Ohio told me of two youngsters discovered in the bushes during recess.

Drugs and alcohol are also seeping into tween culture. The past six years 15 have seen more than a doubling of the number of eighth-graders who smoke marijuana (10 percent today) and those who no longer see it as dangerous. "The stigma isn't there the way it was ten years ago," says Dan Kindlon, assistant professor of psychiatry at Harvard Medical School and co-author with Michael Thompson of *Raising Cain*. "Then it was the fringe group smoking pot. You were looked at strangely. Now the fringe group is using LSD."

Aside from sex, drugs, and rock and roll, another teen problem—eating 16 disorders—is also beginning to affect younger kids. This behavior grows out of premature fashion-consciousness, which has an even more pernicious effect on tweens than on teens, because, by definition, younger kids have a more vulnerable and insecure self-image. Therapists say they are seeing a growing

[2]Crimes against a person. They include assault, robbery, rape, and homicide (editors' note).

number of anorexics and obsessive dieters even among late-elementary-school girls. "You go on Internet chat rooms and find ten- and 11-year-olds who know every [fashion] model and every statistic about them," says Nancy Kolodny, a Connecticut-based therapist and author of *When Food's a Foe: How You Can Confront and Conquer Your Eating Disorder.* "Kate Moss is their god. They can tell if she's lost a few pounds or gained a few. If a powerful kid is talking about this stuff at school, it has a big effect."

What change in our social ecology has led to the emergence of tweens?   17 Many note that kids are reaching puberty at earlier ages, but while earlier physical maturation may play a small role in defining adolescence down, its importance tends to be overstated. True, the average age at which girls begin to menstruate has fallen from 13 to between 11 and 12½ today, but the very gradualness of this change means that 12-year-olds have been living inside near-adult bodies for many decades without feeling impelled to build up a cosmetics arsenal or head for the bushes at recess. In fact, some experts believe that the very years that have witnessed the rise of the tween have also seen the age of first menstruation stabilize. Further, teachers and principals on the front lines see no clear correlation between physical and social maturation. Plenty of budding girls and bulking boys have not put away childish things, while an abundance of girls with flat chests and boys with squeaky voices ape the body language and fashions of their older siblings. . . .

Of course, the causes are complex, and most people working with   18 tweens know it. In my conversations with educators and child psychologists who work primarily with middle-class kids nationwide, two major and fairly predictable themes emerged: a sexualized and glitzy media-driven marketplace and absentee parents. What has been less commonly recognized is that at this age, the two causes combine to augment the authority of the peer group, which in turn both weakens the influence of parents and reinforces the power of the media. Taken together, parental absence, the market, and the peer group form a vicious circle that works to distort the development of youngsters. . . .

Questions for Close Reading

1. What is the selection's thesis? Locate the sentence(s) in which Hymowitz states her main idea. If she doesn't state the thesis explicitly, express it in your own words.
2. According to Hymowitz, what self-image do tweens cultivate? How do they project this image to others?
3. What physically dangerous behavioral trends does Hymowitz link to the tween phenomenon?
4. According to Hymowitz, what are the primary causes of the tween phenomenon?

5. Refer to your dictionary as needed to define the following words used in the selection: *glowering* (1), *Talmudic* (1), *rites* (1), *demographic* (3), *pragmatic* (5), *ideological* (5), *regalia* (8), *donning* (8), *ply* (8), *emblazoned* (10), *de rigueur* (10), *eschewing* (11), *tentative* (14), *proclivities* (14), *connotations* (14), *stigma* (15), *pernicious* (16), *correlation* (17), and *augment* (18).

Questions About the Writer's Craft

1. The pattern. Hymowitz opens her essay with an anecdotal example of tweenhood—her daughter's. What does this example add to her essay?

2. The pattern. What types of examples does Hymowitz provide in her essay? (See pages 142–143 for a discussion of the various forms that examples can take.) Cite at least one example of each type. How does each type of example contribute to her thesis?

3. How would you characterize Hymowitz's tone in the selection? Cite vocabulary that conveys this tone.

4. Other patterns. In paragraph 8, Hymowitz uses clothing as a means of presenting an important *contrast*. What does she contrast in these paragraphs? How does this contribute to her thesis?

Writing Assignments Using Exemplification as a Pattern of Development

1. Hymowitz is troubled and perplexed by her daughter's behavior. Think about an older person, such as a parent or another relative, who finds *your* behavior troubling and perplexing. Write an essay in which you illustrate why your behavior distresses this person. (Or, conversely, think of an elder whose behavior *you* find problematic, and write an essay illustrating why that person evokes this response in you.) You might structure your essay by picking the two or three most irksome characteristics or habits and developing supporting paragraphs around each of them. However you choose to organize your essay, be sure to provide abundant examples throughout.

2. The cultivation of a sophisticated self-image is, according to Hymowitz, a hallmark of tweenhood. Think back to when you were around that age. What was your self-image at that time? Did you think of yourself as worldly or inexperienced? Cool or awkward? Attractive or unappealing? In your journal, freewrite about the traits that you would have identified in yourself as either a tween or an adolescent. Write an essay in which you illustrate your self-image at that age, focusing on two to three dominant characteristics you associated with yourself. It's important that you illustrate each trait with examples of when and how you displayed it. For example, if you saw yourself as "dorky," you might recall an embarrassing time when you tripped and fell in the middle of your school lunchroom. Conclude your essay by reflecting on whether the way you saw yourself at the time was accurate, and whether your feelings about yourself have changed since then. You'd also benefit from reading any of the following authors' musings on their childhood self-perceptions: Gary Soto's "The Jacket" (page 91), Maya Angelou's "Sister Flowers" (page 96), Annie Dillard's "The Chase" (page 113),

Langston Hughes's "Salvation" (page 124), Beth Johnson's "Bombs Bursting in Air" (page 160), and Joseph H. Suina's "And Then I Went to School" (page 271).

Writing Assignments Combining Patterns of Development

3. Hymowitz advances a powerful argument about the alarming contemporary trend of tweenhood. But many would disagree with her entirely pessimistic analysis. Write an essay in which you *argue,* contrary to Hymowitz, that tweens today actually exhibit several *positive* characteristics. You might say, for example, that tweens today are more independent or more socially conscious than kids in the past. In order to develop your argument, you'll need to show how each characteristic you're discussing *contrasts* favorably with that characteristic in a previous generation of kids. Be sure, too, to acknowledge opposing arguments as you proceed. Research conducted in the library and/or on the Internet might help you develop your pro-tween argument.

4. Though she doesn't use the term explicitly, Hymowitz points to peer pressure as a significant factor in tweens' premature maturity. In your journal, take a few moments to reflect on your own experiences with peer pressure, whether as a preteen or teen, or even into adulthood. What are some incidents that stand out in your memory? Write an essay *narrating* a particularly memorable incident of peer pressure in which you were involved. You may have been the object of the pressure, or even perhaps the source. What were the circumstances? Who was involved? How did you respond at the time? How did the episode *affect* you? In retrospect, how do you feel about the incident today? Be sure to use dialogue as well as *descriptive* language in order to make the episode come alive.

Writing Assignment Using a Journal Entry as a Starting Point

5. As a way of illustrating her daughter's evolving tween tastes, Hymowitz cites the "years-in-the-making American Girl doll collection" over which her disaffected daughter has now drawn a sheet. Reviewing what you wrote in your pre-reading journal entry, identify some once-loved childhood items or activities that you distanced yourself from as you got older. Write an essay in which you exemplify your growth into adolescence by identifying two or three childhood possessions or activities that you cast off. You might, for example, discuss building up a beloved rock collection or playing with action figures. As you introduce these items, be sure to describe them and to explain the significance they once held for you, as well as your reasons for leaving them behind. Conclude your essay by offering some reflections on whether you currently regard the childhood items with the same distaste or disinterest you felt as a teen.

Beth Johnson

Beth Johnson (1956–) is a writer, occasional college teacher, and freelance editor. A graduate of Goshen College and Syracuse University, Johnson is the author of several college texts, including *Everyday Heroes* (1996) and *Reading Changed My Life* (2003). Containing profiles of men and women who have triumphed over obstacles to achieve personal and academic success, the books have provided a motivational boost to college students nationwide. She is also the coauthor of the textbook *Voices and Values: A Reader for Writers* (2002). She lives with her husband and three children in Lederach, Pennsylvania. The following piece is one of several that Johnson has written about the complexities and wonders of life.

Pre-Reading Journal Entry

When you were young, did adults acknowledge the existence of life's tragedies, or did they deny such harsh truths? In your journal, list several difficult events that you observed or experienced firsthand as a child. How did the adults in your life explain these hardships? In each case, do you think the adults acted appropriately? If not, how should they have responded?

Bombs Bursting in Air

It's Friday night and we're at the Olympics, the Junior Olympics, that is. 1
My son is on a relay-race team competing against fourth-graders from all over the school district. His little sister and I sit high in the stands, trying to pick Isaac out from the crowd of figures milling around on the field during these moments of pre-game confusion. The public address system sputters to life and summons our attention. "And now," the tinny voice rings out, "please join together in the singing of our national anthem."

"Oh saaay can you seeeeee," we begin. My arm rests around Maddie's 2
shoulders. I am touching her a lot today, and she notices. "Mom, you're *squishing* me," she chides, wriggling from my grip. I content myself with stroking her hair. News that reached me today makes me need to feel her near. We pipe along, squeaking out the impossibly high note of "land of the freeeeeeeee." Maddie clowns, half-singing, half-shouting the lyrics, hitting the "b's" explosively on "bombs bursting in air."

Bombs indeed, I think, replaying the sound of my friend's voice over the 3
phone that afternoon: "Bumped her head sledding. Took her in for an x-ray, just to make sure. There was something strange, so they did more tests . . . a brain tumor . . . Children's Hospital in Boston Tuesday . . . surgery, yes,

right away. . . ." Maddie's playmate Shannon, only five years old. We'd last seen her at Halloween, dressed in her blue princess costume, and we'd talked of Furby and Scooby-Doo and Tootsie Rolls. Now her parents were hurriedly learning a new vocabulary—CAT scans, glioma, pediatric neurosurgery, and frontal lobe.[1] A bomb had exploded in their midst, and, like troops under attack, they were rallying in response.

The games over, the children and I edge our way out of the school parking lot, bumper to bumper with other parents ferrying their families home. I tell the kids as casually as I can about Shannon. "She'll have to have an operation. It's lucky, really, that they found it by accident this way while it's small."   4

"I want to send her a present," Maddie announces. "That'd be nice," I say, glad to keep the conversation on a positive note.   5

But my older son is with us now. Sam, who is thirteen, says, "She'll be OK, though, right?" It's not a question, really; it's a statement that I must either agree with or contradict. I want to say yes. I want to say of course she'll be all right. I want them to inhabit a world where five-year-olds do not develop silent, mysterious growths in their brains, where "malignancy" and "seizure" are words for *New York Times* crossword puzzles, not for little girls. They would accept my assurance; they would believe me and sleep well tonight. But I can't; the bomb that exploded in Shannon's home has sent splinters of shrapnel into ours as well, and they cannot be ignored or lied away. "We hope she'll be just fine," I finally say. "She has very good doctors. She has wonderful parents who are doing everything they can. The tumor is small. Shannon's strong and healthy."   6

"*She'll* be OK," says Maddie matter-of-factly. "In school we read about a little boy who had something wrong with his leg and he had an operation and got better. Can we go to Dairy Queen?"   7

Bombs on the horizon don't faze Maddie. Not yet. I can just barely remember from my own childhood the sense that still surrounds her, that feeling of being cocooned within reassuring walls of security and order. Back then, Monday meant gym, Tuesday was pizza in the cafeteria, Wednesday brought clarinet lessons. Teachers stood in their familiar spots in the classrooms, telling us with reassuring simplicity that World War II happened because Hitler, a very bad man, invaded Poland. Midterms and report cards, summer vacations and new notebooks in September gave a steady rhythm to the world. It wasn't all necessarily happy—through the years there were poor grades, grouchy teachers, exclusion from the desired social group, dateless weekends when it seemed the rest of the world was paired off—but it was familiar territory where we felt walled off from the really bad things that happened to other people.   8

[1]A CAT scan is a computerized cross-sectional image of an internal body structure; a glioma is a tumor in the brain or spinal cord; pediatric neurosurgery is surgery performed on the nerves, brain, or spinal cord of a child; the frontal lobe is the largest section of the brain (editors' note).

There were hints of them, though, even then. Looking back, I recall the   9
tiny shock waves, the tremors from far-off explosions that occasionally rat-
tled our shelter. There was the little girl who was absent for a week and when
she returned wasn't living with her mother and stepfather anymore. There
was a big girl who threw up in the bathroom every morning and then disappeared from school. A playful, friendly custodian was suddenly fired, and
it had something to do with an angry parent. A teacher's husband had a
heart attack and died. These were interesting tidbits to report to our families over dinner, mostly out of morbid interest in seeing our parents bite their
lips and exchange glances.

As we got older, the bombs dropped closer. A friend's sister was arrest-   10
ed for selling drugs; we saw her mother in tears at church that Sunday. A boy
I thought I knew, a school clown with a sweet crooked grin, shot himself in
the woods behind his house. A car full of senior boys, going home from a
dance where I'd been sent into ecstasy when the cutest of them all greeted
me by name, rounded a curve too fast and crashed, killing them. We wept
and hugged each other in the halls. Our teachers listened to us grieve and
tried to comfort us, but their words came out impatient and almost angry. I
realize now that what sounded like anger was a helplessness to teach us
lessons we were still too young or too ignorant to learn. For although our
sorrow was real, we still had some sense of a protective curtain between us
and the bombs. If only, we said. If only she hadn't used drugs. If only he'd
told someone how depressed he was. If only they'd been more careful. *We*
weren't like them; we were careful. Like magical incantations, we recited the
things that we would or wouldn't do in order to protect ourselves from such
sad, unnecessary fates.

And then my best friend, a beautiful girl of sixteen, went to sleep one   11
January night and never woke up. I found myself shaken to the core of my
being. My grief at the loss of my vibrant, laughing friend was great. But what
really tilted my universe was the nakedness of my realization that there was
no "if only." There were no drugs, no careless action, no crime, no accident,
nothing I could focus on to explain away what had happened. She had simply died. Which could only mean that there was no magic barrier separating
me and my loved ones from the bombs. We were as vulnerable as everyone
else. For months the shock stayed with me. I sat in class watching my teachers draw diagrams of Saturn, talk about Watergate,[2] multiply fractions, and
wondered at their apparent cheer and normalcy. Didn't they *know* we were
all doomed? Didn't they know it was only a matter of time until one of us
took a direct hit? What was the point of anything?

[2]In June, 1972, supporters of Republican President Richard Nixon were caught breaking into
the Democratic campaign headquarters in the Watergate office complex in Washington, D.C.
The resulting investigation of the White House connection to the break-in led to President
Nixon's eventual resignation in August, 1974 (editors' note).

But time moved on, and I moved with it. College came and went, grad- 12
uate school, adulthood, middle age. My heightened sense of vulnerability
began to subside, though I could never again slip fully into the soothing
security of my younger days. I became more aware of the intertwining
threads of joy, pain, and occasional tragedy that weave through all our lives.
College was stimulating, exciting, full of friendship and challenge. I fell in
love for the first time, reveled in its sweetness, then learned the painful les-
son that love comes with no guarantee. A beloved professor lost two children
to leukemia, but continued with skill and passion to introduce students to
the riches of literature. My father grew ill, but the last day of his life, when I
sat by his bed holding his hand, remains one of my sweetest memories. The
marriage I'd entered into with optimism ended in bitter divorce, but produced three children whose existence is my daily delight. At every step along
the way, I've seen that the most rewarding chapters of my life have contained
parts that I not only would not have chosen, but would have given much to
avoid. But selecting just the good parts is not an option we are given.

The price of allowing ourselves to truly live, to love and be loved, is (and 13
it's the ultimate irony) the knowledge that the greater our investment in life,
the larger the target we create. Of course, it is within our power to refuse
friendship, shrink from love, live in isolation, and thus create for ourselves a
nearly impenetrable bomb shelter. There are those among us who choose
such an existence, the price of intimacy being too high. Looking about me,
however, I see few such examples. Instead, I am moved by the courage with
which most of us, ordinary folks, continue soldiering on. We fall in love, we
bring our children into the world, we forge our friendships, we give our
hearts, knowing with increasing certainty that we do so at our own risk. Still
we move ahead with open arms, saying yes, yes to life.

Shannon's surgery is behind her; the prognosis is good. Her mother 14
reports that the family is returning to its normal routines, laughing again and
talking of ordinary things, even while they step more gently, speak more quietly, are more aware of the precious fragility of life and of the blessing of
every day that passes without explosion.

Bombs bursting in air. They can blind us, like fireworks at the moment 15
of explosion. If we close our eyes and turn away, all we see is their fiery
image. But if we have the courage to keep our eyes open and welcoming,
even bombs finally fade against the vastness of the starry sky.

Questions for Close Reading

1. What is the selection's thesis? Locate the sentence(s) in which Johnson states her
   main idea. If she doesn't state the thesis explicitly, express it in your own words.
2. In paragraph 2, Johnson describes her "need to feel her [daughter] near." What
   compels her to want to be physically close to her daughter? Why do you think
   Johnson responds this way?

3. In describing her family's responses to Shannon's illness, Johnson presents three reactions: Maddie's, Sam's, and her own. How do these responses differ? In what ways do Maddie's, Sam's, and Johnson's reactions typify the age groups to which they belong?
4. In paragraph 13, Johnson describes two basic ways people respond to life's inevitable "bombs." What are these ways? Which response does Johnson endorse?
5. Refer to your dictionary as needed to define the following words used in the selection: *ferrying* (paragraph 4), *shrapnel* (6), *faze* (8), *cocooned* (8), *tremors* (9), *incantations* (10), *vulnerable* (11), *intertwining* (12), *impenetrable* (13), *soldiering on* (13), *prognosis* (14), and *fragility* (14).

Questions About the Writer's Craft

1. **The pattern.** Although Johnson provides many examples of life's "bombs," she gives more weight to some examples than to others. Which examples does she emphasize? Which ones receive less attention? Why?
2. **Other patterns.** What important *contrast* does Johnson develop in paragraph 6? How does this contrast reinforce the essay's main idea?
3. Writers generally vary sentence structure in an effort to add interest to their work. But in paragraphs 9 and 10, Johnson employs a repetitive sentence structure. Where is the repetition in these two paragraphs? Why do you think she uses this technique?
4. Johnson develops her essay by means of an extended metaphor (see page 75), using bombs as her central image. Identify all the places where Johnson draws upon language and imagery related to bombs and battles. What do you think Johnson hopes to achieve with this sustained metaphor?

Writing Assignments Using Exemplification as a Pattern of Development

1. In paragraphs 9 and 10, Johnson catalogues a number of events that made her increasingly aware of life's bombs. Write an essay of your own, illustrating how you came to recognize the inevitability of painful life events. Start by listing the difficult events you've encountered. Select the three most compelling occurrences, and do some freewriting to generate details about each. Before writing, decide whether you will order your examples chronologically or emphatically; use whichever illustrates more effectively your dawning realization of life's complexity. End with some conclusions about your ability to cope with difficult times.
2. Johnson describes her evolving understanding of life. In an essay of your own, show the way several events combined to change your understanding of a specific aspect of your life. Perhaps a number of incidents prompted you to reconsider career choices, end a relationship, or appreciate the importance of family. Cite only those events that illustrate your emerging understanding. Your decision to use either chronological or emphatic sequence depends on which illustrates more dramatically the change in your perception. To see how other writers describe their journeys of self-discovery, read Maya Angelou's "Sister Flowers" (page 96) and Joseph H. Suina's "And Then I Went to School" (page 271).

Writing Assignments Combining
Patterns of Development

∞ **3.** Johnson explores the lasting impact the death of her friend had on her life. Write an essay about the *effect* of a *single* bomb on your life. You might *recount* getting left back in school, losing a loved one, seeing the dark side of someone you admired, and so on. Your causal analysis should make clear how the event affected your life. Perhaps the event had painful short-term consequences but positive long-term repercussions. Langston Hughes's "Salvation" (page 124) and Joseph H. Suina's "And Then I Went to School" (page 271) provide helpful models for examining the effects of a life-changing event.

⌨ **4.** In an essay, offer readers a *guide* to surviving a specific life calamity. You might, for instance, explain how to survive a pet's death, a painful breakup, a financial hardship. Consider doing some library and/or Internet research on your subject. Combining your own insights with any material gathered through research, *describe* fully the *steps* readers should take to recover from the devastating events.

Writing Assignment Using a Journal
Entry as a Starting Point

∞ **5.** Johnson asserts that painful truths shouldn't "be ignored or lied away" by adults. Do you agree? Write an essay explaining why you think adults should protect children from harsh realities—or why they should present the whole truth, even when it's painful. Review your pre-reading journal entry, searching for strong examples to support your position. Discussing this topic with others will also help you shape your point of view, as will reading Yuh Ji-Yeon's "Let's Tell the Story of All America's Cultures" (page 385).

Barbara Ehrenreich

Barbara Ehrenreich (1941–) has been a college professor, investigative reporter, magazine editor, and social activist. A graduate of Reed College, Ehrenreich received her Ph.D. in biology from Rockefeller University. She has cowritten several books, including *For Her Own Good: 150 Years of the Experts' Advice to Women* (1978), *Remaking Love: The Feminization of Sex* (1986), and *Global Woman* (2003). Her more recent books include *Fear of Falling: The Inner Life of the Middle Class* (1989), *The Worst Years of Our Lives* (1990), *Snarling Citizen: Essays* (1995), *Blood Rites* (1997), *Nickle and Dimed* (2001), and the novel *Kipper's Game* (1993). A regular columnist for *Time, The Guardian,* and *The Nation,* Ehrenreich has published articles in many other magazines, such as *Esquire, Vogue,* and the *New Republic.* "What I've Learned From Men" first appeared in *Ms.* in 1985.

Pre-Reading Journal Entry

Drawing upon childhood experiences and recent observations, reflect in your journal about the way children's gender identity is formed. What traits do parents and society tend to encourage in boys? In girls? How do these gendered characteristics benefit and/or hinder boys and girls later in life?

What I've Learned From Men

For many years I believed that women had only one thing to learn from   1
men: how to get the attention of a waiter by some means short of kicking over the table and shrieking. Never in my life have I gotten the attention of a waiter, unless it was an off-duty waiter whose car I'd accidentally scraped in a parking lot somewhere. Men, however, can summon a maître d' just by thinking the word "coffee," and this is a power women would be well-advised to study. What else would we possibly want to learn from them? How to interrupt someone in mid-sentence as if you were performing an act of conversational euthanasia? How to drop a pair of socks three feet from an open hamper and keep right on walking? How to make those weird guttural gargling sounds in the bathroom?

But now, at mid-life, I am willing to admit that there are some real and   2
useful things to learn from men. Not from all men—in fact, we may have the most to learn from some of the men we like the least. This realization does not mean that my feminist principles have gone soft with age: what I think women could learn from men is how to get *tough.* After more than a decade of consciousness-raising, assertiveness training, and hand-to-hand combat in

the battle of the sexes, we're still too ladylike. Let me try that again—we're just too *damn* ladylike.

Here is an example from my own experience, a story that I blush to recount. A few years ago, at an international conference held in an exotic and luxurious setting, a prestigious professor invited me to his room for what he said would be an intellectual discussion on matters of theoretical importance. So far, so good. I showed up promptly. But only minutes into the conversation—held in all-too-adjacent chairs—it emerged that he was interested in something more substantial than a meeting of minds. I was disgusted, but not enough to overcome 30-odd years of programming in ladylikeness. Every time his comments took a lecherous turn, I chattered distractingly; every time his hand found its way to my knee, I returned it as if it were something he had misplaced. This went on for an unconscionable period (as much as 20 minutes); then there was a minor scuffle, a dash for the door, and I was out—with nothing violated but my self-esteem. I, a full-grown feminist, conversant with such matters as rape crisis counseling and sexual harassment at the workplace, had behaved like a ninny—or, as I now understand it, like a lady. 3

The essence of ladylikeness is a persistent servility masked as "niceness." For example, we (women) tend to assume that it is our responsibility to keep everything "nice" even when the person we are with is rude, aggressive, or emotionally AWOL. (In the above example, I was so busy taking responsibility for preserving the veneer of "niceness" that I almost forgot to take responsibility for myself.) In conversations with men, we do almost all the work: sociologists have observed that in male-female social interactions it's the woman who throws out leading questions and verbal encouragements ("So how did you *feel* about that?" and so on) while the man, typically, says "Hmmmm." Wherever we go, we're perpetually smiling—the on-cue smile, like the now-outmoded curtsy, being one of our culture's little rituals of submission. We're trained to feel embarrassed if we're praised, but if we see a criticism coming at us from miles down the road, we rush to acknowledge it. And when we're feeling aggressive or angry or resentful, we just tighten up our smiles or turn them into rueful little moues. In short, we spend a great deal of time acting like wimps. 4

For contrast, think of the macho stars we love to watch. Think, for example, of Mel Gibson facing down punk marauders in *The Road Warrior* . . . John Travolta swaggering his way through the early scenes of *Saturday Night Fever* . . . or Marlon Brando shrugging off the local law in *The Wild One*. Would they simper their way through tight spots? Chatter aimlessly to keep the conversation going? Get all clutched up whenever they think they might—just might—have hurt someone's feelings? No, of course not, and therein, I think, lies their fascination for us. 5

The attraction of the "tough guy" is that he has—or at least seems to have—what most of us lack, and that is an aura of power and control. In an 6 article, feminist psychiatrist Jean Baker Miller writes that "a woman's using self-determined power for herself is equivalent to selfishness [and] destructiveness"—an equation that makes us want to avoid even the appearance of power. Miller cites cases of women who get depressed just when they're on the verge of success—and of women who do succeed and then bury their achievement in self-deprecation. As an example, she describes one company's periodic meetings to recognize outstanding salespeople: when a woman is asked to say a few words about her achievement, she tends to say something like, "Well, I really don't know how it happened. I guess I was just lucky this time." In contrast, the men will cheerfully own up to the hard work, intelligence, and so on, to which they owe their success. By putting herself down, a woman avoids feeling brazenly powerful and potentially "selfish"; she also does the traditional lady's work of trying to make everyone else feel better ("She's not really so smart, after all, just lucky").

So we might as well get a little tougher. And a good place to start is   7
by cutting back on the small acts of deference that we've been programmed to perform since girlhood. Like unnecessary smiling. For many women—waitresses, flight attendants, receptionists—smiling is an occupational requirement, but there's no reason for anyone to go around grinning when she's not being paid for it. I'd suggest that we save our off-duty smiles for when we truly feel like sharing them, and if you're not sure what to do with your face in the meantime, study Clint Eastwood's expressions—both of them.

Along the same lines, I think women should stop taking responsibility   8
for every human interaction we engage in. In a social encounter with a woman, the average man can go 25 minutes saying nothing more than "You don't say?" "Izzat so?" and, of course, "Hmmmm." Why should we do all the work? By taking so much responsibility for making conversations go well, we act as if we had much more at stake in the encounter than the other party—and that gives him (or her) the power advantage. Every now and then, we deserve to get more out of a conversation than we put into it: I'd suggest not offering information you'd rather not share ("I'm really terrified that my sales plan won't work") and not, out of sheer politeness, soliciting information you don't really want ("Wherever did you get that lovely tie?"). There will be pauses, but they don't have to be awkward for *you*.

It is true that some, perhaps most, men will interpret any decrease in   9
female deference as a deliberate act of hostility. Omit the free smiles and perky conversation-boosters and someone is bound to ask, "Well, what's come over *you* today?" For most of us, the first impulse is to stare at our feet and make vague references to a terminally ill aunt in Atlanta, but we should have as much right to be taciturn as the average (male) taxi driver. If you're taking a vacation from smiles and small talk and some fellow is moved to inquire about what's "bothering" you, just stare back levelly and say, the international debt crisis, the arms race, or the death of God.

There are all kinds of ways to toughen up—and potentially move up— 10
at work, and I leave the details to the purveyors of assertiveness training. But
Jean Baker Miller's study underscores a fundamental principle that anyone
can master on her own. We can stop acting less capable than we actually are.
For example, in the matter of taking credit when credit is due, there's a key
difference between saying "I was just lucky" and saying "I had a plan and it
worked." If you take the credit you deserve, you're letting people know that
you were confident you'd succeed all along, and that you fully intend to do
so again.

Finally, we may be able to learn something from men about what to do 11
with anger. As a general rule, women get irritated: men get *mad*. We make
tight little smiles of ladylike exasperation; they pound on desks and roar. I
wouldn't recommend emulating the full basso profundo male tantrum, but
women do need ways of expressing justified anger clearly, colorfully, and,
when necessary, crudely. If you're not just irritated, but *pissed off*, it might
help to say so.

I, for example, have rerun the scene with the prestigious professor many 12
times in my mind. And in my mind, I play it like Bogart. I start by moving
my chair over to where I can look the professor full in the face. I let him do
the chattering, and when it becomes evident that he has nothing serious to
say, I lean back and cross my arms, just to let him know that he's wasting my
time. I do not smile, neither do I nod encouragement. Nor, of course, do I
respond to his blandishments with apologetic shrugs and blushes. Then, at
the first flicker of lechery, I stand up and announce coolly, "All right, I've
had enough of this crap." Then I walk out—slowly, deliberately, confident-
ly. Just like a man.

Or—now that I think of it—just like a woman. 13

Questions for Close Reading

1. What is the selection's thesis? Locate the sentence(s) in which Ehrenreich states her
   main idea. If she doesn't state the thesis explicitly, express it in your own words.
2. Why did Ehrenreich handle the lecherous professor as she did? In retrospect, how
   does she wish she had dealt with the situation? How does her current perspective
   of the way she should have behaved reinforce her thesis in the essay?
3. What does "behaving like a lady" mean, according to Ehrenreich? What is her
   opinion of "ladylike" behavior?
4. Why, in Ehrenreich's view, do we like "macho stars" (paragraph 5)? What can we
   learn from them?
5. Refer to your dictionary as needed to define the following words used in the selection: *euthanasia* (paragraph 1), *guttural* (1), *lecherous* (3), *distractingly* (3),
   unconscionable (3), *ninny* (3), *servility* (4), *veneer* (4), *moues* (4), *marauders* (5),
   aura (6), *brazenly* (6), *deference* (9), *taciturn* (9), *purveyors* (10), *emulating* (11),
   basso profundo (11), and *blandishments* (12).

Questions About the Writer's Craft

1. **The pattern.** In paragraphs 3 and 12, Ehrenreich uses her own personal experience as a key example. Why do you think she chooses to include this example? Why do you suppose she presents it so early in the essay and then returns to it at the end?

2. **Other patterns.** Locate places in the essay where Ehrenreich uses examples to *contrast* the different responses and behaviors of males and females. How do these contrasts help the writer develop her main idea?

3. Do you think that Ehrenreich is speaking primarily to a male or to a female audience? What in the essay makes you feel this way? Do you think that the author expects her audience to be positive, hostile, or neutral toward her ideas? What in the essay leads you to this conclusion?

4. In her attack on "ladylikeness," Ehrenreich deliberately avoids using a "ladylike" or "nice" tone. Which of her phrases or expressions seem to defy stereotypes about the way "ladies" should express themselves?

Writing Assignments Using Exemplification as a Pattern of Development

1. If, as Ehrenreich suggests, women have much to learn from men, is it also true that men could learn from women? Write an essay illustrating your belief that men would indeed be better off if they acquired some attitudes and behaviors traditionally associated with women. Be sure to provide numerous examples from your own experience and observations. You may take a humorous or serious approach when showing that men should—in some respects—become more like women. Dave Barry's "The Ugly Truth About Beauty" (page 277) may spark some insight into characteristically male and female behavioral patterns.

2. Ehrenreich points to the popularity of several "macho stars": Mel Gibson in *The Road Warrior*, John Travolta in *Saturday Night Fever*, Marlon Brando in *The Wild One*, and Clint Eastwood in anything. Choose several female characters from film or television who you feel provide positive role models for both males and females. Write an essay in which you use these characters as examples of the way that men and women should conduct their lives. Before writing, consider reading Maya Angelou's "Sister Flowers" (page 96), a loving portrait of a memorable female role model.

Writing Assignments Combining Patterns of Development

3. Ehrenreich suggests that some of the problems women experience in relationships and careers are of their own making—they smile too much, are too deferential, and fail to claim their own achievements. Pick one or two areas in which women tend to experience difficulty and write an essay *arguing* either that women sabotage themselves or that they are sabotaged by society's attitudes and expectations. Brainstorm with others to gather ideas and *examples* for your paper. For other perspectives, you may want to read one or more of the following

essays: Dave Barry's "The Ugly Truth About Beauty" (page 277), Camille Paglia's "Rape: A Bigger Danger Than Feminists Know" (page 395), and Susan Jacoby's "Common Decency" (page 401).

∞ **4.** Like Ehrenreich, most of us have been subjected at one time or another to the inappropriate or unpleasant behavior of others: slurs on our abilities, interests, or appearance; derision about our sex or sexual preference; taunts about our race, religion, or ethnic background. Focus on *one category* of insult, and brainstorm with others to identify *ways* for dealing with such an affront. Then write an essay describing different *strategies* for coping with the offensive behavior. Reach some conclusions about which approach is most effective. Caroline Rego's "The Fine Art of Complaining" (page 245) may spark some ideas worth exploring.

Writing Assignment Using a Journal Entry as a Starting Point

🖳 **5.** Drawing upon your pre-reading journal entry, write an essay in which you compare and/or contrast the qualities that parents and the culture at large nurture in boys with those they nurture in girls. Brainstorming with others will help you identify telling examples. Reach some conclusions about the long-term effects on children of these parental and societal influences. Consider supplementing your informal research with library and/or Internet information about the formation of children's gender identity.

Additional Writing Topics

EXEMPLIFICATION

General Assignments

Use examples to develop any one of the following topics into a well-organized essay. When writing the paper, choose enough relevant examples to support your thesis. Organize the material into a sequence that most effectively illustrates the thesis, keeping in mind that emphatic order is often the most compelling way to present specifics.

1. Many of today's drivers have dangerous habits.
2. Drug and alcohol abuse is (or is not) a serious problem among many young people.
3. One rule of restaurant dining is "Management often seems oblivious to problems that are perfectly obvious to customers."
4. Children today are not encouraged to use their imaginations.
5. The worst kind of hypocrite is a religious hypocrite.
6. The best things in life are definitely not free.
7. A part-time job is an important experience that every college student should have.
8. The Internet has resulted in a generation of lazy young people.
9. _____ (name someone you know well) is a _____ (use a quality: open-minded, dishonest, compulsive, reliable, gentle, and so on) person.
10. Television commercials stereotype the elderly (or another minority group).
11. Today, salespeople act as if they're doing you a favor by taking your money.
12. Most people behave decently in their daily interactions with each other.
13. Pettiness, jealousy, and selfishness abound in our daily interactions with each other.
14. You can tell a lot about people by observing what they wear and eat.
15. Too many Americans are overly concerned/completely unconcerned with being physically fit.
16. There are several study techniques that will help a student learn more efficiently.
17. Some teachers seem to enjoy turning tests into ordeals.
18. "How to avoid bad eating habits" is one course all college students should take.
19. More needs to be done to eliminate obstacles faced by the physically handicapped.
20. Some of the best presents are those that cost the least.

Assignments With a Specific Purpose, Audience, and Point of View

On Campus

1. Lately, many people at your college have been experiencing stress. As a member of the Student Life Committee, you've been asked to prepare a pamphlet illustrating

strategies for reducing different kinds of stress. Decide which stresses to discuss, and explain coping strategies for each, providing helpful examples as you go.

2. A friend of yours will be going away to college in an unfamiliar environment—in a bustling urban setting or in a quiet rural one. To help your friend prepare for this new environment, write a letter giving examples of what life on an urban or a rural campus is like. You might focus on the benefits and dangers with which your friend is unlikely to be familiar.

At Home or in the Community

3. Shopping for a new car, you become annoyed at how many safety features are available only as expensive options. Write a letter of complaint to the auto manufacturer, citing at least three examples of such options. Avoid sounding hostile.

4. A pet food company is having an annual contest to choose a new animal to feature in its advertising. To win the contest, you must convince the company that your pet is personable, playful, unique. Write an essay giving examples of your pet's special qualities.

On the Job

5. Assume that you're an elementary school principal planning to give a speech in which you'll try to convince parents that television distorts children's perceptions of reality. Write the speech, illustrating your point with vivid examples.

6. The online publication you work for has asked you to write an article on what you consider to be the "three best consumer products of the past twenty-five years." Support your opinion with lively, engaging specifics that are consistent with the website's offbeat and slightly ironic tone.

6

DIVISION-CLASSIFICATION

WHAT IS DIVISION-CLASSIFICATION?

Imagine what life would be like if this is how an average day unfolded:

> You plan to stop at the supermarket for only five items, but your marketing takes over an hour because all the items in the store are jumbled together. Clerks put new shipments anywhere they please; the milk might be with the vegetables on Monday but with laundry detergent on Thursday. Next, you go to the drugstore to pick up some photos you left to be developed. You don't have time, though, to wait while the cashier roots through the large carton into which all the pickup envelopes have been thrown. You return to your car and decide to stop at the town hall to pay a parking ticket. But the town hall baffles you. The offices are unmarked, and there's not even a directory to tell you on which floor the Violations Bureau can be found. Annoyed, you get back into your car and, minutes later, end up colliding with another car, which is driving toward you in your lane. When you wake up in the hospital, you find there are three other patients in your room: a middle-aged man with a heart problem, a young boy ready to have his tonsils removed, and a woman about to go into labor.

Such a muddled world, lacking the most basic forms of organization, would make daily life chaotic. All of us instinctively look for ways to order our environment. Without systems, categories, or sorting mechanisms, we'd be overwhelmed by life's complexity. An organization such as a college or university, for example, is made manageable by being divided into various schools (Liberal Arts, Performing Arts, Engineering, and so on). The schools are then separated into departments (English, History, Political Science), and each department's offerings are grouped into distinct categories—English, for instance, into Literature and Composition—before being further divided into specific courses.

The kind of ordering system we've been discussing is called *division-classification*, a logical way of thinking that allows us to make sense of a complex world. Division and classification, though separate processes, are often used together as complementary techniques. *Division* involves taking a single unit or concept, breaking the unit down into its parts, and then analyzing the connections among the parts and between the parts and the whole. For instance, if we wanted to organize the chaotic hospital described at the start of the chapter, we might think about how the single concept "a hospital" could be broken down into its components. We might come up with the following breakdown: pediatric wing, cardiac wing, maternity wing, and so on.

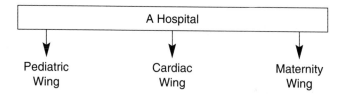

What we have just done involves division: We've taken a single entity (a hospital) and divided it into some of its component parts (wings), each with its own facilities and patients.

In contrast, *classification* brings two or more related items together and categorizes them according to type or kind. If the disorganized supermarket described earlier were to be restructured, the clerks would have to classify the separate items arriving at the loading dock. Cartons of lettuce, tomatoes, cucumbers, butter, yogurt, milk, shampoo, conditioner, and setting lotion would be assigned to the appropriate categories:

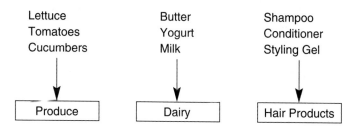

HOW DIVISION-CLASSIFICATION FITS YOUR PURPOSE AND AUDIENCE

The reorganized hospital and supermarket show the way division and classification work in everyday life. But division and classification also come into play during the writing process. Because division involves breaking a subject into parts, it can be a helpful strategy during prewriting, especially if you're analyzing a broad, complex subject: the structure of a film; the motivation of a character in a novel; the problem your community has with vandalism; the controversy surrounding school prayer. An editorial examining a recent hostage crisis, for example, might divide the crisis into three areas: how the hostages were treated by (1) their captors, (2) the governments negotiating their release, and (3) the media. The purpose of the editorial might be to show readers that the governments' treatment of the hostages was particularly exploitative.

Classification can be useful for imposing order on the hodgepodge of ideas generated during prewriting. You examine that material to see which of your rough ideas are alike and which are dissimilar, so that you can cluster related items in the same category. Classification would, then, be a helpful strategy in analyzing topics like these: techniques for impressing teachers; comic styles of talk-show hosts; views on abortion; reasons for the current rise in volunteerism. You might, for instance, use classification in a paper showing that Americans are undermining their health through their obsessive pursuit of various diets. Perhaps you begin by brainstorming all the diets that have gained popularity in recent years (Weight Watchers', Slim-Fast, Jenny Craig, whatever). Then you categorize the diets according to type: high-fiber, low-protein, high-carbohydrate, and so on. Once the diets are grouped, you can discuss the problems within each category, demonstrating to readers that none of the diets is safe or effective.

Division-classification can be crucial when responding to college assignments like the following:

> From your observations, what kinds of appeals do television advertisers use when selling automobiles? In your view, are any of these appeals morally irresponsible?

> Analyze the components that go into being an effective parent. Indicate those you consider most vital for raising confident, well-adjusted children.

> Describe the hierarchy of the typical high school clique, identifying the various parts of the hierarchy. Use your analysis to support or refute the view that adolescence is a period of rigid conformity.

> Many social commentators have observed that discourtesy is on the rise. Indicate whether you think this is a valid observation by characterizing the types of everyday encounters you have with people.

These assignments suggest division-classification through the use of such words as *kinds, components, parts,* and *types.* Generally, though, you won't receive such clear signals to use division-classification. Instead, the broad purpose of the essay—and the point you want to make—will lead you to the analytical thinking characteristic of division-classification.

Sometimes division-classification will be the dominant technique for structuring an essay; other times it will be used as a supplemental pattern in an essay organized primarily according to another pattern of development. Let's look at some examples. Say you want to write a paper *explaining a process* (surviving divorce; creating a hit record; shepherding a bill through Congress; using the Heimlich maneuver on people who are choking). You could *divide* the process into parts or stages, showing, for instance, that the Heimlich maneuver is an easily mastered skill that readers should acquire. Or perhaps you plan to write a light-spirited essay analyzing the *effect* that increased awareness of sexual stereotypes has had on college students' social lives. In such a case, you might use *classification*. To show readers that shifting gender roles make young men and women comically self-conscious, you could categorize the places where students scout each other out: in class, at the library, at parties, in dorms. You could then show how students—not wishing to be macho or coyly feminine—approach each other with laughable tentativeness in these four environments.

Now imagine that you're writing an *argumentation-persuasion* essay urging that the federal government prohibit the use of growth-inducing antibiotics in livestock feed. The paper could begin by *dividing* the antibiotics cycle into stages: the effects of antibiotics on livestock; the short-term effects on humans who consume the animals; the possible long-term effects of consuming antibiotic-tainted meat. To increase readers' understanding of the problem, you might also discuss the antibiotics controversy in terms of an even larger issue: the dangerous ways food is treated before being consumed. In this case, you would consider the various procedures (use of additives, preservatives, artificial colors, and so on), *classifying* these treatments into several types—from least harmful (some additives or artificial colors, perhaps) to most harmful (you might slot the antibiotics here). Such an essay would be developed using both division *and* classification: first, the division of the antibiotics cycle and then the classification of the various food treatments. Frequently, this interdependence will be reversed, and classification will precede rather than follow division.

SUGGESTIONS FOR USING DIVISION-CLASSIFICATION IN AN ESSAY

The following suggestions will be helpful whether you use division-classification as a dominant or a supportive pattern of development.

1. Select a principle of division-classification consistent with your purpose.   Most subjects can be divided or classified according to a *number* *of different principles.* For example, when writing about an ideal vacation, you could divide your subject according to any of these principles: location, cost, recreation available. Similarly, when analyzing students at your college, you could base your classification on a variety of principles: students' majors, their racial or ethnic background, whether they belong to a fraternity or sorority. In all cases, though, the principle of division-classification you select must meet one stringent requirement: It must help you meet your overall purpose and reinforce your central point.

Sometimes a principle of division-classification seems so attractive that you latch on to it without examining whether it's consistent with your purpose. Suppose you want to write a paper asserting that several episodes of a new television comedy are destined to become classics. Here's how you might go wrong.

You begin by doing some brainstorming about the episodes. Then, as you start to organize the prewriting material, you hit on a possible principle of classification: grouping the characters in the show according to the frequency with which they appear (main characters appearing in every show, supporting characters appearing in most shows, and guest characters appearing once or twice). You name the characters and explain which characters fit where. But is this principle of classification significant? Has it anything to do with why the shows will become classics? No, it hasn't. Such an essay would be little more than a meaningless exercise in classifying things just to classify them.

In contrast, a significant principle of classification might involve categorizing a number of shows according to the easily recognized human types portrayed: the Pompous Know-It-All, the Boss Who's Out of Control, the Lovable Grouch, the Surprisingly Savvy Innocent. You might illustrate the way certain episodes offer delightful twists on these stock figures, making such shows models of comic plotting and humor.

When you write an essay that uses division-classification as its primary method of development, a *single principle* of division-classification provides the foundation for each major section of the paper. Imagine you're writing an essay showing that the success of contemporary music groups has less to do with musical talent than with the groups' ability to market themselves to a distinct segment of the listening audience. To develop your point, you might categorize several performers according to the age ranges they appeal to (preteens, adolescents, people in their late twenties) and then analyze the marketing strategies the musicians use to gain their fans' support. The essay's logic would be undermined if you switched, in the middle of your analysis, to another principle of classification—say, the influence of earlier groups on today's music scene.

Don't, however, take this caution to mean that essays can never use more than one principle of division-classification as they unfold. They can—as long as the *shift from one principle to another* occurs in *different parts* of the paper. Imagine you want to write about widespread disillusionment with student government leaders at your college. You could develop this point by breaking down the dissatisfaction into the following: disappointment with the students' qualifications for office; disenchantment with their campaign tactics; frustration with their performance once elected. That section of the essay completed, you might move to a second principle of division—how students can get involved in campus government. Perhaps you break the proposed involvement into the following possibilities: serving on nominating committees; helping to run candidates' campaigns; attending open sessions of the student government.

2. Apply the principle of division-classification logically. In an essay using division-classification, you need to demonstrate to readers that your analysis is the result of careful thought. First of all, your division-classification should be as *complete* as possible. Your analysis should include—within reason—all the parts into which you can divide your subject, or all the types into which you can categorize your subjects. Let's say you're writing an essay showing that where college students live is an important factor in determining how satisfied they are with college life. Keeping your purpose in mind, you classify students according to where they live: with parents, in dorms, in fraternity and sorority houses. But what about all the students who live in rented apartments, houses, or rooms off campus? If these places of residence are ignored, your classification won't be complete; you will lose credibility with your readers because they'll probably realize that you have overlooked several important considerations.

Your division-classification should also be *consistent:* The parts into which you break your subject or the groups into which you place your subjects should be as mutually exclusive as possible. The parts or categories should not be mixed, nor should they overlap. Assume you're writing an essay describing the animals at the zoo in a nearby city. You decide to describe the zoo's mammals, reptiles, birds, and endangered species. But such a classification is inconsistent. You begin by categorizing the animals according to scientific class (mammals, birds, reptiles), then switch to another principle when you classify some animals according to whether they are endangered. Because you drift over to a different principle of classification, your categories are no longer mutually exclusive: Endangered species could overlap with any of the other categories. In which section of the paper, for instance, would you describe an exotic parrot that is obviously a bird but is also nearly extinct? And how would you categorize the zoo's rare mountain gorilla? This impressive creature is a mammal, but it is also an endangered species. Such overlapping categories undercut the logic that gives an essay its integrity.

A helpful tip: A solid outline is invaluable when you use division-classification. The outline encourages you to do the rigorous thinking needed to arrive at divisions and classifications that are logical, complete, and consistent.

3. Prepare an effective thesis.   If your essay uses division-classification as its dominant method of development, it might be helpful to prepare a thesis that does more than signal the paper's subject and suggest your attitude toward that general subject. You might also want the thesis to state the principle of division-classification at the heart of the essay. Furthermore, you might want the thesis to reveal which part or category you regard as most important.

Consider the two thesis statements that follow:

As the observant beachcomber moves from the tidal area to the upper beach to the sandy dunes, rich variations in marine life become apparent.

Although most people focus on the dangers associated with the disposal of toxic waste in the land and ocean, the incineration of toxic matter may pose an even more serious threat to human life.

The first thesis statement makes clear that the writer will organize the paper by classifying forms of marine life according to location. Because the purpose of the essay is to inform as objectively as possible, the thesis doesn't suggest the writer's opinion about which category is most significant.

The second thesis signals that the essay will evolve by dividing the issue of toxic waste according to methods of disposal. Moreover, because the paper takes a stance on a controversial subject, the thesis is worded to reveal which aspect of the topic the writer considers most important. Such a clear statement of the writer's position is an effective strategy in an essay of this kind.

You may have noted that each thesis statement also signals the paper's plan of development. The first essay, for example, will use specific facts, examples, and details to describe the kinds of marine life found in the tidal area, upper beach, and dunes. However, thesis statements in papers developed primarily through division-classification don't have to be so structured. If a paper is well written, your principle of division-classification, your opinion about which part or category is most important, and the essay's plan of development will become apparent as the essay unfolds.

4. Organize the paper logically.   Whether your paper is developed wholly or in part by division-classification, it should have a logical structure. As much as possible, you should try to discuss *comparable points* in each section of the paper. In the essay on seashore life, for example, you might describe life in the tidal area by discussing the mollusks, crustaceans, birds, and amphibians that live or feed there. You would then follow through, as much as you could, with this arrangement in the paper's other sections (upper beach and dune). Forgetting to describe the bird life thriving in the dunes, especially when you had discussed bird life in the tidal and upper-beach areas, would compromise the paper's structure. Of course, perfect parallelism is not always possible—there are no mollusks in the dunes, for instance. You should also use *signal devices* to connect various parts of the paper: "*Another* characteristic of marine life battered by the tides"; "A *final* important trait of both tidal and upper-beach crustaceans"; "*Unlike* the creatures of the tidal area and the upper beach." Such signals clarify the connections among the essay's ideas.

5. State any conclusions or recommendations in the paper's final section.   The analytic thinking that occurs during division-classification often leads to surprising insights. Such insights may be introduced early on, or they may be reserved for the end, where they are stated as conclusions or recommendations. A paper might categorize different kinds of coaches—from inspiring to incompetent—and make the point that athletes learn a great deal about human relations simply by having to get along with their coaches, regardless of the coaches' skills. Such a paper might conclude that participation in a team sport teaches more about human nature than several courses in psychology. Or the essay might end with a proposal: Rookies and seasoned team members should be paired so that novice players can get advice on dealing with coaching eccentricities.

REVISION STRATEGIES

Once you have a draft of the essay, you're ready to revise. The following checklist will help you and those giving you feedback apply to division-classification some of the revision techniques discussed on pages 59–61.

☑ DIVISION-CLASSIFICATION: A REVISION/PEER
REVIEW CHECKLIST

Revise Overall Meaning and Structure

❑ What is the principle of division-classification at the heart of the essay? How does this principle contribute to the essay's overall purpose and thesis?

❑ Does the thesis state the essay's principle of division-classification? Should it? Does the thesis signal which part or category is most important? Should it? Does the thesis reveal the essay's plan of development? Should it?

❑ Is the essay organized primarily through division, classification, or a blend of both?

❑ If the essay is organized mainly through division, is the subject sufficiently complex to be broken down into parts? What are the parts?

❑ If the essay is organized mainly through classification, what are the categories? How does this categorizing reveal similarities and/or differences that would otherwise not be apparent?

Revise Paragraph Development

❏ Are comparable points discussed in each of the paper's sections? What are these points?

❏ In which paragraphs does the division-classification seem illogical, incomplete, or inconsistent? In which paragraphs are parts or categories not clearly explained?

❏ Are the subject's different parts or categories discussed in separate paragraphs? Is there any overlap among categories?

Revise Sentences and Words

❏ What signal devices help integrate the paper? Are there enough signals? Too many?

❏ Where should sentences and words be made more specific in order to clarify the parts and categories being discussed?

STUDENT ESSAY

The following student essay was written by Gail Oremland in response to this assignment:

> In "Propaganda Techniques in Today's Advertising," Ann McClintock describes the flaws in many of the persuasive strategies used by advertisers. Choose another group of people whose job is also to communicate—for example, parents, bosses, teachers. Then, in an essay of your own, divide the group into types according to the flaws they make when communicating.

While reading Gail's paper, try to determine how effectively it applies the principles of division-classification. The annotations on Gail's paper and the commentary following it will help you look at the essay more closely.

The Truth About College Teachers
by Gail Oremland

Introduction   A recent TV news story told about a group of college   1
professors from a nearby university who were hired by a local
school system to help upgrade the teaching in the
community's public schools. The professors were to visit
classrooms, analyze teachers' skills, and then conduct
workshops to help the teachers become more effective at their
jobs. But after the first round of workshops, the superintendent
of schools decided to cancel the whole project. He fired the
learned professors and sent them back to their ivory tower.

Why did the project fall apart? There was a simple reason. The college professors, who were supposedly going to show the public school teachers how to be more effective, were themselves poor teachers. Many college students could have predicted such a disastrous outcome. They know, firsthand, that college teachers are strange. They know that professors often exhibit bizarre behaviors, relating to students in ways that make it difficult for students to stay awake, or--if awake--to learn.

Thesis

One type of professor assumes, legitimately enough, that her function is to pass on to students the vast store of knowledge she has acquired. But because the "Knowledgeable One" regards herself as an expert and her students as the ignorant masses, she adopts an elitist approach that sabotages learning. The Knowledgeable One enters a lecture hall with a self-important air, walks to the podium, places her yellowed-with-age notes on the stand, and begins her lecture at the exact second the class is officially scheduled to begin. There can be a blizzard or hurricane raging outside the lecture hall; students can be running through freezing sleet and howling winds to get to class on time. Will the Knowledgeable One wait for them to arrive before beginning her lecture? Probably not. The Knowledgeable One's time is precious. She's there, set to begin, and that's what matters.

Topic sentence

The first of three paragraphs on the first category of teacher

The first paragraph in a three-part chronological sequence: What happens *before* class

2

Once the monologue begins, the Knowledge-able One drones on and on. The Knowledgeable One is a fact person. She may be the history prof who knows the death toll of every Civil War battle, the biology prof who can diagram all the common biological molecules, the accounting prof who enumerates every clause of the federal tax form. Oblivious to students' glazed eyes and stifled yawns, the Knowledgeable One delivers her monologue, dispensing one dry fact after another. The only advantage to being on the receiving end of this boring monologue is that students do not have to worry about being called on to question a point or provide an opinion; the Knowledgeable One is not willing to relinquish one minute of her time by giving students a voice. Assume for one improbable moment that a student actually manages to stay awake during the monologue and is brave enough to ask a question. In such a case, the Knowledge-able One will address the questioning student as "Mr." or "Miss." This formality does not, as some students mistakenly suppose, indicate respect for the student as a fledgling member of the academic community. Not at all. This impersonality represents the Knowledgeable One's desire to keep as wide a distance as possible between her and her students.

Topic sentence

The second paragraph on the first category of teacher

The second paragraph in the chronological sequence: What happens *during* class

3

The Knowledgeable One's monologue always comes to a close at the precise second the class is scheduled to end. No

Topic sentence

4

<table>
<tr><td>The third paragraph on the first category of teacher</td><td>sooner has she delivered her last forgettable word than the Knowledgeable One packs up her notes and shoots out the door, heading back to the privacy of her office, where she can pursue her specialized academic interests--free of any possible</td></tr>
</table>

The third paragraph on the first category of teacher

The final paragraph in the chronological sequence: What happens *after* class

sooner has she delivered her last forgettable word than the Knowledgeable One packs up her notes and shoots out the door, heading back to the privacy of her office, where she can pursue her specialized academic interests--free of any possible interruption from students. The Knowledgeable One's hasty departure from the lecture hall makes it clear she has no desire to talk with students. In her eyes, she has met her obligations; she has taken time away from her research to transmit to students what she knows. Any closer contact might mean she would risk contagion from students, that great unwashed mass. Such a danger is to be avoided at all costs.

Unlike the Knowledgeable One, the "Leader of Intellectual   5
Discussion" seems to respect students. Emphasizing class discussion, the Leader encourages students to confront ideas ("What is Twain's view of morality?" "Was our intervention in Iraq justified?" "Should big business be given tax breaks?")

Topic sentence ——— and discover their own truths. Then, about three weeks into the semester, it becomes clear that the Leader wants students

Paragraph on the second category of teacher

to discover his version of the truth. Behind the Leader's democratic guise lurks a dictator. When a student voices an opinion that the Leader accepts, the student is rewarded by hearty nods of approval and "Good point, good point." But if a student is rash enough to advance a conflicting viewpoint, the Leader responds with killing politeness: "Well, yes, that's an interesting perspective. But don't you think that . . . ?" Grade-conscious students soon learn not to chime in with their viewpoint. They know that when the Leader, with seeming honesty, says, "I'd be interested in hearing what you think. Let's open this up for discussion," they had better figure out what the Leader wants to hear before advancing their own theories. "Me-tooism" rather than independent thinking, they discover, guarantees good grades in the Leader's class.

Topic sentence ———▶ Then there is the professor who comes across as the   6

Paragraph on the third category of teacher

students' "Buddy." This kind of professor does not see himself as an imparter of knowledge or a leader of discussion but as a pal, just one in a community of equals. The Buddy may start his course this way. "All of us know that this college stuff--grades, degrees, exams, required reading--is a game. So let's not play it, okay?" Dressed in jeans, sweatshirt, and scuffed sneakers, the Buddy projects a relaxed, casual attitude. He arranges the class seats in a circle (he would never take a position in front of the room) and insists that students call him by his first name. He uses no syllabus and gives few tests, believing that such constraints keep students from directing their own learning. A free spirit, the Buddy often teaches courses like "The Psychology of Interpersonal Relations" or "The Social Dynamics of the Family." If students choose to use class time to discuss the course material, that's fine. If they want to discuss something else, that's fine, too. It's the self-expression, the honest dialogue, that counts. In fact, the Buddy seems especially fond of digressions from academic subjects. By talking about his political views, his marital problems, his tendency to drink one too many beers, the Buddy lets students see that he is a regular guy--just like them. At first, students look forward to classes with the Buddy. They enjoy the informality, the chitchat, the lack of pressure. But after a while, they wonder why they are paying for a course where they learn nothing. They might as well stay home and watch the soaps.

Conclusion

Echoes
opening
anecdote

Obviously, some college professors are excellent. They are   7
learned, hardworking, and imaginative; they enjoy their work and like being with students. On the whole, though, college professors are a strange lot. Despite their advanced degrees and their own exposure to many different kinds of teachers, they do not seem to understand how to relate to students. Rather than being hired as consultants to help others upgrade their teaching skills, college professors should themselves hire consultants to tell them what they are doing wrong and how they can improve. Who should these consultants be? That's easy: the people who know them best--their students.

COMMENTARY

Introduction and thesis.   After years of being graded by teachers, Gail took special pleasure in writing an essay that gave her a chance to evaluate her teachers—in this case, her college professors. Even the essay's title, "The Truth About College Teachers," implies that Gail is going to have fun knocking profs down from their ivory towers. To introduce her subject, she uses a timely news story. This brief anecdote leads directly to the essay's *thesis:* "Professors often exhibit bizarre behaviors, relating to students in ways that make it difficult for students to stay awake, or—if awake—to learn." Note that Gail's thesis isn't highly structured; it doesn't, for example, name the specific categories to be discussed. Still, her thesis suggests that the essay is going to *categorize* a range of teaching behaviors, using as a *principle of classification* the strange ways that college profs relate to students.

Purpose.   As with all good papers developed through division-classification, Gail's essay doesn't use classification as an end in itself. Gail uses classification because it helps her achieve a broader *purpose.* She wants to *convince* readers—without moralizing or abandoning her humorous tone—that such teaching styles inhibit learning. In other words, there's a serious underside to her essay. This additional layer of meaning is characteristic of satiric writing.

Categories and topic sentences.   The essay's body, consisting of five paragraphs, presents the three categories that make up Gail's analysis. According to Gail, college teachers can be categorized as the Knowledgeable One (paragraphs 2–4), the Leader of Intellectual Discussion (5), or the Buddy (6). Obviously, there are other ways professors might be classified. But given Gail's purpose, audience, tone, and point of view, her categories are appropriate; they are reasonably *complete, consistent,* and *mutually exclusive.* Note, too, that Gail uses *topic sentences* near the beginning of each category to help readers see which professorial type she's discussing.

Overall organization and paragraph structure.   Gail is able to shift smoothly and easily from one category to the next. How does she achieve such graceful transitions? Take a moment to reread the sentences that introduce her second and third categories (paragraphs 5 and 6). Look at the way each sentence's beginning (in italics here) links back to the preceding category or categories: "*Unlike the Knowledgeable One,* the 'Leader of Intellectual Discussion' seems to respect students"; and "[the Buddy] . . . *does not see himself as an imparter of knowledge or a leader of discussion* but as a pal. . . ."

Gail is equally careful about providing an easy-to-follow structure within each section. She uses a *chronological sequence* to organize her three-paragraph discussion of the Knowledgeable One. The first paragraph deals with the beginning of the Knowledgeable One's lecture; the second, with the lecture itself; the third, with the end of the lecture. And the paragraphs' *topic sentences* clearly indicate this passage of time. Similarly, *transitions* are used in the paragraphs on the Leader of Intellectual Discussion and the Buddy to ensure a logical progression of points: "*Then,* about three weeks into the semester, it becomes clear that the Leader wants students to discover *his* version of the truth" (5) and "*At first,* students look forward to classes with the Buddy. . . . But *after a while,* they wonder why they are paying for a course where they learn nothing" (6).

Tone.   The essay's unity can also be traced to Gail's skill in sustaining her satiric tone. Throughout the essay, Gail selects details that fit her gently mocking attitude. She depicts the Knowledgeable One lecturing from "yellowed-with-age notes . . . , oblivious to students' glazed eyes and stifled yawns," unwilling to wait for students who "run . . . through freezing sleet and howling winds to get to class on time." Then she presents another tongue-in-cheek description, this one focusing on the way the Leader of Intellectual Discussion conducts class: "Good point, good point. . . . Well, yes, that's an interesting perspective. But don't you think that . . . ?" Finally, with similar killing accuracy, Gail portrays the Buddy, democratically garbed in "jeans, sweatshirt, and scuffed sneakers."

Combining patterns of development.   Gail's satiric depiction of her three professorial types employs a number of techniques associated with *narrative* and *descriptive writing*: vigorous images, highly connotative language, and dialogue. *Definition, exemplification, causal analysis,* and *comparison-contrast* also come into play. Gail defines the characteristics of each type of professor; she provides numerous examples to support her categories; she explains the effects of the different teaching styles on students; and, in her description of the Leader of Intellectual Discussion, she contrasts the appearance of democracy with the dictatorial reality.

Unequal development of categories.   Although Gail's essay is unified, organized, and well-developed, you may have felt that the first category outweighs the other two. There is, of course, no need to balance the categories exactly. But Gail's extended treatment of the first category sets up an expectation that the others will be treated as fully. One way to remedy this problem would be to delete some material from the discussion of the Knowledgeable One. Gail might, for instance, omit the last five sentences in the third paragraph (about the professor's habit of addressing students as "Mr." or "Miss"). Such a change could be made without taking the bite out of her portrayal. Even better, Gail could simply switch the order of her sections, putting the portrait of the Knowledgeable One at the essay's end. Here, the extended discussion wouldn't seem out of proportion. Instead, the sections would appear in *emphatic order*, with the most detailed category saved for last.

Revising the first draft.   It's apparent that an essay as engaging as Gail's must have undergone a good deal of revising. That was in fact the case. Gail made many changes in the body of the essay, but it's particularly interesting to review what happened to the introduction as she revised the paper. Reprinted here is Gail's original introduction.

Original Version of the Introduction

Despite their high IQs, advanced degrees, and published papers, some college professors just don't know how to teach. Found in almost any department, in tenured and untenured positions, they prompt student apathy. They fail to convey ideas effectively and to challenge or inspire students. Students thus finish their courses having learned very little. Contrary to popular opinion, these professors' ineptitude is not simply a matter of delivering boring lectures or not caring about students. Many of them care a great deal. Their failure actually stems from their unrealistic perceptions of what a teacher should be. Specifically, they adopt teaching styles or roles that alienate students and undermine learning. Three of the most common ones are "The Knowledgeable One," "The Leader of Intellectual Discussion," and "The Buddy."

When Gail showed the first draft of the essay to her composition instructor, he laughed—and occasionally squirmed—as he read what she had prepared. He was enthusiastic about the paper but felt that there was a problem with the introduction's tone; it was too serious when compared to the playful, lightly satiric mood of the rest of the essay. When Gail reread the paragraph, she agreed, but she was uncertain about the best way to remedy the problem. After revising other sections of the essay, she decided to let the paper sit for a while before going back to rewrite the introduction.

In the meantime, Gail switched on the TV. The timing couldn't have been better; she tuned into a news story about several supposedly learned professors who had been fired from a consulting job because they had turned out to know so little about teaching. This was exactly the kind of item Gail needed to start her essay. Now she was able to prepare a completely new introduction, making it consistent in spirit with the rest of the paper.

With this stronger introduction and the rest of the essay well in hand, Gail was ready to write a conclusion. Now, as she worked on the concluding paragraph, she deliberately shaped it to recall the story about the fired consultants. By echoing the opening anecdote in her conclusion, Gail was able to end the paper with another poke at professors—a perfect way to close her clever and insightful essay.

ACTIVITIES: DIVISION-CLASSIFICATION

Prewriting Activities

1. Imagine you're writing two essays: One is a humorous paper outlining a *process* for impressing college instructors; the other is a serious essay examining the *causes* of the recent rise in volunteerism. What about the topics might you divide and/or classify?

2. Use group brainstorming to identify three principles of division for *one* of the topics in Set A below. Focusing on one of the principles, decide what your thesis might be if you were writing an essay. That done, use group brainstorming to identify three principles of classification that might provide the structure for *one* of the topics in Set B. Focusing on one of the principles, decide what your thesis might be if you were writing an essay.

Set A
- Rock music
- A shopping mall
- A good horror movie

Set B
- Why people get addicted to computers
- How fast-food restaurants affect family life
- Why long-term relationships break up

Revising Activities

3. Following is a scratch outline for an essay developed through division-classification. On what principle of division-classification is the essay based? What

problem do you see in the way the principle is applied? How could the problem be remedied?

Thesis: The same experience often teaches opposite things to different people.

- What working as a fast-food cook teaches: Some learn responsibility; others learn to take a "quick and dirty" approach.
- What a negative experience teaches optimists: Some learn from their mistakes; others continue to maintain a positive outlook.
- What a difficult course teaches: Some learn to study hard; others learn to avoid demanding courses.
- What the breakup of a close relationship teaches: Some learn how to negotiate differences; others learn to avoid intimacy.

4. Following is a paragraph from the first draft of an essay urging that day care centers adopt play programs tailored to children's developmental needs. What principle of division-classification focuses the paragraph? Is the principle applied consistently and logically? Are parts/categories developed sufficiently? Revise the paragraph, eliminating any problems you discover and adding specific details where needed.

> Within a few years, preschool children move from self-absorbed to interactive play. Babies and toddlers engage in solitary play. Although they sometimes prefer being near other children, they focus primarily on their own actions. This is very different from the highly interactive play of the elementary school years. Sometime in children's second year, solitary play is replaced by parallel play, during which children engage in similar activities near one another. However, they interact only occasionally. By age three, most children show at least some cooperative play, a form that involves interaction and cooperative role-taking. Such role-taking can be found in the "pretend" games that children play to explore adult relationships (games of "Mommy and Daddy") and anatomy (games of "Doctor"). Additional signs of youngsters' growing awareness of peers can be seen at about age four. At this age, many children begin showing a special devotion to one other child and may want to play only with that child. During this time, children also begin to take special delight in physical activities such as running and jumping, often going off by themselves to expend their abundant physical energy.

Stephanie Ericsson

Stephanie Ericsson (1953–) is a writer, screenwriter, and ad copywriter who often uses her own life experiences as starting points for her deeply personal work. She wrote *Companion Through the Darkness: Inner Dialogues on Grief* (1993) in response to her husband's sudden death while she was pregnant, and she chronicled her struggles with substance abuse in both *Shamefaced* (1985) and *Women of AA: Recovering Together* (1986). Ericsson's latest book is *Companion into the Dawn: Inner Dialogues on Loving* (1994). A frequent speaker on the subject of loss, she lives in Minneapolis, Minnesota. "The Ways We Lie" was originally published in the *Utne Reader* in 1992.

Pre-Reading Journal Entry

Something that everyone is guilty of, but may not want to admit to, is lying. Think for a moment about times when you told a lie. In your pre-reading journal, begin by listing any episodes of lying you can recall. Then go back and freewrite to a greater extent about these incidents. In each case, why did you tell the lie—what were the circumstances? What was the outcome? Do you now regret having lied, or are you thankful you did it?

The Ways We Lie

The bank called today and I told them my deposit was in the mail, even though I hadn't written a check yet. It'd been a rough day. The baby I'm pregnant with decided to do aerobics on my lungs for two hours, our three-year-old daughter painted the living room couch with lipstick, the IRS put me on hold for an hour, and I was late to a business meeting because I was tired.

I told my client that traffic had been bad. When my partner came home, his haggard face told me his day hadn't gone any better than mine, so when he asked, "How was your day?" I said, "Oh, fine," knowing that one more straw might break his back. A friend called and wanted to take me to lunch. I said I was busy. Four lies in the course of a day, none of which I felt the least bit guilty about.

We lie. We all do. We exaggerate, we minimize, we avoid confrontation, we spare people's feelings, we conveniently forget, we keep secrets, we justify lying to the big-guy institutions. Like most people, I indulge in small falsehoods and still think of myself as an honest person. Sure I lie, but it doesn't hurt anything. Or does it?

I once tried going a whole week without telling a lie, and it was paralyzing. I discovered that telling the truth all the time is nearly impossible. It means living with some serious consequences: The bank charges me $60 in overdraft fees, my partner keels over when I tell him about my travails, my client fires me for telling her I didn't feel like being on time, and my friend takes it personally when I say I'm not hungry. There must be some merit to lying.

But if I justify lying, what makes me any different from slick politicians   5
or the corporate robbers who raided the S&L industry?[1] Saying it's okay to lie one way and not another is hedging. I cannot seem to escape the voice deep inside me that tells me: When someone lies, someone loses.

What far-reaching consequences will I, or others, pay as a result of my   6
lie? Will someone's trust be destroyed? Will someone else pay *my* penance because I ducked out? We must consider the *meaning of our actions*. Deception, lies, capital crimes, and misdemeanors all carry meanings. *Webster's* definition of *lie* is specific:

> 1: a false statement or action especially made with the intent to deceive; 2: anything that gives or is meant to give a false impression.

A definition like this implies that there are many, many ways to tell a lie.   7
Here are just a few.

The White Lie

A man who won't lie to a woman has very little consideration for her feelings.

—Bergen Evans

The white lie assumes that the truth will cause more damage than a   8
simple, harmless untruth. Telling a friend he looks great when he looks like hell can be based on a decision that the friend needs a compliment more than a frank opinion. But, in effect, it is the liar deciding what is best for the lied to. Ultimately, it is a vote of no confidence. It is an act of subtle arrogance for anyone to decide what is best for someone else.

Yet not all circumstances are quite so cut-and-dried. Take, for instance,   9
the sergeant in Vietnam who knew one of his men was killed in action but listed him as missing so that the man's family would receive indefinite compensation instead of the lump-sum pittance the military gives widows and children. His intent was honorable. Yet for twenty years this family kept their hopes alive, unable to move on to a new life.

---

[1]Reference to the savings and loan scandal of the 1980s, in which corrupt owners of bank-like institutions defrauded the federal government of vast amounts of money (editors' note).

Façades

Et tu, Brute?

—Caesar

We all put up façades to one degree or another. When I put on a suit to   10
go to see a client, I feel as though I am putting on another face, obeying the
expectation that serious businesspeople wear suits rather than sweatpants. But
I'm a writer. Normally, I get up, get the kid off to school, and sit at my computer in my pajamas until four in the afternoon. When I answer the phone,
the caller thinks I'm wearing a suit (though the UPS man knows better).

But façades can be destructive because they are used to seduce others   11
into an illusion. For instance, I recently realized that a former friend was a
liar. He presented himself with all the right looks and the right words and
offered lots of new consciousness theories, fabulous books to read, and fascinating insights. Then I did some business with him, and the time came for
him to pay me. He turned out to be all talk and no walk. I heard a plethora
of reasonable excuses, including in-depth descriptions of the big break
around the corner. In six months of work, I saw less than a hundred bucks.
When I confronted him, he raised both eyebrows and tried to convince me
that I'd heard him wrong, that he'd made no commitment to me. A simple
investigation into his past revealed a crowded graveyard of disenchanted former friends.

Ignoring the Plain Facts

Well, you must understand that Father Porter is only human. . . .

—A Massachusetts priest

In the '60s, the Catholic Church in Massachusetts began hearing com-   12
plaints that Father James Porter was sexually molesting children. Rather than
relieving him of his duties, the ecclesiastical authorities simply moved him
from one parish to another between 1960 and 1967, actually providing him
with a fresh supply of unsuspecting families and innocent children to abuse.
After treatment in 1967 for pedophilia, he went back to work, this time in
Minnesota. The new diocese was aware of Father Porter's obsession with children, but they needed priests and recklessly believed treatment had cured
him. More children were abused until he was relieved of his duties a year later.
By his own admission, Porter may have abused as many as a hundred children.

Ignoring the facts may not in and of itself be a form of lying, but con-   13
sider the context of this situation. If a lie is *a false action done with the intent
to deceive,* then the Catholic Church's conscious covering for Porter created
irreparable consequences. The church became a co-perpetrator with Porter.

Deflecting

When you have no basis for an argument, abuse the plaintiff.

—Cicero

I've discovered that I can keep anyone from seeing the true me by being   14
selectively blatant. I set a precedent of being up-front about intimate issues,
but I never bring up the things I truly want to hide; I just let people assume
I'm revealing everything. It's an effective way of hiding.

Any good liar knows that the way to perpetuate an untruth is to deflect   15
attention from it. When Clarence Thomas[2] exploded with accusations that the
Senate hearings were a "high-tech lynching," he simple switched the focus
from a highly charged subject to a radioactive subject. Rather than defending
himself, he took the offensive and accused the country of racism. It was a brilliant maneuver. Racism is now politically incorrect in official circles—unlike
sexual harassment, which still rewards those who can get away with it.

Some of the most skillful deflectors are passive-aggressive[3] people who,   16
when accused of inappropriate behavior, refuse to respond to the accusations. This you-don't-exist stance infuriates the accuser, who, understandably, screams something obscene out of frustration. The trap is sprung and
the act of deflection successful, because now the passive-aggressive person
can indignantly say, "Who can talk to someone as unreasonable as you?" The
real issue is forgotten and the sins of the original victim become the focus.
Feeling guilty of namecalling, the victim is fully tamed and crawls into a hole,
ashamed. I have watched this fighting technique work thousands of times in
disputes between men and women, and what I've learned is that the real culprit is not necessarily the one who swears the loudest.

Omission

The cruelest lies are often told in silence.

—R. L. Stevenson

Omission involves telling most of the truth minus one or two key facts   17
whose absence changes the story completely. You break a pair of glasses that
are guaranteed under normal use and get a new pair, without mentioning
that the first pair broke during a rowdy game of basketball. Who hasn't tried

---

[2]Nominated to the Supreme Court in 1993, Clarence Thomas, an African American jurist, was
accused by former colleague Anita Hill of sexual harassment. Much of Thomas's confirmation
hearing, televised nationwide, focused on this issue (editors' note).

[3]A psychological pattern in which hostility is expressed through an infuriating detachment and
nonresponsiveness (editors' note).

something like that? But what about omission of information that could make a difference in how a person lives his or her life?

For instance, one day I found out that rabbinical legends tell of another 18 woman in the Garden of Eden before Eve. I was stunned. The omission of the Sumerian goddess Lilith from Genesis—as well as her demonization by ancient misogynists as an embodiment of female evil—felt like spiritual robbery. I felt like I'd just found out my mother was really my stepmother. To take seriously the tradition that Adam was created out of the same mud as his equal counterpart, Lilith, redefines all of Judeo-Christian history.

Some renegade Catholic feminists introduced me to a view of Lilith that 19 had been suppressed during many centuries when this strong goddess was seen only as a spirit of evil. Lilith was a proud goddess who defied Adam's need to control her, attempted negotiations, and when this failed, said adios and left the Garden of Eden.

This omission of Lilith from the Bible was a patriarchal strategy to keep 20 women weak. Omitting the strong-woman archetype of Lilith from Western religions and starting the story with Eve the Rib has helped keep Christian and Jewish women believing they were the lesser sex for thousands of years.

Stereotypes and Clichés

Where opinion does not exist, the status quo becomes
stereotyped and all originality is discouraged.

—Bertrand Russell

Stereotype and cliché serve a purpose as a form of shorthand. Our need 21 for vast amounts of information in nanoseconds has made the stereotype vital to modern communication. Unfortunately, it often shuts down original thinking, giving those hungry for the truth a candy bar of misinformation instead of a balanced meal. The stereotype explains a situation with just enough truth to seem unquestionable.

All the "isms"—racism, sexism, ageism, et al.—are founded on and fueled 22 by the stereotype and the cliché, which are lies of exaggeration, omission, and ignorance. They are always dangerous. They take a single tree and make it a landscape. They destroy curiosity. They close minds and separate people. The single mother on welfare is assumed to be cheating. Any black male could tell you how much of his identity is obliterated daily by stereotypes. Fat people, ugly people, beautiful people, old people, large-breasted women, short men, the mentally ill, and the homeless all could tell you how much more they are like us than we want to think. I once admitted to a group of people that I had a mouth like a truck driver. Much to my surprise, a man stood up and said, "I'm a truck driver, and I never cuss." Needless to say, I was humbled.

Groupthink

Who is more foolish, the child afraid of the dark, or the man afraid of the light?

—Maurice Freehill

Irving Janis, in *Victims of Group Think*, defines this sort of lie as a psy- 23
chological phenomenon within decision-making groups in which loyalty to
the group has become more important than any other value, with the result
that dissent and the appraisal of alternatives are suppressed. If you've ever
worked on a committee or in a corporation, you've encountered groupthink.
It requires a combination of other forms of lying—ignoring facts, selective
memory, omission, and denial, to name a few.

The textbook example of groupthink came on December 7, 1941. From 24
as early as the fall of 1941, the warnings came in, one after another, that Japan
was preparing for a massive military operation. The Navy command in Hawaii
assumed Pearl Harbor was invulnerable—the Japanese weren't stupid enough
to attack the United States' most important base. On the other hand, racist
stereotypes said the Japanese weren't smart enough to invent a torpedo effective in less than 60 feet of water (the fleet was docked in 30 feet); after all,
U.S. technology hadn't been able to do it.

On Friday, December 5, normal weekend leave was granted to all the 25
commanders at Pearl Harbor, even though the Japanese consulate in Hawaii
was busy burning papers. Within the tight, good-ole-boy cohesiveness of the
U.S. command in Hawaii, the myth of invulnerability stayed well entrenched.
No one in the group considered the alternatives. The rest is history.

Out-and-Out Lies

The only form of lying that is beyond reproach is lying for its own sake.

—Oscar Wilde

Of all the ways to lie, I like this one the best, probably because I get tired 26
of trying to figure out the real meanings behind things. At least I can trust
the bald-faced lie. I once asked my five-year-old nephew, "Who broke the
fence?" (I had seen him do it.) He answered, "The murderers." Who could
argue?

At least when this sort of lie is told it can be easily confronted. As the 27
person who is lied to, I know where I stand. The bald-faced lie doesn't toy
with my perceptions—it argues with them. It doesn't try to refashion reality, it tries to refute it. *Read my lips* . . . No sleight of hand.[4] No guessing. If

[4]A phrase used by presidential candidate George Bush during the 1988 campaign (and often
parodied thereafter): "Read my lips. . . . No new taxes" (editors' note).

this were the only form of lying, there would be no such things as floating anxiety[5] or the adult, children-of-alcoholics movement.

Dismissal

Pay no attention to that man behind the curtain! I am the Great Oz!

—The Wizard of Oz

Dismissal is perhaps the slipperiest of all lies. Dismissing feelings, perceptions, or even the raw facts of a situation ranks as a kind of lie that can do as much damage to a person as any other kind of lie.   28

The roots of many mental disorders can be traced back to the dismissal of reality. Imagine that a person is told from the time she is a tot that her perceptions are inaccurate. *"Mommy, I'm scared."* "No you're not, darling." *"I don't like that man next door, he makes me feel icky."* "Johnny, that's a terrible thing to say, of course you like him. You go over there right now and be nice to him."   29

I've often mused over the idea that madness is actually a sane reaction to an insane world. Psychologist R. D. Laing supports this hypothesis in *Sanity, Madness and the Family,* an account of his investigations into the families of schizophrenics. The common thread that ran through all of the families he studied was a deliberate, staunch dismissal of the patient's perceptions from a very early age. Each of the patients started out with an accurate grasp of reality, which, through meticulous and methodical dismissal, was demolished until the only reality the patient could trust was catatonia.   30

Dismissal runs the gamut. Mild dismissal can be quite handy for forgiving the foibles of others in our day-to-day lives. Toddlers who have just learned to manipulate their parents' attention sometimes are dismissed out of necessity. Absolute attention from the parents would require so much energy that no one would get to eat dinner. But we must be careful and attentive about how far we take our "necessary" dismissals. Dismissal is a dangerous tool, because it's nothing less than a lie.   31

Delusion

We lie loudest when we lie to ourselves.

—Eric Hoffer

I could write the book on this one. Delusion, a cousin of dismissal, is the tendency to see excuses as facts. It's a powerful lying tool because it filters out information that contradicts what we want to believe. Alcoholics who   32

[5]A psychological condition in which a person feels generalized anxiety for no specific reason (editor's note).

believe that the problems in their lives are legitimate reasons for drinking rather than results of the drinking offer the classic example of deluded thinking. Delusion uses the mind's ability to see things in myriad ways to support what it wants to be the truth.

But delusion is also a survival mechanism we all use. If we were to fully contemplate the consequences of our stockpiles of nuclear weapons or global warming, we could hardly function on a day-to-day level. We don't want to incorporate that much reality into our lives because to do so would be paralyzing.   33

Delusion acts as an adhesive to keep the status quo intact. It shamelessly employs dismissal, omission, and amnesia, among other sorts of lies. Its most cunning defense is that it cannot see itself.   34

• • •

The liar's punishment . . . is that he cannot believe anyone else.

—George Bernard Shaw

These are only a few of the ways we lie. Or are lied to. As I said earlier, it's not easy to entirely eliminate lies from our lives. No matter how pious we may try to be, we will still embellish, hedge, and omit to lubricate the daily machinery of living. But there is a world of difference between telling functional lies and living a lie. Martin Buber once said, "The lie is the spirit committing treason against itself." Our acceptance of lies becomes a cultural cancer that eventually shrouds and reorders reality until moral garbage becomes as invisible to us as water is to a fish.   35

How much do we tolerate before we become sick and tired of being sick and tired? When will we stand up and declare our *right* to trust? When do we stop accepting that the real truth is in the fine print? Whose lips do we read this year when we vote for president? When will we stop being so reticent about making judgments? When do we stop turning over our personal power and responsibility to liars?   36

Maybe if I don't tell the bank the check's in the mail I'll be less tolerant of the lies told me every day. A country song I once heard said it all for me: "You've got to stand for something or you'll fall for anything."   37

Questions for Close Reading

1. What is the selection's thesis? Locate the sentence(s) in which Ericsson states her main idea. If she doesn't state the thesis explicitly, express it in your own words.
2. What did Ericsson discover when she tried to go a whole week without lying?
3. Ericsson classifies as "lies" some behaviors not always considered dishonest. How can "ignoring the plain facts," "deflecting," and "omission" be types of lies? How do "stereotypes and clichés" and "groupthink" qualify as lies?

4. Why doesn't Ericsson easily accept the fact that lies are a necessary part of her life and that of most people?
5. Refer to your dictionary as needed to define the following words used in the selection: *travails* (paragraph 4), *hedging* (5), *penance* (4), *pittance* (9), *façades* (10), *plethora* (11), *disenchanted* (11), *ecclesiastical* (12), *pedophilia* (12), *irreparable* (13), *blatant* (14), *demonization* (18), *misogynists* (18), *embodiment* (18), *archetype* (20), *obliterated* (22), *dissent* (23), *cohesiveness* (25), *invulnerability* (25), *entrenched* (25), *catatonia* (30), and *gamut* (31).

Questions About the Writer's Craft

1. **The pattern.** In paragraph 6, Ericsson asserts that we "must consider the *meaning of our actions*" when deciding whether or not we have lied. How does this principle of classification help her show that each category of behavior discussed is a type of lying?
2. **Other patterns.** In the body of her essay, Ericsson draws upon both personal experience and third-person material to make her point. Her introduction, though, includes only a first-person *narrative*. Why do you suppose Ericsson decided to open the essay with this brief first-person account?
3. Despite the seriousness of her subject, Ericsson's overall tone is informal—almost conversational. Identify at least five instances of this informality. Why do you suppose Ericsson adopted such a tone?
4. **Other patterns.** In her concluding paragraphs (35–37), Ericsson *contrasts* two broad types of lies, saying that "there is a world of difference between telling functional lies and living a lie." How does this contrast help her sum up the essay?

Writing Assignments Using Division-Classification as a Pattern of Development

1. Ericsson takes an often used, seemingly simple word and, by categorizing its various manifestations, shows that it represents a complex phenomenon. Choose another frequently used word—such as *loyalty, excellence, arrogance,* or *hypocrisy*— and show its complexity by categorizing its different types. Before presenting your categories, offer a definition, either yours or the dictionary's, of the word; then provide dramatic examples to illustrate the various categories.
2. In paragraph 23, Ericsson cites Irving Janus's definition of "groupthink." Using this definition as a starting point, analyze several situations involving groupthink that you have observed or heard about. Classify the kinds of groupthink that are revealed in these situations, illustrating each type with at least one vivid example. To deepen your understanding of groupthink, read the following essays before writing your paper: Langston Hughes's "Salvation" (page 124) and John Darley and Bibb Latané's "Why People Don't Help in a Crisis" (page 304).

Writing Assignments Combining Patterns of Development

3. Stereotypes, Ericsson writes, "explain a situation with just enough truth to seem unquestionable." Write a *narrative* about a specific time that you or someone you

know either falsely stereotyped a person or reacted stereotypically to a situation. Include only those details and *examples* that dramatize your narrative point. Before writing, you'll find it helpful to read any of the following essays, which show how pervasive and corrosive stereotypes can be: Joseph H. Suina's "And Then I Went to School" (page 271), William Raspberry's "The Handicap of Definition" (page 345), Roger Wilkins's "Racism Has Its Privileges" (page 406), and Shelby Steele's "Affirmative Action: The Price of Preference" (page 416).

4. Many social commentators call attention, as Ericsson does in paragraph 15, to the growing tendency of individuals to absolve themselves from responsibility for something they've done by claiming that *they* are actually the victims. Gain some background on the issue of victimization by brainstorming with others and locating relevant material in the library and/or on the Internet. (You might find articles and books by Charles Sykes, Shelby Steele, and William Raspberry especially helpful.) Then write an essay *arguing* that we are or are not becoming a nation of victims and crybabies. Discredit the opposing viewpoint as much as possible by drawing upon your own and other people's experiences, as well as the outside sources you've read. And, in the course of your essay, speculate about the *causes* of the behavior you have identified.

Writing Assignment Using a Journal Entry as a Starting Point

5. At the beginning of her essay, Ericsson says that "there are many, many ways to tell a lie." Refer to your pre-reading journal entry, and select *one* memorable incident in which you lied, making sure the incident you select is substantial enough to support an entire essay. Then review Ericsson's ten categories of lying and determine which one best applies to the lie in question. Write an essay in which you *narrate* your episode of lying as a way of *illustrating* that particular category. Be sure, at the beginning of your essay, to briefly cite Ericsson's explanation of the category. As you narrate the incident involving your lie, point out the ways in which it illustrates that category. In addition, you should conclude with some commentary on whether lying was justified in the circumstances. You might benefit, too, from reading Langston Hughes's "Salvation" (page 124), a compelling account of telling a childhood, but not a *childish,* lie.

William Lutz

With a dash of humor, William Lutz (1941–), professor of English at Rutgers University and former editor of the *Quarterly Review of Doublespeak*, writes about a subject he takes very seriously: doublespeak—the use of language to evade, deceive, and mislead. An expert on language, Lutz has appeared on many national television programs, among them the *Today Show, Larry King Live,* and the *MacNeil-Lehrer News Hour*. Lutz, who has both a doctorate in English and a Doctor of Law degree, has written over two dozen articles and is the author or coauthor of fourteen books, including the best-selling *Doublespeak: From Revenue Enhancement to Terminal Living* (1989) as well as its sequels, *Why No One Knows What Anyone's Saying Anymore* (1996) and *Doublespeak Defined: Cut Through the Bull**** and Get to the Point* (1999). He is also the coauthor of *Firestorm at Peshtigo* (2002) about the devastating 1871 fire in a Wisconsin mining town. The following piece is from *Doublespeak*.

Pre-Reading Journal Entry

At one time or another, everyone twists language in order to avoid telling the full truth. In your journal, list several instances which demonstrate that indirect, partially true language ("doublespeak") is sometimes desirable, even necessary. In each case, why was this evasive language used?

Doublespeak

There are no potholes in the streets of Tucson, Arizona, just "pavement deficiencies." The Reagan Administration didn't propose any new taxes, just "revenue enhancement" through new "user's fees." Those aren't bums on the street, just "non-goal oriented members of society." There are no more poor people, just "fiscal underachievers." There was no robbery of an automatic teller machine, just an "unauthorized withdrawal." The patient didn't die because of medical malpractice, it was just a "diagnostic misadventure of a high magnitude." The U.S. Army doesn't kill the enemy anymore, it just "services the target." And the doublespeak goes on.

Doublespeak is language that pretends to communicate but really doesn't. It is language that makes the bad seem good, the negative appear positive, the unpleasant appear attractive or at least tolerable. Doublespeak is language that avoids or shifts responsibility, language that is at variance with its real or purported meaning. It is language that conceals or prevents thought; rather than extending thought, doublespeak limits it. . . .

How to Spot Doublespeak

How can you spot doublespeak? Most of the time you will recognize   3
doublespeak when you see or hear it. But, if you have any doubts, you can
identify doublespeak just by answering these questions: Who is saying what
to whom, under what conditions and circumstances, with what intent, and
with what results? Answering these questions will usually help you identify as
doublespeak language that appears to be legitimate or that at first glance
doesn't even appear to be doublespeak.

First Kind of Doublespeak

There are at least four kinds of doublespeak. The first is the euphemism,   4
an inoffensive or positive word or phrase used to avoid a harsh, unpleasant,
or distasteful reality. But a euphemism can also be a tactful word or phrase
which avoids directly mentioning a painful reality, or it can be an expression
used out of concern for the feelings of someone else, or to avoid directly discussing a topic subject to a social or cultural taboo.

When you use a euphemism because of your sensitivity for someone's   5
feelings or out of concern for a recognized social or cultural taboo, it is not
doublespeak. For example, you express your condolences that someone has
"passed away" because you do not want to say to a grieving person, "I'm
sorry your father is dead." When you use the euphemism "passed away," no
one is misled. Moreover, the euphemism functions here not just to protect
the feelings of another person, but to communicate also your concern for
that person's feelings during a period of mourning. When you excuse yourself to go to the "restroom," or you mention that someone is "sleeping
with" or "involved with" someone else, you do not mislead anyone about
your meaning, but you do respect the social taboos about discussing bodily
functions and sex in direct terms. You also indicate your sensitivity to the
feelings of your audience, which is usually considered a mark of courtesy and
good manners.

However, when a euphemism is used to mislead or deceive, it becomes   6
doublespeak. For example, in 1984 the U.S. State Department announced
that it would no longer use the word "killing" in its annual report on the status of human rights in countries around the world. Instead, it would use the
phrase "unlawful or arbitrary deprivation of life," which the department
claimed was more accurate. Its real purpose for using this phrase was simply
to avoid discussing the embarrassing situation of government-sanctioned
killings in countries that are supported by the United States and have been
certified by the United States as respecting the human rights of their citizens.
This use of a euphemism constitutes doublespeak, since it is designed to mislead, to cover up the unpleasant. Its real intent is at variance with its apparent intent. It is language designed to alter our perception of reality.

The Pentagon, too, avoids discussing unpleasant realities when it refers   7
to bombs and artillery shells that fall on civilian targets as "incontinent ord-
nance." And in 1977 the Pentagon tried to slip funding for the neutron bomb
unnoticed into an appropriations bill by calling it a "radiation enhancement
device."

Second Kind of Doublespeak

A second kind of doublespeak is jargon, the specialized language of a   8
trade, profession, or similar group, such as that used by doctors, lawyers,
engineers, educators, or car mechanics. Jargon can serve an important and
useful function. Within a group, jargon functions as a kind of verbal shorthand that allows members of the group to communicate with each other
clearly, efficiently, and quickly. Indeed, it is a mark of membership in the
group to be able to use and understand the group's jargon.

But jargon, like the euphemism, can also be doublespeak. It can be—and   9
often is—pretentious, obscure, and esoteric terminology used to give an air
of profundity, authority, and prestige to speakers and their subject matter.
Jargon as doublespeak often makes the simple appear complex, the ordinary
profound, the obvious insightful. In this sense it is used not to express but
impress. With such doublespeak, the act of smelling something becomes
"organoleptic analysis," glass becomes "fused silicate," a crack in a metal support beam becomes a "discontinuity," conservative economic policies become
"distributionally conservative notions."

Lawyers, for example, speak of an "involuntary conversion" of property   10
when discussing the loss or destruction of property through theft, accident,
or condemnation. If your house burns down or if your car is stolen, you have
suffered an involuntary conversion of your property. When used by lawyers
in a legal situation, such jargon is a legitimate use of language, since lawyers
can be expected to understand the term.

However, when a member of a specialized group uses its jargon to com-   11
municate with a person outside the group, and uses it knowing that the non-
member does not understand such language, then there is doublespeak. For
example, on May 9, 1978, a National Airlines 727 airplane crashed while
attempting to land at the Pensacola, Florida airport. Three of the fifty-two
passengers aboard the airplane were killed. As a result of the crash, National
made an after-tax insurance benefit of $1.7 million, or an extra 18¢ a share
dividend for its stockholders. Now National Airlines had two problems: It did
not want to talk about one of its airplanes crashing, and it had to account for
the $1.7 million when it issued its annual report to its stockholders. National-
al solved the problem by inserting a footnote in its annual report which
explained that the $1.7 million income was due to "the involuntary conver-
sion of a 727." National thus acknowledged the crash of its airplane and the

subsequent profit it made from the crash, without once mentioning the accident or the deaths. However, because airline officials knew that most stockholders in the company, and indeed most of the general public, were not familiar with legal jargon, the use of such jargon constituted doublespeak.

Third Kind of Doublespeak

A third kind of doublespeak is gobbledygook or bureaucratese. Basically, such doublespeak is simply a matter of piling on words, of overwhelming the audience with words, the bigger the words and the longer the sentences the better. Alan Greenspan, then chair of President Nixon's Council of Economic Advisors, was quoted in *The Philadelphia Inquirer* in 1974 as having testified before a Senate committee that "It is a tricky problem to find the particular calibration in timing that would be appropriate to stem the acceleration in risk premiums created by falling incomes without prematurely aborting the decline in the inflation-generated risk premiums." 12

Nor has Mr. Greenspan's language changed since then. Speaking to the meeting of the Economic Club of New York in 1988, Mr. Greenspan, now Federal Reserve chair, said, "I guess I should warn you, if I turn out to be particularly clear, you've probably misunderstood what I've said." Mr. Greenspan's doublespeak doesn't seem to have held back his career. 13

Sometimes gobbledygook may sound impressive, but when the quote is later examined in print it doesn't even make sense. During the 1988 presidential campaign, vice-presidential candidate Senator Dan Quayle explained the need for a strategic-defense initiative by saying, "Why wouldn't an enhanced deterrent, a more stable peace, a better prospect to denying the ones who enter conflict in the first place to have a reduction of offensive systems and an introduction to defense capability? I believe this is the route the country will eventually go." 14

The investigation into the Challenger disaster in 1986 revealed the doublespeak of gobbledygook and bureaucratese used by too many involved in the shuttle program. When Jesse Moore, NASA's associate administrator, was asked if the performance of the shuttle program had improved with each launch or if it had remained the same, he answered, "I think our performance in terms of the liftoff performance and in terms of the orbital performance, we knew more about the envelope we were operating under, and we have been pretty accurately staying in that. And so I would say the performance has not by design drastically improved. I think we have been able to characterize the performance more as a function of our launch experience as opposed to it improving as a function of time." While this language may appear to be jargon, a close look will reveal that it is really just gobbledygook laced with jargon. But you really have to wonder if Mr. Moore had any idea what he was saying. 15

Fourth Kind of Doublespeak

The fourth kind of doublespeak is inflated language that is designed to   16
make the ordinary seem extraordinary; to make everyday things seem impressive; to give an air of importance to people, situations, or things that would
not normally be considered important; to make the simple seem complex.
Often this kind of doublespeak isn't hard to spot, and it is usually pretty
funny. While car mechanics may be called "automotive internists," elevator
operators members of the "vertical transportation corps," used cars "pre-
owned" or "experienced cars," and black-and-white television sets described
as having "non-multicolor capability," you really aren't misled all that much
by such language.

However, you may have trouble figuring out that, when Chrysler "initi-   17
ates a career alternative enhancement program," it is really laying off five
thousand workers; or that "negative patient care outcome" means the
patient died; or that "rapid oxidation" means a fire in a nuclear power plant.

The doublespeak of inflated language can have serious consequences. In   18
Pentagon doublespeak, "pre-emptive counterattack" means that American
forces attacked first; "engaged the enemy on all sides" means American
troops were ambushed; "backloading of augmentation personnel" means a
retreat by American troops. In the doublespeak of the military, the 1983
invasion of Grenada was conducted not by the U.S. Army, Navy, Air Force,
and Marines, but by the "Caribbean Peace Keeping Forces." But then,
according to the Pentagon, it wasn't an invasion, it was a "predawn vertical
insertion.". . .

The Dangers of Doublespeak

These . . . examples of doublespeak should make it clear that double-   19
speak is not the product of carelessness or sloppy thinking. Indeed, most
doublespeak is the product of clear thinking and is carefully designed and
constructed to appear to communicate when in fact it doesn't. It is language
designed not to lead but mislead. It is language designed to distort reality
and corrupt thought. . . . When a fire in a nuclear reactor building is called
"rapid oxidation," an explosion in a nuclear power plant is called an "energetic disassembly," the illegal overthrow of a legitimate government is
termed "destabilizing a government," and lies are seen as "inoperative statements," we are hearing doublespeak that attempts to avoid responsibility and
make the bad seem good, the negative appear positive, something unpleasant appear attractive; and which seems to communicate but doesn't. It is language designed to alter our perception of reality and corrupt our thinking.
Such language does not provide us with the tools we need to develop,
advance, and preserve our culture and our civilization. Such language breeds
suspicion, cynicism, distrust, and, ultimately, hostility.

Questions for Close Reading

1. What is the selection's thesis? Locate the sentence(s) in which Lutz states his main idea. If he doesn't state the thesis explicitly, express it in your own words.
2. According to Lutz, four questions help people "spot" doublespeak. What are the questions? How do they help people distinguish between legitimate language and doublespeak?
3. Lutz's headings indicate simply "First Kind of Doublespeak," "Second Kind of Doublespeak," and so on. What terms does Lutz use to identify the four kinds of doublespeak? Cite one example of each kind.
4. What, according to Lutz, are the dangers of doublespeak?
5. Refer to your dictionary as needed to define the following words used in the selection: *variance* (paragraph 6), *esoteric* (9), *profundity* (9), *dividend* (11), and *initiative* (14).

Questions About the Writer's Craft

1. **The pattern.** Does Lutz make his four categories of doublespeak mutually exclusive, or does he let them overlap? Cite specific examples to support your answer. Why do you think Lutz took the approach he did?
2. **Other patterns.** What other patterns, besides division-classification, does Lutz use in this selection? Cite examples of at least two other patterns. Explain how each pattern reinforces Lutz's thesis.
3. Lutz quotes Alan Greenspan twice: first in paragraph 12 and again in paragraph 13. What is surprising about Greenspan's second comment (paragraph 13)? Why might Lutz have included this second quotation?
4. How would you characterize Lutz's tone in the essay? What key words indicate his attitude toward the material he discusses? Why do you suppose he chose this particular tone?

Writing Assignments Using Division-Classification as a Pattern of Development

1. According to Lutz, doublespeak "is language designed to alter our perception of reality." Using two of Lutz's categories (or any others you devise), analyze an advertisement or commercial that you think deliberately uses doublespeak to mislead consumers. Before writing your paper, read Ann McClintock's "Propaganda Techniques in Today's Advertising" (page 207). Feel free to include any of McClintock's interpretations in your paper.
2. Select *one* area of life that you know well. Possibilities include life in a college dormitory, the parent-child relationship, the dating scene, and sibling conflicts. Focus on a specific type of speech (for example, gossip, reprimands, flirtation, or criticism) that occurs in this area. Then identify the component parts of that type of speech. You might, for example, analyze dormitory gossip about individual students, couples, and professors. Reach some conclusions about the kinds of speech you discuss. Do you consider them funny, pathetic, or troubling? Your tone should be consistent with the conclusions you reach.

Writing Assignments Combining Patterns of Development

∞ 3. Find a spoken or written *example* of doublespeak that disturbs you. Possibilities include a political advertisement, television commercial, newspaper article, or legal document. Write a letter of complaint to the appropriate person or office, using convincing examples to point out what is misleading about the communication. Pointing out negative impressions or *consequences* resulting from the doublespeak will enhance your position. Caroline Rego's "The Fine Art of Complaining" (page 245) offers guidelines for writing effective letters of complaint.

∞ 4. In his essay, Lutz examines the relationship between language and perception. Identify two closely related terms, and *contrast* the different perceptions of reality represented by each term. For example, you might contrast "African-American" and "Negro," "Ms." and "Miss," "gay" and "homosexual," "dolls" and "action figures," or "pro-life" and "anti-abortion." Interviewing family, friends, and classmates will help you identify ideas and *examples* to explore in the essay. For a discussion of the connection between language and perception, read Ann McClintock's "Propaganda Techniques in Today's Advertising" (page 207).

Writing Assignment Using a Journal Entry as a Starting Point

∞ 5. Select from your pre-reading journal entry two or three compelling instances of *beneficial* doublespeak. Use these examples in an essay arguing that doublespeak isn't always harmful. For each example cited, contrast the positive effects of doublespeak with the potentially negative consequences of *not* using it. Brainstorming with others will help you generate convincing examples. Before you begin writing, consider reading Beth Johnson's "Bombs Bursting in Air" (page 160), which illustrates an instance of well-intentioned doublespeak.

Ann McClintock

Ann McClintock (1946–) was educated at Temple University in Philadelphia and later earned an advanced degree from the University of Pennsylvania. Formerly director of occupational therapy at Ancora State Hospital in New Jersey, she has also worked as a freelance editor and writer. A frequent speaker before community groups, McClintock is especially interested in the effects of advertising on American life. The following selection, revised for this text, is part of a work in progress on the way propaganda techniques are used to sell products and political candidates.

Pre-Reading Journal Entry

How susceptible are you to ads and commercials? Do you consider yourself an easy target, or are you a "hard sell"? Have you purchased any products simply because you were won over by effective advertising strategies? What products have you not purchased because you deliberately didn't let yourself be swayed by advertisers' tactics? In your journal, reflect on these questions.

Propaganda Techniques in Today's Advertising

Americans, adults and children alike, are being seduced. They are being brainwashed. And few of us protest. Why? Because the seducers and the brainwashers are the advertisers we willingly invite into our homes. We are victims, content—even eager—to be victimized. We read advertisers' propaganda messages in newspapers and magazines; we watch their alluring images on television. We absorb their messages and images into our subconscious. We all do it—even those of us who claim to see through advertisers' tricks and therefore feel immune to advertising's charm. Advertisers lean heavily on propaganda to sell products, whether the "products" are a brand of toothpaste, a candidate for office, or a particular political viewpoint. 1

Propaganda is a systematic effort to influence people's opinions, to win them over to a certain view or side. Propaganda is not necessarily concerned with what is true or false, good or bad. Propagandists simply want people to believe the messages being sent. Often, propagandists will use outright lies or more subtle deceptions to sway people's opinions. In a propaganda war, any tactic is considered fair. 2

When we hear the word "propaganda," we usually think of a foreign menace: anti-American radio programs broadcast by a totalitarian regime or 3 brainwashing tactics practiced on hostages. Although propaganda may seem relevant only in the political arena, the concept can be applied fruitfully to the way products and ideas are sold in advertising. Indeed, the vast majority of us are targets in advertisers' propaganda war. Every day, we are bombarded with slogans, print and Internet pop-up ads, commercials, packaging claims, billboards, trademarks, logos, and designer brands—all forms of propaganda. One study reports that each of us, during an average day, is exposed to over *five hundred* advertising claims of various types. This saturation may even increase in the future since current trends include ads on movie screens, shopping carts, videocassettes, even public television.

What kind of propaganda techniques do advertisers use? There are seven basic types: 4

1. *Name Calling*   Name calling is a propaganda tactic in which nega-   5 tively charged names are hurled against the opposing side or competitor. By using such names, propagandists try to arouse feelings of mistrust, fear, and hate in their audiences. For example, a political advertisement may label an opposing candidate a "loser," "fence-sitter," or "warmonger." Depending on the advertiser's target market, labels such as "a friend of big business" or "a dues-paying member of the party in power" can be the epithets that damage an opponent. Ads for products may also use name calling. An American manufacturer may refer, for instance, to a "foreign car" in its commercial— not an "imported" one. The label of foreignness will have unpleasant connotations in many people's minds. A childhood rhyme claims that "names can never hurt me," but name calling is an effective way to damage the opposition, whether it is another car maker or a congressional candidate.

2. *Glittering Generalities*   Using glittering generalities is the opposite   6 of name calling. In this case, advertisers surround their products with attractive—and slippery—words and phrases. They use vague terms that are difficult to define and that may have different meanings to different people: *freedom, democratic, all-American, progressive, Christian,* and *justice.* Many such words have strong, affirmative overtones. This kind of language stirs positive feelings in people, feelings that may spill over to the product or idea being pitched. As with name calling, the emotional response may overwhelm logic. Target audiences accept the product without thinking very much about what the glittering generalities mean—or whether they even apply to the product. After all, how can anyone oppose "truth, justice, and the American way"?

The ads for politicians and political causes often use glittering generali-   7 ties because such "buzz words" can influence votes. Election slogans include high-sounding but basically empty phrases like the following:

"He cares about people." (That's nice, but is he a better candidate than his opponent?)

"Vote for progress." (Progress by *whose* standards?)
"They'll make this country great again." (What does "great" mean?
Does "great" mean the same thing to others as it does to me?)
"Vote for the future." (What kind of future?)
"If you love America, vote for Phyllis Smith." (If I don't vote for Smith,
does that mean I don't love America?)

Ads for consumer goods are also sprinkled with glittering generalities.   8
Product names, for instance, are supposed to evoke good feelings: *Luvs* diapers, *Stayfree* feminine hygiene products, *Joy* liquid detergent, *Loving Care* hair color, *Almost Home* cookies, *Yankee Doodle* pastries. Product slogans lean heavily on vague but comforting phrases: Sears is "Good life. Great price," General Electric "brings good things to life," and Dow Chemical "lets you do great things." Chevrolet, we are told, is the "heartbeat of America," and Chrysler boasts cars that are "built by Americans for Americans."

3. *Transfer*   In transfer, advertisers try to improve the image of a   9
product by associating it with a symbol most people respect, like the American flag or Uncle Sam. The advertisers hope that the prestige attached to the symbol will carry over to the product. Many companies use transfer devices to identify their products: Lincoln Insurance shows a profile of the president; Continental Insurance portrays a Revolutionary War minuteman; Amtrak's logo is red, white, and blue; Liberty Mutual's corporate symbol is the Statue of Liberty; Allstate's name is cradled by a pair of protective, fatherly hands.

Corporations also use the transfer technique when they sponsor prestigious shows on radio and television. These shows function as symbols of   10
dignity and class. Kraft Corporation, for instance, sponsored a "Leonard Bernstein Conducts Beethoven" concert, while Gulf Oil is the sponsor of *National Geographic* specials and Mobil supports public television's *Masterpiece Theater.* In this way, corporations can reach an educated, influential audience and, perhaps, improve their public image by associating themselves with quality programming.

Political ads, of course, practically wrap themselves in the flag. Ads for a   11
political candidate often show either the Washington Monument, a Fourth of July parade, the Stars and Stripes, a bald eagle soaring over the mountains, or a white-steepled church on the village green. The national anthem or "America the Beautiful" may play softly in the background. Such appeals to Americans' love of country can surround the candidate with an aura of patriotism and integrity.

4. *Testimonial*   The testimonial is one of advertisers' most-loved and   12
most-used propaganda techniques. Similar to the transfer device, the testimonial capitalizes on the admiration people have for a celebrity to make the

product shine more brightly—even though the celebrity is not an expert on the product being sold.

Print and television ads offer a nonstop parade of testimonials: here's   13
William Shatner for Priceline.com; here's basketball star Michael Jordan eating Wheaties; a slew of well-known people (including pop star Madonna) advertise clothing from the Gap; and Jerry Seinfeld assures us he never goes anywhere without his American Express card. Testimonials can sell movies, too; newspaper ads for films often feature favorable comments by well-known reviewers. And, in recent years, testimonials have played an important role in pitching books; the backs of paperbacks frequently list complimentary blurbs by celebrities.

Political candidates, as well as their ad agencies, know the value of testi-   14
monials. Barbra Streisand lent her star appeal to the presidential campaign of Bill Clinton, while Arnold Schwarzenegger endorsed George H. W. Bush. Even controversial social issues are debated by celebrities. The nuclear-freeze debate, for instance, starred Paul Newman for the pro side and Charlton Heston for the con.

As illogical as testimonials sometimes are (Pepsi's Michael Jackson, for   15
instance, is a health-food adherent who does not drink soft drinks), they are effective propaganda. We like the *person* so much that we like the *product* too.

5. *Plain Folks*   The plain folks approach says, in effect, "Buy me or vote   16
for me. I'm just like you." Regular folks will surely like Bob Evans's Down on the Farm Country Sausage or good old-fashioned Countrytime Lemonade. Some ads emphasize the idea that "we're all in the same boat." We see people making long-distance calls for just the reasons we do—to put the baby on the phone to Grandma or to tell Mom we love her. And how do these folksy, warmhearted (usually saccharine) scenes affect us? They're supposed to make us feel that AT&T—the multinational corporate giant—has the same values we do. Similarly, we are introduced to the little people at Ford, the ordinary folks who work on the assembly line, not to bigwigs in their executive offices. What's the purpose of such an approach? To encourage us to buy a car built by these honest, hardworking "everyday Joes" who care about quality as much as we do.

Political advertisements make almost as much use of the "plain folks"   17
appeal as they do of transfer devices. Candidates wear hard hats, farmers' caps, and assembly-line coveralls. They jog around the block and carry their own luggage through the airport. The idea is to convince voters that the candidates are average people, not the elite—not wealthy lawyers or executives but common citizens.

6. *Card Stacking*   When people say that "the cards were stacked   18
against me," they mean that they were never given a fair chance. Applied to

propaganda, card stacking means that one side may suppress or distort evidence, tell half-truths, oversimplify the facts, or set up a "straw man"—a false target—to divert attention from the issue at hand. Card stacking is a difficult form of propaganda both to detect and to combat. When a candidate claims that an opponent has "changed his mind five times on this important issue," we tend to accept the claim without investigating whether the candidate had good reasons for changing his mind. Many people are simply swayed by the distorted claim that the candidate is "waffling" on the issue.

Advertisers often stack the cards in favor of the products they are push-   19
ing. They may, for instance, use what are called "weasel words." These are small words that usually slip right past us, but that make the difference between reality and illusion. The weasel words are underlined in the following claims:

> "<u>Helps control</u> dandruff symptoms." (The audience usually interprets this as *stops* dandruff.)
> "Most dentists <u>surveyed</u> recommend sugarless gum for their patients <u>who chew gum</u>." (We hear the "most dentists" and "for their patients," but we don't think about how many were surveyed or whether the dentists first recommended that the patients not chew gum at all.)
> "Sticker price $1,000 lower than <u>most comparable</u> cars." (How many is "most"? What car does the advertiser consider "comparable"?)

Advertisers also use a card stacking trick when they make an unfinished   20
claim. For example, they will say that their product has "twice as much pain reliever." We are left with a favorable impression. We don't usually ask, "Twice as much pain reliever as what?" Or advertisers may make extremely vague claims that sound alluring but have no substance: Toyota's "Oh, what a feeling!"; Vantage cigarettes' "The taste of success"; "The spirit of Marlboro"; Coke's "the real thing." Another way to stack the cards in favor of a certain product is to use scientific-sounding claims that are not supported by sound research. When Ford claimed that its LTD model was "400% quieter," many people assumed that the LTD must be quieter than all other cars. When taken to court, however, Ford admitted that the phrase referred to the difference between the noise level inside and outside the LTD. Other scientific-sounding claims use mysterious ingredients that are never explained as selling points: "Retsyn," "special whitening agents," "the ingredient doctors recommend."

7. *Bandwagon*   In the bandwagon technique, advertisers pressure,   21
"Everyone's doing it. Why don't you?" This kind of propaganda often succeeds because many people have a deep desire not to be different. Political

ads tell us to vote for the "winning candidate." Advertisers know we tend to feel comfortable doing what others do; we want to be on the winning team. Or ads show a series of people proclaiming, "I'm voting for the Senator. I don't know why anyone wouldn't." Again, the audience feels under pressure to conform.

In the marketplace, the bandwagon approach lures buyers. Ads tell us   22
that "nobody doesn't like Sara Lee" (the message is that you must be weird if you don't). They tell us that "most people prefer Brand X two to one over other leading brands" (to be like the majority, we should buy Brand X). If we don't drink Pepsi, we're left out of "the Pepsi generation." To take part in "America's favorite health kick," the National Dairy Council asks us, "Got Milk?" And Honda motorcycle ads, praising the virtues of being a follower, tell us, "Follow the leader. He's on a Honda."

Why do these propaganda techniques work? Why do so many of us buy   23
the products, viewpoints, and candidates urged on us by propaganda messages? They work because they appeal to our emotions, not to our minds. Often, in fact, they capitalize on our prejudices and biases. For example, if we are convinced that environmentalists are radicals who want to destroy America's record of industrial growth and progress, then we will applaud the candidate who refers to them as "treehuggers." Clear thinking requires hard work: analyzing a claim, researching the facts, examining both sides of an issue, using logic to see the flaws in an argument. Many of us would rather let the propagandists do our thinking for us.

Because propaganda is so effective, it is important to detect it and under-   24
stand how it is used. We may conclude, after close examination, that some propaganda sends a truthful, worthwhile message. Some advertising, for instance, urges us not to drive drunk, to become volunteers, to contribute to charity. Even so, we must be aware that propaganda is being used. Otherwise, we have consented to handing over to others our independence of thought and action.

Questions for Close Reading

1. What is the selection's thesis? Locate the sentence(s) in which McClintock states her main idea. If she doesn't state the thesis explicitly, express it in your own words.
2. What is *propaganda*? What mistaken associations do people often have with this term?
3. What are "weasel words"? How do they trick listeners?
4. Why does McClintock believe we should be better informed about propaganda techniques?
5. Refer to your dictionary as needed to define the following words used in the selection: *seduced* (paragraph 1), *warmonger* (5), and *elite* (17).

Questions About the Writer's Craft

1. **The pattern and other patterns.** Before explaining the categories in-to which propaganda techniques can be grouped, McClintock provides a *definition* of propaganda. Is the definition purely informative, or does it have a larger objective? If you think the latter, what is the definition's broader purpose?
2. In her introduction, McClintock uses loaded words such as *seduced* and *brainwashed*. What effect do these words have on the reader?
3. Locate places in the essay where McClintock uses questions. Which are rhetorical and which are genuine queries?
4. What kind of conclusion does McClintock provide for the essay?

Writing Assignments Using Division-Classification as a Pattern of Development

∞ 1. McClintock cautions us to be sensitive to propaganda in advertising. Young children, however, aren't capable of this kind of awareness. With pen or pencil in hand, watch some commercials aimed at children, such as those for toys, cereals, and fast food. Then analyze the use of propaganda techniques in these commercials. Using division-classification, write an essay describing the main propaganda techniques you observed. Support your analysis with examples drawn from the commercials. Remember to provide a thesis that indicates your opinion of the advertising techniques. For additional insight into this issue, read Ellen Goodman's "Family Counterculture" (page 6) and Kay S. Hymowitz's "Tweens: Ten Going on Sixteen" (page 153).
2. Like advertising techniques, television shows can be classified. Avoiding the obvious system of classifying according to game shows, detective shows, and situation comedies, come up with your own original division-classification principle. Possibilities include how family life is depicted, the way work is presented, how male-female relationships are portrayed. Using one such principle, write an essay in which you categorize popular TV shows into three types. Refer to specific shows to support your classification system. Your attitude toward the shows being discussed should be made clear.

Writing Assignments Combining Patterns of Development

∞ 3. McClintock says that card stacking "distort[s] evidence, tell[s] half-truths, over-simpli[fies] the facts" (paragraph 18). Focusing on an extended *example* such as an editorial, a political campaign, a print ad, or a television commercial, analyze the extent to which card stacking is used as a *persuasive* strategy. Reading William Lutz's "Doublespeak" (page 200) will deepen your understanding of the extent to which the truth can be distorted.
4. To increase further your sensitivity to the moral dimensions of propaganda, write a proposal outlining an ad campaign for a real or imaginary product or elected official. The introduction to your proposal should identify who or what is to be promoted, and the thesis or plan of development should indicate the specific

propaganda techniques you suggest. In the paper's supporting paragraphs, explain the *process* by which these techniques would be used to promote your product or candidate and what their desired *effects* would be.

Writing Assignment Using a Journal Entry as a Starting Point

5. Write an essay showing that, on the whole, you are fairly susceptible to *or* are fairly immune to advertising ploys. Drawing upon your pre-reading journal entry, illustrate your position with lively details of advertising campaigns that won you over—or that failed to sway you. Draw upon some of McClintock's terminology when describing advertisers' techniques. Your essay may have a serious or a playful tone.

Additional Writing Topics

DIVISION-CLASSIFICATION

General Assignments

Choose one of the following subjects and write an essay developed wholly or in part through division-classification. Start by determining the purpose of the essay. Do you want to inform, compare and contrast, or persuade? Apply a single, significant principle of division or classification to your subject. Don't switch the principle midway through your analysis. Also, be sure that the types or categories you create are as complete and mutually exclusive as possible.

Division

1. A shopping mall
2. A video and/or stereo system
3. A fruit, such as a pineapple, an orange, or a banana
4. A tax dollar
5. A particular kind of team
6. A word-processing system
7. A human hand
8. A meal
9. A meeting
10. A favorite poem, story, or play
11. A favorite restaurant
12. A school library
13. A basement
14. A playground, gym, or other recreational area
15. A church service
16. A wedding or funeral
17. An eventful week in your life
18. A college campus
19. A television show or movie
20. A homecoming or other special weekend

Classification

1. People in a waiting room
2. Holidays
3. Closets
4. Roommates
5. Salad bars
6. Divorces
7. Beds
8. Students in a class
9. Shoes

10. Summer movies
11. Teachers
12. Neighbors
13. College courses
14. Bosses
15. Computer/Internet users
16. Mothers or fathers
17. Commercials
18. Vacations
19. Trash
20. Relatives

Assignments With a Specific Purpose, Audience, and Point of View

On Campus

1. You're a dorm counselor. During orientation week, you'll be talking to students on your floor about the different kinds of problems they may have with roommates. Write your talk, describing each kind of problem and explaining how to cope with it.

2. As your college newspaper's TV critic, you plan to write a review of the fall shows, most of which—in your opinion—lack originality. To show how stereotypical the programs are, select one type (for example, situation comedies or crime dramas). Then use a specific division-classification principle to illustrate that the same stale formulas are trotted out from show to show.

3. Asked to write an editorial for the campus paper, you decide to do a half-serious piece on taking "mental health" days off from classes. Structure your essay around three kinds of occasions when "playing hooky" is essential for maintaining sanity.

At Home or in the Community

4. Your favorite magazine runs an editorial asking readers to send in what they think are the main challenges facing their particular gender group. Write a letter to the editor in which you identify at least three categories of problems that your sex faces. Be sure to provide lively, specific examples to illustrate each category. In your letter, you may adopt a serious or lighthearted tone, depending on your overall subject matter.

On the Job

5. As a driving instructor, you decide to prepare a lecture on the types of drivers that your students are likely to encounter on the road. In your lecture, categorize drivers according to a specific principle and show the behaviors of each type.

6. A seasoned camp counselor, you've been asked to prepare, for new counselors, an informational sheet on children's emotional needs. Categorizing those needs into types, explain what counselors can do to nurture youngsters emotionally.

7

PROCESS ANALYSIS

WHAT IS PROCESS ANALYSIS?

Perhaps you've noticed the dogged determination of small children when they learn how to do something new. Whether trying to tie their shoelaces or tell time, little children struggle along, creating knotted tangles, confusing the hour with the minute hand. But they don't give up. Mastering such basic skills makes them feel less dependent on the adults of the world—all of whom seem to know how to do everything. Actually, none of us is born knowing how to do very much. We spend a good deal of our lives learning— everything from speaking our first word to balancing our first bank statement. Indeed, the milestones in our lives are often linked to the processes we have mastered: how to cross the street alone; how to drive a car; how to make a speech without being paralyzed by fear.

Process analysis, a technique that explains the steps or sequence involved in doing something, satisfies our need to learn as well as our curiosity about how the world works. All the self-help books flooding the market today (*Managing Stress, How to Make a Million in Real Estate, Ten Days to a Perfect Body*) are examples of process analysis. The instructions on the federal tax form and the recipes in a cookbook are also process analyses. Several television classics, now seen in reruns, also capitalize on our desire to learn how things happen: *The Wild Kingdom* shows how animals survive in faraway lands, and *Mission: Impossible* has great fun detailing elaborate plans for preventing the triumph of evil. Process analysis can be more than merely interesting or entertaining, though; it can be of critical importance. Consider a waiter hurriedly skimming the "Choking Aid" instructions posted on a restaurant wall or an air-traffic controller following emergency procedures in an effort to prevent a midair collision. In these last examples, the consequences could be fatal if the process analyses were slipshod, inaccurate, or confusing.

Undoubtedly, all of us have experienced less dramatic effects of poorly written process analyses. Perhaps you've tried to assemble a bicycle and spent hours sorting through a stack of parts, only to end up with one or two extra pieces never mentioned in the instructions. Or maybe you were baffled when putting up a set of wall shelves because the instructions used unfamiliar terms such as *mitered cleat, wing nut,* and *dowel pin.* No wonder many people stay clear of anything that actually admits "assembly required."

HOW PROCESS ANALYSIS FITS YOUR PURPOSE AND AUDIENCE

You will use process analysis in two types of writing situations: (1) when you want to give step-by-step instructions to readers showing how they can do something, or (2) when you want readers to understand how something happens even though they won't actually follow the steps outlined. The first kind of process analysis is *directional;* the second is *informational.*

When you look at the cooking instructions on a package of frozen vegetables or follow guidelines for completing a job application, you're reading directional process analysis. A serious essay explaining how to select a college and a humorous essay telling readers how to get on the good side of a professor are also examples of directional process analysis. Using a variety of tones, informational process analyses can range over equally diverse subjects; they can describe mechanical, scientific, historical, sociological, artistic, or psychological processes: for example, how the core of a nuclear reactor melts down; how television became so important in political campaigns; how abstract painters use color; how to survive a blind date.

Process analysis, both directional and informational, is often appropriate in *problem-solving situations.* In such cases, you say, "Here's the problem and here's what should be done to solve the problem." Indeed, college assignments frequently take the form of problem-solving process analyses. Consider these examples:

> Community officials have been accused of mismanaging recent unrest over the public housing ordinance. Describe the steps the officials took, indicating why you think their strategy was unwise. Then explain how you think the situation should have been handled.

> Over the years, there have been many reports citing the abuse of small children in day care centers. What can parents do to guard against the mistreatment of their children?

> Because many colleges and universities have changed the eligibility requirements for financial aid, fewer students can depend on loans or scholarships. How can students cope with the increasing costs of obtaining a higher education?

Note that the first assignment asks students to explain what's wrong with the current approach before they present their own step-by-step solution. Problem-solving process analyses are often organized in this way. You may also have noted that none of the assignments explicitly requires an essay response using process analysis. However, the wording of the assignments— "*Describe* the steps," "*What* can parents *do*," "*How* can students *cope*,"—suggests that process analysis would be an appropriate strategy for developing the responses.

Assignments don't always signal the use of process analysis so clearly. But during the prewriting stage, as you generate material to support your thesis, you'll often realize that you can best achieve your purpose by developing the essay—or part of it—using process analysis.

Sometimes process analysis will be the primary strategy for organizing an essay; other times it will be used to help make a point in an essay organized according to another pattern of development. Let's take a look at process analysis as a supporting strategy.

Assume that you're writing a *causal analysis* examining the impact of television commercials on people's buying behavior. To help readers see that commercials create a need where none existed before, you might describe the various stages in an advertising campaign to pitch a new, completely frivolous product. In an essay *defining* a good boss, you could convey the point that effective managers must be skilled at settling disputes by explaining the steps your boss took to resolve a heated disagreement between two employees. If you write an *argumentation-persuasion* paper urging the funding of programs to ease the plight of the homeless, you would have to dramatize for readers the tragedy of these people's lives. To achieve your purpose, you could devote part of the paper to an explanation of how the typical street person goes about the desperate jobs of finding a place to sleep and getting food to eat.

SUGGESTIONS FOR USING PROCESS ANALYSIS IN AN ESSAY

The suggestions that follow will be helpful whether you use process analysis as a dominant or a supportive pattern of development.

1. Identify the desired outcome of the process analysis.   Many papers developed primarily through process analysis have a clear-cut purpose—simply to *inform* readers as objectively as possible about a process: "Here's a way of making french fries at home that will surpass the best served in your favorite fast-food restaurant." But a process analysis essay may also have a *persuasive* edge, with the writer advocating a point of view about the process, perhaps even urging a course of action: "If you don't want your arguments to deteriorate into ugly battles, you should follow a series of foolproof steps for having disagreements that leave friendships intact." Before starting to write, you need to decide if the essay is to be purely factual or if it will include this kind of persuasive dimension.

2. Formulate a thesis that clarifies your attitude toward the process. Like the thesis in any other paper, the thesis in a process analysis should do more than announce your subject. ("Here's how the college's work-study program operates.") It should also state or imply your attitude toward the process: "Enrolling in the college's work-study program has become unnecessarily complicated. The procedure could be simplified if the college adopted the helpful guidelines prepared by the Student Senate."

3. Keep your audience in mind.   Only when you gauge how much your readers already know (or don't know) about the process can you determine how much explanation you'll have to provide. Suppose you've been asked to write an article informing students of the best way to use the university computer center. The article will be published in a newsletter for computer science majors. You would seriously misjudge your audience—and probably put them to sleep—if you explained in detail how to transfer material from disk to disk or how to delete information from a file. However, an article on the same topic prepared for a general audience—your composition class, for instance—would probably require such detailed instructions.

   To determine how much explanation is needed, put yourself in your readers' shoes. Don't assume readers will know something just because you do. Ask questions such as these about your audience: "Will my readers need some background about the process before I describe it in depth?" "Are there technical terms I should define?" "If my essay is directional, should I specify near the beginning the ingredients, materials, and equipment needed to perform the process?" (For more help in analyzing your audience, see the checklist on page 17.)

4. Use prewriting to identify the steps in the process.   To explain a sequence to your readers, you need to think through the process thoroughly, identifying its major parts and subparts, locating possible missteps or trouble spots. With your purpose, thesis, and audience in mind, use the appropriate prewriting techniques (brainstorming and mapping should be especially helpful) to break down the process into its component parts. In prewriting, it's a good idea to start by generating more material than you expect to use. Then the raw material can be shaped and pruned to fit your purpose and the needs of your audience. The amount of work done during the prewriting stage will have a direct bearing on the clarity of your presentation.

5. Identify the directional and informational aspects of the process analysis.   Directional and informational process analyses are not always distinct. In fact, they may be complementary. Your prewriting may reveal that you'll need to provide background information about a process before outlining its steps. For example, in a paper describing a step-by-step approach for losing weight, you might first need to explain how the body burns calories. Or, in a paper on gardening, you could provide some theory about the way organic fertilizers work before detailing a plan for growing vegetables. Although both approaches may be appropriate in a paper, one generally predominates.

The kind of process analysis chosen has implications for the way you will relate to your reader. When the process analysis is *directional,* the reader is addressed in the *second person:* "You should first rinse the residue from the radiator by . . . ," or "Wrap the injured person in a blanket and then. . . ." (In the second example, the pronoun *you* is implied.)

If the process analysis has an *informational* purpose, you won't address the reader directly but will choose from a number of other options. For example, you might use the *first-person* point of view. In a humorous essay explaining how not to prepare for finals, you could cite your own disastrous study habits: "Filled with good intentions, I sit on my bed, pick up a pencil, open my notebook, and promptly fall asleep." The *third-person singular or plural* can also be used in informational process essays: "The door-to-door salesperson walks up the front walk, heart pounding, more than a bit nervous, but also challenged by the prospect of striking a deal," or "The new recruits next underwent a series of important balance tests in what was called the 'horror chamber.'" Whether you use the first, second, or third person, avoid shifting point of view midstream.

You might have noticed that in the third-person examples, the present tense ("walks up") is used in one sentence, the past tense ("underwent") in the other. The past tense is appropriate for events already completed, whereas the present tense is used for habitual or ongoing actions. ("A dominant male goose usually flies at the head of the V-wedge during migration.") The present tense is also effective when you want to lend a sense of dramatic immediacy to a process, even if the steps were performed in the past. ("The surgeon gently separates the facial skin and muscle from the underlying bony skull.") As with point of view, be on guard against changing tenses in the middle of your explanation.

6. Explain the process, one step at a time.   Prewriting helped you identify key stages and sort out the directional and informational aspects of the process. Now you're ready to organize your raw material into an easy-to-follow sequence. At times your purpose will be to explain a process with a *fairly fixed chronological sequence:* how to make pizza, how to pot a plant, how to change a tire. In such cases, you should include all necessary steps, in the correct chronological order. However, if a strict chronological ordering of steps means that a particularly important part of the sequence gets buried in the middle, the sequence probably should be juggled so that the crucial step receives the attention it deserves.

Other times your goal will be to describe a process having *no commonly accepted sequence*. For example, in an essay explaining how to discipline a child or how to pull yourself out of a blue mood, you will have to come up with your own definition of the key steps and then arrange those steps in some logical order. You may also use process analyses to *reject* or *reformulate* a traditional sequence. In this case, you would propose a more logical series of steps: "Our system for electing congressional representatives is inefficient and undemocratic; it should be reformed in the following ways."

Whether the essay describes a generally agreed-on process or one that is not commonly accepted, you must provide all the details needed to explain the process. Your readers should be able to understand, even visualize, the process. There should be no fuzzy patches or confusing cuts from one step to another. Don't, however, go into obsessive detail about minor stages or steps. If you dwell for several hundred words on how to butter the pan, your readers will never stay with you long enough to learn how to make the omelet.

It's not unusual, especially in less defined sequences, for some steps in a process to occur simultaneously and overlap. When this happens, you should present the steps in the most logical order, being sure to tell your readers that several steps are not perfectly distinct and may merge. For example, in an essay explaining how a species becomes extinct, you would have to indicate that overpopulation of hardy strains and destruction of endangered breeds are often simultaneous events. You would also need to clarify that the depletion of food sources both precedes and follows the demise of a species.

7. Provide readers with the help they need to follow the sequence.   As you move through the steps of a process analysis, don't forget to *warn readers about difficulties* they might encounter. For example, when writing a paper on the artistry involved in butterflying a shrimp, you might say something like this:

> Next, make a shallow cut with your sharpened knife along the convex curve of the shrimp's intestinal tract. The tract, usually a faint black line along the outside curve of the shrimp, is faintly visible beneath the translucent flesh. But some shrimp have a thick orange, blue, or gray line instead of a thin black one. In all cases, be careful not to slice too deeply, or you will end up with two shrimp halves instead of one butterflied shrimp.

You have told readers what to look for, citing the exceptions, and have warned them against making too deep a cut. Anticipating spots where communication might break down is a key part of writing an effective process analysis.

Transitional words and phrases are also critical in helping readers understand the order of the steps being described. Time signals such as *first, next, now, while, after, before,* and *finally* provide readers with a clear sense of the sequence. Entire sentences can also be used to link parts of the process, reminding your audience of what has already been discussed and indicating what will now be explained: "Once the panel of experts finishes its evaluation of the exam questions, randomly selected items are field-tested in schools throughout the country."

8. Maintain an appropriate tone.   When writing a process analysis essay, be sure your tone is consistent with your purpose, your attitude toward your subject, and the effect you want to have on the reader. When explaining how fraternities and sororities recruit new members, do you want to use an objective, nonjudgmental tone? To decide, take into account readers' attitudes toward your subject. Does your audience have a financial or emotional investment in the process being described? Does your own interest in the process coincide or conflict with that of your audience? Awareness of your readers' stance can be crucial. Consider another example: Assume you're writing a letter to the director of the student health center proposing a new system to replace the currently chaotic one. You'd do well to be tactful in your criticisms. Offend your reader, and your cause is lost. If, however, the letter is slated for the college newspaper and directed primarily to other students, you could adopt a more pointed, even sarcastic tone. Readers, you would assume, will probably share your view and favor change.

Once you settle on the essay's tone, maintain it throughout. If you're writing a light piece on the way computers are taking over our lives, you wouldn't include a grim step-by-step analysis of the way confidential computerized medical records may become public.

9. Open and close the process analysis effectively.   A paper developed primarily through process analysis should have a strong beginning. The introduction should state the process to be described and imply whether the essay has an informational or directional intent.

If you suspect readers are indifferent to your subject, use the introduction to motivate them, telling them how important the subject is:

> Do you enjoy the salad bars found in many restaurants? If you do, you probably have noticed that the vegetables are always crisp and fresh--no matter how many hours they have been exposed to the air. What are the restaurants doing to make the vegetables look so inviting? There's a simple answer. Many restaurants dip and spray the vegetables with potent chemicals to make them appetizing.

If you think your audience may be intimidated by your subject (perhaps because it's complex or relatively obscure), the introduction is the perfect spot to reassure them that the process being described is not beyond their grasp:

> Studies show that many people willingly accept a defective product just so they won't have to deal with the uncomfortable process of making a complaint. But once a few easy-to-learn basics are mastered, anyone can register a complaint that gets results.

Most process analysis essays don't end as soon as the last step in the sequence is explained. Instead, they usually include some brief final comments that round out the piece and bring it to a satisfying close. This final section of the essay may summarize the main steps in the process—not by repeating the steps verbatim but by rephrasing and condensing them in several concise sentences. The conclusion can also be an effective spot to underscore the significance of the process, recalling what may have been said in the introduction about the subject's importance. Or the essay can end by echoing the note of reassurance that may have been included at the start.

REVISION STRATEGIES

Once you have a draft of the essay, you're ready to revise. The following checklist will help you and those giving you feedback apply to process analysis some of the revision techniques discussed on pages 59–61.

☑ PROCESS ANALYSIS: A REVISION/PEER REVIEW CHECKLIST

Revise Overall Meaning and Structure

❑ What purpose does the process analysis serve—to inform, to persuade, or to do both?

❑ Is the process analysis primarily *directional* or *informational*? How can you tell?

❑ Where does the process seem confusing? Where have steps been left out? Which steps need simplifying?

❑ What is the essay's tone? Is the tone appropriate for the essay's purpose and readers? Where are there distracting shifts in tone?

Revise Paragraph Development

❑ Does the introduction specify the process to be described? Does it provide an overview? Should it?

❑ Which paragraphs are difficult to follow? Have any steps or materials been omitted or explained in too much or too little detail? Which paragraphs should warn readers about potential trouble spots or overlapping steps?

❑ Where are additional time signals needed to clarify the sequence within and between paragraphs? Where does overreliance on time signals make the sequence awkward and mechanical?

❑ Which paragraph describes the most crucial step in the sequence? How has the step been highlighted?

❑ How could the conclusion be more effective?

Revise Sentences and Words

❏ What technical or specialized terms appear in the essay? Have they been sufficiently explained? Where could simpler, less technical language be used?

❏ Are there any places where the essay's point of view awkwardly shifts? How could this problem be corrected?

❏ Does the essay use correct verb tenses—the past tense for completed events, the present tense for habitual or ongoing actions?

❏ Where does the essay use the passive voice ("The hole is dug")? Would the active voice ("You dig the hole") be more effective?

STUDENT ESSAY

The following student essay was written by Robert Barry in response to this assignment:

In "Your New Computer," Bill Bryson suggests that technology can sometimes waste time rather than save it. Identify another example of a technology that has turned out to be unexpectedly time-consuming. Drawing upon your own and other people's experiences, write a light-spirited essay that shows, step by step, how this technology ends up consuming more time than it should.

While reading Robert's paper, try to determine how effectively it applies the principles of process analysis. The annotations on Robert's paper and the commentary following it will help you look at the essay more closely.

Becoming a Videoholic
by Robert Barry

Introduction

Videocassette recorders (VCRs) have been around for   1
quite a few years. At last count, three out of four U.S.
households owned at least one VCR. As a technological
breakthrough, the VCR has been an enormous success—
almost as popular as television itself. You can buy a VCR just
about anywhere, and very affordably. No consumer warning
labels are attached to these rapidly multiplying VCRs, but

Start of two-
sentence thesis — there should be. VCRs can be dangerous. Barely aware of what
is happening, a person can turn into a compulsive videotaper.
The descent from innocent hobby to full-blown addiction
takes place in several stages.

Topic sentence ⟶ In the first innocent stage, the unsuspecting person buys   2
a VCR for occasional use. I was at this stage when I asked my
First stage in   parents if they would buy me a VCR as a birthday gift. With
process (VCR   the VCR, I could tape reruns of <u>Seinfeld</u> and new episodes of
addiction)   <u>The Simpsons</u>, shows that I would otherwise miss on nights I
was at work. The VCR was perfect. I hooked it up to the old TV
in my bedroom, recorded the antics of Jerry, Elaine, George,
and Kramer and the adventures of my favorite cartoon family,
and then watched the tape the next day. Occasionally, I taped
a movie, which my friends and I watched over the weekend. I
had just one cassette, but that was all I needed since I
Beginning   watched every show I recorded and simply taped over the
of analogy   preceding show when I recorded another. In these early days,
to alcoholism ⟶ my use of the VCR was the equivalent of light social drinking.

Topic sentence ⟶ In the second phase on the road to videoholism, an   3
individual uses the VCR more frequently and begins to
Second stage   stockpile tapes rather than watch them. My troubles began in
in process   July when my family and I went to the shore for a week's
vacation. I programmed the VCR to tape all five episodes of
<u>Seinfeld</u> while I was at the beach perfecting my tan. Since I
used the VCR's long-play mode, I could get all five <u>Seinfelds</u> on
one cassette. But that ended up creating a problem. Even I, an
avid Jerry Seinfeld fan, didn't want to watch five shows in one
sitting. I viewed two shows, but the three unwatched shows
tied up my tape, making it impossible to record other shows.
How did I resolve this dilemma? Very easily. I went out and
bought several more blank cassettes. Once I had these
additional tapes, I was free to record as many <u>Seinfelds</u> as I
wanted, plus I could tape reruns of classics like <u>Law & Order</u>
and <u>Buffy the Vampire Slayer</u>. Very quickly, I accumulated
six <u>Seinfelds</u>, four <u>Law & Orders</u>, and three <u>Buffys</u>. Then a
friend—who shall go nameless—told me that only 144
episodes of <u>Buffy</u> existed. Only 144! Excited by the thought
that I could acquire as impressive a collection of tapes as a
Hollywood executive, I continued recording <u>Buffy</u>, even taping
shows while I watched them. Clearly, my once innocent hobby
Continuation   was getting out of control. I was now using the VCR on a
of analogy ⟶ regular basis—the equivalent of several stiff drinks a day.

Topic sentence ⟶ In the third stage of videoholism, the amount of taping   4
increases significantly, which leads to an even more irrational
Third stage   stockpiling of cassettes. The catalyst that propelled me into
in process   this third stage was my parents' decision to get satellite TV.
Selfless guy that I am, I volunteered to move my VCR and hook
it up to the living room TV, where the satellite connection was
located. Now I could tape all the most recent movies and cable
Continuation   specials. With that delightful possibility in mind, I went out
of analogy ⟶ and bought two six-packs of blank tapes. Then, in addition to

my regular lineup, I began to record a couple of additional shows every day. I also went movie-crazy and taped Gangs of New York, Barbershop, and The Godfather I, II, and III. I taped an HBO comedy special with Chris Rock, and an MTV concert featuring Radiohead. Where did I get time to watch all these tapes? I didn't. Taping at this point was more satisfying than watching. Reason and common sense were abandoned. Getting things on tape had become an obsession, and I was taping all the time.

Topic sentence

Fourth stage in process

Continuation of analogy

In the fourth stage, videoholism creeps into other parts of   5 the addict's life, influencing behavior in strange ways. Secrecy becomes commonplace. One day, my mother came into my room and saw my bookcase filled with tapes--rather than with the paperbacks that used to be there. "Robert," she exclaimed, "isn't this getting a bit out of hand?" I assured her it was just a hobby, but I started hiding my tapes, putting them in a suitcase stored in my closet. I also taped at night, slipping downstairs to turn on the VCR after my parents had gone to bed and getting down first thing in the morning to turn off the VCR and remove the cassette before my parents noticed. Also, denial is not unusual during this stage of VCR addiction. At the dinner table, when my younger sister commented, "Robert tapes all the time," I laughingly told everyone--including myself--that the taping was no big deal. I was getting bored with it and was going to stop any day, I assured my family. Obsessive behavior also characterizes the fourth stage of videoholism. Each week, I pulled out the TV magazine from the Sunday paper and went through it carefully, circling in red all the shows I wanted to tape. Another sign of addiction was my compulsive organization of all the tapes I had stockpiled. Working more diligently than I ever had for any term paper, I typed up labels and attached them to each cassette. I also created an elaborate list that showed my tapes broken down into categories such as police dramas, horror movies, and comedies.

Topic sentence

Continuation of analogy

Final stage in process

In the final stage of an addiction, the individual either   6 succumbs completely to the addiction or is able to break away from the habit. I broke my addiction, and I broke it cold turkey. This total withdrawal occurred when I went off to college. There was no point in taking my VCR to school because TVs were not allowed in the freshman dorms. Even though there were many things to occupy my time during the school week, cold sweats overcame me whenever I thought about everything on TV I was not taping. I even considered calling home and asking members of my family to tape things for me, but I knew they would think I was crazy. At the beginning of the semester, I also had to resist the overwhelming desire to

Conclusion

Final references
to analogy

travel the three hours home every weekend so I could get my fix. But after a while, the urgent need to tape subsided. Now, months later, as I write this, I feel detached and sober.

I have no illusions, though. I know that once a videoholic, always a videoholic. Soon I will return home for the holidays, which, as everyone knows, can be a time for excess eating-- and taping. But I will cope with the pressure. I will take each day one at a time. I will ask my little sister to hide my blank tapes from me. And if I feel myself succumbing to the temptations of taping, I will pick up the telephone and dial the videoholics' hot line: 1-800-VCR-TAPE. I will win the battle.

7

COMMENTARY

Purpose, thesis, and tone.   Robert's essay is an example of *informational process analysis;* his purpose is to describe—rather than teach—the process of becoming a "videoholic." The title, with its coined term *videoholic,* tips us off that the essay is going to be entertaining. And the introductory paragraph clearly establishes the essay's playful, mock-serious tone. The tone established, Robert briefly defines the term *videoholic* as a "compulsive videotaper" and then moves to the essay's *thesis:* "Barely aware of what is happening, a person can turn into a compulsive videotaper. The descent from innocent hobby to full-blown addiction takes place in several stages."

Throughout the essay, Robert sustains the introduction's humor by mocking his own motivations and poking fun at his quirks: "Selfless guy that I am, I volunteered to move my VCR" (paragraph 4), and "Working more diligently than I ever had for any term paper, I typed up labels" (5). Robert probably uses a bit of *dramatic license* when reporting some of his obsessive behavior, and we, as readers, understand that he's exaggerating for comic effect. Most likely he didn't break out in a cold sweat at the thought of the TV shows he was unable to tape, and he probably didn't hide his tapes in a suitcase. Nevertheless, this tinkering with the truth is legitimate because it allows Robert to create material that fits the essay's lightly satiric tone.

Organization and topic sentences.   To meet the requirements of the assignment, Robert needed to provide a *step-by-step* explanation of a process. And because he invented the term *videoholism,* Robert also needed to invent the stages in the progression of his addiction. During his prewriting, Robert discovered five stages in his videoholism: Presented *chronologically,* these stages provide the organizing focus for his paper. Specifically, each supporting paragraph is devoted to one stage, with the *topic sentence* for each paragraph indicating the stage's distinctive characteristics.

Transitions.   Although Robert's essay is playful, it is nonetheless a process analysis and so must have an easy-to-follow structure. Keeping this in mind,

Robert wisely includes *transitions* to signal what happened at each stage of his videoholism: "*Once* I had these additional tapes, I was free to record" (paragraph 3); "*Then*, in addition to my regular lineup, I began to record" (4); "*One day*, my mother came into my room" (5); and "*But after a while*, the urgent need to tape subsided" (6). In addition to such transitions, Robert also uses crisp questions to move from idea to idea within a paragraph: "How did I resolve this dilemma? Very easily. I . . . bought several more blank cassettes" (3), and "Where did I get time to watch all these tapes? I didn't" (4).

Combining patterns of development.   Even though Robert's essay is a process analysis, it contains elements of other patterns of development. For example, his paper is unified by an *analogy*—a sustained *comparison* between Robert's video addiction and the obviously more serious addiction to alcohol. Handled incorrectly, the analogy could have been offensive, but Robert makes the comparison work to his advantage. The analogy is stated specifically in several spots: "In these early days, my use of the VCR was the equivalent of light social drinking" (paragraph 2); "I was now using the VCR on a regular basis—the equivalent of several stiff drinks a day" (3). Another place where Robert touches wittily on the analogy occurs in the middle of the fourth paragraph: "I went out and bought two six-packs of blank tapes." To illustrate his progression toward videoholism, Robert depicts the *effects* of his addiction. Finally, he generates numerous lively details or *examples* to illustrate the different stages in his addiction.

Two unnecessary sentences.   Perhaps you noticed that Robert runs into a minor problem at the end of the fourth paragraph. Starting with the sentence "Reason and common sense were abandoned," he begins to ramble and repeat himself. The paragraph's last two sentences fail to add anything substantial. Take a moment to read paragraph 4 aloud, omitting the last two sentences. Note how much sharper the new conclusion is: "Where did I get time to watch all these tapes? I didn't. Taping at this point was more satisfying than watching." This new ending says all that needs to be said.

Revising the first draft.   When it was time to revise, Robert—in spite of his apprehension—showed his paper to his roommate and asked him to read it out loud. Robert knew this strategy would provide a more objective point of view on his work. His roommate, at first an unwilling recruit, nonetheless laughed as he read the essay aloud. That was just the response Robert wanted. But when his roommate got to the conclusion, Robert heard that the closing paragraph was flat and anticlimactic. Here is Robert's original conclusion.

Original Version of the Conclusion

I have no illusions, though, that I am over my videoholism. Soon I will be returning home for the holidays, which can be a time for excess taping. All I can do is ask my little sister to hide my blank tapes. After that, I will hope for the best.

Robert and his roommate brainstormed ways to make the conclusion livelier and more in spirit with the rest of the essay. They decided that the best approach would be to continue the playful, mock-serious tone that characterized earlier parts of the essay. Robert thus made three major changes in the conclusion. First, he tightened the first sentence of the paragraph ("I have no illusions, though, that I am over my videoholism"), making it crisper and more dramatic: "I have no illusions, though." Second, he added a few sentences to sustain the light, self-deprecating tone he had used earlier: "I know that once a videoholic, always a videoholic"; "But I will cope with the pressure"; "I will win the battle." Third, and perhaps most important, he returned to the alcoholism analogy: "I will take each day one at a time. . . . And if I feel myself succumbing to the temptations of taping, I will pick up the telephone and dial the videoholics' hotline. . . ."

These weren't the only changes Robert made while reworking his paper, but they give you some sense of how sensitive he was to the effect he wanted to achieve. Certainly, the recasting of the conclusion was critical to the overall success of this amusing essay.

ACTIVITIES: PROCESS ANALYSIS

Prewriting Activities

1. Imagine you're writing two essays: One *defines* the term "comparison shopping"; the other *contrasts* two different teaching styles. Jot down ways you might use process analysis in each essay.

2. Select *one* of the essay topics that follow and determine what your purpose, tone, and point of view would be for each audience indicated in parentheses. Then use brainstorming, questioning, mapping, or another prewriting technique to identify the points you'd cover for each audience. Finally, organize the raw material, noting the differences in emphasis and sequence for each group of readers.

   a. How to buy a car (*young people who have just gotten a driver's license; established professionals*)
   b. How children acquire their values (*first-time parents; elementary school teachers*)
   c. How to manage money (*grade-school children; college students*)
   d. How loans or scholarships are awarded to incoming students on your campus (*high school graduates applying for financial aid; high school guidance counselors*)

e. How arguments can strengthen relationships (*preteen children; young adults*)

f. How to relax (*college students; parents with young children*)

Revising Activities

3. Below is the brainstorming for a brief essay that describes the steps involved in making a telephone sales call. The paper has the following thesis: "Establishing rapport with customers is the most challenging and the most important part of phone sales." Revise the brainstormed material by deleting anything that undermines the paper's unity and organizing the steps in a logical sequence.

- Keep customers on the phone as long as possible to learn what they need
- The more you know about customers' needs the better
- The tone of the opening comments is very important
- Gently introduce the product
- Use a friendly tone in opening comments
- End on a friendly tone, too
- Don't introduce the product right away
- Growing rudeness in society. Some people hang up right away. Very upsetting.
- Try in a friendly way to keep the person on the phone
- Many people are so lonely they don't mind staying on the phone so they can talk to someone--anyone
- How sad that there's so much loneliness in the world
- Describe the product's advantages--price, convenience, installment plan
- If person is not interested, try in a friendly way to find out why
- Don't tell people that their reasons for not being interested are silly
- Don't push people if they're not interested
- Encourage credit card payment--the product will arrive earlier
- Explain payment--check, money order, or credit card payment

4. Reprinted here is a paragraph from the first draft of a humorous essay advising shy college students how to get through a typical day. Written as a process analysis, the paragraph outlines techniques for surviving class. Revise the paragraph, deleting digressions that disrupt the paragraph's unity, eliminating unnecessary repetition, and sequencing the steps in the proper order. Also correct inappropriate shifts in person and add transitions where needed. Feel free to add any telling details.

Simply attending class can be stressful for shy people. Several strategies, though, can lessen the trauma. Shy students should time their arrival to coincide with that of most other class members--about two minutes before the class is scheduled to begin. If you arrive too early, you may be seen sitting alone, or, even worse, may actually be forced to talk with another early arrival. If you arrive late, all eyes will be upon you. Before heading to class, the shy student should dress in the least conspicuous manner possible--say, in the blue jeans, sweatshirt, and sneakers that 99.9 percent of your classmates wear. That way you won't stand out from everyone else. Take a seat near the back of the room. Don't, however, sit at the very back since professors often take sadistic pleasure in calling on students back there, assuming they chose those seats because they didn't want to be called on. A friend of mine who is far from shy uses just the opposite ploy. In an attempt to get in good with her professors, she sits in the front row and, incredibly enough, volunteers to participate. However, since shy people don't want to call attention to themselves, they should stifle any urge to sneeze or cough. You run the risk of having people look at you or offer you a tissue or cough drop. And of course, never, ever volunteer to answer. Such a display of intelligence is sure to focus all eyes on you. In other words, make yourself as inconspicuous as possible. How, you might wonder, can you be inconspicuous if you're blessed (or cursed) with great looks? Well, . . . have you ever considered earning your degree through the mail?

Bill Bryson

Bill Bryson (1951–) has kept audiences on both sides of the Atlantic chuckling by exposing, in rollicking, down-to-earth fashion, the humor inherent in the world around him. A native of Iowa who resided in England for almost twenty years, Bryson earned fame as a columnist and best-selling author in England before returning to live with his wife and four children in Hanover, New Hampshire. Bryson's cross-cultural sensibility and talent for unearthing the absurd are apparent in his books on language, including *The Mother Tongue* (1990), and in his travel writing, including *In a Sunburned Country* (2000) and *A Walk in the Woods*, his best-selling 1998 account of a hike along the Appalachian trail. Most recently, he tackled explaining the history of the universe up to the present in *A Short History of Nearly Everything* (2003). The following selection first appeared in *I'm a Stranger Here Myself: Notes on Returning to America After 20 Years Away* (1999).

Pre-Reading Journal Entry

Like most people, you've probably found that today's sophisticated technologies often complicate life, rather than making it easier. Take a moment to list in your journal some of the technologies that have added stress to your life. Under each technology, jot down some specifics about the problems you've experienced.

Your New Computer

Congratulations. You have purchased an Edsel[1]/2000 Multimedia 615X 1 Personal Computer with Digital Doo-Dah Enhancer. It will give years of faithful service, if you ever get it up and running. Also included with your PC is a bonus pack of preinstalled software—Lawn Mowing Planner, Mr. Arty-Farty, Blank Screen Saver, and Antarctica Route Finder—which will provide hours of pointless diversion while using up most of your computer's spare memory.

So turn the page and let's get started! 2

Getting Ready

Congratulations. You have successfully turned the page and are ready to 3 proceed.

[1]Short-lived automobile (produced for only three model years, from 1958–1960), built by Ford Motors and named after Henry Ford's son. Its demise owed to the general perception that it was poorly designed and engineered—essentially, a "lemon" (editors' note).

Important meaningless note: The Edsel/2000 is configured to use   4
80386, 214J10, or higher processors running at 2472 Herz on variable
speed spin cycle. Check your electrical installations and insurance policies
before proceeding. Do not machine wash.

To prevent internal heat buildup, select a cool, dry environment for your   5
computer. The bottom shelf of the refrigerator is ideal.

Unpack the box and examine its contents. (Warning: Do not open box if   6
contents are missing or faulty, as this will invalidate your warranty. Return all
missing contents in their original packaging with a note explaining where they
have gone and a replacement will be sent within twelve working months.)

The contents of the box should include some of the following: monitor   7
with mysterious De Gauss[2] button; keyboard; computer unit; miscellaneous
wires and cables not necessarily designed for this model; 2,000-page Owner's
Manual; Short Guide to the Owner's Manual; Quick Guide to the Short
Guide to the Owner's Manual; Laminated Super-Kwik Set-Up Guide for People Who Are Exceptionally Impatient or Stupid; 1,167 pages of warranties,
vouchers, notices in Spanish, and other loose pieces of paper; 292 cubic feet
of Styrofoam packing material.

Something They Didn't Tell You at the Store

Because of the additional power needs of the preinstalled bonus software,   8
you will need to acquire an Edsel/2000 auxiliary software upgrade pack, a
900-volt memory capacitator for the auxiliary software pack, a 50-megaherz
oscillator unit for the memory capacitator, 2,500 mega-gigabytes of additional memory for the oscillator, and an electrical substation.

Setting Up

Congratulations. You are ready to set up. If you have not yet acquired a   9
degree in electrical engineering, now is the time to do so.

Connect the monitor cable (A) to the portside outlet unit (D); attach   10
power offload unit suborbiter (Xii) to the coaxial AC/DC servo channel (G);
plug three-pin mouse cable into keyboard housing unit (make extra hole if
necessary); connect modem (B2) to offside parallel audio/video lineout jack.
Alternatively, plug the cables into the most likely looking holes, switch on,
and see what happens.

Additional important meaningless note: The wires in the ampule modu-   11
lator unit are marked as follows according to international convention: blue
= neutral or live; yellow = live or blue; blue and live = neutral and green;
black = instant death. (Except where prohibited by law.)

---

[2]Refers to neutralizing a magnetic field (something a computer owner would not want to happen to a hard drive) (editors' note).

Switch the computer on. Your hard drive will automatically download. 12
(Allow three to five days.) When downloading is complete, your screen will
say: "Yeah, what?"

Now it is time to install your software. Insert Disc A (marked "Disk D" 13
or "Disk G") into Drive Slot B or J, and type "Hello! Anybody home?" At
the DOS command prompt, enter you License Verification Number. Your
License Verification Number can be found by entering your Certified User
Number, which can be found by entering your License Verification Number.
If you are unable to find your License Verification or Certified User numbers, call the Software Support Line for assistance. (Please have your License
Verification and Certified User numbers handy as the support staff cannot
otherwise assist you.)

If you have not yet committed suicide, then insert Installation Diskette 1 14
in drive slot 2 (or vice versa) and follow the instructions on your screen.
(Note: Owing to a software modification, some instructions will appear in
Turkish.) At each prompt, reconfigure the specified file path, double-click on
the button launch icon, select a single equation default file from the macro
selection register, insert the VGA graphics card in the rear aerofoil, and type
"C:\>" followed by the birthdates of all the people you have ever known.

Your screen will now say: "Invalid file path. Whoa! Abort or continue?" 15
Warning: Selecting "Continue" may result in irreversible file compression and
a default overload in the hard drive. Selecting "Abort," on the other hand,
will require you to start the installation process all over again. Your choice.

When the smoke has cleared, insert disc A2 (marked "Disc A1") and 16
repeat as directed with each of the 187 other discs.

When installation is complete, return to file path, and type your name, 17
address, and credit card numbers and press "SEND." This will automatically
register you for our free software prize, "Blank Screensaver IV: Nighttime in
Deep Space," and allow us to pass your name to lots and lots of computer
magazines, online services, and other commercial enterprises, who will be
getting in touch shortly.

Congratulations. You are now ready to use your computer. Here are 18
some simple exercises to get you off to a flying start.

Writing a Letter

Type "Dear ——" and follow it with a name of someone you know. 19
Write a few lines about yourself, and then write, "Sincerely yours" followed
by your own name. Congratulations.

Saving a File

To save your letter, select File Menu. Choose Retrieve from Sub- 20
Directory A, enter a backup file number, and place an insertion point beside

the macro dialogue button. Select secondary text box from the merge menu, and double-click on the supplementary cleared document window. Assign the tile cascade to a merge file and insert in a text equation box. Alternatively, write the letter out in longhand and put it in a drawer.

Advice on Using the Spreadsheet Facility

Don't.   21

Troubleshooting Section

You will have many, many problems with your computer. Here are some   22
common problems and their solutions.

Problem: My computer won't turn on.   23
Solution: Check to make sure the computer is plugged in; check to make   24
sure the power button is in the ON position; check the cables for damage;
dig up underground cables in your yard and check for damage; drive out into
country and check electricity pylons for signs of fallen wires; call hotline.

Problem: My keyboard doesn't seem to have any keys.   25
Solution: Turn the keyboard the right way up.   26

Problem: My mouse won't drink its water or go on the spinning wheel.   27
Solution: Try a high-protein diet or call your pet shop support line.   28

Problem: I keep getting a message saying: "Non-System General Protection 29
Fault."
Solution: This is probably because you are trying to use the computer.   30
Switch the computer to OFF mode and any annoying messages will disappear.

Problem: My computer is a piece of useless junk.   31
Correct—and congratulations. You are now ready to upgrade to an   32
Edsel/3000 Turbo model, or go back to pen and paper.

Questions for Close Reading

1. What is the selection's thesis? Locate the sentence(s) in which Bryson states his main idea. If he doesn't state the thesis explicitly, express it in your own words.
2. Paragraphs 6 and 13 target a similar flaw in computer manuals. What unfortunate tendency do the paragraphs ridicule?
3. Using humor to make a serious point, in paragraph 8 Bryson levels a not-so-funny charge against computer manufacturers. What accusation does he make? What support for this accusation does he provide?
4. Which Edsel model does Bryson cite at the beginning of the essay? Which does he refer to at the end? In what way do these two references reinforce Bryson's thesis?
5. Refer to your dictionary as needed to define the following words used in the selection: *diversion* (paragraph 1), *configured* (4), *invalidate* (6), *miscellaneous* (7), *auxiliary* (8), *convention* (11), and *pylons* (24).

Questions About the Writer's Craft

1. **The pattern.** Is Bryson's process analysis *directional* or *informational* (see pages 218–219)? How do you know? What *purpose* (see page 217) do you think Bryson had in mind when writing the piece? Explain.
2. Although Bryson voices serious complaints about computers, their manufacturers, and computer manuals, he uses wry humor to do so. Why do you think Bryson uses humor rather than angry accusation to voice his grievances?
3. Bryson's essay is a *parody;* it mimics and ridicules the instructional manuals that come with computers. How does Bryson's use of subheads contribute to the effectiveness of his parody?
4. Bryson repeats the word "Congratulations" several times in the essay. Identify each place the word appears. What effect do you think Bryson hoped this word would have each time he used it?

Writing Assignments Using Process Analysis as a Pattern of Development

1. With lightly barbed humor, Bryson shows how needlessly frustrating it can be to set up a computer. Write a humorous essay of your own explaining to the uninitiated how to do something that is supposedly easy but in practice is unnecessarily complicated. You might explain how to correct an erroneous credit card charge, how to apply for a scholarship or loan, how to register for classes, and so on. Like Bryson, devise several tongue-in-cheek headings that convey your attitude about the absurd complexities of the process. To see how another writer uses humor and/or irony in a how-to piece, read Clifford Stoll's "Cyberschool" (page 239).

2. In his essay, Bryson ironically suggests actions that in reality should *not* be done in order to get a computer functioning—for example, typing "the birthdates of all the people you have ever known" (paragraph 14). Taking a similarly ironic stance, write your own how-*not*-to guide to doing something. You could, for example, explain how *not* to get a raise, how *not* to pass a college course, how *not* to pass a driver's test. Adopt whatever tone you wish, though a lighthearted one seems particularly appropriate for this essay. For another model of a how-*not*-to guide, see Clifford Stoll's "Cyberschool" (page 239).

Writing Assignments Combining Patterns of Development

3. Write an essay exploring the *impact* that a relatively recent technological development has had on your life. You might focus on ATMs, answering machines, cell phones, beepers, or satellite television. To *illustrate* how this technology has *affected* you personally, *contrast* your life *before* and *after* the introduction of the innovation. Your essay may have a serious or a lighthearted tone. Before you begin writing, consider reading Jay Walljasper's "Our Schedules, Our Selves" (page 311) an essay exploring technology's impact on daily life.

4. Bryson uses humor to express his frustration with computers. But some people don't regard computers with amusement; they are upset about threats posed by computer technology. Brainstorm with others to identify some of the concerns

people have about computers. They may, for example, be disturbed about unauthorized access to computerized personal information or about children's exposure to Internet pornography. Review your brainstormed material and select *one category* of concern that seems especially compelling. Also consider doing some library and/or Internet research to gain further insight into the issue. Then write an essay in which you provide dramatic *examples* to illustrate the validity of people's concerns. End by briefly describing steps that could be taken to minimize these problems.

Writing Assignment Using a Journal Entry as a Starting Point

5. Write an essay showing how technologies that are supposed to make life easier actually create stress. Review your pre-reading journal entry, selecting one or two technologies to write about. Draw upon the material in your journal as well as discussions with other people about their frustrating encounters with today's technologies. Your essay may have a serious or a lighthearted tone.

Clifford Stoll

An astronomer at the University of California at Berkeley, Clifford Stoll (1950–) is also a lecturer, commentator on MSNBC, and occasional visiting teacher of astronomy in elementary, middle, and high schools. He is the best-selling author of *The Cuckoo's Egg: Tracking a Spy Through the Maze of Computer Espionage* (1990) and *Silicon Snake Oil: Second Thoughts on the Information Superhighway* (1995), both of which address the complications of the computer age. As he reveals in the preface of *High-Tech Heretic: Reflections of a Computer Contrarian* (1999), despite having programmed and used computers since the mid-sixties, Stoll seeks to inject "a few notes of skepticism into the utopian dreams of a digital wonderland." According to his website, he is a "stay-at-home daddy" who lives with his family in the San Francisco Bay Area. The following essay appears as a chapter in *High-Tech Heretic.*

Pre-Reading Journal Entry

Over the past several years, the Internet has become increasingly popular as an educational resource. What do you think are the merits and the drawbacks of including the Internet as part of school assignments? Is your response affected by the age of the students in question? Record in your journal the pros and cons of requiring students—at the elementary, high school, and college levels, respectively—to access the Net as part of their studies.

Cyberschool

Welcome to the classroom of the future! Complete with electronic links to the world, it'll revolutionize education. Students will interact with information infrastructures and knowledge processors to learn group work and telework, whatever that means. You'll be enriched, empowered, and enabled by the digital classroom; immersed in an optimal learning environment. Yee-ha! 1

Worried that things rarely turn out as promised? Well, let me present a pessimal[1] view of the schoolroom of the future. 2

Suppose you're a harried school board member. Voters complain about high taxes. Teachers' unions strike for higher wages and smaller classes. Parents worry about plummeting scores on standardized tests. Newspapers criticize backward teaching methods, outdated textbooks, and security problems. Unruly students cut classes and rarely pay attention. Instructors teach topics which aren't in the curriculum or, worse, inject their own opinions into subject matter. 3

---

[1]The opposite of optimal?

Sound like a tough call? Naw—it's easy to solve all these problems, pla-   4
cate the taxpayers, and get re-elected. High technology!

First, the school district buys a computer for every student. Sure, this'll   5
set back the budget—maybe a few hundred dollars per student. Quantity dis-
counts and corporate support should keep the price down, and classroom savings will more than offset the cost of the equipment.

Next buy a pile of CD-ROMs for the students, each preprogrammed   6
with fun edutainment[2] programs. The educational games will exactly cover
the curriculum . . . for every paragraph in the syllabus, the game will have an
interactive aspect. As students climb to more advanced levels, the game naturally becomes more challenging and rewarding. But always fun.

Every student will work at her own pace. The youngest will watch happy   7
cartoon characters and exciting animations. The kid that likes horses will listen to messages from a chatty pony; the child that dreams of fire engines will
hear from Fred the Firefighter. High schoolers get multimedia images of film
stars and rock and roll celebrities. With access to interactive video sessions,
chat rooms, and e-mail, students can collaborate with each other. It's the ultimate in individualized, child-centered instruction.

Naturally, the edu-games will be programmed so that students become   8
adept at standardized tests. No reason to teach anything that's not on the
ACT, PSAT, or SAT exams. And the students will have fun because all this
information will be built into games like Myst, Dungeon, or Doom. They'll
master the games, and automatically learn the material.

Meanwhile, the computers will keep score, like pinball machines. They'll   9
send e-mail to parents and administrators . . . scores that will become part of
each kid's permanent record. No more subjectivity in grading: The principal
will know instantly how each child's doing. And if a student gets confused
or falls behind, automated help will be just a mouse click away.

We'll update crowded classrooms, too. Replace desks with individual   10
cubicles, comfortable chairs, and multimedia monitors. With no outside
interruptions, kids' attention will be directed into the approved creative
learning experiences, built into the software. Well compartmentalized, students will hardly ever see other . . . neatly ending classroom discipline
problems.

Naturally, teachers are an unnecessary appendix at this cyberschool. No   11
need for 'em when there's a fun, multimedia system at each student's finger-
tips. Should students have a question, they can turn to the latest on-line
encyclopedia, enter an electronic chat room, or send e-mail to a professional educator. Those laid-off teachers can be retrained as data entry clerks.

As librarians and teachers become irrelevant, they'll be replaced by a   12
cadre of instructional specialists, consultants, and professional hall monitors.

[2]A term, coined by Stoll, combining the words *education* and *entertainment* (editors' note).

Any discipline problems could be handled by trained security guards, who'd monitor the cubicles via remote video links.

Effect? With no more wasted time on student-teacher interactions or off-topic discussions, education will become more efficient. Since the computers' content would be directed at maximizing test performance, standardized test scores will zoom.   13

Eliminating teachers and luxuries such as art lessons and field trips will save enough to recoup the cost of those fancy computers. With little effort, this electronic education could even become a profit center. Merely sell advertising space in the edutainment programs. Corporate sponsors, eager to market their messages to impressionable minds, would pay school systems to plug their products within the coursework.   14

Concerned that such a system might be dehumanizing? Not to worry. Interactive chat sessions will encourage a sense of community and enhance kids' social skills. Should a student have questions, the Internet will put her in instant touch with a trained support mentor. When necessary, real-time instructors will appear on the distance learning displays, available to interact via two-way video.   15

The Cyberschool will showcase technology and train students for the upcoming electronic workplace. As local employment prospects change, the school board will issue updates to the curriculum over its interactive website. And the school board will monitor what each student learns—without idiosyncratic teachers to raise unpopular topics or challenge accepted beliefs.   16

Advanced students can sign up for on-line extracurricular activities—perhaps joining the Virtual Compassion Corps. There, students will be paired up across racial, gender, and class lines. Our children would offer foreigners advice and even arrange interviews with prospective employers. In this way, students will perform community service and mentor others, while displaying their cultural awareness over the network. All without ever having to shake hands with a real person, travel to a distant country, or (gasp!) face the real problems of another culture.[3] Simple, safe, and sterile.   17

Should parents worry about Johnny's progress, they need only log in over the Internet to see their son's latest test scores. In addition, they'll receive e-mailed reports summarizing their child's work. And at any time, they can click on an icon to see live images of their young scholar, automatically uploaded by a school video camera.   18

Yep, just sign up for the future: the parent-pleasin', tax-savin', teacher-firin', interactive-educatin', child-centerin' Cyberschool. No stuffy classrooms. No more teacher strikes. No outdated textbooks. No expensive   19

[3]An actual proposal from the director of MIT's Laboratory for Computer Science, Michael Dertouzos.

clarinet lessons. No boring homework. No learning. Coming soon to a
school district near you.[4]

---

[4]Idea for a computer game: Cyberschool Superintendent. Players score by saving money. They
could eliminate teachers, close libraries, or blow up music studios. Competitors advance by
wiring schools, adding computers, and plugging in multimedia systems. Evil monstors might
appear in the form of teachers, scholars, and librarians who insist that you read a book. Bonus
points, labeled Pilot Project Grants, would be awarded for writing vapid press releases.

Questions for Close Reading

1. What is the selection's thesis? Locate the sentence(s) in which Stoll states his main
   idea. If he doesn't state the thesis explicitly, express it in your own words.
2. What process does Stoll describe in the essay? What are the basic steps of this
   process? What is Stoll's underlying attitude toward these measures?
3. What specific group of people does Stoll imagine as being especially in favor of the
   "cyberschool"? According to Stoll, how do these individuals justify using computers to teach children?
4. What role does Stoll indicate teachers will play in the "cyberschool"? What attitude does he convey about this role? Explain.
5. Refer to your dictionary as needed to define the following words used in the selection: *infrastructures* (paragraph 1), *optimal* (1), *harried* (3), *placate* (4), *adept* (8),
   standardized (8), *cubicles* (10), *compartmentalized* (10), *cadre* (12), *recoup* (14),
   and *idiosyncratic* (16).

Questions About the Writer's Craft

1. **The pattern.** Is Stoll's process analysis primarily directional or primarily informational? Explain. To what extent does Stoll try to persuade readers that the
   process he describes should be followed?
2. Focusing on his word choices, how would you characterize Stoll's tone in his
   essay? In your opinion, does his tone enhance or detract from the point he's trying
   to make? Explain.
3. **Other patterns.** Underlying Stoll's process analysis is an *argument* against a particular form of education. To write an effective argument, writers need to establish
   their own credibility. Based on what you learned about Stoll in his biography
   (page 239), what makes him appear qualified to write about his subject?
4. **Other patterns.** In his persona of pro-cyberschool spokesman, Stoll addresses
   opposition to idea of the cyberschool in paragraph 15. How does Stoll represent
   and rebut the *arguments* against the cyberschool? Are his arguments effective, in
   your opinion?

Writing Assignments Using Process-Analysis as a Pattern of Development

1. In his essay, Stoll offers a cynical recipe for creating an "optimal learning environment." Write an essay in which you present a process analysis of concrete ways the

school you currently attend or one you have attended in the past could realistically be improved. You might, for instance, discuss physical improvements such as updating the equipment in the computer lab, or less tangible measures such as cultivating a more interactive classroom environment. Brainstorm on your own or with others to generate specific ideas to include in your process.

2. In his essay, Stoll ironically suggests a course of action that he implies should not be taken in order to improve children's education. Taking a similarly ironic stance, write an essay *mis*guiding readers on how to "improve" some other significant institution or serious condition. For instance, you might discuss ways to increase the efficiency of a particular government agency, how to even out inequities between classes or races of people, how to protect the environment, and so on—all the while presenting steps that would work to the contrary. Like Stoll, you should ultimately reveal your true position in the concluding paragraph, preferably in a subtle way. You should consider reading Bill Bryson's "Your New Computer" (page 233) to see how another writer recommends a course of action that is antithetical to what he initially seems to advocate.

Writing Assignments Combining Patterns of Development

3. According to Stoll, computers serve as a distraction to students rather than a legitimate learning tool. What are other kinds of distractions students face? Write an essay in which you *classify* the different types of distractions that can make learning difficult. You may adopt a serious tone and address categories such as, for example, problems at home and pressure from peers. Or you might adopt a humorous tone and discuss distractions that include interest in the opposite sex and the temptation of computer games. Provide vivid *examples* to illustrate each of the categories you create. For an additional viewpoint about the pressures to which students are subject, read Joseph H. Suina's "And Then I Went to School" (page 271).

4. With the increasing popularity of the Internet, the future of traditional printed materials—such as books, magazines, and newspapers—has come into question. Write an essay in which you *compare* and *contrast* using printed materials with using the Internet in order to perform research. Be sure to provide at least one extended example or a few briefer examples to *illustrate* the differences and/or similarities you're pointing out. Your best source of information might be a "hands-on" approach: to research a topic using both methods in order to see for yourself what the differences are. By the end of your essay, make clear to your reader which of the two methods you find preferable, and why.

Writing Assignment Using a Journal Entry as a Starting Point

5. In an indirect way, Stoll argues against the wholesale computerization of the classroom. Write an essay in which you argue that the Internet in specific should *or* should not play a significant role in the education of *one* particular age group of students (elementary, high school, or college). In formulating your argument,

refer to the material you generated in your pre-reading journal entry. For additional perspectives on this issue, you might consider doing some research on this topic in the library and/or on the Internet. In writing your essay, you should acknowledge and rebut opposing points of view.

Caroline Rego

Caroline Rego was born in 1950 in Edmond, Oklahoma. A graduate of the University of Oklahoma, she began her journalistic career as a police reporter for a daily newspaper in Montana. Later, while filling in for a vacationing colleague in the features section of another newspaper, she found her true calling: writing consumer-affairs articles that teach readers how to protect themselves against shoddy service, dangerous products, and inefficiency. A sought-after public speaker, Rego talks frequently to students and community groups on strategies for becoming an informed consumer. The following selection is part of a work in progress on consumer empowerment.

Pre-Reading Journal Entry

When you're disappointed with someone or something, how do you typically react—passively, assertively, or in some other way? In your journal, list a few disappointments you've experienced. How did you respond on each occasion? In retrospect, are you happy with your responses? Why or why not?

The Fine Art of Complaining

You waited forty-five minutes for your dinner, and when it came it was 1
cold—and not what you ordered in the first place. You washed your supposedly machine-washable, preshrunk T-shirt (the one the catalogue claimed was "indestructible"), and now it's the size of a napkin. Your new car broke down a month after you bought it, and the dealer says the warranty doesn't apply.

Life's annoyances descend on all of us—some pattering down like gen- 2
tle raindrops, others striking with the bruising force of hailstones. We dodge the ones we can, but inevitably, plenty of them make contact. And when they do, we react fairly predictably. Many of us—most of us, probably—grumble to ourselves and take it. We scowl at our unappetizing food but choke it down. We stash the shrunken T-shirt in a drawer, vowing never again to order from a catalogue. We glare fiercely at our checkbooks as we pay for repairs that should have been free.

A few of us go to the other extreme. Taking our cue from the crazed 3
newscaster in the 1976 movie *Network,* we go through life mad as hell and unwilling to take it anymore. In offices, we shout at hapless receptionists when we're kept waiting for appointments. In restaurants, we make scenes that have fellow patrons craning their necks to get a look at us. In stores, we argue with salespeople for not waiting on us. We may notice after a while that our friends seem reluctant to venture into public with us, but hey—we're just standing up for our rights. Being a patsy doesn't get you anywhere in life.

It's true—milquetoasts live unsatisfying lives. However, people who go   4
through the day in an eye-popping, vein-throbbing state of apoplectic rage
don't win any prizes either. What persons at both ends of the scale need—
what could empower the silent sufferer and civilize the Neanderthal—is a
course in the gentle art of *effective* complaining.

Effective complaining is not apologetic and half-hearted. It's not mak-   5
ing one awkward attempt at protest—"Uh, excuse me, I don't think I
ordered the squid and onions"—and then slinking away in defeat. But neither is it roaring away indiscriminately, attempting to get satisfaction through
the sheer volume of our complaint.

Effective complainers are people who act businesslike and important.   6
Acting important doesn't mean puffing up your chest and saying, "Do you
know who I am?"—an approach that would tempt anyone to take you down
a peg or two. It doesn't mean shouting and threatening—techniques that
will only antagonize the person whose help you need. It *does* mean making
it clear that you know your request is reasonable and that you are confident
it will be taken care of. People are generally treated the way they expect to
be treated. If you act like someone making a fair request, chances are that
request will be granted. Don't beg, don't explain. Just state your name, the
problem, and what you expect to have done. Remain polite. But be firm.
"My car has been in your garage for three days, and a mechanic hasn't even
looked at it yet," you might say. "I want to know when it is going to be
worked on." Period. Now it is up to them to give you a satisfactory response.
Don't say, "Sorry to bother you about this, but . . ." or "I, uh, was sort of
expecting. . . ." You're only asking people to remedy a problem, after all; that
is not grounds for apology.

If your problem requires an immediate response, try to make your   7
complaint in person; a real, live, in-the-flesh individual has to be dealt with
in some way. Complaining over the telephone, by contrast, is much less
effective. When you speak to a disembodied voice, when the person at the
other end of the line doesn't have to face you, you're more likely to get a
runaround.

Most importantly, complain to the right person. One of the greatest   8
frustrations in complaining is talking to a clerk or receptionist who cannot
solve your problem and whose only purpose seems to be to drive you crazy.
Getting mad doesn't help; the person you're mad at probably had nothing
to do with your actual problem. And you'll have to repeat everything you've
said to the clerk once you're passed along to the appropriate person. So make
sure from the start that you're talking to someone who can help—a manager or supervisor.

If your problem doesn't require an immediate response, complaining by   9
letter is probably the most effective way to get what you want. A letter of
complaint should be brief, businesslike, and to the point. If you have a new
vacuum cleaner that doesn't work, don't spend a paragraph describing how

your Uncle Joe tried to fix the problem and couldn't. As when complaining in person, be sure you address someone in a position of real authority. Here's an example of an effective letter of complaint.

Ms. Anne Lublin   10
Manager
Mitchell Appliances
80 Front Street
Newton, MA 02159

Dear Ms. Lublin: 11

First section: Explain the problem. Include facts to back up your story.   12

On August 6, I purchased a new Perma-Kool freezer from your store (a copy of   13
my sales receipt is enclosed). In the two weeks I have owned the freezer, I have
had to call your repair department three times in an attempt to get it running
properly. The freezer ran normally when it was installed, but since then it has
repeatedly turned off, causing the food inside to spoil. My calls to your repair
department have not been responded to promptly. After I called the first time, on
August 10, I waited two days for the repair person to show up. It took three days
to get a repair person here after my second call, on August 15. The freezer
stopped yet again on August 20. I called to discuss this recent problem, but no
one has responded to my call.

Second section: Tell how you trust the company and are confident that your   14
reader will fix the problem. This is to "soften up" the reader a bit.

I am surprised to receive such unprofessional service and poor quality from Mitchell   15
Appliances since I have been one of your satisfied customers for fifteen years. In
the past, I have purchased a television, air conditioner, and washing machine
from your company. I know that you value good relations with your customers,
and I'm sure you want to see me pleased with my most recent purchase.

Third section: Explain exactly what you want to be done—repair, replacement,   16
refund, etc.

Although your repair department initially thought that the freezer needed only   17
some minor adjustments, the fact that no one has been able to permanently fix
the problem convinces me that the freezer has some serious defect. I am
understandably unwilling to spend any more time having repairs made.
Therefore, I expect you to exchange the freezer for an identical model by the end
of this week (August 30). Please call me to arrange for the removal of the
defective freezer and the delivery of the new one.

Sincerely,   18

Janice Becker

P.S. (Readers always notice a P.S.) State again when you expect the problem to　19
be taken care of, and what you will do if it isn't.

P.S. I am confident that we can resolve this problem by August 30. If the　20
defective freezer is not replaced by then, however, I will report this incident to
the Better Business Bureau.

Notice that the P.S. says what you'll do if your problem isn't solved. In other　21
words, you make a threat—a polite threat. Your threat must be reasonable
and believable. A threat to burn down the store if your purchase price isn't
refunded is neither reasonable nor believable—or if it *were* believed, you
could end up in jail. A threat to report the store to a consumer-protection
agency, such as the Better Business Bureau, however, is credible.

　　Don't be too quick to make one of the most common—and commonly　22
empty—threats: "I'll sue!" A full-blown lawsuit is more trouble, and more
expensive, than most problems are worth. On the other hand, most areas
have a small-claims court where suits involving modest amounts of money
are heard. These courts don't use complex legal language or procedures, and
you don't need a lawyer to use them. A store or company will often settle
with you—if your claim is fair—rather than go to small-claims court.

　　Whether you complain over the phone, in person, or by letter, be persis-　23
tent. One complaint may not get results. In that case, keep on complaining,
and make sure you keep complaining to the same person. Chances are he or
she will get worn out and take care of the situation, if only to be rid of you.

　　Someday, perhaps, the world will be free of the petty annoyances that　24
plague us all from time to time. Until then, however, toasters will break
down, stores will refuse to honor rainchecks, and bills will include items that
were never purchased. You can depend upon it—there will be grounds for
complaint. You might as well learn to be good at it.

Questions for Close Reading

1. What is the selection's thesis? Locate the sentence(s) in which Rego states her main idea. If she doesn't state the thesis explicitly, express it in your own words.
2. In Rego's opinion, what types of actions and statements are *not* helpful when making a complaint?
3. What should be included in a letter of complaint? What should be omitted?
4. What does Rego suggest doing if a complaint is ignored?
5. Refer to your dictionary as needed to define the following words used in the selection: *hapless* (paragraph 3), *venture* (3), *patsy* (3), *milquetoasts* (4), *apoplectic* (4), *Neanderthal* (4), *indiscriminately* (5), *disembodied* (7), and *credible* (21).

Questions About the Writer's Craft

1. **The pattern.** Is Rego's process analysis primarily directional or primarily informational? Explain. To what extent does Rego try to persuade readers to follow her process?

2. **Other patterns.** Where does Rego include *narrative* elements in her essay? What do these brief narratives add to the piece?

3. **Other patterns.**   Numerous oppositions occur throughout the essay. How do these *contrasts* enliven the essay and help Rego persuade readers to adopt her suggestions?

4. Reread the essay, noting where Rego shifts point of view. Where does she use the second-person (*you*), the first-person-plural (*we*), and the third-person-plural (*they*) points of view? How does her use of multiple points of view add to the essay's effectiveness?

Writing Assignments Using Process Analysis as a Pattern of Development

1. Write an essay explaining to college students how to register—with someone in a position of authority—an effective complaint about a campus problem. You could show, for example, how to complain to a professor about a course's grading policy, to the bookstore manager about the markup on textbooks, to security about the poorly maintained college parking lots. Feel free to adapt some of Rego's recommendations, but be sure to invent several strategies of your own. In either case, provide—as Rego does—lively examples to illustrate the step-by-step procedure for registering an effective complaint with a specific authority figure on campus.

2. Rego argues that "people who go through the day in an eye-popping, vein-throbbing state of apoplectic rage don't win any prizes." But sometimes, getting mad can be appropriate—even productive. Write an essay explaining the best process for expressing anger effectively. Explain how to vent emotion safely, communicate the complaint in a nonthreatening way, encourage more honest interaction, and prompt change for the better. Illustrate the process by drawing upon your own experiences and observations. Consider reading Barbara Ehrenreich's "What I've Learned From Men" (page 166), which provides some insight into the dynamics of anger and resentment.

Writing Assignments Combining Patterns of Development

3. Think about a service or product that failed to live up to your expectations. Perhaps you were disgruntled about your mechanic's car repair, a store's return policy, or a hotel's accommodations. Using Rego's suggestions, write a letter of complaint in which you *describe* the problem, convey confidence in the reader's ability to resolve the problem, and state your request for specific action. Remember that a firm but cordial tone will *persuade* your reader that you have legitimate grounds for seeking the resolution you propose.

4. Rego shows that events often don't turn out as we had hoped. In an essay, *contrast* how you thought a specific situation would be with the way it actually turned out. Was the unexpected outcome better or worse than what you had expected? Did you have trouble adjusting, or did you adapt with surprising ease? Provide vivid *specifics* about the unforeseen turn of events and your *reaction* to it. Before writing, you might read Gary Soto's "The Jacket" (page 91), a professional writer's account of an experience that dramatically departed from his expectations.

Writing Assignment Using a Journal
Entry as a Starting Point

∞ 5. Write an essay contrasting the way you reacted to a specific disappointment with the way you wish you had reacted. Reread your pre-reading journal entry, and select *one* incident that illustrates this discrepancy most dramatically. Use vigorous narrative details to make the contrast vivid and real. In your conclusion, indicate what you've learned in hindsight. Before writing, consider reading three other essays that document personal reactions to life's minor—and major—calamities: Langston Hughes's "Salvation" (page 124), Adam Mayblum's "The Price We Pay" (page 128), and Beth Johnson's "Bombs Bursting in Air" (page 160).

Additional Writing Topics

PROCESS ANALYSIS

General Assignments

Develop one of the following topics through process analysis. Explain the process one step at a time, organizing the steps chronologically. If there's no agreed-on sequence, design your own series of steps. Use transitions to ease the audience through the steps in the process. You may use any tone you wish, from serious to light.

Directional: How to Do Something

1. How to improve a course you have taken
2. How to drive defensively
3. How to get away with _____
4. How to succeed at a job interview
5. How to relax
6. How to show appreciation to others
7. How to get through school despite personal problems
8. How to be a responsible pet owner
9. How to conduct a garage or yard sale
10. How to look fashionable on a limited budget
11. How to protect a home from burglars
12. How to meet more people
13. How to improve the place where you work
14. How to gain or lose weight
15. How to get over a disappointment

Informational: How Something Happens

1. How a student becomes burned out
2. How a library's card catalog or computerized catalog organizes books
3. How a dead thing decays (or how some other natural process works)
4. How the college registration process works
5. How *Homo sapiens* chooses a mate
6. How a VCR (or some other machine) works
7. How a bad habit develops
8. How people fall into debt
9. How someone becomes an Internet addict/junkie
10. How a child develops a love of reading

Assignments With a Specific Purpose, Audience, and Point of View

On Campus

1. As an experienced campus tour guide for prospective students, you've been asked by your school's Admissions Office to write a pamphlet explaining to new tour

guides how to conduct a tour of your school's campus. When explaining the process, keep in mind that tour guides need to portray the school in its best light.

2. You write an "advice to the lovelorn" column for the campus newspaper. A correspondent writes saying that he or she wants to break up with a steady girlfriend/boyfriend but doesn't know how to do this without hurting the person. Give the writer guidance on how to end a meaningful relationship with a minimal amount of pain.

At Home or in the Community

3. To help a sixteen-year-old friend learn how to drive, explain a specific driving maneuver one step at a time. You might, for example, describe how to make a three-point turn, parallel park, or handle a skid. Remember, your friend lacks self-confidence and experience.

4. Your best friend plans to move into his or her own apartment but doesn't know the first thing about how to choose one. Explain the process of selecting an apartment—where to look, what to investigate, what questions to ask before signing a lease.

On the Job

5. As a staff writer for a consumer magazine, you've been asked to write an article on how to shop for a certain product. Give specific steps explaining how to save money, buy a quality product, and the like.

6. An author of books for elementary school children, you want to show children how to do something—take care of a pet, get along with siblings, keep a room clean. Explain the process in terms a child would understand yet not find condescending.

8

COMPARISON-CONTRAST

WHAT IS COMPARISON-CONTRAST?

We frequently try to make sense of the world by finding similarities and differences in our experiences. Seeing how things are alike (comparing) and seeing how they are different (contrasting) helps us impose meaning on experiences that otherwise might remain fragmented and disconnected. Barely aware of the fact that we're comparing and contrasting, we may think to ourselves, "I woke up in a great mood this morning, but now I feel uneasy and anxious. I wonder why I feel so different." This inner questioning, which often occurs in a flash, is just one example of the way we use comparison and contrast to understand ourselves and our world.

Comparing and contrasting also helps us make choices. We compare and contrast everything—from two brands of soap we might buy to two colleges we might attend. We listen to a favorite radio station, watch a preferred nightly news show, select a particular dessert from a menu—all because we have done some degree of comparing and contrasting. We often weigh these alternatives in an unstudied, casual manner, as when we flip from one radio station to another. But when we have to make important decisions, we tend to think rigorously about how things are alike or different: Should I live in a dorm or rent an apartment? Should I accept the higher-paying job or the lower-paying one that offers more challenges? Such a deliberate approach to comparison-contrast may also provide us with needed insight into complex contemporary issues: Is television's coverage of political campaigns more or less objective than it used to be? What are the merits of the various positions on abortion?

HOW COMPARISON-CONTRAST FITS YOUR PURPOSE AND AUDIENCE

When is it appropriate in writing to use the comparison-contrast method of development? Comparison-contrast works well if you want to demonstrate any of the following: (1) that one thing is better than another (the first example below); (2) that things which seem different are actually alike (the second example below); (3) that things which seem alike are actually different (the third example below).

> Compare and contrast the way male and female relationships are depicted in *Cosmopolitan, Ms., Playboy,* and *Esquire.* Which publication has the most limited view of men and women? Which has the broadest perspective?

> Football, basketball, and baseball differ in the ways they appeal to fans. Describe the unique drawing power of each sport, but also reach some conclusions about the appeals the three sports have in common.

> Studies show that both college students and their parents feel that post-secondary education should equip young people to succeed in the marketplace. Yet the same studies report that the two groups have a very different understanding of what it means to succeed. What differences do you think the studies identify?

Other assignments will, in less obvious ways, lend themselves to comparison-contrast. For instance, although words like *compare, contrast, differ,* and *have in common* don't appear in the following assignments, essay responses to the assignments could be organized around the comparison-contrast format:

> The emergence of the two-career family is one of the major phenomena of our culture. Discuss the advantages and disadvantages of having both parents work, showing how you feel about such two-career households.

> Some people believe that the 1950s, often called the golden age of television, produced several never-to-be-equaled comedy classics. Do you agree that such shows as *I Love Lucy* and *The Honeymooners* are superior to the situation comedies aired on television today?

> There has been considerable criticism recently of the news coverage by the city's two leading newspapers, the *Herald* and the *Beacon.* Indicate whether you think the criticism is valid by discussing the similarities and differences in the two papers' news coverage.

Note: The last assignment shows that a comparison-contrast essay may cover similarities *and* differences, not just one or the other.

As you have seen, comparison-contrast can be the key strategy for achieving an essay's purpose. But comparison-contrast can also be a supplemental method used to help make a point in an essay organized chiefly around another pattern of development. A serious, informative essay intended for lay-people might *define* clinical depression by contrasting that state of mind with ordinary run-of-the-mill blues. Writing humorously about the exhausting *effects* of trying to get in shape, you might dramatize your plight for readers by contrasting the leisurely way you used to spend your day with your current rigidly compulsive exercise regimen. Or, in an urgent *argumentation-persuasion* essay on the need for stricter controls over drug abuse in the workplace, you might provide readers with background by comparing several companies' approaches to the problem.

SUGGESTIONS FOR USING COMPARISON-CONTRAST IN AN ESSAY

The following suggestions will be helpful whether you use comparison-contrast as a dominant or a supportive pattern of development.

1. Be sure your subjects are at least somewhat alike.   Unless you plan to develop an *analogy* (see below), the subjects you choose to compare or contrast should share some obvious characteristics or qualities. It makes sense to compare different parts of the country, two comedians, or several college teachers. But a reasonable paper wouldn't result from, let's say, a comparison of a television game show with a soap opera. Your subjects must belong to the same general group so that your comparison-contrast stays within good logical bounds and doesn't veer off into pointlessness.

2. Stay focused on your purpose.   When writing, remember that comparison-contrast isn't an end in itself. That is, your objective isn't to turn an essay into a mechanical list of "how A differs from B" or "how A is like B." Like the other patterns of development discussed in this book, comparison-contrast is a strategy for making a point or meeting a larger purpose.

Consider the assignment on page 254 about the two newspapers. Your purpose here might be simply to *inform*, to present information as objectively as possible: "This is what the *Herald*'s news coverage is like. This is what the *Beacon*'s news coverage is like."

More frequently, though, you'll use comparison-contrast to *evaluate* your subjects' pros and cons, your goal being to reach a conclusion or make a judgment: "Both the *Herald* and the *Beacon* spend too much time reporting local news," or "The *Herald*'s analysis of the recent hostage crisis was more insightful than the *Beacon*'s." Comparison-contrast can also be used to *persuade* readers to take action: "People interested in thorough coverage of international events should read the *Herald* rather than the *Beacon*." Persuasive essays may also propose a change, contrasting what now exists with a more ideal situation: "For the *Beacon* to compete with the *Herald*, it must assign more reporters to international stories."

Yet another purpose you might have in writing a comparison-contrast essay is to *clear up misconceptions* by revealing previously hidden similarities or differences. For example, perhaps your town's two newspapers are thought to be sharply different. However, a comparison-contrast analysis might reveal that—although one paper specializes in sensationalized stories while the other adopts a more muted approach—both resort to biased, emotionally charged analyses of local politics. Or the essay might illustrate that the tabloid's treatment of the local arts scene is surprisingly more comprehensive than that of its competitor.

Comparing and contrasting also make it possible to *draw an analogy* between two seemingly unrelated subjects. An analogy is an imaginative comparison that delves beneath the surface differences of subjects in order to expose their significant and often unsuspected similarities or differences. Your purpose may be to show that singles bars and zoos share a number of striking similarities. Or you may want to illustrate that wolves and humans raise their young in much the same way, but that wolves go about the process in a more civilized manner. The analogical approach can make a complex subject easier to understand—as when the national deficit is compared to a household budget gone awry. Analogies are often dramatic and instructive, challenging you and your audience to consider subjects in a new light. But analogies don't speak for themselves. You must make clear to the reader how the analogy demonstrates your purpose.

3. Formulate a strong thesis. An essay developed primarily through comparison-contrast should be focused by a solid thesis. Besides revealing your attitude, the thesis will often do the following:

- Name the subjects being compared and contrasted.
- Indicate whether the essay focuses on the subjects' similarities, differences, or both.
- State the essay's main point of comparison or contrast.

Not all comparison-contrast essays need thesis statements as structured as those that follow. Even so, these examples can serve as models of clarity. Note that the first thesis statement signals similarities, the second differences, and the last both similarities and differences:

Middle-aged parents are often in a good position to empathize with adolescent children because the emotional upheavals experienced by the two age groups are much the same.

The priorities of most retired people are more conducive to health and happiness than the priorities of most young professionals.

College students in their thirties and forties face many of the same pressures as younger students, but they are better equipped to withstand these pressures.

4. Select the points to be discussed.   Once you have identified the essay's subjects, purpose, and thesis, you need to decide which aspects of the subjects to compare or contrast. College professors, for instance, could be compared and contrasted on the basis of their testing methods, ability to motivate students, confidence in front of a classroom, personalities, level of enthusiasm, and so forth.

Brainstorming, freewriting, and mapping are valuable for gathering possible points to cover. Whichever prewriting technique you use, try to produce more raw material than you'll need, so that you have the luxury of narrowing the material down to the most significant points.

When selecting points to cover, be sure to consider your audience. Ask yourself: "Will my readers be familiar with this item? Will I need it to get my message across? Will my audience find this item interesting or convincing?" What your readers know, what they don't know, and what you can predict about their reactions should influence your choices. And, of course, you need to select points that support your thesis. If your essay explains the differences between healthy, sensible diets and dangerous crash diets, it wouldn't be appropriate to talk about aerobic exercise. Similarly, imagine you want to write an essay making the point that, despite their differences, hard rock of the 1960s and punk rock of the 1970s both reflected young people's disillusionment with society. It wouldn't make much sense to contrast the long, uncombed hairstyle of the 1960s with the short, spikey cuts of the 1970s. But contrasting song lyrics (protest versus nihilistic messages) would help support your thesis and lead to interesting insights.

5. Organize the points to be discussed.   After deciding which points to include, you should use a systematic, logical plan for presenting those ideas. If the points aren't organized, your essay will be little more than a confusing jumble of ideas. There are two common ways to organize an essay developed wholly or in part by comparison-contrast: the one-side-at-a-time method and the point-by-point method. Although both strategies may be used in a paper, one method usually predominates.

In the *one-side-at-a-time method* of organization, you discuss everything relevant about one subject before moving to another subject. For example, responding to the earlier assignment that asked you to analyze the news coverage in two local papers, you might first talk about the *Herald*'s coverage of international, national, and local news; then you would discuss the *Beacon*'s coverage of the same categories. Note that the areas discussed should be the same for both newspapers. It wouldn't be logical to review the *Herald*'s coverage of international, national, and local news and then to detail the *Beacon*'s magazine supplements, modern living section, and comics page. Moreover, the areas compared and contrasted should be presented in the same order.

This is how you would organize the essay using the one-side-at-a-time method:

Everything about A	*Herald*'s news coverage:
	• International
	• National
	• Local
Everything about B	*Beacon*'s news coverage:
	• International
	• National
	• Local

In the *point-by-point method* of organization, you alternate from one aspect of the first subject to the same aspect of your other subject(s). For example, to use this method when comparing or contrasting the *Herald* and the *Beacon*, you would first discuss the *Herald*'s international coverage, then the *Beacon*'s international coverage; next the *Herald*'s national coverage, then the *Beacon*'s; and finally, the *Herald*'s local coverage, then the *Beacon*'s.

Using the point-by-point method, this is how the essay would be organized:

First aspect of A and B	*Herald:* International coverage
	Beacon: International coverage
Second aspect of A and B	*Herald:* National coverage
	Beacon: National coverage
Third aspect of A and B	*Herald:* Local coverage
	Beacon: Local coverage

Deciding which of these two methods of organization to use is largely a personal choice, though there are several factors to consider. The one-side-at-a-time method tends to convey a more unified feeling because it highlights broad similarities and differences. It is, therefore, an effective approach for subjects that are fairly uncomplicated. This strategy also works well when essays are brief; the reader won't find it difficult to remember what has been said about subject A when reading about subject B.

Because the point-by-point method permits more extensive coverage of similarities and differences, it is often a wise choice when subjects are complex. This pattern is also useful for lengthy essays since readers would probably find it difficult to remember, let's say, ten pages of information about subject A while reading the next ten pages about subject B. The point-by-point approach, however, may cause readers to lose sight of the broader picture, so remember to keep them focused on your central point.

6. Supply the reader with clear transitions.   Although a well-organized comparison-contrast format is important, it doesn't guarantee that readers will be able to follow your line of thought easily. *Transitions*—especially those signaling similarities or differences—are needed to show readers where they have been and where they are going. Such cues are essential in all writing, but they're especially crucial in a paper using comparison-contrast. By indicating clearly when subjects are being compared or contrasted, the transitions help weave the discussion into a coherent whole.

The transitions (in boldface) in the following examples could be used to *signal similarities* in an essay discussing the news coverage in the *Herald* and the *Beacon:*

- The *Beacon* **also** allots only a small portion of the front page to global news.
- **In the same way**, the *Herald* tries to include at least three local stories on the first page.
- **Likewise**, the *Beacon* emphasizes the importance of up-to-date reporting of town meetings.
- The *Herald* is **similarly** committed to extensive coverage of high school and college sports.

The transitions (in boldface) in these examples could be used to *signal differences:*

- **By way of contrast**, the *Herald's* editorial page deals with national matters on the average of three times a week.
- **On the other hand**, the *Beacon* does not share the *Herald's* enthusiasm for interviews with national figures.
- The *Beacon,* **however**, does not encourage its reporters to tackle national stories the way the *Herald* does.
- **But** the *Herald's* coverage of the Washington scene is much more comprehensive than its competitor's.

REVISION STRATEGIES

Once you have a draft of the essay, you're ready to revise. The following checklist will help you and those giving you feedback apply to comparison-contrast some of the revision techniques discussed on pages 59–61.

☑ COMPARISON-CONTRAST: A REVISION/PEER
REVIEW CHECKLIST

Revise Overall Meaning and Structure

❏ Are the subjects sufficiently alike for the comparison-contrast to be
logical and meaningful?

❏ What purpose does the essay serve—to inform, to evaluate, to persuade readers to accept a viewpoint, to eliminate misconceptions, or
to draw a surprising analogy?

❏ What is the essay's thesis? How could the thesis be stated more
effectively?

❏ Is the overall essay organized primarily by the one-side-at-a-time
method or by the point-by-point method? Why is that the best strategy for this essay?

❏ Are the same features discussed for each subject? Are they discussed
in the same order?

❏ Which points of comparison and/or contrast need further development? Which points should be deleted? Where do significant points
seem to be missing? How has the most important similarity or difference been emphasized?

Revise Paragraph Development

❏ If the essay uses the one-side-at-a-time method, which paragraph
marks the switch from one subject to another?

❏ If the essay uses the point-by-point method, do paragraphs consistently alternate between subjects? If this alternation becomes too elaborate or predictable, what could be done to eliminate the problem?

❏ If the essay uses both methods, which paragraph marks the switch
from one method to the other? If the switch is confusing, how could
it be made less so?

❏ Where would signal devices make it easier to see similarities and differences between the subjects being discussed?

Revise Sentences and Words

❏ Where do too many signal devices make sentences awkward and
mechanical?

❏ Which sentences and words fail to convey the intended tone?

STUDENT ESSAY

The following student essay was written by Carol Siskin in response to this
assignment:

In "The Ugly Truth About Beauty," Dave Barry humorously contrasts two attitudes toward personal appearance, finding merit in the one normally considered less praiseworthy. In an essay of your own, contrast two personality types, lifestyles, or stages of life, showing that the one most people consider inferior is actually superior.

While reading Carol's paper, try to determine how well it applies the principles of comparison-contrast. The annotations on Carol's paper and the commentary following it will help you look at the essay more closely.

The Virtues of Growing Older
by Carol Siskin

The first of a two-paragraph introduction → Our society worships youth. Advertisements convince us to buy Grecian Formula and Oil of Olay so we can hide the gray in our hair and smooth the lines on our face. Television shows feature attractive young stars with firm bodies, perfect complexions, and thick manes of hair. Middle-aged folks work out in gyms and jog down the street, trying to delay the effects of age. 1

The second introductory paragraph → Wouldn't any person over thirty gladly sign with the devil just to be young again? Isn't aging an experience to be dreaded? Perhaps it is un-American to say so, but I believe the answer is "No." *Thesis* Being young is often pleasant, but being older has distinct advantages. 2

First half of topic sentence for point 1: Appearance → When young, you are apt to be obsessed with your appearance. *Start of what it's like being young* When my brother Dave and I were teens, we worked feverishly to perfect the bodies we had. Dave lifted weights, took megadoses of vitamins, and drank a half-dozen milkshakes a day in order to turn his wiry adolescent frame into some muscular ideal. And as a teenager, I dieted constantly. No matter what I weighed, though, I was never satisfied with the way I looked. My legs were too heavy, my shoulders too broad, my waist too big. When Dave and I were young, we begged and pleaded for the "right" clothes. If our parents didn't get them for us, we felt our world would fall apart. How could we go to school wearing loose-fitting overcoats when everyone else would be wearing fitted leather jackets? We would be considered freaks. I often wonder how *Second half of topic sentence for point 1* my parents, and parents in general, manage to tolerate their children during the adolescent years. Now, however, Dave and I are beyond such adolescent agonies. *Start of what it's like being older* My rounded figure seems fine, and I don't deny myself a slice of pecan pie if I feel in the mood. Dave still works out, but he has actually become fond of his tall, lanky frame. The two of us enjoy wearing fashionable clothes, but we are no longer slaves to style. And women, I'm embarrassed to admit, even more than men, have 3 always seemed to be at the mercy of fashion. Now my clothes--and my brother's--are attractive yet easy to wear. We no longer feel anxious about what others will think. As long as we feel good about how we look, we are happy.

Being older is preferable to being younger in another way. Obviously, I still have important choices to make about my life, but I have already made many of the critical decisions that confront those just starting out. I chose the man I wanted to marry. I decided to have children. I elected to return to college to complete my education. But when you are young, major decisions await you at every turn. "What college should I attend? What career should I pursue? Should I get married? Should I have children?" These are just a few of the issues facing young people. It's no wonder that, despite their carefree facade, they are often confused, uncertain, and troubled by all the unknowns in their future.

But the greatest benefit of being forty is knowing who I am. The most unsettling aspect of youth is the uncertainty you feel about your values, goals, and dreams. Being young means wondering what is worth working for. Being young means feeling happy with yourself one day and wishing you were never born the next. It means trying on new selves by taking up with different crowds. It means resenting your parents and their way of life one minute and then feeling you will never be as good or as accomplished as they are. By way of contrast, forty is sanity. I have a surer self-concept now. I don't laugh at jokes I don't think are funny. I can make a speech in front of a town meeting or complain in a store because I am no longer terrified that people will laugh at me; I am no longer anxious that everyone must like me. I no longer blame my parents for my every personality quirk or keep a running score of everything they did wrong raising me. Life has taught me that I, not they, am responsible for who I am. We are all human beings--neither saints nor devils.

Most Americans blindly accept the idea that newer is automatically better. But a human life contradicts this premise. There is a great deal of happiness to be found as we grow older. My own parents, now in their sixties, recently told me that they are happier now than they have ever been. They would not want to be my age. Did this surprise me? At first, yes. Then it gladdened me. Their contentment holds out great promise for me as I move into the next--perhaps even better--phase of my life.

Margin annotations:
- First half of topic sentence for point 2: Life choices
- Start of what it's like being older
- Second half of topic sentence for point 2
- Start of what it's like being younger
- Topic sentence for point 3: Self-concept
- Start of what it's like being younger
- Start of what it's like being older
- Conclusion

Paragraph numbers: 4, 5, 6

COMMENTARY

Purpose and thesis.   In her essay, Carol disproves the widespread belief that being young is preferable to being old. The *comparison-contrast* pattern allows her to analyze the drawbacks of one and the merits of the other, thus providing the essay with an *evaluative purpose*. Using the title to indicate her point of view, Carol places the *thesis* at the end of her two-paragraph introduction: "Being young is often pleasant, but being older has distinct advantages." Note that the thesis accomplishes several things. It names the two subjects to be discussed and clarifies Carol's point of view about her subjects. The thesis also implies that the essay will focus on the contrasts between these two periods of life.

Points of support and overall organization.   To support her assertion that older is better, Carol supplies examples from her own life and organizes the examples around three main points: attitudes about appearance, decisions about life choices, and questions of self-concept. Using the *point-by-point method* to organize the overall essay, she explores each of these key ideas in a separate paragraph. Each paragraph is further focused by one or two sentences that serve as a topic sentence.

Sequence of points, organizational cues, and paragraph development. Let's look more closely at the way Carol presents her three central points in the essay. She obviously considers appearance the least important of a person's worries, life choices more important, and self-concept the most critical. So she uses *emphatic order* to sequence the supporting paragraphs, with the phrase "But the greatest benefit" signaling the special significance of the last issue. Carol is also careful to use *transitions* to help readers follow her line of thinking: "*Now, however,* Dave and I are beyond such adolescent agonies" (paragraph 3); "*But* when you are young, major decisions await you at every turn" (4); and "*By way of contrast,* forty is sanity" (5).

Although Carol has worked hard to write a well-organized paper—and has on the whole been successful—she doesn't feel compelled to make the paper fit a rigid format. As you've seen, the essay as a whole uses the point-by-point method, but each supporting paragraph uses the *one-side-at-a-time* method—that is, everything about one age group is discussed before there is a shift to the other age group. Notice too that the third and fifth paragraphs start with young people and then move to adults, whereas the fourth paragraph reverses the sequence by starting with older people.

Combining patterns of development.   Carol uses the comparison-contrast format to organize her ideas, but other patterns of development also come into play. To illustrate her points, she makes extensive use of *exemplification,* and her discussion also contains elements typical of *causal analysis.* Throughout the essay, for instance, she traces the effect of being a certain age on her brother, herself, and her parents.

A problem with unity.   As you read the third paragraph, you might have noted that Carol's essay runs into a problem. Two sentences in the paragraph disrupt the *unity* of Carol's discussion: "I often wonder how my parents, and parents in general, manage to tolerate their children during the adolescent years," and "women, I'm embarrassed to admit . . . have always seemed to be at the mercy of fashion." These sentences should be deleted because they don't develop the idea that adolescents are overly concerned with appearance.

Conclusion.   Carol's final paragraph brings the essay to a pleasing and interesting close. The conclusion recalls the point made in the introduction: Americans overvalue youth. Carol also uses the conclusion to broaden the scope of her discussion. Rather than continuing to focus on herself, she briefly mentions her parents and the pleasure they take in life. By bringing her parents into the essay, Carol is able to make a gently philosophical observation about the promise that awaits her as she grows older. The implication is that a similarly positive future awaits us, too.

Revising the first draft.   To help guide her revision, Carol asked her husband to read her first draft aloud. As he did, Carol took notes on what she sensed were the paper's strengths and weaknesses. She then jotted down her observations, as well as her husband's, on the draft. Keeping these comments in mind, Carol made a number of changes in her paper. You'll get a good sense of how she proceeded if you compare the original introduction reprinted here with the final version in the full essay.

Original Version of the Introduction

America is a land filled with people who worship youth. We admire dynamic young achievers; our middle-aged citizens work out in gyms; all of us wear tight tops and colorful sneakers--clothes that look fine on the young but ridiculous on aging bodies. Television shows revolve around perfect-looking young stars, while commercials entice us with products that will keep us young.

Wouldn't every older person want to be young again? Isn't aging to be avoided? It may be slightly unpatriotic to say so, but I believe the answer is "No." Being young may be pleasant at times, but I would rather be my forty-year-old self. I no longer have to agonize about my physical appearance, I have already made many of my crucial life decisions, and I am much less confused about who I am.

After hearing her original two-paragraph introduction read aloud, Carol was dissatisfied with what she had written. Although she wasn't quite sure how to proceed, she knew that the paragraphs were flat and that they failed to open the essay on a strong note. She decided to start by whittling down the opening sentence, making it crisper and more powerful: "Our society worships youth." That done, she eliminated two bland statements ("We admire dynamic young achievers" and "all of us wear tight tops and colorful sneakers") and made several vague references more concrete and interesting.

For example, "Commercials entice us with products that will keep us young" became "Grecian Formula and Oil of Olay . . . hide the gray in our hair and smooth the lines on our face"; "perfect-looking young stars" became "attractive young stars with firm bodies, perfect complexions, and thick manes of hair." With the addition of these specifics, the first paragraph became more vigorous and interesting.

Carol next made some subtle changes in the two questions that opened the second paragraph of the original introduction. She replaced "Wouldn't every older person want to be young again?" and "Isn't aging to be avoided?" with two more emphatic questions: "Wouldn't any person over thirty gladly sign with the devil just to be young again?" and "Isn't aging an experience to be dreaded?" Carol also made some changes at the end of the original second paragraph. Because the paper is relatively short and the subject matter easy to understand, she decided to omit her somewhat awkward *plan of development* ("I no longer have to agonize about my physical appearance, I have already made many of my crucial life decisions, and I am much less confused about who I am"). This deletion made it possible to end the introduction with a clear statement of the essay's thesis.

Once these revisions were made, Carol was confident that her essay got off to a stronger start. Feeling reassured, she moved ahead and made changes in other sections of her paper. Such work enabled her to prepare a solid piece of writing that offers food for thought.

ACTIVITIES: COMPARISON-CONTRAST

Prewriting Activities

1. Imagine you're writing two essays: One explores the *effects* of holding a job while in college; the other explains a *process* for budgeting money wisely. Jot down ways you might use comparison-contrast in each essay.

2. Using your journal or freewriting, jot down the advantages and disadvantages of two ways of doing something (for example, watching movies in the theater versus watching them on a DVD player at home; following trends versus ignoring them; dating one person versus playing the field; and so on). Reread your prewriting and determine what your thesis, purpose, audience, tone, and point of view might be if you were to write an essay. Make a scratch list of the main ideas you would cover. Would a point-by-point or a one-side-at-a-time method of organization work more effectively?

Revising Activities

3. Of the statements that follow, which would *not* make effective thesis statements for comparison-contrast essays? Identify the problem(s) in the faulty statements and revise them accordingly.

a. Although their classroom duties often overlap, teacher aides are not as equipped as teachers to handle disciplinary problems.
b. This college provides more assistance to its students than most schools.
c. During the state's last congressional election, both candidates relied heavily on television to communicate their messages.
d. There are many differences between American and foreign cars.

4. The following paragraph is from the draft of an essay detailing the qualities of a skillful manager. How effective is this comparison-contrast paragraph? What revisions would help focus the paragraph on the point made in the topic sentence? Where should details be added or deleted? Rewrite the paragraph, providing necessary transitions and details.

A manager encourages creativity and treats employees courteously, while a boss discourages staff resourcefulness and views it as a threat. At the hardware store where I work, I got my boss's approval to develop a system for organizing excess stock in the storeroom. I shelved items in roughly the same order as they were displayed in the store. The system was helpful to all the salespeople, not just to me, since everyone was stymied by the boss's helter-skelter system. What he did was store overstocked items according to each wholesaler, even though most of us weren't there long enough to know which items came from which wholesaler. His supposed system created chaos. When he saw what I had done, he was furious and insisted that we continue to follow the old slapdash system. I had assumed he would welcome my ideas the way my manager did last summer when I worked in a drugstore. But he didn't and I had to scrap my work and go back to his eccentric system. He certainly could learn something about employee relations from the drugstore manager.

Rachel Carson

Once accused of being a fearmonger, biologist Rachel Carson (1907–64) is now recognized as one of the country's first environmentalists. She was the author of three popular books about the marine world: *The Sea Around Us* (1951), *Under the Sea Wind* (1952), and *The Edge of the Sea* (1955). But it was the publication of *Silent Spring* (1962), Carson's alarming study of the use of pesticides and herbicides, that brought her special attention and established her reputation as a passionate advocate for a clean environment. The following selection is taken from *Silent Spring*.

Pre-Reading Journal Entry

Take a few minutes to record in your journal your impressions of a place that has special meaning for you—but that is being threatened in one way or another. Jot down sensory details about the place, focusing on those specifics that capture its unique qualities.

A Fable for Tomorrow

There was once a town in the heart of America where all life seemed to live in harmony with its surroundings. The town lay in the midst of a checkerboard of prosperous farms, with fields of grain and hillsides of orchards where, in spring, white clouds of bloom drifted above the green fields. In autumn, oak and maple and birch set up a blaze of color that flamed and flickered across a backdrop of pines. Then foxes barked in the hills and deer silently crossed the fields, half hidden in the mists of the fall mornings.

Along the roads, laurel, viburnum and alder, great ferns and wildflowers delighted the traveler's eye through much of the year. Even in winter the roadsides were places of beauty, where countless birds came to feed on the berries and on the seed heads of the dried weeds rising above the snow. The countryside was, in fact, famous for the abundance and variety of its bird life, and when the flood of migrants was pouring through in spring and fall people traveled from great distances to observe them. Others came to fish the streams, which flowed clear and cold out of the hills and contained shady pools where trout lay. So it had been from the days many years ago when the first settlers raised their houses, sank their wells, and built their barns.

Then a strange blight crept over the area and everything began to change. Some evil spell had settled on the community: mysterious maladies swept the flocks of chickens; the cattle and sheep sickened and died. Everywhere was a shadow of death. The farmers spoke of much illness among their families. In the town the doctors had become more and more puzzled by new kinds of sickness appearing among their patients. There had been several sudden and unexplained deaths, not only among adults but even among children, who would be stricken suddenly while at play and die within a few hours.

There was a strange stillness. The birds, for example—where had they   4
gone? Many people spoke of them, puzzled and disturbed. The feeding stations in the backyards were deserted. The few birds seen anywhere were moribund; they trembled violently and could not fly. It was a spring without voices. On the mornings that had once throbbed with the dawn chorus of robins, catbirds, doves, jays, wrens, and scores of other bird voices there was now no sound; only silence lay over the fields and woods and marsh.

On the farms the hens brooded, but no chicks hatched. The farmers   5
complained that they were unable to raise any pigs—the litters were small and the young survived only a few days. The apple trees were coming into bloom but no bees droned among the blossoms, so there was no pollination and there would be no fruit.

The roadsides, once so attractive, were now lined with browned and   6
withered vegetation as though swept by fire. These, too, were silent, deserted by all living things. Even the streams were now lifeless. Anglers no longer visited them, for all the fish had died.

In the gutters under the eaves and between the shingles of the roofs, a   7
white granular powder still showed a few patches; some weeks before it had fallen like snow upon the roofs and the lawns, the fields and streams.

No witchcraft, no enemy action had silenced the rebirth of new life in   8
this stricken world. The people had done it themselves.

This town does not actually exist, but it might easily have a thousand   9
counterparts in America or elsewhere in the world. I know of no community that has experienced all the misfortunes I describe. Yet every one of these disasters has actually happened somewhere, and many real communities have already suffered a substantial number of them. A grim specter has crept upon us almost unnoticed, and this imagined tragedy may easily become a stark reality we all shall know.

Questions for Close Reading

1. What is the selection's thesis? Locate the sentence(s) in which Carson states her main idea. If she doesn't state the thesis explicitly, express it in your own words.
2. What are some of the delights of Carson's beautiful, healthy countryside?
3. When Carson writes of "a strange blight," an "evil spell" (paragraph 3), whose point of view is she adopting?
4. What are the effects of the blight?
5. Refer to your dictionary as needed to define the following words used in the selection: *viburnum* (paragraph 2), *alder* (2), *moribund* (4), and *specter* (9).

Questions About the Writer's Craft

1. The pattern. To develop her essay, Carson uses the one-side-at-a-time method of comparison-contrast. What does this method enable her to do that the point-by-point approach would not?

2. Other patterns. Throughout the essay, Carson appeals to the reader's senses of sight and hearing. Which paragraphs are developed primarily through visual or auditory *description?* How do the sensory images in these paragraphs reinforce Carson's thesis?

3. Carson's diction (word choice) and sentence rhythm often resemble those of the Bible. For example, we read, "So it had been from the days many years ago" (paragraph 2), "a strange blight crept over the area" (3), and "Everywhere was a shadow of death" (3). Why do you suppose Carson chose to echo the Bible in this way?

4. How does Carson's approach to her subject change in the last paragraph? What is the effect of this change?

Writing Assignments Using Comparison-Contrast as a Pattern of Development

1. Carson imagines a fictional town that has changed for the worse. Consider a place you know well that has changed for the *better.* You might focus on a renovated school, a rehabilitated neighborhood, a newly preserved park. Write an essay contrasting the place before and after the change. At the end of your essay, describe briefly the effects of the change.

2. In her essay, Carson provides descriptive details unique to particular seasons. For example, she writes that "in autumn, oak and maple and birch set up a blaze of color that flamed and flickered across a backdrop of pines" (paragraph 1). Choosing a place you know well, contrast its sights, sounds, and smells during one season with those you've noticed during another time of year. Use rich sensory details to convey the differences between the two seasons.

Writing Assignments Combining Patterns of Development

3. Carson cites "white granular powder" (paragraph 7) as the cause of the blight. Write an essay about a time you noticed a visible environmental problem—say, smog blurring a city skyline, soot coating a window, or medical syringes discarded on the beach. Use vivid *narrative details* to capture the effect of the experience on you.

4. Carson graphically shows the effects of herbicides and pesticides on the environment. Focus on some other less global environmental problem: graffiti on a public building; vandalized trees and shrubs; beer cans thrown in a neighborhood park, for example. Discuss the *effects* of this situation on the physical environment and on people's attitudes and actions. Conclude with suggestions about possible *strategies* for remedying the problem. Gordon Parks's "Flavio's Home" (page 83) will help you appreciate the interaction between the environment and human behavior.

Writing Assignment Using a Journal
Entry as a Starting Point

5. Write an essay describing an endangered place that is very important to you.
Describe the potential threat either at the beginning or at the end of the essay, and
paint such a vivid picture of the place in the rest of the essay that readers understand why the potential threat is so unfortunate. Select from your pre-reading
journal entry only those details that convey the special qualities of the place,
adding more texture and specifics where needed.

Joseph H. Suina

Still living on the Cochiti Pueblo Reservation in New Mexico where he grew up, former U.S. Marine Joseph H. Suina (1944–) teaches in the Multicultural Teacher Education Program at the University of New Mexico. Suina's work as an educator led to his coauthoring a book for teachers, *The Learning Environment: An Instructional Strategy* (1982). The following selection first appeared in *Linguistic and Cultural Influences on Learning Mathematics,* edited by Rodney Cocking and Jose Mestre (1988).

Pre-Reading Journal Entry

Bilingualism—instruction in a student's native language as well as in English—remains an important educational issue in many parts of the country. Do you think non-English-speaking students should be forced to speak only English when they start school, or should they for a time be taught in their native tongue as well? Use your journal to reflect on your beliefs about this question.

And Then I Went to School

I lived with my grandmother from the ages of five through nine. It was the early 1950s when electricity had not yet invaded the homes of the Cochiti Indians. The village day school and health clinic were first to have it and to the unsuspecting Cochitis this was the approach of a new era in their uncomplicated lives. 1

Transportation was simple then. Two good horses and a sturdy wagon met most needs of a villager. Only five or six individuals possessed an automobile in the Pueblo of 300. A flatbed truck fixed with wooden rails and a canvas top made a regular Saturday trip to Santa Fe. It was always loaded beyond capacity with Cochitis taking their wares to town for a few staples. With an escort of a dozen barking dogs, the straining truck made a noisy exit, northbound from the village. 2

During those years, Grandmother and I lived beside the plaza in a one-room house. It consisted of a traditional fireplace, a makeshift cabinet for our few tin cups and dishes, and a wooden crate that held our two buckets of all-purpose water. At the far end of the room were two rolls of bedding we used as comfortable sitting "couches." Consisting of thick quilts, sheepskin, and assorted blankets, these bed rolls were undone each night. A wooden pole the length of one side of the room was suspended about 10 inches from the ceiling beams. A modest collection of colorful shawls, blankets, and sashes was draped over the pole making this part of the room most interesting. In 3 one corner was a bulky metal trunk for our ceremonial wear and a few valuables. A dresser, which was traded for some of my grandmother's well-known pottery, held the few articles of clothing we owned and the "goody bag." Grandmother always had a flour sack filled with candy, store bought cookies, and Fig Newtons. These were saturated with a sharp odor of moth balls. Nevertheless, they made a fine snack with coffee before we turned in for the night. Tucked securely in my blankets, I listened to one of her stories or accounts of how it was when she was a little girl. These accounts seemed so old fashioned compared to the way we lived. Sometimes she softly sang a song from a ceremony. In this way I fell asleep each night.

Earlier in the evening we would make our way to a relative's house if   4
someone had not already come to visit us. I would play with the children while the adults caught up on all the latest. Ten-cent comic books were finding their way into the Pueblo homes. For us children, these were the first link to the world beyond the Pueblo. We enjoyed looking at them and role playing as one of the heroes rounding up the villains. Everyone preferred being a cowboy rather than an Indian because cowboys were always victorious. Sometimes, stories were related to both children and adults. These get-togethers were highlighted by refreshments of coffee and sweet bread or fruit pies baked in the outdoor oven. Winter months would most likely include roasted pinon nuts or dried deer meat for all to share. These evening gatherings and sense of closeness diminished as the radios and televisions increased over the following years. It was never to be the same again.

The winter months are among my fondest recollections. A warm fire   5
crackled and danced brightly in the fireplace and the aroma of delicious stew filled our one-room house. To me the house was just right. The thick adobe walls wrapped around the two of us protectingly during the long freezing nights. Grandmother's affection completed the warmth and security I will always remember.

Being the only child at Grandmother's, I had lots of attention and plen-   6
ty of reasons to feel good about myself. As a pre-schooler, I already had the chores of chopping firewood and hauling in fresh water each day. After "heavy work," I would run to her and flex what I was certain were my gigantic biceps. Grandmother would state that at the rate I was going I would soon attain the status of a man like the adult males in the village. Her shower of praises made me feel like the Indian Superman of all times. At age five, I suppose I was as close to that concept of myself as anyone.

In spite of her many years, Grandmother was still active in the village   7
ceremonial setting. She was a member of an important women's society and attended all the functions, taking me along to many of them. I would wear one of my colorful shirts she handmade for just such occasions. Grandmother taught me the appropriate behavior at these events. Through modeling she taught me to pray properly. Barefooted, I would greet the sun each

morning with a handful of cornmeal. At night I would look to the stars in wonderment and let a prayer slip through my lips. I learned to appreciate cooperation in nature and my fellowmen early in life. About food and material things, Grandmother would say, "There is enough for everyone to share and it all comes from above, my child." I felt very much a part of the world and our way of life. I knew I had a place in it and I felt good about me.

At age six, like the rest of the Cochiti six-year-olds that year, I had to begin my schooling. It was a new and bewildering experience. One I will not forget. The strange surroundings, new concepts about time and expectations, and a foreign tongue were overwhelming to us beginners. It took some effort to return the second day and many times thereafter.

To begin with, unlike my grandmother, the teacher did not have pretty brown skin and a colorful dress. She was not plump and friendly. Her clothes were one color and drab. Her pale and skinny form made me worry that she was very ill. I thought that explained why she did not have time just for me and the disappointed looks and orders she seemed to always direct my way. I didn't think she was so smart because she couldn't understand my language. "Surely that was why we had to leave our 'Indian' at home." But then I did not feel so bright either. All I could say in her language was "yes teacher," "my name is Joseph Henry," and "when is lunch time." The teacher's odor took some getting used to also. In fact, many times it made me sick right before lunch. Later, I learned from the girls that this odor was something she wore called perfume.

The classroom too had its odd characteristics. It was terribly huge and smelled of medicine like the village clinic I feared so much. The walls and ceiling were artificial and uncaring. They were too far from me and I felt naked. The fluorescent light tubes were eerie and blinked suspiciously above me. This was quite a contrast to the fire and sunlight that my eyes were accustomed to. I thought maybe the lighting did not seem right because it was man-made, and it was not natural. Our confinement to rows of desks was another unnatural demand from our active little bodies. We had to sit at these hard things for what seemed like forever before relief (recess) came midway through the morning and afternoon. Running carefree in the village and fields was but a sweet memory of days gone by. We all went home for lunch because we lived within walking distance of the school. It took coaxing and sometimes bribing to get me to return and complete the remainder of the school day.

School was a painful experience during those early years. The English language and the new set of values caused me much anxiety and embarrassment. I could not comprehend everything that was happening but yet I could understand very well when I messed up or was not doing so well. The negative aspect was communicated too effectively and I became unsure of myself more and more. How I wished I could understand other things just as well in school.

The value conflict was not only in school performance but in other areas   12
of my life as well. For example, many of us students had a problem with head
lice due to "the lack of sanitary conditions in our homes." Consequently, we
received a severe shampooing that was rough on both the scalp and the ego.
Cleanliness was crucial and a washing of this type indicated to the class how
filthy a home setting we came from. I recall that after one such treatment I
was humiliated before my peers with a statement that I had "She'na" (lice)
so tough that I must have been born with them. Needless to say, my Super
Indian self-image was no longer intact.

My language, too, was questionable from the beginning of my school   13
career. "Leave your Indian (language) at home" was like a trademark of
school. Speaking it accidentally or otherwise was a sure reprimand in the
form of a dirty look or a whack with a ruler. This punishment was for speaking the language of my people which meant so much to me. It was the language of my grandmother and I spoke it well. With it, I sang beautiful songs
and prayed from my heart. At that young and tender age, comprehending
why I had to part with it was most difficult for me. And yet at home I was
encouraged to attend school so that I might have a better life in the future.
I knew I had a good village life already but this was communicated less and
less each day I was in school. . . .

I had to leave my beloved village of Cochiti for my education beyond   14
Grade 6. I left to attend a Bureau of Indian Affairs boarding school 30 miles
from home. Shined shoes and pressed shirt and pants were the order of the
day. I managed to adjust to this just as I had to most of the things the school
shoved at me or took away from me. Adjusting to leaving home and the village was tough indeed. It seemed the older I got, the further away I became
from the ways I was so much a part of. Because my parents did not own an
automobile, I saw them only once a month when they came up in the community truck. They never failed to come supplied with "eats" for me. I enjoyed
the outdoor oven bread, dried meat, and tamales they usually brought. It
took a while to get accustomed to the diet of the school. I longed for my
grandmother and my younger brothers and sisters. I longed for my house. I
longed to take part in a Buffalo Dance. I longed to be free.

I came home for the four-day Thanksgiving break. At first, home did not   15
feel right anymore. It was much too small and stuffy. The lack of running
water and bathroom facilities were too inconvenient. Everything got dusty so
quickly and hardly anyone spoke English. I did not realize I was beginning to
take on the white man's ways, the ways that belittled my own. However, it did
not take long to "get back with it." Once I established my relationships with
family, relatives, and friends I knew I was where I came from and where I
belonged.

Leaving for the boarding school the following Sunday evening was one   16
of the saddest events in my entire life. Although I enjoyed myself immense-
ly the last few days, I realized then that life would never be the same again.

I could not turn back the time just as I could not do away with school and the ways of the white man. They were here to stay and would creep more and more into my life. The effort to make sense of both worlds together was painful and I had no choice but to do so. The schools, television, automobiles, and other white man's ways and values had chipped away at the simple cooperative life I grew up in. The people of Cochiti were changing. The winter evening gatherings, exchanging of stories, and even the performing of certain ceremonies were already only a memory that someone commented about now and then. Still the demands of both worlds were there. The white man's was flashy, less personal, but comfortable. The Indian was both attracted and pushed toward these new ways that he had little to say about. There was no choice left but to compete with the white man on his terms for survival. For that I knew I had to give up a part of my life.

Determined not to cry, I left for school that dreadfully lonely night. My right hand clutched tightly the mound of cornmeal Grandmother placed there and my left hand brushed away a tear as I made my way back to school.   17

Questions for Close Reading

1. What is the selection's thesis? Locate the sentence(s) in which Suina states his main idea. If he doesn't state the thesis explicitly, express it in your own words.
2. How did the Cochiti instill their values and native culture in their children? How was the Cochiti approach different from the teaching methods used in the white school Suina attended?
3. What non-native influences appear in Suina's town and life before he starts attending school?
4. Why is Suina forced to attend a white school and learn about the whites' lifestyle and language? What does he find confusing about school? How does school change him?
5. Refer to your dictionary as needed to define the following words used in the selection: *adobe* (paragraph 5), *ego* (12), and *belittled* (15).

Questions About the Writer's Craft

1. **The pattern.** Comparison-contrast essays organize material according to the point-by-point or one-side-at-a-time method. Which method predominates in this essay? Why do you think Suina uses this method? Locate places where Suina uses the other method of organization.
2. **Other patterns.** Suina uses *description* to evoke the simple, emotional warmth of the Native American lifestyle as well as the sterile, stark coldness of the white school. Locate places in the essay where Suina provides sensory details to help readers understand the differences between the two cultures.
3. Consider Suina's word choice in the opening paragraph. How do the words *invade* and *unsuspecting* help establish the essay's overall tone? What do these terms reveal about Suina's attitude toward the transformation of Native American culture?

4. Where in paragraph 14 does Suina use repetition? What is the effect of the repetition?

Writing Assignments Using Comparison-Contrast as a Pattern of Development

1. As a Native American, Suina is made to feel like an outsider in the white school. But cultural differences aren't the only factors that cause children to feel uncomfortable in school. For example, they may have trouble fitting in because they have a learning disability, are shy, are extroverted, or need more (or less) structure than the school provides. Focusing on *one* such problem, write an essay comparing and contrasting present-day education with the way it should be. For a poignant account of one young "outsider," consider reading Gary Soto's "The Jacket" (page 91).

2. After attending boarding school for a few months, Suina reappraises his home and earlier lifestyle. In a similar way, separation can cause the rest of us to view our home, our school, another institution, or an individual in a more positive or a more negative light. Write an essay comparing and contrasting the feelings you had for a person, place, or institution with your attitude after being separated for a while. Provide vigorous details to show why your attitude changed.

Writing Assignments Combining Patterns of Development

3. Suina reports that his grandmother showered him with praise and made him feel like a "Superman." However, once he entered school, the constant scoldings, dirty looks, and ruler slaps eroded his self-esteem. Write an essay *illustrating* how a person *affected* your view of yourself, either by praising or by criticizing your efforts. Provide several dramatic examples or a single, richly detailed example to show how this person affected you. Before writing, read Maya Angelou's "Sister Flowers" (page 96), an essay that illustrates the influence of a powerful individual.

4. Everyone, at some level of his or her education, has felt anxious about the first day of school. Write an essay in which you explain *steps* that a student can take to reduce the nervousness associated with beginning his or her first semester in college. Where appropriate, *illustrate* the steps with vivid examples. You may adopt a serious or a lighthearted tone in your essay.

Writing Assignment Using a Journal Entry as a Starting Point

5. In school, Suina is pressured to abandon his native language and to speak only English. Refer to your pre-reading journal essay, and conduct some research in the library and/or on the Internet on the subject of bilingualism in education. Then write an essay arguing that schools either should *or* should not teach non-English-speaking students in their own language until they become sufficiently proficient in English to join regular classes. At some point, you should acknowledge and perhaps refute opposing views.

Dave Barry

Pulitzer Prize–winning humorist Dave Barry (1947–) began his writing career covering—as he puts it—"incredibly dull municipal meetings" for the *Daily Local News* of West Chester, Pennsylvania. Next came an eight-year stint trying to teach businesspeople not to write sentences like "Enclosed please find the enclosed enclosures." In 1983, Barry joined the staff of the *Miami Herald,* where his rib-tickling commentary on the absurdities of everyday life quickly brought him a legion of devoted fans. Barry's column is now syndicated in more than 150 newspapers. A popular guest on television and radio, Barry has written dozens of books, including *Dave Barry's Complete Guide to Guys* (1995), *Dave Barry in Cyberspace* (1996), *Big Trouble* (1999), *Dave Barry Hits Below the Beltway* (2001), and *Boogers Are My Beat* (2003), as well as the comic mystery novel *Tricky Business* (2002). The father of two, he lives in Miami with his wife. The essay below first appeared in the *Miami Herald* in 1998.

Pre-Reading Journal Entry

To what extent would you say our images of personal attractiveness are influenced by TV commercials and magazine advertisements? Think of commercials and ads you've seen recently. What physical traits are typically identified as attractive in women? In men? List as many as you can. What assumptions does each trait suggest? Use your journal to respond to these questions.

The Ugly Truth About Beauty

If you're a man, at some point a woman will ask you how she looks. 1

"How do I look?" she'll ask. 2

You must be careful how you answer this question. The best technique 3 is to form an honest yet sensitive opinion, then collapse on the floor with some kind of fatal seizure. Trust me, this is the easiest way out. Because you will never come up with the right answer.

The problem is that women generally do not think of their looks in the 4 same way that men do. Most men form an opinion of how they look in the seventh grade, and they stick to it for the rest of their lives. Some men form the opinion that they are irresistible stud muffins, and they do not change this opinion even when their faces sag and their noses bloat to the size of eggplants and their eyebrows grow together to form what appears to be a giant forehead-dwelling tropical caterpillar.

Most men, I believe, think of themselves as average-looking. Men will think 5 this even if their faces cause heart failure in cattle at a range of 300 yards. Being average does not bother them; average is fine, for men. This is why men never ask anybody how they look. Their primary form of beauty care is to shave them-selves, which is essentially the same form of beauty care that they give to their lawns. If, at the end of his four-minute daily beauty regimen, a man has man-aged to wipe most of the shaving cream out of his hair and is not bleeding too badly, he feels that he has done all he can, so he stops thinking about his appear-ance and devotes his mind to more critical issues, such as the Super Bowl.

Women do not look at themselves this way. If I had to express, in three   6
words, what I believe most women think about their appearance, those words would be: "not good enough." No matter how attractive a woman may appear to be to others, when she looks at herself in the mirror, she thinks: woof. She thinks that at any moment a municipal animal-control offi-cer is going to throw a net over her and haul her off to the shelter.

Why do women have such low self-esteem? There are many complex   7
psychological and societal reasons, by which I mean Barbie. Girls grow up playing with a doll proportioned such that, if it were human, it would be seven feet tall and weigh 81 pounds, of which 53 pounds would be bosoms. This is a difficult appearance standard to live up to, especially when you con-trast it with the standard set for little boys by their dolls . . . excuse me, by their action figures. Most of the action figures that my son played with when he was little were hideous-looking. For example, he was very fond of an action figure (part of the He-Man series) called "Buzz-Off," who was part human, part flying insect. Buzz-Off was not a looker. But he was extremely self-confident. You could not imagine Buzz-Off saying to the other action figures: "Do you think these wings make my hips look big?"

But women grow up thinking they need to look like Barbie, which for   8
most women is impossible, although there is a multibillion-dollar beauty industry devoted to convincing women that they must try. I once saw an Oprah show wherein supermodel Cindy Crawford dispensed makeup tips to the studio audience. Cindy had all these middle-aged women applying beau-ty products to their faces; she stressed how important it was to apply them in a certain way, using the tips of their fingers. All the women dutifully did this, even though it was obvious to any sane observer that, no matter how carefully they applied these products, they would never look remotely like Cindy Crawford, who is some kind of genetic mutation.

I'm not saying that men are superior. I'm just saying that you're not   9
going to get a group of middle-aged men to sit in a room and apply cos-metics to themselves under the instruction of Brad Pitt, in hopes of looking more like him. Men would realize that this task was pointless and demean-ing. They would find some way to bolster their self-esteem that did not require looking like Brad Pitt. They would say to Brad: "Oh YEAH? Well what do you know about LAWN CARE, pretty boy?"

Of course many women will argue that the reason they become obsessed   10
with trying to look like Cindy Crawford is that men, being as shallow as a drop of spit, WANT women to look that way. To which I have two responses:

1. Hey, just because WE'RE idiots, that does not mean YOU have to be; and   11

2. Men don't even notice 97 percent of the beauty efforts you make   12
anyway. Take fingernails. The average woman spends 5,000 hours per year
worrying about her fingernails; I have never once, in more than 40 years
of listening to men talk about women, heard a man say, "She has a nice set
of fingernails!" Many men would not notice if a woman had upward of
four hands.

Anyway, to get back to my original point: If you're a man, and a woman   13
asks you how she looks, you're in big trouble. Obviously, you can't say she
looks bad. But you also can't say that she looks great, because she'll think
you're lying, because she has spent countless hours, with the help of the multibillion-dollar beauty industry, obsessing about the differences between herself
and Cindy Crawford. Also, she suspects that you're not qualified to judge anybody's appearance. This is because you have shaving cream in your hair.

Questions for Close Reading

1. What is the selection's thesis? Locate the sentence(s) in which Barry states his main idea. If he doesn't state the thesis explicitly, express it in your own words.
2. Barry tells us that most men consider themselves to be "average-looking" (paragraph 5). Why, according to Barry, do men feel this way?
3. When Barry writes that most women think of themselves as "not good enough" (6), what does he mean? What, according to Barry, causes women to develop low opinions of themselves?
4. Barry implies that women could have a more rational response to the "difficult appearance standard" that pervades society (7). What would that response be?
5. Refer to your dictionary as needed to define the following words used in the selection: *regimen* (paragraph 5), *municipal* (6), *societal* (7), *dispensed* (8), *genetic* (8), *mutation* (8), *demeaning* (9), and *bolster* (9).

Questions About the Writer's Craft

1. **The pattern.** Which comparison-contrast method of organization (point-by-point or one-side-at-a-time) does Barry use to develop his essay? Why might he have chosen this pattern?
2. Barry uses exaggeration, a strategy typically associated with humorous writing. Locate instances of exaggeration in the selection. Why do you think he uses this strategy?
3. **Other patterns.** Barry demonstrates a series of *cause-effect* chains in his essay. Locate some of the cause-effect series. How do they help Barry reinforce his thesis?
4. Barry's title involves an *oxymoron*—a contradiction in terms. What does this title imply about Barry's attitude toward his subject?

Writing Assignments Using Comparison-Contrast as a Pattern of Development

∞ 1. Examine the pitches made in magazines and on TV for the male and female versions of *one* kind of grooming product. Possibilities include deodorant, hair dye, soap, and so on. Then write an essay contrasting the persuasive appeals that the product makes to men with those it makes to women. (Don't forget to examine the assumptions behind the appeals.) To gain insight into advertising techniques, you'll find it helpful to read Ann McClintock's "Propaganda Techniques in Today's Advertising" (page 207). For useful perspectives on gender issues, consider reading Barbara Ehrenreich's "What I've Learned From Men" (page 166), Camille Paglia's "Rape: A Bigger Danger Than Feminists Know" (page 395), and Susan Jacoby's "Common Decency" (page 401).

2. Barry contrasts women's preoccupation with looking good to men's lack of concern about their appearance. Now consider the flip side—something men care about deeply that women virtually ignore. Write an essay contrasting men's stereotypical fascination with *one* area to women's indifference. You might, for example, examine male and female attitudes toward sports, cars, tools, even lawn care. Following Barry's example, adopt a playful tone in your essay, illustrating the absurdity of the obsession you discuss.

Writing Assignments Combining Patterns of Development

3. Barry implies that most men, unaffected by the "multibillion-dollar beauty industry," are content to "think of themselves as average looking." Do you agree? Conduct your own research into whether or not Barry's assertions about men are true. Begin by interviewing several male friends, family members, and classmates to see how these men feel about their physical appearance. In addition, in the library or online, research magazines such as *People, Gentlemen's Quarterly,* or *Men's Health* for articles describing how everyday men as well as male celebrities view their looks. Then write an essay *refuting or defending* the view that being average-looking doesn't bother most men. Start by acknowledging the opposing view; then support your assertion with convincing *examples* and other evidence drawn from your research.

4. Barry blames Barbie dolls for setting up "a difficult appearance standard" for girls to emulate. Many would *argue* that the toys that *boys* play with also teach negative, ultimately damaging values. Write an essay exploring the values that are conveyed to boys through their toys. Brainstorm with others, especially males, about the toys of their youth or the toys that boys have today. Identify two to three key negative values to write about, *illustrating* each with several examples of toys.

Writing Assignment Using a Journal Entry as a Starting Point

5. Review your pre-reading journal entry. Focusing on the characteristics of male *or* female attractiveness conveyed by the mass media, identify two to three assumptions suggested by these standards. Illustrate each assumption with examples from TV commercials and/or magazine advertisements. Be sure to make clear how you feel about these assumptions.

Additional Writing Topics

COMPARISON-CONTRAST

General Assignments

Using comparison-contrast, write an essay on one of the following topics. Your thesis should indicate whether the two subjects are being compared, contrasted, or both. Organize the paper by arranging the details in a one-side-at-a-time or point-by-point pattern. Remember to use organizational cues to help the audience follow your analysis.

1. Living at home versus living in an apartment or dorm
2. Two-career family versus one-career family
3. Two approaches for dealing with problems
4. Children's pastimes today and yesterday
5. Life before the Internet versus after the Internet
6. Neighborhood stores versus shopping malls
7. Two characters in a novel or other literary work
8. Two attitudes toward money
9. A sports team then and now
10. Watching a movie on television versus viewing it in a theater
11. Two attitudes about a controversial subject
12. Two approaches to parenting
13. A typical fan of one type of music versus another
14. Marriage versus living together
15. The atmosphere in two classes
16. Two approaches to studying
17. The place where you live and the place where you would like to live
18. Two comedians
19. The coverage of an event on television versus the coverage in a newspaper
20. Significant trend versus passing fad
21. Two horror or adventure movies
22. Handwriting a letter versus sending an e-mail message
23. Two candidates for an office
24. Your attitude before and after getting to know someone
25. Two friends with different lifestyles

Assignments With a Specific Purpose, Audience, and Point of View

On Campus

1. You would like to change your campus living arrangements. Perhaps you want to move from a dormitory to an off-campus apartment or from home to a dorm. Before you do, though, you'll have to convince your parents (who are paying

most of your college costs) that the move will be beneficial. Write out what you would say to your parents. Contrast your current situation with your proposed one, explaining why the new arrangement would be better.

2. Write a guide on "Passing Exams" for first-year college students, contrasting the right and wrong ways to prepare for and take exams. Although your purpose is basically serious, write the selection on how *not* to approach exams with some humor.

At Home or in the Community

3. As president of your local Neighbors' Association, you're concerned about the way your local government is dealing with a particular situation (for example, an increase in robberies, muggings, graffiti, and so on). Write a letter to your mayor contrasting the way your local government handles the situation with another city or town's approach. In your conclusion, point out the advantages of adopting the other neighborhood's strategy.

4. Your old high school has invited you back to make a speech before an audience of seniors. The topic will be "how to choose the college that is right for you." Write your speech in the form of a comparison-contrast analysis. Focus on the choices available (two-year versus four-year schools, large versus small, local versus faraway, and so on), showing the advantages and/or disadvantages of each.

On the Job

5. As store manager, you decide to write a memo to all sales personnel explaining how to keep customers happy. Compare and/or contrast the needs and shopping habits of several different consumer groups (by age, spending ability, or sex), and show how to make each group comfortable in your store.

6. You work as a volunteer for a mental health hot line. Many people call simply because they feel "stressed out." Do some research on the subject of stress management, and prepare a brochure for these people, recommending a "Type B" approach to stressful situations. Focus the brochure on the contrast between "Type A" and "Type B" personalities: the former is nervous, hard-driving, competitive; the latter is relaxed and noncompetitive. Give specific examples of how each type tends to act in stressful situations.

9

CAUSE-EFFECT

WHAT IS CAUSE-EFFECT?

Superstition has it that curiosity killed the cat. Maybe so. Yet our science, technology, storytelling, and fascination with the past and future all spring from our determination to know "Why" and "What if." Seeking explanations, young children barrage adults with endless questions: "Why do trees grow tall?" "What would happen if the sun didn't shine?" But children aren't the only ones who wonder in this way. All of us think in terms of cause and effect, sometimes consciously, sometimes unconsciously: "Why did they give me such an odd look?" we wonder, or "How would I do at another college?" we speculate. This exploration of reasons and results is also at the heart of most professions: "What led to our involvement in Vietnam?" historians question; "What will happen if we administer this experimental drug?" scientists ask.

Cause-effect writing, often called *causal analysis,* is rooted in this elemental need to make connections. Because the drive to understand reasons and results is so fundamental, causal analysis is a common kind of writing. An article analyzing the unexpected outcome of an election, a report linking poor nutrition to low academic achievement, an editorial analyzing the impact of a proposed tax cut—all are examples of cause-effect writing.

Done well, cause-effect pieces can uncover the subtle and often surprising connections between events or phenomena. By rooting out causes and projecting effects, causal analysis enables us to make sense of our experiences, revealing a universe that is somewhat less arbitrary and chaotic.

HOW CAUSE-EFFECT FITS YOUR PURPOSE AND AUDIENCE

Many assignments and exam questions in college involve writing essays that analyze causes, effects, or both. Sometimes, as in the following examples, you'll be asked to write an essay developed primarily through the cause-effect pattern:

> Although divorces have leveled off in the last few years, the number of marriages ending in divorce is still greater than it was a generation ago. What do you think are the causes of this phenomenon?

> Political commentators were surprised that so few people voted in the last election. Discuss the probable causes of this weak voter turnout.

> Americans never seem to tire of gossip about the rich and famous. What effect has this fascination with celebrities had on U.S. culture?

> The federal government is expected to pass legislation that will significantly reduce the funding of student loans. Analyze the possible effects of such a cutback.

Other assignments and exam questions may not explicitly ask you to address causes and effects, but they may use words that suggest causal analysis would be appropriate. Consider these examples, paying special attention to the words in boldface:

> In contrast to the socially involved youth of the 1960s, many young people today tend to remove themselves from political issues. What do you think are the **sources** of the political apathy found among 18- to 25-year-olds? (*cause*)

> A number of experts forecast that drug abuse will be the most significant factor affecting U.S. productivity in the coming decade. Evaluate the validity of this observation by discussing the **impact** of drugs in the workplace. (*effect*)

> According to school officials, a predictable percentage of entering students drop out of college at some point during their first year. What **motivates** students to drop out? What **happens** to them once they leave? (*cause and effect*)

In addition to serving as the primary strategy for achieving an essay's purpose, causal analysis can also be a supplemental method used to help make a point in an essay developed chiefly through another pattern of development. Assume, for example, that you want to write an essay *defining* the term *the homeless*. To help readers see that unfavorable circumstances can result in nearly anyone becoming homeless, you might discuss some of the unavoidable, everyday factors causing people to live on streets and in subway stations. Similarly, in a *persuasive* proposal urging your college administration to institute an honors program, you would probably spend some time analyzing the positive effect of such a program on students and faculty.

SUGGESTIONS FOR USING CAUSE-EFFECT IN AN ESSAY

The following suggestions will be helpful whether you use causal analysis as a dominant or a supportive pattern of development.

1. Stay focused on the purpose of your analysis.   When writing a causal analysis, don't lose sight of your overall purpose. Consider, for example, an essay on the causes of widespread child abuse. If you're concerned primarily with explaining the problem of child abuse to your readers, you might take a purely *informative* approach:

> Although parental stress is the immediate cause of child abuse, the more compelling reason for such behavior lies in the way parents were themselves mistreated in their own families.

Or you might want to *persuade* the audience about some point or idea concerning child abuse:

> The tragic consequences of child abuse provide strong support for more aggressive handling of such cases by social workers and judges.

Then again, you could choose a *speculative* approach, your main purpose being to suggest possibilities:

> Psychologists disagree about the potential effect on youngsters of all the media attention to child abuse. Will children exposed to this media coverage grow up assertive, self-confident, and able to protect themselves? Or will they become fearful and distrustful?

These examples illustrate that an essay's causal analysis may have more than one purpose. For instance, although the last example points to a paper with a primarily speculative purpose, the essay would probably start by informing readers of experts' conflicting views. The paper would also have a persuasive slant if it ended by urging readers to complain to the media about their sensationalized treatment of the child-abuse issue.

2. Adapt content and tone to your purpose and readers.   Your purpose and audience determine what supporting material and what tone will be most effective in a cause-effect essay. Assume you want to direct your essay on child abuse to general readers who know little about the subject. To *inform* readers, you might use facts, statistics, and expert opinion to provide an objective discussion of the causes of child abuse. Your analysis might show the following: (1) adults who were themselves mistreated as children tend to abuse their own offspring; (2) marital stress contributes to the mistreatment of children; and (3) certain personality disorders increase the likelihood of child abuse. Sensitive to what your readers would and wouldn't understand, you would stay away from a technical or formal tone. Rather than writing "Pathological preabuse symptomatology predicts adult transference of high aggressivity," you would say "Psychologists can often predict, on the basis of family histories, who will abuse children."

Now imagine that your purpose is to *convince* future social workers that the failure of social service agencies to act authoritatively in child-abuse cases often has tragic consequences. Hoping to encourage more responsible behavior in the prospective social workers, you would adopt a more emotional tone in the essay, perhaps citing wrenching case histories that dramatize what happens when child abuse isn't taken seriously.

3. Think rigorously about causes and effects.   To write a meaningful causal analysis, you should do some careful thinking about the often complex relationship between causes and effects. Children tend to oversimplify causes and effects ("Mommy and Daddy are getting divorced because I was bad the other day"), and adults' arguments can be characterized by hasty, often slipshod thinking ("All these immigrants willing to work cheaply have made us lose our jobs"). But imprecise thinking has no place in essay writing. You should be willing to dig for causes, to think creatively about effects. You should examine your subject in depth, looking beyond the obvious and superficial.

Brainstorming, freewriting, and mapping will help you explore causes and effects thoroughly. No matter which prewriting technique you use, generate as many explanations as possible by asking yourself questions like these:

> *Causes:* What happened? What are the possible reasons? Which are most likely? Who was involved? Why?
>
> *Effects:* What happened? Who was involved? What were the observable results? What are some possible future consequences? Which consequences are negative? Which are positive?

If you remain open and look beyond the obvious, you'll discover that a cause may have many effects. Imagine that you're writing a paper on the effects of cigarette smoking. Prewriting would probably generate a number of consequences that could be discussed, some less obvious but perhaps more interesting than others: increased risk of lung cancer and heart disease, harm traced to secondhand smoke, legal battles regarding the rights of smokers and nonsmokers, lower birth weights in babies of mothers who smoke, and developmental problems experienced by such underweight infants.

In the same way, prewriting will help you see that an effect may have multiple causes. An essay analyzing the reasons for world hunger could discuss many causes, again some less evident but perhaps more thought-provoking than others: climatic changes, inefficient use of land, cultural predispositions for large families, and poor management of international relief funds.

Your analysis may also uncover a *causal chain* in which one cause (or effect) brings about another, which, in turn, brings about another, and so on. Here's an example of a causal chain: Prohibition went into effect; bootleggers and organized crime stepped in to supply public demand for alcoholic beverages; ordinary citizens began breaking the law by buying illegal alcohol and patronizing speakeasies; disrespect for legal authority became widespread and acceptable. As you can see, a causal chain often leads to interesting points. In this case, the subject of Prohibition leads not just to the obvious (illegal consumption of alcohol) but also to the more complex issue of society's decreasing respect for legal authority.

Don't grapple with so complex a chain, however, that you become hopelessly entangled. If your subject involves multiple causes and effects, limit what you'll discuss. Identify which causes and effects are *primary* and which are *secondary*. How extensively you cover secondary factors will depend on your purpose and audience. In an essay intended to inform a general audience about the harmful effects of pesticides, you would most likely focus on everyday dangers—polluted drinking water, residues in food, and the like. You probably wouldn't include a discussion of more long-range consequences (evolution of resistant insects, disruption of the soil's acid-alkaline balance).

Similarly, decide whether to focus on *immediate,* more obvious causes and effects, or on less obvious, more *remote* ones. Or perhaps you need to focus on both. In an essay about a faculty strike at your college, should you attribute the strike simply to the faculty's failure to receive a salary increase? Or should you also examine other factors: the union's failure to accept a salary package that satisfied most professors; the administration's inability to coordinate its negotiating efforts? It may be more difficult to explore more remote causes and effects, but it can also lead to more original and revealing essays. Thoughtful analyses take these less obvious considerations into account.

When developing a causal analysis, be careful to avoid the *post hoc fallacy*. Named after the Latin phrase *post hoc, ergo propter hoc,* meaning "after this, therefore because of this," this kind of faulty thinking occurs when you assume that simply because one event *followed* another, the first event *caused* the second. For example, if the Republicans win a majority of seats in Congress and, several months later, the economy collapses, can you conclude that the Republicans caused the collapse? A quick assumption of "Yes" fails the test of logic, for the timing of events could be coincidental and not indicative of any cause-effect relationship. The collapse may have been triggered by uncontrolled inflation that began well before the congressional elections. (For more information on the *post hoc* fallacy, see pages 287–288.)

Also, be careful not to mistake *correlation* for *causation*. Two events correlate when they occur at about the same time. Such co-occurrence, however, doesn't guarantee a cause-effect relationship. For instance, while the number of ice cream cones eaten and the instances of heat prostration both increase during the summer months, this doesn't mean that eating ice-cream causes heat prostration! A third factor—in this case, summer heat—is the actual cause. When writing causal analyses, then, use with caution words that imply a causal link (such as *therefore* and *because*). Words that express simply time of occurrence (like *following* and *previously*) are safer and more objective.

Finally, keep in mind that a rigorous causal analysis involves more than loose generalizations about causes and effects. Creating plausible connections may require library research, interviewing, or both. Often you'll need to provide facts, statistics, details, personal observations, or other corroborative material if readers are going to accept the reasoning behind your analysis.

4. Write a thesis that focuses the paper on causes, effects, or both.   The thesis in an essay developed through causal analysis often indicates whether the essay will deal mostly with causes, effects, or both. Here, for example, are three thesis statements for causal analyses dealing with the public school system. You'll see that each thesis signals that essay's particular emphasis:

> Our school system has been weakened by an overemphasis on trendy electives. *(causes)*

> An ineffectual school system has led to crippling teachers' strikes and widespread disrespect for the teaching profession. *(effects)*

> Bureaucratic inefficiency has created a school system unresponsive to children's emotional, physical, and intellectual needs. *(causes and effects)*

Note that the thesis statement—in addition to signaling whether the paper will discuss causes or effects or both—may also point to the essay's plan of development. Consider the last thesis statement; it makes clear that the paper will discuss children's emotional needs first, their physical needs second, and their intellectual needs last.

The thesis statement in a causal analysis doesn't have to specify whether the essay will discuss causes, effects, or both. Nor does the thesis have to be worded in such a way that the essay's plan of development is apparent. But when first writing cause-effect essays, you may find that a highly focused thesis will keep your analysis on track.

5. Choose an organizational pattern. There are two basic ways to organize the points in a cause-effect essay: You may use a chronological or an emphatic sequence. If you select a *chronological order,* you discuss causes and effects in the order in which they occur or will occur. Suppose you're writing an essay on the causes for the popularity of imported cars. These causes might be discussed in chronological sequence: American plant workers became frustrated and dissatisfied on the job; some workers got careless while others deliberately sabotaged the production of sound cars; a growing number of defective cars hit the market; consumers grew dissatisfied with American cars and switched to imports.

Chronology might also be used to organize a discussion about effects. Imagine you want to write an essay about the need to guard against disrupting delicate balances in the country's wildlife. You might start the essay by discussing what happened when the starling, a non-native bird, was introduced into the American environment. Because the starling had few natural predators, the starling population soared out of control; the starlings took over food sources and habitats of native species; the bluebird, a native species, declined and is now threatened with extinction.

Although a chronological pattern can be an effective way to organize material, a strict time sequence can present a problem if your primary cause or effect ends up buried in the middle of the sequence. In such a case, you might use *emphatic order,* reserving the most significant cause or effect for the end. For example, time order could be used to present the reasons behind a candidate's unexpected victory: Less than a month after the candidate's earlier defeat, a full-scale fund-raising campaign for the next election was started; the candidate spoke to many crucial power groups early in the campaign; the candidate did exceptionally well in the pre-election debates; good weather and large voter turnout on election day favored the candidate. However, if you believe that the candidate's appearance before influential groups was the key factor in the victory, it would be more effective to emphasize that point by saving it for the end. This is what is meant by emphatic order—saving the most important point for last.

Emphatic order is an especially effective way to sequence cause-effect points when readers hold what, in your opinion, are mistaken or narrow views about a subject. To encourage readers to look more closely at the issues, you present what you consider the erroneous or obvious views first, show why they are unsound or limited, then present what you feel to be the actual causes and effects. Such a sequence nudges the audience into giving further thought to the causes and effects you have discovered. Here are informal outlines for two causal analyses using this approach.

Subject: The causes of the riot at the rock concert

1. Some commentators blame the excessively hot weather.
2. Others cite drug use among the concertgoers.
3. Still others blame the liquor sold at the concessions.
4. But the real cause of the disaster was poor planning by the concert promoters.

Subject: The effects of campus crime

1. Immediate problems
   a. Students feel insecure and fearful.
   b. Many nighttime campus activities have been curtailed.
2. More significant long-term problems
   a. Unfavorable publicity about campus crime will affect future student enrollments.
   b. Hiring faculty will become more difficult.

When using emphatic order in a causal analysis, you might want to word the thesis in such a way that it signals which point your essay will stress. Look at the following thesis statements:

Although many immigrants arrive in this country without marketable skills, their most pressing problem is learning how to make their way in a society whose language they don't know.

The space program has led to dramatic advances in computer technology and medical science. Even more important, though, the program has helped change many people's attitudes toward the planet we live on.

These thesis statements reflect an awareness of the complex nature of cause-effect relationships. While not dismissing secondary issues, the statements establish which points the writer considers most noteworthy. The second thesis, for instance, indicates that the paper will touch on the technological and medical advances made possible by the space program but will emphasize the way the program has changed people's attitudes toward the earth.

Whether you use a chronological or emphatic pattern to organize your essay, you'll need to provide clear *signals* to identify when you're discussing causes and when you're discussing effects. Expressions such as "Another reason" and "A final outcome" help readers follow your line of thought.

6. Use language that hints at the complexity of cause-effect relationships.
Because it's difficult—if not impossible—to identify causes and effects with certainty, you should avoid such absolutes as "It must be obvious" and "There is no doubt." Instead, try phrases like "Most likely" or "It's probable that." Using such language is not indecisive; rather, it reflects your understanding

of the often tangled nature of causes and effects. Be careful, though, of going to the other extreme and being reluctant to take a stand on the issues. If you've thought carefully about causes and effects, you have a right to state your analysis with conviction. Don't undercut the hard work you've done by writing as if your ideas were unworthy of your reader's attention.

REVISION STRATEGIES

Once you have a draft of the essay, you're ready to revise. The following checklist will help you and those giving you feedback apply to cause-effect some of the revision techniques discussed on pages 59–61.

☑ CAUSE-EFFECT: A REVISION/PEER REVIEW CHECKLIST

Revise Overall Meaning and Structure

❏ Is the essay's purpose informative, persuasive, speculative, or a combination of these?

❏ What is the essay's thesis? Is it stated specifically or implied? Where? Could it be made any clearer? How?

❏ Does the essay focus on causes, effects, or both? How do you know?

❏ Where has correlation been mistaken for causation? Where is the essay weakened by *post hoc* thinking?

❏ Where does the essay distinguish between primary and secondary causes and effects? Do the most critical causes and effects receive special attention?

❏ Where does the essay dwell on the obvious?

Revise Paragraph Development

❏ Are the essay's paragraphs sequenced chronologically or emphatically? Could they be sequenced more effectively? How?

❏ Where would signal devices make it easier to follow the progression of thought within and between paragraphs?

❏ Which paragraphs would be strengthened by vivid examples (such as statistics, facts, anecdotes, or personal observations) that support the causal analysis?

Revise Sentences and Words

❏ Where do expressions like *as a result, because,* and *therefore* mislead the reader by implying a cause-effect relationship? Would words such as *following* and *previously* eliminate the problem?

❏ Do any words or phrases convey an arrogant or dogmatic tone (*there is no question, undoubtedly, always, never*)? What other expressions (*most likely, probably*) would improve credibility?

STUDENT ESSAY

The following student essay was written by Carl Novack in response to this assignment:

> In "Our Schedules, Our Selves," Jay Walljasper examines the way Palm Pilots, cell phones, e-mail, and other technologies have resulted in our "overbooking" our daily lives. Think of another aspect of everyday life that has changed recently, and discuss those factors that you believe are responsible for the change.

While reading Carl's paper, try to determine how well it applies the principles of causal analysis. The annotations on Carl's paper and the commentary following it will help you look at the essay more closely.

Americans and Food
by Carl Novack

Introduction

1   An offbeat but timely cartoon recently appeared in the local newspaper. The single panel showed a gravel-pit operation with piles of raw earth and large cranes. Next to one of the cranes stood the owner of the gravel pit--a grizzled, tough-looking character, hammer in hand, pointing proudly to the new sign he had just tacked up. The sign read, "Fred's Fill Dirt and Croissants." The cartoon illustrates an interesting phenomenon: the changing food habits of Americans. Our meals used to consist of something like home-cooked pot roast, mashed potatoes laced with butter and salt, a thick slice of apple pie topped with a healthy scoop of vanilla ice cream--plain, heavy meals, cooked from scratch, and eaten leisurely at home.

Thesis —

But America has changed, and as it has, so have what we Americans eat and how we eat it.

Topic sentence:
Background
paragraph —

2   We used to have simple, unsophisticated tastes and looked with suspicion at anything more exotic than hamburger. Admittedly, we did adopt some foods from the various immigrant groups who flocked to our shores. We learned to eat Chinese food, pizza, and bagels.

Topic sentence:
Three causes
answer the
question —

But in the last few years, the international character of our diet has grown tremendously. We can walk into any mall in Middle America and buy pita sandwiches, quiche, and tacos. Such foods are often changed on their journey from exotic imports to ordinary "American" meals (no Pakistani, for example, eats frozen-on-a-stick boysenberry-flavored yogurt), but the imports are still a long way from hamburger on a bun.

First cause —

3   Why have we become more worldly in our tastes? For one thing, television blankets the country with information about

new food products and trends. Viewers in rural Montana know that the latest craving in Washington, D.C., is Cajun cooking or that something called tofu is now available in the local

Second cause — supermarket. Another reason for the growing international flavor of our food is that many young Americans have traveled abroad and gotten hooked on new tastes and flavors. Backpacking students and young professionals vacationing in Europe come home with cravings for authentic French bread

Third cause — or German beer. Finally, continuing waves of immigrants settle in the cities where many of us live, causing significant changes in what we eat. Vietnamese, Haitians, and Thais, for instance, bring their native foods and cooking styles with them and eventually open small markets or restaurants. In time, the new food will become Americanized enough to take its place in our

Topic sentence: national diet.

Another cause → Our growing concern with health has also affected the 4 way we eat. For the last few years, the media have warned us about the dangers of our traditional diet, high in salt and fat, low in fiber. The media also began to educate us about the

Start of a dangers of processed foods pumped full of chemical additives.

causal chain → As a result, consumers began to demand healthier foods, and manufacturers started to change some of their products. Many foods, such as lunch meat, canned vegetables, and soups, were made available in low-fat, low-sodium versions. Whole-grain cereals and higher-fiber breads also began to appear on the grocery shelves. Moreover, the food industry started to produce all-natural products--everything from potato chips to ice cream--without additives and preservatives. Not surprisingly, the restaurant industry responded to this switch to healthier foods, luring customers with salad bars, broiled

Topic sentence: fish, and steamed vegetables.

Another cause → Our food habits are being affected, too, by the rapid 5 increase in the number of women working outside the home. Sociologists and other experts believe that two important factors triggered this phenomenon: the women's movement and a changing economic climate. Women were assured that it was acceptable, even rewarding, to work outside the home; many women also discovered that they had to work just to keep up with the cost of living. As the traditional role of homemaker changed, so did the way families ate. With Mom working, there wasn't time for her to prepare the traditional three square meals a day. Instead, families began looking for

Start of a alternatives to provide quick meals. What was the result? For

causal chain — one thing, there was a boom in fast-food restaurants. The suburban or downtown strip that once contained a lone McDonald's now features Wendy's, Roy Rogers, Taco Bell, Burger King, and Pizza Hut. Families also began to depend on frozen foods as another time-saving alternative. Once again, though, demand changed the kind of frozen food available. Frozen foods no longer consist of foil trays divided into greasy fried chicken, watery corn niblets, and lumpy mashed potatoes. Supermarkets now stock a range of supposedly gourmet frozen dinners--from fettucini in cream sauce to braised beef en brochette.

Conclusion   It may not be possible to pick up a ton of fill dirt and a half-   6
dozen croissants at the same place, but America's food habits are definitely changing. If it is true that "you are what you eat," then America's identity is evolving along with its diet.

COMMENTARY

Title and introduction.   Asked to prepare a paper analyzing the reasons behind a change in our lives, Carl decided to write about a shift he had noticed in Americans' eating habits. The title of the essay, "Americans and Food," identifies Carl's subject but could be livelier and more interesting.

Despite his rather uninspired title, Carl starts his *causal analysis* in an engaging way—with the vivid description of a cartoon. He then connects the cartoon to his subject with the following sentence: "The cartoon illustrates an interesting phenomenon: the changing food habits of Americans." To back up his belief that there has been a revolution in our eating habits, Carl uses the first paragraph to summarize the kind of meal that people used to eat. He then moves into his *thesis:* "But America has changed, and as it has, so have what Americans eat and how we eat it." The thesis implies that Carl's paper will focus on both causes and effects.

Purpose.   Carl's *purpose* was to write an *informative* causal analysis. But before he could present the causes of the change in eating habits, he needed to show that such a change had, in fact, taken place. He therefore uses the second paragraph to document one aspect of this change—the internationalization of our eating habits.

Topic sentences.   At the beginning of the third paragraph, Carl uses a question—"Why have we become more worldly in our tastes?"—to signal that his discussion of causes is about to begin. This question also serves as the paragraph's *topic sentence,* indicating that the paragraph will focus on reasons for the increasingly international flavor of our food. The next two paragraphs, also focused by topic sentences, identify two other major reasons for the change in eating habits: "Our growing concern with health has also affected the way we eat" (paragraph 4), and "Our food habits are being affected, too, by the rapid increase in the number of women working outside the home" (5).

Combining patterns of development.   Carl draws on two patterns—comparison-contrast and exemplification—to develop his causal analysis. At the heart of the essay is a basic *contrast* between the way we used to eat and the way we eat now. And throughout his essay, Carl provides convincing *examples* to demonstrate the validity of his points. Consider for a moment the third paragraph. Here Carl asserts that one reason for our new eating habits is our growing exposure to international foods. He then presents concrete evidence to show that we have indeed become more familiar with international cuisine: Television exposes rural Montana to Cajun cooking; students traveling abroad take a liking to French bread; urban dwellers enjoy the exotic fare served by numerous immigrant groups. The fourth and fifth paragraphs use similarly specific evidence (for example, "low-fat, low-sodium versions" of "lunch meat, canned vegetables, and soups") to illustrate the soundness of key ideas.

Causal chains.   Let's look more closely at the evidence in the essay. Not satisfied with obvious explanations, Carl thought through his ideas carefully and even brainstormed with friends to arrive at as comprehensive an analysis as possible. Not surprisingly, much of the evidence Carl uncovered took the form of *causal chains*. In the fourth paragraph, Carl writes, "The media also began to educate us about the dangers of processed foods pumped full of chemical additives. As a result, consumers began to demand healthier foods, and manufacturers started to change some of their products." And the next paragraph shows how the changing role of American women caused families to search for alternative ways of eating. This shift, in turn, caused the restaurant and food industries to respond with a wide range of food alternatives.

Making the paper easy to follow.   Although Carl's analysis digs beneath the surface and reveals complex cause-effect relationships, he wisely limits his pursuit of causal chains to *primary causes and effects*. He doesn't let the complexities distract him from his main purpose: to show why and how the American diet is changing. Carl is also careful to provide his essay with abundant *connecting devices,* making it easy for readers to see the links between points. Consider the use of *transitions* (signaled by italics) in the following sentences: "*Another* reason for the growing international flavor of our food is that many young Americans have traveled abroad" (paragraph 3); "*As a result,* consumers began to demand healthier foods" (4); and "*As* the traditional role of homemaker changed, so did the way families ate" (5).

A problem with the essay's close.   When reading the essay, you probably noticed that Carl's conclusion is a bit weak. Although his reference to the cartoon works well, the rest of the paragraph limps to a tired close. Ending an otherwise vigorous essay with such a slight conclusion undercuts the effectiveness of the whole paper. Carl spent so much energy developing the body of his essay that he ran out of the stamina needed to conclude the piece more forcefully. Careful budgeting of his time would have allowed him to prepare a stronger concluding paragraph.

Revising the first draft.   When Carl was ready to revise, he showed the first draft of his essay to several classmates during a peer review session. Listening carefully to what they said, he jotted down their most helpful comments and eventually transferred them, numbered in order of importance, to his draft. Comparing Carl's original version of his fourth paragraph (shown here) with his final version in the essay will show you how he went about revising.

Original Version of the Fourth Paragraph

A growing concern with health has also affected the way we eat, especially because the media have sent us warnings the last few years about the dangers of salt, sugar, food additives, high-fat and low-fiber diets. We have started to worry that our traditional meals may have been shortening our lives. As a result, consumers demanded healthier foods and manufacturers started taking some of the salt and sugar out of canned foods. "All-natural" became an effective selling point, leading to many preservative-free products. Restaurants, too, adapted their menus, luring customers with light meals. Because we now know about the link between overweight and a variety of health problems, including heart attacks, we are counting calories. In turn, food companies made fortunes on diet beer and diet cola. Sometimes, though, we seem a bit confused about the health issue; we drink soda that is sugar-free but loaded with chemical sweeteners. Still, we believe we are lengthening our lives through changing our diets.

On the advice of his classmates, Carl decided to omit all references to the way our concern with weight has affected our eating habits. It's true, of course, that calorie-counting has changed how we eat. But as soon as Carl started to discuss this point, he got involved in a causal chain that undercut the paragraph's unity. He ended up describing the paradoxical situation in which we find ourselves. In an attempt to eat healthy, we stay away from sugar and use instead artificial sweeteners that probably aren't very good for us. This is an interesting issue, but it detracts from the point Carl wants to make: that our concern with health has affected our eating habits in a *positive* way.

Carl's peer reviewers also pointed out that the fourth paragraph's first sentence contained too much material to be an effective topic sentence. Carl corrected the problem by breaking the overlong sentence into two short ones: "Our growing concern with health has also affected the way we eat. For the last few years, the media have warned us about the dangers of our traditional diet, high in salt and fat, low in fiber." The first of these sentences serves as a crisp topic sentence that focuses the rest of the paragraph.

Finally, Carl agreed with his classmates that the fourth paragraph lacked convincing specifics. When revising, he changed "manufacturers started taking some of the salt and sugar out of canned foods" to the more specific "Many foods, such as lunch meats, canned vegetables, and soups, were made available in low-fat, low-sodium versions." Similarly, generalizations about "light meals" and "all-natural products" gained life through the addition of concrete examples: restaurants lured "customers with salad bars, broiled fish, and steamed vegetables," and the food industry produced "everything from potato chips to ice cream—without additives and preservatives."

Carl did an equally good job revising other sections of his paper. With the exception of the weak spots already discussed, he made the changes needed to craft a well-reasoned essay, one that demonstrates his ability to analyze a complex phenomenon.

ACTIVITIES: CAUSE-EFFECT

Prewriting Activities

1. Imagine you're writing two essays: One *argues* the need for high school courses in personal finance (how to budget money, balance a checkbook, and the like); the other explains a *process* for showing appreciation. Jot down ways you might use cause-effect in each essay.

2. Use mapping, collaborative brainstorming, or another prewriting technique to generate possible causes and/or effects for *one* of the topics below. Be sure to keep in mind the audience indicated in parentheses. Next, devise a thesis and decide whether your purpose would be informative, persuasive, speculative, or some combination of these. Finally, organize your raw material into a brief outline, with related causes and effects grouped in the same section.
   a. Pressure on students to do well (*high school students*)
   b. Children's access to pornography on the Internet (*parents*)
   c. Being physically fit (*those who are out of shape*)
   d. Spiraling costs of a college education (*college officials*)

Revising Activities

3. Explain how the following statements demonstrate *post hoc* thinking and confuse correlation and cause-effect.
   a. Our city now has many immigrants from Latin American countries. The crime rate in our city has increased. Latin American immigrants are the cause of the crime wave.
   b. The divorce rate has skyrocketed. More women are working outside the home than ever before. Working outside the home destroys marriages.
   c. A high percentage of people in Dixville have developed cancer. The landfill, used by XYZ Industries, has been located in Dixville for twenty years. The XYZ landfill has caused cancer in Dixville residents.

4. The following paragraph is from the first draft of an essay arguing that technological advances can diminish the quality of life. How solid is the paragraph's causal analysis? Which causes and/or effects should be eliminated? Where is the analysis simplistic? Where does the writer make absolute claims even though cause-effect relationships are no more than a possibility? Keeping these questions in mind, revise the paragraph.

How did the banking industry respond to inflation? It simply introduced a new technology--the automated teller machine (ATM). By making money more available to the average person, the ATM gives people the cash to buy inflated goods--whether or not they can afford them. Not surprisingly, automated teller machines have had a number of negative consequences for the average individual. Since people know they can get cash at any time, they use their lunch hours for something other than going to the bank. How do they spend this newfound time? They go shopping, and machine-vended money means more impulse buying, even more than with a credit card. Also, because people don't need their checkbooks to withdraw money, they can't keep track of their accounts and therefore develop a casual attitude toward financial matters. It's no wonder children don't appreciate the value of money. Another problem is that people who would never dream of robbing a bank try to trick the machine into dispensing money "for free." There's no doubt that this kind of fraud contributes to the immoral climate in the country.

Stephen King

Probably the best-known living horror writer, Stephen King (1947–) is the author of more than thirty books. Before earning fame through his vastly popular books, including *Carrie* (1974), *The Shining* (1977), *Cujo* (1981), and *Tommyknockers* (1987), King worked as a high school English teacher and an industrial laundry worker. Much of King's prolific output has been adapted for the screen; movies based on King's work include *Misery* (1990), *Stand By Me* (1986), and *The Green Mile* (1999). More recent works include *Dreamcatcher* (2001), *Everything's Eventual* (2002), *From a Buick 8* (2002), and Volumes V, VI, and VII in the *Dark Tower* series (published in 2003, 2004, and 2004, respectively). His book *On Writing: A Memoir of the Craft* (2000) offers insight into the writing process and examines the role that writing has played in King's own life—especially following a near-fatal accident in 1999. King lives with his wife in Bangor, Maine, and has three adult children. The following essay first appeared in *Playboy* in 1982.

Pre-Reading Journal Entry

Several forms of entertainment, besides horror movies, are highly popular despite what many consider a low level of quality. In your journal, list as many "low-brow" forms of entertainment as you can. Possibilities include professional wrestling, aggressive video games, Internet chat rooms, and so on. Review your list, and respond to the following question in your journal: What is it about each form of entertainment that attracts such popularity—and inspires such criticism?

Why We Crave Horror Movies

1   I think that we're all mentally ill: those of us outside the asylums only hide it a little better—and maybe not all that much better, after all. We've all known people who talk to themselves, people who sometimes squinch their faces into horrible grimaces when they believe no one is watching, people who have some hysterical fear—of snakes, the dark, the tight place, the long drop . . . and, of course, those final worms and grubs that are waiting so patiently underground.

2   When we pay our four or five bucks and seat ourselves at tenth-row center in a theater showing a horror movie, we are daring the nightmare.

3   Why? Some of the reasons are simple and obvious. To show that we can, that we are not afraid, that we can ride this roller coaster. Which is not to say that a really good horror movie may not surprise a scream out of us at some point, the way we may scream when the roller coaster twists through

a complete 360 or plows through a lake at the bottom of the drop. And horror movies, like roller coasters, have always been the special province of the young; by the time one turns 40 or 50, one's appetite for double twists or 360-degree loops may be considerably depleted.

We also go to re-establish our feelings of essential normality; the horror   4
movie is innately conservative, even reactionary. Freda Jackson as the horrible melting woman in *Die, Monster, Die!* confirms for us that no matter how far we may be removed from the beauty of a Robert Redford or a Diana Ross, we are still light-years from true ugliness.

And we go to have fun.   5

Ah, but this is where the ground starts to slope away, isn't it? Because   6
this is a very peculiar sort of fun indeed. The fun comes from seeing others menaced—sometimes killed. One critic has suggested that if pro football has become the voyeur's version of combat, then the horror film has become the modern version of the public lynching.

It is true that the mythic, "fairytale" horror film intends to take away the   7
shades of gray. . . . It urges us to put away our more civilized and adult penchant for analysis and to become children again, seeing things in pure blacks and whites. It may be that horror movies provide psychic relief on this level because this invitation to lapse into simplicity, irrationality and even outright madness is extended so rarely. We are told we may allow our emotions a free rein . . . or no rein at all.

If we are all insane, then sanity becomes a matter of degree. If your   8
insanity leads you to carve up women like Jack the Ripper or the Cleveland Torso Murderer, we clap you away in the funny farm (but neither of those two amateur-night surgeons was ever caught, heh-heh-heh); if, on the other hand your insanity leads you only to talk to yourself when you're under stress or to pick your nose on the morning bus, then you are left alone to go about your business . . . though it is doubtful that you will ever be invited to the best parties.

The potential lyncher is in almost all of us (excluding saints, past and   9
present; but then, most saints have been crazy in their own ways), and every now and then, he has to be let loose to scream and roll around in the grass. Our emotions and our fears form their own body, and we recognize that it demands its own exercise to maintain proper muscle tone. Certain of these emotional muscles are accepted—even exalted—in civilized society; they are, of course, the emotions that tend to maintain the status quo of civilization itself. Love, friendship, loyalty, kindness—these are all the emotions that we applaud, emotions that have been immortalized in the couplets of Hallmark cards. . . .

When we exhibit these emotions, society showers us with positive rein-   10
forcement; we learn this even before we get out of diapers. When, as children, we hug our rotten little puke of a sister and give her a kiss, all the aunts

and uncles smile and twit and cry, "Isn't he the sweetest little thing?" Such coveted treats as chocolate-covered graham crackers often follow. But if we deliberately slam the rotten little puke of a sister's fingers in the door, sanctions follow—angry remonstrance from parents, aunts and uncles; instead of a chocolate-covered graham cracker, a spanking.

But anticivilization emotions don't go away, and they demand periodic   11
exercise. We have such "sick" jokes as, "What's the difference between a truckload of bowling balls and a truckload of dead babies?" (You can't unload a truckload of bowling balls with a pitchfork . . . a joke, by the way, that I heard originally from a ten-year-old.) Such a joke may surprise a laugh or a grin out of us even as we recoil, a possibility that confirms the thesis: If we share a brotherhood of man, then we also share an insanity of man. None of which is intended as a defense of either the sick joke or insanity but merely as an explanation of why the best horror films, like the best fairy tales, manage to be reactionary, anarchistic, and revolutionary all at the same time.

The mythic horror movie, like the sick joke, has a dirty job to do. It   12
deliberately appeals to all that is worst in us. It is morbidity unchained, our most base instincts let free, our nastiest fantasies realized . . . and it all happens, fittingly enough, in the dark. For those reasons, good liberals often shy away from horror films. For myself, I like to see the most aggressive of them—*Dawn of the Dead,* for instance—as lifting a trap door in the civilized forebrain and throwing a basket of raw meat to the hungry alligators swimming around in that subterranean river beneath.

Why bother? Because it keeps them from getting out, man. It keeps   13
them down there and me up here. It was Lennon and McCartney who said that all you need is love, and I would agree with that.

As long as you keep the gators fed.   14

Questions for Close Reading

1. What is the selection's thesis? Locate the sentence(s) in which King states his main idea. If he doesn't state the thesis explicitly, express it in your own words.
2. In what ways do King's references to "Jack the Ripper" and the "Cleveland Torso Murderer" (paragraph 8) support his thesis?
3. What does King mean in paragraph 4 when he says that horror movies are "innately conservative, even reactionary"? What does he mean in paragraph 11 when he calls them "anarchistic, and revolutionary"?
4. In paragraphs 12 and 14, King refers to "alligators" and "gators." What does the alligator represent? What does King mean when he says that all the world needs is love—"[a]s long as you keep the gators fed"?
5. Refer to your dictionary as needed to define the following words used in the selection: *hysterical* (paragraph 1), *reactionary* (4), *voyeur's* (6), *lynching* (6), *penchant* (7), *immortalized* (9), *anarchistic* (11), and *morbidity* (12).

Questions About the Writer's Craft

1. **The pattern.** Does King's causal analysis have an essentially informative, speculative, or persuasive (see pages 285–286) purpose? What makes you think so? How might King's profession as a horror writer have influenced his purpose?
2. **Other patterns.** King *compares* and *contrasts* horror movies to roller coasters (3), public lynchings (6), and sick jokes (11–12). How do these comparisons and contrasts reinforce King's thesis about horror movies?
3. **Other patterns.** Throughout the essay, King uses several *examples* involving children. Identify these instances. How do these examples help King develop his thesis?
4. What is unusual about paragraphs 2, 5, and 14? Why do you think King might have designed these paragraphs in this way?

Writing Assignments Using Cause-Effect as a Pattern of Development

1. King argues that horror movies have "a dirty job to do": they feed the hungry monsters in our psyche. Write an essay in which you put King's thesis to the test. Briefly describe the first horror movie you ever saw; then explain its effect on you. Like King, speculate about the nature of your response—your feelings and fantasies—while watching the movie.
2. Many movie critics claim that horror movies nowadays are more violent and bloody than they used to be. Write an essay about *one* other medium of popular culture that you think has changed for the worse. You might consider action movies, televised coverage of sports, men's or women's magazines, radio talk shows, TV sitcoms, and so on. Briefly describe key differences between the medium's past and present forms. Analyze the reasons for the change, and, at the end of the essay, examine the effects of the change. For reflections on another questionable cultural practice, read Joan Didion's "Marrying Absurd" (page 442).

Writing Assignments Combining Patterns of Development

3. King advocates the horror movie precisely because "It deliberately appeals to all that is worst in us." Write an essay in which you rebut King. *Argue* instead that horror movies should be avoided precisely *because* they satisfy monstrous feelings in us. To refute King, provide strong *examples* drawn from your own and other people's experience. Consider supplementing your informal research with material gathered in the library and/or on the Internet.
4. Write an essay in which you *illustrate*, contrary to King, that humans are by nature essentially benevolent and kind. Brainstorm with others to generate vivid *examples* in support of your thesis.

Writing Assignment Using a Journal Entry as a Starting Point

5. King believes that horror movies involve "a very peculiar sort of fun." Review your pre-reading journal entry, and select *one* other form of popular entertainment that

you think provides its own strange kind of enjoyment. Like King, write an essay in which you analyze the causes of people's enjoyment of this type of entertainment. Brainstorm with others to identify convincing examples. You may, like King, endorse the phenomenon you examine—or you may condemn it. For discussion of another strange source of people's enjoyment, read Joan Didion's "Marrying Absurd" (page 442).

John M. Darley
Bibb Latané

Harvard graduate John M. Darley (1938–) is professor of psychology at Princeton University, where he studies the principles of moral judgment in children and adults. Bibb Latané (1937–), the former director of the Behavioral Sciences Laboratory at Ohio State University, is professor of psychology at Florida Atlantic University. A doctoral graduate of the University of Minnesota, Latané is interested in social impact and group influence theory. Darley and Latané are coauthors of *The Unresponsive Bystander: Why Doesn't He Help* (1970) and *Help in a Crisis: Bystander Response to an Emergency* (1976). Based on their research into the origins of noninvolvement, "Why People Don't Help in a Crisis? (1968) was awarded an essay prize from the American Association for the Advancement of Science.

Pre-Reading Journal Entry

Faced with a challenging or difficult situation, people sometimes choose *not* to get involved—and then later regret this decision. Such situations might include, for example, helping an injured stranger, standing up for someone being bullied, and letting in a stray animal on a cold day. In your journal, write about one or more times when you faced a difficult situation and failed to respond in a way that you now believe you should have.

Why People Don't Help in a Crisis

Kitty Genovese is set upon by a maniac as she returns home from work   1
at 3 A.M. Thirty-eight of her neighbors in Kew Gardens, N.Y., come to their windows when she cries out in terror; not one comes to her assistance, even though her assailant takes half an hour to murder her. No one so much as calls the police. She dies.

Andrew Mormille is stabbed in the head and neck as he rides in a New   2
York City subway train. Eleven other riders flee to another car as the 17-year-old boy bleeds to death; not one comes to his assistance, even though his attackers have left the car. He dies.

Eleanor Bradley trips and breaks her leg while shopping on New York   3
City's Fifth Avenue. Dazed and in shock, she calls for help, but the hurrying stream of people simply parts and flows past. Finally, after 40 minutes, a taxi driver stops and helps her to a doctor.

How can so many people watch another human being in distress and do   4
nothing? Why don't they help?

Since we started research on bystander responses to emergencies, we   5
have heard many explanations for the lack of intervention in such cases. "The
megalopolis in which we live makes closeness difficult and leads to the alien-
ation of the individual from the group," says the psychoanalyst. "This sort of
disaster," says the sociologist, "shakes the sense of safety and sureness of the
individuals involved and causes psychological withdrawal." "Apathy," says
others. "Indifference."

All of these analyses share one characteristic: they set the indifferent wit-   6
ness apart from the rest of us. Certainly not one of us who reads about these
incidents in horror is apathetic, alienated or depersonalized. Certainly these
terrifying cases have no personal implications for us. We needn't feel guilty,
or re-examine ourselves, or anything like that. Or should we?

If we look closely at the behavior of witnesses to these incidents, the   7
people involved begin to seem less inhuman and a lot more like the rest of
us. They were not indifferent. The 38 witnesses of Kitty Genovese's murder,
for example, did not merely look at the scene once and then ignore it. They
continued to stare out of their windows, caught, fascinated, distressed,
unwilling to act but unable to turn away.

Why, then, didn't they act?   8

There are three things the bystander must do if he is to intervene in an   9
emergency: *notice* that something is happening; *interpret* that event as an emergency; and decide that he has *personal responsibility* for intervention. As we shall
show, the presence of other bystanders may at each stage inhibit his action.

The Unseeing Eye

Suppose that a man has a heart attack. He clutches his chest, staggers to   10
the nearest building and slumps sitting to the sidewalk. Will a passerby come
to his assistance? First, the bystander has to notice that something is happening. He must tear himself away from his private thoughts and pay attention. But Americans consider it bad manners to look closely at other people
in public. We are taught to respect the privacy of others, and when among
strangers we close our ears and avoid staring. In a crowd, then, each person
is less likely to notice a potential emergency than when alone.

Experimental evidence corroborates this. We asked college students to   11
an interview about their reactions to urban living. As the students waited
to see the interviewer, either by themselves or with two other students,
they filled out a questionnaire. Solitary students often glanced idly about
while filling out their questionnaires: those in groups kept their eyes on
their own papers.

As part of the study, we staged an emergency: smoke was released into   12
the waiting room through a vent. Two thirds of the subjects who were alone
noticed the smoke immediately, but only 25 percent of those waiting in

groups saw it as quickly. Although eventually all the subjects did become aware of the smoke—when the atmosphere grew so smoky as to make them cough and rub their eyes—this study indicates that the more people present, the slower an individual may be to perceive an emergency and the more likely he is not to see it at all.

Seeing Is Not Necessarily Believing

Once an event is noticed, an onlooker must decide if it is truly an emergency. Emergencies are not always clearly labeled as such; "smoke" pouring into a waiting room may be caused by fire, or it may merely indicate a leak in a steam pipe. Screams in the street may signal an assault or a family quarrel. A man lying in a doorway may be having a coronary—or he may simply be sleeping off a drunk.   13

A person trying to interpret a situation often looks at those around him to see how he should react. If everyone else is calm and indifferent, he will tend to remain so; if everyone else is reacting strongly, he is likely to become aroused. This tendency is not merely slavish conformity; ordinarily we derive much valuable information about new situations from how others around us behave. It's a rare traveler who, in picking a roadside restaurant, chooses to stop at one where no other cars appear in the parking lot.   14

But occasionally the reactions of others provide false information. The studied nonchalance of patients in a dentist's waiting room is a poor indication of their inner anxiety. It is considered embarrassing to "lose your cool" in public. In a potentially acute situation, then, everyone present will appear more unconcerned that he is in fact. A crowd can thus force inaction on its members by implying, through its passivity, that an event is not an emergency. Any individual in such a crowd fears that he may appear a fool if he behaves as though it were.   15

To determine how the presence of other people affects a person's interpretation of an emergency, Latané and Judith Rodin set up another experiment. Subjects were paid $2 to participate in a survey of game and puzzle preferences conducted at Columbia University by the Consumer Testing Bureau. An attractive young market researcher met them at the door and took them to the testing room, where they were given questionnaires to fill out. Before leaving, she told them that she would be working next door in her office, which was separated from the room by a folding room-divider. She then entered her office, where she shuffled papers, opened drawers and made enough noise to remind the subjects of her presence. After four minutes she turned on a high-fidelity tape recorder.   16

On it, the subjects heard the researcher climb up on a chair, perhaps to reach for a stack of papers on the bookcase. They heard a loud crash and a scream as the chair collapsed and she fell, and they heard her moan, "Oh, my   17

foot . . . I . . . I . . . can't move it Oh, I . . . can't get this . . . thing off me."
Her cries gradually got more subdued and controlled.

Twenty-six people were alone in the waiting room when the "accident" 18
occurred. Seventy percent of them offered to help the victim. Many pushed
back the divider to offer their assistance; others called out to offer their help.

Among those waiting in pairs, only 20 percent—8 out of 40—offered to 19
help. The other 32 remained unresponsive. In defining the situation as a
nonemergency, they explained to themselves why the other member of the
pair did not leave the room; they also removed any reason for action themselves. Whatever had happened, it was believed to be not serious. "A mild
sprain," some said. "I didn't want to embarrass her." In a "real" emergency,
they assured us, they would be among the first to help.

The Lonely Crowd

Even if a person defines an event as an emergency, the presence of other 20
bystanders may still make him less likely to intervene. He feels that his
responsibility is diffused and diluted. Thus, if your car breaks down on a busy
highway, hundreds of drivers whiz by without anyone's stopping to help—
but if you are stuck on a nearly deserted country road, whoever passes you
first is likely to stop.

To test this diffusion-of-responsibility theory, we simulated an emer- 21
gency in which people overheard a victim calling for help. Some thought
they were the only person to hear the cries; the rest believed that others
heard them, too. As with the witnesses to Kitty Genovese's murder, the subjects could not *see* one another or know what others were doing. The kind
of direct group inhibition found in the other two studies could not operate.

For the simulation, we recruited 72 students at New York University to 22
participate in what was referred to as a "group discussion" of personal problems in an urban university. Each student was put in an individual room
equipped with a set of headphones and a microphone. It was explained that
this precaution had been taken because participants might feel embarrassed
about discussing their problems publicly. Also, the experimenter said that he
would not listen to the initial discussion, but would only ask for reactions
later. Each person was to talk in turn.

The first to talk reported that he found it difficult to adjust to New York 23
and his studies. Then, hesitantly and with obvious embarrassment, he mentioned that he was prone to nervous seizures when he was under stress.
Other students then talked about their own problems in turn. The number
of people in the "discussion" varied. But whatever the apparent size of the
group—two, three or six people—only the subject was actually present; the
others, as well as the instructions and the speeches of the victim-to-be, were
present only on a pre-recorded tape.

When it was the first person's turn to talk again, he launched into the   24
following performance, becoming louder and having increasing speech difficulties: "I can see a lot of er of er how other people's problems are similar to
mine because er I mean er they're not er e-easy to handle sometimes and er
I er um I think I I need er if if could er er somebody er er er give me give
me a little er give me a little help here because er I er *uh* I've got a a one of
the er seiz-er er things coming *on* and and er uh uh (choking sounds) . . ."

Eighty-five percent of the people who believed themselves to be alone   25
with the victim came out of their room to help. Sixty-two percent of the
people who believed there was *one* other bystander did so. Of those who
believed there were four other bystanders, only 31 percent reported the fit.
The responsibility-diluting effect of other people was so strong that single
individuals were more than twice as likely to report the emergency as those
who thought other people also knew about it.

The Lesson Learned

People who failed to report the emergency showed few signs of the apa-   26
thy and indifference thought to characterize "unresponsive bystanders."
When the experimenter entered the room to end the situation, the subject
often asked if the victim was "all right." Many of them showed physical signs
of nervousness; they often had trembling hands and sweating palms. If anything, they seemed more emotionally aroused than did those who reported
the emergency. Their emotional behavior was a sign of their continuing conflict concerning whether to respond or not.

Thus, the stereotype of the unconcerned, depersonalized *homo urbanus*,   27
blandly watching the misfortunes of others, proves inaccurate. Instead, we
find that a bystander to an emergency is an anguished individual in genuine
doubt, wanting to do the right thing but compelled to make complex decisions under pressure of stress and fear. His reactions are shaped by the
actions of others—all too frequently by their inaction.

And we are that bystander. Caught up by the apparent indifference of   28
others, we may pass by an emergency without helping or even realizing that
help is needed. Once we are aware of the influence of those around us, however, we can resist it. We can choose to see distress and step forward to
relieve it.

Questions for Close Reading

1. What is the selection's thesis? Locate the sentence(s) in which Darley and Latané
   state their main idea. If they don't state the thesis explicitly, express it in your own
   words.
2. According to the authors, what three factors prevent people in a crowd from helping victims during an emergency?

3. Why did Darley and Latané isolate the subjects in separate rooms during the staged emergency described in paragraphs 21–26?

4. What kind of person, according to the authors, would tend to ignore or bypass a person experiencing a problem? What might encourage this person to act more responsibly?

5. Refer to your dictionary as needed to define the following words used in the selection: *megalopolis* (paragraph 5), *apathy* (5), *indifference* (5), *alienated* (6), *depersonalized* (6), *inhibit* (9), *corroborates* (11), *coronary* (13), *slavish* (14), *nonchalance* (15), *diffused* (20), and *blandly* (27).

Questions About the Writer's Craft

1. The pattern. What techniques do Darley and Latané use to help readers focus on the causes of people's inaction during an emergency?

2. Other patterns. The three brief *narratives* that open the essay depict events that happened well before Darley and Latané wrote their essay. Why might the authors have chosen to recount these events in the present tense rather than in the past tense?

3. Locate places where Darley and Latané describe the experiments investigating bystander behavior. How do the authors show readers the steps—and the implications—of each experiment?

4. What purpose do you think the authors had in mind when writing the selection? How do you know?

Writing Assignments Using Cause-Effect as a Pattern of Development

1. Write an essay showing the "responsibility-diluting effect" that can occur when several people witness a critical event. Brainstorm with others to gather examples of this effect; then select two or three dramatic situations as the basis of your essay. Be sure to acknowledge other factors that may have played a role in inhibiting people's ability to act responsibly.

2. Although Darley and Latané focus on times when individuals fail to act responsibly, people often respond with moral heroism during difficult situations. Brainstorm with others to identify occasions in which people have taken the initiative to avert a crisis. Focusing on two or three compelling instances, write an essay in which you analyze the possible motives for people's responsible behavior. Also show how their actions affected the other individuals involved. To gain additional insight into the psychology of heroism, read Adam Mayblum's "The Price We Pay" (page 128).

Writing Assignments Combining Patterns of Development

3. How could families or schools or communities or religious organizations encourage children to act rather than withdraw when confronted by someone in difficulty? Focusing on *one* of these situations, talk with friends, classmates, and family members to gather their experiences and recommendations. Then consider doing some research on this subject in the library and/or on the Internet. Select the most provocative ideas, and write an essay explaining the *steps* that this particular institution could take to help develop children's sense of responsibility to others. Develop your points with specific *examples* of what has been done and what could be done.

∞ 4. Darley and Latané cite social critics who believe that the United States has become a nation of strangers, alienated and withdrawn from one another. Write an essay *refuting* this claim by presenting several vivid *instances* of small acts of everyday kindness—examples in which people demonstrate their sense of connectedness to those around them. Generate examples by drawing on your own and other people's experiences. Before writing, you might want to read Maya Angelou's "Sister Flowers" (page 96) for a portrait of an individual who shows—in small, quiet ways—that she cares for others.

Writing Assignment Using a Journal Entry as a Starting Point

∞ 5. Though the authors don't state so directly, they suggest that unresponsive bystanders often may regret their inaction later on. Reviewing the material you generated in your journal entry, select the most compelling or profound of the incidents you described. Then write an essay in which you narrate *one* situation in which you chose not to get involved but now realize you should have. Be sure to provide dialog and vivid descriptive details to bring the incident to life for your readers. Conclude your essay with a brief reflection on what you wish you had done and how your failure to respond properly has affected you. You might also begin by reading Gordon Parks's "Flavio's Home" (page 83), which conveys the author's impulse to get involved when he witnesses the desperate circumstances of another.

Jay Walljasper

Jay Walljasper (1955–), a graduate of the University of Iowa, is editor and editorial director of the *Utne Reader* and of *Utne Reader Books*. He also writes a series for *The Nation* magazine about positive social and political initiatives as well as a column on political and environmental topics for *Resurgence, Shambhala Sun,* and *Conscious Choice* magazines. His work has been published in a number of other alternative and mainstream publications, including *Mother Jones,* the *New Age Journal,* the *Chicago Tribune Magazine,* the *Philadelphia Inquirer Magazine,* the *Toronto Star,* and the *L.A. Weekly.* He lives in Minneapolis with his wife and son. The following essay appeared in the January/February 2003 issue of the *Utne Reader.*

Pre-Reading Journal Entry

You've probably observed that people today have such full schedules, they often do several things at once. What examples of "multitasking" have you seen in yourself and in others? What do you think about the tendency to multitask? Do you consider it productive? Do you think it overcomplicates life? Does the quality of the tasks accomplished tend to suffer? Use your journal to respond to these questions.

Our Schedules, Our Selves

DAMN! You're 20 minutes—no, more like half an hour—late for your breakfast meeting, which you were hoping to scoot out of early to make an 8:30 seminar across town. And, somewhere in there, there's that conference call. Now, at the last minute, you have to be at a 9:40 meeting. No way you can miss it. Let's see, the afternoon is totally booked, but you can probably push back your 10:15 appointment and work through lunch. That would do it. Whew! The day has barely begun and already you are counting the hours until evening, when you can finally go home and happily, gloriously, triumphantly, do nothing. You'll skip yoga class, blow off the neighborhood meeting, ignore the piles of laundry and just relax. Yes! . . . No! Tonight's the night of the concert. You promised Nathan and Mara weeks ago that you would go. *DAMN!*

Welcome to daily grind circa 2003—a grueling 24-7 competition against the clock that leaves even the winners wondering what happened to their lives. Determined and sternly focused, we march through each day obeying the orders of our calendars. The idle moment, the reflective pause, serendipity of any sort have no place in our plans. Stopping to talk to someone or slowing down to appreciate a sunny afternoon will only make you late for your next round of activities. From the minute we rise in the morning, most of us have our day charted out. The only surprise is if we actually get everything done that we had planned before collapsing into bed at night.

On the job, in school, at home, increasing numbers of North Americans   3
are virtual slaves to their schedules. Some of what fills our days are onerous obligations, some are wonderful opportunities, and most fall in between, but taken together they add up to too much. Too much to do, too many places to be, too many things happening too fast, all mapped out for us in precise quarter-hour allotments on our Palm Pilots or day planners. We are not leading our lives, but merely following a dizzying timetable of duties, commitments, demands, and options. How did this happen? Where's the luxurious leisure that decades of technological progress was supposed to bestow upon us?

The acceleration of the globalized economy, and the accompanying   4
decline of people having any kind of a say over wages and working conditions, is a chief culprit. Folks at the bottom of the socio-economic ladder feel the pain most sharply. Holding down two or three jobs, struggling to pay the bills, working weekends, no vacation time, little social safety net, they often feel out of control about everything happening to them. But even successful professionals, people who seem fully in charge of their destinies, feel the pinch. Doctors, for example, working impossibly crowded schedules under the command of HMOs,[1] feel overwhelmed. Many of them are now seeking union representation, traditionally the recourse of low-pay workers.

The onslaught of new technology, which promised to set us free, has   5
instead ratcheted up the rhythms of everyday life. Cell phones, e-mail, and laptop computers instill expectations of instantaneous action. While such direct communication can loosen our schedules in certain instances (it's easier to shift around an engagement on short notice), overall they fuel the trend that every minute must be accounted for. It's almost impossible to put duties behind you now, when the boss or committee chair can call you at a rap show or sushi restaurant, and documents can be e-mailed to you on vacation in Banff[2] or Thailand. If you are never out of the loop, then are you ever not working?

Our own human desire for more choices and new experiences also plays   6
a role. Just like hungry diners gathering around a bountiful smorgasbord, it's hard not to pile too many activities on our plates. An expanding choice of cultural offerings over recent decades and the liberating sense that each of us can fully play a number of different social roles (worker, citizen, lover, parent, artist, etc.) has opened up enriching and exciting opportunities. Spanish lessons? Yes. Join a volleyball team? Why not. Cello and gymnastics classes for the kids? Absolutely. Tickets to a blues festival, food and wine

---

[1]Health management organizations, or corporations whose member physicians provide services to enrolled patients within certain (often strict) limits (editors' note).
[2]A popular winter resort town in southwest Alberta, Canada (editors' note).

expo, and political fundraiser? Sure. And we can't forget to make time for school events, therapy sessions, protest rallies, religious services, and dinner with friends.

Yes, these can all add to our lives. But with only 24 hours allotted to us   7
each day, something is lost too. You don't just run into a friend anymore and decide to get coffee. You can't happily savor an experience because your mind races toward the next one on the calendar. In a busy life, nothing happens if you don't plan it, often weeks in advance. Our "free" hours become just as programmed as the work day. What begins as an idea for fun frequently turns into an obligation obstacle course. Visit that new barbecue restaurant. *Done!* Go to tango lessons. *Done!* Fly to Montreal for a long weekend. *Done!*

We've booked ourselves so full of prescheduled activities there's no time   8
left for those magic, spontaneous moments that make us feel most alive. We seldom stop to think of all the experiences we are eliminating from our lives when we load up our appointment book. Reserving tickets for a basketball game months away could mean you miss out on the first balmy evening of spring. Five p.m. skating lessons for your children fit so conveniently into your schedule that you never realize it's the time all the other kids in the neighborhood gather on the sidewalk to play.

A few years back, radical Brazilian educator Paulo Freire was attending a   9
conference of Midwestern political activists and heard over and over about how overwhelmed people felt about the duties they face each day. Finally, he stood up and, in slow, heavily accented English, declared, "We are bigger than our schedules." The audience roared with applause.

Yes, we are bigger than our schedules. So how do we make sure our lives   10
are not overpowered by an endless roster of responsibilities? Especially in an age where demanding jobs, two-worker households or single-parent families make the joyous details of everyday life—cooking supper from scratch or organizing a block party—seem like an impossible dream? There is no set of easy answers, despite what the marketers of new convenience products would have us believe. But that doesn't mean we can't make real steps to take back our lives.

Part of the answer is political. So long as Americans work longer hours   11
than any other people on Earth we are going to feel hemmed in by our schedules. Expanded vacation time for everyone, including part-time and minimum wage workers, is one obvious and overdue solution. Shortening the work week, something the labor movement and progressive politicians successfully accomplished in the early decades of the 20th century, is another logical objective. There's nothing preordained about 40 hours on the job; Italy, France, and other European nations have already cut back working hours. An opportunity for employees outside academia to take a sabbatical every decade or so is another idea whose time has come. And how about more vacation and paid holidays? Let's start with Martin Luther King's birthday, Susan B.

Anthony's birthday, and your own! Any effort to give people more clout in their workplaces—from strengthened unions to employee ownership—could help us gain much-needed flexibility in our jobs, and our lives.

On another front, how you think about time can make a big difference 12 in how you feel about your life . . . Note how some of your most memorable moments occurred when something in your schedule fell through. The canceled lunch that allows you to spend an hour strolling around town. Friday night plans scrapped for a bowl of popcorn in front of the fireplace. Don't be shy about shucking your schedule whenever you can get away with it. And with some experimentation, you may find that you can get away with it a lot more than you imagined.

Setting aside some time on your calendar for life to just unfold in its own 13 surprising way can also nurture your soul. Carve out some nonscheduled hours (or days) once in a while and treat them as a firm commitment. And resist the temptation to turn every impulse or opportunity into another appointment. It's neither impolite nor inefficient to simply say, "let me get back to you on that tomorrow" or "let's check in that morning to see if it's still a good time." You cannot know how crammed that day may turn out to be, or how uninspired you might feel about another engagement, or how much you'll want to be rollerblading or playing chess or doing something else at that precise time.

In our industrialized, fast-paced society, we too often view time as just 14 another mechanical instrument to be programmed. But time possesses its own evershifting shape and rhythms, and defies our best efforts to corral it within the tidy lines of our Palm Pilots or datebooks. Stephan Rechtschaffen, author of *Time Shifting,* suggests you think back on a scary auto collision (or near miss), or spectacular night of lovemaking. Time seemed almost to stand still. You can remember everything in vivid detail. Compare that to an overcrammed week that you recall now only as a rapid-fire blur. Keeping in mind that our days expand and contract according to their own patterns is perhaps the best way to help keep time on your side.

Questions for Close Reading

1. What is the selection's thesis? Locate the sentence(s) in which Walljasper states his main idea. If he doesn't state the thesis explicitly, express it in your own words.
2. In the essay, Walljasper lists some of the technological devices people have come to rely upon. Name some of these devices. What, according to Walljasper, are their advantages and disadvantages?
3. What, according to Walljasper's analysis, are the three principal reasons why we have become so prone to overscheduling our lives? What does he observe are the effects of this problem?
4. In paragraph 4, Walljasper briefly addresses the issue of socioeconomic class as it relates to the problem of overscheduling. In his view, how are different classes of people affected? Do you agree with his analysis? Explain.

5. Refer to your dictionary as needed to define the following words used in the selection: *circa* (paragraph 2), *grueling* (2), *serendipity* (2), *virtual* (3), *onerous* (3), *allotments* (3), *onslaught* (5), *ratcheted* (5), *instill* (5), *smorgasbord* (6), *roster* (10), *preordained* (11), *sabbatical* (11), *clout* (11), and *shucking* (12).

Questions About the Writer's Craft

1. **The pattern.** Reread the discussion in paragraphs 4 through 6 of what is causing overscheduling. What organizational pattern (see pages 289–290) does Walljasper use to arrange his causal analysis? How can you tell? What benefit might this organizational pattern offer over another?
2. What seems to be Walljasper's purpose in pointing out that our lives are overscheduled? Is his purpose mainly informative, speculative, or persuasive? How do you know?
3. **Other patterns.** Walljasper peppers his essay with an abundance of undeveloped *examples*, as seen in paragraphs 1, 6, and 7. What might have been his reason for presenting examples in this way?
4. At various points in the essay, Walljasper adopts different points of view, alternating between first, second, and third person. Why do you think he uses different points of view in different instances? Do you think his choice was an effective one, or do you think he should have adopted a single, consistent point of view? Explain.

Writing Assignments Using Cause-Effect as a Pattern of Development

∞ 1. Though he doesn't say so explicitly, Walljasper implies that stress is a major result of overscheduling. Consider the issue of stress in your own life. What are the things in your life that "stress you out"? Brainstorm on this question for a few minutes. After reviewing what you've written and discussing it with friends and family, write an essay in which you analyze the two or three main causes of stress in your life. Your sources of stress might be immediate and concrete, such as having to pay an unexpected bill or passing a particularly challenging course. Or you might describe more constant and abstract stressors, such as living up to family expectations or finding a "soul mate." Consider ending your essay by briefly discussing what you can do to make these aspects of your life less stressful. For an additional perspective on stress in contemporary life, read Alexandra Robbins and Abby Wilner's "What Is the Quarterlife Crisis?" (page 337).

∞ 2. Walljasper cites as one of the main causes of overscheduling the "onslaught of new technology." In all likelihood, you know someone who hasn't been seduced by recent technological devices. Perhaps the person resists having voice mail, owning a cell phone, or using the Internet. Write an essay exploring possible reasons why this individual hasn't been lured by one or more technological advancements. Examine, too, the effect on others of the person's decision. Your essay may be lighthearted or serious. Whatever your tone, be sure to indicate, explicitly or implicitly, how you feel about the person's reluctance to embrace technology. For insight into why many people avoid computer technology, read Bill Bryson's spirited essay "Your New Computer" (page 233).

Writing Assignments Combining Patterns of Development

📖 **3.** Walljasper contends that technology has helped render us "slaves to our schedules." Focusing on one or two specific technologies, write an essay in which you *argue* against this view. Show instead that technology can enhance life experiences and free people to pursue personal interests. Be sure, though, to acknowledge Walljasper's viewpoint near the beginning of the essay to provide a context for your argument. Like Walljasper, support your position with heartfelt commentary and lively *examples.* You might also find it helpful to supplement your observations with information gathered in the library and/or on the Internet.

4. Many would agree with Walljasper that people today—especially young people— increasingly exhibit an overreliance on new technologies in their day-to-day lives. Identify several activities that you participated in as a child and teenager but that you think young people experience differently nowadays because of technology's dominant role in the culture. Possibilities include dating, doing homework, shopping, and celebrating holidays with family. Write an essay *illustrating* how technology has changed young people's experience of these activities. To illustrate the change, *contrast* your childhood *or* adolescent experience of these activities with the experience of children *or* teenagers today. Be sure to convey whether you think the change has or has not been for the better.

Writing Assignments Using a Journal Entry as a Starting Point

5. Though Walljasper doesn't explicitly discuss it, a phenomenon related to over-scheduling is "multitasking"—doing more than one thing at a time. Write an essay illustrating the advantages and disadvantages of multitasking. To develop your discussion, draw upon the examples in your pre-reading journal entry and upon the experiences and observations of others. Your essay should indicate whether, on the whole, you think multitasking is a positive or negative phenomenon.

Additional Writing Topics

CAUSE-EFFECT

General Assignments

Write an essay that analyzes the causes and/or effects of one of the following topics. Determine your purpose before beginning to write: Will the essay be informative, persuasive, or speculative? As you prewrite, think rigorously about causes and effects; try to identify causal chains. Provide solid evidence for the thesis and use either chronological or emphatic order to organize your supporting points.

1. Sleep deprivation
2. Having the parents you have
3. Lack of communication in a relationship
4. Overexercising or not exercising
5. A particular TV or rock star's popularity
6. Skill or ineptitude in sports
7. A major life decision
8. Stiffer legal penalties for drunken driving
9. Changing attitudes toward protecting the environment
10. A particular national crisis
11. The mass movement of women into the workforce
12. Choosing to attend this college
13. "Back to basics" movement in schools
14. Headaches
15. An act of violence
16. A natural event: leaves turning, birds migrating, animals hibernating, an eclipse occurring
17. Pesticide use
18. Use of computers in the classroom
19. Banning disposable cans and bottles
20. A bad habit
21. A fear of _____
22. Legalizing drugs
23. Abolishing the F grade
24. Joining a particular organization
25. Owning a pet

Assignments With a Specific Purpose, Audience, and Point of View

On Campus

1. A debate about the prominence of athletics at colleges and universities is going to be broadcast on the local cable station. For this debate, prepare a speech

pointing out either the harmful or the beneficial effects of "big-time" college athletic programs.

2. Why do students "flunk out" of college? Write an article for the campus newspaper outlining the main causes of failure. Your goal is to steer students away from dangerous habits and situations that lead to poor grades or dropping out.

At Home or in the Community

3. Write a letter to the editor of your favorite newspaper analyzing the causes of the country's current "trash crisis." Be sure to mention the nationwide love affair with disposable items and the general disregard of the idea of thrift. Conclude by offering brief suggestions for how people in your community can begin to remedy this problem.

4. Write a letter to the mayor of your town or city suggesting a "Turn Off the TV" public relations effort, convincing residents to stop watching television for a month. Cite the positive effects that "no TV" would have on parents, children, and the community in general.

On the Job

5. As the manager of a store or office, you've noticed that a number of employees have negative workplace habits and/or attitudes. Write a memo for your employees in which you identify these negative behaviors and show how they affect the workplace environment. Be sure to adopt a tone that will sound neither patronizing nor overly harsh.

6. Why do you think teenage suicide is on the rise? You're a respected psychologist. Write a fact sheet for parents of teenagers and for high school guidance counselors describing the factors that could make a young person desperate enough to attempt suicide. At the end, suggest what parents and counselors can do to help confused, unhappy young people.

10
DEFINITION

WHAT IS DEFINITION?

In Lewis Carroll's wise and whimsical tale *Through the Looking Glass,* Humpty Dumpty proclaims, "When *I* use a word . . . , it means just what I choose it to mean—neither more nor less." If the world were filled with characters like Humpty Dumpty, all of them bending words to their own purposes and accepting no challenges to their personal definitions, communication would be an exercise in frustration. You would say a word, and it would mean one thing to you but perhaps something completely different to a close friend. Without a common understanding, the two of you would talk at cross-purposes, missing each other's meanings as you blundered through a conversation.

For language to communicate, words must have accepted *definitions.* Dictionaries, the sourcebooks for accepted definitions, are compilations of current word meanings, enabling speakers of a language to understand one another. But as you might suspect, things are not as simple as they first appear. We all know that a word like *discipline* has a standard dictionary definition. We also know, though, that parents argue over what constitutes "discipline" and that controversies about the meaning of "discipline" rage within school systems year after year. Moreover, many of the wrenching moral debates of our time also boil down to questions of definition. Much of the controversy over abortion, for instance, centers on what is meant by "life" and when it "begins."

Words can, in short, be slippery. Each of us has unique experiences, attitudes, and values that influence the way we use words and the way we interpret the words of others. Lewis Carroll may have been exaggerating, but Humpty Dumpty's attitude exists—in a very real way—in all of us.

In addition to the idiosyncratic interpretations that may attach to words, some words may shift in meaning over time. The word *pedagogue,* for instance, originally meant "a teacher or leader of children." However, with time, *pedagogue* has come to mean "a dogmatic, pedantic teacher." And, of course, we invent other words (*modem, byte*) as the need arises.

Writing a definition, then, is no simple task. Primarily, the writer tries to answer basic questions: "What does _____ mean?" and "What is the special or true nature of _____?" The word to be defined may be an object, a concept, a type of person, a place, or a phenomenon. Potential subjects might be the "user-friendly" computer, animal rights, a model teacher, cabin fever. As you will see, there are various strategies for expanding definitions far beyond the single-word synonyms or brief phrases that dictionaries provide.

HOW DEFINITION FITS YOUR PURPOSE AND AUDIENCE

Many times, short-answer exam questions call for definitions. Consider the following examples:

Define the term *mob psychology.*

What is the difference between a metaphor and a simile?

How would you explain what a religious cult is?

In such cases, a good response might involve a definition of several sentences or several paragraphs.

Other times, definition may be used in an essay organized mainly around another pattern of development. In this situation, all that's needed is a brief formal definition or a short definition given in your own words. For instance, a *process analysis* showing readers how computers have revolutionized the typical business office might start with a textbook definition of the term *artificial intelligence.* In an *argumentation-persuasion* paper urging students to support recent efforts to abolish fraternities and sororities, you could refer to the definitions of *blackballing* and *hazing* found in the university handbook. Or your personal definition of *hero* could be the starting point for a *causal analysis* that explains to readers why there are few real heroes in today's world.

But the most complex use of definition, and the one we are primarily concerned with in this chapter, involves exploring a subject through an *extended definition.* Extended definition allows you to apply a personal interpretation to a word, to make a case for a revisionist view of a commonly accepted meaning, to analyze words representing complex or controversial issues. "Pornography," "gun control," "secular humanism," and "right-to-life" would be excellent subjects for extended definition—each is multifaceted, often misunderstood, and fraught with emotional meaning. "Junk food," "anger," "leadership," "anxiety" could make interesting subjects, especially if the extended definition helped readers develop a new understanding of the word. You might, for example, define "anxiety" not as a negative state to be avoided but as a positive force that propels us to take action.

An extended definition could perhaps run several paragraphs or a few pages. Keep in mind, however, that an extended definition may require a chapter or even an entire book to develop. If this seems unlikely, remember that theologians, philosophers, and pop psychologists have devoted entire texts to such concepts as "evil" and "love."

SUGGESTIONS FOR USING DEFINITION IN AN ESSAY

The following suggestions will be helpful whether you use definition as a dominant or a supportive pattern of development.

1. Stay focused on the essay's purpose, audience, and tone.   Since your purpose for writing an extended definition shapes the entire paper, you need to keep that objective in mind when developing your definition. Suppose you decide to write an essay defining *jazz*. The essay could be purely *informative* and discuss the origins of jazz, its characteristic tonal patterns, and some of the great jazz musicians of the past. Or the essay could move beyond pure information and take on a *persuasive* edge. It might, for example, argue that jazz is the only contemporary form of music worth considering seriously.

Just as your purpose in writing will vary, so will your tone. A strictly informative definition will generally assume a detached, objective tone ("Apathy is an emotional state characterized by listlessness and indifference"). By way of contrast, a definition essay with a persuasive slant might be urgent in tone ("To combat student apathy, we must design programs that engage students in campus life"), or it might take a satiric approach ("An apathetic stance is a wise choice for any thinking student").

As you write, keep thinking about your audience as well. Not only do your readers determine what terms need to be defined (and in how much detail), but they also keep you focused on the essay's purpose and tone. For instance, you probably wouldn't write a serious, informative piece for the college newspaper about the "mystery meat" served in the campus cafeteria. Instead, you would adopt a light tone as you defined the culinary horror and might even make a persuasive pitch about improving the food prepared on campus.

2. Formulate an effective definition.   A definition essay sometimes begins with a brief *formal definition*—the dictionary's, a textbook's, or the writer's—and then expands that initial definition with supporting details. Formal definitions are traditionally worded as three-part statements that consist of the following: the *term*, the *class* to which the term belongs, and the *characteristics* that distinguish the term from other members of its class.

Term	Class	Characteristics
The peregrine falcon,	an endangered bird,	is the world's fastest flyer.
A bodice-ripper	is a paperback book	that deals with highly charged romance in exotic places and faraway times.
Back to basics	is a trend in education	that emphasizes skill mastery through rote learning.

A definition that meets these guidelines will clarify what your subject *is* and what it *is not*. These guidelines also establish the boundaries of your definition, removing unlike items from consideration in your (and your reader's) mind. For example, defining "back to basics" as a trend that emphasizes rote learning signals a certain boundary; it lets readers know that other educational trends, such as those that emphasize children's social or emotional development, will not be part of the essay's definition.

If you decide to include a formal definition, avoid tired openers like "the dictionary says" or "according to Webster." Such weak starts are just plain boring and often herald an unimaginative essay. You should also keep in mind that a strict dictionary definition may actually confuse readers. Suppose you're writing a paper on the way all of us absorb ideas and values from the media. Likening this automatic response to the process of osmosis, you decide to open the paper with a dictionary definition. If you write, "Osmosis is the tendency of a solvent to disperse through a semipermeable membrane into a more concentrated medium," readers are apt to be baffled, even hostile. Remember: The purpose of a definition is to clarify meaning, not obscure it.

You should also stay clear of ungrammatical "is when" definitions: "Blind ambition is when you want to get ahead, no matter how much other people are hurt." Instead, write "Blind ambition is wanting to get ahead, no matter how much other people are hurt." A final pitfall to avoid in writing formal definitions is *circularity*, saying the same thing twice and therefore defining nothing: "A campus tribunal is a tribunal composed of various members of the university community." Circular definitions like this often repeat the term being defined (*tribunal*) or use words having the same meaning (*campus; university community*). In this case, we learn nothing about what a campus tribunal is; the writer says only that "X is X."

3. Develop the extended definition.   You can choose from a variety of patterns when formulating an extended definition. Description, narration, process analysis, and comparison-contrast can be used—alone or in combination. Imagine that you're planning to write an extended definition of "robotics." You might develop the term by providing *examples* of the ways robots are currently being used in scientific research; by *comparing* and *contrasting* human and robot capabilities; or by *classifying* robots, starting with the most basic and moving to the most advanced or futuristic models.

Which patterns of development to use will often become apparent during the prewriting stage. Here is a list of prewriting questions as well as the pattern of development implied by each question.

Question	Pattern of Development
How does X look, taste, smell, feel, and sound?	Description
What does X do? When? Where?	Narration
What are some typical instances of X?	Exemplification
What are X's component parts? What different forms can X take?	Division-classification
How does X work?	Process analysis
What is X like or unlike?	Comparison-contrast
What leads to X? What are X's consequences?	Cause-effect

Those questions yielding the most material often suggest the effective pattern(s) for developing an extended definition.

4. Organize the material that develops the definition.   If you use a single pattern to develop the extended definition, apply the principles of organization suited to that pattern, as described in the appropriate chapter of this book. Assume that you're defining "fad" by means of *process analysis*. You might organize your paragraphs according to the steps in the process: a fad's slow start as something avant-garde or eccentric; its wildfire acceptance by the general public; the fad's demise as it becomes familiar or tiresome. If you want to define "character" by means of a single *narration*, you would probably organize paragraphs chronologically.

In a definition essay using several methods of development, you should devote separate paragraphs to each pattern. A definition of "relaxation," for instance, might start with a paragraph that *narrates* a particularly relaxing day; then it might move to a paragraph that describes several *examples* of people who find it difficult to unwind; finally, it might end with a paragraph that explains a *process* for relaxing the mind and body.

5. Write an effective introduction.   It can be helpful to provide—near the beginning of a definition essay—a brief formal definition of the term you're going to develop in the rest of the paper. Beyond this basic element, the introduction may include a number of other features. You might explain the *origin* of the term being defined: "Acid rock is a term first coined in the

1960s to describe music that was written or listened to under the influence of the drug LSD." Similarly, you could explain the *etymology*, or linguistic origin, of the key word that focuses the paper. "The term *vigilantism* is derived from the Latin word meaning 'to watch and be awake.'"

You may also use the introduction to clarify what the subject is *not*. Such *definition by negation* can be an effective strategy at the beginning of a paper, especially if readers don't share your view of the subject. In such a case, you might write something like this: "The gorilla, far from being the vicious killer of jungle movies and popular imagination, is a sedentary, gentle creature living in a closely knit family group." Such a statement provides the special focus of your essay and signals some of the misconceptions or fallacies soon to be discussed.

In addition, you may include in the introduction a *stipulative definition*, one that puts special restrictions on a term: "Strictly defined, a mall refers to a one- or two-story enclosed building containing a variety of retail shops and at least two large anchor stores. Highway-strip shopping centers or downtown centers cannot be considered true malls." When a term has multiple meanings, or when its meaning has become fuzzy through misuse, a stipulative definition sets the record straight right at the start, so that readers know exactly what is, and is not, being defined.

Finally, the introduction may end with a *plan of development* that indicates how the definition essay will unfold. A student who returned to school after having raised a family decided to write a paper defining the *midlife crisis* that led to her enrollment in college. After providing a brief formal definition of "midlife crisis," the student rounded off her introduction with this sentence: "Such a midlife crisis starts with vague misgivings, turns into depression, and ends with a significant change in lifestyle."

REVISION STRATEGIES

Once you have a draft of the essay, you're ready to revise. The following checklist will help you and those giving you feedback apply to definition some of the revision techniques discussed on pages 59–61.

☑ DEFINITION: A REVISION/PEER REVIEW CHECKLIST

Revise Overall Meaning and Structure

❑ Is the essay's purpose informative, persuasive, or both?

❑ Is the term being defined clearly distinguished from similar terms?

❑ Where does a circular definition cloud meaning? Where are technical, nonstandard, or ambiguous terms a source of confusion?

❑ Where would a word's historical or linguistic origin clarify meaning? Where would a formal definition, stipulative definition, or definition by negation help?

❑ Which patterns of development are used to develop the definition? How do these help the essay achieve its purpose?

❑ If the essay uses only one pattern, is the essay's method of organization suited to that pattern (step-by-step for process analysis, chronological for narration, and so on)?

❑ Where could a dry formal definition be deleted without sacrificing overall clarity?

Revise Paragraph Development

❑ If the essay uses several patterns of development, where would separate paragraphs for different patterns be appropriate?

❑ Which paragraphs are flat or unconvincing? How could they be made more compelling?

Revise Sentences and Words

❑ Which sentences and words are inconsistent with the essay's tone?

❑ Where should overused phrases like "the dictionary says" and "according to Webster's" be replaced by more original wording?

❑ Have "is when" definitions been avoided?

STUDENT ESSAY

The following student essay was written by Laura Chen in response to this assignment:

In "Entropy," K. C. Cole takes a scientific term from physics and gives it a broader definition and a wider application. Choose another specialized term and define it in such a way that you reveal something significant about contemporary life.

While reading Laura's paper, try to determine how well it applies the principles of definition. The annotations on Laura's paper and the commentary following it will help you look at the essay more closely.

Physics in Everyday Life
by Laura Chen

Introduction   A boulder sits on a mountainside for a thousand years.   1
The boulder will remain there forever unless an outside force intervenes. Suppose a force does affect the boulder—an earthquake, for instance. Once the boulder begins to thunder down the mountain, it will remain in motion and head in one

direction only--downhill--until another force interrupts its progress. If the boulder tumbles into a gorge, it will finally come to rest as gravity anchors it to the earth once more. In both

Formal definition cases, the boulder is exhibiting the physical principle of inertia: the tendency of matter to remain at rest or, if moving, to keep moving in one direction unless affected by an outside force.

Thesis ⟶ Inertia, an important factor in the world of physics, also plays a crucial role in the human world. Inertia affects our individual

Plan of development lives as well as the direction taken by society as a whole.

Topic sentence ⟶ Inertia often influences our value systems and personal   2
growth. Inertia is at work, for example, when people cling to certain behaviors and views. Like the boulder firmly fixed to the mountain, most people are set in their ways. Without thinking, they vote Republican or Democratic because they have always voted that way. They regard with suspicion a couple having no children, simply because everyone else in the neighborhood has a large family. It is only when an outside

Start of a series of causes and effects force--a jolt of some sort--occurs that people change their views. A white American couple may think little about racial discrimination, for instance, until they adopt an Asian child and must comfort her when classmates tease her because she looks different. Parents may consider promiscuous any unmarried teenage girl who has a baby until their seventeen-year-old honor student confesses that she is pregnant. Personal jolts like these force people to think, perhaps for the first time, about issues that now affect them directly.

Topic sentence ⟶ To illustrate how inertia governs our lives, it is helpful to   3
compare the world of television with real life. On TV, inertia

Start of a series of contrasts does not exist. Television shows and commercials show people making all kinds of drastic changes. They switch brands of coffee or try a new hair color with no hesitation. In one car commercial, an ambitious young accountant abandons her career with a flourish and is seen driving off into the sunset as she heads for a small cabin by the sea to write poetry. In a soap opera, a character may progress from homemaker to hooker to nun in a single year. But in real life, inertia rules. People tend to stay where they are, to keep their jobs, to be loyal to products. A second major difference between television and real life is that, on television, everyone takes prompt and dramatic action to solve problems. The construction worker with a thudding headache is pain-free at the end of the sixty-second commercial; the police catch the murderer within an hour; the family learns to cope with their son's life-threatening drug addiction by the time the made-for-TV movie ends at eleven. But in the real world, inertia persists, so that few problems are solved neatly or quickly. Illnesses drag on, few crimes are solved, and family conflicts last for years.

Topic sentence ———————→ Inertia is, most importantly, a force at work in the life of   4
our nation. Again, inertia is two-sided. It keeps us from
moving and, once we move, it keeps us pointed in one
direction. We find ourselves mired in a certain path, accepting

Start of a series ——— the inferior, even the dangerous. We settle for toys that break,
of examples   winter coats with no warmth, and rivers clogged with
pollution. Inertia also compels our nation to keep moving in
one direction--despite the uncomfortable suspicion that it is
the wrong direction. We are not sure if manipulating genes is
a good idea, yet we continue to fund scientific projects in
genetic engineering. More than fifty years ago, we were
shaken when we saw the devastation caused by an atomic
bomb. But we went on to develop weapons hundreds of times
more destructive. Although warned that excessive television
viewing may be harmful, we continue to watch hours of
television each day.

Conclusion   We have learned to defy gravity, one of the basic laws of   5
physics; we fly high above the earth, even float in outer space.
But most of us have not learned to defy inertia. Those special
individuals who are able to act when everyone else seems
paralyzed are rare. But the fact that such people do exist
means that inertia is not all-powerful. If we use our reasoning
ability and our creativity, we can conquer inertia, just as we
have conquered gravity.

COMMENTARY

Introduction.   As the title of her essay suggests, Laura has taken a scientific term (*inertia*) from a specialized field and drawn on the term to help explain some everyday phenomena. Using the *simple-to-complex* approach to structure the introduction, she opens with a vivid *descriptive* example of inertia. This description is then followed by a *formal definition* of inertia: "the tendency of matter to remain at rest or, if moving, to keep moving in one direction unless affected by an outside force." Laura wisely begins the paper with the easy-to-understand description rather than with the more-difficult-to-grasp scientific definition. Had the order been reversed, the essay would not have gotten off to nearly as effective a start. She then ends her introductory paragraph with a *thesis*, "Inertia, an important factor in the world of physics, also plays a crucial role in the human world," and with a *plan of development*, "Inertia affects our individual lives as well as the direction taken by society as a whole."

Organization.   To support her definition of inertia and her belief that it can rule our lives, Laura generates a number of compelling examples. She organizes these examples by grouping them into three major points, each point signaled by a *topic sentence* that opens each of the essay's three supporting paragraphs (2–4).

A definite organizational strategy determines the sequence of Laura's three central points. The essay moves from the way inertia affects the individual to the way it affects the nation. The phrase "most importantly" at the beginning of the fourth paragraph shows that Laura has arranged her points emphatically, believing that inertia's impact on society is most critical.

A weak example.   When reading the fourth paragraph, you might have noticed that Laura's examples aren't sequenced as effectively as they could be. To show that we, as a nation, tend to keep moving in the same direction, Laura discusses our ongoing uneasiness about genetic engineering, nuclear arms, and excessive television viewing. The point about nuclear weapons is most significant, yet it gets lost because it's sandwiched in the middle. The paragraph would be stronger if it ended with the point about nuclear arms. Moreover, the example about excessive television viewing doesn't belong in this paragraph since, at best, it has limited bearing on the issue being discussed.

Combining patterns of development.   In addition to using numerous *examples* to illustrate her points, Laura draws on several other patterns of development to show that inertia can be a powerful force. In the second and fourth paragraphs, she uses *causal analysis* to explain how inertia can paralyze people and nations. The second paragraph indicates that only "an outside force—a jolt of some sort—" can motivate inert people to change. To support this view, Laura provides two examples of parents who experience such jolts. Similarly, in the fourth paragraph, she contends that inertia causes the persistence of specific national problems: shoddy consumer goods and environmental pollution.

Another pattern, *comparison-contrast,* is used in the third paragraph to highlight the differences between television and real life: on television, people zoom into action, but in everyday life, people tend to stay put and muddle through. The essay also contains a distinct element of *argumentation-persuasion,* since Laura clearly wants readers to accept her definition of inertia and her view that it often governs human behavior.

Conclusion.   Laura's *conclusion* rounds off the essay nicely and brings it to a satisfying close. Laura refers to another law of physics, one with which we are all familiar—gravity. By creating an *analogy* between gravity and inertia, she suggests that our ability to defy gravity should encourage us to defy inertia. The analogy enlarges the scope of the essay; it allows Laura to reach out to her readers by challenging them to action. Such a challenge is, of course, appropriate in a definition essay having a persuasive bent.

Revising the first draft.   When it was time to rework her essay, Laura began by reading her paper aloud. She noted in the margin of her draft the problems she detected, numbering them in order of importance. After reviewing her notes, she started to revise in earnest, paying special attention to her third paragraph. The first draft of that paragraph is reprinted here:

Original Version of the Third Paragraph

The ordinary actions of daily life are, in part, determined by inertia. To understand this, it is helpful to compare the world of television with real life, for, in the TV-land of ads and entertainment, inertia does not exist. For example, on television, people are often shown making all kinds of drastic changes. They switch brands of coffee or try a new hair color with no hesitation. In one car commercial, a young accountant leaves her career and sets off for a cabin by the sea to write poetry. In a soap opera, a character may progress from homemaker to hooker to nun in a single year. In contrast, inertia rules in real life. People tend to stay where they are, to keep their jobs, to be loyal to products (wives get annoyed if a husband brings home the wrong brand or color of bathroom tissue from the market). Middle-aged people wear the hairstyles or makeup that suited them in high school. A second major difference between television and real life is that, on TV, everyone takes prompt and dramatic action to solve problems. A woman finds the solution to dull clothes at the end of a commercial; the police catch the murderer within an hour; the family learns to cope with a son's disturbing lifestyle by the time the movie is over. In contrast, the law of real-life inertia means that few problems are solved neatly or quickly. Things, once started, tend to stay as they are. Few crimes are actually solved. Medical problems are not easily diagnosed. Messy wars in foreign countries seem endless. National problems are identified, but Congress does not pass legislation to solve them.

After rereading what she had written, Laura realized that her third paragraph rambled. To give it more focus, she removed the last two sentences ("Messy wars in foreign countries seem endless" and "National problems are identified, but Congress does not pass legislation. . . .") because they referred to national affairs but were located in a section focusing on the individual. Then, she eliminated two flat, unconvincing examples: wives who get annoyed when their husbands bring home the wrong brand of bathroom tissue and middle-aged people whose hairstyles and makeup are outdated. Condensing the two disjointed sentences that originally opened the paragraph also helped tighten this section of the essay. Note how much crisper the revised sentences are: "To illustrate how inertia rules our lives, it is helpful to compare the world of television with real life. On TV, inertia does not exist."

Laura also worked to make the details and the language in the paragraph more specific and vigorous. The vague sentence "A woman finds the solution to dull clothes at the end of the commercial" is replaced by the more dramatic "The construction worker with a thudding headache is pain-free at the end of the sixty-second commercial." Similarly, Laura changed a "son's disturbing lifestyle" to a "son's life-threatening drug addiction"; "by the time the movie is over" became "by the time the made-for-TV movie ends at eleven"; and "a young accountant leaves her career and sets off for a cabin by the sea to write poetry" was changed to "an ambitious young accountant abandons her career with a flourish and is seen driving off into the sunset as she heads for a small cabin by the sea to write poetry."

After making these changes, Laura decided to round off the paragraph with a powerful summary statement highlighting how real life differs from television: "Illnesses drag on, few crimes are solved, and family conflicts last for years."

These third-paragraph revisions are similar to those that Laura made elsewhere in her first draft. Her astute changes enabled her to turn an already effective paper into an especially thoughtful analysis of human behavior.

ACTIVITIES: DEFINITION

Prewriting Activities

1. Imagine you're writing two essays: one explains the *process* for registering a complaint that gets results; the other *contrasts* the styles of two stand-up comics. Jot down ways you might use definition in each essay.

2. Select a term whose meaning varies from person to person or one for which you have a personal definition. Some possibilities include:

success	femininity	a liberal
patriotism	affirmative action	a housewife
individuality	pornography	intelligence

   Brainstorm with others to identify variations in the term's meaning. Then examine your prewriting material. What thesis comes to mind? If you were writing an essay, would your purpose be informative, persuasive, or both? Finally, prepare a scratch list of the points you might cover.

Revising Activities

3. Explain why each of the following is an effective or ineffective definition. Rewrite those you consider ineffective.
   a. *Passive aggression* is when people show their aggression passively.
   b. A *terrorist* tries to terrorize people.
   c. *Being assertive* means knowing how to express your wishes and goals in a positive, noncombative way.
   d. *Pop music* refers to music that is popular.
   e. *Loyalty* is when someone stays by another person during difficult times.

4. The following introductory paragraph is from the first draft of an essay contrasting walking and running as techniques for reducing tension. Although intended to be a definition paragraph, it actually doesn't tell us anything we don't already know. It also relies on the old-hat "*Webster's* says." Rewrite the paragraph so it is more imaginative. You might use a series of anecdotes or one extended example to define *tension* and introduce the essay's thesis more gracefully.

According to Webster's, tension is "mental or nervous strain, often accompanied by muscular tightness or tautness." Everyone feels tense at one time or another. It may occur when there's a deadline to meet. Or it could be caused by the stress of trying to fulfill academic, athletic, or social goals. Sometimes it comes from criticism by family, bosses, or teachers. Such tension puts wear and tear on our bodies and on our emotional well-being. Although some people run to relieve tension, research has found that walking is a more effective tension reducer.

K. C. Cole

K. C. Cole's writings about science, especially physics, have made a great deal of specialized knowledge available to the general public. A graduate of Barnard College, Cole has contributed numerous articles to such publications as the *New York Times,* the *Washington Post,* and *Long Island Newsday,* and writes a regular column for *Discover* magazine. Her work with the Exploratorium, a San Francisco science museum, led her to write several books on the exhibits there. In 1985, Cole published a collection of essays, *Sympathetic Vibrations: Reflections on Physics as a Way of Life.* Other books include *What Only a Mother Can Tell You About Having a Baby* (1986), *The Universe and the Teacup* (1998), *First You Build a Cloud* (1999), *The Hole in the Universe* (2000), and *Mind Over Matter* (2003). She is currently a science writer and editor at the *L.A. Times.* The following selection was first published as a "Hers" column in the *New York Times* in 1982.

Pre-Reading Journal Entry

Do you consider yourself an orderly or a disorderly person? What about those around you? What are the benefits and the drawbacks of being orderly? Of being disorderly? Use your journal to reflect on these questions.

Entropy

It was about two months ago when I realized that entropy was getting the better of me. On the same day my car broke down (again), my refrigerator conked out and I learned that I needed root-canal work in my right rear tooth. The windows in the bedroom were still leaking every time it rained and my son's baby sitter was still failing to show up every time I really needed her. My hair was turning gray and my typewriter was wearing out. The house needed paint and I needed glasses. My son's sneakers were developing holes and I was developing a deep sense of futility.

After all, what was the point of spending half of Saturday at the Laundromat if the clothes were dirty all over again the following Friday?

Disorder, alas, is the natural order of things in the universe. There is even a precise measure of the amount of disorder, called entropy. Unlike almost every other physical property (motion, gravity, energy), entropy does not work both ways. It can only increase. Once it's created it can never be destroyed. The road to disorder is a one-way street.

Because of its unnerving irreversibility, entropy has been called the arrow of time. We all understand this instinctively. Children's rooms, left on their own, tend to get messy, not neat. Wood rots, metal rusts, people wrinkle and flowers wither. Even mountains wear down; even the nuclei of atoms decay. In the city we see entropy in the rundown subways and worn-out sidewalks and torn-down buildings, in the increasing disorder of our lives. We know, without asking, what is old. If we were suddenly to see the paint jump back on an old building, we would know that something was wrong. If we saw an egg unscramble itself and jump back into its shell, we would laugh in the same way we laugh at a movie run backward.

Entropy is no laughing matter, however, because with every increase in entropy energy is wasted and opportunity is lost. Water flowing down a mountainside can be made to do some useful work on its way. But once all the water is at the same level it can work no more. That is entropy. When my refrigerator was working, it kept all the cold air ordered in one part of the kitchen and warmer air in another. Once it broke down the warm and cold mixed into a lukewarm mess that allowed my butter to melt, my milk to rot and my frozen vegetables to decay.   5

Of course the energy is not really lost, but it has diffused and dissipated into a chaotic caldron of randomness that can do us no possible good. Entropy is chaos. It is loss of purpose.   6

People are often upset by the entropy they seem to see in the haphazardness of their own lives. Buffeted about like so many molecules in my tepid kitchen, they feel that they have lost their sense of direction, that they are wasting youth and opportunity at every turn. It is easy to see entropy in marriages, when the partners are too preoccupied to patch small things up, almost guaranteeing that they will fall apart. There is much entropy in the state of our country, in the relationships between nations—lost opportunities to stop the avalanche of disorders that seems ready to swallow us all.   7

Entropy is not inevitable everywhere, however. Crystals and snowflakes and galaxies are islands of incredibly ordered beauty in the midst of random events. If it was not for exceptions to entropy, the sky would be black and we would be able to see where the stars spend their days; it is only because air molecules in the atmosphere cluster in ordered groups that the sky is blue.   8

The most profound exception to entropy is the creation of life. A seed soaks up some soil and some carbon and some sunshine and some water and arranges it into a rose. A seed in the womb takes some oxygen and pizza and milk and transforms it into a baby.   9

The catch is that it takes a lot of energy to produce a baby. It also takes energy to make a tree. The road to disorder is all downhill but the road to creation takes work. Though combating entropy is possible, it also has its price. That's why it seems so hard to get ourselves together, so easy to let ourselves fall apart.   10

Worse, creating order in one corner of the universe always creates more disorder somewhere else. We create ordered energy from oil and coal at the price of the entropy of smog.   11

I recently took up playing the flute again after an absence of several   12
months. As the uneven vibrations screeched through the house, my son covered his ears and said, "Mom, what's wrong with your flute?" Nothing was
wrong with my flute, of course. It was my ability to play it that had atrophied, or entropied, as the case may be. The only way to stop that process
was to practice every day, and sure enough my tone improved, though only
at the price of constant work. Like anything else, abilities deteriorate when
we stop applying our energies to them.

That's why entropy is depressing. It seems as if just breaking even is an   13
uphill fight. There's a good reason that this should be so. The mechanics of
entropy are a matter of chance. Take any ice-cold air molecule milling
around my kitchen. The chances that it will wander in the direction of my
refrigerator at any point are exactly 50-50. The chances that it will wander
away from my refrigerator are also 50-50. But take billions of warm and cold
molecules mixed together, and the chances that all the cold ones will wander
toward the refrigerator and all the warm ones will wander away from it are
virtually nil.

Entropy wins not because order is impossible but because there are   14
always so many more paths toward disorder than toward order. There are so
many more different ways to do a sloppy job than a good one, so many more
ways to make a mess than to clean it up. The obstacles and accidents in our
lives almost guarantee that constant collisions will bounce us on to random
paths, get us off the track. Disorder is the path of least resistance, the easy
but not the inevitable road.

Like so many others, I am distressed by the entropy I see around me   15
today. I am afraid of the randomness of international events, of the lack of
common purpose in the world; I am terrified that it will lead into the ultimate entropy of nuclear war. I am upset that I could not in the city where I
live send my child to a public school; that people are unemployed and inflation is out of control; that tensions between sexes and races seem to be
increasing again; that relationships everywhere seem to be falling apart.

Social institutions—like atoms and stars—decay if energy is not added to   16
keep them ordered. Friendships and families and economies all fall apart
unless we constantly make an effort to keep them working and well oiled.
And far too few people, it seems to me, are willing to contribute consistently to those efforts.

Of course, the more complex things are, the harder it is. If there were   17
only a dozen or so air molecules in my kitchen, it would be likely—if I waited a year or so—that at some point the six coldest ones would congregate
inside the freezer. But the more factors in the equation—the more players in
the game—the less likely it is that their paths will coincide in an orderly way.
The more pieces in the puzzle, the harder it is to put back together once
order is disturbed. "Irreversibility," said a physicist, "is the price we pay for
complexity."

Questions for Close Reading

1. What is the selection's thesis? Locate the sentence(s) in which Cole states her main idea. If she doesn't state the thesis explicitly, express it in your own words.
2. How does entropy differ from the other properties of the physical world? Is the image "the arrow of time" helpful in establishing this difference?
3. Why is the creation of life an exception to entropy? What is the relationship between entropy and energy?
4. Why does Cole say that entropy "is no laughing matter"? What is so depressing about the entropy she describes?
5. Refer to your dictionary as needed to define the following words used in the selection: *futility* (paragraph 1), *dissipated* (6), *buffeted* (7), *tepid* (7), and *atrophied* (12).

Questions About the Writer's Craft

1. **The pattern.** What is Cole's underlying purpose in defining the scientific term *entropy?* What gives the essay its persuasive edge?
2. What tone does Cole adopt to make reading about a scientific concept more interesting? Identify places in the essay where her tone is especially prominent.
3. Cole uses such words as *futility, loss,* and *depressing.* How do these words affect you? Why do you suppose she chose such terms? Find similar words in the essay.
4. **Other patterns.** Many of Cole's sentences follow a two-part pattern involving a *contrast:* "The road to disorder is all downhill but the road to creation takes work" (paragraph 10). Find other examples of this pattern in the essay. Why do you think Cole uses it so often?

Writing Assignments Using Definition as a Pattern of Development

1. Write an essay in which you define *order* or *disorder* by applying the term to a system that you know well—for example, your school, dorm, family, or workplace. Develop your definition through any combination of writing patterns: by supplying examples, by showing contrasts, by analyzing the process underlying the system.
2. Choose, as Cole does, a technical term that you think will be unfamiliar to most readers. In a humorous or serious paper, define the term as it is used technically; then show how the term can shed light on some aspect of your life. For example, the concept in astronomy of a *supernova* could be used to explain your sudden emergence as a new star on the athletic field, in your schoolwork, or on the social scene. Here are a few suggested terms:

symbiosis	volatility	resonance
velocity	erosion	catalyst
neutralization	equilibrium	malleability

Writing Assignments Combining Patterns of Development

3. Can one person make much difference in the amount of entropy—disorder and chaos—in the world? *Argue* your position in an essay. Use *examples* of people who

have tried to overcome the tendency of things to "fall apart." Make clear whether you think these people succeeded or failed in their attempts.

∞ 4. Cole claims that we humans are "buffeted about like so many molecules." Write an essay *arguing* that people either do or do not control their own fates. Support your point with a series of specific *examples*. For different perspectives on the issue, you might want to read Gary Soto's "The Jacket" (page 91), Maya Angelou's "Sister Flowers" (page 96), and Joseph H. Suina's "And Then I Went to School" (page 271).

Writing Assignment Using a Journal Entry as a Starting Point

5. Write an essay arguing that disorder can be liberating *or* that it can be stifling. Review your pre-reading journal entry, and select strong, compelling examples that support your position. Aim to refute as many opposing arguments as possible. Your essay may have a serious or a humorous tone.

Alexandra Robbins
Abby Wilner

A contributing editor at *Mademoiselle* magazine, Alexandra Robbins (1976–) has written for such publications as the *New Yorker*, the *Atlantic Monthly*, the *Washington Post, Salon*, and *USA Today*. Soon after graduating from Yale University, she began to work on the book *Quarterlife Crisis: The Unique Challenges of Life in Your Twenties* (2001) with her high school friend Abby Wilner (1976–), a Washington University of St. Louis alumna. The book, which became a *New York Times* best-seller, grew out of the two authors' own post-college experiences as well as interviews with several hundred peers. The success of *Quarterlife Crisis* led to its authors appearing on national and international television and radio programs, including *The Today Show, The Oprah Winfrey Show, CNN Daybreak*, and *BBC Breakfast News*. Abby Wilner has since developed a series of quarterlife crisis workshops and seminars and serves as administrator of the www.quarterlifecrisis.com website. Alexandra Robbins went on to write *Secrets of the Tomb: Skull and Bones, the Ivy League, and the Hidden Paths of Power* (2002), an investigative report on Yale University's infamous secret society. Both women live in Washington, D.C. The following essay is the first chapter of *Quarterlife Crisis*.

Pre-Reading Journal Entry

When you look ahead to your future after graduation, what are some of the things you fear? In your pre-reading journal, brainstorm a list of the various concerns you see looming on the horizon. Once you've completed your list, create categories grouping together similar kinds of fears. What are the resulting categories?

What Is the Quarterlife Crisis?

Jim, the neighbor who lives in the three-story colonial down the block, has recently turned 50. You know this because Jim's wife threw him a surprise party about a month ago. You also know this because, since then, Jim has dyed his hair blond, purchased a leather bomber jacket, traded in his Chevy Suburban for a sleek Miata, and ditched the wife for a girlfriend half her size and age. 1

Yet, aside from the local ladies' group's sympathetic clucks for the scorned wife, few neighbors are surprised at Jim's instant lifestyle change. Instead, they nod their heads understandingly. "Oh, Jim," they say. "He's just going through a midlife crisis. Everyone goes through it." Friends, colleagues, and family members excuse his weird behavior as an inevitable effect 2 of reaching this particular stage of life. Like millions of other middle-aged people, Jim has reached a period during which he believes he must ponder the direction of his life—and then alter it.

Chances are . . . you're not Jim. You know this because you can't afford a leather bomber jacket, you drive your parents' Volvo (if you drive a car at all), and, regardless of your gender, you would happily marry Jim's wife if she gets to keep the house. But Jim's midlife crisis is relevant to you nonetheless, because it is currently the only age-related crisis that is widely recognized as a common, inevitable part of life. This is pertinent because, despite all of the attention lavished on the midlife crisis, despite the hundreds of books, movies, and magazine articles dedicated to explaining the sometimes traumatic transition through middle age and the ways to cope with it, the midlife crisis is not the only age-related crisis that we experience. As Yoda whispered to Luke Skywalker, "There is another."

This other crisis can be just as, if not more, devastating than the midlife crisis. It can throw someone's life into chaotic disarray or paralyze it completely. It may be the single most concentrated period during which individuals relentlessly question their future and how it will follow the events of their past. It covers the interval that encompasses the transition from the academic world to the "real" world—an age group that can range from late adolescence to the mid-thirties but is usually most intense in twentysomethings. It is what we call the quarterlife crisis, and it is a real phenomenon.

The quarterlife crisis and the midlife crisis stem from the same basic problem, but the resulting panic couldn't be more opposite. At their cores, both the quarterlife and the midlife crisis are about a major life change. Often, for people experiencing a midlife crisis, a sense of stagnancy sparks the need for change. During this period, a middle-aged person tends to reflect on his past, in part to see if his life to date measures up to the life he had envisioned as a child (or as a twentysomething). The midlife crisis also impels a middle-aged person to look forward, sometimes with an increasing sense of desperation, at the time he feels he has left.

In contrast, the quarterlife crisis occurs precisely because there is none of that predictable stability that drives middle-aged people to do unpredictable things. After about twenty years in a sheltered school setting—or more if a person has gone on to graduate or professional school—many graduates undergo some sort of culture shock. In the academic environment, goals were clear-cut and the ways to achieve them were mapped out distinctly. To get into a good college or graduate school, it helped if you graduated with honors; to graduate with honors, you needed to get good grades; to get good grades, you had to study hard. If your goals were athletic, you worked your way up from junior varsity or walk-on to varsity by practicing skills, working out in the weight broom, and gelling with teammates and coaches. The better you were, the more playing time you got, the more impressive your statistics could become.

But after graduation, the pathways blur. In that crazy, wild nexus that 7
people like to call the "real world," there is no definitive way to get from
point A to point B, regardless of whether the points are related to a career,
financial situation, home, or social life (though we have found through several unscientific studies that offering to pay for the next round of drinks can
usually improve three out of the four). The extreme uncertainty that twentysomethings experience after graduation occurs because what was once a solid
line that they could follow throughout their series of educational institutions
has now disintegrated into millions of different options. The sheer number
of possibilities can certainly inspire hope—that is why people say that twentysomethings have their whole lives ahead of them. But the endless array of
decisions can also make a recent graduate feel utterly lost.

So while the midlife crisis revolves around a doomed sense of stagnancy, 8
of a life set on pause while the rest of the world rattles on, the quarterlife
crisis is a response to overwhelming instability, constant change, too many
choices, and a panicked sense of helplessness. Just as the monotony of a
lifestyle stuck in idle can drive a person to question himself intently, so, too,
can the uncertainty of a life thrust into chaos. The transition from childhood
to adulthood—from school to the world beyond—comes as a jolt for which
many of today's twentysomethings simply are not prepared. The resulting
overwhelming senses of helplessness and cluelessness, of indecision and
apprehension, make up the real and common experience we call the quarterlife crisis. Individuals who are approaching middle age at least know what is
coming. Because the midlife crisis is so widely acknowledged, people who
undergo it are at the very least aware that there are places where they can go
for help, such as support groups, books, movies, or Internet sites. Twentysomethings, by contrast, face a crisis that hits them with a far more powerful
force than they ever expected. The slam is particularly painful because
today's twentysomethings believe that they are alone and that they are having a much more difficult transition period than their peers—because the
twenties are supposed to be "easy," because no one talks about these problems, and because the difficulties are therefore so unexpected. And at the
fragile, doubt-ridden age during which the quarterlife crisis occurs, the ramifications can be extremely dangerous.

Why Worry About a Quarterlife Crisis?

The whirlwind of new responsibilities, new liberties, and new choices 9
can be entirely overwhelming for someone who has just emerged from the
shelter of twenty years of schooling. We don't mean to make graduates
sound as if they have been hibernating since they emerged from the womb;
certainly it is not as if they have been slumbering throughout adolescence
(though some probably tried). They have in a sense, however, been encased
in a bit of a cocoon, where someone or something—parents or school, for

example—has protected them from a lot of the scariness of their surroundings. As a result, when graduates are let loose into the world, their dreams and desires can be tinged with trepidation. They are hopeful, but at the same time they are also, to put it simply, scared silly.

Some might say that because people have had to deal with the rite of 10 passage from youth to adulthood since the beginning of time, this crisis is not really a "crisis" at all, given that historically this transitional period has, at various times, been marked with ceremonial rituals involving things like spears and buffalo dung. Indeed, it may not always have been a crisis.

But it has become one . . .   11

Although hope is a common emotion for twentysomethings, hopeless- 12 ness has become just as widespread. The revelation that life simply isn't easy—a given for some twentysomethings, a mild inconvenience for others, but a shattering blow for several—is one of the most distressing aspects of the quarterlife crisis, particularly for individuals who do not have large support networks or who doubt themselves often. It is in these situations that the quarterlife crisis becomes not just a common stage—it can become hazardous. Not everyone at the age of the quarterlife encounters some sort of depression. . . . But we are addressing depression as one common result of the quarterlife crisis here so that we can illustrate why it is so important to acknowledge this transition period.

After interviewing dozens of twentysomethings who said they were 13 depressed because of the transition, we ran our conclusions by Robert DuPont, a Georgetown Medical School professor of psychology who wrote *The Anxiety Cure.* "Based on my experience," DuPont said, "I have found that there is a high rate of all forms of disorder in this age group, including addiction, anxiety, depression, and many other kinds of problems because of the high stress associated with the transition from being a child to being an adult. And that has gotten more stressful as the road map has become less used. The old way of doing this was to get out and get it done right away. There was an economic imperative to doing it. It's not like that anymore. And as the road map has disappeared, the stress has gone up. People have to invent their own road map. It used to be that it came with the college graduation. Now you have to go out and figure it out yourself."

These high rates of disorders, however, have gone virtually unacknowl- 14 edged. That's why we can't bog you down with statistics on this age group. They don't exist. Psychological research on twentysomethings, including statistics on depression and suicide, has not been performed. We asked major national mental health associations such as the National Institutes of Mental Health, the American Psychiatric Association, and the National Depressive and Manic Depressive Association for any information they had on people in their twenties. They didn't have any. As one psychologist told us, associations don't cut the data to incorporate this age group. "It's not a subject that's interesting to them. They just lump everybody together," he said. . . .

Another way the quarterlife crisis can show up, particularly in the mid- to late twenties, is in a feeling of disappointment, of "This is all there is?" Maybe the job turns out to be not so glamorous after all, or maybe it just doesn't seem to lead anywhere interesting. Perhaps the year of travel in Europe was more of a wallet buster than previously imagined—even with nights in youth hostels and meals of ramen. Or maybe the move to a hip, new city just didn't turn out to be as fabulous a relocation as expected. 15

While these are, according to older generations, supposed to be the best years of their lives, twentysomethings also feel that the choices they make during this period will influence their thirties, forties, fifties, and on, in an irreparable domino effect. As a result, twentysomethings frequently have the unshakable belief that this is the time during which they have to nail down the meaning in their lives, which explains why they often experience a nagging feeling that somehow they need to make their lives more fulfilling. This is why there are so many drastic life changes at this point in life: an investment banker breaks off his engagement and volunteers for the Peace Corps; a consultant suddenly frets that consulting may not really have that much influence on other people's lives; a waiter chucks the steady paycheck to live in his car and try to make it in Hollywood; a law school graduate decides she doesn't want to be a lawyer after all and seeks a job in technology. 16

The changes hurtling toward a young adult, as well as the potential for more changes ahead, can be excruciatingly overwhelming for someone who is trying so hard to figure out how to feel fulfilled. A lot of people don't realize just how suffocating this pressure can be. The prevalent belief is that twentysomethings have it relatively easy because they do not have as many responsibilities as older individuals. But it is precisely this reduced responsibility that renders the vast array of decisions more difficult to make. For instance, if there were, say, a family to consider, a mother might not be as inclined to take a risk on the stock market. If a guy's elderly father were sick, he probably wouldn't take that year off to travel in South America. Twentysomethings, for the most part, just aren't at those stages yet, which is why they are sometimes envied. But because their choices aren't narrowed down for them by responsibilities, they have more decisions to make. And while this isn't necessarily bad, it can make things pretty complex. Figuring out which changes to make in order to make life more fulfilling is hard enough. But deciding to make a change and then following through with it requires an extraordinary amount of strength, which is sometimes hard to come by for a recent graduate who has not had to rely solely on himself for very long. 17

The most widespread, frightening, and quite possibly the most difficult manifestation of the quarterlife crisis is a feeling that can creep up on a twentysomething whether he is unemployed, living at home, and friendless, or in an interesting job, with a great apartment, and dozens of buddies. Regardless of their levels of self-esteem, confidence, and overall well-being, twentysomethings are particularly vulnerable to doubts. They doubt their decisions, 18 their abilities, their readiness, their past, present, and future . . . but most of all, they doubt themselves. The twenties comprise a period of intense questioning—of introspection and self-development that young adults often feel they are not ready for. The questions can range from seemingly trivial choices—"Should I really have spent $100 to join that fantasy baseball league?"—to irrefutably mammoth decisions—"When is the right time for me to start a family?" It is healthy, of course, for people to question themselves some; an occasional self-assessment or life inventory is a natural part of the quest for improvement. But if the questioning becomes constant and the barrage of doubts never seems to cease, twentysomethings can feel as if it is hard to catch their breath, as if they are spiraling downward. Many times the doubts increase because twentysomethings think it is abnormal to have them in the first place. No one talks about having doubts at this age, so when twentysomethings do find that they are continuously questioning themselves, they think something is wrong with them.

Questions for Close Reading

1. What is the selection's thesis? Locate the sentence(s) in which Robbins and Wilner state their main idea. If they don't state the thesis explicitly, express it in your own words.
2. People can be affected by the quarterlife crisis when they are in what age range? What age group is typically most vulnerable to it?
3. According to the authors, how is the quarterlife crisis similar to its midlife counterpart? How is it different?
4. At the end of the essay, Robbins and Wilner discuss the "most difficult manifestation" of the quarterlife crisis. What is this manifestation? What is so bad about it?
5. Refer to your dictionary as needed to define the following words used in the selection: *pertinent* (paragraph 3), *chaotic* (4), *disarray* (4), *interval* (4), *phenomenon* (4), *stagnancy* (5), *nexus* (7), *monotony* (8), *ramifications* (8), *trepidation* (9), *virtually* (14), *ramen* (15), *excruciatingly* (17), *manifestation* (18), and *barrage* (18).

Questions About the Writer's Craft

1. **The pattern.** What is Robbins and Wilner's underlying purpose in defining the term *quarterlife crisis?* Is their purpose mainly informative, speculative, or persuasive? How do you know?
2. **Other patterns.** The essay opens with a *narrative* anecdote about "Jim." Why do you think the authors chose to begin the essay this way? How does this anecdote relate to the paragraphs that follow it?
3. **Other patterns.** A central component in Robbins and Wilner's definition of the quarterlife crisis is a *causal analysis* of this phenomenon. What are the causes and effects they identify? How does this causal analysis contribute to the shaping of their definition?
4. **Other patterns.** In developing their definition of *quarterlife crisis,* the authors *compare and contrast* it to midlife crisis. What signal devices do they use to organize and clarify the comparisons and contrasts they identify?

Writing Assignments Using Definition as a Pattern of Development

1. In their essay and in the book in which it appears, Robbins and Wilner coin and define a kind of crisis they've observed or even experienced. Write an essay in which you coin the term for and define another kind of crisis. You might, for example, discuss the exam-cram crisis, the blind-date crisis, or the empty-fridge crisis. Be sure you give an "official" name to your crisis, and go on to develop your definition with specific examples and illustrations. A humorous or a mock-serious tone is likely to be most appropriate for your essay.

∞ 2. Underlying the quarterlife crisis, Robbins and Wilner imply, is a young person's anxiety about having to "grow up." But the meaning of growing up can vary widely from person to person. Write an essay in which you define what you think it means to "grow up." Here are some key questions you might ask yourself in formulating your definition: What new concerns and responsibilities are involved in growing up? What old priorities are left behind? At what point should people grow up? Is growing up a desirable objective? Do you feel you've reached this stage yet? Discussing these issues with friends and family before you begin writing might help you clarify your ideas. And for additional perspectives on the subject of growing up—especially growing up *too soon*—you should consult Ellen Goodman's "Family Counterculture" (page 6) and Kay S. Hymowitz's "Tweens: Ten Going on Sixteen" (page 200).

Writing Assignments Combining Patterns of Development

∞ 3. The classic definition of the word *crisis* is "turning point," though today the word generally carries the connotation of "distressing event." Think about a significant crisis you experienced at some point in your life, and write an essay *narrating* this event. Be sure in the course of your essay to examine the *causes* and *effects* of the crisis, paying special attention to whether and how you still feel its effects. Other accounts of personal crisis you might want to read before you write include any of the following: Gary Soto's "The Jacket" (page 91), Langston Hughes's "Salvation" (page 124), Adam Mayblum's "The Price We Pay" (page 128), Beth Johnson's "Bombs Bursting in Air" (page 160), and Joseph H. Suina's "And Then I Went to School" (page 271).

4. One of the causes of the quarterlife crisis, according to the authors, is that the single clear path of education has "disintegrated into millions of different options." Write an essay in which you *divide* and *classify* three options for your future that you have considered (or are still considering). For instance, you might discuss becoming a teacher, going to law school, pursuing a performance art, enlisting in the military, creating an Internet start-up—any three possibilities you have envisioned, no matter how impractical. Discuss each career option in at least one separate paragraph, detailing your *causes* for considering that career and speculating on the possible *effects* of selecting that path. If appropriate, you might consider doing some research in the library and/or on the Internet into projected trends—economic, social, and so on—regarding your career choices as a way of helping explain your selections.

Writing Assignment Using a Journal
Entry as a Starting Point

5. Write an essay in which you identify the three main *categories* of worries you have about the future. Such categories might include career, relationship, environmental, geopolitical, and so on. For each category of worry, be sure to present a variety of specific *examples* and explanations of why these issues concern you. For instance, if you discuss the category of economic worries, you might explain that your anxiety stems from having to pay off student loans and other debts, not earning enough money in your job, needing to support a family, and so on. For additional perspectives on this issue, you might also consider talking about these issues with friends and family.

William Raspberry

Journalist William Raspberry was born in Okolona, Mississippi. From his mother, an English teacher and poet, Raspberry learned to care "about the rhythm and grace of words." His father, a shop teacher, taught him "that neither end tables nor arguments are worthwhile unless they stand solidly on all four legs." Raspberry graduated from Indiana Central College and later joined the staff of the Indianapolis *Recorder* as a reporter and editor. Following a two-year stint in the army, he was hired by the *Washington Post*, where his nationally syndicated column has originated since 1971. His coverage of the Watts race riots in 1965 won him the Capital Press Club Journalist of the Year award, and he later went on to win the Pulitzer Prize for commentary in 1994. *Looking Backward at Us*, a collection of Raspberry's columns, was published in 1991. He currently teaches Communication and Journalism at Duke University. He and his wife live in Washington, D.C., and have three children. The following selection appeared in Raspberry's *Washington Post* column in 1982.

Pre-Reading Journal Entry

Which do you think plays a more important role in determining what a person accomplishes: innate talent or belief in oneself? Take a few minutes to respond to this question in your journal, jotting down examples drawn from your experiences and observations.

The Handicap of Definition

I know all about bad schools, mean politicians, economic deprivation and racism. Still, it occurs to me that one of the heaviest burdens black Americans—and black children in particular—have to bear is the handicap of definition: the question of what it means to be black.

Let me explain quickly what I mean. If a basketball fan says that the Boston Celtics' Larry Bird plays "black," the fan intends it—and Bird probably accepts it—as a compliment. Tell pop singer Tom Jones he moves "black" and he might grin in appreciation. Say to Teena Marie or the Average White Band that they sound "black" and they'll thank you.

But name one pursuit, aside from athletics, entertainment or sexual performance, in which a white practitioner will feel complimented to be told he does it "black." Tell a white broadcaster he talks "black" and he'll sign up for diction lessons. Tell a white reporter he writes "black" and he'll take a writing course. Tell a white lawyer he reasons "black" and he might sue you for slander.

What we have here is a tragically limited definition of blackness, and it   4
isn't only white people who buy it.

Think of all the ways black children can put one another down with   5
charges of "whiteness." For many of these children, hard study and hard
work are "white." Trying to please a teacher might be criticized as acting
"white." Speaking correct English is "white." Scrimping today in the interest of tomorrow's goals is "white." Educational toys and games are "white."

An incredible array of habits and attitudes that are conducive to success   6
in business, in academia, in the nonentertainment professions are likely to be
thought of as somehow "white." Even economic success, unless it involves
such "black" undertakings as numbers banking, is defined as "white."

And the results are devastating. I wouldn't deny that blacks often are   7
better entertainers and athletes. My point is the harm that comes from too
narrow a definition of what is black.

One reason black youngsters tend to do better at basketball, for instance,   8
is that they assume they can learn to do it well, and so they practice constantly to prove themselves right.

Wouldn't it be wonderful if we could infect black children with the notion   9
that excellence in math is "black" rather than white, or possibly Chinese?
Wouldn't it be of enormous value if we could create the myth that morality, strong families, determination, courage and love of learning are traits
brought by slaves from Mother Africa and therefore quintessentially black?

There is no doubt in my mind that most black youngsters could develop   10
their mathematical reasoning, their elocution and their attitudes, the way they
develop their jump shots and their dance steps: by the combination of sustained, enthusiastic practice and the unquestioned belief that they can do it.

In one sense, what I am talking about is the importance of developing   11
positive ethnic traditions. Maybe Jews have an innate talent for communication; maybe the Chinese are born with a gift for mathematical reasoning;
maybe blacks are naturally blessed with athletic grace. I doubt it. What is at
work, I suspect, is assumption, inculcated early in their lives, that this is a
thing our people do well.

Unfortunately, many of the things about which blacks make this assump-   12
tion are things that do not contribute to their career success—except for that
handful of the truly gifted who can make it as entertainers and athletes. And
many of the things we concede to whites are the things that are essential to
economic security.

So it is with a number of assumptions black youngsters make about what   13
it is to be a "man": physical aggressiveness, sexual prowess, the refusal to
submit to authority. The prisons are full of people who, by this perverted
definition, are unmistakably men.

But the real problem is not so much that the things defined as "black"   14
are negative. The problem is that the definition is much too narrow.

Somehow, we have to make our children understand that they are intel- 15
ligent, competent people, capable of doing whatever they put their minds to
and making it in the American mainstream, not just in a black subculture.

What we seem to be doing, instead, is raising up yet another generation 16
of young blacks who will be failures—by definition.

Questions for Close Reading

1. What is the selection's thesis? Locate the sentence(s) in which Raspberry states his
   main idea. If he doesn't state the thesis explicitly, express it in your own words.
2. In paragraph 14, Raspberry emphasizes that the word *black* presents a problem
   not because it's negative but because it has become "much too narrow." According to Raspberry, what limitations have become associated with the term *black*?
   What negative consequences does he see resulting from these limitations?
3. In paragraph 11, Raspberry talks about "positive ethnic traditions." What does he
   mean by this term? What examples does he provide?
4. In Raspberry's opinion, what needs to be done to ensure the future success of
   African-American children?
5. Refer to your dictionary as needed to define the following words used in the selection: *diction* (paragraph 3), *scrimping* (5), *array* (6), *quintessentially* (9), *elocution*
   (10), *inculcated* (11), and *concede* (12).

Questions About the Writer's Craft

1. **The pattern.** Raspberry is primarily concerned with showing how limited the
   definition of *black* has come to be in our society. In the course of the essay,
   though, he also defines three other terms. Locate these terms and their definitions. How do the definitions and the effects of the definitions help Raspberry
   make his point about the narrowness of the term *black*?
2. **Other patterns.** In his opening paragraph, Raspberry uses the *argumentation*
   technique of refutation. What does he refute? What does he achieve by using this
   strategy at the very beginning of the essay?
3. A black journalist, Raspberry writes a nationally syndicated column that originates
   in the *Washington Post*, a major newspaper serving the nation's capital and the
   nation as a whole. Consider these facts when examining Raspberry's use of the
   pronouns *I, we,* and *our* in the essay. What do these pronouns seem to imply about
   Raspberry's intended audience? What is the effect of these pronouns?
4. Raspberry has chosen a relatively abstract topic to write about—the meaning of
   the term *black*. What techniques does he use to draw in readers and keep them
   engaged? Consider his overall tone, choice of examples, and use of balanced sentence structure.

Writing Assignments Using Definition as a Pattern of Development

1. Raspberry points out how restrictive the definitions of *black* and *white* can be.
   Do you think that the definitions of *male* and *female* can be equally restrictive?

Focusing on the term *male* or *female,* write an essay showing how the term was defined as you were growing up. Considering the messages conveyed by your family, the educational system, and society at large, indicate whether you came to perceive the term as limiting or liberating. Before planning your paper, you may want to read one or more of the following essays, all of which deal with the way gender roles influence behavior: Barbara Ehrenreich's "What I've Learned From Men" (page 166), Dave Barry's "The Ugly Truth About Beauty" (page 277), Camille Paglia's "Rape: A Bigger Danger Than Feminists Know" (page 395), and Susan Jacoby's "Common Decency" (page 401).

2. In paragraph 15, Raspberry seems to define *success* as "making it in the American mainstream," but not everyone would agree that this is what constitutes success. Write an essay in which you offer your personal definition of *success.* One way to proceed might be to contrast what you consider success with what you consider failure. Or you might narrate the success story of a person you respect highly. No matter how you proceed, be sure to provide telling specifics that support your definition.

Writing Assignments Combining Patterns of Development

3. Like most people, you've probably had a *"defining"* term applied to you at one time or another. Perhaps you've been called "shy" or "stubborn" or "the class clown" or "the athlete in the family." Focusing on one such label that's been applied to you, write an essay showing the *effect* of this term on your life. Be sure to explain why you got the label and how you felt about it. The following essays will give you additional perspectives on the ways that labels and names affect people's lives and self-image: Joseph H. Suina's "And Then I Went to School" (page 271) and Shelby Steele's "Affirmative Action: The Price of Preference (page 416).

4. In his conclusion, Raspberry makes a plea for providing the younger generation with a more positive, more expansive definition of *black.* Consider the beliefs and principles that today's older generation seems to impart to the younger generation. Write an essay *arguing* which aspects of this value system seem helpful and valid and which do not. Also explain what additional values and convictions the older generation should be passing on, providing *examples* along the way. How should parents, teachers, and others convey these precepts? For a discussion of some obstacles to children's moral instruction, read Ellen Goodman's "Family Counterculture" (page 6) and Kay S. Hymowitz's "Tweens: Ten Going on Sixteen (page 153).

Writing Assignment Using a Journal Entry as a Starting Point

5. Developing the material in your pre-reading journal entry, write an essay arguing that an individual's innate talent *or* self-confidence is the critical factor in determining achievement. Consider brainstorming with others to generate examples in support of your contention. At some point in the essay, you should acknowledge the opposing viewpoint, dismantling as much of it as you can.

Additional Writing Topics

DEFINITION

General Assignments

Use definition to develop any of the following topics. Once you fix on a limited subject, decide if the essay has an informative or a persuasive purpose. The paper might begin with the etymology of the term, a stipulative definition, or a definition by negation. You may want to use a number of writing patterns—such as description, comparison, narration, process analysis—to develop the definition. Remember, too, that the paper doesn't have to be scholarly and serious. There is no reason it can't be a lighthearted discussion of the meaning of a term.

1. Fads
2. A family fight
3. Helplessness
4. An epiphany
5. A workaholic
6. A Pollyanna
7. A con artist
8. A stingy person
9. A team player
10. A Yiddish term like *mensch, klutz,* or *chutzpah,* or a term from some other ethnic group
11. Adolescence
12. Fast food
13. A perfect day
14. Hypocrisy
15. Inner peace
16. Obsession
17. Generosity
18. Exploitation
19. Depression
20. A double bind

Assignments With a Specific Purpose, Audience, and Point of View

On Campus

1. You've been asked to write part of a pamphlet for students who come to the college health clinic. For this pamphlet, define *one* of the following conditions and its symptoms: *depression, stress, burnout, test anxiety, addiction* (to alcohol, drugs, or TV), *workaholism.* Part of the pamphlet should describe ways to cope with the condition described.

2. One of your responsibilities as a peer counselor in the student counseling center involves helping students communicate more effectively. To assist students, write a definition of some term that you think represents an essential component of a strong interpersonal relationship. You might, for example, define *respect, sharing, equality,* or *trust.* Part of the definition should employ definition by negation, a discussion of what the term is *not.*

At Home or in the Community

3. *Newsweek* magazine runs a popular column called "My Turn," consisting of readers' opinions on subjects of general interest. Write a piece for this column defining *today's college students.* Use the piece to dispel some negative stereotypes (for example, that college students are apathetic, ill-informed, self-centered, and materialistic).

4. In your apartment building, several residents have complained about their neighbors' inconsiderate and rude behavior. You're president of the Residents' Association, and it's your responsibility to address this problem at your next meeting. Prepare a talk in which you define *courtesy,* the quality you consider most essential to neighborly relations. Use specific examples of what courtesy is and isn't to illustrate your definition.

On the Job

5. You're an attorney arguing a case of sexual harassment—a charge your client has leveled against an employer. To win the case, you must present to the jury a clear definition of exactly what *sexual harassment* is and isn't. Write such a definition for your opening remarks in court.

6. A new position has opened in your company. Write a job description to be sent to employment agencies that will screen candidates. Your description should define the job's purpose, state the duties involved, and outline essential qualifications.

11

ARGUMENTATION-
PERSUASION

WHAT IS ARGUMENTATION-PERSUASION?

"You can't possibly believe what you're saying."
"Look, I know what I'm talking about, and that's that."

Does this heated exchange sound familiar? Probably. When we hear the word *argument,* most of us think of a verbal battle propelled by stubbornness and irrational thought, with one person pitted against the other.

Argumentation in writing, though, is a different matter. Using clear thinking and logic, the writer tries to convince readers of the soundness of a particular opinion on a controversial issue. If, while trying to convince, the writer uses emotional language and dramatic appeals to readers' concerns, beliefs, and values, then the piece is called *persuasion.* Besides encouraging acceptance of an opinion, persuasion often urges readers (or another group) to commit themselves to a course of action. Assume you're writing an essay protesting the federal government's policy of offering aid to those suffering from hunger in other countries while many Americans go hungry. If your purpose is to document, coolly and objectively, the presence of hunger in the United States, you would prepare an argumentation essay. Such an essay would be filled with statistics, report findings, and expert opinion to demonstrate how widespread hunger is nationwide. If, however, your purpose is to shake up readers, even motivate them to write letters to their congressional representatives and push for a change in policy, you would write a persuasive essay. In this case, your essay might contain emotional accounts of undernourished children, ill-fed pregnant women, and nearly starving elderly people.

Because people respond rationally *and* emotionally to situations, argumentation and persuasion are usually *combined*. Suppose you decide to write an article for the campus newspaper advocating a pre–Labor Day start for the school year. Your audience includes the college administration, students, and faculty. The article might begin by *arguing* that several schools starting the academic year earlier were able to close for the month of January and thus reduce heating and other maintenance expenses. Such an argument, supported by documented facts and figures, would help convince the administration. Realizing that you also have to gain student and faculty support for your idea, you might argue further that the proposed change would mean that students and faculty could leave for winter break with the semester behind them—papers written, exams taken, grades calculated and recorded. To make this part of your argument especially compelling, you could adopt a *persuasive* strategy by using emotional appeals and positively charged language: "Think how pleasant it would be to sleep late, spend time with family and friends, toast the New Year—without having to worry about work awaiting you back on campus."

When argumentation and persuasion blend in this way, emotion *supports* rather than *replaces* logic and sound reasoning. Although some writers resort to emotional appeals to the exclusion of rational thought, when you prepare argumentation-persuasion essays, you should advance your position through a balanced appeal to reason and emotion.

HOW ARGUMENTATION-PERSUASION FITS YOUR PURPOSE AND AUDIENCE

You probably realize that argumentation, persuasion, or a combination of the two is everywhere: an editorial urging the overhaul of an ill-managed literacy program; a commercial for a new shampoo; a scientific report advocating increased funding for AIDS research. Your own writing involves argumentation-persuasion as well. When you prepare a *causal analysis, descriptive piece, narrative,* or *definition essay,* you advance a specific point of view: MTV has a negative influence on teens' view of sex; Cape Cod in winter is imbued with a special kind of magic; a disillusioning experience can teach people much about themselves; *character* can be defined as the willingness to take unpopular positions on difficult issues. Indeed, an essay organized around any of the patterns of development described in this book may have a persuasive intent. You might, for example, encourage readers to try out a *process* you've explained, or to see one of the two movies you've *compared.*

Argumentation-persuasion, however, involves more than presenting a point of view and providing evidence. Unlike other forms of writing, it assumes controversy and addresses opposing viewpoints. Consider the following assignments, all of which require the writer to take a position on a controversial issue:

In parts of the country, communities established for older citizens or childless couples have refused to rent to families with children. How do you feel about this situation? What do you think are the rights of the parties involved?

Citing the fact that the highest percentage of automobile accidents involve young men, insurance companies consistently charge their highest rates to young males. Is this policy fair? Why or why not?

Some colleges and universities have instituted a "no pass, no play" policy for athletes. Explain why this practice is or is not appropriate.

It's impossible to predict with absolute certainty what will make readers accept the view you advance or take the action you propose. But the ancient Greeks, who formulated our basic concepts of logic, isolated three factors crucial to the effectiveness of argumentation-persuasion: *logos, pathos,* and *ethos.*

Your main concern in an argumentation-persuasion essay should be with the *logos,* or soundness, of your argument: the facts, statistics, examples, and authoritative statements you gather to support your viewpoint. This supporting evidence must be unified, specific, adequate, accurate, and representative (see pages 33–37). Imagine, for instance, you want to convince people that a popular charity misappropriates the money it receives from the public. Your readers, inclined to believe in the good works of the charity, will probably dismiss your argument unless you can substantiate your claim with valid, well-documented evidence that enhances the *logos* of your position.

Sensitivity to *pathos,* or the emotional power of language, is another key consideration for writers of argumentation-persuasion essays. *Pathos* appeals to readers' needs, values, and attitudes, encouraging them to commit themselves to a viewpoint or course of action. The *pathos* of a piece derives partly from the writer's language. *Connotative* language—words with strong emotional overtones—can move readers to accept a point of view and may even spur them to act.

Advertising and propaganda generally rely on *pathos* to the exclusion of logic, using emotion to influence and manipulate. Consider the following pitches for a man's cologne and a woman's perfume. The language—and the attitudes to which it appeals—is different in each case:

Brawn: Experience the power. Bold. Yet subtle. Clean. Masculine. The scent for the man who's in charge.

Black Lace is for you—the woman who dresses for success but who dares to be provocative, slightly naughty. Black Lace. Perfect with pearls by day and with diamonds by night.

The appeal to men plays on the impact that words like *Brawn, bold, power,* and *in charge* may have for some males. Similarly, the charged words *Black Lace, provocative, naughty,* and *diamonds* are intended to appeal to business women who—in the advertiser's mind, at least—may be looking for ways to reconcile sensuality and professionalism. (For more on slanted language, read Ann McClintock's "Propaganda Techniques in Today's Advertising," page 207.)

Like an advertising copywriter, you must select language that reinforces your message. In a paper supporting an expanded immigration policy, you might use evocative phrases like "land of liberty," "a nation of immigrants," and "America's open-door policy." However, if you were arguing for strict immigration quotas, you might use language like "save jobs for unemployed Americans," "flood of unskilled labor," and "illegal aliens." Remember, though: Such language should support, not supplant, clear thinking.

Finally, whenever you write an argumentation-persuasion essay, you should establish your *ethos,* or credibility and integrity. You cannot expect readers to accept or act on your viewpoint unless you convince them that you know what you're talking about and that you're worth listening to. Be sure, then, to tell readers about any experiences you've had that make you knowledgeable about the issue being discussed. You will also come across as knowledgeable and trustworthy if you present a logical, reasoned argument that takes opposing views into account. And make sure that your appeals to emotion aren't excessive. Overwrought emotionalism undercuts credibility. Remember, too, that *ethos* isn't constant. A writer may have credibility on one subject but not on another: An army general might be a reliable source for information on military preparedness but not for information on federal funding of day care.

Writing an effective argumentation-persuasion essay involves an interplay of *logos, pathos,* and *ethos.* The exact balance among these factors is determined by your audience and purpose (that is, whether you want the audience simply to agree with your view or whether you also want them to take action). More than any other kind of writing, argumentation-persuasion requires that you *analyze your readers* and tailor your approach to them. You need to determine how much they know about the issue, how they feel about you and your position, what their values and attitudes are, what motivates them.

In general, most readers will fall into one of three broad categories: supportive, wavering, or hostile. Each type of audience requires a different blend of *logos, pathos,* and *ethos* in an argumentation-persuasion essay.

1. A supportive audience.   If your audience agrees with your position and trusts your credibility, you don't need a highly reasoned argument dense with facts, examples, and statistics. Although you may want to solidify support by providing additional information (*logos*), you can rely primarily on *pathos*—a strong emotional appeal—to reinforce readers' commitment to your shared viewpoint. Assume that you belong to a local fishing club and have volunteered to write an article encouraging members to support threatened fishing rights in state parks. You might begin by stating that fishing strengthens the fish population by thinning out overcrowded streams. Since your audience would certainly be familiar with this idea, you wouldn't need to devote much discussion to it. Instead, you would attempt to move them emotionally. You might evoke the camaraderie in the sport, the pleasure of a perfect cast, the beauty of the outdoors, and perhaps conclude with "If you want these enjoyments to continue, please make a generous contribution to our fund."

2. A wavering audience.   At times, readers may be open to what you have to say but may not be committed fully to your viewpoint. Or perhaps they're not as informed about the subject as they should be. In either case, you don't want to risk alienating them with a heavy-handed emotional appeal. Concentrate instead on *ethos* and *logos,* bolstering your image as a reliable source and providing the evidence needed to advance your position. If you want to convince an audience of high school seniors to take a year off to work between high school and college, you might establish your credibility by recounting the year you spent working and by showing the positive effects it had on your life (*ethos*). In addition, you could cite studies indicating that delayed entry into college is related to higher grade point averages. A year's savings, you would explain, allows students to study when they might otherwise need to hold down a job to earn money for tuition (*logos*).

3. A hostile audience.   An apathetic, skeptical, or hostile audience is obviously most difficult to convince. With such an audience, you should avoid emotional appeals because they might seem irrational, sentimental, or even comical. Instead, weigh the essay heavily in favor of logical reasoning and hard-to-dispute facts (*logos*). Assume your college administration is working to ban liquor from the student pub. You plan to submit to the campus newspaper an open letter supporting this generally unpopular effort. To sway other students, you cite the positive experiences of schools that have gone dry. Many colleges, you explain, have found their tavern revenues actually increase because all students—not just those of drinking age—can now support the pub. With the greater revenues, some schools have upgraded the food served in the pubs and have hired disc jockeys or musical groups to provide entertainment. Many schools have also seen a sharp reduction in alcohol-related vandalism. Readers may not be won over to your side, but your sound, logical argument may encourage them to be more tolerant of your viewpoint. Indeed, such increased receptivity may be all you can reasonably expect from a hostile audience. (For more help in analyzing your audience, see pages 17–18.)

SUGGESTIONS FOR USING ARGUMENTATION-PERSUASION IN AN ESSAY

1. At the beginning of the paper, identify the controversy surrounding the issue and state your position in the thesis.   Your introduction should clarify the controversy about the issue. In addition, it should provide as much background information as your readers are likely to need.

The thesis of an argumentation-persuasion paper is often called the *assertion* or *proposition*. Occasionally, the proposition appears at the paper's end, but it is usually stated at the beginning. If you state the thesis right away, your audience knows where you stand and is better able to evaluate the evidence presented.

Remember: Argumentation-persuasion assumes conflicting viewpoints. Be sure your proposition focuses on a controversial issue and indicates your view. Avoid a proposition that is merely factual; what is demonstrably true allows little room for debate. To see the difference between a factual statement and an effective thesis, examine the two statements that follow:

> *Fact:* In the past decade, the nation's small farmers have suffered financial hardships.

> *Thesis:* Inefficient management, rather than competition from agricultural conglomerates, is responsible for the financial plight of the nation's small farmers.

The first statement is certainly true. It would be difficult to find anyone who believes that these are easy times for small farmers. Because the statement invites little opposition, it can't serve as the focus of an argumentation-persuasion essay. The second statement, though, takes a controversial stance on a complex issue. Such a proposition is a valid starting point for a paper intended to argue and persuade. However, don't assume that such advice means that you should take a highly opinionated position in your thesis. A dogmatic, overstated proposition ("Campus security is staffed by overpaid, badge-flashing incompetents") is bound to alienate some readers.

Remember also to keep the proposition narrow and specific, so you can focus your thoughts in a purposeful way. Consider the following statements:

> *Broad thesis:* The welfare system has been abused over the years.

> *Narrow thesis:* Welfare payments should be denied to unmarried teenage girls who have more than one child out of wedlock.

If you tried to write a paper based on the first statement, you would face an unmanageable task—showing all the ways that welfare has been abused. Your readers would also be confused about what to expect in the paper: Will it discuss unscrupulous bureaucrats, fraudulent bookkeeping, dishonest recipients? In contrast, the revised thesis is limited and specific. It signals that the paper will propose severe restrictions on welfare payments. Such a proposal will surely have opponents and is thus appropriate for argumentation-persuasion.

The thesis in an argumentation-persuasion essay can simply state your opinion about an issue, or it can go a step further and call for some action:

> *Opinion:* The lack of affordable day care centers discriminates against lower-income families.

> *Call for action:* The federal government should support the creation of more day care centers in low-income neighborhoods.

In either case, your stand on the issue must be clear to your readers.

2. Provide readers with strong support for the thesis. Finding evidence that relates to the readers' needs, values, and experience is a crucial part of writing an effective argumentation-persuasion essay. Readers will be responsive to evidence that is *unified, adequate, specific, accurate,* and *representative* (see pages 33–37). It might consist of personal experiences or observations. Or it could be gathered from outside sources—statistics; facts; examples; or expert authority taken from books, articles, reports, interviews, and documentaries. A paper arguing that elderly Americans are better off than they used to be might incorporate the following kinds of evidence:

- *Personal observation or experience:* A description of the writer's grandparents who are living comfortably on Social Security and pensions.
- *Statistics from a report:* A statement that the per capita after-tax income of older Americans is $335 greater than the national average.
- *Fact from a newspaper article:* The point that the majority of elderly Americans do not live in nursing homes or on the streets; rather, they have their own houses or apartments.
- *Examples from interviews:* Accounts of several elderly couples living comfortably in well-managed retirement villages in Florida.
- *Expert opinion cited in a documentary:* A statement by Dr. Marie Sanchez, a specialist in geriatrics: "An over-sixty-five American today is likely to be healthier, and have a longer life expectancy, than a fifty-year-old living only a decade ago."

As you seek outside evidence, you may—perhaps to your dismay—come across information that undercuts your argument. Resist the temptation to ignore such material; instead, use the evidence to arrive at a more balanced, perhaps somewhat qualified viewpoint. Conversely, don't blindly accept points made by sources agreeing with you. Retain a healthy skepticism, analyzing the material as rigorously as if it were advanced by the opposing side.

Also, keep in mind that outside sources aren't infallible. They may have biases that cause them to skew evidence. So be sure to evaluate your sources. If you're writing an essay supporting a woman's right to abortion, the National Abortion Rights Action League (NARAL) can supply abundant statistics, case studies, and reports. But realize that NARAL most likely won't give you the complete picture; it will probably present evidence that supports its "pro-choice" position only. To counteract such bias, you should review what those with differing opinions have to say. You should, for example, examine material published by such "pro-life" organizations as the National Right-to-Life Committee—keeping in mind, of course, that this material is also bound to present support for its viewpoint only. Remember, too, that there are more than two sides to a complex issue. To get as broad a perspective as possible, you should also track down sources that have no axe to grind—that is, sources that make a deliberate effort to examine all sides of the issue. For example, published proceedings from a debate on abortion or an in-depth article that aims to synthesize various views on abortion would broaden your understanding of this controversial subject.

Whatever sources you use, be sure to *document* (give credit to) that material. Otherwise, readers may dismiss your evidence as nothing more than your subjective opinion, or they may conclude that you have *plagiarized*—tried to pass off someone else's ideas as your own. (Documentation isn't necessary when material is commonly known or is a matter of historical or scientific record.) In brief informal papers, documentation may consist of simple citations like "Psychologist Aaron Beck believes depression is the result of distorted thoughts" or "*Time* (Dec. 4, 2000) reports a decline in the enrollment of male students in colleges across the country." In longer, more formal papers, documentation is more detailed (see Appendix A, "A Concise Guide to Finding and Documenting Sources"). One additional point: Because documentation lends a note of objectivity to writing, it may not be appropriate in a paper that cites sources to use the first-person point of view ("I, like many college students, agree with the government report that . . ."). To be on the safe side, check with your instructor to see if you should use the third-person point of view ("Many college students agree with the government report that . . .") instead.

3. Seek to create goodwill.   To avoid alienating readers with views different from your own, stay away from condescending expressions like "Anyone can see that . . ." or "It's obvious that . . ." Also, guard against personalizing the debate and being confrontational: "*My opponents* find the law ineffective" sounds adversarial, whereas "*Those opposed* to the law find it ineffective" or

"*Opponents* of the law find it ineffective" is more evenhanded. The last two statements also focus—as they should—on the issue, not on the people involved in the debate.

Goodwill can also be established by finding a *common ground*—some points on which all sides can agree, despite their differences. Assume a township council has voted to raise property taxes. The additional revenues will be used to preserve, as parkland, a wooded area that would otherwise be sold to developers. Before introducing its tax-hike proposal, the council would do well to remind homeowners of everyone's shared goals: maintaining the town's beauty and preventing the community's overdevelopment. This reminder of the common values shared by the town council and homeowners will probably make residents more receptive to the tax hike. (For more on establishing common ground, see pages 361–362.)

4. Organize the supporting evidence.   The support for an argumentation-persuasion paper can be organized in a variety of ways. Any of the patterns of development described in this book (description, narration, definition, causal analysis, and so on) may be used—singly or in combination—to develop the essay's proposition. Imagine you're writing a paper arguing that car racing should be banned from television. Your essay might contain a *description* of a horrifying accident that was televised in graphic detail; you might devote part of the paper to a *causal analysis* showing that the broadcast of such races encourages teens to drive carelessly; you could include a *process analysis* to explain how young drivers "soup up" their cars in a dangerous attempt to imitate the racers seen on television. If your essay includes several patterns, you may need a separate paragraph for each.

When presenting evidence, arrange it so you create the strongest possible effect. In general, you should end with your most compelling point, leaving readers with dramatic evidence that underscores your proposition's validity.

5. Use Rogerian strategy to acknowledge differing viewpoints.   If your essay has a clear thesis and strong logical support, you've taken important steps toward winning readers over. However, because argumentation-persuasion focuses on controversial issues, you should also consider contrary points of view. A good argument seeks out and acknowledges conflicting viewpoints. Such a strategy strengthens your argument in several ways. It helps you anticipate objections, alerts you to flaws in your own position, and makes you more aware of the other sides' weaknesses. Further, by acknowledging dissenting views, you come across as reasonable and thorough—qualities that may disarm readers and leave them more receptive to your argument. You may not convince them to surrender their views, but you can enlarge their perspectives and encourage them to think about your position.

Psychologist Carl Rogers took the idea of acknowledging contrary viewpoints a step further. He believed that argumentation's goal should be to *reduce conflict,* rather than to produce a "winner" and a "loser." But he recognized that people identify so strongly with their opinions that they experience any challenge to those opinions as highly threatening. Such a challenge feels like an attack on their very identity. And what's the characteristic response to such a perceived attack? People become defensive; they dig in their heels and become more adamant than ever about their position. Indeed, when confronted with solid information that calls their opinion into question, they devalue that evidence rather than allow themselves to be persuaded. The old maxim about the power of first impressions demonstrates this point. Experiments show that after people form a first impression of another person, they are unlikely to let future conflicting information affect that impression. If, for example, they initially perceive someone to be unpleasant and disagreeable, they tend to reject subsequent evidence that casts the person in a more favorable light.

Taking into account this tendency to cling tenaciously to opinions in the face of a challenge, Rogerian strategy rejects the adversarial approach that often characterizes argumentation. It adopts, instead, a respectful, conciliatory posture—one that demonstrates a real understanding of opposing views, one that emphasizes shared interests and values. Such an approach makes it easier to negotiate differences and arrive at—ideally—a synthesis: a new position that both parties find at least as acceptable as their original positions.

How can you apply Rogerian strategy in your writing? Simply follow the steps in the following checklist.

☑ USING ROGERIAN STRATEGY: A CHECKLIST

❑ Begin by making a conscientious effort to *understand* the viewpoints of those with whom you disagree. As you listen to or read about their opinions, try to put yourself in their shoes; focus on *what they believe* and *why they believe* it, rather than on how you will challenge their beliefs.

❑ Open your essay with an unbiased, even-handed *restatement of opposing points of view.* Such an objective summary shows that you're fair and open-minded—and not so blinded by the righteousness of your own position that you can't consider any other. Typically, people respond to such a respectful approach by lowering their defenses. Because they appreciate your ability to understand what they have to say, they become more open to your point of view.

❑ When appropriate, *acknowledge the validity* of some of the arguments raised by those with differing views. What should you do if they make a well-founded point? You'll enhance your credibility if you concede that point while continuing to maintain that, overall, your position is stronger.

❑ Point out areas of *common ground* (see page 359) by focusing on interests, values, and beliefs that you and those with opposing views share. When you say to them, "Look at the beliefs we share. Look at our common concerns," you communicate that you're not as unlike them as they first believed.

❑ Finally, *present evidence* for your position. Since those not agreeing with you have been "softened up" by your non-combative stance and disarmed by the realization that you and they share some values and beliefs, they're more ready to consider your point of view.

Let's consider, more specifically, how you might draw upon essentially Rogerian strategy when writing an argumentation-persuasion essay. In the following paragraphs, we discuss three basic strategies. As you read about each strategy, keep in mind this key point: The earlier you acknowledge alternate viewpoints, the more effective your argument will be. Establishing— right at the outset—your awareness of opposing positions shows you to be fair-minded and helps reduce resistance to what you have to say.

First, you may acknowledge the opposing viewpoint in a two-part proposition consisting of a subordinate clause followed by a main clause. The *first part of the proposition* (the subordinate clause) *acknowledges opposing opinions;* the *second part* (the main clause) *states your opinion* and implies that your view stands on more solid ground. (When using this kind of proposition, you may, but don't have to, discuss opposing opinions.) The following thesis illustrates this strategy (the opposing viewpoint is underlined once; the writer's position is underlined twice):

Although some instructors think that standardized finals restrict academic freedom, such exams are preferable to those prepared by individual professors.

Second, *in the introduction,* you may provide—separate from the proposition—a *one- or two-sentence summary of the opposing viewpoint.* Suppose you're writing an essay advocating a ten-day waiting period before an individual can purchase a handgun. Before presenting your proposition at the end of the introductory paragraph, you might include sentences like these: "Opponents of the waiting period argue that the ten-day delay is worthless without a nationwide computer network that can perform background checks. Those opposed also point out that only a percentage of states with a waiting period have seen a reduction in gun-related crime."

Third, you can take *one or two body paragraphs* near the beginning of the essay to *present in greater detail arguments raised by opposing viewpoints.* After that, you *grant* (when appropriate) the validity of some of those points ("It may be true that . . . ," "Granted, . . ."). Then you go on to *present evidence* for your position ("Even so . . . ," "Nevertheless . . ."). Imagine you're preparing an editorial for your student newspaper arguing that fraternities and sororities on your campus should be banned. Realizing that many students don't agree with you, you "research" the opposing viewpoint by seeking out supporters of Greek organizations and listening respectfully to the points they raise. When it comes time to write the editorial, you decide not to begin with arguments for your position; instead, you start by summarizing the points made by those supporting fraternities and sororities. You might, for example, mention their argument that Greek organizations build college spirit, contribute to worthy community causes, and provide valuable contacts for entry into the business world. Following this summary of the opposing viewpoint, you might concede that the point about the Greeks' contributions to community causes is especially valid; you could then reinforce this conciliatory stance by stressing some common ground you share—perhaps you acknowledge that you share your detractors' belief that enjoyable social activities with like-minded people are an important part of campus life. Having done all that, you would be in a good position to present arguments why you nevertheless think fraternities and sororities should be banned. Because you prepared readers to listen to your opinion, they would tend to be more receptive to your argument.

6. Refute differing viewpoints.   There will be times, though, that acknowledging opposing viewpoints and presenting your own case won't be enough. Particularly when an issue is complex and when readers strongly disagree with your position, you may have to refute all or part of the *dissenting views. Refutation* means pointing out the problems with opposing viewpoints, thereby highlighting your own position's superiority. You may focus on the opposing sides' inaccurate or inadequate evidence, or you may point to their faulty logic. (Some common types of illogical thinking are discussed on pages 364–365, 366–367, and 370–372.)

Let's consider how you could refute a competing position in an essay you're writing that supports sex education in public schools. Adapting the Rogerian approach to suit your purposes, you might start by acknowledging the opposing viewpoint's key argument: "Sex education should be the prerogative of parents." After granting the validity of this view in an ideal world, you might show that many parents don't provide such education. You could present statistics on the number of parents who avoid discussing sex with their children because the subject makes them uncomfortable; you could cite studies revealing that children in single-parent homes are apt to receive even less parental guidance about sex; and you could give examples of young people whose parents provided sketchy, even misleading information.

There are various ways to develop a paper's refutation section. The best method to use depends on the paper's length and the complexity of the issue. Two possible sequences are outlined here:

First Strategy
- State your proposition.
- Cite opposing viewpoints and the evidence for those views.
- Refute opposing viewpoints by presenting counterarguments.

Second Strategy
- State your proposition.
- Cite opposing viewpoints and the evidence for those views.
- Refute opposing viewpoints by presenting counterarguments.
- Present additional evidence for your proposition.

In the first strategy, you simply refute all or part of the opposing positions' arguments. The second strategy takes the first one a step further by presenting *additional evidence* to support your proposition. In such a case, the additional evidence *must be different* from the points made in the refutation. The additional evidence may appear at the essay's end (as in the preceding outline), or it may be given near the beginning (after the proposition); it may also be divided between the beginning and end.

No matter which strategy you select, you may refute opposing views *one side at a time* or *one point at a time*. When using the one-side-at-a-time approach, you cite all the points raised by the opposing side and then present your counterargument to each point. When using the one-point-at-a-time strategy, you mention the first point made by the opposing side, refute that point, then move on to the second point and refute that, and so on. (For more on comparing and contrasting the sides of an issue, see pages 255–260.)

Throughout the essay, be sure to provide clear signals so that readers can distinguish your arguments from the other side's: "Despite the claims of those opposed to the plan, many think that . . ." and "Those not in agreement think that . . . ."

7. Use induction or deduction to think logically about your argument.

The line of reasoning used to develop an argument is the surest indicator of how rigorously you have thought through your position. There are two basic ways to think about a subject: *inductively* and *deductively*. Though the following discussion treats induction and deduction as separate processes, the two often overlap and complement each other.

Inductive reasoning involves examination of specific cases, facts, or examples. Based on these specifics, you then draw a conclusion or make a generalization. This is the kind of thinking scientists use when they examine evidence (the results of experiments, for example) and then draw a *conclusion*: "Smoking increases the risk of cancer." All of us use inductive reasoning in everyday life.

We might think the following: "My head is aching" (evidence); "My nose is stuffy" (evidence); "I'm coming down with a cold" (conclusion). Based on the conclusion, we might go a step further and take some action: "I'll take an aspirin."

With inductive reasoning, the conclusion reached can serve as the proposition for an argumentation essay. (Of course, the essay will most likely include elements of persuasion since strict argumentation—with no appeal to emotions—is uncommon.) If the paper advances a course of action, the proposition often mentions the action, signaling an essay with a distinctly persuasive purpose.

Let's suppose that you're writing a paper about a crime wave in the small town where you live. You might use inductive thinking to structure the essay's argument:

> Several people were mugged last month while shopping in the center of town. (*evidence*)
>
> Several homes and apartments were burglarized in the past few weeks. (*evidence*)
>
> Several cars were stolen from people's driveways over the weekend. (*evidence*)
>
> The police force hasn't adequately protected town residents. (*conclusion, or proposition, for an argumentation essay with probable elements of persuasion*)
>
> The police force should take steps to upgrade its protection of town residents. (*conclusion, or proposition, for an argumentation essay with a clearly persuasive intent*)

This inductive sequence highlights a possible structure for the essay. After providing a clear statement of your proposition, you might detail recent muggings, burglaries, and car thefts. Then you could move to the opposing viewpoint: a description of the steps the police say they have taken to protect town residents. At that point, you would refute the police's claim, citing additional evidence that shows the measures taken have not been sufficient. Finally, if you wanted your essay to have a decidedly persuasive purpose, you could end by recommending specific action the police department should take to improve its protection of the community.

As in all essays, your evidence should be *specific, unified, adequate,* and *representative* (see pages 33–37). These last two characteristics are critical when you think inductively; they guarantee that your conclusion would be equally valid even if other evidence were presented. Insufficient or atypical evidence often leads to *hasty generalizations* that mar the essay's logic. For example, you might think the following: "Some elderly people are very wealthy and do not need Social Security checks" (evidence), and "Some Social Security recipients illegally collect several checks" (evidence). If you then conclude, "Social Security is a waste of taxpayers' money," your conclusion is invalid and hasty because it's based on only a few atypical examples. Millions of Social Security recipients aren't wealthy and don't abuse the system. If you've failed to consider the full range of evidence, any action you propose ("The Social Security system should be disbanded") will probably be considered suspect by thoughtful readers. It's possible, of course, that Social Security should be disbanded, but the evidence leading to such a conclusion must be sufficient and representative.

When reasoning inductively, you should also be careful that the evidence you collect is both *recent* and *accurate*. No valid conclusion can result from dated or erroneous evidence. To ensure that your evidence is sound, you also need to evaluate the reliability of your sources. When a person who is legally drunk claims to have seen a flying saucer, the evidence is shaky, to say the least. But if two respected scientists, both with 20/20 vision, saw the saucer, their evidence is worth considering.

Finally, it's important to realize that there's always an element of uncertainty in inductive reasoning. The conclusion can never be more than an *inference*, involving what logicians call an *inductive leap*. There could be other explanations for the evidence cited and thus other positions to take and actions to advocate. For example, given a small town's crime wave, you might conclude not that the police force has been remiss but that residents are careless about protecting themselves and their property. In turn, you might call for a different kind of action—perhaps that the police conduct public workshops in self-defense and home security. In an inductive argument, your task is to weigh the evidence, consider alternative explanations, then choose the conclusion and course of action that seem most valid.

Unlike inductive reasoning, which starts with a specific case and moves toward a generalization or conclusion, *deductive reasoning* begins with a generalization that is then applied to a specific case. This movement from general to specific involves a three-step form of reasoning called a *syllogism*. The first part of a syllogism is called the *major premise*, a general statement about an entire group. The second part is the *minor premise*, a statement about an individual within that group. The syllogism ends with a *conclusion* about that individual.

Just as you use inductive thinking in everyday life, you use deductive thinking—often without being aware of it—to sort out your experiences. When trying to decide which car to buy, you might think as follows:

Major premise: In an accident, large cars are safer than small cars.

Minor premise: The Turbo Titan is a large car.

Conclusion: In an accident, the Turbo Titan will be safer than a small car.

Based on your conclusion, you might decide to take a specific action, buying the Turbo Titan rather than the smaller car you had first considered.

To create a valid syllogism and thus arrive at a sound conclusion, you need to avoid two major pitfalls of deductive reasoning. First, be sure not to start with a *hasty generalization* (see page 364) as your *major premise*. Second, don't accept as truth a *faulty conclusion*. Let's look at each problem.

Sweeping major premise.   Perhaps you're concerned about a trash-to-steam incinerator scheduled to open near your home. Your thinking about the situation might follow these lines:

Major premise:	Trash-to-steam incinerators have had serious problems and pose significant threats to the well-being of people living near the plants.
Minor premise:	The proposed incinerator in my neighborhood will be a trash-to-steam plant.
Conclusion:	The proposed trash-to-steam incinerator in my neighborhood will have serious problems and pose significant threats to the well-being of people living near the plant.

Having arrived at this conclusion, you might decide to join organized protests against the opening of the incinerator. But your thinking is somewhat illogical. Your *major premise* is a *sweeping* one because it indiscriminately groups all trash-to-steam plants into a single category. It's unlikely that you're familiar with the operations of all trash-to-steam incinerators in this country and abroad; it's probably not true that *all* such plants have had serious difficulties that endangered the public. For your argument to reach a valid conclusion, the major premise must be based on repeated observations or verifiable facts. You would have a better argument, and thus reach a more valid conclusion, if you restricted or qualified the major premise, applying it to some, not all, of the group:

Major premise:	A number of trash-to-steam incinerators have had serious problems and posed significant threats to the well-being of people living near the plants.
Minor premise:	The proposed incinerator in my neighborhood will be a trash-to-steam plant.
Conclusion:	It's possible that the proposed trash-to-steam incinerator in my neighborhood will run into serious

> problems and pose significant threats to the well-being of people living near the plant.

This new conclusion, the result of more careful reasoning, would probably encourage you to learn more about trash-to-steam incinerators in general and about the proposed plant in particular. If further research still left you feeling uncomfortable about the plant, you would probably decide to join the protest. On the other hand, your research might convince you that the plant has incorporated into its design a number of safeguards that have been successful at other plants. This added information could reassure you that your original fears were unfounded. In either case, the revised deductive process would lead to a more informed conclusion and course of action.

Faulty conclusion.   Your syllogism—and thus your reasoning—would also be invalid if your *conclusion reverses the "if . . . then" relationship implied in the major premise*. Assume you plan to write a letter to the college newspaper urging the resignation of the student government president. Perhaps you pursue a line of reasoning that goes like this:

Major premise: Students who plagiarize papers must appear before the Faculty Committee on Academic Policies and Procedures.

Minor premise: Yesterday, Jennifer Kramer, president of the student government, appeared before the Faculty Committee on Academic Policies and Procedures.

Conclusion: Jennifer must have plagiarized a paper.

Action: Jennifer should resign her position as president of the student government.

Such a chain of reasoning is illogical and unfair. Here's why. *If* students plagiarize their papers and are caught, *then* they must appear before the committee. However, the converse isn't necessarily true—that *if* students appear before the committee, *then* they must have plagiarized. In other words, not *all* students appearing before the committee have been called up on plagiarism charges. For example, Jennifer could have been speaking on behalf of another student; she could have been protesting some action taken by the committee; she could have been seeking the committee's help on an article she plans to write about academic honesty. The conclusion doesn't allow for these other possible explanations.

Now that you're aware of potential problems associated with deductive reasoning, let's look at the way you can use a syllogism to structure an argumentation-persuasion essay. Suppose you decide to write a paper advocating support for a projected space mission. You know that controversy surrounds the space program, especially since seven astronauts died in a 1986 launch. Confident that the tragedy has led to more rigorous controls, you want to argue that the benefits of an upcoming mission outweigh its risks. A deductive pattern could be used to develop your argument. In fact, outlining your thinking as a syllogism might help you formulate a proposition, organize your evidence, deal with opposing viewpoints, and—if appropriate—propose a course of action:

Major premise:	Space programs in the past have led to important developments in technology, especially in medical science.
Minor premise:	The Cosmos Mission is the newest space program.
Proposition (essay might be persuasive):	The Cosmos Mission will most likely lead to important developments in technology, especially in medical science.
Proposition (essay clearly is persuasive):	Congress should continue its funding of the Cosmos Mission.

Having outlined the deductive pattern of your thinking, you might begin by stating your proposition and then discuss some new procedures developed to protect the astronauts and the rocket system's structural integrity. With that background established, you could detail the opposing claim that little of value has been produced by the space program so far. You could then move to your refutation, citing significant medical advances derived from former space missions. Finally, the paper might conclude on a persuasive note, with a plea to Congress to continue funding the latest space mission.

8. Use Toulmin logic to establish a strong connection between your evidence and your thesis.   Whether you use an essentially inductive or deductive approach, your argument depends on strong evidence. In *The Uses of Argument,* Stephen Toulmin describes a useful approach for strengthening the connection between evidence and thesis. Toulmin divides a typical argument into three parts:

- **Claim**—The thesis, proposition, or conclusion.
- **Data**—The evidence (facts, statistics, examples, observations, expert opinion) used to convince readers of the claim's validity.
- **Warrant**—The underlying assumption that justifies moving from evidence to claim.

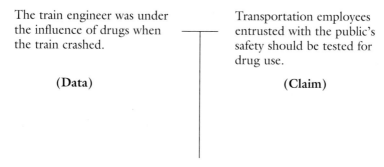

The train engineer was under the influence of drugs when the train crashed.		Transportation employees entrusted with the public's safety should be tested for drug use.
(Data)		**(Claim)**

Transportation employees entrusted with the public's safety should not be allowed on the job if they use drugs.

(Warrant)

As Toulmin explains in his book, readers are more apt to consider your argument valid if they know what your warrant is. Sometimes your warrant will be so obvious that you won't need to state it explicitly; an *implicit warrant* will be sufficient. Assume you want to argue that the use of live animals to test product toxicity should be outlawed. To support your claim, you cite the following evidence: first, current animal tests are painful and usually result in the animal's death; second, human cell cultures frequently offer more reliable information on how harmful a product may be to human tissue; and third, computer simulations often can more accurately rate a substance's toxicity. Your warrant, although not explicit, is nonetheless clear: "It is wrong to continue product testing on animals when more humane and valid test methods are available."

Other times, you'll do best to make your warrant *explicit*. Suppose you plan to argue that students should be involved in deciding which faculty members are granted tenure. To develop your claim, you present some evidence. You begin by noting that, currently, only faculty members and administrators review candidates for tenure. Next, you call attention to the controversy surrounding two professors, widely known by students to be poor teachers, who were nonetheless granted tenure. Finally, you cite a decision, made several years ago, to discontinue using student evaluations as part of the tenure process; you emphasize that since that time complaints about teachers' incompetence have risen dramatically. Some readers, though, still might wonder how you got from your evidence to your claim. In this case, your argument could be made stronger by stating your warrant explicitly: "Since students are as knowledgeable as the faculty and administrators about which professors are competent, they should be involved in the tenure process."

The more widely accepted your warrant, Toulmin explains, the more likely it is that readers will accept your argument. If there's no consensus about the warrant, you'll probably need to *back it up*. For the preceding example, you might mention several reports that found students evaluate faculty fairly (most students don't, for example, use the ratings to get back at professors against whom they have a personal grudge); further, students' ratings correlate strongly with those given by administrators and other faculty.

Toulmin describes another way to increase receptivity to an argument: *qualify the claim*—that is, explain under what circumstances it might be invalid or restricted. For instance, you might grant that most students know little about their instructors' research activities, scholarly publications, or participation in professional committees. You could, then, qualify your claim this way: "Because students don't have a comprehensive view of their instructors' professional activities, they should be involved in the tenure process but play a less prominent role than faculty and administrators."

As you can see, Toulmin's approach provides strategies for strengthening an argument. So, when prewriting or revising, take a few minutes to ask yourself the questions listed below.

☑ QUESTIONS FOR USING TOULMIN LOGIC: A CHECKLIST

- ❏ What data (*evidence*) should I provide to support my claim (*thesis*)?
- ❏ Is my warrant clear? Should I state it explicitly? What backup can I provide to justify my warrant?
- ❏ Would qualifying my claim make my argument more convincing?

Your responses to these questions will help you structure a convincing and logical argument.

9. Recognize logical fallacies. When writing an argumentation-persuasion essay, you need to recognize *logical fallacies* both in your own argument and in points raised by opposing sides. Work to eliminate such gaps in logic from your own writing and, when they appear in opposing arguments, try to expose them in your refutation. Logicians have identified many logical fallacies—including the sweeping or hasty generalization and the faulty conclusion discussed on pages 364 and 366. Other logical fallacies are described in Ann McClintock's "Propaganda Techniques in Today's Advertising" (page 207) and in the paragraphs that follow.

The *post hoc fallacy* (short for a Latin phrase meaning "after this, therefore because of this") occurs when you conclude that a cause-effect relationship exists simply because one event preceded another. Let's say you note the growing number of immigrants settling in a nearby city, observe the city's economic decline, and conclude that the immigrants' arrival caused the decline. Such a chain of thinking is faulty because it assumes a cause-effect relationship based purely on co-occurrence. Perhaps the immigrants' arrival was a factor in the economic slump, but there could also be other reasons: the lack of financial incentives to attract business to the city, restrictions on the size of the city's manufacturing facilities, citywide labor disputes that make companies leery of settling in the area. Your argument should also consider these possibilities. (For more on the *post hoc* fallacy, see pages 287–288.)

The *non sequitur fallacy* (Latin for "it does not follow") is an even more blatant muddying of cause-effect relationships. In this case, a conclusion is drawn that has no logical connection to the evidence cited: "Millions of Americans own cars, so there is no need to fund public transportation." The faulty conclusion disregards the millions of Americans who don't own cars; it also ignores pollution and road congestion, both of which could be reduced if people had access to safe, reliable public transportation.

An *ad hominem argument* (from the Latin meaning "to the man") occurs when someone attacks a person rather than a point of view. Suppose your college plans to sponsor a physicians' symposium on the abortion controversy. You decide to write a letter to the school paper opposing the symposium. Taking swipes at two of the invited doctors who disapprove of abortion, you mention that one was recently involved in a messy divorce and that the other is alleged to have a drinking problem. By hurling personal invective, you avoid discussing the issue. Mudslinging is a poor substitute for reasoned argument.

Appeals to questionable or faulty authority also weaken an argument. Most of us have developed a healthy suspicion of phrases like *sources close to, an unidentified spokesperson states, experts claim,* and *studies show.* If these people and reports are so reliable, they should be clearly identified.

Begging the question involves failure to establish proof for a debatable point. The writer expects readers to accept as given a premise that's actually controversial. For instance, you would have trouble convincing readers that prayer should be banned from public schools if you based your argument on the premise that school prayer violates the U.S. Constitution. If the Constitution does, either explicitly or implicitly, prohibit prayer in public education, your essay must demonstrate that fact. You can't build a strong argument if you pretend there's no controversy surrounding your premise.

A *false analogy* wrongly implies that because two things share *some* characteristics, they are therefore *alike in all respects.* You might, for example, compare nicotine and marijuana. Both, you could mention, involve health risks and have addictive properties. If, however, you go on to conclude, "Driving while smoking a cigarette isn't illegal, so driving while smoking marijuana shouldn't be illegal either," you're employing a false analogy. You've overlooked a major difference between nicotine and marijuana: Marijuana impairs perception and coordination—important aspects of driving—while there's no evidence that nicotine does the same.

The *either-or fallacy* occurs when you assume that a particular viewpoint or course of action can have only one of two diametrically opposed outcomes—either totally this or totally that. Say you argue as follows: "Unless colleges continue to offer scholarships based solely on financial need, no one who is underprivileged will be able to attend college." Such a statement ignores the fact that bright, underprivileged students could receive scholarships based on their potential or their demonstrated academic excellence.

Finally, a *red herring argument* is an intentional digression from the issue—a ploy to deflect attention from the matter being discussed. Imagine that you're arguing that condoms shouldn't be dispensed to high school students. You would introduce a red herring if you began to rail against parents who fail to provide their children with any information about sex. Most people would agree that parents *should* provide such information. However, the issue being discussed is not parents' irresponsibility but the pros and cons of schools' distributing condoms to students.

REVISION STRATEGIES

Once you have a draft of the essay, you're ready to revise. The following checklist will help you and those giving you feedback apply to argumentation-persuasion some of the revision techniques discussed on pages 59–61.

☑ ARGUMENTATION-PERSUASION: A REVISION/PEER REVIEW CHECKLIST

Revise Overall Meaning and Structure

❏ What issue is being discussed? What is controversial about it?

❏ What is the essay's thesis? How does it differ from a generalization or mere statement of fact?

❏ What is the essay's purpose—to win readers over to a point of view, to spur readers to some type of action?

❏ For what audience is the essay written? What strategies are used to make readers receptive to the essay's thesis?

❏ What tone does the essay project? Is the tone likely to win readers over?

❏ If the essay's argument is essentially deductive, is the major premise sufficiently restricted? What evidence is the premise based on? Are the minor premise and conclusion valid? If not, how could these problems be corrected?

❏ Where is the essay weakened by hasty generalizations, a failure to weigh evidence honestly, or a failure to draw the most valid conclusion?

❏ Where does the essay commit any of the following logical fallacies: Concluding that a cause-effect relationship exists simply because one event preceded another? Attacking a person rather than an issue? Drawing a conclusion that isn't logically related to the evidence? Failing to establish proof for a debatable point? Relying on questionable or vaguely specified authority? Drawing a false analogy? Resorting to *either/or* thinking? Using a *red herring* argument?

Revise Paragraph Development

❏ How apparent is the link between the evidence (data) and the thesis (claim)? How could an explicit warrant clarify the connection? How would supporting the warrant or qualifying the claim strengthen the argument?

❏ Which paragraphs lack sufficient evidence (facts, examples, statistics, and expert opinion)?

❏ Which paragraphs lack unity? How could they be made more focused? In which paragraph(s) does evidence seem bland, overly general, unrepresentative, or inaccurate?

❏ Which paragraphs take opposing views into account? Are these views refuted? How? Which counterarguments are ineffective?

❏ Where do outside sources require documentation?

Revise Sentences and Words

❏ What words and phrases help readers distinguish the essay's arguments from those advanced by the opposing side?

❏ Which words carry strong emotional overtones? Is this connotative language excessive? Where does emotional language replace rather than reinforce clear thinking?

❏ Where might dogmatic language ("Anyone can see that . . ." and "Obviously, . . .") alienate readers?

STUDENT ESSAY

The following student essay was written by Mark Simmons in response to this assignment:

> Camille Paglia's "Rape: A Bigger Danger Than Feminists Know" invites controversy by claiming that fundamental gender differences limit the everyday decisions women can make. Select another controversial issue, one that you feel strongly about. Conduct library research to gather evidence in support of your position, and brainstorm with others to identify some points that might be raised by those who oppose your view. Then, using logic and formal, documented evidence, convince readers that your viewpoint is valid.

Your instructor may not ask you to include research in your essay. But, if you're asked—as Mark was—to research your paper and to provide *formal documentation,* you'll want to pay special attention to the way Mark credits his sources. (In *your* paper, the Works Cited list should be double-spaced—along with the rest of the paper—and placed at the end on a separate page.) You'll also find it helpful to refer to the Appendix, "A Concise Guide to Finding and Documenting Sources" (page 445). If your instructor wants you to research your paper but will accept *informal documentation,* the material on page 358 should come in handy.

Whether or not you include research in your paper, the annotations on Mark's essay and the comments following it will help you determine how well it applies the principles of argumentation-persuasion.

Compulsory National Service
by Mark Simmons

Beginning of two-paragraph introduction	Our high school history class spent several weeks studying the events of the 1960s. The most interesting thing about that decade was the spirit of service and social commitment among young people. In the '60s, young people thought about issues beyond themselves; they joined the Peace Corps, worked in poverty-stricken Appalachian communities, and participated in freedom marches against segregation. Most young people today, despite their concern with careers and getting ahead, would also like an opportunity to make a worthwhile contribution to society.	1
Common knowledge: No need to document	Convinced that many young adults are indeed eager for such an opportunity, President Bill Clinton's administration implemented in 1994 a pilot program of voluntary national service. The following year, the program was formalized, placed under the management of the Corporation for National Service (CNS), and given the name AmeriCorps. In the years 1994–2003, approximately 250,000 AmeriCorps volunteers provided varied assistance in communities across the country ("AmeriCorps:	2
Parenthetic citation of unpaged anonymous material obtained through the Internet	Who We Are"). Such voluntary national service was also endorsed by President George W. Bush. Following the devastating terrorist attacks on September 11, 2001, President Bush urged Americans to volunteer as a way of assisting in the nation's recovery and of demonstrating a spirit of national unity. He issued an executive order in early 2002 establishing USA Freedom Corps, an organization seeking to persuade Americans to perform 4,000 hours of volunteer service over a lifetime (Hutcheson A2). In general, programs such as USA Freedom Corps and the more established AmeriCorps hold out so much promise that it seems only natural to go one step further and make young people's participation in these	
Start of two-sentence thesis	programs or some kind of national service mandatory. By	

instituting a program of compulsory national service, the country could tap youth's idealistic desire to make a difference. Such a system would yield significant benefits.

Definition paragraph

What exactly is meant by compulsory national service? Traditionally, it has tended to mean that everyone between the ages of seventeen and twenty-five would serve the country for two years. These young people could choose between two major options: military service or a public-service corps. They could serve their time at any point within an eight-year span. The unemployed or the uncertain could join immediately after high school; college-bound students could complete their education before joining the national service. Years ago, Senator Sam Nunn and Representative Dave McCurdy gave a new twist to the definition of compulsory national service. They proposed a plan that would require all high school graduates applying for federal aid for college tuition to serve either in the military or in a Citizens Corps. Anyone in the Citizens Corps would be required to work full-time at public-service duties for one or two years. During that time, participants would receive a weekly stipend, and, at the end, be given a voucher worth $10,000 for each year of civilian service. The voucher could then be applied toward college credit, employment training, or a down payment on a house (Sudo 9).

Beginning of summary of a source's ideas

Parenthetic citation—page number *and* author are given since the author is not cited earlier in the sentence

The traditional plan for compulsory national service and the one proposed by Nunn and McCurdy are just two of many variations that have been discussed over the years. While this country debates the concept, some nations such as France have gone ahead and accepted it enthusiastically. The idea could be workable in this country too. Unfortunately, opponents are doing all they can to prevent the idea from taking hold. They contend, first of all, that the program would cost too much. A great deal of money, they argue, would be spent administering the program, paying young people's wages, and providing housing for participants. Another argument against compulsory national service is that it would demoralize young people; supposedly, the plan would prevent the young from moving ahead with their careers and would make them feel as though they were engaged in work that offered no personal satisfaction. A third argument is that compulsory service would lay the groundwork for a dictatorship. The picture is painted of an army of young people, controlled by the government, much like the Hitler Youth of World War II.

Topic sentence

Beginning of summary of three points made by the opposing viewpoint

Topic sentence: Refutation of first point

Despite opponents' claims that compulsory national service would involve exorbitant costs, the program would not have to be that expensive to run. AmeriCorps has already provided an excellent model for achieving substantial benefits at reasonable cost. For example, a study conducted by

3

4

5

Information comes from two sources. Sources, separated by a semicolon, are given in the order they appear in the Works Cited list. First source is unpaged electronic text. No page given for second source because it runs only one page.

Topic sentence: Refutation of second point

Attribution giving author's full name and area of expertise

Full-sentence quotation is preceded by a comma and begins with a capital letter

Where secondary source was quoted

Quotation is blended into the sentence (no comma and the quotation begins with a lowercased word)

Quotation with ellipsis

Just the page number is provided because the author's name is cited in the preceding attribution

Parenthetic citation for electronic source having two authors. No page given since electronic text is unpaged.

universities in Iowa and Michigan showed that each dollar spent on AmeriCorps programs yielded $2.60 in reduced welfare costs, increased earnings, and other benefits (Garland 120). Also, the sums required for wages and housing could be reduced considerably through payments made by the towns, cities, and states using the corps' services. And the economic benefits of the program could be significant. AmeriCorps's official website gives an idea of the current scope of the program's activities. Volunteers provide crucial services including building affordable homes for families, reducing crime in neighborhoods, responding to natural disasters, and tutoring children ("AmeriCorps"). A compulsory national corps could also clean up litter, provide day care services, staff libraries, immunize children, and care for the country's growing elderly population (Clinton; Eng). All these projects would help solve many of the problems that plague our nation, and they would probably cost less than if they were handled by often inefficient government bureaucracies.

Also, rather than undermining the spirit of young people, as opponents contend, the program would probably boost their morale. Many young people feel enormous pressure and uncertainty; they are not sure whether they want to find a job or further their education. Compulsory national service could give these young people much-needed breathing space. As Edward Lewis, president of St. Mary's College, says, "Many students are not ready for college at seventeen or eighteen. This kind of program responds to that need" (qtd. in Fowler 3). Robert Coles, psychiatrist and social activist, argues that a public service stint enriches participants' lives in yet another way. Coles points out that young people often have little sense of the job market. When they get involved in community service, though, they frequently "discover an area of interest . . . that launches them on a career" (93). Equally important, compulsory national service can provide an emotional boost for the young; all of them would experience the pride that comes from working hard, reaching goals, acquiring skills, and handling responsibilities (Waldman and Wofford). A positive mind-set would also result from the sense of community that would be created by serving in the national service. All young people--rich or poor, educated or not, regardless of sex and social class--would come together and perceive not their differences but their common interests and similarities (Waldman and Wofford). As President Clinton proclaimed at the Year 2000 swearing-in of AmeriCorps's recruits in Philadelphia, AmeriCorps gives volunteers a chance "to tear down barriers of distrust and misunderstanding and old-fashioned ignorance, and build a genuine American community" (Clinton).

6

Topic sentence: ──────▶ Finally, in contrast to what opponents claim, compulsory 7
Refutation of national service would not signal the start of a dictatorship.
third point Although the service would be required, young people would
have complete freedom to choose any two years between the
ages of seventeen and twenty-five. They would also have
complete freedom to choose the branch of the military or
public service corps that suits them best. And the corps would
not need to be outfitted in military uniforms or to live in
barrack-like camps. It could be set up like a regular job, with
young people living at home as much as possible, following a
nine-to-five schedule, enjoying all the personal freedoms that
would ordinarily be theirs. Also, a dictatorship would no more
likely emerge from compulsory national service than it has
from our present military system. We would still have a series
of checks and balances to prohibit the taking of power by one
group or individual. We should also keep in mind that our
system is different from that of fascist regimes; our long
tradition of personal liberty makes improbable the seizing of
absolute power by one person or faction. A related but even
more important point to remember is that freedom does not
mean people are guaranteed the right to pursue only their
individual needs. That is mistaking selfishness for freedom.

Beginning of And, as everyone knows, selfishness leads only to misery. The
two-paragraph national service would not take away freedom. On the
conclusion ── contrary, serving in the corps would help young people grasp
this larger concept of freedom, a concept that is badly needed
Attribution to counteract the deadly "look out for number one" attitude
leading to a long that is spreading like a poison across the nation.
quotation. Attri-
bution is followed ──────▶ Perhaps there will never be a time like the 1960s when so 8
by a colon since many young people were concerned with remaking the world.
the lead-in is a Still, a good many of today's young people want meaningful
full sentence. If work. They want to feel that what they do makes a difference.
the lead-in isn't A program of compulsory national service would harness this
a full sentence, idealism and help young people realize the best in themselves.
use a comma after Such a program would also help resolve some of the country's
the attribution. ┐ most critical social problems.

Long quotation Almost two decades ago, political commentator Donald 9
is indented ten Eberly expressed his belief in the power of national service.
spaces. Don't Urging the inauguration of such a program, Eberly wrote the
leave any extra following:
space within,
above, or below ── ──────▶ The promise of national service can be manifested
the quotation. in many ways: in cleaner air and fewer forest fires;
in well-cared-for infants and old folks; in a better-
For an indented educated citizenry and better-satisfied work force;
quotation, the perhaps in a more peaceful world. National service
period is placed has a lot of promise. It's a promise well worth
before the paren- keeping. (651)
thetic citation. ─┐

In *your* paper, the Works Cited list would be double-spaced like the rest of the paper, with no extra space after the heading or between entries. Also, in *your* paper, the Works Cited would start on a *separate* page.

Several years later, President Clinton took office, gave his support to the concept, and AmeriCorps was born. This advocacy of public service was then championed, at least in word, by President Bush. During his administration, however, AmeriCorps was threatened by deep budget cuts advocated by opponents of the program and its Clintonian legacy. Fortunately, despite these measures, Congress voted in 2003 with overwhelming bipartisan support to save AmeriCorps and salvage a portion of its budget ("Timely Help"). In the words of a Philadelphia Inquirer editorial, "The civic yield from that investment is incalculable" ("Ill Served"). An efficient and successful program of voluntary service, AmeriCorps has paved the way. Now seems to be the perfect time to expand the concept and make compulsory national service a reality.

Anonymous material obtained on the Internet. Names of website and of sponsoring organization appear. Electronic text is 5 paragraphs long. Web address always required.

Authored material on the Internet. Dates the material was published and accessed, respectively, are provided.

Book by one author

Published speech

Newspaper article whose text is only one page

Article from weekly magazine

Internet article with unnumbered paragraphs or pages

Works Cited

"AmeriCorps: Who We Are." AmeriCorps. The Corporation for National Service. 11 July 2003: 5 pars. 26 Jan. 2004 <http://www.americorps.org/whoweare.html>.

Clinton, William. "Remarks by the President to AmeriCorps." AmeriCorps. The Corporation for National Service. 11 Oct. 2000: 28 pars. 7 Jan. 2004 <http://www.americorps.org/news/pr/potus_remarks101100.html>.

Coles, Robert. The Call of Service. Boston: Houghton Mifflin, 1993.

Eberly, Donald. "What the President Should Do About National Service." Vital Speeches of the Day 15 Aug. 1989: 561–63.

Eng, Lily. "Congressional Pressure Puts AmeriCorps Under the Gun." Philadelphia Inquirer 18 Apr. 1996, late ed.: B1.

Fowler, Margaret. "New Interest in National Youth Corps." New York Times 16 May 1989, natl. ed.: A25.

Garland, Susan B. "A Social Program CEOs Want to Save." Business Week 19 June 1996: 120–21.

Hutcheson, Ron. "Bush Moves to Establish His New Volunteer Program." Philadelphia Inquirer 31 Jan. 2002: A2.

"Ill Served." Editorial. Philadelphia Inquirer Online 27 June 2003. 1 Mar. 2004 <http://www.philly.com/mld/inquirer/news/editorial/6180250.htm>.

Sudo, Phil. "Mandatory National Service?" <u>Scholastic Update</u>
23 Feb. 1990: 9.

"Timely Help for AmeriCorps." Editorial. <u>New York Times</u>
<u>Online</u> 17 July 2003: 4 pars. 28 Feb 2004 <http://
www.nytimes.com/2003/07/17/opinion/17THU4.html>.

Article (by two → Waldman, Steven, and Harris Wofford. "AmeriCorps the
authors) from
scholarly journal
on CD-ROM
Beautiful? Habitat for Conservative Values." <u>Policy</u>
<u>Review</u> Sept.–Oct. 1997: 49 pars. CD-ROM.
EBSCOhost.

COMMENTARY

Blend of argumentation and persuasion.   In his essay, Mark tackles a controversial issue. He takes the position that compulsory national service would benefit both the country as a whole and its young people in particular. Mark's essay is a good example of the way argumentation and persuasion often mix: Although the paper presents Mark's position in a logical, well-reasoned manner (argumentation), it also appeals to readers' personal values and suggests a course of action (persuasion).

Audience analysis.   When planning the essay, Mark realized that his audience—his composition class—would consist largely of two kinds of readers. Some, not sure of their views, would be inclined to agree with him if he presented his case well. Others would probably be reluctant to accept his view. Because of this mixed audience, Mark knew he couldn't depend on *pathos* (an appeal to emotion) to convince readers. Rather, his argument had to rely mainly on *logos* (reason) and *ethos* (credibility). So Mark organized his essay around a series of logical arguments—many of them backed by expert opinion—and he evoked his own authority by drawing on his knowledge of history and his "inside" knowledge of young people.

Introduction and thesis.   Mark introduces his subject by discussing an earlier decade when large numbers of young people worked for social change. Mark's references to the Peace Corps, community work, and freedom marches reinforce his image as a knowledgeable source and establish a context for his position. These historical references, combined with the comments about AmeriCorps, the program of voluntary national service, lead into the two-sentence thesis at the end of the two-paragraph introduction: "By instituting a program of compulsory national service, the country could tap youth's idealistic desire to make a difference. Such a system would yield significant benefits."

The second paragraph in the introduction also illustrates Mark's first use of outside sources. Because the assignment called for research in support of an argument, Mark went to the library and online and identified sources that helped him defend his position. If Mark's instructor had required extensive investigation of an issue, Mark would have been obligated both to dig more deeply into his subject and to use more scholarly and specialized sources. But given the instructor's requirements, Mark proceeded just as he should have: He searched out expert opinion that supported his viewpoint; he presented that evidence clearly; he documented his sources carefully.

Background paragraph and use of outside sources.   The third paragraph provides a working *definition* of compulsory national service by presenting two common interpretations of the concept. Such background information guarantees that Mark's readers will share his understanding of the essay's central concept.

Acknowledging the opposing viewpoint.   Having explained the meaning of compulsory national service, Mark is now in a good position to launch his argument. Even though he wasn't required to research the opposing viewpoint, Mark wisely decided to get together with some friends to brainstorm some issues that might be raised by the dissenting view. He acknowledges this position in the *topic sentence* of the essay's fourth paragraph: "Unfortunately, opponents are doing all they can to prevent the idea from taking hold." Next he summarizes the main points the dissenting opinion might advance: compulsory national service would be expensive, demoralizing to young people, and dangerously authoritarian. Mark uses the rest of the essay to counter these criticisms.

Refutation.   The next three paragraphs (5–7) *refute* the opposing stance and present Mark's evidence for his position. Mark structures the essay so that readers can follow his *counterargument* with ease. Each paragraph argues against one opposing point and begins with a *topic sentence* that serves as Mark's response to the dissenting view. Note the way the italicized portion of each topic sentence recalls a dissenting point cited earlier: "Despite opponents' claims that *compulsory national service would involve exorbitant costs,* the program would not have to be that expensive to run" (paragraph 5); "Also, rather than *undermining the spirit of young people,* as opponents contend, the program would probably boost their morale" (6); "Finally, in contrast to what opponents claim, *compulsory national service would not signal the start of a dictatorship"* (7). Mark also guides the reader through the various points in the refutation by using *transitions* within paragraphs: "*And* the economic benefits . . . could be significant" (5); "*Equally important,* compulsory national service could provide an emotional boost . . ." (6); "*Also,* a dictatorship would no more likely emerge . . ." (7).

Throughout the three-paragraph refutation, Mark uses outside sources to lend power to his argument. If the assignment had called for in-depth research, he would have cited facts, statistics, and case studies to develop this section of his essay. Given the nature of the assignment, though, Mark's reliance on expert opinion is perfectly acceptable.

Mark successfully incorporates material from these outside sources into his refutation. He doesn't, for example, string one quotation numbingly after another; instead he usually develops his refutation by *summarizing* expert opinion and saves *direct quotations* for points that deserve emphasis. Moreover, whenever Mark quotes or summarizes a source, he provides clear signals to indicate that the material is indeed borrowed. (If you'd like some suggestions for citing outside sources in an essay of your own, see pages 364 and 459–464.)

Some problems with the refutation.   Overall, Mark's three-paragraph refutation is strong, but it would have been even more effective if the paragraphs had been resequenced. As it now stands, the last paragraph in the refutation (7) seems anticlimactic. Unlike the preceding two paragraphs, which are developed through fairly extensive reference to outside sources, paragraph 7 depends entirely on Mark's personal feelings and interpretations for its support. Of course, Mark was under no obligation to provide research in all sections of the paper. Even so, the refutation would have been more persuasive if Mark had placed the final paragraph in the refutation in a less emphatic position. He could, for example, have put it first or second in the sequence, saving for last either of the other two more convincing paragraphs.

You may also have felt that there's another problem with the third paragraph in the refutation. Here, Mark seems to lose control of his counterargument. Beginning with "And, as everyone knows . . . ," Mark falls into the *logical fallacy* called *begging the question.* He shouldn't assume that everyone agrees that a selfish life inevitably brings misery. He also indulges in charged emotionalism when he refers—somewhat melodramatically—to the "deadly 'look out for number one' attitude that is spreading like a poison across the nation."

Inductive reasoning.   In part, Mark arrived at his position *inductively*, through a series of *inferences* or *inductive leaps.* He started with some personal *observations* about the nation and its young people. Then, to support those observations, he added his friends' insights as well as information gathered through research. Combined, all this material led him to the general *conclusion* that compulsory national service would be both workable and beneficial.

Combining patterns of development.   To develop his argument, Mark draws on several patterns of development. The third paragraph relies on *definition* to clarify what is meant by compulsory national service. The first paragraph of both the introduction and conclusion *compares* and *contrasts* young people of the 1960s with those of today. And, to support his position, Mark uses a kind of *causal analysis;* he both speculates on the likely consequences of compulsory national service and cites expert opinion to illustrate the validity of some of those speculations.

Conclusion.   Despite some problems in the final section of his refutation, Mark comes up with an effective two-paragraph conclusion for his essay. In the first closing paragraph, he echoes the point made in the introduction about the 1960s and restates his thesis. That done, he moves to the second paragraph of his conclusion. There, he quotes a dramatic statement from a knowledgeable source, cites efforts to undermine AmeriCorps, and ends by pointing out that AmeriCorps has earned the respect of some unlikely supporters. All that Mark does in this final paragraph lends credibility to the crisp assertion and suggested course of action at the very end of his essay.

Revising the first draft.   Given the complex nature of his argument, Mark found that he had to revise his essay several times. One way to illustrate some of the changes he made is to compare his final introduction with the original draft reprinted here:

Original Version of the Introduction

"There's no free lunch." "You can't get something for nothing." "You have to earn your way." In America, these sayings are not really true. In America, we gladly take but give back little. In America, we receive economic opportunity, legal protection, the right to vote, and, most of all, a personal freedom unequaled throughout the world. How do we repay our country for such gifts? In most cases, we don't. This unfair relationship must be changed. The best way to make a start is to institute a system of national compulsory service for young people. This system would be of real benefit to the country and its citizens.

When Mark met with a classmate for a peer review session, he found that his partner had a number of helpful suggestions for revising various sections of the essay. But Mark's partner focused most of her comments on the essay's introduction because she felt it needed special attention. Following his classmate's suggestion, Mark deleted the original introduction's references to Americans in general. He made this change because he wanted readers to know—from the very start of the essay—that the paper would focus not on all Americans but on American youth. To reinforce this emphasis, he also added the point about the social commitment characteristic of young people in the 1960s. This reference to an earlier period gave the discussion an important historical perspective and lent a note of authority to Mark's argument. The decision to mention the '60s also helped Mark realize that his introduction should point out more recent developments—specifically, the promise of AmeriCorps. Mark was pleased to see that adding this new material not only gave the introduction a sharper focus, but it also provided a smoother lead-in to his thesis.

These are just a few of the many changes Mark made while reworking his essay. Because he budgeted his time carefully, he was able to revise thoroughly. With the exception of some weak spots in the refutation, Mark's essay is well-reasoned and convincing.

ACTIVITIES: ARGUMENTATION-PERSUASION

Prewriting Activities

1. Imagine you're writing two essays: One *defines* hypocrisy; the other *contrasts* license and freedom. Identify an audience for each essay (college students, professors, teenagers, parents, employers, employees, or some other group). Then jot down how each essay might argue the merits of certain ways of behaving.

2. Following are several thesis statements for argumentation-persuasion essays. For each thesis, determine whether the three audiences indicated in parentheses are apt to be supportive, wavering, or hostile. Then select *one* thesis and use group brainstorming to identify, for each audience, specific points you would make to persuade each group.

   a. Students should not graduate from college until they have passed a comprehensive exam in their majors (*college students, their parents, college officials*).

   b. Abandoned homes owned by the city should be sold to low-income residents for a nominal fee (*city officials, low-income residents, general citizens*).

   c. The town should pass a law prohibiting residents who live near the reservoir from using pesticides on their lawns (*environmentalists, homeowners, members of the town council*).

   d. Faculty advisors to college newspapers should have the authority to prohibit the publication of articles that reflect negatively on the school (*alumni, college officials, student journalists*).

Revising Activities

3. Each set of statements that follows contains at least one of the logical fallacies described earlier in the chapter and in Ann McClintock's essay "Propaganda Techniques in Today's Advertising" (page 207). Identify the fallacy or fallacies in each set and explain why the statements are invalid.

   a. Grades are irrelevant to learning. Students are in college to get an education, not good grades. The university should eliminate grading altogether.

   b. The best policy is to put juvenile offenders in jail so that they can get a taste of reality. Otherwise, they will repeat their crimes again and again.

c. So-called sex education programs do nothing to decrease the rate of teenage pregnancy. Further expenditures on these programs should be curtailed.

d. If we allow abortion, people will think it's acceptable to kill the homeless or pull the plug on sick people—two groups that are also weak and frail.

e. The curfews that some towns impose on teenagers are as repressive as the curfews in totalitarian countries.

4. Following is the introduction from the first draft of an essay advocating the elimination of mandatory dress codes in public schools. Revise the paragraph, being sure to consider these questions: How effectively does the writer deal with the opposing viewpoint? Does the paragraph encourage those who might disagree with the writer to read on? Why or why not? Do you see any logical fallacies in the writer's thinking? Where? Does the writer introduce anything that veers away from the point being discussed? Where? Before revising, you may find it helpful to do some brainstorming—individually or in a group—to find ways to strengthen the paragraph.

   After reworking the paragraph, take a few minutes to consider how the rest of the essay might unfold. What persuasive strategies could be used? How could Rogerian argument win over readers? What points could be made? What action could be urged in the effort to build a convincing argument?

   In three nearby towns recently, high school administrators joined forces to take an outrageously strong stand against students' constitutional rights. Acting like fascists, they issued an edict in the form of a preposterous dress code that prohibits students from wearing expensive jewelry, designer jeans, leather jackets--anything that the administrators, in their supposed wisdom, consider ostentatious. Perhaps the next thing they'll want to do is forbid students to play rock music at school dances. What prompted the administrators' dictatorial prohibition against certain kinds of clothing? Somehow or other, they got it into their heads that having no restrictions on the way students dress creates an unhealthy environment, where students vie with each other for the flashiest attire. Students and parents alike should protest this and any other dress code. If such codes go into effect, we might as well throw out the Constitution.

Yuh Ji-Yeon

At the age of five, Yuh Ji-Yeon (1965–) immigrated from Seoul, Korea, to the United States, settling in Chicago with her parents. After graduating from Stanford University, she worked as a reporter for the *Omaha World-Herald* and *New York Newsday*. She received a doctorate from the University of Pennsylvania following her dissertation examining the experiences of Korean women immigrating to the United States as wives of U.S. soldiers, which she expanded into her book *Beyond the Shadow of Camptown* (2002). Nearly all of Yuh's writing reflects the concerns of people struggling for liberation in the face of oppression. She currently teaches history at Northwestern University. The following selection first appeared in the *Philadelphia Inquirer* in 1991.

Pre-Reading Journal Entry

Which events in American history do you consider shameful? List these events in your journal. For each, jot down what your teachers taught you about the event when you were a child. Does what you were taught as a child differ from what you know now? In what way? If you did later on learn harsher truths about these events, how did you feel? Do you believe that you should have been told the truth from the beginning? Why or why not?

Let's Tell the Story of All America's Cultures

I grew up hearing, seeing and almost believing that America was white— 1
albeit with a little black tinge here and there—and that white was best.

The white people were everywhere in my 1970s Chicago childhood: 2
Founding Fathers, Lewis and Clark, Lincoln, Daniel Boone, Carnegie, presidents, explorers and industrialists galore. The only black people were slaves. The only Indians were scalpers.

I never heard one word about how Benjamin Franklin was so impressed 3
by the Iroquois federation of nations that he adapted that model into our system of state and federal government. Or that the Indian tribes were systematically betrayed and massacred by a greedy young nation that stole their land and called it the United States.

I never heard one word about how Asian immigrants were among the 4
first to turn California's desert into fields of plenty. Or about Chinese immigrant Ah Bing, who bred the cherry now on sale in groceries across the nation. Or that plantation owners in Hawaii imported labor from China, Japan, Korea and the Philippines to work the sugar cane fields. I never

learned that Asian immigrants were the only immigrants denied U.S. citizenship, even though they served honorably in World War I. All the immigrants in my textbook were white.

I never learned about Frederick Douglass, the runaway slave who   5
became a leading abolitionist and statesman, or about black scholar W.E.B. Du Bois. I never learned that black people rose up in arms against slavery. Nat Turner wasn't one of the heroes in my childhood history class.

I never learned that the American Southwest and California were already   6
settled by Mexicans when they were annexed after the Mexican-American War. I never learned that Mexico once had a problem keeping land-hungry white men on the U.S. side of the border.

So when other children called me a slant-eyed chink and told me to go   7
back where I came from, I was ready to believe that I wasn't really an American because I wasn't white.

America's bittersweet legacy of struggling and failing and getting another   8
step closer to democratic ideals of liberty and equality and justice for all wasn't for the likes of me, an immigrant child from Korea. The history books said so.

Well, the history books were wrong.   9

Educators around the country are finally realizing what I realized as a   10
teenager in the library, looking up the history I wasn't getting in school. America is a multicultural nation, composed of many people with varying histories and varying traditions who have little in common except their humanity, a belief in democracy and a desire for freedom.

America changed them, but they changed America too.   11

A committee of scholars and teachers gathered by the New York State   12
Department of Education recognizes this in their recent report, "One Nation, Many Peoples: A Declaration of Cultural Interdependence."

They recommend that public schools provide a "multicultural educa-   13
tion, anchored to the shared principles of a liberal democracy."

What that means, according to the report, is recognizing that America   14
was shaped and continues to be shaped by people of diverse backgrounds. It calls for students to be taught that history is an ongoing process of discovery and interpretation of the past, and that there is more than one way of viewing the world.

Thus, the westward migration of white Americans is not just a heroic set-   15
tling of an untamed wild, but also the conquest of indigenous peoples. Immigrants were not just white, but Asian as well. Blacks were not merely passive slaves freed by northern whites, but active fighters for their own liberation.

In particular, according to the report, the curriculum should help chil-   16
dren "to assess critically the reasons for the inconsistencies between the ideals of the U.S. and social realities. It should provide information and intellectual tools that can permit them to contribute to bringing reality closer to the ideals."

In other words, show children the good with the bad, and give them the   17
skills to help improve their country. What could be more patriotic?

Several dissenting members of the New York committee publicly worry   18
that America will splinter into ethnic fragments if this multicultural curriculum is adopted. They argue that the committee's report puts the focus on
ethnicity at the expense of national unity.

But downplaying ethnicity will not bolster national unity. The history of   19
America is the story of how and why people from all over the world came to
the United States, and how in struggling to make a better life for themselves,
they changed each other, they changed the country, and they all came to call
themselves Americans.

E pluribus unum. Out of many, one.   20

This is why I, with my Korean background, and my childhood tormentors,   21
with their lost-in-the-mist-of-time European backgrounds, are all Americans.

It is the unique beauty of this country. It is high time we let all our chil-   22
dren gaze upon it.

Questions for Close Reading

1. What is the selection's thesis? Locate the sentence(s) in which Yuh states her main
   idea. If she doesn't state the thesis explicitly, express it in your own words.
2. Yuh makes the rather shocking claim that "the history books were wrong" (paragraph 9). Why does she make this statement? What evidence does she offer to support it?
3. According to Yuh, what changes are needed in U.S. history courses?
4. Why does Yuh feel it is critical that U.S. students receive more than the traditional whites-only version of our nation's history? Who will be served by making history books more multicultural?
5. Refer to your dictionary as needed to define the following words used in the selection: *albeit* (paragraph 1), *tinge* (1), *galore* (2), *multicultural* (10, 13, 18), *interdependence* (12), *indigenous* (15), *dissenting* (18), *ethnicity* (18), and *bolster* (19).

Questions About the Writer's Craft

1. **The pattern.** Where in her argument does Yuh present the opposing viewpoint?
   Why do you suppose she waits so long to deal with the dissenting opinion? What
   effect does this delay have on her argument's effectiveness?
2. **Other patterns.** Why might Yuh have decided to use so many *examples* in paragraphs 2 through 6? How do these examples contribute to the persuasiveness of her
   position? Why might she have placed these examples before her thesis statement?
3. Yuh mixes the subjective and the objective in her argument. Where does she use
   specifics from her own life? How do these personal details help persuade readers
   to accept her viewpoint?
4. Yuh often uses parallelism and repetition of phrases, particularly in paragraphs 1
   through 6 and paragraph 15. What effect do you think she intended these two
   stylistic devices to have on her readers?

Writing Assignments Using Argumentation-Persuasion as a Pattern of Development

1. Using the resources of the library and/or Internet, read several articles about the ongoing debate over multiculturalism's role in contemporary education. In addition to locating coverage of the 1991 New York State Department of Education Study (cited by Yuh in paragraph 12) and historian Arthur Schlesinger's *Time* essay "The Cult of Ethnicity: Good and Bad" (July 8, 1991), you should review many more recent sources on this issue. Review your research, and decide whether or not you support the idea of a multicultural curriculum. Then write an essay in which you argue your position, refuting as many of the opposing views as possible. Draw upon your own experiences as well as your research when developing your point of view.

2. Yuh cites a problem she encountered in her education. What problems or insufficiencies have you found in your own education? Perhaps you perceive an overemphasis on athletics, a reliance on rote memorization, a tendency to discourage female students from pursuing an interest in math and science. Select a single problem at one level of education, and brainstorm with others to gather material about the problem. Then write an essay directed at those who think all is well in our educational system. Be sure your argument illustrates the inaccuracy of these individuals' overly positive view. Before writing your paper, you may want to read Clifford Stoll's "Cyberschool" (page 239), Joseph H. Suina's "And Then I Went to School" (page 271), and James Barszcz's "Can You Be Educated From a Distance?" (page 390) because they offer critiques of U.S. education.

Writing Assignments Combining Patterns of Development

3. Because the mainstream culture they lived in didn't recognize the presence of minorities, the author's classmates considered Yuh an outsider, almost a nonbeing. To what extent, in your opinion, does television contribute to the dehumanization of minorities? For several days, watch a variety of television shows, noting how a particular ethnic or minority group (such as African-Americans, Hispanic-Americans, or the elderly) is portrayed. Then write an essay *arguing* that the depiction of this group on television is either accurate *or* distorted. Support your main idea with plentiful *examples* of specific television shows, including newscasts, situation comedies, talk shows, and so forth.

4. In her essay, Yuh refers to a report issued by the New York State Department of Education. The report argues that curriculum should encourage students to examine "the reasons for the inconsistencies between the ideals of the U.S. and social realities." Like most people, you probably detected such disparities when you were growing up. Perhaps as a youngster, you heard an admired neighbor brag about "scamming" the government or a business of owed money. As a high school student, you might have learned that an esteemed coach took kickbacks from college recruiters. Focus on one such clash between the ethical ideal and the everyday reality, and write about the incident's *effect* on you. Provide dramatic *details* to show how you reacted, what you did to explain the discrepancy to yourself, and whether you asked adults to help you understand the situation. At the

end, reach some conclusions about the way children can be helped to deal with such collisions between ideals and reality. Before writing your paper, you may want to read Langston Hughes's "Salvation" (page 124), a powerful essay that explores a child's disillusionment with adult realities.

Writing Assignment Using a Journal Entry as a Starting Point

5. Write an essay in which you argue for *or* against schools' revealing harsh historical realities to children. Review your pre-reading journal entry, and select *one* historical event to focus on. Provide plentiful reasons to support your position, whenever possible pointing out weaknesses in opposing viewpoints. To deepen your understanding of the issue, consider reading Beth Johnson's "Bombs Bursting in Air" (page 160), an essay exploring parents' quandary between protecting their children and educating them about life's painful realities.

James Barszcz

After earning his doctoral degree in English at Rutgers University, James Barszcz (1955–) taught college for several years. He is now employed at a major telecommunications company and pursues writing and independent scholarship in his spare time. In addition to issues related to technology and the classroom, his research interests include nineteenth-century American literature, especially Hawthorne, Melville, and Emerson. He lives with his wife and two children in Maplewood, New Jersey.

Pre-Reading Journal Entry

While many students readily acknowledge the practical reasons for attending college, fewer consider the intangible opportunity for personal development that higher education can provide. Take a few moments to consider what personal qualities you seek to cultivate in the course of your college education. Freewrite about this subject in your pre-reading journal, listing the various characteristics you hope to develop by the time you get your diploma. Discussing your thoughts with peers might help broaden your perspective on this question.

Can You Be Educated From a Distance?

By almost any measure, there is a boom in Internet-based instruction. In just a few years, thirty-four percent of American colleges and universities have begun offering some form of what's called "distance learning" (DL), and among the larger schools, it's closer to ninety percent. If you doubt the popularity of the trend, you probably haven't heard of the University of Phoenix. It grants degrees entirely on the basis of online instruction. It enrolls 90,000 students, a statistic used to support its claim to be the largest private university in the country.

While the kinds of instruction offered in these programs will differ, DL usually signifies a course in which the instructors post syllabi, reading assignments, and schedules on websites, and students send in their written assignments by e-mail. Other forms of communication often come into play, such as threaded messaging, which allows for posting questions and comments that are publicly viewable, as a bulletin board would, as well as chat rooms for real-time interchanges. Generally speaking, face-to-face communication with an instructor is minimized or eliminated altogether.

The attraction for students might at first seem obvious. Primarily, there's the convenience promised by courses on the Net: you can do the work, as they say, in your pajamas. But figures indicate that the reduced effort results in a reduced commitment to the course. While the attrition rate for all freshmen at American universities is around twenty percent, the rate for on-line students is thirty-five percent. Students themselves seem to understand the weaknesses inherent in the setup. In a survey conducted for eCornell, the DL division of Cornell University, less than a third of the respondents expect-ed the quality of the online course to be as good as the classroom course.

Clearly, from the schools' perspective, there's a lot of money to be saved.   4 Although some of the more ambitious programs require new investments in servers and networks to support collaborative software, most DL courses can run on existing or minimally upgraded systems. The more students who enroll in a course but don't come to campus, the more the school saves on keeping the lights on in the classrooms, paying custodians, and maintaining parking lots. And, while there's evidence that instructors must work harder to run a DL course for a variety of reasons, they won't be paid any more, and might well be paid less.

But as a rule, those who champion distance learning don't base their   5 arguments on convenience or cost savings. More often, they claim DL signals an advance in the effectiveness of education. Consider the vigorous case made by Fairleigh Dickinson University (FDU), in Madison, New Jersey, where students—regardless of their expectations or desires—are now required to take one DL course per year. By setting this requirement, FDU claims that it recognizes the Internet as "a premier learning tool" of the current tech-nological age. Skill in using online resources "prepares our students, more than others, for life-long learning—for their jobs, their careers, and their per-sonal growth." Moreover, Internet-based courses will connect FDU students to a "global virtual faculty," a group of "world-class scholars, experts, artists, politicians, and business leaders around the world."

Sounds pretty good. But do the claims make much sense? First, it should   6 be noted that students today and in the future might well use the Internet with at least as much facility as the faculty. It's not at all clear that they need to be taught such skills. More to the point, how much time and effort do you suppose "world-class scholars" (much less politicians and business leaders) will expend for the benefit of students they never meet or even see? Probably a lot less than they're devoting to the books, journal articles, and position papers that are already available to anyone with access to a library.

Another justification comes from those who see distance learning as the   7 next step in society's progress toward meritocracy. A recent article in *Forbes* magazine cites Professor Roger Schank of Northwestern University, who predicts that soon "students will be able to shop around, taking a course from any institution that offers a good one. . . . Quality education will be available to all. Students will learn what they want to learn rather than what some faculty committee decided was the best practical compromise." In sum, says Professor Schank, who is also chairman of a distance-learning enterprise called CognitiveArts, "Education will be measured by what you know rather than by whose name appears on your diploma."

Statements like these assume education consists in acquiring information   8
("what you know"). Accept that and it's hard to disagree with the conclusions. After all, what does it matter how, or through what medium, you get
the information? But few truly educated people hold such a mechanistic view.
Indeed, traditionally, education was aimed at cultivating intellectual and
moral values, and the "information" you picked up was decidedly secondary.
It was commonplace for those giving commencement speeches to note that,
based on etymology, education is a drawing out, not a putting in. That is, a
true education *educes,* or draws out, from within a person qualities of intellect
and character that would otherwise have remained hidden or dormant.

Exactly how this kind of educing happens is hard to pin down. Only in   9
part does it come from watching professors in the classroom present material and respond to student questions, the elements of education that can be
translated to the Net with reasonable fidelity. Other educational experiences
include things like watching how professors joke with each other (or not!) in
the hallways, seeing what kinds of pictures are framed in a professor's office,
or going out for coffee after class with people in your dorm. Such experiences, and countless others, are sometimes labeled (and dismissed) as "social
life on campus." But they also contribute invaluably to education. Through
them, you learn a style, in the noblest sense of that term, a way of regarding
the information you acquire and the society you find yourself in. This is what
the philosopher Alfred North Whitehead meant when he called style the ultimate acquisition of a cultivated mind. And it's the mysterious ways of cultivating that style that the poet Robert Frost had in mind when he said that
all that a college education requires is that you "hang around until you catch
on." Hang around campus, that is, not lurk on the Net.

Questions for Close Reading

1. What is the selection's thesis? Locate the sentence(s) in which Barszcz states his
   main idea. If he doesn't state the thesis explicitly, express it in your own words.
2. According to Barszcz, what primarily attracts students and schools to distance
   learning?
3. What does Barszcz say are the most common arguments made by proponents of
   distance learning?
4. How does Barszcz define *education?* Do you agree with his definition, or do you
   see education functioning in a different way? Explain.
5. Refer to your dictionary as needed to define the following words used in the selection: *attrition* (3), *virtual* (5), *facility* (6), *meritocracy* (7), *mechanistic* (8), *etymology* (8), *dormant* (8), and *fidelity* (9).

Questions About the Writer's Craft

1. **The pattern.**   What sort of audience—supportive, wavering, or hostile (see
   pages 354–355)—does Barszcz seem to have geared his argument toward? How
   can you tell?

2. **Other patterns.** Barszcz develops paragraph 2 through *division-classification*. What larger topic does he divide into categories? What are these categories? What organizational order does he use in this paragraph?

3. Barszcz quotes literature from Fairleigh Dickinson University (FDU) in some detail. Considering that FDU's position represents an opposing point of view, why do you think he quotes FDU at such length? What is the effect of this quoting?

4. **Other patterns.** In paragraphs 2 and 8, Barszcz provides two *definitions* that fundamentally differ in purpose and tone. Describe the differences.

Writing Assignments Using Argumentation-Persuasion as a Pattern of Development

∞ 1. Barszcz posits that a central component of education should be the cultivation of "moral values." Do you agree? Take the case of public elementary schools. Write an essay in which you argue that these schools should *or* should not instruct students in morality as part of the curriculum. Be sure as you develop your argument to acknowledge and refute opposing points of view. You might benefit from reading Yuh Ji-Yeon's "Let's Tell the Story of All America's Cultures" (page 385), in which the author advocates a certain type of moral education.

2. Barszcz suggests that the true motivation of some who champion distance learning is financial. Think of some other phenomenon—say, the invasion of one country by another, the marketing of a new medication, advertisements for life insurance—and write an essay *arguing* that a financial motive underlies lofty rhetoric ("We will liberate the people of . . . ," "We care about your health," "Invest in your children's future"). Support your case with at least three major *examples* that *illustrate* your assertion. You should also consider citing facts, statistics, and/or expert opinions derived from visiting the library and/or going online to lend additional authority to your position.

Writing Assignments Combining Patterns of Development

∞ 3. In Barszcz's view, educated people are intellectually and morally cultivated. Write an essay *describing* someone you know (or know of) who, in your view, epitomizes an educated person. What are the person's intellectual qualities? What are his or her character traits? What are his or her moral values and tastes? As you answer these questions about the person, provide vivid *examples* to *illustrate* the characteristics you're describing. You might begin by reading "Sister Flowers" (page 96), in which Maya Angelou lovingly conveys the portrait of a very cultivated lady.

4. As Barszcz indicates, on-campus experiences contribute to college students' education. In an essay of your own, *narrate* a school-related experience from any time in your life that left you significantly better educated. The experience you describe, though school-related, need not be strictly academic. For example, you might discuss developing a friendship with someone from a different culture, coming to appreciate an initially disliked instructor, participating in an inspiring class, and so on. *Describe* those details that convey what made the experience so enlightening. How did the experience make you more understanding, aware, critical, sensitive, or appreciative? How did it alter your worldview?

Writing Assignment Using a Journal
Entry as a Starting Point

∞ 5. A "true education," according to Barszcz, "*educes,* or draws out, from within a person qualities of intellect and character that would otherwise have remained hidden or dormant" (8). What personal qualities do you hope a college education will educe from you? Reviewing what you wrote in your pre-reading journal entry, write an essay in which you identify at least two or three qualities you hope to nurture during your college years and explain why you hope to do so. For instance, you might discuss your aspiration to become more intellectually objective, more assertive, more articulate, and so on. And, in order to demonstrate the progress you hope to make, for each quality, you should *contrast* yourself at the outset of your college education with where you hope to be by the end. For some general reflections on the role of education in students' lives, read any of the following: Clifford Stoll's "Cyberschool" (page 239), Joseph H. Suina's "And Then I Went to School" (page 271), and Yuh Ji-Yeon's "Let's Tell the Story of All America's Cultures" (page 385).

Camille Paglia

Before 1990, Camille Paglia, professor of humanities at Philadelphia's University of the Arts, was known primarily for her electrifying performance in the classroom. Then came the publication of Paglia's *Sexual Personae: Art and Decadence From Nefertiti to Emily Dickinson,* a sweeping book that moves with dizzying speed from the days of cave art to the nineteenth century. *Sexual Personae* makes the case that man creates art as a defensive response to woman's terrifying cosmic power—specifically, her sexual and procreative force. Suddenly Paglia became an international celebrity and had many opportunities to express her controversial views. She has been both revered and reviled for making statements like these: "Male aggression and lust are the energizing factors in culture" and "If I ever got into a dating situation where I was overpowered and raped, I would say, 'Oh well, I misread the signals.'" Born in 1947, Paglia earned her doctorate from Yale University, where her Ph.D. thesis was an early version of *Sexual Personae. Sex, Art, and American Culture: Essays* (1992), *Vamps and Tramps: New Essays* (1994), and *Alfred Hitchcock's "The Birds"* (1998) are Paglia's latest works. Formerly a columnist for *Salon* online magazine, she is a contributing editor to *Interview* magazine and appears frequently on television programs to provide commentary on pop culture and gender issues. The following selection, written in Paglia's characteristically provocative style, first appeared in *New York Newsday* in 1991.

Pre-Reading Journal Entry

How would you define "date rape"? Use your journal to formulate a preliminary definition. Working as quickly as you can, jot down your preliminary thoughts about what it is and what it isn't.

Rape: A Bigger Danger Than Feminists Know

Rape is an outrage that cannot be tolerated in civilized society. Yet feminism, which has waged a crusade for rape to be taken more seriously, has put young women in danger by hiding the truth about sex from them. 1

In dramatizing the pervasiveness of rape, feminists have told young women that before they have sex with a man, they must give consent as explicit as a legal contract's. In this way, young women have been convinced that they have been the victims of rape. On elite campuses in the Northeast and on the West Coast, they have held consciousness-raising sessions, petitioned administrations, demanded inquests. At Brown University, outraged, panicky "victims" have scrawled the names of alleged attackers 2 on the walls of women's rest rooms. What marital rape was to the '70s, "date rape" is to the '90s.

The incidence and seriousness of rape do not require this kind of exag-   3
geration. Real acquaintance rape is nothing new. It has been a horrible problem for women for all of recorded history. Once, father and brothers protected women from rape. Once, the penalty for rape was death. I come from à fierce Italian tradition where, not so long ago in the motherland, a rapist would end up knifed, castrated, and hung out to dry.

But the old clans and small rural communities have broken down. In our   4
cities, on our campuses far from home, young women are vulnerable and defenseless. Feminism has not prepared them for this. Feminism keeps saying the sexes are the same. It keeps telling women they can do anything, go anywhere, say anything, wear anything. No, they can't. Women will always be in sexual danger.

One of my male students recently slept overnight with a friend in a pas-   5
sageway of the Great Pyramid in Egypt. He described the moon and sand, the ancient silence and eerie echoes. I am a woman. I will never experience that. I am not stupid enough to believe I could ever be safe there. There is a world of solitary adventure I will never have. Women have always known these somber truths. But feminism, with its pie-in-the-sky fantasies about the perfect world, keeps young women from seeing life as it is.

We must remedy social injustice whenever we can. But there are some   6
things we cannot change. There are sexual differences that are based in biology. Academic feminism is lost in a fog of social constructionism. It believes we are totally the product of our environment. This idea was invented by Rousseau.[1] He was wrong. Emboldened by dumb French language theory, academic feminists repeat the same hollow slogans over and over to each other. Their view of sex is naive and prudish. Leaving sex to the feminists is like letting your dog vacation at the taxidermist's.

The sexes are at war. Men must struggle for identity against the over-   7
whelming power of their mothers. Women have menstruation to tell them they are women. Men must do or risk something to be men. Men become masculine only when other men say they are. Having sex with a woman is one way a boy becomes a man.

College men are at their hormonal peak. They have just left their moth-   8
ers and are questing for their male identity. In groups, they are dangerous. A woman going to a fraternity party is walking into Testosterone Flats, full of prickly cacti and blazing guns. If she goes, she should be armed with resolute alertness. She should arrive with girlfriends and leave with them. A girl who lets herself get dead drunk at a fraternity party is a fool. A girl who goes upstairs alone with a brother at a fraternity party is an idiot. Feminists call this "blaming the victim." I call it common sense.

[1] A French political writer and philosopher (1712–78) (editors' note).

For a decade, feminists have drilled their disciples to say, "Rape is a crime   9
of violence but not of sex." This sugar-coated Shirley Temple nonsense has
exposed young women to disaster. Misled by feminism, they do not expect
rape from the nice boys from good homes who sit next to them in class.

Aggression and eroticism, in fact, are deeply intertwined. Hunt, pursuit   10
and capture are biologically programmed into male sexuality. Generation
after generation, men must be educated, refined, and ethically persuaded
away from their tendency toward anarchy and brutishness. Society is not the
enemy, as feminism ignorantly claims. Society is woman's protection against
rape. Feminism, with its solemn Carry Nation[2] repressiveness, does not see
what is for men the eroticism or fun element in rape, especially the wild,
infectious delirium of gang rape. Women who do not understand rape cannot defend themselves against it.

The date-rape controversy shows feminism hitting the wall of its own   11
broken promises. The women of my '60s generation were the first respect-
able girls in history to swear like sailors, get drunk, stay out all night—in
short, to act like men. We sought total sexual freedom and equality. But as
time passed, we woke up to cold reality. The old double standard protected
women. When anything goes, it's women who lose.

Today's young women don't know what they want. They see that femi-   12
nism has not brought sexual happiness. The theatrics of public rage over date
rape are their way of restoring the old sexual rules that were shattered by my
generation. Yet nothing about the sexes has really changed. The comic film
Where the Boys Are (1960), the ultimate expression of '50s man-chasing, still
speaks directly to our time. It shows smart, lively women skillfully anticipating and fending off the dozens of strategies with which horny men try to get
them into bed. The agonizing date-rape subplot and climax are brilliantly
done. The victim, Yvette Mimieux, makes mistake after mistake, obvious to
the other girls. She allows herself to be lured away from her girlfriends and
into isolation with boys whose character and intentions she misreads. *Where
the Boys Are* tells the truth. It shows courtship as a dangerous game in which
the signals are not verbal but subliminal.

Neither militant feminism, which is obsessed with politically correct lan-   13
guage, nor academic feminism, which believes that knowledge and experience
are "constituted by" language, can understand preverbal or nonverbal communication. Feminism, focusing on sexual politics, cannot see that sex exists
in and through the body. Sexual desire and arousal cannot be fully translated
into verbal terms. This is why men and women misunderstand each other.

Trying to remake the future, feminism cut itself off from sexual history.   14
It discarded and suppressed the sexual myths of literature, art and religion.
Those myths show us the turbulence, the mysteries and passions of sex. In
mythology we see men's sexual anxiety, their fear of woman's dominance.

---

[2]A nineteenth-century reformer who advocated the abolition of alcohol (editors' note).

Much sexual violence is rooted in men's sense of psychological weakness toward women. It takes many men to deal with one woman. Woman's voracity is a persistent motif. Clara Bow,[3] it was rumored, took on the USC[4] football team on weekends. Marilyn Monroe, singing "Diamonds Are a Girl's Best Friend," rules a conga line of men in tuxes. Half-clad Cher, in the video for "If I Could Turn Back Time," deranges a battleship of screaming sailors and straddles a pink-lit cannon. Feminism, coveting social power, is blind to woman's cosmic sexual power.

To understand rape, you must study the past. There never was and never   15
will be sexual harmony. Every woman must be prudent and cautious about where she goes and with whom. When she makes a mistake, she must accept the consequences and, through self-criticism, resolve never to make that mistake again. Running to mommy and daddy on the campus grievance committee is unworthy of strong women. Posting lists of guilty men in the toilet is cowardly, infantile stuff.

The Italian philosophy of life espouses high-energy confrontation. A   16
male student makes a vulgar remark about your breasts? Don't slink off to whimper with the campus shrinking violets. Deal with it. On the spot. Say, "Shut up, you jerk! And crawl back to the barnyard where you belong!" In general, women who project this take-charge attitude toward life get harassed less often. I see too many dopey, immature, self-pitying women walking around like melting sticks of butter. It's the Yvette Mimieux syndrome: make me happy. And listen to me weep when I'm not.

The date-rape debate is already smothering in propaganda churned out   17
by the expensive Northeastern colleges and universities, with their over-concentration of boring, uptight academic feminists and spoiled, affluent students. Beware of the deep manipulativeness of rich students who were neglected by their parents. They love to turn the campus into hysterical psychodramas of sexual transgression, followed by assertions of parental authority and concern. And don't look for sexual enlightenment from academe, which spews out mountains of books but never looks at life directly.

As a fan of football and rock music, I see in the simple, swaggering mas-   18
culinity of the jock and in the noisy posturing of the heavy-metal guitarist certain fundamental, unchanging truths about sex. Masculinity is aggressive, unstable, combustible. It is also the most creative cultural force in history. Women must reorient themselves toward the elemental powers of sex, which can strengthen or destroy.

The only solution to date rape is female self-awareness and self-control. A   19
woman's number-one line of defense against rape is herself. When a real rape occurs, she should report it to the police. Complaining to college committees because the courts "take too long" is ridiculous. College administrations are

---

[3]A movie star from the Roaring Twenties era (editors' note).
[4]University of Southern California (editors' note).

not a branch of the judiciary. They are not equipped or trained for legal inquiry. Colleges must alert incoming students to the problems and dangers of adulthood. Then colleges must stand back and get out of the sex game.

Questions for Close Reading

1. What is the selection's thesis? Locate the sentence(s) in which Paglia states her main idea. If she doesn't state the thesis explicitly, express it in your own words.
2. In Paglia's opinion, why are women more "vulnerable and defenseless" now than in the past?
3. According to Paglia, what "truth about sex" has feminism hidden from young women?
4. What does Paglia believe is "the only solution to date rape"?
5. Refer to your dictionary as needed to define the following words used in the selection: *inquests* (paragraph 2), *testosterone* (8), *constituted* (13), *grievance* (15), and *judiciary* (19).

Questions About the Writer's Craft

1. **The pattern.** Examine the way Paglia develops her argument in paragraphs 6 and 8. Which of her assertions in these paragraphs can be assumed to be true without further proof? Why do you think Paglia includes these essentially incontestable statements? Conversely, which of her assertions in paragraphs 6 and 8 require further proof before their truth can be demonstrated? Does Paglia provide such support? Explain.
2. **Other patterns.** How does Paglia use the *comparison-contrast* pattern to develop her argument?
3. Paglia's style is frequently characterized by short sentences strung together with few transitions. Locate some examples of this style. Why might Paglia have chosen this style? What is its effect?
4. Where does Paglia use emotional, highly connotative language? Where does she employ strongly worded absolute statements? Do you think that this use of pathos makes Paglia's argument more or less convincing? Explain.

Writing Assignments Using Argumentation-Persuasion as a Pattern of Development

1. Read Susan Jacoby's "Common Decency" (page 401), an essay that takes exception to Paglia's view of date rape. Decide which writer presents her case more convincingly. Then write an essay arguing that the *other writer* has trouble making a strong case for her position. Consider the merits and flaws (including any logical fallacies) in the argument, plus such issues as the writer's credibility, strategies for dealing with the opposing view, and use of emotional appeals. Throughout, support your opinion with specific examples drawn from the selection. Keep in mind that you're critiquing the effectiveness of the writer's argument. It's not appropriate, then, simply to explain why you agree or disagree with the writer's position or merely to summarize what the writer says.

∞ 2. Paglia criticizes those who claim that the environment, or social climate, is primarily responsible for shaping gender differences. She believes that such differences "are based in biology." Write an essay arguing your own position about the role that environment and biology play in determining sex-role attitudes and behavior. Remembering to acknowledge opposing views, defend your own viewpoint with plentiful examples based on your experiences and observations. You may also need to conduct some library research to gather support for your position. The following essays will provide insights that you may want to draw upon in your paper: Barbara Ehrenreich's "What I've Learned From Men" (page 166) and Dave Barry's "The Ugly Truth About Beauty" (page 277).

Writing Assignments Combining Patterns of Development

3. Paglia writes in paragraph 7 that "men become masculine only when other men say they are. Having sex with a woman is one way a boy becomes a man." Write an essay constructing your own *definition* of masculinity. Comment on the extent to which you feel being sexually active is an important criterion, but also include other hallmarks and *examples* of masculinity.

4. Date rape seems to be on the rise. Brainstorm with others to identify what may be leading to its growing occurrence. Focusing on several related *factors*, write an essay showing how these factors contribute to the problem. Possible factors include the following: the way males and females are depicted in the media (advertisements, movies, television, rock videos); young people's use of alcohol; the emergence of coed college dorms. At the end of the essay, offer some recommendations about *steps* that can be taken to create a safer climate for dating. You should consider supporting your speculations with information about date rape gathered in the library and/or on the Internet.

Writing Assignment Using a Journal Entry as a Starting Point

5. Drawing upon the material in your pre-reading journal entry, write an essay in which you present a carefully considered definition of the term "date rape." Explain clearly what constitutes date rape and what doesn't. To deepen your understanding of this thorny issue, consider brainstorming with others as well as conducting research in the library and/or on the Internet. One issue to consider: Do males and females define the term differently? If so, how do they define it, and why might their definitions differ?

Susan Jacoby

In her first job as a newspaper reporter, Susan Jacoby (1945–) carefully avoided doing "women's stories," believing that such features weren't worthy of a serious journalist. However, Jacoby's opinion changed with the times, especially as women's issues began to gain increasing attention. Indeed, many of her essays—including those in the *New York Times* and *McCall's*—have dealt with women's concerns. Several of Jacoby's essays have been collected in *The Possible She* (1979) and *Money, Manners, and Morals* (1993). In 1994, she coauthored the biography *Soul to Soul: A Black Russian American Family 1865–1992.* Jacoby's most recent books include *Body* and *Geotrivia Sports,* both published in 1996; *Half-Jew: A Daughter's Search for Her Family's Buried Past* (2000); and *Freethinkers: A History of American Secularism* (2004). The following selection, published in the *New York Times* in April 1991, was written in response to the book *Sexual Personae* by Camille Paglia (see page 395).

Pre-Reading Journal Entry

The phrase "boys will be boys" is often cited to explain certain types of male behavior. What kinds of actions typically fall into this category? List a few of these in your journal. Which behaviors are positive? Why? Which are negative? Why?

Common Decency

She was deeply in love with a man who was treating her badly. To assuage 1
her wounded ego (and to prove to herself that she could get along nicely
without him), she invited another man, an old boyfriend, to a dinner *à deux*
in her apartment. They were on their way to the bedroom when, having realized that she wanted only the man who wasn't there, she changed her mind.
Her ex-boyfriend was understandably angry. He left her apartment with a
not-so-politely phrased request that she leave him out of any future plans.

And that is the end of the story—except for the fact that he was eventu- 2
ally kind enough to accept her apology for what was surely a classic case of
"mixed signals."

I often recall this incident, in which I was the embarrassed female par- 3
ticipant, as the controversy over "date rape"—intensified by the assault that
William Kennedy Smith[1] has been accused of—heats up across the nation.

---

[1]William Kennedy Smith, the nephew of John, Robert, and Edward Kennedy, was accused of
raping a woman in 1991. Kennedy was acquitted, but the trial, broadcast on television, created
a national furor and generated heated debate on the issue of date rape (editors' note).

What seems clear to me is that those who place acquaintance rape in a different category from "stranger rape"—those who excuse friendly social rapists on grounds that they are too dumb to understand when "no" means no—are being even more insulting to men than to women.

These apologists for date rape—and some of them are women—are really saying that the average man cannot be trusted to exercise any impulse control. Men are nasty and men are brutes—and a woman must be constantly on her guard to avoid giving a man any excuse to give way to his baser instincts.   4

If this view were accurate, few women would manage to get through life without being raped, and few men would fail to commit rape. For the reality is that all of us, men as well as women, send and receive innumerable mixed signals in the course of our sexual lives—and that is as true in marital beds at age fifty as in the back seats of cars at age fifteen.   5

Most men somehow manage to decode these signals without using superior physical strength to force themselves on their partners. And most women manage to handle conflicting male signals without, say, picking up carving knives to demonstrate their displeasure at sexual rejection. This is called civilization.   6

Civilized is exactly what my old boyfriend was being when he didn't use my muddleheaded emotional distress as an excuse to rape me. But I don't owe him excessive gratitude for his decent behavior—any more than he would have owed me special thanks for not stabbing him through the heart if our situations had been reversed. Most date rapes do not happen because a man honestly mistakes a woman's "no" for a "yes" or a "maybe." They occur because a minority of men—an ugly minority, to be sure—can't stand to take "no" for an answer.   7

This minority behavior—and a culture that excuses it on grounds that boys will be boys—is the target of the movement against date rape that has surfaced on many campuses during the past year.   8

It's not surprising that date rape is an issue of particular importance to college-age women. The campus concentration of large numbers of young people, in an unsupervised environment that encourages drinking and partying, tends to promote sexual aggression and discourage inhibition. Drunken young men who rape a woman at a party can always claim they didn't know what they were doing—and a great many people will blame the victim for having been there in the first place.   9

That is the line adopted by antifeminists like Camille Paglia,[2] author of the controversial *Sexual Personae: Art and Decadence From Nefertiti to Emily Dickinson*. Paglia, whose views strongly resemble those expounded twenty years ago by Norman Mailer[3] in *The Prisoner of Sex*, argues that feminists have   10

---

[2]For information on Camille Paglia, see page 395 (editors' note).
[3]An American essayist and novelist (editors' note).

deluded women by telling them they can go anywhere and do anything without fear of rape. Feminism, in this view, is both naïve and antisexual because it ignores the power of women to incite uncontrollable male passions.

Just to make sure there is no doubt about a woman's place, Paglia also   11
links the male sexual aggression that leads to rape with the creative energy of art. "There is no female Mozart," she has declared, "because there is no female Jack the Ripper." According to this "logic," one might expect to discover the next generation of composers in fraternity houses and dorms that have been singled out as sites of brutal gang rapes.

This type of unsubtle analysis makes no distinction between sex as an   12
expression of the will to power and sex as a source of pleasure. When domination is seen as an inevitable component of sex, the act of rape is defined not by a man's actions but by a woman's signals.

It is true, of course, that some women (especially the young) initially   13
resist sex not out of real conviction but as part of the elaborate persuasion and seduction rituals accompanying what was once called courtship. And it is true that many men (again, especially the young) take pride in the ability to coax a woman a step further than she intended to go.

But these mating rituals do not justify or even explain date rape. Even   14
the most callow youth is capable of understanding the difference between resistance and genuine fear; between a halfhearted "no, we shouldn't" and tears or screams; between a woman who is physically free to leave a room and one who is being physically restrained.

The immorality and absurdity of using mixed signals as an excuse for   15
rape is cast in high relief when the assault involves one woman and a group of men. In cases of gang rape in a social setting (usually during or after a party), the defendants and their lawyers frequently claim that group sex took place but no force was involved. These upright young men, so the defense invariably contends, were confused because the girl had voluntarily gone to a party with them. Why, she may have even displayed sexual interest in *one* of them. How could they have been expected to understand that she didn't wish to have sex with the whole group?

The very existence of the term "date rape" attests to a slow change in   16
women's consciousness that began with the feminist movement of the late 1960s. Implicit in this consciousness is the conviction that a woman has the right to say no at any point in the process leading to sexual intercourse—and that a man who fails to respect her wishes should incur serious legal and social consequences.

The other, equally important half of the equation is respect for men. If   17
mixed signals are the real cause of sexual assault, it behooves every woman to regard every man as a potential rapist.

In such a benighted universe, it would be impossible for a woman (and,   18
let us not forget, for a man) to engage in the tentative emotional and physical

exploration that eventually produces a mature erotic life. She would have to make up her mind right from the start in order to prevent a rampaging male from misreading her intentions.

Fortunately for everyone, neither the character of men nor the general   19 quality of relations between the sexes is that crude. By censuring the minority of men who use ordinary socializing as an excuse for rape, feminists insist on sex as a source of pure pleasure rather than as a means of social control. Real men want an eager sexual partner—not a woman who is quaking with fear or even one who is ambivalent. Real men don't rape.

Questions for Close Reading

1. What is the selection's thesis? Locate the sentence(s) in which Jacoby states her main idea. If she doesn't state the thesis explicitly, express it in your own words.
2. Why does Jacoby feel that she doesn't owe her old boyfriend a great deal of gratitude, even though she sent mixed signals about what type of relationship she wanted?
3. What does Jacoby mean in paragraph 6 by her comment, "This is called civilization"? How does this comment support her thesis?
4. Why does Jacoby think that it's insulting to men to accept Paglia's notion that men are ruled by uncontrollable passions?
5. Refer to your dictionary as needed to define the following words used in the selection: *apologists* (paragraph 4), *deluded* (10), *unsubtle* (12), *implicit* (16), *benighted* (18), *erotic* (18), *rampaging* (18), and *ambivalent* (19).

Questions About the Writer's Craft

1. **The pattern.** One way to refute an idea is to carry it to its logical extreme, thus revealing its inherent falsity or absurdity. This technique is called *reduction ad absurdum*. Examine paragraphs 4–5 and 15 and explain how Jacoby uses this technique to refute Paglia's position on date rape.
2. **Other patterns.** Locate places in the essay where Jacoby *compares* and *contrasts* male and female behavior or the behavior of rapists and nonrapists. How does her use of comparison-contrast help her build her argument?
3. What introduction technique (see pages 52–54) does Jacoby use to begin the essay? How does this type of introduction help her achieve her persuasive goal?
4. How would you characterize Jacoby's tone? Identify specific sentences and words that convey this tone. What effect might Jacoby have hoped this tone would have on readers?

Writing Assignments Using Argumentation-Persuasion as a Pattern of Development

∞ 1. Jacoby feels that Camille Paglia and others "excuse . . . rapists." If you haven't already done so, read "Rape: A Bigger Danger Than Feminists Know" (page 395) to see what Paglia says about who bears primary responsibility for preventing rape.

Then decide to what degree you feel men who commit date rape should be held accountable for their actions. Argue your position in an essay, making reference to both Jacoby's and Paglia's ideas to support your case. Also include reasons and evidence of your own.

2. Determine what your campus is doing about date rape. Does it have a formal policy defining date rape, a hearing process, ongoing workshops, discussions during orientation for incoming students? Write a paper explaining how your college deals with date rape. Then argue either that more attention should be devoted to this issue or that your college has adopted fair and comprehensive measures to deal with the problem. If you feel the college should do more, indicate what additional steps should be taken.

Writing Assignments Combining Patterns of Development

3. Jacoby acknowledges that males and females often send "mixed signals" and cause each other confusion. Select one time that you found "mixed signals" with a person of the opposite sex to be a problem. For example, you might have conflicted because of different ways of expressing anger or because of dissimilar styles in asking for support. In an essay of your own, *recount* what happened and explore the reason(s) why you think such mixed signals occurred.

4. Interview some people, both males and females, to determine their definition of date rape. In an essay, discuss any differences between the two sexes' perspectives. That done, present your own definition of date rape, explaining what it is and what it isn't.

Writing Assignment Using a Journal Entry as a Starting Point

5. Some people believe that "boys-will-be-boys" behavior is potentially dangerous and therefore not acceptable. Others argue that it is perfectly innocent and therefore permissible. What do you think? Drawing upon your pre-reading journal entry, write an essay taking a position on this issue. Provide persuasive examples to support your viewpoint, refuting as much of the opposing argument as you can. Discussing the topic with others and doing some research in the library and/or on the Internet will broaden your understanding of this complex issue.

Roger Wilkins

Pulitzer Prize–winning journalist Roger Wilkins (1932–) is the author of many works, including *A Man's Life: An Autobiography* (1982), *Quiet Riots: Race and Poverty in the U.S.* (1988), and *Jefferson's Pillow* (2001). A member of the editorial board at *The Nation* and publisher of the NAACP's journal, *Crisis,* Wilkins is professor of history at George Mason University in Virginia. Senior advisor to Jesse Jackson during Jackson's presidential campaigns, Wilkins also served as assistant attorney general under President Lyndon Johnson and as national coordinator of the visit that South African president Nelson Mandela made to the United States in 1988. The following essay was first published in *The Nation* in 1995.

Pre-Reading Journal Entry

Do you think schools should engage in discussions of racism, a sensitive and painful topic? Why do you feel as you do? Would such discussions be appropriate at some levels of schooling but not at others? Take some time to explore these questions in your journal.

Racism Has Its Privileges

The storm that has been gathering over affirmative action for the past few years has burst. Two conservative California professors are leading a drive to place an initiative on the state ballot in 1996 that will ask Californians to vote affirmative action up or down.[1] Since the state is beloved in political circles for its electoral votes, advance talk of the initiative has put the issue high on the national agenda. Three Republican presidential contenders—Bob Dole, Phil Gramm and Lamar Alexander—have already begun taking shots at various equal opportunity programs. Congressional review of the Clinton Administration's enforcement of these programs has begun. The President has started his own review, promising adherence to principles of nondiscrimination and full opportunity while asserting the need to prune those programs that are unfair or malfunctioning.

It is almost an article of political faith that one of the major influences in last November's election was the backlash against affirmative action among "angry white men," who are convinced it has stacked the deck against them. Their attitudes are shaped and their anger heightened by unquestioned and

---

[1]Approved by 54 percent of the voters in California, Proposition 209 took effect in August 1997, ending affirmative action efforts in the state (editors' note).

virtually uncheckable anecdotes about victimized whites flooding the culture. For example, *Washington Post* columnist Richard Cohen recently began what purported to be a serious analysis and attack on affirmative action by recounting that he had once missed out on a job someplace because they "needed a woman."

Well, I have an anecdote too, and it, together with Cohen's, offers some   3
important insights about the debate that has flared recently around the issues of race, gender and justice. Some years ago, after watching me teach as a visiting professor for two semesters, members of the history department at George Mason University invited me to compete for a full professorship and endowed chair. Mason, like other institutions in Virginia's higher education system, was under a court order to desegregate. I went through the appropriate application and review process and, in due course, was appointed. A few years later, not long after I had been honored as one of the university's distinguished professors, I was shown an article by a white historian asserting that he had been a candidate for that chair but that at the last moment the job had been whisked away and handed to an unqualified black. I checked the story and discovered that this fellow had, in fact, applied but had not even passed the first threshold. But his "reverse discrimination" story is out there polluting the atmosphere in which this debate is taking place.

Affirmative action, as I understand it, was not designed to punish anyone;   4
it was, rather—as a result of a clear-eyed look at how America actually works—an attempt to enlarge opportunity for *everybody*. As amply documented in the 1968 Kerner Commission report on racial disorders, when left to their own devices, American institutions in such areas as college admissions, hiring decisions and loan approvals had been making choices that discriminated against blacks. That discrimination, which flowed from doing what came naturally, hurt more than blacks: it hurt the entire nation, as the riots of the late 1960s demonstrated. Though the Kerner report focused on blacks, similar findings could have been made about other minorities and women.

Affirmative action required institutions to develop plans enabling them to   5
go beyond business as usual and search for qualified people in places where they did not ordinarily conduct their searches or their business. Affirmative action programs generally require some proof that there has been a good-faith effort to follow the plan and numerical guidelines against which to judge the sincerity and the success of the effort. The idea of affirmative action is *not* to force people into positions for which they are unqualified but to encourage institutions to develop realistic criteria for the enterprise at hand and then to find a reasonably diverse mix of people qualified to be engaged in it. Without the requirements calling for plans, good-faith efforts and the setting of broad numerical goals, many institutions would do what they had always done: assert that they had looked but "couldn't find anyone qualified," and then go out and hire the white man they wanted to hire in the first place.

Affirmative action has done wonderful things for the United States by   6
enlarging opportunity and developing and utilizing a far broader array of the
skills available in the American population than in the past. It has not out-
lived its usefulness. It was never designed to be a program to eliminate
poverty. It has not always been used wisely, and some of its permutations do
have to be reconsidered, refined or, in some cases, abandoned. It is not a
quota program, and those cases where rigid numbers are used (except under
a court or administrative order after a specific finding of discrimination) are
a bastardization of an otherwise highly beneficial set of public policies.

President Clinton is right to review what is being done under present   7
laws and to express a willingness to eliminate activities that either don't work
or are unfair. Any program that has been in place for thirty years should be
reviewed. Getting rid of what doesn't work is both good government and
good politics. Gross abuses of affirmative action provide ammunition for its
opponents and undercut the moral authority of the entire effort. But the
President should retain—and strengthen where required—those programs
necessary to enlarge social justice.

What makes the affirmative action issue so difficult is that it engages   8
blacks and whites exactly at those points where they differ the most. There
are some areas, such as rooting for the local football team, where their experiences and views are virtually identical. There are others—sometimes including work and school—where their experiences and views both overlap and
diverge. And finally, there are areas such as affirmative action and inextricably related notions about the presence of racism in society where the diver-
gences draw out almost all the points of difference between the races.

This Land Is My Land

Blacks and whites experience America very differently. Though we often   9
inhabit the same space, we operate in very disparate psychic spheres.

Whites have an easy sense of ownership of the country; they feel they   10
are entitled to receive all that is best in it. Many of them believe that their
country—though it may have some faults—is superior to all others and
that, as Americans, they are superior as well. Many of them think of this as
a white country and some of them even experience it that way. They think
of it as a land of opportunity—a good place with a lot of good people in
it. Some suspect (others *know*) that the presence of blacks messes everything up. . . .

For most blacks, America is either a land of denied opportunity or one   11
in which the opportunities are still grudgingly extended and extremely limited. For some—that one-third who are mired in poverty, many of them
isolated in dangerous ghettos—America is a land of desperadoes and desperation. In places where whites see a lot of idealism, blacks see, at best,
idealism mixed heavily with hypocrisy. Blacks accept America's greatness

but are unable to ignore ugly warts that many whites seem to need not to see. I am reminded here of James Baldwin's searing observation from *The Fire Next Time:*

> The American Negro has the great advantage of having never believed that collection of myths to which white Americans cling: that their ancestors were all freedom-loving heroes, that they were born in the greatest country the world has ever seen, or that Americans are invincible in battle and wise in peace, that Americans have always dealt honorably with Mexicans and Indians and all other neighbors or inferiors, that American men are the world's most direct and virile, that American women are pure.

It goes without saying, then, that blacks and whites remember America   12 differently. The past is hugely important since we argue a lot about who we are on the basis of who we think we have been, and we derive much of our sense of the future from how we think we've done in the past. In a nation in which few people know much history these are perilous arguments, because in such a vacuum, people tend to weave historical fables tailored to their political or psychic needs.

Blacks are still recovering the story of their role in America, which so   13 many white historians simply ignored or told in a way that made black people ashamed. But in a culture that batters us, learning the real history is vital in helping blacks feel fully human. It also helps us understand just how deeply American we are, how richly we have given, how much has been taken from us and how much has yet to be restored. Supporters of affirmative action believe that broad and deep damage has been done to American culture by racism and sexism over the whole course of American history and that they are still powerful forces today. We believe that minorities and women are still disadvantaged in our highly competitive society and that affirmative action is absolutely necessary to level the playing field. . . .

The Politics of Denial

The successful public relations assault on affirmative action flows on a   14 river of racism that is as broad, powerful and American as the Mississippi. And, like the Mississippi, racism can be violent and deadly and is a permanent feature of American life. But while nobody who is sane denies the reality of the Mississippi, millions of Americans who are deemed sane—some of whom are powerful and some even thought wise—deny, wholly or in part, that racism exists.

It is critical to understand the workings of denial in this debate because   15 it is used to obliterate the facts that created the need for the remedy in the first place. One of the best examples of denial was provided recently by the nation's most famous former history professor, House Speaker Newt Gingrich. According to *The Washington Post,* "Gingrich dismissed the argument that the beneficiaries of affirmative action, commonly African Americans, have been subjected to discrimination over a period of centuries. 'That is true of virtually every American,' Gingrich said, noting that the Irish were discriminated against by the English, for example."

That is breathtaking stuff coming from somebody who should know   16
that blacks have been on this North American continent for 375 years and that for 245 the country permitted slavery. Gingrich should also know that for the next hundred years we had legalized subordination of blacks, under a suffocating blanket of condescension and frequently enforced by night-riding terrorists. We've had only thirty years of something else.

That something else is a nation trying to lift its ideals out of a thick,   17
often impenetrable slough of racism. Racism is a hard word for what over the centuries became second nature in America—preferences across the board for white men and, following in their wake, white women. Many of these men seem to feel that it is un-American to ask them to share anything with blacks—particularly their work, their neighborhoods or "their" women. To protect these things—apparently essential to their identity—they engage in all forms of denial. For a historian to assert that "virtually every American" shares the history I have just outlined comes very close to lying.

Denial of racism is much like the denials that accompany addictions to   18
alcohol, drugs or gambling. It is probably not stretching the analogy too much to suggest that many racist whites are so addicted to their unwarranted privileges and so threatened by the prospect of losing them that all kinds of defenses become acceptable. . . .

"Those People" Don't Deserve Help

Before the 1950s, whites who were busy denying that the nation was   19
unfair to blacks would simply assert that we didn't deserve equal treatment because we were *inferior.* These days it is not permissible in most public circles to say that blacks are inferior, but it is perfectly acceptable to target the *behavior* of blacks, specifically poor blacks. . . .

While I don't hold the view that all blacks who behave badly are blame-   20
less victims of a brutal system, I do believe that many poor blacks have, indeed, been brutalized by our culture, and I know of *no* blacks, rich or poor, who haven't been hurt in some measure by the racism in this country. The current mood (and, in some cases like the Speaker's, the cultivated ignorance) completely ignores the fact that some blacks never escaped the straight line of oppression that ran from slavery through the semislavery of sharecropping to the late mid-century migration from Southern farms into isolated pockets of urban poverty. Their families have always been excluded, poor and without

skills, and so they were utterly defenseless when the enormous American economic dislocations that began in the mid-1970s slammed into their communities, followed closely by deadly waves of crack cocaine. One would think that the double-digit unemployment suffered consistently over the past two decades by blacks who were *looking for work* would be a permanent feature of the discussions about race, responsibility, welfare and rights.

But people's attention is kept trained on the behavior of some poor blacks   21
by politicians and television news shows, reinforcing the stereotypes of blacks as dangerous, as threats, as unqualified. Frightened whites direct their rage at pushy blacks rather than at the corporations that export manufacturing operations to low-wage countries, or at the Federal Reserve, which imposes interest rate hikes that slow down the economy.

Who Benefits? We All Do

There is one final denial that blankets all the rest. It is that only society's   22
"victims"—blacks, other minorities and women (who should, for God's sake, renounce their victimological outlooks)—have been injured by white male supremacy. Viewed in this light, affirmative action remedies are a kind of zero-sum game in which only the "victims" benefit. But racist and sexist whites who are not able to accept the full humanity of other people are themselves badly damaged—morally stunted—people. The principal product of a racist and sexist society is damaged people and institutions—victims and victimizers alike. Journalism and education, two enterprises with which I am familiar, provide two good examples.

Journalistic institutions often view the nation through a lens that bends   23
reality to support white privileges. A recent issue of *U.S. News & World Report* introduced a package of articles on these issues with a question on its cover: "Does affirmative action mean NO WHITE MEN NEED APPLY?" The words "No white men need apply" were printed in red against a white background and were at least four times larger than the other words in the question. Inside, the lead story was illustrated by a painting that carries out the cover theme, with a wan white man separated from the opportunity ladders eagerly being scaled by women and dark men. And the story yielded up the following sentence: "Affirmative action poses a conflict between two cherished American principles: the belief that all Americans deserve equal opportunities and the idea that hard work and merit, not race or religion or gender or birthright, should determine who prospers and who does not."

Whoever wrote that sentence was in the thrall of one of the myths that   24
Baldwin was talking about. The sentence suggests—as many people do when talking about affirmative action—that America is a meritocratic society. But what kind of meritocracy excludes women and blacks and other minorities from all meaningful competition? And even in the competition among white

men, money, family and connections often count for much more than merit, test results (for whatever they're worth) and hard work.

The *U.S. News* story perpetuates and strengthens the view that many of   25
my white students absorb from their parents: that white men now have few chances in this society. The fact is that white men still control virtually everything in America except the wealth held by widows. According to the Urban Institute, 53 percent of black men aged 25–34 are either unemployed or earn too little to lift a family of four from poverty.

Educational institutions that don't teach accurately about why America   26
looks the way it does and why the distribution of winners and losers is as it is also injure our society. Here is another anecdote.

A warm, brilliant young white male student of mine came in just before   27
he was to graduate and said that my course in race, law and culture, which he had just finished, had been the most valuable and the most disturbing he had ever taken. I asked how it had been disturbing.

"I learned that my two heroes are racists," he said.   28

"Who are your heroes and how are they racists?" I asked.   29

"My mom and dad," he said. "After thinking about what I was learning,   30
I understand that they had spent all my life making me into the same kind of racists they were."

Affirmative action had brought me together with him when he was 22.   31
Affirmative action puts people together in ways that make that kind of revelation possible. Nobody is a loser when that happens. The country gains.

And that, in the end, is the case for affirmative action. The arguments   32
supporting it should be made on the basis of its broad contributions to the entire American community. It is insufficient to vilify white males and to skewer them as the whiners that journalism of the kind practiced by *U.S. News* invites us to do. These are people who, from the beginning of the Republic, have been taught that skin color is destiny and that whiteness is to be revered. Listen to Jefferson, writing in the year the Constitution was drafted:

> The first difference that strikes us is that of colour. . . . And is the difference of no importance? Is it not the foundation of a greater or less share of beauty in the two races? Are not the fine mixtures of red and white . . . in the one, preferable to that eternal monotony, which reigns in the countenances, that immoveable veil of black which covers all the emotions of the other race? Add to these, flowing hair, a more elegant symmetry of form, their own judgment in favor of the whites, declared by their preference for them, as uniformly as is the preference of the Oran-ootan for the black women over those of his own species. The circumstance of superior beauty, is thought worthy attention in the propagation of our horses, dogs, and other domestic animals; why not in that of man?

In a society so conceived and so dedicated, it is understandable that white males would take their preferences as a matter of natural right and consider any alteration of that a primal offense. But a nation that operates in that way abandons its soul and its economic strength, and will remain mired in ugliness and moral squalor because so many people are excluded from the possibility of decent lives and from forming any sense of community with the rest of society. . . .

It may be that we will need affirmative action until most white males are 33 really ready for a color-blind society—that is, when they are ready to assume "the rank of a mere citizen." As a nation we took a hard look at that special favoritism thirty years ago. Though the centuries of cultural preference enjoyed by white males still overwhelmingly skew power and wealth their way, we have in fact achieved a more meritocratic society as a result of affirmative action than we have ever previously enjoyed in this country.

If we want to continue making things better in this society, we'd better 34 figure out ways to protect and defend affirmative action against the confused, the frightened, the manipulators and, yes, the liars in politics, journalism, education and wherever else they may be found. In the name of longstanding American prejudice and myths and in the service of their own narrow interests, power-lusts or blindness, they are truly victimizing the rest of us, perverting the ideals they claim to stand for and destroying the nation they pretend to serve.

Questions for Close Reading

1. What is the selection's thesis? Locate the sentences in which Wilkins states his main idea. If he doesn't state the thesis explicitly, express it in your own words.
2. How does Wilkins define *affirmative action?* What must an affirmative-action program include in order to be successful?
3. According to Wilkins, what "myths" do White people believe? How have these myths prevented White people from seeing the need for affirmative action?
4. How, in Wilkins's opinion, does affirmative action benefit *all* Americans?
5. Refer to your dictionary as needed to define the following words used in the selection: *initiative* (paragraph 1), *adherence* (1), *purported* (2), *permutations* (6), *bastardization* (6), *inextricably* (8), *disparate* (9), *invincible* (11), *obliterate* (15), *meritocratic* (24), *perpetuates* (25), *vilify* (32), and *skew* (33).

Questions About the Writer's Craft

1. **The pattern.** Where in his argument does Wilkins acknowledge conflicting viewpoints? What is his attitude toward these opposing views? How does this attitude help Wilkins reinforce his thesis?
2. **Other patterns.** Why do you suppose Wilkins places the *anecdote* about his being hired at George Mason University (paragraph 3) near the beginning of his essay? How does this anecdote add to the effectiveness of his argument?

3. **Other patterns.** Locate places in the essay where Wilkins uses *comparison-contrast*. How do these comparisons and contrasts help Wilkins develop his central argument?

4. Sometimes Wilkins uses provocative language, as when he refers to the beliefs of those opposed to affirmative action as "myths." What other emotionally loaded words does he use? What assumptions about his audience might have motivated Wilkins to employ this charged language?

Writing Assignments Using Argumentation-Persuasion as a Pattern of Development

∞ 1. Wilkins argues that "affirmative action is absolutely necessary to level the playing field" for minorities in this country. Do you agree? Focusing on a specific minority group, write an essay in which you support or challenge Wilkins's argument. To ensure that your position is more than a reflexive opinion, conduct some library research on the group in question, and read Shelby Steele's "Affirmative Action: The Price of Preference" (page 416), an essay that is in sharp opposition to Wilkins's. No matter which side you take, assume that some readers are opposed to your point of view. Acknowledge and try to dismantle as many of their objections as possible. Refer, whenever it's relevant, to Steele's argument in your paper.

∞ 2. Wilkins suggests that it is appropriate for schools to celebrate the admirable and heroic aspects of our history. But, he believes, schools must also be willing to acknowledge the "ugly warts" in that history. Do you agree? Write an essay arguing that schools should *or* should not teach students about the non-heroic aspects of our national story. Your essay should acknowledge and refute as many opposing arguments as possible. To broaden your understanding of the issue, interview classmates, family members, friends, and instructors. Also read "And Then I Went to School" (page 271) by Joseph H. Suina and "Let's Tell the Story of All America's Cultures" (page 385) by Yuh Ji-Yeon.

Writing Assignments Combining Patterns of Development

∞ 3. Wilkins believes that people who consider themselves victims should "renounce their victimological outlooks." Select a group that you believe perceives itself as being victimized. Possibilities include a specific racial, ethnic, or religious group; the disabled; the overweight; those in abusive relationships. Write an essay explaining the *steps* these individuals could take to overthrow their victimhood. End the paper by discussing the *effects* of abandoning a victimological perspective. What would be gained? What might be lost? Before writing, read one or more of the following essays to sharpen your understanding of the concept of victimhood: Maya Angelou's "Sister Flowers" (page 96), William Raspberry's "The Handicap of Definition" (page 345), and Camille Paglia's "Rape: A Bigger Danger Than Feminists Know" (page 395).

4. One student told Wilkins that the course Wilkins taught was "the most valuable . . . he had ever taken." Write an essay showing how a course or school experience *caused* you, like Wilkins's student, to realize something important about yourself,

society, or life in general. Develop your essay by *contrasting* what you were like before with what you were like after the educational experience.

Writing Assignment Using a Journal
Entry as a Starting Point

∞ 5. Write an essay arguing that schools should *or* should not encourage students to discuss the issue of racism. Review your pre-reading journal entry, and select a specific level of schooling to focus on before taking a position. Supplement the material in your journal by gathering the opinions, experiences, and observations of friends, family, and classmates. No matter which position you take, remember to cite opposing arguments, refuting as many of them as you can. Before writing, consider reading "Let's Tell the Story of All America's Cultures" (page 385), in which Yuh Ji-Yeon forcefully argues the need for honest discussion of race and ethnicity in the classroom.

Shelby Steele

Currently a professor of English at San Jose State University, Shelby Steele (1946–) was born in Chicago and earned his doctoral degree at the University of Utah. The recipient of a National Magazine Award in 1989, Steele has published widely. His writing on racial issues has appeared in publications including *Harper's,* the *New York Times,* the *Washington Post,* and *American Scholar.* One of his pieces on race was selected for *The Best American Essays 1989,* and a number of his most compelling essays were published in *The Content of Our Character: A New Vision of Race in America* (1990). Most recently, he wrote *A Dream Deferred: The Second Betrayal of Black Freedom in America* (1998). The following essay, which originally appeared in the *New York Times Magazine* (1990), is reprinted from *The Content of Our Character.*

Pre-Reading Journal Entry

What do you think would happen if college affirmative-action admission policies were ruled illegal and were subsequently outlawed? What positive effects might there be? What negative effects? Take some time to respond to these questions in your journal.

Affirmative Action:
The Price of Preference

In a few short years, when my two children will be applying to college, 1
the affirmative-action policies by which most universities offer black students
some form of preferential treatment will present me with a dilemma. I am
a middle-class black, a college professor, far from wealthy, but also well
removed from the kind of deprivation that would qualify my children for the
label "disadvantaged." Both of them have endured racial insensitivity from
whites. They have been called names, have suffered slights and have experienced first hand the peculiar malevolence that racism brings out of people.
Yet they have never experienced racial discrimination, have never been
stopped by their race on any path they have chosen to follow. Still, their society now tells them that if they will only designate themselves as black on their
college applications, they will probably do better in the college lottery than if
they conceal this fact. I think there is something of a Faustian[1] bargain in this.

Of course many blacks and a considerable number of whites would say 2
that I was sanctimoniously making affirmative action into a test of character.

---

[1]A reference to the legend of Faust, a scholar who sold his soul to the devil in return for unlim-
ited power. Faust later regretted the bargain (editors' note).

They would say that this small preference is the meagerest recompense for centuries of unrelieved oppression. And to these arguments other very obvious facts must be added. In America, many marginally competent or flatly incompetent whites are hired every day—some because their white skin suits the conscious or unconscious racial preference of their employers. The white children of alumni are often grandfathered[2] into elite universities in what can only be seen as a residual benefit of historic white privilege. Worse, white incompetence is always an individual matter, but for blacks it is often confirmation of ugly stereotypes. Given that unfairness cuts both ways, doesn't it only balance the scales of history, doesn't this repay, in a small way, the systematic denial under which my children's grandfather lived out his days?

In theory, affirmative action certainly has all the moral symmetry that fairness requires. It is reformist and corrective, even repentant and redemptive. And I would never sneer at these good intentions. Born in the late 1940s in Chicago, I started my education (a charitable term, in this case) in a segregated school, and suffered all the indignities that come to blacks in a segregated society. My father, born in the South, made it only to the third grade before the white man's fields took permanent priority over his formal education. And though he educated himself into an advanced reader with an almost professorial authority, he could only drive a truck for a living, and never earned more than $90 a week in his entire life. So yes, it is crucial to my sense of citizenship, to my ability to identify with the spirit and the interests of America, to know that this country, however imperfectly, recognizes its past sins and wishes to correct them. 3

Yet good intentions can blind us to the effects they generate when implemented. In our society affirmative action is, among other things, a testament to white good will and to black power, and in the midst of these heavy investments its effects can be hard to see. But after 20 years of implementation I think that affirmative action has shown itself to be more bad than good and that blacks—whom I will focus on in this essay—now stand to lose more from it than they gain. 4

In talking with affirmative-action administrators and with blacks and whites in general, I found that supporters of affirmative action focus on its good intentions and detractors emphasize its negative effects. It was virtually impossible to find people outside either camp. The closest I came was a white male manager at a large computer company who said, "I think it amounts to reverse discrimination, but I'll put up with a little of that for a little more diversity." But this only makes him a half-hearted supporter of affirmative action. I think many people who don't really like affirmative action support it to one degree or another anyway. 5

[2]Permitted to enter on the basis of longtime association with an institution without having to satisfy existing entrance requirements (editors' note).

I believe they do this because of what happened to white and black   6
Americans in the crucible of the 1960s,[3] when whites were confronted with
their racial guilt and blacks tasted their first real power. In that stormy time
white absolution and black power coalesced into virtual mandates for society. Affirmative action became a meeting ground for those mandates in the
law. At first, this meant insuring equal opportunity. The 1964 civil-rights bill
was passed on the understanding that equal opportunity would not mean
racial preference. But in the late 60's and early 70's, affirmative action underwent a remarkable escalation of its mission from simple anti-discrimination
enforcement to social engineering by means of quotas, goals, timetables, set-
asides and other forms of preferential treatment.

Legally, this was achieved through a series of executive orders and Equal   7
Employment Opportunity Commission guidelines that allowed racial imbalances in the workplace to stand as proof of racial discrimination. Once it
could be assumed that discrimination explained racial imbalances, it became
easy to justify group remedies to presumed discrimination rather than the
normal case-by-case redress.

Even though blacks had made great advances during the 60's without   8
quotas, the white mandate to achieve a new racial innocence and the black
mandate to gain power, which came to a head in the very late 60's, could no
longer be satisfied by anything less than racial preferences. I don't think
these mandates, in themselves, were wrong, because whites clearly needed to
do better by blacks and blacks needed more real power in society. But as they
came together in affirmative action, their effect was to distort our understanding of racial discrimination. By making black the color of preference,
these mandates have reburdened society with the very marriage of color and
preference (in reverse) that we set out to eradicate. . . .

I think one of the most troubling effects of racial preferences for blacks   9
is a kind of demoralization. Under affirmative action, the quality that earns
us preferential treatment is an implied inferiority. However this inferiority is
explained—and it is easily enough explained by the myriad deprivations that
grew out of our oppression—it is still inferiority. There are explanations and
then there is the fact. And the fact must be borne by the individual as a condition apart from the explanation, apart even from the fact that others like
himself also bear this condition. In integrated situations in which blacks must
compete with whites who may be better prepared, these explanations may
quickly wear thin and expose the individual to racial as well as personal self-
doubt. (Of course whites also feel doubt, but only personally, not racially.)

What this means in practical terms is that when blacks deliver themselves   10
into integrated situations they encounter a nasty little reflex in whites, a

---

[3]A decade characterized by both nonviolent and violent civil rights protests that forced mainstream America finally to acknowledge the injustices endured by Black Americans (editors' note).

mindless, atavistic reflex that responds to the color black with negative stereotypes, such as intellectual ineptness. I think this reflex embarrasses most whites today and thus it is usually quickly repressed. On an equally atavistic level, the black will be aware of the reflex his color triggers and will feel a stab of horror at seeing himself reflected in this way. He, too, will do a quick repression, but a lifetime of such stabbings is what constitutes his inner realm of racial doubt. Even when the black sees no implication of inferiority in racial preferences, he knows that whites do, so that—consciously or unconsciously—the result is virtually the same. The effect of preferential treatment—the lowering of normal standards to increase black representation—puts blacks at war with an expanded realm of debilitating doubt, so that the doubt itself becomes an unrecognized preoccupation that undermines their ability to perform, especially in integrated situations.

I believe another liability of affirmative action comes from the fact that it indirectly encourages blacks to exploit their own past victimization. Like implied inferiority, victimization is what justifies preference, so that to receive the benefits of preferential treatment one must, to some extent, become invested in the view of one's self as a victim. In this way, affirmative action nurtures a victim-focused identity in blacks and sends us the message that there is more power in our past suffering than in our present achievements. 11

When power itself grows out of suffering, blacks are encouraged to expand the boundaries of what qualifies as racial oppression, a situation that can lead us to paint our victimization in vivid colors even as we receive the benefits of preference. The same corporations and institutions that give us preference are also seen as our oppressors. At Stanford University, minority-group students—who receive at least the same financial aid as whites with the same need—recently took over the president's office demanding, among other things, more financial aid. 12

But I think one of the worst prices that blacks pay for preference has to do with an illusion. I saw this illusion at work recently in the mother of a middle-class black student who was going off to his first semester of college: "They owe us this, so don't think for a minute that you don't belong there." This is the logic by which many blacks, and some whites, justify affirmative action—it is something "owed," a form of reparation. But this logic overlooks a much harder and less digestible reality, that it is impossible to repay blacks living today for the historic suffering of the race. If all blacks were given a million dollars tomorrow it would not amount to a dime on the dollar for three centuries of oppression, nor would it dissolve the residues of that oppression that we still carry today. The concept of historic reparation grows out of man's need to impose on the world a degree of justice that simply does not exist. Suffering can be endured and overcome, it cannot be repaid. To think otherwise is to prolong the suffering. . . . 13

But if not preferences, what? The impulse to discriminate is subtle and   14
cannot be ferreted out unless its many guises are made clear to people. I
think we need social policies that are committed to two goals: the educational and economic development of disadvantaged people regardless of race
and the eradication from our society—through close monitoring and severe
sanctions—of racial, ethnic or gender discrimination. Preferences will not get
us to either of these goals, because they tend to benefit those who are not
disadvantaged—middle-class white women and middle-class blacks—and
attack one form of discrimination with another. Preferences are inexpensive
and carry the glamour of good intentions—change the numbers and the
good deed is done. To be against them is to be unkind. But I think the
unkindest cut is to bestow on children like my own an undeserved advantage
while neglecting the development of those disadvantaged children in the
poorer sections of my city who will most likely never be in a position to benefit from a preference. Give my children fairness; give disadvantaged children
a better shot at development—better elementary and secondary schools, job
training, safer neighborhoods, better financial assistance for college and so
on. A smaller percentage of black high school graduates go to college today
than 15 years ago; more black males are in prison, jail or in some other way
under the control of the criminal-justice system than in college. This despite
racial preferences.

The mandates of black power and white absolution out of which prefer-   15
ences emerged were not wrong in themselves. What was wrong was that both
races focused more on the goals of those mandates than on the means to the
goals. Blacks can have no real power without taking responsibility for their own
educational and economic development. Whites can have no racial innocence
without earning it by eradicating discrimination and helping the disadvantaged to develop. Because we ignored the means, the goals have not been
reached and the real work remains to be done.

Questions for Close Reading

1. What is the selection's thesis? Locate the sentence(s) in which Steele states his
   main idea. If he doesn't state the thesis explicitly, express it in your own words.
2. Why doesn't Steele want his children to designate themselves as Black on their college applications? Why does he call such labeling "a Faustian bargain"?
3. Why does Steele believe that affirmative action "demoralizes" Blacks?
4. What does Steele suggest as an alternative to affirmative action in hiring and in
   education?
5. Refer to your dictionary as needed to define the following words used in the selection: *malevolence* (paragraph 1), *sanctimoniously* (2), *meagerest* (2), *recompense* (2),
   residual (2), *symmetry* (3), *diversity* (5), *absolution* (6), *mandates* (6), *eradicate*
   (8), *demoralization* (9), *myriad* (9), *ineptness* (10), *debilitating* (10), *reparation*
   (13), and *residues* (13).

Questions About the Writer's Craft

1. **The pattern.** Which of the two possible strategies for organizing a refutation (see pages 363–364) does Steele use in his essay? Do you consider the points he makes in the refutation sufficiently persuasive? Explain.
2. **Other patterns.** Why do you suppose Steele begins with the *example* of his own children? How does this example prepare readers for his argument?
3. Steele often uses "I think" or "I believe" when making his points. (One example is at the end of the first paragraph.) Find additional instances elsewhere in the essay. Why do you think he uses these expressions so frequently?
4. In paragraph 9, which two key words does Steele repeat? Why might he have used this repetition?

Writing Assignments Using Argumentation-Persuasion as a Pattern of Development

∞ 1. To support his argument that affirmative action has negative effects, Steele makes a number of key points, including the following:

- Preferential treatment implies an inherent inferiority and thus leads to corrosive self-doubt.
- Preferential treatment fosters a feeling of victimhood that strips people of the ability to take strong action on their own behalf.
- Preferential treatment creates a dangerous illusion of entitlement that ultimately works to the detriment of those who feel they are owed something.

Focusing on a specific minority group, write an essay defending or challenging *one* of these points (or any other that Steele makes). Remember to acknowledge and, when possible, to refute opposing opinions. Before formulating your position, read William Raspberry's "The Handicap of Definition" (page 345) and Roger Wilkins's "Racism Has Its Privileges" (page 406). Raspberry provides additional evidence for Steele's viewpoint, while Wilkins presents a sharply divergent point of view. Where appropriate, refer to Raspberry and/or Wilkins in your paper.

∞ 2. Choose another social program or common practice with which you are familiar, and write an essay arguing—as Steele does—that it has had an effect very different from that which was intended. Like Steele, include specific examples of the program's ill effects, making sure to acknowledge the views of those who support the program. For additional insight into the way practices can have unintended negative consequences, read Clifford Stoll's "Cyberschool" (page 239), Jay Walljasper's "Our Schedules, Our Selves" (page 311), and James Barszcz's "Can You Be Educated From a Distance?" (page 390).

Writing Assignments Combining Patterns of Development

3. Imagine what your life might be like if you were a member of another race, religion, or ethnic group. Or consider what life might be like if you were the

opposite sex. Then write an essay in which you provide *examples* showing how your life would *or* would *not* change if you did indeed have another identity. Reach some conclusions about the overall *effect* of having this new identity, including whether life would be easier or more difficult.

∞ **4.** Steele states that "Blacks can have no real power without taking responsibility for their own . . . development." The same could be said for all people. Write an essay *recounting* a time that you took charge of your life at a difficult point. Perhaps you rallied your strength to end a painful relationship or insisted on furthering your education even though others believed additional schooling was unnecessary. Provide vivid narrative details to show how hard you worked to take responsibility for your life. End by explaining how this concerted effort on your own behalf *affected* you and those who are important to you. Maya Angelou's "Sister Flowers" (page 96), Adam Mayblum's "The Price We Pay" (page 128), and William Raspberry's "The Handicap of Definition" (page 345) should spark ideas worth exploring.

Writing Assignment Using a Journal Entry as a Starting Point

5. In June 2003, the Supreme Court (in *Gratz v. Bollinger*) ruled that the University of Michigan's procedure of granting admissions "points" based on minority students' race was unconstitutional. While this ruling did not altogether ban affirmative action, it did undermine the practice, forcing universities to place less emphasis on race considerations in admissions. Considering these recent developments, write an essay exploring the positive and negative consequences that might ensue if colleges nationwide were required to dismantle their affirmative-action admission programs. To develop your discussion, draw upon the material in your pre-reading journal entry as well as the opinions of friends, classmates, and family members. Consider supplementing your informal research with material gathered in the library and/or on the Internet about the University of Michigan case and other pertinent data and evidence. At the end of your essay, indicate whether you think disbanding affirmative-action admission policies would be a good idea or a bad one.

Additional Writing Topics

ARGUMENTATION-PERSUASION

General Assignments

Using argumentation-persuasion, develop one of the topics below in an essay. After choosing a topic, think about your purpose and audience. Remember that the paper's thesis should state the issue under discussion as well as your position on the issue. As you work on developing evidence, you might want to do some outside research. Keep in mind that effective argumentation-persuasion usually means that some time should be spent acknowledging and perhaps refuting opposing points of view. Be careful not to sabotage your argument by basing your case on a logical fallacy.

1. Euthanasia
2. Hiring or college-admissions quotas
3. Giving birth-control devices to teenagers
4. Prayer in the schools
5. Living off campus
6. The drinking age
7. Spouses sharing housework equally
8. Smoking in public places
9. Big-time sports in college
10. Pornography on the Internet
11. Single parents with young children
12. Acid rain
13. Drugs on campus
14. Political campaigns
15. Requiring college students to pass a comprehensive exam in their majors before graduating
16. Reinstating the military draft
17. Putting elderly parents in nursing homes
18. An optional pass-fail system for courses
19. The homeless
20. Nonconformity in a neighborhood: allowing a lawn to go wild, keeping many pets, painting a house an odd color, or some other atypical behavior

Assignments With a Specific Purpose, Audience, and Point of View

On Campus

1. Your college's Financial Aid Department has decided not to renew your scholarship for next year, citing a drop in your grades last semester and an unenthusiastic recommendation from one of your instructors. Write a letter to the director of financial aid arguing for the renewal of your scholarship.

2. You strongly believe that a particular policy or regulation on campus is unreasonable or unjust. Write a letter to the dean of students (or other appropriate administrator) arguing that the policy needs to be, if not completely revoked, amended in some way. Support your contention with specific examples showing how the regulation has gone wrong. End by providing constructive suggestions for how the policy problem can be solved.

At Home or in the Community

3. You and one or more family members don't agree on some aspect of your romantic life (you want to live with your boyfriend/girlfriend and they don't approve; you want to get married and they want you to wait; they simply don't like your partner). Write a letter explaining why your preference is reasonable. Try hard to win your family member(s) over to your side.

4. Assume you're a member of a racial, ethnic, religious, or social minority. You might, for example, be a Native American, an elderly person, a female executive. On a recent television show or in a TV commercial, you saw something that depicts your group in an offensive way. Write a letter (to the network or the advertiser) expressing your feelings and explaining why you feel the material should be taken off the air.

On the Job

5. As a staff writer for an online pop-culture magazine, you've been asked to nominate the "Most Memorable TV Moment of the Last 50 Years" to be featured as the magazine's lead article. Write a letter to your supervising editor in support of your nominee.

6. As a high school teacher, you support some additional restriction on students. The restriction might be "no radios in school," "no T-shirts," "no food in class," "no smoking on school grounds." Write an article for the school newspaper, justifying this new rule to the student body.

12
COMBINING THE PATTERNS

Throughout this book, you've studied the patterns of development—narration, process analysis, definition, and so on—in depth. You've seen how the patterns are used as strategies for generating, developing, and organizing ideas for essays. You've also learned that, in practice, most types of writing combine two or more patterns. The two sections that follow provide additional information about these important points. The rest of the chapter then gives you an opportunity to look more closely at the way several writers use the patterns of development in their work.

THE PATTERNS IN ACTION: DURING THE WRITING PROCESS

The patterns of development come into play throughout the composing process. In the prewriting stage, awareness of the patterns encourages you to think about your subject in fresh, new ways. Assume, for example, that you've been asked to write an essay about the way children are disciplined in school. However, you draw a blank as soon as you try to limit this general subject. To break the logjam, you could apply one or more patterns of development to your subject. *Comparison-contrast* might prompt you to write an essay investigating the differences between your parents' and your own feelings about school discipline. *Division-classification* might lead you to another paper—one that categorizes the kinds of discipline used in school. And *cause-effect* might point to still another essay—one that explores the way students react to being suspended.

Further along in the writing process—after you've identified your limited subject and your thesis—the patterns of development can help you generate your paper's evidence. Imagine that your thesis is "Teachers shouldn't discipline students publicly just to make an example of them." You're not sure, though, how to develop this thesis. Calling upon the patterns might spark some promising possibilities. *Narration* might encourage you to recount the disastrous time you were singled out and punished for the misdeeds of an entire class. Using *definition,* you might explain what is meant by an *autocratic* disciplinary style. *Argumentation-persuasion* might prompt you to advocate a new plan for disciplining students fairly and effectively.

The patterns of development also help you organize your ideas by pointing the way to an appropriate framework for a paper. Suppose you plan to write an essay for the campus newspaper about the disturbingly high incidence of shoplifting among college students; your purpose is to persuade young people not to get involved in this tempting, supposedly victimless crime. You believe that many readers will be deterred from shoplifting if you tell them about the harrowing *process* set in motion once a shoplifter is detected. With this step-by-step explanation in mind, you can now map out the essay's content: what happens when a shoplifter is detained by a salesperson, questioned by store security personnel, led to a police car, booked at the police station, and tried in a courtroom.

THE PATTERNS IN ACTION:
IN AN ESSAY

Although this book devotes a separate chapter to each of the nine patterns of development, all chapters emphasize the same important point: Most writing consists of several patterns, with the dominant pattern providing the piece's organizational framework. To reinforce this point, each chapter contains a section, "How [the Pattern] Fits Your Purpose and Audience," that shows how a writer's purpose often leads to a blending of patterns. Also, the commentary following each student essay talks about the way the paper mixes patterns. Similarly, at least one of the "Questions About the Writer's Craft" following each professional selection asks you to analyze the piece's combination of patterns. Further, the "Writing Assignments Combining Patterns of Development" encourage you to experiment with mixing patterns in your own writing. In short, all through *The Longman Reader: Brief Edition* we emphasize that the patterns of development are far from being mechanical formulas. On the contrary: They are practical strategies that open up options in every stage of the composing process.

Now you'll have a chance to focus on the way student and professional writers combine patterns in their essays. In the pages ahead, you'll find one student essay and three professional selections, one by each of the following writers: Virginia Woolf; Martin Luther King, Jr.; and Joan Didion. As you read the student and professional essays, ask yourself these questions:

1. What are the writer's *purpose* and *thesis?*
2. What *pattern of development dominates* the essay? How does this pattern help the writer support the essay's thesis and fulfill the essay's purpose?

3. What *other patterns appear* in the essay? How do these secondary patterns help the writer support the essay's thesis and fulfill the essay's purpose?

Your responses to these three questions will reward you with a richer understanding of the way writers work. To give you an even clearer sense of how writers mix patterns, we have annotated the student essay (Tasha Walker's "The Super-Sizing of America's Kids" below) and the first professional essay (Virginia Woolf's "The Death of the Moth" on page 433). The preceding three questions served as our guide when we prepared the annotations. By making your own annotations on these essays and then comparing them to ours, you can measure your ability to analyze writers' use of the patterns. You can further evaluate your analysis of the pieces by answering the three questions on your own and then comparing your responses to ours on pages 431–432 and 436–437.

STUDENT ESSAY

The following student essay was written by Tasha Walker in response to this assignment:

> In the essay "Tweens: Ten Going on Sixteen," Kay S. Hymowitz explores an alarming trend among children: the tendency of preteens to act much older than they are. Write an essay analyzing the causes and effects of another significant problem among young people today. Conclude your essay by offering possible solutions for the problem you've examined.

The annotations on the essay will help you look at the way Tasha uses various patterns of development to achieve her purpose and develop her thesis.

The Super-Sizing of America's Kids
by Tasha Walker

Introduction has *narrative* and *descriptive* elements Examples of foods *contrast* with *examples* later in ¶ *Contrast* between average breakfast in the 1950s and today	Picture this scene from the 1950s. A couple of kids wake up, get dressed, and sit down for breakfast before leaving for school. They're greeted by an array of healthy choices: a glass of orange juice, a bowl of cornflakes or oatmeal with a healthy serving of milk, perhaps a plateful of scrambled eggs and toast. Now fast-forward a few decades to the present. The situation is very different. If kids sit down for breakfast at all, they gulp down a bowl of rainbow-colored sugary bits with a dollop of milk. Or, racing out the door, they grab a syrupy jumbo cinnamon bun or a glazed, fudge-filled toaster tart.

1

Exemplification in the form of facts and statistics ——

Causal analysis (main pattern) begins with *effects* of problem

Statement of purpose/thesis: ⌐ Need to end increasing childhood obesity; emotional language urging action reinforces essay's *persuasive* ⌐ intent

Causal analysis shifts to several *causes* of problem⌐

Transition signals first *cause* of problem ——

Transition signals second *cause* of problem——

Transition signals most important *cause* of problem ——

What's the harm, you might ask, in giving kids tasty, convenient food options? After all, kids burn so much energy; they shouldn't have to worry about their diet until they're adults. Right? Wrong, says the latest information on obesity in the United States. According to several recent studies cited by the magazine Children's Health (October 2003), the number of overweight American kids has more than doubled in the last thirty years. As many as 22 percent of today's children are considered dangerously obese. Many are developing diet-related diabetes, a disease that used to be seen almost exclusively in adults. When California's students (grades 5 through 12) were given a basic fitness test, almost eight out of ten failed. These statistics point to a clear conclusion: There's a growing problem of childhood obesity in this country, a dire trend that must be stopped in its tracks.

Whether they're called big-boned, chubby, husky, or plus-sized, kids are becoming heavier at younger ages and less physically fit than ever before. But why? Like most serious problems, this one has a number of causes. One factor is the massive impact of electronic entertainment on kids' lives. Kids used to go outside to play because it was more fun than sitting around the house. Today, kids at home have access to cable TV channels, the Internet, DVD players, and a dizzying assortment of video games, all of which diminish the lure of outdoor play.

Another cause is the lack of parental supervision. Decades ago, most kids had an adult at home encouraging them to play outdoors. Now, a large number of American families have two working parents or a working single parent. For most of the daylight hours, parents aren't around to make sure their kids get some exercise. Parents who can't be home may feel guilty; one way to relieve this guilt is to buy kids the game system of their dreams and a nice wide-screen TV to play it on, almost guaranteeing that kids will sit idle rather than participate in vigorous physical activity.

But more than any other factor, fast-food restaurants and other sources of calorie-laden junk have dramatically contributed to the fattening of America's kids. To many of today's kids, normal dinnertime equals McDonald's, Domino's, Taco Bell, or Kentucky Fried Chicken. And increasingly, lunchtime at school means those foods too since a good number of schools have sold chain restaurants the right to put their food items on the lunch line. Many schools also allow candy and soft-drink vending machines on their campuses. Given the choice between an apple and a candy bar, how many kids would choose the apple?

2

3

4

5

Start of *secondary causal analysis* (*effects* of fast food on kids)

Exemplification — in the form of facts and statistics

Emotional language reinforces essay's *persuasive* intent

Exemplification in the form of facts and statistics

End of secondary causal analysis

Emotional language reinforces essay's *persuasive* intent

Argumentation presents several possible solutions to problem

Transitions signal several solutions

6   Whether for breakfast, lunch, or dinner, when fast food becomes the staple of young people's diets, it's the kids who become Whoppers. And it has become the staple for many. Children's Health reports that nationwide, kids get 40 percent of their meals from fast-food chains and convenience stores. And what makes the situation even worse is the increasingly huge portions sold by fast-food restaurants. In the 1950s, the standard meal at McDonald's consisted of a hamburger, two ounces of French fries, and a 12-ounce Coke. That meal provided 590 calories. But today's customers are encouraged to say "Super-size that!" For very little extra money, diners end up with a quarter-pound burger, extra-large fries, and gigantic cup of Coke, all adding up to 1,550 calories. A whole generation of kids is growing up believing that this massive shot of fat, sugar, and sodium equals a "normal portion." Kids' perception of what's normal is also distorted by the size of the drinks sold by fast-food and convenience stores. The drinks, often sporting names like the "Big Gulp" or "Super Thirst Quencher," are huge in both size and popularity. Every day, the average adolescent chugs enough soda and fruit beverages to equal the sugar content of fifty chocolate-chip cookies. No wonder kids are becoming "super-sized" themselves.

7   The fast-food franchises push youngsters to overeat in other ways too. Plunking themselves down in front of the TV to watch after-school and Saturday-morning cartoons, children see at least an hour of commercials for every five hours of programming. On Saturday mornings, nine out of ten of those TV ads are for sugary cereals, fast foods, and other non-nutritious junk. Watching those commercials makes the kids hungry--or at least makes them think they are. So they snack as they sit in front of the TV set. Then at mealtime, they beg for the junk food they've seen televised all day long. The result? Kids get bigger, and bigger, and bigger.

8   There's no overnight solution to the problem of American children's increasing weight. But there are some remedies that could be put into place easily. To begin, fast-food meals and junk-food vending machines should be banned from schools, as some states have started to do. Second, food companies should reduce serving sizes and lower the fat and sugar content of the snack items that children eat most often. (Kraft Foods has recently begun to take such steps.) Third, commercials for junk food should be prohibited from being aired on TV during children's viewing time, specifically Saturday mornings. Fourth, parents and schools need to educate kids about the benefits of healthy foods and moderate

portion size--and about the drawback of huge meals of junk food. Schools could, for example, mount an educational effort equivalent to the school-based anti-smoking campaign of the 1980s and 1990s. Fifth, fast-food restaurants should be required to do something like what tobacco companies have to do: clearly display health warnings on their products. If young people learned in school and at home about healthy eating, they might think twice about ordering a Double Whopper with cheese, an extra-large order of fries and a king-size Dr. Pepper, especially if they read something like this:

Exemplification in the form of hypothetical situation

- Your meal provides 2030 calories, 860 of those calories from fat.
- Your recommended daily intake is 2000 calories, with no more than 600 of those calories coming from fat.

At a glance, they could see that in one fast-food meal, they would be taking in more calories and fat than they should consume in an entire day.

Transition signals final solution

Finally, parents need to curb their reliance on fast food   9 to nourish their children. Making fast food an occasional treat rather than an everyday habit can make a significant difference. Parents may argue that they simply don't have time to cook healthy, well-balanced meals, particularly during the week. The answer may be to get the whole family involved in preparing meals ahead of time. (Younger kids, whose attitudes are still in the formative stage, love helping out in the kitchen.) Letting kids assist in preparing, packaging, and freezing their own nutritious, reasonably sized individual servings for later use can go a long way toward helping youngsters develop more healthy attitudes toward food.

Restatement of purpose/thesis; emotional language urging action reinforces essay's *persuasive* intent

Such efforts, challenging as they may be, are well worth   10 the trouble. Why? Because overweight kids today become overweight adults tomorrow. Overweight adults are at increased risk for heart disease, diabetes, stroke, and cancer. Schools, fast-food restaurants, and the media are contributing to a public-health disaster in the making. Anything that decreases the role that super-sized junk food plays in kids' lives needs to be done, and done quickly.

The following answers to the questions on pages 427–428 will help you analyze Tasha Walker's use of the patterns of development in her essay "The Super-Sizing of America's Kids."

1. *What are the writer's purpose and thesis?*

Tasha's general purpose, clearly indicated in the assignment, is to explore the causes and effects of a significant problem among young people today. Tasha chooses to address the problem of increasing obesity among children. She expresses her thesis in the final sentence of paragraph 2: "There's a growing problem of childhood obesity in this country, a dire trend that must be stopped in its tracks." Over the course of her essay, Tasha marshals compelling evidence of the obesity problem, explores its causes and effects, and concludes with thoughts on how this problem might be rectified.

2. *What pattern of development dominates the essay? How does this pattern help the writer support the essay's thesis and fulfill the essay's purpose?*

As the assignment required, Tasha uses *causal analysis* as her essay's principal pattern of development. To establish the severity of the childhood obesity problem, Tasha presents, in paragraph 2, a battery of statistics pointing to obesity's dire and pervasive *effects*. She then shifts gears in paragraph 3 to consider the *causes* of this obesity. The phrase "Like most serious problems, this one has a number of causes" announces that Tasha will discuss a series of causes. She uses various signal phrases, including "One factor" (3), "Another cause" (4), and "But more than any other factor" (5), to direct readers' attention to each factor under consideration. This clear, easy-to-follow presentation—first of effects and then of causes— allows Tasha to develop her thesis and meet her writing objectives. Along the way, several *secondary causal analyses* buttress her overarching examination of causes and effects. Consider paragraphs 5–7. There, Tasha begins by citing fast-food restaurants as the most significant cause of kids' poor eating habits; that done, she examines how the fast-food industry affects kids—how it distorts their perception of portion size and uses enticing commercials to increase their reliance on "calorie-laden junk" (5).

3. *What other patterns appear in the essay? How do these secondary patterns help the writer support the essay's thesis and fulfill the essay's purpose?*

Although Tasha's essay is primarily a causal analysis, it contains a strong element of *argumentation-persuasion*. For one thing, Tasha's thesis takes the form of an *argument:* The "dire trend [of childhood obesity] . . . must be stopped in its tracks" (2). Careful to support her argument with solid reasoning, Tasha uses facts and statistics throughout the essay. She also employs strong language to enhance the argument's *persuasiveness*. Note, for example, the way she's worded her thesis to convey a sense of urgency. Note, too, the way she forcefully restates her core argument at various points in the essay. In paragraph 3, she asserts that "kids are becoming heavier at younger ages and less physically fit than ever before," and later she argues, "No wonder kids are becoming 'super-sized' themselves" (6) and "Kids get bigger, and bigger, and bigger" (7). The essay's last sentence ("Anything that decreases the role that super-sized junk food plays in kids' lives needs to be done, and done quickly") echoes the feeling of urgency expressed in the thesis.

Tasha's essay draws upon other patterns of development as well. The introductory anecdote, *narrative* and *descriptive* in structure, *contrasts* kids' waking up to breakfast in the 1950s with what happens nowadays. Vivid contrasting *examples* ("a bowl of . . . oatmeal" versus a "bowl of rainbow-colored sugary bits") help Tasha establish her key point: that childhood obesity is a contemporary trend that didn't exist in the past. Tasha continues to use exemplification in the form of facts (6 and 8), statistics (2 and 7), and hypothetical situations (8 and 9). Taken together, all these patterns help Tasha make her point about the importance of reversing the dangerous trend of childhood obesity.

Now that you've seen the way one student writer brings together several patterns of development in an essay, it will be helpful to look at the way a renowned prose stylist, Virginia Woolf, does the same in her classic essay "The Death of the Moth."

Virginia Woolf

Virginia Woolf is considered one of the most innovative writers of the twentieth century. Born in 1882 in London, Woolf was educated at home by her father, Leslie Stephen, a well-known biographer, critic, and scholar. Along with her sister, Woolf became a key member of the Bloomsbury Group, a circle of writers and artists committed to the highest standards in art and literature. Woolf married a fellow Bloomsbury member, author and publisher Leonard Woolf. Together, they established Hogarth Press, which went on to publish Woolf's ground-breaking writings, including the novels *Mrs. Dalloway* (1923) and *To the Lighthouse* (1927), as well as the collection of essays *A Room of One's Own* (1920). Woolf's experimentation with point of view and her use of stream of consciousness earned her a place as a pivotal figure in English literature. Although Woolf's work met with critical acclaim and her collaboration with her husband was productive, Woolf was troubled all her life by severe depression. She committed suicide in 1941. "The Death of the Moth" appeared in the volume *The Death of the Moth and Other Essays* (1948).

The Death of the Moth

Description of the moth

Definition (by negation): How this moth differs from the usual kind

Part of implied purpose/thesis: Nature's energy

Description of nature's energy here *contrasts* with *description* of nature in ¶5 (part of purpose/thesis)

Moths that fly by day are not properly to be called moths; they do not excite that pleasant sense of dark autumn nights and ivy-blossom which the commonest yellow-underwing asleep in the shadow of the curtain never fails to rouse in us. They are hybrid creatures, neither gay like butterflies nor sombre like their own species. Nevertheless the present specimen, with his narrow hay-coloured wings, fringed with a tassel of the same colour, seemed to be content with life. It was a pleasant morning, mid-September, mild, benignant, yet with a keener breath than that of the summer months. The plough was already scoring the field opposite the window, and where the share had been, the earth was pressed flat and gleamed with moisture. Such vigour came rolling in from the fields and the down beyond that it was difficult to keep the eyes strictly turned upon the book. The rooks too were keeping one of their annual festivities; soaring round the tree tops until it looked as if a vast net with thousands of black knots in it had been cast up

1

into the air; which, after a few moments, sank slowly down upon the trees until every twig seemed to have a knot at the end of it. Then, suddenly, the net would be thrown into the air again in a wider circle this time, with the utmost clamour and vociferation, as though to be thrown into the air and settle slowly down upon the tree tops were a tremendously exciting experience.

Comparison between nature's energy and the moth's strong life force (part of purpose/thesis)

The same energy which inspired the rooks, the plough- 2 men, the horses, and even, it seemed, the lean bare-backed downs, sent the moth fluttering from side to side of his square of the window-pane. One could not help watching him. One was, indeed, conscious of a queer feeling of pity for him. The possibilities of pleasure seemed that morning so enormous and so various that to have only a moth's part in life, and a day moth's at that, appeared a hard fate, and his zest in enjoying his meagre opportunities to the full, pathetic. He flew vigorously to one corner of his compartment, and, after waiting there a second, flew across to the other. What remained for him but to fly to a third corner and then to a fourth? That was all he could do, in spite of the size of the downs, the width of the sky, the far-off smoke of houses, and the romantic voice, now and then, of a steamer out at sea. What he could do he did. Watching him, it seemed as if a fibre, very thin but pure, of the enormous energy of the world had been thrust into his frail and diminutive body. As often as he crossed the pane, I could fancy that a thread of vital light became visible. He was little or nothing but life.

Start of *narrative* (main pattern) about the moth's plight

Start of *narrative* about Woolf's reaction to the moth's plight

Description of moth's strong life force—despite its small size (these two contrasting qualities are part of purpose/thesis)

Part of purpose/thesis: The moth represents life

Yet, because he was so small, and so simple a form of 3 the energy that was rolling in at the open window and driving its way through so many narrow and intricate corridors in my own brain and in those of other human beings, there was something marvellous as well as pathetic about him. It was as if someone had taken a tiny bead of pure life and decking it as lightly as possible with down and feathers, had set it dancing and zigzagging to show us the true nature of life. Thus displayed one could not get over the strangeness of it. One is apt to forget all about life, seeing it humped and bossed and garnished and cumbered so that it has to move with the greatest circumspection and dignity. Again, the thought of all that life might have been had he been born in any other shape caused one to view his simple activities with a kind of pity.

Narrative about Woolf's reaction continues

Restatement of part of purpose/thesis: The moth's two contrasting qualities

Restatement of part of purpose/thesis: The moth represents life

Narrative about the moth's plight continues; tension builds

Narrative about Woolf's reaction continues

Hint of the resolution of the *narrative* about the moth

Narrative about Woolf's reaction continues

Description of nature's indifference here *contrasts* with *description* of nature in ¶1 (part of purpose/thesis)

Restatement of part of purpose/thesis: The strength of the moth's life force—despite small size

Part of purpose/thesis: Death's inevitability

Narrative about moth continues

Narrative about Woolf's reaction continues

Restatement of part of purpose/thesis: The strength of the moth's life force—despite its size

4   After a time, tired by his dancing apparently, he settled on the window ledge in the sun, and, the queer spectacle being at an end, I forgot about him. Then, looking up, my eye was caught by him. He was trying to resume his dancing, but seemed either so stiff or so awkward that he could only flutter to the bottom of the window-pane; and when he tried to fly across it he failed. Being intent on other matters I watched these futile attempts for a time without thinking, unconsciously waiting for him to resume his flight, as one waits for a machine, that has stopped momentarily, to start again without considering the reason of its failure. After perhaps a seventh attempt he slipped from the wooden ledge and fell, fluttering his wings, on to his back on the window sill. The helplessness of his attitude roused me. It flashed upon me that he was in difficulties; he could no longer raise himself; his legs struggled vainly. But, as I stretched out a pencil, meaning to help him to right himself, it came over me that the failure and awkwardness were the approach of death. I laid the pencil down again.

5   The legs agitated themselves once more. I looked as if for the enemy against which he struggled. I looked out of doors. What had happened there? Presumably it was midday, and work in the fields had stopped. Stillness and quiet had replaced the previous animation. The birds had taken themselves off to feed in the brooks. The horses stood still. Yet the power was there all the same, massed outside, indifferent, impersonal, not attending to anything in particular. Somehow it was opposed to the little hay-coloured moth. It was useless to try to do anything. One could only watch the extraordinary efforts made by those tiny legs against an oncoming doom which could, had it chosen, have submerged an entire city, not merely a city, but masses of human beings; nothing, I knew, had any chance against death. Nevertheless after a pause of exhaustion the legs fluttered again. It was superb, this last protest, and so frantic that he succeeded at last in righting himself. One's sympathies, of course, were all on the side of life. Also, when there was nobody to care or to know, this gigantic effort on the part of an insignificant little moth, against a power of such magnitude, to retain what no one else valued or desired to keep, moved one strangely. Again, somehow, one saw life, a pure bead. I lifted the pencil again, useless though I knew it to be. But even as I did so, the unmistakable tokens of death

Resolution of
the *narrative*
about the moth ⌡
showed themselves. The body relaxed, and instantly grew stiff. The struggle was over. The insignificant little creature now knew death. As I looked at the dead moth, this minute wayside triumph of so great a force over so mean an antagonist filled me with wonder. Just as life had been strange a few minutes before, so death was now as strange. The moth having righted himself now lay most decently and uncomplainingly composed. O yes, he seemed to say, death is stronger than I am.

Restatement of
part of purpose/
thesis: Death's
inevitability

The following answers to the questions on pages 427–428 will help you analyze Virginia Woolf's use of the patterns of development in the essay "The Death of the Moth."

1. *What are the writer's purpose and thesis?*

   Woolf's *purpose* is to show that the tiny moth's courageous but ultimately futile battle to cling to life embodies the struggle at the very heart of all existence. Woolf achieves her purpose by relating the story of the moth's efforts to resist death. Her *thesis* might be expressed this way: Although living creatures may make "extraordinary efforts" (paragraph 5) to hold onto life, these attempts aren't strong enough to defy death. Nothing, Woolf writes, has "any chance against death" (5).
   Woolf's purpose and thesis first become apparent at the end of paragraph 2. There she shows that the moth, with his "frail and diminutive body," represents "nothing but life." Although "small . . . and . . . simple" (3), the moth is suffused with the same extraordinary energy that is evident in the natural world beyond Woolf's window. This energy, combined with the moth's tiny size, makes the creature both "marvellous" and "pathetic" (3)—two qualities that are particularly apparent during the moth's final struggles. During those moments, the moth makes a final "superb" (5) protest against death, but ultimately the "insignificant" (5) creature—like all forms of life—must cease his valiant struggle and die.

2. *What pattern of development dominates the essay? How does this pattern help the writer support the essay's thesis and fulfill the essay's purpose?*

   Although the essay's first paragraph is largely descriptive, it becomes clear by paragraph 2 that the description is in service of a larger narrative about the moth's struggles. It's this narrative that dominates the essay.
   At the beginning, the moth is imbued with vitality, as he flies "vigorously" (paragraph 2) and with "zest" (2) from one side of the window to the other. But narrative tension begins to build in paragraph 4. There Woolf writes that the moth tries once again to cross the windowpane, fails repeatedly, and slips "on to his back," seemingly defeated. However, even then, the moth doesn't abandon his hold on life, for—as Woolf relates in paragraph 5—he tries, despite exhaustion, to right himself. Against all odds, he finally succeeds, but his frantic struggle to hold onto life takes its toll, and the tiny creature soon dies. This detailed story of the moth's futile battle against death is presented as an emblem of the fate of all life. Through this

narrative, Woolf achieves her purpose and thesis: to convey the power of nature and the inability of living creatures—despite heroic efforts—to defy this power.

Paralleling the tale of the moth's struggle is another *narrative*: the story of Woolf's changing understanding of the event that unfolds before her. When the moth is "dancing" (3), energetic, and vital, Woolf "could not help watching him" (2) and feels a kind of wonderment at this "tiny bead of pure life" (3). Then in paragraph 4, Woolf writes that she forgets about the moth for a while until she happens to look up and see his "futile attempts" to "resume . . . dancing." For a few moments, she watches the moth's "stiff" and "awkward" efforts to fly, expecting him to demonstrate the same vitality as before. Suddenly, she understands that the moth is "in difficulties" and can no longer lift himself up. She tries to help but abandons her efforts when she realizes that the moth's labored efforts signify the "approach of death." Paragraph 5 presents the final stage of Woolf's interior narrative. She looks outside her window for an explanation of the moth's plight. But now she finds that the forces of nature—earlier so exuberant and vibrant—are, if anything, "opposed to the little hay-coloured moth." With that, her attention is once again drawn to the moth and the fluttering of his legs. Although drained, the tiny creature makes one last effort to resist death—and, improbably enough, picks himself up one more time. Struck by the sheer power of the moth's life force, Woolf is prompted, as before, to help the creature, even though she recognizes the futility. But then the "unmistakable tokens of death" appear, and the moth gives up his struggle, succumbing—as all forms of life must—to the forces of nature. With the moth lying "uncomplainingly composed," Woolf comes to accept the fact that death is stronger than life.

3. *What other patterns appear in the essay? How do these secondary patterns help the writer support the essay's thesis and fulfill the essay's purpose?*

Although the essay is predominantly a narrative, it also contains other patterns. The *descriptive* passage at the beginning of the essay includes a brief *definition by negation* in which Woolf explains how the creature she is observing differs from the usual, more colorful night moth. The rest of paragraph 1 draws upon description to evoke the sense of early autumn and nature's extraordinary energy. This description of the natural world's vibrancy and abundance, exemplified by the rooks and plowed earth, *contrasts* with Woolf's later characterization of the natural world in paragraph 5. There she writes, "Stillness and quiet . . . replaced the previous animation," and she senses not that nature fosters vitality, but that it is "indifferent, impersonal, not attending to anything in particular."

Shifting her focus in paragraph 2 from the natural world to the moth, Woolf exercises her *descriptive* powers to convey the moth's extraordinary zest as he flies across the windowpane. In this paragraph, Woolf also draws upon *comparison-contrast* to show that despite *differences* in their sizes, the tiny moth and the vast natural world embody the *same* primal energy. Woolf's consideration of this elemental similarity leads her to the basic *contrast* at the heart of the essay: While the moth's tiny size makes him "pathetic," his formidable life spirit makes him "marvellous." He may be small and lightweight, but he is abuzz with vitality. When contrasted to the enormous power of nature, the moth—like all forms of life—may be puny, but his impulse to defy such power inspires awe and reverence.

Martin Luther King, Jr.

More than thirty years after his assassination, Martin Luther King, Jr. (1929–68), is still recognized as the towering figure in the struggle for civil rights in the United States. Born in Atlanta, Georgia, King earned doctorates from Boston University and Chicago Theological Seminary and served as pastor of a Baptist congregation in Montgomery, Alabama. Advocating a philosophy of nonviolent resistance to racial injustice, he led bus boycotts, marches, and sit-ins that brought about passage of the 1964 Civil Rights Act and the Voting Rights Act of 1965. Dr. King was awarded the Nobel Peace Prize in 1964. The following selection by King is taken from *Where Do We Go From Here: Community or Chaos?* (1967).

Where Do We Go From Here: Community or Chaos?

A final problem that mankind must solve in order to survive in the world 1 house that we have inherited is finding an alternative to war and human destruction. Recent events have vividly reminded us that nations are not reducing but rather increasing their arsenals of weapons of mass destruction. The best brains in the highly developed nations of the world are devoted to military technology. The proliferation of nuclear weapons has not been halted, in spite of the limited-test-ban treaty.

In this day of man's highest technical achievement, in this day of daz- 2 zling discovery, of novel opportunities, loftier dignities and fuller freedoms for all, there is no excuse for the kind of blind craving for power and resources that provoked the wars of previous generations. There is no need to fight for food and land. Science has provided us with adequate means of survival and transportation, which make it possible to enjoy the fullness of this great earth. The question now is, do we have the morality and courage required to live together as brothers and not be afraid?

One of the most persistent ambiguities we face is that everybody talks 3 about peace as a goal, but among the wielders of power peace is practically nobody's business. Many men cry "Peace! Peace!" but they refuse to do the things that make for peace.

The large power blocs talk passionately of pursuing peace while expand- 4 ing defense budgets that already bulge, enlarging already awesome armies and devising ever more devastating weapons. Call the roll of those who sing the glad tidings of peace and one's ears will be surprised by the responding sounds. The heads of all the nations issue clarion calls for peace, yet they come to the peace table accompanied by bands of brigands each bearing unsheathed swords.

The stages of history are replete with the chants and choruses of the con-   5 querors of old who came killing in pursuit of peace. Alexander, Genghis Khan, Julius Caesar, Charlemagne and Napoleon were akin in seeking a peaceful world order, a world fashioned after their selfish conceptions of an ideal existence. Each sought a world at peace which would personify his egotistic dreams. Even within the life span of most of us, another megalomaniac strode across the world stage. He sent his blitzkrieg-bent legions blazing across Europe, bringing havoc and holocaust in his wake. There is grave irony in the fact that Hitler could come forth, following nakedly aggressive expansionist theories, and do it all in the name of peace.

So when in this day I see the leaders of nations again talking peace while   6 preparing for war, I take fearful pause. When I see our country today intervening in what is basically a civil war, mutilating hundreds of thousands of Vietnamese children with napalm, burning villages and rice fields at random, painting the valleys of that small Asian country red with human blood, leaving broken bodies in countless ditches and sending home half-men, mutilated mentally and physically; when I see the unwillingness of our government to create the atmosphere for a negotiated settlement of this awful conflict by halting bombings in the North and agreeing unequivocally to talk with the Vietcong—and all this in the name of pursuing the goal of peace—I tremble for our world.[1] I do so not only from dire recall of the nightmares wreaked in the wars of yesterday, but also from dreadful realization of today's possible nuclear destructiveness and tomorrow's even more calamitous prospects.

Before it is too late, we must narrow the gaping chasm between our   7 proclamations of peace and our lowly deeds which precipitate and perpetuate war. We are called upon to look up from the quagmire of military programs and defense commitments and read the warnings on history's signposts.

One day we must come to see that peace is not merely a distant goal that   8 we seek but a means by which we arrive at that goal. We must pursue peaceful ends through peaceful means. How much longer must we play at deadly war games before we heed the plaintive pleas of the unnumbered dead and maimed of past wars?

President John F. Kennedy said on one occasion, "Mankind must put an   9 end to war or war will put an end to mankind." Wisdom born of experience should tell us that war is obsolete. There may have been a time when war served as a negative good by preventing the spread and growth of an evil

---

[1]Only after more than 58,000 Americans had been killed did the United States withdraw from Vietnam. The war then continued until the North Vietnamese, aided by the Vietcong, took over all of Vietnam (editors' note).

force, but the destructive power of modern weapons eliminates even the possibility that war may serve any good at all. If we assume that life is worth living and that man has a right to survive, then we must find an alternative to war. In a day when vehicles hurtle through outer space and guided ballistic missiles carve highways of death through the stratosphere, no nation can claim victory in war. A so-called limited war will leave little more than a calamitous legacy of human suffering, political turmoil and spiritual disillusionment. A world war will leave only smoldering ashes as mute testimony of a human race whose folly led inexorably to ultimate death. If modern man continues to flirt unhesitatingly with war, he will transform his earthly habitat into an inferno such as even the mind of Dante[2] could not imagine.

Therefore I suggest that the philosophy and strategy of nonviolence   10
become immediately a subject for study and for serious experimentation in every field of human conflict, by no means excluding the relations between nations. It is, after all, nation-states which make war, which have produced the weapons that threaten the survival of mankind and which are both genocidal and suicidal in character.

We have ancient habits to deal with, vast structures of power, indescrib-   11
ably complicated problems to solve. But unless we abdicate our humanity altogether and succumb to fear and impotence in the presence of the weapons we have ourselves created, it is as possible and as urgent to put an end to war and violence between nations as it is to put an end to poverty and racial injustice.

The United Nations is a gesture in the direction of nonviolence on a   12
world scale. There, at least, states that oppose one another have sought to do so with words instead of with weapons. But true nonviolence is more than the absence of violence. It is the persistent and determined application of peaceable power to offenses against the community—in this case the world community. As the United Nations moves ahead with the giant tasks confronting it, I would hope that it would earnestly examine the uses of nonviolent direct action.

I do not minimize the complexity of the problems that need to be faced   13
in achieving disarmament and peace. But I am convinced that we shall not have the will, the courage and the insight to deal with such matters unless in this field we are prepared to undergo a mental and spiritual re-evaluation, a change of focus which will enable us to see that the things that seem most real and powerful are indeed now unreal and have come under sentence of death. We need to make a supreme effort to generate the readiness, indeed the eagerness, to enter into the new world which is now possible, "the city which hath foundation, whose Building and Maker is God."

---

[2]In *The Divine Comedy* (1321), Italian poet Dante depicts the burning torments of hell endured by a lost soul before it can attain salvation (editors' note).

It is not enough to say, "We must not wage war." It is necessary to love   14
peace and sacrifice for it. We must concentrate not merely on the eradication
of war but on the affirmation of peace. A fascinating story about Ulysses and
the Sirens[3] is preserved for us in Greek literature. The Sirens had the ability
to sing so sweetly that sailors could not resist steering toward their island.
Many ships were lured upon the rocks, and men forgot home, duty and honor
as they flung themselves into the sea to be embraced by arms that drew them
down to death. Ulysses, determined not to succumb to the Sirens, first decided to tie himself tightly to the mast of his boat and his crew stuffed their ears
with wax. But finally he and his crew learned a better way to save themselves:
They took on board the beautiful singer Orpheus, whose melodies were
sweeter than the music of the Sirens. When Orpheus sang, who would bother
to listen to the Sirens?

So we must see that peace represents a sweeter music, a cosmic melody   15
that is far superior to the discords of war. Somehow we must transform the
dynamics of the world power struggle from the nuclear arms race, which no
one can win, to a creative contest to harness man's genius for the purpose of
making peace and prosperity a reality for all the nations of the world. In
short, we must shift the arms race into a "peace race." If we have the will and
determination to mount such a peace offensive, we will unlock hitherto
tightly sealed doors of hope and bring new light into the dark chambers of
pessimism.

[3]Ulysses and the Sirens, as well as Orpheus (mentioned later in the paragraph), are all figures in
Greek mythology (editors' note).

Joan Didion

Known for her taut prose style and sharp social commentary, Joan Didion (1934–)
graduated from the University of California at Berkeley. Her essays have appeared in
the *Saturday Evening Post,* the *American Scholar,* and the *National Review,* as well as
in three collections: *Slouching Towards Bethlehem* (1969), *The White Album* (1979),
and *After Henry* (1992). *Salvador* (1983) is a book-length essay about a 1982 visit
to Central America. The coauthor of several screenplays (including *A Star Is Born* in
1976 and *Up Close and Personal* in 1996), Didion has also written novels, including
Run River (1963), *A Book of Common Prayer* (1977), *Democracy* (1984), *The Last
Thing He Wanted* (1996), and *Where I Was From* (2003), as well as *Fixed Ideas:
America Since 9.11* (2003), a book of political commentary. The following selection
is from *Slouching Towards Bethlehem*.

Marrying Absurd

To be married in Las Vegas, Clark County, Nevada, a bride must swear   1
that she is eighteen or has parental permission and a bridegroom that he is
twenty-one or has parental permission. Someone must put up five dollars for
the license. (On Sundays and holidays, fifteen dollars. The Clark County
Courthouse issues marriage licenses at any time of the day or night except
between noon and one in the afternoon, between eight and nine in the
evening, and between four and five in the morning.) Nothing else is required.
The State of Nevada, alone among these United States, demands neither a
premarital blood test nor a waiting period before or after the issuance of a
marriage license. Driving in across the Mojave from Los Angeles, one sees
the signs way out on the desert, looming up from that moonscape of rattle-
snakes and mesquite, even before the Las Vegas lights appear like a mirage on
the horizon: "GETTING MARRIED? Free License Information First Strip Exit."
Perhaps the Las Vegas wedding industry achieved its peak operational efficiency between 9:00 P.M. and midnight of August 26, 1965, an otherwise
unremarkable Thursday which happened to be, by Presidential order,[1] the last
day on which anyone could improve his draft status merely by getting married. One hundred and seventy-one couples were pronounced man and wife
in the name of Clark County and the State of Nevada that night, sixty-seven
of them by a single justice of the peace, Mr. James A. Brennan. Mr. Brennan
did one wedding at the Dunes and the other sixty-six in his office, and

---

[1]Refers to a declaration made by President Lyndon Johnson regarding the draft for the Vietnam
conflict (editors' note).

charged each couple eight dollars. Once bride lent her veil to six others. "I got it down from five to three minutes," Mr. Brennan said later of his feat. "I could've married them *en masse,* but they're people, not cattle. People expect more when they get married."

What people who get married in Las Vegas actually do expect—what, in   2
the largest sense, their "expectations" are—strikes one as a curious and self-contradictory business. Las Vegas is the most extreme and allegorical of American settlements, bizarre and beautiful in its venality and in its devotion to immediate gratification, a place the tone of which is set by mobsters and call girls and ladies' room attendants with amyl nitrite poppers[2] in their uniform pockets. Almost everyone notes that there is no "time" in Las Vegas, no night and no day and no past and no future (no Las Vegas casino, however, has taken the obliteration of the ordinary time sense quite so far as Harold's Club in Reno, which for a while issued, at odd intervals in the day and night, mimeographed "bulletins" carrying news from the world outside); neither is there any logical sense of where one is. One is standing on a highway in the middle of a vast hostile desert looking at an eighty-foot sign which blinks "STARDUST" or "CAESAR'S PALACE." Yes, but what does that explain? This geographical implausibility reinforces the sense that what happens there has no connection with "real" life; Nevada cities like Reno and Carson City are ranch towns, Western towns, places behind which there is some historical imperative. But Las Vegas seems to exist only in the eye of the beholder. All of which makes it an extraordinarily stimulating and interesting place, but an odd one in which to want to wear a candlelight satin Priscilla of Boston wedding dress with Chantilly lace insets, tapered sleeves and a detachable modified train.

And yet the Las Vegas wedding business seems to appeal to precisely that   3
impulse. "Sincere and Dignified Since 1954," one wedding chapel advertises. There are nineteen such wedding chapels in Las Vegas, intensely competitive, each offering better, faster, and, by implication, more sincere services than the next: Our Photos Best Anywhere, Your Wedding on A Phonograph Record, Candlelight with Your Ceremony, Honeymoon Accommodations, Free Transportation from Your Motel to Courthouse to Chapel and Return to Motel, Religious or Civil Ceremonies, Dressing Rooms, Flowers, Rings, Announcements, Witnesses Available, and Ample Parking. All of these services, like most others in Las Vegas (sauna baths, payroll-check cashing, chinchilla coats for sale or rent) are offered twenty-four hours a day, seven days a week, presumably on the premise that marriage, like craps, is a game to be played when the table seems hot.

But what strikes one most about the Strip chapels, with their wishing   4
wells and stained-glass paper windows and their artificial bouvardia, is that so much of their business is by no means a matter of simple convenience, of

[2]An illegal liquid drug, inhaled through the nose, that originally came in small capsules that would "pop" upon opening. Known for heightening sexual arousal, it also causes dizziness and sometimes a blackout (editors' note).

late-night liaisons between show girls and baby Crosbys. Of course there is some of that. (One night about eleven o'clock in Las Vegas I watch a bride in an orange minidress and masses of flame-colored hair stumble from a Strip chapel on the arm of her bridegroom, who looked the part of the expendable nephew in the movies like *Miami Syndicate*.[3] "I gotta get the kids," the bride whimpered. "I gotta pick up the sitter, I gotta get to the midnight show." "What you gotta get," the bridegroom said, opening the door of a Cadillac Coupe de Ville and watching her crumple on the seat, "is sober.") But Las Vegas seems to offer something other than "convenience"; it is merchandising "niceness," the facsimile of proper ritual, to children who do not know how else to find it, how to make the arrangements, how to do it "right." All day and evening long on the Strip, one sees actual wedding parties, waiting under the harsh lights at a crosswalk, standing uneasily in the parking lot of the Frontier while the photographer hired by The Little Church of the West ("Wedding Place of the Stars") certifies the occasion, takes the picture: the bride in a veil and white satin pumps, the bridegroom usually in a white dinner jacket, and even an attendant or two, a sister or a best friend in hot-pink *peau de soie,* a flirtation veil, a carnation nosegay. "When I Fall in Love It Will Be Forever," the organist plays, and then a few bars of *Lohengrin.* The mother cries; the stepfather, awkward in his role, invites the chapel hostess to join them for a drink at the Sands. The hostess declines with a professional smile; she has already transferred her interest to the group waiting outside. One bride out, another in, and again the sign goes up on the chapel door: "One moment please—Wedding."

I sat next to one such wedding party in a Strip restaurant the last time I 5
was in Las Vegas. The marriage had just taken place; the bride still wore her dress, the mother her corsage. A bored waiter poured out a few swallows of pink champagne ("on the house") for everyone but the bride, who was too young to be served. "You'll need something with more kick than that," the bride's father said with heavy jocularity to his new son-in-law; the ritual jokes about the wedding night had a certain Panglossian character, since the bride was clearly several months pregnant. Another round of pink champagne, this time not on the house, and the bride began to cry. "It was just as nice," she sobbed, "as I hoped and dreamed it would be."

[3]The actual title is *The Miami Story,* a 1954 film about a group of citizens destroying a crime syndicate with the help of a reformed criminal (editors' note).

Appendix A
A CONCISE GUIDE
TO FINDING AND
DOCUMENTING SOURCES

Many assignments in *The Longman Reader: Brief Edition* suggest that you might want to do some research in the library and/or on the Internet. Such research enlarges your perspective and enables you to move beyond off-the-top-of-your-head opinions to those that are firmly supported. This appendix will be useful if you do decide to draw upon outside sources when preparing a paper. The appendix explains how to (1) use the library to find books, reference works, and periodicals on a subject; (2) research a topic using the Internet; and (3) document print and electronic sources.

USING THE LIBRARY TO FIND BOOKS ON YOUR SUBJECT

To locate books on a specific topic, go to your college's *library catalog*, which lists all the books in the library. Although most college libraries have a *computerized catalog* of their book holdings, some use a *card catalog*, a list of alphabetically arranged cards in a series of drawers. Library technology is changing rapidly. With each passing year, a greater number of college (and local) libraries can be accessed online. That means that you can check—at any time of the day or night—a library's book holdings from your home or dorm computer.

Searching the Library Catalog by Author, Title, or Subject

Whether you use your own computer to visit a library's holdings online or use the library's computerized (or card) catalog, you need to familiarize yourself with the three ways to look up a book: by author, title, or subject. To locate a specific book, you can do either an *author* or a *title search*. To search by author, look up the book under the author's last name; to search by title, use the first word in the title, or the second word if the first is *A, An,* or *The.* To identify books on a specific topic, do a *subject search.* Following are some strategies for searching a computerized catalog by subject. (If your library's holdings aren't computerized, it's easy to adapt the suggestions to card-catalog research.) For a subject search, type in a word or phrase that summarizes your topic. You may have to try several key terms to discover under which term(s) the computer lists sources on your topic. Assume you're conducting research to identify classroom strategies that undermine student success. You might start by typing the word "Education." But that word would probably yield so many possibilities that you wouldn't know where to start. You might narrow your search by entering "teaching techniques," "classroom practices," or "academic failure." For help in identifying appropriate key terms, speak with your college librarian. He or she will probably have you consult the *Library of Congress Subject Headings* or a bound or on-screen thesaurus of headings used in your library's database.

When you search for a book by subject, the screen usually indicates narrower subheadings under that topic. When you click on one of those subheads, a list of books on that subject will appear. To get complete bibliographic information about a specific book, follow the computer's instructions. The book's publisher, publication date, call number (see below), and so on will then appear on the screen. Most computerized catalogs also indicate the status of a book—whether it is available, on reserve, out on loan, overdue, lost, or available through an interlibrary loan system. (If all copies of the book are checked out, fill out a form to be notified when the book is returned.) On the next page is one college's computerized catalog display for a book on how bias in educational materials affects students' education.

Once the computer identifies books on your subject, you can copy down the authors, titles, and call numbers of promising books; or, in many libraries, you can direct the computer to print out a list. Mastering your library's computerized catalog enables you to identify in minutes sources that once might have taken you several hours to track down.

Locating Books in the Stacks

Most college libraries contain several floors of bookshelves (called *stacks*). There you'll find fiction, nonfiction, periodicals, microfilm and microfiche files, reserved books, government documents, reference works (see below), and special collections. To locate a book in the stacks, use its *call number* (a number used to classify a book and indicate its location in the library). The call number appears both in the catalog entry and on the spine of the book. There are two major systems of call numbers in use in the United States—the

Other subject headings to look under to find additional relevant books. The underlining indicates that these are links to related subjects in the computerized catalog.

AUTHOR:	Ravitch, Diane.
TITLE:	The Language Police: How Pressure Groups Restrict What Students Learn
PUBLICATION INFO:	New York: A.A. Knopf, 2003.
PAGING AND SIZE:	255p.; 25 cm.
SUBJECTS:	Education, Textbooks--Censorship-- United States. Test Bias--United States. Censorship--United States.

1. CALL NUMBER: LB3045.7.R38 2003--STACKS--Checked Out

2. CALL NUMBER: LB3045.7.R38 2003--STACKS--Available

Indicates the book's call number, location, and availability in the library. In this case, the library owns two copies, one checked out, the other available.

Dewey Decimal and the *Library of Congress.* Once you have a book's call number, consult a map or list (usually posted near the front desk) to see where in the library you'll find the book. For example, to track down Diane Ravitch's *The Language Police,* you'd need to find where the library shelves books with the call number *LB3045.7.R38 2003.* If your library has closed stacks, make out a call slip, and a member of the staff will get the book for you.

USING THE LIBRARY TO FIND REFERENCE WORKS ON YOUR SUBJECT

Though they present highly condensed information, *reference works* can be helpful, especially in the early stages of your research. Some reference volumes cover a wide range of subjects (*Encyclopedia Britannica* and the *World Almanac and Book of Facts*), while others are more specialized (*Mathematics*

Dictionary and *Dance Encyclopedia*). Many reference volumes are available on CD-ROM or can be accessed online. Those that aren't are most likely arranged on library shelves alphabetically by subject ("Art," "Economics," "History"), makes it easy to browse for useful reference volumes. Keep in mind that reference materials can't be checked out; you must consult them while in the library. The following box lists representative reference books found in most college libraries. Check with the librarian to see if any you're interested in are available electronically.

Representative Reference Works

Biography: *International Who's Who, Who's Who in America*

Business/Economics: *Dictionary of Banking and Finance, Encyclopedia of Economics*

Fine Arts: *New Grove Dictionary of American Music, The Oxford Companion to Art*

Literature: *Benét's Reader's Encyclopedia, The Oxford Companion to American Literature*

History/Political Science: *Editorials on File, Facts on File, A Political Handbook of the World*

Philosophy/Religion: *The Encyclopedia of American Religions, An Encyclopedia of Philosophy*

Science/Technology/Mathematics: *McGraw-Hill Encyclopedia of Science and Technology, A Dictionary of Mathematics*

Psychology/Education: *Encyclopedia of Education, Encyclopedia of Psychology*

Social Sciences: *International Encyclopedia of the Social Sciences, Encyclopedia of Crime and Justice*

Women's/Ethnic Studies: *Encyclopedia of Feminism, Harvard Encyclopedia of American Ethnic Groups*

USING THE LIBRARY TO FIND ARTICLES ON YOUR SUBJECT

Periodicals are publications issued at intervals throughout the year. Generally, periodicals contain material that is more recent than that found in books or reference works. There are three broad types of periodicals: general, scholarly, and serious. Written for the average reader, *general periodicals* (daily newspapers and magazines such as *Time* and *Newsweek*) contain articles that provide background information rather than comprehensive coverage of a subject. Intended for readers with specialized knowledge, *scholarly publications* (such as the *Journal of Experimental Child Psychology* and the *Journal of Renaissance*

Drama) provide in-depth analyses written by authorities in the field. Designed for well-educated laypeople rather than those having specialized knowledge, *serious publications* (for example, *Scientific American* and *Smithsonian*) develop subjects with less depth than scholarly publications.

Using Periodical Indexes, Abstracts, and Bibliographies

Periodical indexes are cumulative directories that list articles published in specific journals, newspapers, and magazines. (Major newspapers, such as the *New York Times,* publish their own directories.) Most periodical indexes list articles under subject headings. Beneath the headings, individual articles are organized alphabetically by authors' last names.

When you were in high school, you may have used the *Readers' Guide to Periodical Literature,* which lists highly accessible, general-interest articles published by popular newsstand magazines like *U.S. News & World Report* and *Sports Illustrated*. The college equivalents of the *Readers' Guide* are the *Humanities Index* and the *Social Sciences Index*. To locate articles appropriate for college-level research, you'll need to consult these indexes as well as those listing articles from more academic, professional, and specialized publications.

Some specialized indexes provide brief descriptions of the articles they list. These indexes are usually called *abstracts*. Examples are *Abstracts of Folklore Studies* and *Psychological Abstracts*. Abstracts usually contain fewer listings than other types of indexes and are restricted to a limited field. In contrast to indexes that list only articles, *bibliographies* like the *Modern Language Association International Bibliography* list books as well as articles.

You shouldn't end your search for appropriate material until you've consulted the most pertinent indexes and bibliographies. For a paper on the psychology of child abuse, you might start with the *New York Times Index* and then move to more specialized volumes, such as *Psychological Abstracts, Child Development Abstracts,* and *Mental Health Book Review Index*. To ensure that you don't miss current developments in your subject area, start with the most recent years and work your way back.

Most college libraries offer computerized databases of the major periodical indexes, abstracts, and bibliographies. The databases, which group directories alphabetically by subject, can be accessed through the library's computer terminals—and often through a campus-wide computer network, making it possible for you to conduct part of your research from your own room. In most libraries, periodical databases are maintained in the same system as the computerized catalog for books. (If your school library isn't computerized, you'll probably find the periodical indexes located in the periodicals section, arranged alphabetically by title. Simply scan the shelves to find the index you want.)

The following box lists a small sample of the indexes, abstracts, and bibliographies found in most college libraries. Check with the librarian to see which can be accessed electronically.

Representative Indexes, Abstracts, and Bibliographies

General: *Academic Search FullTEXT, Dialog, EBSCOhost, Humanities Index, InfoTrac Academic Index, Magazine Index Plus, National Newspaper Index, NewsBank, Readers' Guide to Periodical Literature, Social Sciences Index*

Education: *Education Abstracts, Education Index, ERIC (Educational Resources Information Center)*

History, Political Science, Government: *Government Publications Index, Historical Abstracts, Monthly Index to United States Government Publications, Political Science Bibliographies, Public Affairs Information Service*

Philosophy/Religion: *Philosopher's Index, Religion Index*

Psychology/Sociology: *Psychological Abstracts, Sociological Abstracts*

Sciences: *Applied Science and Technology Index, Biological Abstracts, Botanical Bibliographies, Chemical Abstracts, Engineering Index Annual, Environment Index, International Computer Bibliography*

Women's/Ethnic Studies: *Bibliography on Women, Ethnic Newswatch, Hispanic American Periodicals Index, Index to Periodical Articles by and About Blacks*

Whether a periodicals directory is in computerized or print form, you identify titles of relevant articles by looking under keywords that describe your subject. If you don't find your subject listed in a printed index, or if a computerized database yields no titles when you type in keywords, try alternate terms for your topic. Suppose you're researching the subject of business ethics. In addition to using "Business ethics" as keywords, you might try "Bribery" or "Fraud" to find relevant articles. Computerized and print indexes also show cross-references. By looking under "Business ethics," you might see suggested search terms such as "Advertising ethics," "Banking, ethical aspects," and "Commercial crime." In many libraries, the computer terminals at which you view database listings are hooked up to printers, enabling you to print out the listings rather than record them from the screen, or they allow you to e-mail listings to yourself. Some online and CD-ROM databases offer access to the full text of selected articles or books. These texts may be read on screen and, if the computer terminal connects to a printer, printed out.

Here's an entry from the computerized database EBSCOhost. The entry gives all the information you need to track down the article in the library.

EBSCOhost

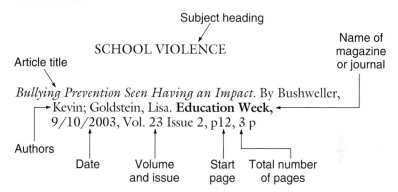

In the event of any puzzling abbreviations or symbols in computerized guides, ask your librarian either to explain their meaning or to direct you to a printed key for an explanation.

Locating a Specific Issue of a Periodical

If you don't have the option of printing out the text of relevant online articles, you'll need to obtain the original text. To do so, you have to determine whether the library owns the specific periodicals and issues you want. If your library catalogs its periodicals online, search for a periodical by typing in its name. Does that particular name appear on screen? If it does, your library owns issues of that publication. With a few additional keystrokes, you can obtain more detailed information—such as which issues of the periodical the library holds and their location in the library.

If your library doesn't catalog its periodicals online, look for a card catalog of holdings. The library probably has a separate periodicals card catalog in the periodicals section. Look up the periodicals by name. A periodical card will usually tell you the issues owned by the library and their location.

Recent issues of magazines, newspapers, and journals are kept in the library's periodicals section, where they are arranged alphabetically by title. Less current issues can be found in bound volumes in the periodicals section, in the stacks, or on microfilm. Usually, periodicals must be read in the library. Back issues of major newspapers are generally stored on microfilm filed in cabinets in a separate location.

USING THE INTERNET TO RESEARCH YOUR SUBJECT

Computer technology isn't, of course, limited to college libraries. It's everywhere. Nothing demonstrates the staggering impact of the computer revolution more powerfully than the growth of the Internet. This global network of interlinked computer systems puts a massive storehouse of information within the reach of anyone with access to a personal computer and an Internet connection. Such a wealth of material presents obvious research benefits to you as a student. However, when faced with the task of using the Internet, you may feel overwhelmed and unsure of how to proceed. The following pages will introduce you to the Internet, show you how to access its resources, and offer pointers on evaluating the material you find there.

The Internet is the catch-all term for the global network that links individual computers throughout the world. The *World Wide Web* refers to a global information system existing *within* the Internet. The Web consists of uncounted millions of *websites*. Some websites feature text only; others also contain graphics; still others include audio and video components. Although there's great variation in the content and design of websites, all contain a *home page* that provides the site's title, descriptive material about the site, and a menu consisting of *links* to the information that can be accessed at the site. A link is a stepping stone to other pages on the site or to a related website. You can jump from the first location to the next just by clicking on the link. (For more on links, see page 454.)

Accessing the Web

Access to the Web is provided through a software program called a *web browser.* Internet Explorer, Netscape, and Apple Safari are several widely used browsers. If you attend one of the many colleges or universities providing Web access to students, you'll probably use one of these browsers. At these schools, you can do your research online by accessing the library's catalog of holdings, its databases, and other resources. If your school doesn't offer Web access and you have a computer and Internet connection at home, you can subscribe to a commercial online service, such as America Online or Earthlink, both of which have their own browsers.

The Advantages and Limitations of the Web

The World Wide Web offers a collection of data that surpasses anything else the world has seen. With the click of a mouse, you can read electronic versions of the *Washington Post* or the *Times of London;* you can check the temperature in Cairo or get up-to-the-minute stock quotes; you can read reviews of a best-selling novel or learn about alternative treatments for arthritis. Because the Web (unlike a library) *doesn't have a centralized organizational structure,* you're automatically—and somewhat haphazardly—exposed to this staggering array of material.

Keep in mind, too, that anyone—from Nobel Prize winners to members of extreme fringe groups—can post material on the Web at any time. Not surprisingly, then, the quality of information found on the Web ranges from authoritative to speculative to fraudulent. Unlike sources in the library, which may be dated or even no longer accurate, online material is generally up-to-date because it can be posted on the Web as soon as it's created (though, increasingly, online materials can also be outdated). Yet the instantaneous nature of Web postings can create problems. Library materials certainly aren't infallible, but most have gone through a process of editorial review before being published. This is often *not* the case with material on the Web. Given this basic limitation, it's not a good idea to rely solely on the Web when you research a topic. Consider using the Web as a supplement to, rather than a substitute for, library research. (For more about evaluating the currency and validity of material on the Web, see pages 457–458.)

Using Online Time Productively

Whether you access the Web through a university service or a commercial provider, the following suggestions will help you use online time productively. First, just as you do when conducting library research (see pages 445–451), be sure to record accurate and sufficient information about your online source so you can provide full documentation when it comes time to write your paper. Specifically, be sure to record the material's title and date, as well as the date of your retrieval. You also need to copy the source's full *URL* (*uniform resource locator*), or Internet *address*. Here, for example, is the address for the *Boston Globe* newspaper: *www.boston.com/ globe*. Having the address makes it possible for you—and the reader of your research paper—to return to this page in the future. Type the address *exactly* as it appears on the website's home page. Don't capitalize something that originally was in lowercase letters, and don't leave extra space between elements in the address. Typing even slight changes in the address usually makes it impossible to access the site. Second, when you find a helpful website that you may want to visit again, use your browser's *Bookmark* or *Favorite Places* option. After you "bookmark" a site, its address is saved in your personal file, so you can click on its name and instantly return to the site, without having to remember (or type) its address.

Using the Internet to Find Books on Your Topic

Assume that you've used your library's computerized catalog to track down several books on your subject. Now you'd like to go online to see if there are additional books—especially brand-new or forthcoming releases— you might find helpful. In such a case, you could access the site of one or both of the following national booksellers: Amazon (at *www.amazon.com*) and Barnes and Noble (at *www.bn.com*). At either site, you would use the

"Browse Subjects" box on the bookseller's home page to identify relevant books. Let's say you want to investigate how the experience of childhood poverty affected the politics of certain American presidents. Using the "Browse Subjects" box, you note that one of the subject listings is "Biography." Clicking on "Biography," you see that one of the subcategories is "Presidents." Click on "Presidents," and a list of books on American presidents appears. By clicking on specific titles from the list, you obtain information about each book, including reviewer and reader comments. With this information, you can usually determine which books are appropriate for your purpose. At that point, you check the availability of those books in the library or, if you wish, purchase them online.

Online booksellers can also help you narrow your topic. Perhaps you want to research the topic of illiteracy. As soon as you type the word "illiteracy" in the "Search" box on the bookseller's home page, you receive a long list of books on the subject. Simply looking at the range of titles can help you narrow your research. You might, for example, decide to focus on illiteracy in the workplace, teenagers' declining reading scores, or programs that teach marginally literate parents how to read to their children.

Using the Internet to Find Articles and Other Materials on Your Topic

What do you do if you want to go online to track down articles, speeches, legislation, TV transcripts, and so on about your subject? How, given the array of online material, can you identify pertinent sources? Search directories and search engines will help.

Search Directories.   A *search directory,* a service that organizes websites by subject categories, will point you in the right direction. If you're not sure how to narrow your topic, seeing the search directory's categories may help you by identifying directions you wouldn't have thought of on your own. New search directories crop up regularly, but one of the most popular and user friendly is Google. On page 623 is an approximation of what you'll see when you go to Google's home page and click on "Directory." (Bear in mind that websites change constantly. What appears on your computer screen may not be identical to what's presented here.)

As you see, Google divides websites into sixteen categories: Arts, Business, and so on. Each category is presented as a *link* (see page 452). Typically, a link shows up as an underlined word or phrase that's a different color from the type elsewhere on the page. When you click on a link, you're automatically transported to a related site. There you're presented with a more focused list of websites to choose from. As you move from link to link, you go from the general topic to more specific aspects of the topic. For example, say you're

researching how product recalls are communicated to consumers. You notice that there's a section titled "Consumers" under the category "Home." Click on "Consumers" and you're presented with a screen that lists several dozen consumer-related links, from "Advocacy and Protection" to "Travel." When you see the link "Recalls," you know you're on the right track. As soon as you click on "Recalls," links to related sites appear on screen. From those, you select the sites you think will be most useful in your research.

Search Engines.   Search directories are wonderful tools when you begin exploring your topic. But when you're refining your investigation, you'll want to use another kind of resource—the *search engine*. Search engines comb through the vast amount of information on the Web for sites that match your research needs. You activate a search engine by entering key words or phrases that tell the engine what to look for. Increasingly, search engines and search directories are combined, making it possible to access both from the site's home page. The following box lists some popular search directories and search engines and their addresses.

Popular Search Directories and Engines

About at *www.about.com*

AltaVista at *www.altavista.com*

Excite! at *www.excite.com*

Google at *www.google.com*

Lycos at *www.lycos.com*

Refdesk at *www.refdesk.com*

Yahoo! at *www.yahoo.com*

Tips for Using Search Engines.   When you reach the home page of a search engine, it's a good idea to click on the "Help" or "Tips" button. When you do, you'll receive specific guidelines for using that particular search engine efficiently. As you proceed, don't forget to "bookmark" (see page 453) the search engines you use so you can return to them easily at a later date.

Return to the example of a Google home page (page 455). Note that at the top, there's an empty box beside "Google Search." That's where you enter in keyword(s) describing your research topic. After you click on "Google Search" (or whatever your search engine calls its "search" command), the engine scans the Web for your keyword(s). It then provides you with a list of "hits," or links, to websites where your keyword is found. Most search engines also provide a brief description of each site.

The success of your search depends on how carefully you follow your search engine's guidelines and on how specific and descriptive your search terms are. For example, say you're doing research on college financial aid. Depending upon your search engine, if you simply enter the words *college financial aid* in the search box, the engine may provide a list of *every* document that contains the word *college* or *financial* or *aid*—hundreds of thousands of hits. To limit the number of hits you get, follow with great care your search engine's specific guidelines. If no guidelines are provided or if the guidelines are confusing, try the suggestions described below.

☑ FOCUSING A WEB SEARCH: A CHECKLIST

❏ Put quotation marks around the phrase you are searching for—in this case, "college financial aid." Many search engines interpret the quotation marks to mean you want only those documents that include the complete phrase *college financial aid*. If you don't include the quotation marks, you may receive listings for each word.

❑ To focus your search further, use the plus (+) and minus (–) signs, leaving no space before or after the signs. Say you're interested in college financial aid as it applies to grants. Try typing this in the search box:

"college financial aid" + grants

The + sign between *college financial aid* and *grants* instructs the search engine to locate items that contain both sets of keywords. A minus (–) sign has the opposite effect. If you want information about college financial aid, *excluding* information about grants, you would type your search phrase like this:

"college financial aid" – grants

❑ Use the Boolean[1] operative words AND, OR, and NOT to limit your search. When you investigate a topic via a search engine that recognizes Boolean logic (the search tips will indicate if it does, or you can experiment on your own as you type in search phrases), using these operatives between key terms broadens or narrows the range of your search. For example, assume you typed the following: reggae music AND Rastafarians AND Jamaica. Using the operative AND instructs the search engine to return only those documents containing all three search terms.

Evaluating Internet Materials

You need to take special care to evaluate the worth of material you find on the Web. Electronic documents often seem to appear out of nowhere and can disappear without a trace. And anyone—from scholar to con artist—can create a Web page. How, then, do you know if an Internet source is credible? The following checklist provides some questions to ask when you work with online material.

☑ EVALUATING INTERNET MATERIALS: A CHECKLIST

❑ Who is the author of the material? Does the author offer his or her credentials in a résumé or biographical note? Do these credentials qualify the author to provide reliable information on the topic? Does the author provide an e-mail address so you can request more information? The less you know about an author, the more suspicious you should be about using the data.

❑ Can you verify the accuracy of the information presented? Does the author refer to studies or to other authors you can investigate? If the

[1]Named for George Boole, a nineteenth-century mathematician, Boolean logic modifies search items through the use of the "operators" AND, OR, and NOT.

author doesn't cite other works or other points of view, that may suggest the document is opinionated and one-sided. In such a case, it's
important to track down material addressing alternative points of view.

❏ Who's sponsoring the website? Many sites are established by organizations—businesses, agencies, lobby groups—as well as by individuals. If a sponsor pushes a single point of view, you should use the
material with great caution. Once again, make an extra effort to locate
material addressing other sides of the issue.

❏ Is the cited information up-to-date? Being on the Internet doesn't
guarantee that information is current. To assess the timeliness of
Internet materials, check at the top or bottom of the document for
copyright date, publication date, and/or revision date. Having those
dates will help you determine whether the material is recent enough
for your purposes.

DOCUMENTING SOURCES

In Chapter 11, you learned the importance of *documentation*—giving credit
to the print and electronic sources whose words and ideas you borrow in an
essay (see page 358). That earlier discussion showed you how to document
sources in informal papers. The following pages will show you how to use the
documentation system of the Modern Language Association (MLA)[2] when
citing sources in more formal papers.

The discussion here covers key features of the MLA system. For more
detailed coverage, you may want to consult a recent composition handbook
or the latest edition of the *MLA Handbook for Writers of Research Papers*. For
a sample paper that uses MLA documentation, turn to the student essay on
pages 373–378.

WHAT TO DOCUMENT

You may inadvertently fall into the trap of *plagiarizing*—passing off someone
else's ideas as your own—if you're not sure when you need to acknowledge
outside sources in an essay. To avoid plagiarism, you must provide documentation in the following situations:

---

[2]MLA documentation is appropriate in papers written for humanities courses, such as your composition class. If you're writing a paper for a course in the social sciences (for example, psychology, economics, or sociology), your professor will probably expect you to use the citation
format developed by the American Psychological Association (APA). For information about
APA documentation, consult *The Longman Writer* or the most recent edition of the *Publication
Manual of the American Psychological Association*.

- When you include *word-for-word quotations* from a source.
- When you *summarize or restate in your own words* ideas or information from a source, unless that material is *commonly known* or is a *matter of historical or scientific record.*
- When you *combine a summary and a quotation.*

An important note: On the whole, you should try to state borrowed material in your own words. A string of quotations signals that you haven't sufficiently evaluated and distilled your sources. Use quotations sparingly; draw upon them only when they dramatically illustrate key points you want to make. Also, keep in mind that quotations won't, by themselves, make your case for you. You need to interpret and comment on them, showing how they support your points.

HOW TO DOCUMENT

The MLA documentation system uses the *parenthetic reference,* a brief note in parentheses inserted into the text after borrowed material. The parenthetic reference doesn't provide full bibliographic information, but it presents enough so that readers can turn to the Works Cited list (see page 464) at the end of the paper for complete information. If the method of documentation you learned in high school involved footnotes or endnotes, you will be happy to know that parenthetic documentation—currently the preferred method— is much easier to use. While it is now accepted by most college professors, be sure to check with your professors to determine their documentation preferences.

Whenever you quote or summarize material from an outside source, you must do two things: (1) *identify the author* and (2) *specify the page(s)* in your source on which the material appears. The author's name may be given *either* in a lead-in sentence (often called the *attribution*) *or* in the parentheses following the borrowed material. The page number *always* appears in parentheses. The examples below illustrate the MLA documentation style and are based on the following excerpt from page 8 of Julian Stamp's book *The Homeless and History:*

> The key to any successful homeless program requires a clear understanding of just who are the homeless in our country. Since fifty percent of shelter residents have drug and alcohol addictions, programs need to provide not only a place to sleep but also comprehensive substance-abuse treatment. Since roughly one-third of the homeless population is mentally ill, programs need to offer psychiatric care, even institutionalization, not just housing subsidies. Since the typical head of a homeless family often lacks the know-how

needed to maintain a job and a home, programs need to supply employment and life skills training.

When we switch our focus to larger *economic* issues, we see that homelessness cannot be resolved solely at the level of the individual. Since the 1980s, the gap between the rich and the poor has widened, buying power has stagnated, jobs have fled overseas, and funding for low-cost housing has been almost eliminated. Given these developments, homelessness begins to look like a product of history, and only by addressing shifts in the American economy can we begin to find effective solutions.

Using Parentheses Only

Counseling and support services are not enough to solve the problem of homelessness; proposed solutions must also address the complex economic issues at the heart of homelessness (Stamp 8).

If we look beyond the problems of homelessness, to "larger economic issues, we see that homelessness cannot be resolved solely at the level of the individual" (Stamp 8).

Given the fact that a significant percentage of the homeless suffer from mental illness, "programs need to offer psychiatric care . . ., not just housing subsidies" (Stamp 8).

Using Parentheses and Attributions

Julian Stamp argues that homelessness must be addressed in terms of economics, not simply in terms of individual counseling, addiction therapy, or job training (8).

As Stamp explains, "The key to any successful homeless policy requires a clear understanding of just who are the homeless. . . ." (8).

Because half of those taking refuge in shelters have problems with drugs and alcohol, Stamp reasons that "programs need to provide not only a place to sleep but also comprehensive substance-abuse treatment" (8).

One historian points out that "homelessness cannot be resolved solely at the level of the individual" (Stamp 8).

According to statistics, half of the homeless individuals living in shelters are substance abusers (Stamp 8).

In The Homeless and History, Stamp maintains that economic issues, rather than difficulties in people's personal lives, are at the core of the homeless problem (8).

Glance back at the above examples and note the following:

- An attribution may specify the author's name (*Julian Stamp argues that; As Stamp explains*) or it may refer to a source more generally (*One historian points out; According to statistics*). If you want to call attention to a specific author, use an attribution indicating the author's name. Otherwise, use a more general attribution and a parenthetic citation that includes the name along with the page number (as in the fourth and fifth examples above).
- The first time an author is referred to in the text, the author's full name is provided; afterward, only the last name is given.
- When the author's name is provided in the text, the name is not repeated in the parentheses. (Later nonparenthetic references to the same author give only the last name.)

Sometimes, to inform readers of an author's expertise, you may identify that person by profession (*The historian Julian Stamp*). Don't, however, use such personal titles as *Mr.* or *Ms.* And as part of an attribution, you may mention your source's title (*In* The Homeless and History, *Stamp maintains that . . .*).

When providing the necessary information, try to avoid such awkward constructions as these: "According to Julian Stamp, he says that . . ." and "In the book by Julian Stamp, he argues that . . ." Instead, follow these hints for writing smooth, graceful attributions. First, don't always place attributions at the beginning of the sentence; experiment by placing them in the middle (*The key to any successful homeless policy,* **Stamp explains,** *"requires a clear understanding of just who are the homeless"*) or at the end (*Half of homeless individuals living in shelters are substance abusers,* **according to statistics.**) Second, try not to use a predictable subject-verb sequence (*Stamp argues that, Stamp explains that*) in all your attributions. Aim for variations like the following:

The information compiled by Stamp shows . . .

In Stamp's opinion, . . .

Stamp's study reveals that . . .

Finally, rather than repeatedly using the verbs *says* or *writes* in your attributions, seek out more vigorous verbs, making sure the verbs you select are appropriate to the tone and content of the piece you're quoting. The boxed list that follows offers a number of options.

acknowledges	demonstrates	reports
adds	endorses	responds
admits	grants	reveals
argues	implies	says
asserts	insists	shows
believes	maintains	speculates
compares	notes	states
confirms	points out	suggests
contends	questions	wonders
declares	reasons	writes

Key Points to Remember

Take a moment to look again at the preceding examples and note the points presented in the following checklist.

☑ CITING SOURCES: A CHECKLIST

❑ The parenthetic reference is placed *immediately after* the borrowed material, at a natural pause in the sentence or at the end of the sentence.

❑ The parenthetic reference is placed *before* any *internal punctuation* (a comma or semicolon) as well as *before* any *terminal punctuation* (a period or question mark).

❑ If you want to call attention to a specific author, use an attribution indicating the author's name.

❑ When the author's name is provided in the attribution, the name is *not* repeated in the parentheses.

❑ The first time an author is referred to in an attribution, the author's *full name* is given; afterwards, only the *last name* is provided.

❑ Sometimes, to inform readers of an author's area of expertise, the person may be identified by profession ("the historian Julian Stamp argues that . . ."), title, or affiliation.

❑ When the author's name is provided in the parentheses, only the last name is given.

❑ The page number comes directly after the author's name. (If the source is only one page long, only the author's name is needed.)

❑ There is no punctuation between the author's name and the page number.

❑ There is no *p.* or *page* preceding the page number.

❑ Words may be deleted from a quotation as long as the author's original meaning isn't changed. In such a case, three spaced periods—called an *ellipsis* (. . .)—are inserted in place of the deleted words.[3] An ellipsis is not needed when material is omitted from the start of a quotation.

Three Other Important Points

Here are three additional situations you may encounter when documenting sources.

1. More than one source by the same author.   When your paper includes references to more than one work by the same author, you must specify—either in the parentheses or in the attribution—the particular work being cited. You do this by providing the *title*, as well as the author's name and the page(s). As with the author's name, the title may be given in *either* the attribution *or* the parenthetic citation. Here are some examples:

In The Language and Thought of the Child, Jean Piaget states that "discussion forms the basis for a logical point of view" (240).

Piaget considers dialogue essential to the development of logical thinking (Language and Thought 240).

The Child's Conception of the World shows that young children think that the name of something can never change (Piaget 81).

Young children assume that everything has only one name and that no others are possible (Piaget, Child's Conception 81).

Notice that when a work is named in the attribution, the full title appears; when a title is given in the parenthetic citation, though, only the first few significant words appear. (However, don't use the ellipsis to indicate that some words have been omitted from the title; the ellipsis is used only in actual quotations.)

2. Long quotations.   A quotation extending beyond four typed lines starts on a new line and is indented ten spaces from the left margin throughout. Since this so-called *block format* already indicates a quotation, quotation

---

[3]The 1999 edition of the *MLA Handbook for Writers of Research Papers* called for the use of brackets with ellipsis points. Earlier editions and the current require only the ellipses. Check with your instructors to see which guidelines they want you to follow.

marks are not used. Double-space the block quotation, as you do the rest of your paper. Don't leave extra space above or below the quotation. Long quotations, which should be used sparingly, require a lead-in. A lead-in that *isn't* a full sentence is followed by a comma, while a lead-in that *is* a full sentence (as in the accompanying example) is followed by a colon:

Stamp cites changing economic conditions as the key to a national homeless policy:

> Since the 1980s, the gap between the rich and the poor has widened, buying power has stagnated, jobs have fled overseas, and funding for low-cost housing has been almost eliminated. Given these developments, homelessness begins to look like a product of history, and only by addressing shifts in the American economy can we begin to find effective solutions. (8)

Notice that the page number appears in parentheses, just as in a short quotation. But in a long quotation, the parenthetic citation is placed two spaces *after* the period that ends the quotation.

3. Quoting or summarizing a source within a source.   If you quote or summarize a *secondhand source* (someone whose ideas come to you only through another source), you need to make this clear. The parenthetic documentation should indicate "as quoted in" with the abbreviation *qtd. in:*

According to Sherman, "Recycling has, in several communities, created unanticipated expenses" (qtd. in Pratt 3-4).

Sherman explains that recycling can be surprisingly costly (qtd. in Pratt 3-4).

Your Works Cited list would include the source you actually read (Pratt), rather than the source you refer to secondhand (Sherman).

LIST OF WORKS CITED

A documented paper ends with a list of Works Cited, which includes only those sources you actually acknowledge in the paper. Placed on its own page, the Works Cited list provides the reader with full bibliographic information about the sources cited in the parenthetic references (see pages 459–461). By referring to the Works Cited list that appears at the end of the student essay on pages 373–378, you will notice the following:

- The list is organized alphabetically by authors' last names. Entries without an author are alphabetized by the first major word in the title (that is, not *A, An,* or *The*).

- Entries are not numbered.
- If an entry runs longer than one line, each additional line is indented five spaces. Entries are double-spaced with no extra space between entries.

Sample Works Cited Entries

Listed here are sample Works Cited entries for the most commonly used kinds of sources. Refer to these samples when you prepare your own Works Cited list, taking special care to reproduce the punctuation and spacing exactly. If you don't spot an entry for the kind of source you need to document, consult the latest edition of the *MLA Handbook* for more comprehensive examples.

CITING BOOKS

Book by One Author

List the author's last name followed by a comma, the first name, and a period. Then give the title (underlined),[4] followed by a period, and city of publication, followed by a colon and the shortened version of the publisher's name (for example, use UP for "University Press" and Norton for "W.W. Norton & Co."). End with the year of publication and a period.

Ridley, Matt. Nature Via Nurture: Genes, Experience, and What Makes Us Human. New York: Harper, 2003.

Book by Two or Three Authors

Provide all the authors' names in the order they appear on the title page of the book, but reverse only the first author's name.

Thernstrom, Abigail, and Stephan Ternstrom. No Excuses: Closing the Racial Gap in Learning. New York: Simon, 2003.

Gunningham, Neil A., Robert Kagan, and Dorothy Thornton. Shades of Green: Business, Regulation, and Environment. Palo Alto: Stanford UP, 2003.

---

[4]*Important note:* According to MLA guidelines, underlining titles is generally preferred to italicizing them because of the greater visibility of underlines; if you'd like to use italics instead, check with your instructor. (For a review of when titles should be underlined and when they should appear in quotation marks, see pages 483–484, the "Misuse of Italics and Underlining" section of Appendix B.)

Book by Four or More Authors

For a work by four or more authors, give only the first author's name followed by a comma and *et al.* (Latin for "and others").

Brown, Michael K., et al. Whitewashing Race: The Myth of a Color-Blind Society.
    Berkeley: U of California P, 2003.

Two or More Works by the Same Author

If you use more than one work by the same author, list each book separately. Give the author's name in the first entry only; begin the entries for other books by that author with three hyphens followed by a period. Arrange the works alphabetically by title.

Cahill, Thomas. Sailing the Wine-Dark Sea: Why the Greeks Matter. New York:
    Doubleday, 2003.

- - -. How the Irish Saved Civilization: The Untold Story of Ireland's Heroic Role
    from the Fall of Rome to the Rise of Medieval Europe. New York:
    Doubleday, 1995.

Revised Edition

Indicate a revised edition (*Rev. ed.*, *2nd ed.*, *3rd ed.*, *4th ed.*, and so on) after the title.

Zinn, Howard. A People's History of the United States: 1492–Present. Rev. ed.
    New York: Perennial, 2003.

Book With an Editor or Translator

Following the title, type *Ed.* or *Trans.*, followed by the name of the editor or translator.

Douglass, Frederick. My Bondage and My Freedom. Ed. John David Smith. New
    York: Penguin, 2003.

Anthology or Compilation of Works by Different Authors

List anthologies according to the editor or editors' names, followed by *ed.*

Brown, Wesley, and Amy Ling, ed. Visions of America: Personal Narratives from
    the Promised Land. New York: Persea, 2002.

Section of an Anthology or Compilation

Begin this entry with the author and title of the selection (in quotation marks), followed by the title of the anthology. The editors' names are listed after the anthology title and are preceded by *Ed.* Note that the entry ends with the page numbers on which the selection appears.

Cofer, Judith Ortiz. "Silent Dancing." Visions of America: Personal Narratives from the Promised Land. Ed. Wesley Brown and Amy Ling. New York: Persea, 2002. 179–86.

Section or Chapter in a Book by One Author

Simmons, Rachel. "The Bully in the Mirror." Odd Girl Out: The Hidden Culture of Aggression in Girls. New York: Harcourt, 2002. 129–54.

Reference Work

"Temperance Movements." Columbia Encyclopedia. 6th ed. New York: Columbia UP, 2000.

Book by an Institution or Corporation

Give the name of the institution or corporation in the author position, even if the same institution is the publisher.

Food and Agriculture Organization of the United Nations. Organic Agriculture, Environment, and Food Security. Eds. Nadia El-Hage Scialabba and Caroline Hattam. Rome: Food and Agriculture Organization of the United Nations, 2002.

CITING PERIODICALS

Article in a Weekly or Biweekly Magazine

Provide the author's name (if the article is signed), article title (in quotation marks), periodical name (underlined and with *no* period), and date of publication, followed by a colon and page number(s) of the article.

Tyranziel, Josh. "Building a Better Pop Star." Newsweek 13 Oct. 2003: 72–76.

Article in a Monthly or Bimonthly Magazine

Willmore, Alison. "Spoofing Big Brother with Spam." Wired July 2003: 43–48.

Article in a Daily Newspaper

If the article is printed on multiple, nonconsecutive pages, simply list the first page (including both section and page numbers or letters) followed by a plus sign (+). (Note: Omit the initial *The* from newspaper names.)

Doolin, Joseph. "Immigrants Deserve a Fair Deal." Boston Globe 19 Aug. 2003: A19+.

Editorial, Letter to the Editor, or Reply to a Letter

List as you would any signed or unsigned article, but indicate the type of piece after the article's title.

"Playing Fair with Nuclear Cleanup." Editorial. Seattle Times 5 Oct. 2003: D2.

Article in a Scholarly Journal

Some journals are paged continuously; the first issue of each year starts with page 1, and each subsequent issue picks up where the previous one left off. For such journals, use numerals to indicate the volume number after the title, and then indicate the year in parentheses. Note that neither *volume* nor *vol.* is used. The article's page(s) appear at the end, separated from the year by a colon.

Previti, Denise, and Paul R. Amato. "Why Stay Married? Rewards, Barriers, and Marital Stability." Journal of Marriage & the Family 65 (2003): 561–73.

For a journal that pages each issue separately, use numerals to indicate the *volume and issue numbers;* separate the two with a period but leave no space after the period.

Shackelford, William G. "The Changing Definition of Workplace Diversity." Black Collegian 33.2 (2003): 53–57.

CITING ELECTRONIC SOURCES

Article in an Online Periodical

For an article obtained online, supply the same information you would for printed text: author's name, selection's title, source, and (when available) publication date and page or paragraph numbers. When page or paragraph numbers are provided, list them after the date of publication (using *pp.* for "pages" or *par.* for "paragraphs").

Complete your listing with the date on which you accessed the material, followed by the exact address of the website (in angle brackets) and then a final period. (Since online material can be revised at any time, it's critical that you provide your date of access to identify the version you retrieved.) Note that long Web addresses should be broken up only after slashes.

Song, Sora. "The High Cost of Teen Drinking." Time Online. 22 Sept. 2003. 19 May 2004 <http://www.time.com/time/magazine/article/ 0,9171,1101030922-485760,00.html>.

Schultz, Jason. "File sharing must be made legal." Salon 12 Sept. 2003: 8 pars. 27 Mar. 2004 <http://archive.salon.com/tech/feature/2003/09/12/ file_sharing_two/>.

Article in a Full-Text Online Periodicals Index

For full-text articles accessed through an online index (generally only available to libraries by subscription), begin with the same information as for online periodicals. After the publication information (issue, date, and page numbers), list the title of the index (underlined), its vendor, and the library through which you gained access to it. Complete the entry with the date you accessed the index and the index's Web address.

Casella, Ronnie. "Zero Tolerance Policy in Schools: Rationale, Consequences, Alternatives." Teachers College Record 105.5 (June 2003): 872–92. EBSCOhost. MasterFILE Premier. Camden County Lib., Voorhees. 17 Apr. 2004 <http://web5.epnet.com>.

Online Book

When it's available, include the book's original publication information between the book's title and the underlined database name. Also include (when available) the name of the site's editor, its electronic publication date, its sponsoring organization, your date of access, and the Web address.

Franklin, Benjamin. The Autobiography of Benjamin Franklin. London, 1793. Electronic Text Center. Ed. David Seaman. 1998. U. of Virginia Lib. 16 Jan. 2004 <http://etext.lib.virginia.edu>.

Online Reference Work

"Salem Witch Trials." Encyclopaedia Britannica Online. 2003. Encyclopaedia Britannica Premium Service. 8 Oct. 2003 <http://www.britannica.com/ eb/article?eu=66735>.

Professional or Personal Website

You'll note that in the first entry below, *Uncle Tom's Cabin* is *not* under-lined. It's a title that would ordinarily be underlined, but since the rest of the website title is underlined, the book title is set off by a *lack* of underlining.

Harriet Beecher Stowe's Uncle Tom's Cabin & American Culture: A Multi-Media Archive. Ed. Stephen Railton. 20 Jan. 2003. Dept. of English, U of Virginia. 2 Mar. 2004 <http://www.iath.virginia.edu/utc/>.

Finney, Dee. Native American Culture. 21 July 2003. 17 Feb. 2004 <http://www.greatdreams.com/native.htm>.

Computer Software

Cite the following information (when available): author of the software, title (underlined), medium (CD-ROM or diskette), version, publication city, publisher, and year of publication.

World Book Encyclopedia 2004 Edition. CD-ROM. 2004 ed. Renton: Topics Entertainment, 2004.

E-mail Message

Bernard, Lynn. "New Developments in Early Childhood Education." E-mail to Ronnie Hotis. 30 Aug. 2004.

CITING OTHER NONPRINT SOURCES

Television or Radio Program

"A Matter of Choice? Gay Life in America." Nightline. Narr. Ted Koppel. Part 4 of 5. ABC. WPVI-TV, Philadelphia. 23 May 2002.

Movie, Recording, Videotape, DVD, Filmstrip, or Slide Program

Provide the author or composer of the piece (if appropriate); title (under-lined); director, conductor, or performer; medium; distributor; and year of release.

Frida. Dir. Julie Taymor. DVD. Miramax, 2003.

Personal or Phone Interview

Langdon, Paul. Personal interview. 26 Jan. 2004.

Lecture

Blacksmith, James. "Urban Design in the New Millennium." Cityscapes Lecture Series. Urban Studies Institute. Metropolitan College, Washington, DC. 18 Apr. 2004.

Papa, Andrea. "Reforming the Nation's Tax Structure." Lecture. Accounting 302, Cypress College. Astoria, New York. 3 May 2004.

Appendix B
AVOIDING TEN COMMON
WRITING ERRORS

Many students consider grammar a nuisance. Taking the easy way out, they cross their fingers and hope they haven't made too many mistakes. They assume that their meaning will come across, even if their writing contains some errors—perhaps a misplaced comma here or a dangling modifier there. Not so. Surface errors annoy readers and may confuse them. Such errors also weaken a writer's credibility because they defy language conventions, customs that readers expect writers to honor. By mastering grammar, punctuation, and spelling conventions, students can increase their power and versatility as writers.

This concise appendix, Avoiding Ten Common Writing Errors, will help you brush up on the most useful rules and conventions of writing. It's organized according to the broad skill areas, listed below, that give writers the most trouble. (For more extensive instruction in grammar and style, refer to the Handbook section of *The Longman Writer.*) Throughout this appendix, grammatical terminology is kept to a minimum. Although we assume that you know the major parts of speech (noun, verb, pronoun, and so on), we do, when appropriate, provide on-the-spot definitions of more technical grammatical terms.

Here are the ten common writing errors covered:

1. Fragments
2. Comma Splices and Run-ons
3. Faulty Subject-Verb Agreement
4. Faulty Pronoun Agreement
5. Misplaced and Dangling Modifiers
6. Faulty Parallelism
7. Comma Misuse

8. Apostrophe Misuse
9. Confusing Homonyms
10. Misuse of Italics and Underlining

---

1 FRAGMENTS

A full *sentence* satisfies two conditions: (1) it has a subject and a verb, and (2) it can stand alone as a complete thought. Although a *fragment* is punctuated like a full sentence, it doesn't satisfy these two requirements.

NO   Meteorologists predict a drought this summer. *In spite of heavy spring rains.*
NO   *A victim of her own hypocrisy.* The senator lost the next election.

Some Easy Ways to Correct Fragments

A. Attach the fragment to the beginning or end of the preceding (or following) sentence, changing punctuation and capitalization as needed.

YES   In spite of heavy spring rains, meteorologists predict a drought this summer.
or
Meteorologists predict a drought this summer, in spite of heavy spring rains.

B. Attach the fragment to a newly created sentence.

YES   Meteorologists predict a drought this summer. *They do so* in spite of heavy spring rains.

C. Insert the fragment into the preceding (or following) sentence, adding commas as needed.

YES   The senator, *a victim of her own hypocrisy,* lost the next election.

D. Supply the missing subject and/or verb, changing other words as necessary.

YES   *The senator became* a victim of her own hypocrisy. *She* lost the next election.

---

2 COMMA SPLICES AND RUN-ONS

Consider the following faulty sentences:

NO   The First Amendment cannot be taken for granted, it is the bedrock of our democracy.
NO   The First Amendment cannot be taken for granted it is the bedrock of our democracy.

The first example is a *comma splice:* a comma used to join, or splice together, two complete thoughts, even though the comma alone is not strong enough to connect the two independent ideas. The second example is a *run-on,* or fused, sentence: two sentences run together without any punctuation indicating where the first sentence ends and the second begins.

Some Easy Ways to Correct Comma Splices and Run-ons

A. Place a period, question mark, or exclamation point at the end of the first sentence, and capitalize the first letter of the second sentence.

YES   The First Amendment cannot be taken for *granted. It* is the bedrock of our democracy.

B. Use a semicolon to mark where the first sentence ends and the second begins.

YES   The First Amendment cannot be taken for *granted; it* is the bedrock of our democracy.

C. Turn one of the sentences into a dependent phrase.

YES   *Because* it is the bedrock of our democracy, the First Amendment cannot be taken for granted.

D. Keep or add a comma at the end of the first sentence, but follow the comma with a coordinating conjunction (*and, but, for, nor, or, so, yet*).

YES   The First Amendment cannot be taken for granted, *for* it is the bedrock of our democracy.

---

3 FAULTY SUBJECT-VERB AGREEMENT

A verb should match its subject in number. If the subject is singular (one person, place, or thing), the verb should have a singular form. If the subject is plural (two or more persons, places, or things), the verb should have a plural form. Always determine the verb's subject and make sure that the verb agrees with it, rather than with some other word in the sentence.

NO   The *documents* from the court case *was* unsealed for the first time in three decades.

YES   The *documents* from the court case *were* unsealed for the first time in three decades.

Some Easy Ways to Correct Faulty Subject-Verb Agreement

A. When there are two or more subjects (joined by *and*) in a sentence, use a plural verb. (However, when the word *or* joins the subjects, use a *singular* verb.)

YES   A sprawling maple *and* a lush rose bush *flank* [not *flanks*] my childhood home.

B. When the subject and verb are separated by a prepositional phrase, be sure to match the verb to its subject—not to a word in the prepositional phrase that comes between them.

YES   The *quality* of student papers *has* [not *have*] been declining over the past semester.

C. When the words *either . . . or* or *neither . . . nor* connect two subjects, use the verb form (singular or plural) that agrees with the subject *closer* to the verb.

YES   *Neither* the employees *nor* the store *owner was* [not *were*] aware of the theft.
YES   *Neither* the store owner *nor* her *employees were* [not *was*] aware of the theft.

D. When using the indefinite pronouns *anybody, anyone, anything, each, either, everyone, everybody, everyone, everything, neither, nobody, none, no one, nothing, one, somebody, someone,* or *something,* use a *singular* verb.

YES   *Neither* of the candidates *is* [not *are*] willing to address the issue.

When you use the indefinite pronouns *all, any, most, none,* or *some,* use a *singular* or a *plural* verb, depending on whether the pronoun refers to one thing or to a number of things.

YES   The spokesperson announced that only *some* of the *report has* been confirmed.

In the above sentence, *some* refers to a single report and therefore takes a *singular* verb. In the following sentence, *some* refers to *multiple* reports and therefore takes a *plural* verb.

YES   The spokesperson announced that only *some* of the *reports have* been confirmed.

E. When the subject of a sentence refers to a group acting as a unit, use a *singular* verb.

YES   The local baseball *team is* [not *are*] boycotting the new sports stadium.

F.   When words such as *here, there, how, what, when, where, which, who,* and *why* invert normal sentence order—so that the verb comes before the subject—look ahead for the subject and make sure that it and the verb agree.

YES   There *is* [not *are*] a *series* of things to consider before deciding on a college major.

YES   What *are* [not *is*] the *arguments* against energy conservation?

---

4 FAULTY PRONOUN AGREEMENT

A *pronoun* must agree in number with its *antecedent*—the noun or pronoun it replaces or refers to. If the antecedent is singular, the pronoun must be singular. If the antecedent is plural, the pronoun must be plural.

Some Easy Ways to Correct Faulty Pronoun Agreement

A.   A compound subject (two or more nouns joined by *and*) requires plural pronouns.

YES   Both the car *manufacturers* and the tire *company* had trouble restoring *their* reputations after losing the class-action lawsuit.

However, when the nouns are joined by *or* or *nor*, the verb form (singular or plural) should agree with the noun that is *closer* to the verb.

YES   Neither the car manufacturers *nor* the tire *company* restored *its* reputation after losing the class-action lawsuit.

YES   Neither the tire company *nor* the car *manufacturers* restored *their* reputations after losing the class-action lawsuit.

B.   A subject that is a *collective noun* (referring to a group that acts as a unit) takes a singular pronoun.

YES   The *orchestra* showed *its* appreciation by playing a lengthy encore.

Or, if a singular pronoun sounds awkward, simply make the antecedent plural.

YES   The orchestra *members* showed *their* appreciation by playing a lengthy encore.

C. The indefinite pronouns *anybody, anyone, anything, each, either, everybody, everyone, everything, neither, nobody, none, no one, nothing, one,*

somebody, someone, and *something* are singular and therefore take singular pronouns.

YES   *Each* of the buildings had *its* [not *their*] roof replaced.
YES   *Neither* of the executives resigned *his* [not *their*] position after the revelations.

Using the singular form with indefinite pronouns can be awkward or sexist when the pronoun encompasses both male and female. To avoid these problems, you can make the antecedent plural and use a plural pronoun.

AWK   *Anyone* who exhibits symptoms should see her or his doctor immediately.
YES   *Individuals* who exhibit symptoms should see *their* doctor immediately.

D. Within a sentence, pronouns should be in the same *person* (point of view) as their antecedents.

NO   To register to vote, *citizens* [third person] can visit the state government's website, where *you* [second person] can download the appropriate forms.
YES   To register to vote, *citizens* [third person] can visit the state government's website, where *they* [third person] can download the appropriate forms.

5 MISPLACED AND DANGLING MODIFIERS

A *modifier* is a word or group of words that describes something else. Sometimes sentences are written in such a way that modifiers are misplaced. Here is an example of a *misplaced modifier:*

NO   Television stations carried the story of the disastrous tornado *throughout the nation.* [The tornado was throughout the nation?]
YES   Television stations *throughout the nation* carried the story of the disastrous tornado.

Modifiers are commonly misused in another way. An introductory modifier must modify the subject of the sentence. If it doesn't, it may be a **dangling modifier.** Here's an example:

NO   *Faded and brittle with age,* archaeologists unearthed a painted clay pot near the riverbank. [The archaeologists were faded and brittle with age?]
YES   Archaeologists unearthed a painted clay pot, *faded and brittle with age,* near the riverbank.
    or
    Faded and brittle with age, a painted clay pot was unearthed near the riverbank by archaeologists.

An Easy Way to Correct Misplaced Modifiers

A. Place the modifier next to the word(s) it describes.

NO   Passengers complained about the flight at the customer service desk, *which was turbulent and delayed.* [The customer service desk was turbulent and delayed?]

YES   Passengers complained about the flight, *which was turbulent and delayed,* at the customer service desk.

NO   Because he repeatedly failed, the judge's son *almost* retook the bar exam ten times. [He nearly retook the exam but didn't actually do so at all?]

YES   Because he repeatedly failed, the judge's son retook the bar exam *almost* ten times.

Some Easy Ways to Correct Dangling Modifiers

The following dangling modifier can be corrected in one of two ways, discussed below.

NO   *Leaping gracefully across the stage,* spectators were in awe of the agile dancer.

A. Rewrite the sentence by adding to the modifying phrase the word that is being described.

YES   *As the agile dancer leaped* gracefully across the stage, spectators were in awe of him.

B. Rewrite the sentence so that the word being modified becomes the subject.

YES   Leaping gracefully across the stage, *the agile dancer awed* the spectators.

---

6 FAULTY PARALLELISM

Words in a pair or in a series should be phrased in *parallel* (matching) grammatical structures. Otherwise, *faulty parallelism* results.

NO   After hiking all day, the campers were *exhausted, hungry,* and *experienced soreness.* [Of the three items in the series, the first two are adjectives, but the last is a verb plus a noun.]

YES   After hiking all day, the campers were *exhausted, hungry,* and *sore.*

Words that follow *correlative conjunctions—either . . . or, neither . . . nor, both . . . and, not only . . . but also—*should also be parallel.

NO   Every road to the airport is **either** *jammed* **or** *is closed* for repairs. [The word *either* is followed by an adjective (*jammed*), but *or* is followed by a verb and adjective (*is closed*).]

YES   Every road to the airport is **either** *jammed* **or** *closed* for repairs.

An Easy Way to Correct Faulty Parallelism

A. Use the *same grammatical structure* for each item in a pair or series.

NO   The finalists for the sales job possess *charismatic personalities, excellent references,* and *they are extensively experienced.*

YES   The finalists for the sales job possess *charismatic personalities, excellent references,* and *extensive experience.*

NO   We knew that autumn was on its way because *the leaves were changing color, the sun was setting earlier,* and *there was a chill in the air.*

YES   We knew that autumn was on its way because *the leaves were changing color, the sun was setting earlier,* and *the air was becoming chillier.*

NO   The romantic comedy that premiered last night was neither *romantic* nor *was it funny.*

YES   The romantic comedy that premiered last night was neither *romantic* nor *funny.*

---

7 COMMA MISUSE

The *comma* is so frequent in writing that mastering its use is essential. By dividing a sentence into its parts, commas clarify meaning. The following are the most common uses of commas.

Most Common Uses of the Comma

A. When two complete sentences are joined with a coordinating conjunction (*and, but, for, nor, or, so, yet*), a comma is placed *before* the conjunction.

YES   Many attended the political rally, *but* few demonstrated enthusiasm for the cause.

B. Introductory material, which precedes a sentence's main subject and verb, usually is followed by a comma.

YES   *Like most kids,* the children in the study were powerfully influenced by TV advertisements.

Similarly, material attached to the *end* of a sentence may be preceded by a comma.

YES   The children in the study were powerfully influenced by TV advertisements, *which peddled expensive toys and unhealthy snacks.*

C. When a word or phrase describes a noun but isn't crucial for identifying that noun, it is set off from the rest of the sentence with a comma.

YES   First-year film students are required to analyze *Metropolis,* a late-1920s film that exhibited important artistic innovations.

D. When words or phrases inserted into the body of a sentence can be removed without significant loss of meaning, such elements are considered *interrupters.* Interrupters should be preceded and followed by commas when they occur midsentence.

YES   Dr. Gene Nome, *a leading genetic researcher,* testified before Congress on the need for increased funding.

E. In a list of *three or more* items in a series, the items should be separated by commas.

YES   The writing process usually entails *prewriting, drafting,* and *revising.*

F. A comma should be inserted between a short quotation and a phrase that indicates the quotation's source.

YES   One voter commented, "This is the first candidate I've voted for enthusiastically."
or
"This is the first candidate I've voted for enthusiastically," one voter commented.
or
"This is the first candidate," one voter commented, "I've voted for enthusiastically."

G. Commas are placed between the numbers in a date and between the elements of the address with the exception that no comma precedes a Zip code.

YES   On November 17, 2003, the fourth graders mailed "Dear President" letters to The White House, 1600 Pennsylvania Avenue, Washington, DC 20500.

8 APOSTROPHE MISUSE

Like the comma, the *apostrophe* is a commonly used—and misused—punctuation mark. The following are its most common uses.

Most Common Uses of the Apostrophe

A. In standard contractions, an apostrophe replaces any omitted letters.

YES   can't, don't, I'm, she's, we've

B. The possessive form of most singular nouns requires adding *'s*.

YES   Senator Ross**'s** position is that health care is every person**'s** right.

For *plural nouns* ending in *s,* an apostrophe only is added to show possession.

YES   The twelve senators**'** position on Native Americans**'** rights is clear.

Plural nouns that do not end in *s* need *'s* to show possession.

YES   Improvement in the children**'s** test scores enabled the school to rise in rank.

However, an apostrophe is *not* used to form the simple plural of a noun.

NO   The central role of *radio's* in American homes has declined in recent decades.
YES   The central role of *radios* in American homes has declined in recent decades.

C. Beware of confusing possessive pronouns with contractions. The possessive forms of personal pronouns do *not* include an apostrophe. Here are the correct forms:

YES   mine, yours, his, hers, its, ours, theirs

Note that *its* (*without* an apostrophe) is the possessive form of *it,* whereas *it's* (*with* an apostrophe) means "it is" or "it has."

YES   The factory closed *its* [not *it's*] doors last week.
YES   The company president determined that *it's* [for it *is*] time to close down the factory.

Similarly, *whose* (*without* an apostrophe) is the possessive form of *who,* whereas *who's* (*with* an apostrophe) means "who is" or "who has."

YES   The sculptor *whose* [not *who's*] work is being exhibited just arrived at the gallery.

YES   The sculptor *who's* [for *who is*] exhibiting his work just arrived at the gallery.

---

9 CONFUSING HOMONYMS

Homonyms are words that sound alike but have different spellings and meanings. Here are some of the most troublesome.

Accept means "receive" or "agree to." **Except** means "but" or "excluding."

YES   *Except* for your position on mandatory school uniforms, I *accept* your ideas about changing the education system.

Affect means "influence" (verb). **Effect** means "result" (noun) or "bring about" (verb).

YES   It's amazing how much a hurricane's *effects* can *affect* a region's economy.

Its means "belonging to it." **It's** means "it is" or "it has."

YES   *It's* been years since the factory produced *its* last car.

Principal means either "main" or "the person in charge of a school." **Principle** means "a law or concept."

YES   The *principal* topic you should study for your midterm is the *principle* of gravity.

Than is a word used in comparisons. **Then** means "at that time."

YES   The insurance agent assessed the house and *then* wrote a report stating that the damage was worse *than* expected.

Their means "belonging to them." **There** refers to a place other than "here." **They're** means "they are."

YES   *They're* planning to drop off *their* donations for the food drive in the bin over *there*.

To can be part of a verb (as in *to smile* or *came to*) or a preposition meaning "toward." **Too** means "overly" (as in *too hot*) or "also." **Two** refers to the number 2.

YES   *Two* of my coworkers go outside *to* eat lunch every day; today they invited me, *too.*

Whose means "belonging to someone or something." **Who's** means "who is" or "who has."

YES   We're trying to determine *who's* going to call my aunt, *whose* son was injured in an accident.

Your means "belonging to you." **You're** means "you are."

YES   When *your* mother calls you by *your* first, middle, and last name, you know *you're* in trouble.

---

10 MISUSE OF ITALICS AND UNDERLINING

Computers and other printing innovations have allowed italics (*slanted type*) to replace underlining (underlined type) in printed text. The following are the most common uses of italics (or of underlining, if you're writing by hand or using a typewriter).

A. The titles of works that are published (or, in the case of visual works, displayed) individually should be italicized or underlined. Such works, which are often lengthy, include books, magazines, journals, newspapers, movies, TV programs, musical recordings, plays, paintings, and sculptures.

Note: The titles of shorter works—such as poems, short stories, articles, essays, songs, and TV episodes—published as part of a magazine, anthology, or other collection are *not* italicized; use quotation marks for such titles.

YES   After reading Anne Sexton's poem "The Starry Night" from the collection *All My Pretty Ones,* the students went online to look at Van Gogh's painting *The Starry Night.*
YES   The Discovery Channel program *The Beatles: The Later Years* focused primarily on the band's albums *Sgt. Pepper's Lonely Hearts Club Band* and *Abbey Road.*

B. Foreign words not fully incorporated into mainstream English should be italicized or underlined.

YES   The labor union leaders sought a *tête-à-tête* with the company's executives in order to resolve a work strike.

C. Words that you wish to emphasize should be italicized or underlined. However, this should be done sparingly at the risk of actually *weakening* emphasis.

YES   Users of the new computer program report that they don't like it. They *love* it.

D. When a word is being referred to *as a word* or as a *defined term*, it should be italicized or underlined.

YES   When writing, avoid using a word like *conflagration* when *fire* will do.
YES   The word *conflagration* actually means "fire."

GLOSSARY

Abstract and concrete language refers to two different qualities of words. Abstract words and phrases convey concepts, qualities, emotions, and ideas that we can think and talk about but not actually see or experience directly. Examples of abstract words are *conservatism, courage, avarice, joy,* and *hatred.* Words or phrases whose meanings are directly seen or experienced by the senses are concrete terms. Examples of phrases using concrete words are *split-level house, waddling penguin,* and *short pink waitress uniform.*

Adequate—see *Evidence.*

Ad hominem **argument**—see *Logical fallacies.*

Analogy refers to an imaginative comparison between two subjects that seem to have little in common. Often a complex idea or topic can be made understandable by comparing it to a more familiar subject, and such an analogy can be developed over several paragraphs or even an entire essay. For example, to explain how the economic difficulties of farmers weaken an entire nation, a writer might create an analogy between failing farms and a cancer that slowly destroys a person's life.

Argumentation-persuasion tries to encourage readers to accept a writer's point of view on some controversial issue. In *argumentation,* a writer uses objective reasoning, facts, and hard evidence to demonstrate the soundness of a position. In *persuasion,* the writer uses appeals to the readers' emotions and value systems, often in the hope of encouraging them to take a specific action. Argumentation and persuasion are frequently used together in an essay. For example, a writer might argue for the construction of a highway through town by pointing out that the road would bring new business, create new jobs, and lighten traffic.

The writer also might try to persuade readers to vote for a highway appropriations bill by appealing to their emotions, claiming that the highway would allow people to get home faster, thus giving them more time for family life and leisure activities. A whole essay can be organized around argumentation-persuasion, or an essay developed chiefly through another pattern may contain elements of argumentation-persuasion.

Assertion refers to the *thesis* of an *argumentation-persuasion* essay. The assertion, or *proposition*, is a point of view or opinion on a controversial issue or topic. The assertion cannot be merely a statement of a fact. Such statements as "Women still experience discrimination in the job market," "General Rabb would make an ideal mayor for our town," and "This university should devote more funds to raising the quality of the food services" are examples of assertions that could serve as theses for argumentation-persuasion essays.

Audience refers to a writer's intended readers. In planning the content and tone of an essay, you should identify your audience and consider its needs. How similar are the members of your audience to you in knowledge and point of view? What will they need to know for you to achieve your *purpose?* What *tone* will make them open to receiving your message? For example, if you were to write a description of a trip to Disney World, you would have to explain a lot more to an eighty-year-old grandmother who had never seen a theme park than to a young parent who has probably visited several. If you wrote about the high cost of clothing for an economics professor, you would choose a serious, analytic tone and supply statistical evidence for your points. If you wrote about the same topic for the college newspaper, you might use a tone tinged with humor and provide helpful hints on finding bargain clothing.

Begging the question—see *Logical fallacies.*

Brainstorming is a technique used in the *prewriting* stage. It helps you discover the limited subject you can successfully write about and also generates raw material— ideas and details—to develop that subject. In brainstorming, you allow your mind to play freely with the subject. You try to capture fleeting thoughts about it, no matter how random, minor, or tangential, and jot them down rapidly before they disappear from your mind.

Causal analysis—see *Cause-effect.*

Causal chain refers to a series of causes and effects, in which the result or effect of a cause becomes itself the cause of a further effect, and so on. For example, a person's alarm clock failing to buzz might begin a causal chain by causing the person to oversleep. Oversleeping then causes the person to miss the bus, and missing the bus causes the person to arrive late to work. Arriving late causes the person to miss an important phone call, which causes the person to lose a chance at a lucrative contract.

Cause-effect, sometimes called *causal analysis,* involves analyzing the reasons for or results of an event, action, decision, or phenomenon. Writers develop an essay through an analysis of causes whenever they attempt to answer such questions as "Why has this happened?" or "Why does this exist?" When writers explore such questions as "What happens or would happen if a certain change occurs?" or "What will happen if a condition continues?" their essays involve a discussion of effects. Some cause-effect essays concentrate on the causes of a situation, some focus on the effects, and others present both causes and effects. Causal analysis can be an essay's central pattern, or it can be used to help support a point in an essay developed primarily through another pattern.

Characteristics—see *Formal definition*.

Chronological sequence—see *Narrative sequence* and *Organization*.

Circularity is an error in *formal definition* resulting from using variations of the to-be-defined word in the definition. For example, "A scientific hypothesis is a hypothesis made by a scientist about the results of an experiment" is circular because the unknown term is used to explain itself.

Class—see *Formal definition*.

Coherence refers to the clear connection among the various parts of an essay. As a writer, you can draw upon two key strategies to make writing coherent. You can use a clear *organizational format* (for example, a chronological, spatial, emphatic, or simple-to-complex sequence). You can also provide *appropriate signaling* or *connecting devices* (transitions, bridging sentences, repeated words, synonyms, and pronouns).

Comparison-contrast means explaining the similarities and/or differences between events, objects, people, ideas, and so on. The comparison-contrast format can be used to meet a purely factual purpose ("This is how A and B are alike or different"). But usually writers use comparison-contrast to make a judgment about the relative merits of the subjects under discussion. Sometimes a writer will concentrate solely on similarities *or* differences. For instance, when writing about married versus single life, you would probably devote most of your time to discussing the differences between these lifestyles. Other times, comparison and contrast are found together. In an essay analyzing two approaches to U.S. foreign policy, you would probably discuss the similarities *and* the differences in the goals and methods characteristic of each approach. Comparison-contrast can be the dominant pattern in an essay, or it can help support a point in an essay developed chiefly through another pattern.

Conclusion refers to the one or more paragraphs that bring an essay to an end. Effective conclusions give the reader a sense of completeness and finality. Writers often use the conclusion as a place to reaffirm the *thesis* and to express a final thought about the subject. Methods of conclusion include summarizing main points, using a quotation, predicting an outcome, and recommending an action.

Conflict creates tension in the readers of a *narration*. It is produced by the opposition of characters or other forces in a story. Conflict can occur between individuals, between a person and society or nature, or within a person. Readers wonder how a conflict will be resolved and read on to find out.

Connotative and denotative language describe the ability of language to emphasize one or another aspect of a word's range of meaning. *Denotative language* stresses the dictionary meaning of words. *Connotative language* emphasizes the echoes of feeling that cluster around some words. For example, the terms *weep, bawl, break down,* and *sob* all denote the same thing: to cry. But they have different associations and call up different images. A writer employing the connotative resources of language would choose the term among these that suggested the appropriate image.

Controlling idea—see *Thesis*.

Deductive reasoning is a form of logical thinking in which general statements believed to be true are applied to specific situations or cases. The result of deduction is a conclusion or prediction about the specific situation. Deduction is often expressed in a three-step pattern called a *syllogism*. The first part of the syllogism is a general statement about a large class of items or situations, the *major premise*. The second part is the *minor premise,* a more limited statement about a specific item or case. The third part is the *conclusion,* drawn from the major premise, about that specific case or item. Deductive reasoning is very common in everyday thinking. For example, you might use deduction when car shopping:

In an accident, large cars are safer than small cars. (*major premise*)

The Turbo Titan is a large car. (*minor premise*)

In an accident, the Turbo Titan will be safer than a small car. (*conclusion*)

Definition explains the meaning of a word or concept. The brief formal definitions found in the dictionary can be useful if you need to clarify or restrict the meaning of a term used in an essay. In such cases, the definition is short and to the point. But you may also use an *extended definition* in an essay, taking several paragraphs, even the entire piece, to develop the meaning of a term. You may use extended definition to convey a personal slant on a well-known term, to refute a commonly held interpretation of a word, or to dissect a complex or controversial issue. Definition can be the chief method of development in an essay, or it can help support a point in an essay organized around another pattern.

Definition by negation is a method of defining a term by first explaining what the term is *not,* and then going on to explain what it is. For example, you might begin a critical essay about television with a definition by negation: "Television, far from being a medium that dispenses only light, insubstantial fare, actually disseminates a dangerously distorted view of family life." Definition by negation can provide a stimulating introduction to an essay.

Denotative language—see *Connotative and denotative language.*

Description involves the use of vivid word pictures to express what the five senses have experienced. The subject of a descriptive essay can be a person, a place, an object, or an event. Description can be the dominant pattern in an essay, or it can be used as a supplemental method in an essay developed chiefly through another pattern.

There are two main types of description. In an *objective description,* a writer provides details about a subject without conveying the emotions the subject arouses. For example, if you were involved in a traffic accident, your insurance agent might ask you to write an objective description of the events leading up to and during the crash. But in a *subjective description,* the writer's goal is to evoke in the reader the emotions felt during the experience. For example, in a cautionary letter to a friend who has a habit of driving dangerously, you might write a subjective description of your horrifyingly close call with death during a car accident.

Development—see *Evidence.*

Dialogue is the writer's way of directly presenting the exact words spoken by characters in a *narration*. By using dialogue, writers can convey people's individuality and also add drama and immediacy to an essay.

Directional process analysis—see *Process analysis.*

Division-classification refers to a logical method for analyzing a single subject or several related subjects. Though often used together in an essay, division and classification are separate processes. *Division* involves breaking a subject or idea into its component parts. For instance, the concept "an ideal vacation" could be divided according to its destination, accommodations, or cost. *Classification* involves organizing a number of related items into categories. For example, in an essay about the overwhelming flow of paper in our everyday lives, you might classify the typical kinds of mail most people receive: personal mail (letters, birthday cards, party invitations), business mail (bills, bank statements, charge-card receipts), and junk mail (flyers about bargain sales, solicitations to donate, contest announcements). Division-classification can be the dominant pattern in a paper, or it may be used to support a point in an essay organized chiefly around another pattern of development.

Dominant impression refers to the purpose of a descriptive essay. While some descriptive essays have a thesis, others do not; instead, they convey a dominant impression or main point. For example, one person writing a descriptive essay about New York City might use its architectural diversity as a focal point. Another person writing a description of Manhattan might concentrate on the overpowering sense of hustle and speed about everyone and everything in the city. Both writers would select only those details that supported their dominant impressions.

Dramatic license refers to the writer's privilege, when writing a narrative, to alter facts or details to strengthen the support of the *thesis* or *narrative point*. For example, a writer is free to flesh out the description of an event whose specific details may be partially forgotten or to modify or omit details of a narrative that do not contribute to the meaning the writer wishes to convey.

Either-or fallacy—see *Logical fallacies.*

Emphatic sequence—see *Organization.*

Ethos refers to a writer's reliability or credibility. Such an image of trustworthiness is particularly important to readers of an *argumentation-persuasion* essay or piece. Writers establish their *ethos* by using reason and logic, by being moderate in their appeals to emotions, by avoiding a hostile tone, and by demonstrating overall knowledgeability of the subject. The most effective argumentation-persuasion involves an interplay of *ethos, logos,* and *pathos.*

Etymology refers to the history of a word or term. All English words have their origins in other, often ancient, languages. Giving a brief etymology of a word can help a writer establish the context for developing an *extended definition* of the word. For example, the word *criminal* is derived from a Latin word meaning "accusation" or "accused." Today, our word *criminal* goes beyond the concept of "accused" to mean "guilty."

Evidence lends substance to a writer's main ideas and thus helps the reader to accept the writer's viewpoint. Evidence should meet several criteria. First of all, it should be *unified,* in the sense that all supporting ideas and details should relate directly to the key point the writer is making. Second, evidence should be *adequate;*

there should be enough evidence to convince the reader to agree with the thesis. Third, evidence should be *specific;* that is, vivid and detailed rather than vague and general. Fourth, evidence must be *accurate* and not overstate or understate information. Fifth, evidence should be *representative,* relying on the typical rather than the atypical to make a point. The bulk of an essay is devoted to supplying evidence. Supporting the thesis with solid evidence is the third stage in the writing process.

Exemplification, at the heart of all effective writing, involves using concrete specifics to support generalizations. In exemplification, writers provide examples or instances that support or clarify broader statements. You might support the thesis statement "I have a close-knit family" by using such examples as the following: "We have a regular Sunday dinner at my grandmother's house with at least ten family members present"; "My sisters and brothers visit my parents every week"; "I spend so much time on the phone talking with my sisters that sometimes I have trouble finding time for my new college friends." Exemplification may be an essay's central pattern, or it may supplement another pattern.

Extended definition—see *Definition.*

Fallacies—see *Logical fallacies.*

False analogy—see *Logical fallacies.*

Figures of speech are imaginative comparisons between two things usually thought of as dissimilar. Some major figures of speech are *simile, metaphor,* and *personification. Similes* are comparisons that use the signal words *like* or *as:* "Superman was as powerful as a locomotive." *Metaphors,* which do not use signal words, directly equate unlike things: "The boss is a tiger when it comes to landing a contract." "The high-powered pistons of the boxer's arms pummeled his opponent." *Personification* attributes human characteristics to inanimate things or nonhuman beings: "The angry clouds unleashed their fury on the town"; "The turtle shyly poked his head out of his shell."

First draft refers to the writer's first try at producing a basic, unpolished version of the whole essay. It is often referred to as the "rough" draft, and nothing about it is final or unchangeable. The process of writing the first draft often brings up new ideas or details. Writers sometimes break off writing the draft to *brainstorm* or *freewrite* as new ideas occur to them and then return to the draft with new inspiration. You shouldn't worry about spelling, grammar, or style in the first-draft stage; instead, you should keep focused on casting your ideas into sentence and paragraph form. Writing the first draft is the fifth stage in the writing process.

Flashback—see *Narrative sequence.*

Flashforward—see *Narrative sequence.*

Formal definition involves stating a definition in a three-part pattern of about one sentence in length. In presenting a formal definition, a writer puts the *term* in a *class* and then lists the *characteristics* that separate the term from other members of its class. For example, a formal definition of a word processor might be, "A word processor (term) is an electronic machine (class) that is used to write, edit, store, and produce typewritten documents (characteristics)." Writers often use a formal definition to prepare a reader for an extended definition that follows.

Freewriting is most often used during the *prewriting* stage to help writers generate ideas about a limited topic. To use this method, write nonstop for five or ten minutes about everything your topic brings to mind. Disregard grammar, spelling, and organization as you keep your pen and mind moving. Freewriting is similar to *brainstorming,* except that the result is a rambling, detail-filled paragraph rather than a list. Freewriting can also be used to generate ideas during later stages of the writing process.

Gender-biased language gives the impression that one sex is more important, powerful, or valuable than the other. When writing, you should work to replace such sexist language with *gender-neutral* or *nonsexist* terms that convey no sexual prejudice. First of all, try to avoid *sexist vocabulary* that demeans or excludes one of the sexes: *stud, jock, chick, fox,* and so on. Also, just as adult males should be called *men,* adult females should be referred to as *women,* not *girls.* And men shouldn't be empowered with professional and honorary titles (*President* Clinton) while professional women—such as congressional representatives—are assigned only personal titles (*Mrs.* Shroeder). Here are some examples of the way you can avoid words that exclude women: Change "chairman" to *chairperson,* "layman" to *layperson,* "congressman" to *congressional representative,* "workmen" to *workers,* the "average guy" to the *average person.* Second, be aware of the fact that indefinite singular nouns—those representing a general group of people consisting of both genders—can lead to *sexist pronoun use:* for example, "On *his* first day of school, a young child often experiences separation anxiety." This sentence excludes female children from consideration, although the situation being described applies equally to them. Third, recognize that indefinite pronouns like *anyone, each,* and *everybody* may also pave the way to sexist pronoun use. Although such pronouns often refer to a number of individuals, they're considered singular. So, wanting to be grammatically correct, you may write a sentence like the following: "Everybody wants *his* favorite candidate to win." The sentence, however, is sexist because *everybody* is certainly not restricted to men. One way to avoid this type of sexist construction is to use both male and female pronouns: "Everybody wants *his* or *her* favorite candidate to win." Another approach is to use *s/he* in place of *he.* A third possibility is to use the gender-neutral pronouns *they, their,* or *themselves:* "Everybody wants *their* favorite candidate to win." Be warned, though. Some people object to using these plural pronouns with singular indefinite pronouns, even though the practice is common in everyday speech. Two alternative strategies enable you to eliminate the need for *any* gender-marked singular pronouns. First, you can change singular general nouns or indefinite pronouns to their plural equivalents and then use nonsexist plural pronouns. For example, you may change "A *workaholic* feels anxious when *he* isn't busy" to "*Workaholics* feel anxious when *they're* not busy" and "*Everyone* in the room expressed *his* opinion freely" to "*Those* in the room expressed *their* opinions freely." Second, you can recast the sentence to omit the singular pronoun: For instance, you may change "A *manager* usually spends part of each day settling squabbles among *his* staff" to "A manager usually spends part of each day settling *staff squabbles*" and "No *one* wants *his* taxes raised" to "No one wants *to pay more taxes.*"

Hasty generalization—see *Logical fallacies.*

Inductive reasoning is a form of logical thinking in which specific cases and facts are examined to draw a wider-ranging conclusion. The result of inductive reasoning is a generalization that is applied to situations or cases similar to the ones examined. Induction is typical of scientific investigation and of everyday thinking. For example, on the basis of specific experiences, you may have concluded that when you feel chilly in a room where everyone else is comfortable, you are likely to develop a cold and fever in the next day or two. In an *argumentation-persuasion* essay, the conclusion reached by induction would be your *assertion* or *thesis*.

Inference is the term for a conclusion based on *inductive reasoning*. Because the reasoning behind specific cases may not be simple, there is usually an element of uncertainty in an inductive conclusion. Choosing the correct explanation for specific cases is a matter of carefully weighing and selecting alternative conclusions.

Informational process analysis—see *Process analysis.*

Introduction refers to the first paragraph or several paragraphs of an essay. The introduction serves three purposes. It informs readers of the general subject of the essay, it catches their attention, and it presents the controlling idea or thesis. The methods of introducing an essay include the use of an anecdote, a quotation or surprising statistic or fact, and questions. Or you may narrow your discussion down from a broad subject to a more iimited one.

Irony occurs when a writer or speaker implies (rather than states directly) a discrepancy or incongruity of some kind. *Verbal irony,* which is often tongue-in-cheek, involves a discrepancy between the literal words and what's actually meant ("I know you must be unhappy about receiving the highest grade in the course"). If the ironic comment is designed to be hurtful or insulting, it qualifies as *sarcasm* ("Congratulations! You failed the final exam"). In *situational irony,* the circumstances are themselves incongruous. For example, although their constitutional rights were violated when the federal government detained them in internment camps, Japanese-Americans nevertheless played American football, sang American songs, and saluted the American flag during their imprisonment.

Journal writing is a form of prewriting in which writers make daily entries in a private journal, much as they would in a diary. Whether they focus on one topic or wander freely, journal writers jot down striking incidents, images, and ideas encountered in the course of a day. Such journal material can produce ideas for future essays.

Logical fallacies are easily committed mistakes in reasoning that writers must avoid, especially when writing *argumentation-persuasion* essays. There are many kinds of logical fallacies. Here are several:

Ad hominem argument occurs when someone attacks another person's point of view by criticizing that person, not the issue. Often called "mudslinging," *ad hominem* arguments try to invalidate a person's ideas by revealing unrelated, past or present, personal or ethical flaws. For example, to claim that a person cannot govern the country well because it can be proven he or she has little sense of humor is to use an *ad hominem* argument.

Begging the question is a fallacy in which the writer assumes the truth of something that needs to be proven. Imagine a writer argues the following: "A law should be passed requiring dangerous pets like German shepherds and Doberman pinschers to be restrained by fences, leashes, and muzzles." Such an argument begs the question since it assumes readers will automatically accept the view that such dogs are indeed dangerous.

Either-or fallacies occur when it's argued that a complex situation can be resolved in only one of two possible ways. Here's an example: "If the administration doesn't grant striking professors more money, the college will never be able to attract outstanding teachers in years ahead." Such an argument over-simplifies matters. Excellent teachers might be attracted to a college for a variety of reasons, not just because of good salaries: the school's location, research facil-ities, reputation for scholarship, hardworking students, and so on.

False analogy erroneously suggests that because two things are alike in some regards, they are similar in all ways. In the process, significant differences between the two are disregarded. If you argue that a woman prosecuting a rapist is subjected to a second rape in court, you're guilty of a false analogy. As embarrassing, painful, and hurtful as the court proceedings may be, the woman is not physically assaulted, as she was when she was raped. Also, as difficult as her decision to seek justice might be, she's in court by choice and not against her will.

Hasty generalizations are unsound *inductive inferences* based on too few instances of a behavior, situation, or process. For example, it would be a hasty generalization to conclude that you're allergic to a food such as curry because you once ate it and became ill. There are several other possible explanations for your illness, and only repetitions of this experience or a lab test could prove con-clusively that you're allergic to this spice.

Non sequiturs are faulty conclusions about cause and effect. Here's an example: "Throughout this country's history, most physicians have been male. Women apparently have little interest in becoming doctors." The faulty conclu-sion accords one factor—the possible vocational preferences of women—the status of sole cause. The conclusion fails to consider pressures on women to devote themselves to homemaking and to avoid an occupation sexually stereo-typed as "masculine."

Post hoc thinking results when it's presumed that one event caused another just because it occurred first. For instance, if your car broke down the day after you lent it to your brother, you would be committing the *post hoc* fallacy if you blamed him, unless you knew he did something to your car's engine.

Questionable authority, revealed by such phrases as "studies show" and "experts claim," undercuts a writer's credibility. Readers become suspicious of such vague and unsubstantial appeals to authority. Writers should demonstrate the reliability of their sources by citing them specifically.

Red herring arguments are deliberate attempts to focus attention on a peripheral matter rather than examine the merits of the issue under discussion. Imagine that a local environmental group advocates stricter controls for employees at a nearby chemical plant. The group points out that plant employ-ees are repeatedly exposed to high levels of toxic chemicals. If you respond, "Many of the employees are illegal aliens and shouldn't be allowed to take jobs from native-born townspeople," you're throwing in a red herring. By bringing in immigration policies, you sidetrack attention from the matter at hand: the toxic level to which plant employees—illegal aliens or not—are exposed.

Logos is a major factor in creating an effective argument. It refers to the soundness of *argumentation,* as created by the use of facts, statistics, information, and com-mentary by authoritative sources. The most effective arguments involve an interplay among *logos, pathos,* and *ethos.*

Major premise—see *Deductive reasoning.*

Minor premise—see *Deductive reasoning.*

MLA documentation is the system developed by the Modern Language Association for citing sources in a paper. When you quote or summarize source material, you must do two things within your paper's text: (1) identify the author and (2) specify the pages on which the material appears. You may provide the author's name in a lead-in sentence or within parentheses following the borrowed material; the page number always appears in parentheses, inserted in the text after the borrowed material. The material in the parentheses is called a *parenthetic reference*. A paper using MLA documentation ends with a *Works Cited* list, which includes only those sources actually acknowledged in the paper. Entries are organized alphabetically by authors' last names. Entries without an author are alphabetized by the first major word in the title.

Narration means recounting an event or a series of related events to make a point. Narration can be an essay's principal pattern of development, or it can be used to supplement a paper organized primarily around another pattern. For instance, to persuade readers to avoid drug use, a writer might use the narrative pattern by recounting the story of an abuser's addiction and recovery.

Narrative point refers to the meaning the writer intends to convey to a reader by telling a certain story. This narrative point might be a specific message, or it might be a feeling about the situation, people, or place of the story. This underlying meaning is achieved by presenting details that support it and eliminating any that are nonessential. For example, in an essay about friendship, a writer's point might be that friendships change when one of the friends acquires a significant partner of the opposite sex. The writer would focus on the details of how her close female friend had less time for her, changed their usual times of getting together, and confided in her less. The writer would omit judgments of the friend's choice of boyfriend and her friend's declining grades because these details, while real for the writer, would distract the reader from the essay's narrative point.

Narrative sequence refers to the order in which a writer recounts events. When you follow the order of the events as they happened, you're using *chronological sequence*. This sequence, in which you begin at the beginning and end with the last event, is the most basic and commonly used narrative sequence. If you interrupt this flow to present an event that happened before the beginning of the narrative sequence, you're employing a *flashback*. If you skip ahead to an event later than the one that comes next in your narrative, you're using the *flashforward* technique.

Non sequiturs—see *Logical fallacies*.

Objective description—see *Description*.

One-side-at-a-time method refers to one of the two techniques for organizing a *comparison-contrast* essay. In using this method, a writer discusses all the points about one of the compared and contrasted subjects before going on to the other. For example, in an essay titled "Single or Married?" a writer might first discuss single life in terms of amount of independence, freedom of career choice, and companionship. Then the writer would, within reason, discuss married life in terms of these same three subtopics. The issues the writer discusses in each half of the essay would be identical and presented in the same order. See also *Point-by-point method*.

Organization refers to the process of arranging evidence to support a thesis in the most effective way. When organizing, a writer decides what ideas come first, next, and last. In *chronological* sequence, details are arranged according to occurrence in time. In *spatial* sequence, details appear in the order in which they occur in space. In *emphatic* order, ideas are sequenced according to importance, with the most significant, outstanding, or convincing evidence being reserved for last. In *simple-to-complex* order, easy-to-grasp material is presented before more-difficult-to-comprehend information. Organizing is the fourth stage of the writing process.

Outlining involves making a formal plan before writing a *first draft*. Writing an outline helps you determine whether your supporting evidence is logical and adequate. As you write, you can use the outline to keep yourself on track. Many writers use the indentation system of Roman numerals, letters, and Arabic numbers to outline; sometimes writers use a less formal system.

Paradox refers to a statement that seems impossible, contrary to common sense, or self-contradictory, yet that can—after consideration—be seen to be plausible or true. For example, Oscar Wilde produced a paradox when he wrote "When the gods wish to punish us, they answer our prayers." The statement doesn't contradict itself because often, Wilde believes, that which we wish for turns out to be the very thing that will bring us the most pain.

Parenthetic reference—see *MLA documentation.*

Pathos refers to the emotional power of an *argumentation-persuasion* essay. By appealing to the needs, values, and attitudes of readers and by using *connotative language,* writers can increase the chances that readers will come to agree with the ideas in an essay. Although *pathos* is an important element of persuasion, such emotional appeals should reinforce rather than replace reason. The most effective argumentation-persuasion involves an interplay among *pathos, logos,* and *ethos.*

Peer review is the critical reading of another person's writing with the intention of suggesting changes. To be effective, peer review calls for readers who are objective, skilled, and tactful enough to provide useful feedback. Begin by giving your readers a clear sense of what you expect from the review. To promote specific responses, ask the reviewers targeted (preferably written) questions. Following the review, rank the problems and solutions that the reviewers identified. Then enter your own notes for revising in the margins of your draft so that you'll know exactly what changes need to be made in your draft as you rework it.

Plan of development refers to a technique whereby the writer supplies the reader with a brief map of the main points to be covered in an essay. If used, the plan of development occurs as part of the *thesis* or in a sentence following the thesis. In it, the main ideas are mentioned in the order in which they'll appear in the supporting paragraphs. Longer essays and term papers usually need a plan of development to maintain unity, but shorter papers may do without one.

Point-by-point method refers to one of the two techniques for organizing a *comparison-contrast* essay. A writer using this method moves from one aspect of one subject to the same aspect of another subject before going on to the second aspect of each subject. For example, in an essay titled "Single or Married?" a writer might first discuss the amount of independence a person has when single and when married. Then, the writer might go on to discuss how much freedom of career choice a person has when single and when married. Finally, the writer might discuss, in turn, the amount of companionship available in each of the two lifestyles. See also *One-side-at-a-time method.*

Point of view refers to the perspective a writer chooses when writing about a subject. If you narrate events as you experience them, you're using the *first-person* point of view. You might say, for example, "*I* noticed jam on the child's collar and holes in her shirt." If you relate the events from a distance—as if you observed them but did not experience them personally—you're using the *third-person* point of view; for instance, "Jam splotched the child's collar, and her shirt had several holes in it." The point of view should be consistent throughout an essay.

Post hoc **thinking**—see *Logical fallacies.*

Prewriting is the first stage of the writing process. During prewriting, you jot down rough ideas about your subject without yet moving to writing a draft of your essay. Your goals at this stage are to (1) understand the boundaries of the assignment, (2) discover the limited subject you could write about, (3) generate raw material about the limited subject, and (4) organize the raw material into a very rough *scratch outline.* If you keep in mind that prewriting is "unofficial," it can be a low-pressure, even enjoyable activity.

Process analysis refers to writing that explains the steps involved in doing something or the sequence of stages in an event or behavior. There are two types of process analysis. In *directional process analysis,* readers are shown how to do something step by step. Cookbook recipes, tax form instructions, and how-to books are some typical uses of directional process analysis. In *informational process analysis,* the writer explains how something is done or occurs, without expecting the reader to attempt the process. "A Senator's Road to Political Power," "How a Bee Makes Honey," and "How a Convict Gets Paroled" would be titles of essays developed through informational process analysis. Process analysis can be the dominant mode in an essay, as in these examples, or it may help make a point in an essay developed chiefly through another pattern. For example, in a cause-effect essay that explores the impact of the two-career family, process analysis might be used to explain how parents arrange for day care.

Proofreading involves rereading a final draft carefully to catch any errors in spelling, grammar, punctuation, or typing that have slipped by. While such errors are minor, a significant number of them can seriously weaken the effectiveness of an essay. Proofreading is the last stage in the writing process.

Proposition—see *Assertion.*

Purpose is the reason a writer has for preparing a particular essay. Usually, writers frame their purposes in terms of the effect they wish to have on their *audience.* They may wish to explore the personal meaning of a subject or experience, explain an idea or process, provide information, influence opinion, or entertain. Many essays combine purposes, with one purpose predominating and providing the essay's focus.

Red herring argument—see *Logical fallacies.*

Refutation is an important strategy in *argumentation-persuasion.* In refutation, writers acknowledge that there are opposing views on the subject under discussion and then go on to do one of two things. Sometimes they may admit that the opposing views are somewhat valid but assert that their own position has more merit and devote their essay to demonstrating that merit. For example, a writer might assert, "Business majors often find interesting and lucrative jobs. However, in the long run, liberal arts graduates have many more advantages in the job market because the breadth of their background helps them think better, learn faster, and communicate more effectively." This writer would concentrate on proving the advantages that liberal arts graduates have. At other times, writers may choose to argue actively against an opposing position by dismantling that view point by point. Such refutation of opposing views can strengthen the writer's own arguments.

Repeated words, synonyms, and pronouns—see *Signaling devices.*

Revision means, literally, "reseeing" a *first draft* with a fresh eye, as if the writer had not actually prepared the draft. When revising, you move from more global issues (like clarifying meaning and organization) to more specific matters (like fine-tuning sentences and word choice). While revising, you make whatever changes are necessary to increase the essay's effectiveness. You might strengthen your thesis, resequence paragraph order, or add more transitions. Such changes often make the difference between mediocre and superior writing. Revision, itself a multi-stage process, is the last stage of the writing process.

Satire is a humorous form of social criticism usually aimed at society's institutions or human behavior. Often irreverent as well as witty, satire is serious in purpose: to point out evil, injustice, and absurdity and bring about change through an increase in awareness. Satire ranges widely in tone: it may be gentle or biting; it may sarcastically describe a real situation or use fictional characters and events to spoof reality. Satire often makes use of *irony.*

Scratch outline refers to your first informal plan for an essay, devised at the end of the *prewriting* stage. In making a scratch outline, you select ideas and details from your raw material for inclusion in your essay and discard the rest. You also arrange these ideas in an order that makes sense and that will help you achieve your *purpose.* A scratch outline is tentative and flexible, and can be reshaped as needed.

Sensory description vividly evokes the sights, smells, tastes, sounds, and physical feelings of a scene or event. For example, if a writer carefully chooses words and images, readers can see the vibrant reds and oranges of falling leaves, taste the sourness of an underripe grapefruit, hear the growling of motorcycles as a gang sweeps through a town, smell the spicy aroma of a grandmother's homemade tomato soup, and feel the pulsing pain of a jaw after Novocain wears off. Sensory description is particularly important in writing *description* or *narration.*

Sentence variety adds interest to the style of an essay or paragraph. In creating sentence variety, writers mix different kinds of sentences and sentence patterns. For example, you might vary the way your sentences open or intersperse short sentences with long ones, simple sentences with complex ones. Repetitive sentence patterns tend to make readers lose interest.

Signaling devices indicate the relationships among ideas in an essay. They help the reader follow the train of thought from sentence to sentence and from paragraph to paragraph. There are three types of connectives. *Transitions* are words that clarify flow of meaning. They can signal an additional or contrasting point, an enumeration of ideas, the use of an example, or other movement of ideas. *Linking sentences* summarize a point just made and then introduce a follow-up point. *Repeated words, synonyms,* and *pronouns* create a sense of flow by keeping important concepts in the mind of the reader.

Spatial sequence—see *Organization.*

Specific—see *Evidence.*

Stipulative definition is a way of restricting a term for the purposes of discussion. Many words have multiple meanings that can get in the way of clarity when a writer is creating an *extended definition.* For example, you might stipulate the following definition of *foreign car:* "While many American automobiles use parts or even whole engines made by foreign car manufacturers, for the purposes of discussion, 'foreign car' refers only to those automobiles designed and manufactured wholly by a company based in another country. By this definition, a European vehicle made in Pennsylvania is *not* a foreign car."

Subjective description—see *Description.*

Support—see *Evidence.*

Syllogism—see *Deductive reasoning.*

Term—see *Formal definition.*

Thesis is the central idea in any essay, usually expressed in a one- or two-sentence *thesis statement.* Writers accomplish two things by providing a thesis statement in an essay: They indicate the essay's limited subject and express an attitude about that subject. Also called the *controlling idea,* the thesis statement consists of a particular slant, angle, or point of view about the limited subject. Stating the thesis is the second stage of the writing process.

Tone conveys your attitude toward yourself, your purpose, your topic, and your readers. As in speaking, tone in writing may be serious, playful, sarcastic, and so on. Generally, readers detect tone more by how you say something (that is, through your sentence structure and word choice) than by what you say.

Topic sentence is the term for the sentence(s) that convey the main idea of a paragraph. Such sentences are often, but not always, found at the start of a paragraph. They provide a statement of the subject to be discussed and an indication of the writer's attitude toward that subject. Writers usually concern themselves with topic sentences during the writing of the first draft, the fifth stage of the writing process.

Transitions—see *Signaling devices.*

Unified—see *Evidence.*

Works Cited—see *MLA documentation.*

ACKNOWLEDGMENTS

Angelou, Maya, "Sister Flowers." From *I Know Why the Caged Bird Sings* by Maya Angelou. Copyright © 1969 and renewed 1997 by Maya Angelou. Used by permission of Random House, Inc.

Barry, Dave, "The Ugly Truth About Beauty." From *Philadelphia Inquirer Magazine,* February 8, 1998. Copyright © 1998 by Dave Barry. Reprinted by permission of Tribune Media Services International.

Barszcz, James, "Can You Be Educated From a Distance?" Reprinted by permission of the author.

Bryson, Bill, "Your New Computer." From *I'm a Stranger Here Myself* by Bill Bryson. Copyright © 1999 by Bill Bryson. Used by permission of Broadway Books, a division of Random House, Inc.

Carson, Rachel, "A Fable for Tomorrow." From *Silent Spring* by Rachel Carson. Copyright © 1962 by Rachel L. Carson, renewed 1990 by Roger Christie. Reprinted by permission of Houghton Mifflin Co. All rights reserved.

Cole, K. C., "Entropy." From *The New York Times,* March 18, 1982. Copyright © 1982 by K. C. Cole. Reprinted by permission.

Darley, John M., and Bibb Latané, "Why People Don't Help in a Crisis?" From *Psychology Today.* Copyright © 1985 by Sussex Publishers, Inc. Reprinted with permission from Psychology Today Magazine.

Didion, Joan, "Marrying Absurd" from *Slouching Towards Bethlehem* by Joan Didion. Copyright © 1966, 1968, renewed 1996 by Joan Didion. Reprinted by permission of Farrar, Straus and Giroux, LLC.

Dillard, Annie, "The Chase." From *An American Childhood* by Annie Dillard. Copyright © 1987 by Annie Dillard. Reprinted by permission of HarperCollins Publishers, Inc.

Ehrenreich, Barbara, "What I've Learned From Men." from *Ms.* Magazine, August 1985. Reprinted by permission of *Ms.* Magazine, © 1985.

Ericsson, Stephanie, "The Ways We Lie." From *The Utne Reader,* 1992. Copyright © 1992 by Stephanie Ericsson. Reprinted by permission of Dunham Literary as agents for the author.

Goodman, Ellen, "Family Counterculture." From *Value Judgments* (originally appeared in *The Boston Globe,* August 16, 1991). © 1991, The Washington Post Writers Group. Reprinted with permission.

Hughes, Langston, "Salvation." From *The Big Sea* by Langston Hughes. Copyright © 1940 by Langston Hughes. Copyright renewed © 1968 by Arna Bontemps and George Houston Bass. Reprinted by permission of Hill and Wang, a division of Farrar, Straus and Giroux, LLC.

Hymowitz, Kay S., "Tweens: Ten Going on Sixteen." Reprinted from the Autumn 1998 issue (vol. 8, no. 4) of the Manhattan Institute's *City Journal* (www.city-journal.org).

Jacoby, Susan, "Common Decency." Copyright © 1991 by Susan Jacoby. From *The New York Times.* Reprinted by permission of Georges Borchardt, Inc. for the author.

Johnson, Beth, "Bombs Bursting in Air." Reprinted by permission of the author. Beth Johnson lives in Lederach, PA.

King, Martin Luther, Jr., "Where Do We Go From Here: Community or Chaos?" Reprinted by arrangement with the Estate of Martin Luther King, Jr., c/o Writers House, New York, NY, as agent for the proprietor. Copyright 1967 by Martin Luther King, Jr., copyright renewed 1991 by Coretta Scott King.

King, Stephen, "Why We Crave Horror Movies." Originally appeared in *Playboy,* 1982. Reprinted with permission. Copyright © Stephen King. All rights reserved.

Lutz, William, "Doublespeak." From *Doublespeak: From Revenue Enhancement to Terminal Living* by William Lutz, Harper Collins. Copyright © 1989 by William D. Lutz.

Mayblum, Adam, "The Price We Pay." From *Doubletake Magazine,* Special Edition, 2001. Reprinted by permission of the author.

McClintock, Ann, "Propaganda Techniques in Today's Advertising." Reprinted by permission of the author.

Paglia, Camille, "Rape: A Bigger Danger Than Feminists Know." Reprinted by permission of the author.

Parks, Gordon, "Flavio's Home." From *Voices in the Mirror* by Gordon Parks. Copyright © 1990 by Gordon Parks. Used by permission of Doubleday, a division of Random House, Inc.

Raspberry, William, "The Handicap of Definition." Copyright © 1982, The Washington Post Writers Group. Reprinted with permission.

Rego, Caroline, "The Fine Art of Complaining." Reprinted by permission of the author.

Robbins, Alexandra, and Abby Wilner, "What Is the Quarterlife Crisis?" Introduction from *Quarterlife Crisis* by Alexandra Robbins and Abby Wilner, Copyright © 2001 by Alexandra Robbins and Abby Wilner. Used by permission of Jeremy P. Tarcher, an imprint of Penguin Group (USA) Inc.

Soto, Gary, "The Jacket." From *Small Faces,* from *The Effects of Knut Hamsun on a Fresno Boy: Recollections and Short Essays* by Gary Soto. Copyright © 1983, 2001 by Gary Soto. Reprinted by permission of Persea Books, Inc. (New York).

Steele, Shelby, "Affirmative Action: The Price of Preference." From *The Content of Our Character: A New Vision of Race in America* by Shelby Steele. Copyright © 1990 by Shelby Steele. Reprinted by permission of St. Martin's Press, LLC.

Stoll, Clifford, "Cyberschool." From *High-Tech Heretic* by Clifford Stoll. Copyright © 1990 by Clifford Stoll. Used by permission of Doubleday, a division of Random House, Inc.

Suina, Joseph H., "And Then I Went to School." From *Linguistic and Cultural Influences on Learning Mathematics* by Joseph H. Suina. Reprinted by permission of the author and Lawrence Earlbaum Associates, Inc.

Walljasper, Jay, "Our Schedules, Our Selves." From *The Utne Reader,* January/February 2003. Reprinted from Utne Magazine.

Wilkins, Roger, "Racism Has Its Privileges." Reprinted with permission from the March 27, 1995, issue of *The Nation.*

Woolf, Virginia, "The Death of the Moth." From *The Death of the Moth and Other Essays* by Virginia Woolf. Copyright 1942 by Harcourt, Inc., and renewed 1970 by Marjorie T. Parsons, Executrix. Reprinted by permission of the publisher.

Yuh, Ji-Yeon, "Let's Tell the Story of All America's Cultures." From *The Philadelphia Inquirer,* June 30, 1991. Reprinted by permission of the author.

INDEX

To the Student
From the Authors

By now, you realize that almost all writing goes through a series of revisions. The same was true for this book. *The Longman Reader,* Seventh Edition, Brief Edition, has been reworked a number of times, with each revision taking into account students' and instructors' reactions to drafts of material.

Before we prepare the eighth edition of *The Longman Reader,* Brief Edition, we'd like to know how you, the student, feel about the book. We hope you'll spend a few minutes completing this brief questionnaire. You can be sure that your responses will help shape subsequent editions. Please send your completed survey to the College English Editor, Longman Publishers, 1185 Avenue of the Americas, New York, NY 10036.

Thanks for your time.

College _____ City and state _____

Course title _____ Instructor _____

	I really liked it.	It was okay.	I didn't like it.	I didn't read it.
DESCRIPTION				
Parks, *Flavio's Home*	___	___	___	___
Soto, *The Jacket*	___	___	___	___
Angelou, *Sister Flowers*	___	___	___	___
NARRATION				
Dillard, *The Chase*	___	___	___	___
Hughes, *Salvation*	___	___	___	___
Mayblum, *The Price We Pay*	___	___	___	___
EXEMPLIFICATION				
Hymowitz, *Tweens: Ten Going on Sixteen*	___	___	___	___
Johnson, *Bombs Bursting in Air*	___	___	___	___
Ehrenreich, *What I've Learned From Men*	___	___	___	___

DIVISION-CLASSIFICATION

	I really liked it.	It was okay.	I didn't like it.	I didn't read it.
Ericsson, *The Ways We Lie*	___	___	___	___
Lutz, *Doublespeak*	___	___	___	___
McClintock, *Propaganda Techniques in Today's Advertising*	___	___	___	___

PROCESS ANALYSIS

Bryson, *Your New Computer*	___	___	___	___
Stoll, *Cyberschool*	___	___	___	___
Rego, *The Fine Art of Complaining*	___	___	___	___

COMPARISON-CONTRAST

Carson, *A Fable for Tomorrow*	___	___	___	___
Suina, *And Then I Went to School*	___	___	___	___
Barry, *The Ugly Truth About Beauty*	___	___	___	___

CAUSE-EFFECT

King, *Why We Crave Horror Movies*	___	___	___	___
Darley & Latané, *Why People Don't Help in a Crisis*	___	___	___	___
Walljasper, *Our Schedules, Our Selves*	___	___	___	___

DEFINITION

Cole, *Entropy*	___	___	___	___
Robbins & Wilner, *What Is the Quarterlife Crisis?*	___	___	___	___
Raspberry, *The Handicap of Definition*	___	___	___	___

ARGUMENTATION-PERSUASION

	I really liked it.	It was okay.	I didn't like it.	I didn't read it.
Yuh, *Let's Tell the Story of All America's Cultures*	——	——	——	——
Barszcz, *Can You Be Educated From a Distance?*	——	——	——	——
Paglia, *Rape: A Bigger Danger Than Feminists Know*	——	——	——	——
Jacoby, *Common Decency*	——	——	——	——
Wilkins, *Racism Has Its Privileges*	——	——	——	——
Steele, *Affirmative Action: The Price of Preference*	——	——	——	——

COMBINING THE PATTERNS

Woolf, *The Death of the Moth*	——	——	——	——
King, *Where Do We Go From Here: Community or Chaos?*	——	——	——	——
Didion, *Marrying Absurd*	——	——	——	——

Any general comments or suggestions?

Name _____ Date _____

Address _____

THANKS AGAIN!